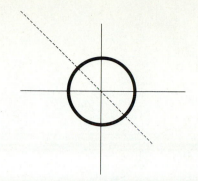

THE DESIGN OF ADVERTISING

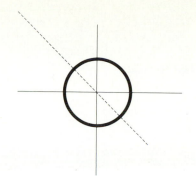

THE DESIGN OF ADVERTISING

7TH EDITION

ROY PAUL NELSON
UNIVERSITY OF OREGON

Boston, Massachusetts   Burr Ridge, Illinios   Dubuque, Iowa
Madison, Wisconsin   New York, New York   San Francisco, California   St. Louis, Missouri

McGraw·Hill

A Division of The **McGraw·Hill** Companies

Book Team

Executive Editor *Stan Stoga*
Developmental Editor *Mary E. Rossa*
Production Editor *Marlys Nekola*
Designer *Eric Engelby*
Art Editor/Processor *Joyce E. Watters*
Photo Editor *Karen Hostert*
Visuals/Design Developmental Consultant *Marilyn A. Phelps*
Visuals/Design Freelance Specialist *Mary L. Christianson*
Publishing Services Specialist *Sherry Padden*
Marketing Manager *Carla J. Aspelmeier*
Advertising Manager *Jodi Rymer*

Executive Vice President/General Manager *Thomas E. Doran*
Vice President/Editor in Chief *Edgar J. Laube*
Vice President/Sales and Marketing *Eric Ziegler*
Director of Production *Vickie Putman Caughron*
Director of Custom and Electronic Publishing *Chris Rogers*

President and Chief Executive Officer *G. Franklin Lewis*
Corporate Senior Vice President and Chief Financial Officer *Robert Chesterman*
Corporate Senior Vice President and President of Manufacturing *Roger Meyer*

Cover by Eric Jacobson/NYC

Interior layout by Roy Paul Nelson

By Roy Paul Nelson
The Design of Advertising
Publication Design
Editing the News (with Roy H. Copperud)
The Fourth Estate (with John L. Hulteng)
Articles and Features
Humorous Illustrations and Cartooning
Comic Art and Caricature
Cartooning
Visits with 30 Magazine Art Directors
Fell's Guide to Commercial Art (with Byron Ferris)
Fell's Guide to the Art of Cartooning
The Cartoonist (a novel)

Cover Concept
The cover was prepared using a simple operation of selective ghosting
with the Macintosh computer-based program Photoshop. The image was
then saved and brought into the Macintosh-based program FreeHand,
where the type and graphics elements were assembled.

Library of Congress Catalog Card Number: 92–74978

ISBN 0-697-38766-6

Printed in the United States of America

10 9 8

To Willis L. Winter, Jr.

CONTENTS

14

POSTERS AND DISPLAYS 316

15

LONG-TERM DESIGN   332

16

CAREERS   358

PREFACE

This seventh edition of *The Design of Advertising* continues to serve journalism, business, art, and graphic design students interested in the creative side of advertising, especially its design aspects. The book assumes that its readers have only modest backgrounds in art, typography, design, and production, and so it goes into those subjects in considerable detail. But it sets the stage first with information about advertising in general. One early chapter deals exclusively and extensively with copywriting.

Although the book puts its emphasis on design, it reminds readers continually that what an ad says is what's really important, and how good it looks is secondary to how well it sells.

A look back at the earlier editions of the book provides startling evidence of the changes that have taken place in advertising and its design since the publication of the first edition in 1967. The current edition bears little resemblance to that first edition and, in fact, less resemblance than might be expected to the last edition, published in 1989. Desktop publishing then had just taken hold in advertising agencies and departments and design studios, and many designers were wary of it. Now it is the rare workspace that is not equipped with computers and desktop systems.

The Design of Advertising makes the necessary adjustments in this edition, discussing computers and software programs throughout, reordering the chapters, combining two of them, adding sections, eliminating others, introducing all kinds of new material, tossing out illustrations no longer useful, and bringing in new ones—more than 160 of them—from a variety of sources.

Not that the book's emphasis on established design principles has been abandoned. That emphasis is still here—and needed, especially in an age when some people in the business think that good graphic design comes from merely working a keyboard and clicking a mouse.

The temptation was to drop all references to board work and the use of traditional tools of design. But the book retains some references to these because electronic layout, design, and pasteup evolved from them, using many of the approaches and, in fact, some of the terminology. Moreover, some graphic designers have not made the switch. Some move back and forth between the drawing board and the computer. And not all classrooms where layout is taught are equipped with computers.

Because much of this book deals with principles rather than methods, what's said applies to design however it's produced. As Ken O'Connell, head of the University of Oregon Department of Fine and Applied Arts and an expert in computer graphics, said in the previous edition, "Just because you have the equipment doesn't mean you can become an artist or designer. . . . The computer is an incredible tool, but [first] you have to develop coordination as a visual thinker."

This is what this book attempts to do for the reader.

A number of professors who have adopted *The Design of Advertising* as a textbook over the years prompted some of the changes made in this new edition. The author thanks those professors for their suggestions. He thanks especially Professor Jack C. Quinton of San Jose State University and Professor Alan Dennis of The University of Alabama, picked by the publisher to officially review the sixth edition. He thanks, too, Marie F. Nelson and Chris Lawrence for their editorial help and the hundreds of agencies, clients, art directors, artists, and designers, many of them named in text and captions, for permission to reproduce their ads and creative works. Finally, the author thanks his colleagues in advertising and graphic design at the University of Oregon for their help and advice, and the editors at Brown & Benchmark Publishers for their professionalism and patience.

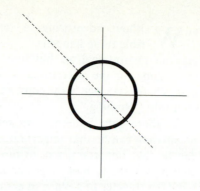

THE DESIGN OF ADVERTISING

1

THE WORLD OF ADVERTISING

"Without advertising, a terrible thing happens . . . ," says an institutional ad building a good name for the advertising business. There is a space in the copy, and then this: "Nothing."

To those with something to sell, advertising can be that important. It can be that important, too, to those who only want to buy. A poster directs the traveler to a place to eat or spend the night. A direct-mail piece invites the reader to subscribe to a magazine. A classified ad announces a garage sale or a job opening.

But advertising can also set up false hopes and get people to buy things they don't need or shouldn't buy. Like lawyers, ad makers work for the unworthy as well as the worthy. Through advertising, every side gets a hearing. In the end, the reader or listener or viewer of the advertising renders the verdict.

Advertising sells not only products but also services and ideas. It can do a job for both profit and nonprofit organizations. Government agencies rank among the big users of advertising. Among government bodies doing advertising are the postal service, the armed forces, and Amtrak. One of the most widely recognized advertising symbols is the U.S. Forest Service's Smokey Bear (not Smokey *the* Bear, we are told in a recent campaign).

Professions like medicine and law tend to avoid advertising, but with increased competition, they, too, find it necessary to buy time and space in the media, if only to announce office openings. With law schools turning out graduates in record numbers, some new law firms sponsor advertising campaigns that could just as well sell soap or cigarettes. Naturally, old-line firms look askance at such campaigns. "What's a Law Firm Doing in an Advertisement?" one firm asks, a bit self-consciously. The second line of the headline answers: "A Service." The copy starts off like this: "Advertisements by law firms are surprising to some people. They shouldn't be. After all, practicing law is a business, as well as a profession."

Churches, especially the evangelical ones, have long regarded advertising as one more tool to use to reach the unsaved. Even the mainline denominations have capitulated. The First Methodist Church of Cleveland hired an advertising agency, Robert Carter & Associates, to help build its attendance. Headlines like "Look Into Our Master's Program," "Summertime and Religion Is Easy," and "Rush at East 30th and Euclid. We Don't Have a Hell Week" were written to appeal to college-age people, whose ranks in the congregation had dwindled. Attendance increased dramatically, although some church members felt that the ads were irreverent.

An ad prepared by the Fallon McElligott agency in Minneapolis for the Episcopal Church carried a picture of Henry VIII and the headline "In the Church Started by a Man Who Had Six Wives, Forgiveness Goes Without Saying."

Categories of products to be advertised know no limits these days. Contraceptive makers once stayed clear of consumer advertising, but gradually they began taking out ads in men's and women's magazines, and, with the AIDS scare, condoms became the subject not only of ads but of promotions of all kinds, including songs. The New York City government ran a campaign with the slogan "Don't Go Out Without Your Rubbers."

We value his opinion as much as any of our other employees.

This is Rex. He works for us at our nutritional headquarters in Illinois. Along with 500 others just like him. To keep developing superior food for dogs, we need their expertise. To test nutritional levels. Monitor diets. And find out if the meals we're producing taste as good as we think they do.

Their hard work has enabled us to offer a variety of foods that have been satisfying dogs' needs for nearly 60 years. From the nutritional benefits of Cycle® Dog Food for each stage of their lives. The rich gravy in Gravy Train® Dog Food. The great-tasting Gaines.burgers® and Top Choice® Dog Foods (which have made us #1 in the soft-moist category). To new products like Tast-tee Chunks® snacks for dogs.

But Rex and his pals don't earn their keep just by eating once a day. They keep busy assisting us in developing other products on the side. Like books and seminars that help care for dogs beyond dinnertime. In return, Rex gets a great place to live. Lots of time to spend with friends.

And plenty of love and devotion from all of us at Gaines. And why not? He works like a dog for it.

Gaines® Sharing your love for dogs

© Gaines Foods, Inc. 1986

This Gaines ad directed to readers of *Canine Practice* magazine is designed to influence veterinarians, who in turn will influence dog owners. The copy quickly explains the surprise in the headline, set in a close-fitting Times Roman. Agency: Chiat/Day. Art director: Leslie Sweet. Copywriter: Nat Whitten. Photographer: Cailor-Resnick.

In an informative institutional ad, Chevron finds a correlation between environmental balance in Tanzania and environmental balance at home. The well-written and well-designed ad, as an aside, tells readers about an upcoming Public Television program, underwritten by Chevron. Agency: J. Walter Thompson. Art director: Tom Burgess. Designer: Nancy O'Hanian. Copywriter: Francis Frazier.

Early ads tended to crowd a lot of type and art into limited space. But an occasional ad like the one for Nestor Cigarettes (in a 1902 issue of *Puck*) was more posterlike.

In the 1930s and 1940s designers often relied on overlaps to bring various elements together. In this newspaper ad for Sunkist (1945), a pattern of oranges overlaps a grocer; a black rectangle overlaps the oranges; a white rectangle for copy overlaps the black rectangle; an orange slice and glass overlap the white rectangle; a small black rectangle overlaps the orange slice and glass.

Advertisers spend well over $130 billion dollars a year to reach customers and potential customers in the United States. The average person sees or hears some 400 ads each day. The people at J. Walter Thompson, the advertising agency, have referred to advertising as "America's Fifth Estate," the Fourth Estate being the press itself.

Advertising people in the United States often point to what's being done in Europe and Japan as superior to what's being done in their country. Overseas advertising tends to be more subtle, sometimes more shocking, and often better infused with humor. The visual becomes more important in advertising in Great Britain and on the continent. The sell is softer.

With its emphasis on "New!" and "Improved!" the advertising industry has not placed much emphasis on its past. Most ad people remember and honor the early Volkswagen ads and admire the creation of the Marlboro cowboy, but yesterday's ads quickly move aside to make room for newer versions echoing the fads and fashions of the day.

To give advertising itself a better image by giving it a history, the Portland Advertising Federation and interested advertising people in 1986 set up the first American Advertising Museum. Its 6,000 square feet of exhibit space in the Old Town section of Oregon's largest city gives visitors a chance to see and appreciate old ads in all media. One exhibit shows continuous TV commercials. Another shows classic packaging and signs. The emphasis is on national, not local, advertising, and the museum attracts visitors, including scholars, from all over the United States.

The Smithsonian's Center for Advertising History in Washington, D.C. and the Museum of Broadcasting in New York also gather advertisements of various kinds to preserve them for scholars and others interested in them as cultural artifacts.

Kinds of Advertising

Advertising takes many forms and uses many approaches. People sometimes confuse advertising with publicity and public relations. Advertising differs from these in that it usually involves the *buying* of space or time. Publicity and public re-

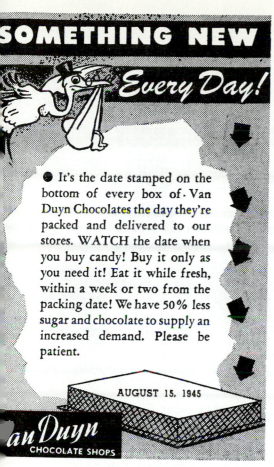

Also popular in the 1940s were black bars into which headlines could be reversed, arrows, black dots in front of paragraphs, and mortises cut in irregular shapes. These devices made a comeback with the advent of desktop publishing and its enabling software.

lations depend upon being noticed by the media and being incorporated into regular news and editorial columns or programs. The space and time they get, in that sense, is free.

From the standpoint of intended audiences, advertising falls into six categories:

■ *National advertising.* Another name for it is "brand-name advertising." The audience consists of potential customers for products sold in stores. The emphasis in the advertising is on the product rather than on the place where it may be purchased. Price usually is not mentioned. National advertising is found mostly in slick magazines and the broadcast media, although some of it appears in newspapers.

■ *Retail advertising.* Another name for it is "local advertising." Its purpose is to get potential customers into particular stores. Price is always mentioned. Retail advertising appears not only in newspapers but also on radio and television stations. Some retail advertising appears in regional editions of national magazines.

■ *Mail-order advertising.* Its practitioners prefer the term "direct-marketing advertising" or "direct-response advertising," but whatever it is called, it asks that the product be ordered by letter, coupon, or phone; the product arrives later by mail or some other carrier. Mail-order advertising is a $200-billion-a-year business.

This kind of advertising combines elements of both national and retail advertising. It uses mostly magazines and direct mail, but it also makes use of radio and television. Orders are often taken on an 800 phone number, charged to credit cards, and sent out by United Parcel Service. *Time* magazine estimates that UPS handles about 90 percent of "mail-order" packages.

Mail-order advertising is sponsored by retailers not readily accessible to customers.

An appeal of mail order is that the customer has already paid for the item by the time it arrives. Getting it is like receiving a gift. Almost everybody likes getting something through the mail. Many people either do not like going out to shop or do not have time to do it. Another appeal of mail order is that, because selling costs are low, prices listed in a catalog can be lower than prices at the store.

■ *Trade advertising.* The audience for this kind of advertising consists of retailers, wholesalers, or brokers. They are "customers," too—customers for products which they in turn sell to others. Instead of stressing the benefits of the product, this kind of advertising stresses the profits that can be made from stocking and selling it.

A maker of lawn mowers and other power equipment runs this headline on a full-page, full-color ad showing various models: "Snapper. Engineered for Profit." The headline and copy are designed to convince retailers—readers of *Farm Store Merchandising,* where the ad appears—to stock the Snapper line. If anything, the ad, stressing "profit opportunities," is the antithesis of what an ad directed to ordinary customers would be.

■ *Industrial advertising.* In buying raw materials and machines to use in their manufacturing processes, manufacturers become customers, too. The audiences for both trade and industrial advertising are reached, in the main, through trade magazines and direct-mail advertising (not to be confused with mail-order advertising).

■ *Professional advertising.* This is advertising directed to physicians, architects, and others who advise people what to buy. Like national advertising, it stresses benefits to the user. The media in which these ads appear include professional and trade magazines and direct mail.

More elaborate design ideas and expensive production techniques are employed in national, industrial, and professional advertising than in the other types. This is because audiences are larger (or more exclusive), space or time is more expensive, and, generally, stakes are higher.

Institutional Advertising

The primary purpose of advertising is to sell products or services. But sometimes it is designed to do something else: to win an audience over to a point of view. We call such advertising *institutional* or *corporate advertising*. It can be national or local; it can address itself to any kind of audience; it can use any medium. In its design it often resembles editorial matter in the newspapers and magazines. An obvious example of institutional advertising is a full-page, mostly-copy ad in the Sunday New York *Times* urging some political action or appealing for funds.

Institutional advertising often is prepared by public relations rather than advertising people. Advertising becomes just one of many tools available to public relations people. "The beauty of advertising [to do a PR job] is that it's the one form of communication which can't be edited [by outsiders]," says Richard Pruitt, executive creative director of Ogilvy & Mather, Hong Kong. "It can be as big as you can buy. You can run it as often as you can afford. You can tell your side of the story without interruptions. I believe that every corporation has a right—and in some cases a responsibility—to tell its side of the story."[1]

Institutional advertising often is an exercise in self-praise. It attempts to build a favorable image for its sponsor.

Companies or organizations that feel the sting of media criticism often turn to institutional advertising to tell their sides of stories. The tobacco industry has fought hard to discredit reports of the connection between smoking and disease. Liquor companies take out ads to preach moderation.

After *Time* ran a cover article unfavorable to Scientology, the organization took out a series of ads in *USA Today* to fight back. "What Magazine Gets It Wrong in 1991?" one headline asked, and then answered: "The Same One That Was Wrong in 1940—*Time*." The ad cited the magazine's praise of Mussolini in 1940. Also in response to *Time*'s article, the organization published a booklet, "Fact vs. Fiction," which it distributed to business leaders and the media.[2]

If an attempt to sell a product creeps into institutional advertising, it does so noiselessly. A direct-mail piece McDonnell Douglas offers to travel agents to make available to their customers (there is a place on the back panel where agents can stamp their names) tells people how to tell one jetliner from another. *A Plane-Watcher's Guide to the World's Great Jetliners* shows them all, with "objective" descriptions under each. The DC-9 is described as "Simple and dependable, adaptable, and comfortable . . . flown by more than forty airlines around the world." Descriptions of non-McDonnell Douglas planes in this folder tend to deal only with appearances. In a friendly gesture at the end, the folder says, after its listing of "Tips for Air Travelers," that "above all, [you should] talk with your travel agent. That's the best source of good advice on the whole world of flying!"

But there is no overt attempt to sell McDonnell Douglas planes to anyone (patrons of travel bureaus are not likely buyers) or even to convince people that they should buy tickets on airlines using McDonnell Douglas planes.

Related to institutional advertising is *advocacy advertising*. The difference between the two types is that in advocacy advertising the sponsor pushes a point of view that may have nothing to do with selling the product or building an image. ". . . Corporations have taken to advocacy advertising because they feel they are not getting a fair shake from what they believe to be a generally hostile press; and because they are convinced that the business world can make significant contributions to public debate on issues of great importance—energy, nuclear power, conservation, environment, taxation, and free enterprise, among others," says Professor Robert Shayon of the University of Pennsylvania Annenberg School of Communications.[3]

Where Advertising Originates

The people in advertising generally fall into three categories: the "wrists" (those who design and lay out the ads), the "wordsmiths" (those who write the copy), and the "suits" (those who run the business and interact with the clients). In-

The American Red Cross addresses the most often asked questions about AIDS and the workplace:

CAN AN EMPLOYEE WITH AIDS INFECT OTHER EMPLOYEES?

The AIDS virus cannot be spread by everyday contact in the workplace. An employee with AIDS can infect another employee only if they have sexual contact or share intravenous drug needles.

CAN THE AIDS VIRUS BE SPREAD BY USING A TELEPHONE OR WATER FOUNTAIN?

No. The AIDS virus is not spread through air, water, or on surfaces, such as telephones, door knobs, or office machines. The virus is spread mainly through an exchange of body fluids during sexual activity, or the exchange of blood as occurs through sharing contaminated IV drug needles.

SHOULD I PROVIDE OR DESIGNATE SEPARATE BATHROOM FACILITIES FOR EMPLOYEES WITH AIDS?

There is no need to. The AIDS virus is not spread through ordinary use of toilets, sinks, or other bathroom facilities.

CAN I TELL IF SOMEONE IS INFECTED WITH THE AIDS VIRUS?

There are many *carriers* of the virus who do not have the symptoms or signs of the disease and may or may not develop the disease. A carrier of the AIDS

SHOULD YOU WORRY ABOUT AIDS AND THE WORK-PLACE?

virus can infect other people but not through ordinary workplace contact.

WHAT IF I TOUCH A COWORKER WITH AIDS WHO HAS A BLEEDING CUT?

There is no reason to believe that AIDS could be spread this way. Whether a person has AIDS or not, all open, bleeding cuts should be taken care of by observing good health and hygiene practices.

HOW SHOULD EMPLOYEES WITH AIDS BE TREATED?

On a day-to-day basis, treat them normally. You and your employees should learn about AIDS, and when dealing with their problem, use compassion and understanding.

Above all, remember...

AIDS IS HARD TO CATCH.

This information is based upon data from the U.S. Public Health Service. For more information, call your local health department, the Public Health Service Hotline (1-800-342-AIDS) or your local Red Cross Chapter.

Or, if you're interested in an educational program about AIDS for your company, call your local health department or your local Red Cross Chapter.

WE WANT YOU TO KNOW AS MUCH ABOUT AIDS AS WE DO.

✚ American Red Cross

The Advertising Council, using volunteer agencies, creates ads for various charity and service organizations, and the media run the ads when space is available. *Sound Management* magazine, published by the Radio Advertising Bureau, ran this ad for the American Red Cross. The bold handling of the headline, the white space, and the setting off of the subheads with ruled lines make art unnecessary.

dustry jargon often puts "wrists" and "wordsmiths" together under the general heading "creatives." Of course, there are some renaissance people in the business who do it all. And in this computer age, the lines separating ad makers become less distinct. One person can design and write an ad, set the type, click in the art, and send the package to the printer or directly to film or even plate production.

Advertising can originate in the advertising department of the advertiser, in the advertising department of the medium that carries the advertising, or in an advertising agency.

In situations in which numerous deadlines and copy changes take place, as with ads for a large department store, a full advertising department is necessary. An outside agency may not be flexible enough or accessible enough to respond quickly to changing demands. If the advertiser is not big enough to support an advertising department, as with a small, locally owned specialty store, the medium—the newspaper or broadcast station—often will produce the advertising. The fee for such a service may be built into the space or time rates.

National advertisers, of course, use advertising agencies, which not only create the advertising but also place it with the media. Even if a national advertiser has an agency, it may have a department of its own to handle some of the advertising, such as direct mail, and to coordinate the agency's efforts. A number of large national advertisers have established "in-house" agencies to create and place their advertising. An in-house agency is more elaborate and offers more services than an advertising department does.

A big company may employ several agencies to handle separate products or divisions. Procter & Gamble, the nation's biggest advertiser, works with nearly twenty agencies.

Some small, local advertisers use agencies, too. Such advertisers are likely to pay a monthly fee for the agency's services. But typically an agency's compensation comes largely from commissions earned on advertising placed with various media. A medium charges the agency a rate that is 15 percent less than the stated rate for time or space; the agency in turn bills the client the full rate.

The commission system has its critics. There is the temptation for the agency to recommend expensive media simply because, with 15 percent of the cost going to the agency, the agency makes more money. A television commercial designed for repeated network showing brings more revenue to an agency than an ad in a magazine. Ted Morgan, in a *New York Times Magazine* article, imagines the following exchange taking place in an advertising agency:

Account supervisor: "Last year I raised my client's sales by 10 percent. I took

With a revival of interest in fountain pens, Parker joins other high-end makers in stepping up its advertising, in this case suggesting that its pens are "mightier than others." Because "a Parker Pen can cost a considerable sum of money," the company uses an unusual amount of copy in this magazine ad along with photographs of historic treaty signings involving Parker pens. Agency: Lowe Tucker Metcalf. Art director: Dennis D'Amico. Copywriter: David Metcalf.

Kids, a line of toiletry products for children, says in this ad that its shampoo was tested not in a laboratory but a bathtub. In the spirit of the times, the ad also points out that ". . . we're proud to say [our products] . . . don't contain animal ingredients and they aren't tested on animals." Agency: Ketchum, L. A. Art director: Mark Erwin. Copywriter: Sam Avery. Photographer: Dennis Manarchy.

them out of TV and put them into print at a saving of 50 percent in their ad budget."

Agency boss: "That's marvelous. You're fired."[4]

Not all advertising is commissionable. Direct mail, for instance, is not. No outside medium is involved. Some large national advertisers have worked out fee systems with their agencies to replace the commission system for all their advertising.

Some agencies specialize in financial advertising, some in direct-mail advertising, some in recruitment advertising, some in travel advertising, and some in health and medicine. Some specialize in advertising to special markets such as blacks and Hispanics.

To give their clients more variety, to exploit talent not available on the staff, and to break a logjam of work, advertising agencies often farm out jobs to art and design studios or to freelancers. Much of the collateral material gets done in this way.

Often an art director has to adapt a basic format to a different space. Here is the single-page version of the Kids ad.

Agencies face much shifting of clients, as clients become restless and dissatisfied with how business is going. To name one client: Gallo, the winemaker, went through thirty agencies in thirty years.

Often an agency executive leaves to start a new agency, and some clients may go along. Sometimes an agency resigns an account because it is no longer profitable or because the agency finds the client's people hard to work with. Agencies develop personalities. Some become known as "creative shops." Others are known for the solid research that goes into their campaigns. By studying looks and content, people in the business often are able to tell which agency created an ad.

The images agencies develop for themselves—images that are amplified in agency-sponsored ads in the advertising trade press that ask for more business—are not necessarily deserved. And an agency known for its creativity might also be strong in research and marketing strategy.

Some agencies specialize. Franklin Spier and Sussman & Sugar are two agencies that create advertising exclusively for book publishers. Some general agencies handle book-publisher accounts, although such accounts are considered more prestigious than profitable, and some publishers have in-house agencies.

Agency mergers and acquisitions dominated advertising news in the 1980s, and the people of advertising—the creative geniuses—seemed less important than in the past. Pricing and discounts in the industry became more important than advertising. "The introduction of the new models of the great brand-name cars was once one of the rituals of fall, like the World Series, trumpeted with spreads in the newspapers, color extravaganzas in the magazines, specials on television," wrote Martin Mayer in *Whatever Happened to Madison Avenue,* his 1991 follow-

The first page (not shown) of this three-page ad directed to retailers says, "There's a Limit to What Today's Parents Will Spend on Their Children." The copy ends on this note: ". . . there may be a limit to how much consumers spend, but with Kids there's really no limit to how much of it you'll get." Agency: Ketchum, L. A. Art director: Mark Erwin. Copywriter: Sam Avery. Photographer: Gary McGuire.

up to his bestselling *Madison Avenue U.S.A.,* published in 1958. "Now the cars come off the assembly lines with rebates attached."[5]

Mergers, when they perpetuate all the names involved, result in cumbersome logos and convoluted phone answerings. No wonder many of the agencies go to initials. Some agencies start out with cute if not memorable names: Advertising Au Gratin, Midnight Oil & Ink, Great Scott Advertising, Designed Marketing. A Los Angeles agency took its name from its phone number: 213–827–9695 & Associates.

The 1990s saw a trend that brought the marketing and advertising processes together. Young & Rubicam developed an "integrated marketing" system for its clients to coordinate all aspects of marketing, including advertising. The agency called its program "The Whole Egg."

Media of Advertising

To reach their audiences, advertisers use a wide variety of media: newspapers (still the number-one medium in dollars spent), television, radio, magazines, outdoor and transportation posters, point-of-purchase materials (displays where customers do their buying), direct mail (leaflets, folders, booklets, brochures, and so on), and short films for showing in theaters. The package the product comes in is a form of advertising. When displayed, the product itself also is a form of advertising.

Advertisers write their names in smoke in the sky, sew them onto shirt and pants pockets and on the fronts or sides of swimming suits, and spell them out in giant letters on the backs of pickup trucks and on tires.

The Goodyear blimp continues to do a job for a tire-maker in America. And National Aerial Advertising offers advertisers the "world's largest flying billboards" for showing over athletic stadiums and wherever else masses of people are gathered. The latter firm offers "picture-perfect computer graphics" as well as "custom-painted bi-planes."

The computer itself has become a medium for advertisers. Sandoz Pharmaceuticals Corp., East Hanover, N.J., sends its salespeople out with laptops and a disk to sell physicians on Triminic Nite Light, a pediatric cough and cold treatment. The sales program provides for a "hot key" that can be punched to allow the salesperson or physician to go to any part of the four-minute presentation to find answers to specific questions. "Physicians are engaged by the computer and

We Let Earthy Instincts Run Wild.

Masland

therefore give it more attention than they give a brochure," says Vince Ippolito, product manager.[6]

The reverse side of grocery-store cash register receipts provide another medium for advertisers. Register Tape Advertising, Inc., puts together the rolls of small ads and coupons sponsored by restaurants, video rental stores, car-lube establishments, and other businesses.

For a couple of decades, the lowly T-shirt and other items of clothing have appeared to be America's most popular advertising medium. "Millions of young Americans—who love to parade as antibusiness snobs—are doing their parading dressed in Budweiser hats, Warner Bros. T-shirts, Olympia beer bikinis—and even *Jaws* underwear," observed an amused *Forbes* magazine back when all this got started. Some companies are in it for the money, but only some. Product makers like Coca-Cola and the cigarette companies just try to break even; the profit comes indirectly through all the free advertising they get from the walking, talking billboards.

The cardboard sun shields for automobile windshields that began appearing on the American market in the mid-1980s provide still another medium for advertisers. Auto Shade Inc., Van Nuys, California, manufactures the sun shields with business logos. The businesses give them away as promotions.

Advertisers, unless restricted by law, place their messages anywhere they find blank space or an intermission in time. The best advertising may be the showing of a product in the course of a regular movie or TV program. The showing often is neither innocent nor accidental; it is planned. It is planned by organizations—"product placers"—like Associated Film Promotions.

Fees paid by clients, who are guaranteed a certain number of showings, are said to be close to what regular commercials would cost, if you consider the audiences. Product placers succeed because they are readily available to film directors to supply whatever props might be needed. The organizations often see scripts before filming begins and look for ways to work in their products. It used to be that Hollywood hid brands or insisted on generic labels, but modern audiences apparently want more realism. It was inevitable that deals would be made.

"We Let Earthy Instincts Run Wild," says Masland Carpet in a two-page ad in *Architectural Digest,* and demonstrates the concepts with a stampede across an earth-colors landscape. The in-and-out-of-the-picture device, made possible with the aid of a computer, along with the several short columns of body copy, set in italics, give this ad an unusual design flavor. The two carpet swatches are enough to tell the reader it's carpet, not animal life, that's behind the ad.

Some media exist solely to serve narrow or specialized audiences. For instance, many radio stations and newspapers, and about twenty magazines serve specifically the black population in this country. Another group of media serves the Spanish-speaking population. It is hard to think of any group that doesn't have its own media.

Agencies develop media mixes for their clients to reach the greatest number of prospects at the lowest cost; but sometimes concentrating on one medium gives the advertiser the best results for the money spent. Media tend to build specific audiences, and such audiences can be particularly responsive to the appeal of particular products. Some companies believe that, as a general rule, 80 percent of their output is consumed by 20 percent of their customers.[7]

The Audience for Advertising

Advertisers generally recognize the young—and especially young couples—as the people most responsive to advertising. Most magazines try to build their circulation among these groups. Newspapers, realizing that they are dealing with a generation raised on TV, do all they can to include features that will appeal to young buyers.

Probably no group in history has been so targeted by advertising people as the baby boomers born during and after World War II. "Boomers have been in the cross hairs of every scheming advertising genius to come along since we were old enough to badger our parents," says one of them, Joe Urschel, a columnist for *USA Today.*

The 1990s saw many advertisers moving over to another group which held out promise as big spenders: aging yuppies, or "grumpies," as some are calling them. (Grown-up mature professionals.) Products directed to this group included jeans with wider seats, girdles with frills, and bifocals without telltale lines in the lenses. RJR Nabisco introduced miniature Oreo cookies to remind baby boomers of their childhood and tempt them without expanding their waistlines.[8]

Even the elderly, with their leisure time and retirement incomes, looked attractive to many advertisers.

Looking for bargains became fashionable in the 1990s, and bragging about finding bargains replaced showing off designer labels. Advertising stressed durability and value.

And yet, emotion rather than logic continued to underlie most advertising messages. The visual in advertising took on added importance. J. Craig Ma-

Michelin tires picks a compelling theme—safety of youngsters—for its advertising campaign. The copy admits that the tires cost more than others to buy but says "you may find, as many Michelin buyers do, they end up costing less to own." Agency: DDB Needham Worldwide. Art director: Jack Mariucci. Copywriter: Barry Greenspun. Photographer: Henry Sandbank.

thiesen, president of Ketchum Advertising, Los Angeles, uses the term "Unique Image Position" to describe what advertising these days tries to establish. It's UIP now instead of USP (Unique Selling Proposition).[9]

Advertisers don't like to call the public's attention to their targeting activities. The leak to the press about its plan to advertise Dakota cigarettes to uneducated young females proved embarrassing to R&R Nabisco in 1990. Earlier it had dropped plans to market Uptown cigarettes to blacks. The entire industry faced new threats to limit its advertising; not many people believed the industry's claim that rather than trying to get young people to start smoking, it was simply trying to get confirmed smokers to switch brands.

Advertising's Job

The trade paper *New Product News* reports a constant stream of new products in supermarkets and drug stores. In the early 1990s, the typical supermarket exhibited some 30,000 products on its shelves. A cosmetic center in the Washington, D.C., area carried 1,500 kinds and sizes of hair care products. "Taken individually, most choices are manageable and, for some sectors of the population, a pleasure," observes Steven Waldman, a writer for *The New Republic*. "Stereo buffs love being able to select the finest woofers. But spend the optimal amount of time on each decision and pretty soon you run out of life."[10]

Advertising to the rescue.

All the advertising textbooks tell us that an ad has several jobs to do:

- *Attract attention to itself.*
- *Enlist reader interest.*
- *Create desire—or capitalize on existing desire—for the product or service being advertised.*
- *Persuade readers to buy the products or services or accept the ideas being advanced.*
- *Show readers how and where they can buy the products or services or direct readers to specific courses of action.*

Art and headline combine to attract attention to an ad. The headline generally states the ad's theme. Readers taking in only these two parts of the ad can at least get the gist of the message. If the art and headline combine to do their job properly, they also lure readers into the copy.

The lead sentence provides a bridge between the headline and the remainder of the copy. If the bridge spans too wide a gulf, the ad may need a second "deck" or "bank"—a headline between the main headline and the copy block.

The bulk of the copy elaborates on the promise of the theme and works to prove its case. In some cases the copy uses logic or rationalization. A good example of the latter is a slogan of used-car dealers: "Everybody drives a used car." That is pretty hard to refute.

The ending calls for action of some sort. In mail-order advertising, the ending often includes a coupon, to make the action as effortless as possible.

The call for action in an ad should be clear, but it need not be direct. Erwin Wasey, Ruthrauff and Ryan came up with an ad for Cheese of Holland showing a photograph of a cut-into ball of Edam cheese. The copy read:

Pâté costs more than liverwurst.
Bisque costs more than soup.
Stroganoff costs more than stew.
This cheese costs more than other Edam.
Life is short.

Complaints Against Advertising

The complaints against advertising center not only on its manipulative powers but also on its tendency to build and perpetuate stereotypes. Every kind of pressure group seems concerned about its image as presented in the ads. Some of the

MICHELIN ANNOUNCES ANOTHER SMALL ADVERTISING CAMPAIGN.

This year over 150 million potential tire buyers will see more small ideas from Michelin; a new package of "Baby" commercials that capitalizes on the tremendous success of last year's campaign.

Research indicates that the Michelin Babies really talk to consumers. And have become synonymous with outstanding performance, mileage, and value.

Of course, we have a better barometer than marketing research: The marketplace.

Last year our Babies brought customers into your stores pre-sold on Michelin quality. Ready to spend a little extra.

This year, expect more of the same. Plus powerful in-store displays that build on the national campaign.

So get ready for a little help from Michelin. Because in advertising it's the little things that count.

MICHELIN. BECAUSE SO MUCH IS RIDING ON YOUR TIRES.

Michelin's advertising to dealers tells of its consumer advertising, using a variation of the child-with-tire art and playing with the word *small*. The copy points to the success of the "Baby" commercials that the year before "brought customers into your stores pre-sold on Michelin quality. . . . This year, expect more of the same. Plus powerful in-store displays that build on the national campaign." Agency: DDB Needham Worldwide. Art director: Jack Mariucci. Copywriter: Mike Rogers. Photographer: Henry Sandbank.

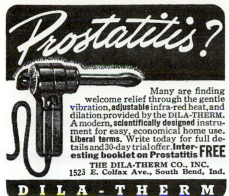

Many early ads, and later ads, too, promised relief from symptoms if not recovery from diseases. An ad from the November 1942 issue of *The Boilermakers Journal* suggested that men with prostate problems could get "welcome relief" with vibrations from the rather formidable device that was pictured.

One of the reasons people criticize advertising is false comparison. If the leather coats are "REG. TO $200.00," why are they now *from* rather than *to* some price? And why do the former prices have zeros after the period while the new prices do not? Whatever happened to parallel construction? Anyway, try to get one of the $200 coats for $79.

demands made by pressure groups brought about changes. Alka-Seltzer found it necessary to withdraw its amusing "Mamma Mia. That'sa Some Spicy Meatball" commercial because of complaints from the Italian Civil Rights League. Pressure from another group forced the "Frito Bandito" animated cartoon character out of his selling job.

When Quaker Oatmeal adopted the comic-strip characters Popeye and Olive Oyl for its advertising and packaging in 1990, it ran into criticism from a Quaker religious organization. Popeye has been a brawler and Olive Oyl has been too submissive a woman. Although the cereal maker had no connection with religious Quakers, it promised to rethink its use of the characters.

Probably the most telling pressure against advertising came from the feminist movement, which did not like the depiction of women as brainless housewives concerned only with the taste of the coffee they served or the power of the laundry detergents they used. Nor did feminists approve of the depiction of women as sex objects.[11]

Feminist activities against advertising ranged from confrontations with the people who prepare advertising (and even revolts within agencies) to the defacing of subway ads with stickers saying "This ad insults women." Women Against Pornography gave a "Plastic Pig" award to Maidenform in 1982 for an ad that put a woman clad in lingerie into the role of a doctor checking a patient's pulse. The company later changed its advertising approach, putting its necessarily scantily clad women in more appropriate settings.

Reflecting new attitudes about the sexes, ad agencies began showing women in previously unfamiliar roles. Barbara Lippert in *Adweek* traces the change to 1973 when Charlie fragrance began showing in its ads a "confident young model in a pantsuit, striding resolutely alone."[12] Later, women in commercials for other products began performing daring deeds previously assigned only to men.

This kind of advertising had two advantages. It met—or at least it appeared to meet—objections that had been raised about sexist advertising. And it often carried an element of surprise. A race car driver removed a helmet and with a shake of the head allowed flowing curls to fall into place. Surprisingly, it was a *woman* who was driving.

Often this early advertising was able to establish the fact that the woman in a "male" role could still maintain her identity as a woman. In a Pepsi commercial, "Sam" was unhappy over the fact that the boys would not let her play ball because she was a girl. Sam's father trained her, and she then showed up the boys (all within the allotted thirty seconds); but when she returned to the bench to her Pepsi reward, she corrected an admiring boy teammate who called her "Sam," telling him that her name was Samantha.

In the 1980s many women appearing in commercials everywhere were older—some in their mid-thirties—and holding down professional rather than menial jobs. No longer did women have to be empty-headed baby-doll types. In fact, there was some worry that the models were so successful, so self-confident that some women viewers would not be able to identify with them.

Meanwhile, helpless bumbling men, along with a few who could qualify as "hunks," overpopulated ads and commercials, causing some critics to conclude that the pendulum had swung too far in the opposite direction. Instead of purely domestic females or females acting out their roles as sex objects, we had men standing by, looking for help, including mechanical help, from women, along with men baring their chests and showing off their rears to sell jeans and underwear. ". . . advertisers have switched bimbos," *Newsweek* reported in 1988. "The woman's movement raised consciousness in the ad business as to how women can be depicted," Fred Danzig, *Advertising Age* editor, observed. "The thought now is, if we can't have women in these old-fashioned traditional roles, at least we can have men being dummies."[13]

When advertising moves into politics, it becomes particularly susceptible to criticism. John O'Toole, chairman of the board at Foote, Cone & Belding Communications, Inc., finds "new depths of distortion and misrepresentation" in TV spots for politicians. He blames the low state of political commercials on "media consultants" called in to produce them. "Political commercials are not like product commercials. If a product commercial lies, the customer may be fooled once but doesn't buy again. But the person fooled by a political commercial has no recourse after buying a candidate."[14]

Some complaints against advertising center on unintended misinformation. Sears Roebuck & Co. had to revise a tire commercial that showed a newborn baby being driven home in its mother's arms instead of in a safety carrier as required by many states.

Other complaints center on what's being sold, not on how it's sold. Nine percent of all magazine advertising involves tobacco products. As America's attitude about smoking changes, criticism of tobacco advertising in all media increases. The American Medical Association thinks tobacco advertising should be banned in the print media as it has been on television.[15]

With cigarette advertising in mind, Martin Mayer says that ". . . advertising people who believe that their work adds value to the brands they advertise must take the next step, and believe also that these values will lure their neighbors— and their neighbors' children—to an addiction that causes sickness and death."[16]

The *Journal of the American Medical Association* in 1991 reported a study that showed children as familiar with Camel cigarettes' "Old Joe" cigarette-smoking cartoon camel as they were with Mickey Mouse. "Old Joe" often appeared in advertising in *Spin,* a rock music magazine, as well as other publications. Critics saw Camel advertising as directly aimed at a young audience. Research showed that the brand held about a third of the pre-teen cigarette market.[17]

The "Old Joe" controversy was enough to prompt Tom Toles, syndicated editorial cartoonist for the Buffalo *News,* to draw a cartoon showing a tobacco executive displaying an ad that showed a little boy, smoking, walking away with a big present from Santa Claus. The "ad" was drawn in a primitive, child's style. Santa was saying "Sorry" to a sad little girl, sitting in his lap, who was *not* smoking. The headline said: "If You Don't Smoke Our Brand, Santa Won't Bring You Any Presents." The executive was saying, "It is *not* aimed at children."

Barbara Lippert in *Ad Week* observed that the face of "Old Joe" looked like a scrotum and wondered why R. J. Reynolds would want that imagery. She criticized all cigarette advertising. "Industry executives still claim that they're not creating smokers, but only getting established smokers to switch brands. In the cases of many older brands, however, they're just trying to replace the smokers who've died."[18]

Criticism sometimes comes from within the family. When the Stroh Brewery in 1991 ran a commercial showing men on a fishing trip drinking beer and saying, as usual, that "It doesn't get any better than this," a Swedish Bikini Team arrives, and, in the words of columnist George Will, "they're not dressed for high tea." Five female employees at the St. Paul brewery sued the company, charging that the commercial encouraged sexual harassment at the workplace. The company's contention that the commercial was a parody did not mollify the litigants.

The Center for Science in the Public Interest on behalf of various consumer groups gives out Harlan Page Hubbard Lemon Awards to advertisers with the most misleading advertising. Volvo drew fire in 1990, for instance, for its commercial showing one of its cars withstanding the weight of a heavy truck running over it. The roof of the car had been reinforced for the commercial. Philip Morris was cited for its Bill of Rights campaign, designed subtlely to defeat government restrictions on tobacco promotion.

The awards were named after Harlan Page Hubbard, the turn-of-the-century promoter of Lydia Pinkham's Vegetable Compound that was advertised as a cure for most diseases, including cancer.

A shocker headline for a full-page institutional ad defending advertising stops readers and then boldly lists the promised lies. After making its points, the ad's copy ends on this note: "And that's the truth." Sponsored by the American Association of Advertising Agencies. Agency: Fallon McElligott.

The Greening of American Advertising

Advertising faces restrictions set up by government agencies, including the Federal Trade Commission, the Food and Drug Administration, the Federal Communications Commission, the U.S. Postal Service, the Securities and Exchange Commission, and the Alcohol and Tax Division of the Internal Revenue Service. It faces additional restrictions from state and local agencies as well as from the media running the ads.

As a protective measure, the industry itself in 1971 set up the National Advertising Review Board (NARB) to apply pressure against agencies and advertisers to get misleading ads out of circulation and off the air. The National Advertising Division (NAD) of the Council of Better Business Bureaus performs a similar function.

Of course, by the time ads change, the damage may be done. The advertiser may have been ready to move on to another theme anyway. Some observers criticize self-regulation as nothing more than window dressing and image building. Still, the activity does show that the industry—at least some segments of it—is concerned about its responsibility to readers, listeners, and viewers.

The most blatant bad practices often come from fringe operators who are more ambitious than sensitive—people who do not have much to lose when they resort to questionable tactics.

On the positive side, to the Advertising Council, in collaboration with advertising agencies, produces free institutional advertising for selected public service organizations.

Advertisers now are quick to reflect societal changes. With fathers sharing more family responsibilities, many of the ads for household products show fathers caring for kids. "Mothers like to see fathers being involved in baby care," explains Glyn Harper, brand manager for Scott Paper Co.[19]

Esprit, a trendy San Francisco-based clothing company, in one of its catalogs, asked its young customers, "If you could change the world, what would you do?" and used answers as part of its later TV and print-media ads.

Benetton, another apparel maker, gained press notice with a campaign that went beyond merely selling merchandise. One ad showed a man dying of AIDS. The company said the ad would warn people about the disease. In earlier ads the company showed a priest and nun kissing, a black man handcuffed to a white man, and a black woman nursing a white baby. An AP writer noted that "The company concedes the ads are designed to improve consumer awareness of the brand but said it wants to raise issues such as ethnic harmony as well."[20]

Some critics saw the Benetton campaign as one to shock rather than to merchandise, and some magazines refused to run the ads.

Many companies make it a point in their advertising to establish themselves as environmentally friendly. In an ad directed to publishers of Yellow Pages directories, Stevens Graphics, Atlanta, Georgia, says that it prints "environmentally friendly directories produced with soy inks, water soluble glues and recycled, uncoated groundwood papers."

Universities, especially, like to pack a number of social and environmental guarantees into advertising, especially direct mail. At the bottom of a direct-mail panel the reader is likely to find a union bug, a recycling insignia, and a line in small type asserting that "The University of _____ is an equal opportunity, affirmative action institution committed to cultural diversity." Another notation may tell the reader that the ink used is soy-based.

A canning company decides not to buy tuna from suppliers who trap dolphins as part of their fishing operations and notes this prominently on its tuna can labels. In its catalogue, Eddie Bauer offers pitch-saturated kindling wood "felled by lightning or other natural causes." The Body Shop sells "natural" cosmetics and offers customers recycled paper bags bearing messages for Amnesty International. Ben & Jerry's puts socially conscious messages on its ice cream cartons.

A demure woman in a TV commercial tells viewers that she has just discovered another reason to use O.B. tampons: There is no applicator to throw away.

One "green" manufacturer and merchandiser, Tom's of Main, uses recyclable packaging carrying printed homey notes from "Your friends, Tom and Kate," who founded the company in 1970. The company takes pride in the fact that its detergent, soap, toothpaste, and other products are biodegradable, that they contain nothing artificial, and that they are not tested on animals.

The Council on Economic Priorities publishes *Shopping for a Better World,* an annual guide for making sound environmental choices among products.

Two subtle ads in a series for Levi's (note the tiny logos at the right edge of each photo) run in music magazines and one women's magazine, *Elle,* in Great Britain. Client: Levi Strauss. Agency: Bartle Bogle Hegarty. Art director: Rooney Carruthers. Copywriter: Larry Barker. Photographer: Elliot Erwitt.

The Designer's Role

Everyone from the person in charge of a church bulletin to the head of a large corporation has tried doing layouts, and sometimes such layouts work well enough. But in most cases a layout needs the touch of someone with an art or design background. The people who do layouts professionally carry various titles.

Layout artist is a beginning title. Traditionally, a layout artist:

- *Sketched clearly enough for the client to see, before the ad appeared in print, what kind of illustrations would be used.*
- *Lettered well enough that the printer could tell, just by looking at the rough, what size and what style of type to set for the ad.*
- *Understood enough about the principles of design to produce an attractive arrangement of what often were inflexible elements in an assigned space.*
- *Knew enough about printing, platemaking, and typesetting to get the best possible effects with the least cost.*
- *Did some thinking as well as arranging.*
- *Shared the client's interest in selling.*

Today, much of what the layout artist does involves the computer, which speeds up the process and makes the work more polished and flexible.

FAITHFUL TILL THE END.

A proficient layout artist who takes on more elaborate and long-term projects becomes a *graphic designer* (or just plain *designer*). A designer does much more than arrange elements and render them. A designer often plans the ads, chooses typefaces, and conceives the art and arranges for its execution. Eventually the designer becomes an *art director*.

The terms cause confusion. "For years," said designer Saul Bass, "[my mother] wondered what I do; that is, what I *really* do. She knew I did art work—and actually she was very happy about it despite some vagueness that surrounded the matter. Her only concern was that I should make a living, and I seemed to be doing all right. But finally her curiosity overcame her timidity, and, I think with some prompting from the neighbors, she finally asked me what it was that I *really* did."

He continued: "I pulled out a proof of an ad that I had designed and I showed it to her and said, 'Mom, that's what I do.' She looked at this and said, 'Oh, I see . . .' and she pointed to a photograph in the ad and said, '*That's* what you do?' I said, 'Oh, no, you see, there are photographers—they are specialists—they know all about cameras and things of this kind, and they make the photographs.'

" 'Oh,' she said, disappointed, 'Then *this* is what you do?' I said, 'No, that's typography. You see there are special organizations who do nothing but set type— you know, Garamond, Caslon, etc. . . . these people do that.' Again she was a little disappointed. She pointed to the lettering and we went through this again. Finally she looked at me somewhat concerned, and said, 'Well, now, what do *you* do?' I said, 'Well, you see, I conceive the whole thing, and then I get all these people together and get them to carry out the process.' She looked at me very coyly, and said, 'Oh—you devil!' "[21]

Marc Trieb, professor of architecture at the University of California at Berkeley and a designer, has another way of describing the designer's job. "Once, when pressed to explain to a somewhat uninformed and bewildered client what exactly

There are people more famous we insure.
But none more important.

In this country, there are 7.7 million women who are sole heads of household. Their need for life insurance has always been obvious.

Of course, there are also millions of married working women who are joint heads of household. It's only been in recent years that the economic value of the housewife or the working mother has even been talked about.

The Travelers and its independent agents, though, have not been Jane-come-latelies in life insurance for women. As evidenced by the fact we were one of the first major companies to offer lower life insurance rates for women.

To get in touch with an independent Travelers agent, check your local Yellow Pages. They are there to help you; whether or not you even need insurance.

Women don't need any more help from insurance companies than men. Just the same help.

THE TRAVELERS

We offer life, health, auto, and homeowners insurance, and mutual funds and variable annuities for individuals, and virtually all forms of insurance for businesses. The Travelers Insurance Company, The Travelers Indemnity Company, Travelers Equities Sales Inc., and other Affiliated Companies of The Travelers Corporation, Hartford, Connecticut 06115.

This ad was designed to appeal to women who are heads of households. It appeared in *Black Enterprise*. The only color (red) appeared as the working part of the umbrella, a symbol of protection promoted by the Travelers Insurance Company. Agency: Ally & Gargano, New York. Art director: Mike Tesch. Copywriter: Tom Messner.

graphic designers do . . . , I offered that designers left out most of what non-designers left in and lined up what was left."[22]

What a designer or art director does *is* hard to pin down, not only for lay people, but also for the people in advertising.

An art director in one agency may be mostly an executive, in another agency more a performer. If an executive, the art director supervises the work of assistant art directors, layout artists, pasteup artists, illustrators, photographers, lettering artists, typographers, platemakers, and printers. Some art directors are able to do finished work themselves—illustrations, lettering, pasteups. Other art directors don't even do rough layouts.

Some art directors become *creative directors,* in charge of both art directing and copywriting.

Jerry Fields, head of a placement agency in communications, has commented on "the increasing stature art directors have achieved in the eyes of management in the past several years." He said: "Being an art director is no longer a roadblock to the top job of agencies."[23]

For its Bicep herbicide for corn fields, Ciba-Geigy Corporation, Greensboro, North Carolina, sponsors a two-page, full-color ad in *Farm Futures,* a farm business magazine. The design works on the principle that less is more. Art director Steve Stone uses a familiar symbol for frustration—a broken pencil—but allows a more-than-generous amount of white space to isolate it. That the copy block is confined to a corner box adds to the impact. A box unites the two pages. With the understated color, the reader is aware only of the yellow in the pencil and in the area behind the headline and the green in the label. Agency: Ketchum Advertising. Art director: Steve Stone. Copywriter: Galen Wright.

"The same drive for control and autonomy that takes an art director from sketchman to creative director ultimately takes him to agency ownership," said Peter Adler, a partner in the Adler, Schwartz agency, Englewood Cliffs, New Jersey. "For me, it was never enough to be given a sheet of manuscript copy and a tentative layout. I had to be part of the creative process from its inception."[24]

Art directors who became agency chiefs include George Lois of Lois Pitts Gershon; Tony Cappiello of Ries Cappiello Colwell; Bob Dolobowsky of Warren, Muller, Dolobowsky; Gene Federico of Lord, Geller, Federico, Einstein; Sam Scali of Scali, McCabe, Sloves; Arnold Arlow of Martin Landey, Arlow Advertising; and Ralph Ammirati of Ammirati & Puris. "A great agency can't be ruled by businessmen alone," says Lois, who has run several different agencies.

To simplify things, this book will refer to the person doing layouts as a *designer.* The term will remind readers that layout at its best is not just arranged; it is designed.

The designer may work for the advertiser (the manufacturer, wholesaler, retailer, service organization) if the advertiser has a large enough operation to merit an advertising department; for a medium (newspaper, magazine, television station, network, outdoor plant) doing work for smaller advertisers who do not have their own staffs or agencies; for an advertising agency; for an art or design studio; for a "creative" printer who does a job for small advertisers similar to what an agency does. Or the designer may freelance.

Nobody cares whether the designer is male or female, and that has almost always been true. In the field of design, women have not faced the discrimination they have faced in many other fields.

Style in Advertising

To some, advertising is largely a matter of style.

Designer Dugald Stermer says, "Preceded by 'in,' style becomes a near synonym for fashion; in other contexts, it is a word meaning *method, approach* or *personality,* as in describing the way a musician plays, a football player runs, or a designer uses type. In its best, if most illusory, sense, it has no synonym that I know of, nor is it easy to define with any precision."[25]

Designer Steve Heller calls style "a personal imprint, a cultural metaphor and a conventional and effective means of communicating. . . . Style is degraded when used to subvert or bypass the product it is required to serve." He adds that when style becomes an end in itself it is "simply a candy coating, a waste of energy and perhaps immoral as well."[26]

"Too many writers, art directors, even entire agencies, try to get a certain style to their work. It's a big turn-on for them—and a big turn-off for the people they want to reach," says Lois Korey, creative director for Needham Harper & Steers Advertising. "I don't think you can let style get in the way of the message. . . .

The best . . . advertising . . . seems to the reader to have no style; it's simply an intelligent, believable presentation of the facts."[27]

"Beauty and style are qualities I count as secondary," adds Helmut Krone, a member of the Art Directors Hall of Fame. "If they are in the work, they come

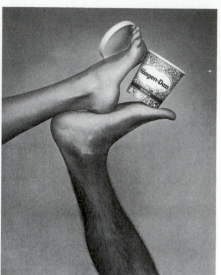

Evocative photography and imaginative typography make a series of black and gold ads for Häagen-Dazs ice cream stand out in weekend newspaper supplements and leisure publications in Great Britain. Agency: Bartle Bogle Hegarty, London. Art director: Rooney Carruthers. Copywriter: Larry Barker. Photographer: Barry Lategan.

along for the ride. The only quality I really appreciate is *newness,* to see something no one has ever seen before. . . ."

Krone sees an ad page as a package for the product. It should look like the product. "Every company, every product needs its own package."[28]

The style of a layout distinguishes it from other layouts. Style may be formal or informal. It may be traditional or modern. Style preferences change, but any style can be resurrected and, if it fits the mood of an ad, used to good effect by a competent designer.

An understanding of style in layout and a highly developed sense of taste more naturally come from art training than from journalism and business training. For this reason, art students enter into a course dealing with advertising design with considerably more poise and self-assurance than students from other disciplines. In addition, they already have some familiarity with the tools necessary to do the job.

But a layout is not an end in itself. It is a plan. The plan takes into account the nature of elements in the ad and how they can best be reproduced. It is the student from the journalism department, with training in production and an understanding of the media, who comes on strong in this area. Also, that student brings to the job of layout a deeper appreciation of the relationship of layout to the ad's copy.

Then there is the business or marketing major, who usually understands better than the art or journalism student the psychology of selling, and who sees the relationship of the ad to what the advertising textbooks call the "marketing mix."

Each of these students brings to a course in advertising design peculiar abilities and interests. Each can contribute to class discussion. Each can benefit from class exchange, from the instructor's comments and criticism—and, if the author has done what he set out to do, from a study of this book.

Sometimes, as a result of taking courses in advertising design, students reorder their college programs. If the students are from outside the journalism school or department, if that is where the courses are being offered, they decide to take additional journalism courses, especially in writing and production. Journalism or business students taking the course may discover in themselves art and design talent they did not know they had. A few in this latter category may consider transferring to an art school or going to one upon graduation.

Designer John Sayles of Sayles Graphic Design, Inc., Des Moines, Iowa, develops a design style incorporating aspects of Art Deco, high tech, and repeating pattern, centering everything but a slogan reversed in a tilted box, to make a small-space ad stand out. The design of the ad is partially inspired by the logo, shown in the top center. Sponsored by the Merle Hay Mall, a shopping center, the ad uses abstract art that suggests buildings and a shopping bag or purse. The ad ran in *Shopping Centers Today* to interest stores in locating at the mall. Art director: John Sayles. Copywriter: Mary Langen-Goldstein.

CHAPTER

2

THE CREATIVE PROCESS

"**B**reakthrough creative" describes an ad or commercial that is especially innovative or daring. Some agencies build their reputations on this kind of advertising. Hal Riney & Partners, with its widely admired Bartles & James wine cooler advertising, among other campaigns, has been one of them. "Hal Riney's patent mixture of small-town realism and shrewdly soft wit are redefining a business known previously for its hard-sell tactics and its obsession with market research," a writer for *The New York Times Magazine* noted in 1986.[1] Hal Riney: the man whose advertising, some say, put Ronald Reagan in the White House.

But "First and foremost, advertising is a business," observes Steven C. Kopcha, chief creative officer of D'Arcy Masius Benton & Bowes. "And when we talk about creativity, what we really mean is applied creativity. An ad has to cause something to happen in the market place—stimulate interest in a product, influence attitudes, make people buy."

"An advertisement can't just entertain. That's what novelists and tap dancers are for."[2]

In his *Advertising Realities,* Wes Perrin tells how creativity helped a German chain saw manufacturer, Sachs-Dolmar, line up dealers in a trade magazine ad. The ad pretended to include a coupon, but actually the ad was preprinted with a die-cut to eliminate the coupon. With "editorial matter" printed on the reverse side, the ad, on regular stock, was then bound into the magazine. Readers thought someone had gotten to the magazine before they did, and stormed the advertiser with questions and requests. "The several hundred leads obtained became the basis for setting up the client's U.S. Dealer network."[3]

Steven Penchina, executive creative director of Ketchum Advertising, says "We've been preoccupied with how [advertising] looks rather than what it says. We've substituted technique for concept, production values for ideas, implicitness for explicitness, glitzy camera angles and quick cuts for innovative thinking." As a result, he says, advertising all looks the same.

"We need to come to the realization that execution is not a substitute for a powerful idea." Penchina asks where the advertising is today to match the advertising of the 1960s and 1970s produced by agencies like Carl Ally, Inc.; Doyle Dane Bernbach; Wells, Rich, Green; Tinker; Scalli, McCabe; Needham; and Leo Burnett. These agencies "had the ability to come up with intrusive, innovative, provocative and memorable ideas that were so powerful you couldn't forget them, even if you tried. . . . And they created warm, human, emotional campaigns that seemed to last forever." He mentions, among others, the campaigns sponsored by Volkswagen, Avis, Braniff, and IBM.[4]

Creativity: What It Is

In an interview in 1991, David Ogilvy, the advertising genius who years ago created classic campaigns for Hathaway shirts and Rolls Royce in *The New Yorker,* said, "Each advertisement I have written has only had . . . one purpose: to sell the product."

"Today, the people who are paid to write advertising are not interested in selling. They consider advertising an art form. And they talk about creativity all the time."

"I'm supposed to be the world's most creative advertising man; I don't even know what creativity is."[5]

"I really don't know how I come up with anything," designer Milton Glaser admits. "It's all muck in the back of your mind and you just wait for some of it to leak out. The best things you ever do are not susceptible to very much analysis."[6]

Like humor, creativity does not lend itself to dissection. Too much analysis of creativity by the creative person could dry up the source of new ideas. As Franz Schoenberner observed in *Confessions of a European Intellectual:* "The centipede, when asked with which foot he started to walk, became paralyzed." Hilaire Belloc made a similar observation about the water beetle: If it stopped to think, it would sink.

Adman John S. Straiton tried to define creativity by telling what creativity is not. It is not showing off to other ad people, he observed. It is not amateurism. It is not "beads and beards." It is not being funny. It is not being "with it." "When someone else is dancing, the best way to be noticed is to stand still."[7]

"As far as I'm concerned, . . . [the] heart [of creativity] is *discipline,*" said the late William Bernbach of Doyle Dane Bernbach. The discipline, as Bernbach saw it, breaks down into four activities:

■ *Discipline to find the product's advantage.*
■ *Discipline to produce an ad that is sophisticated and aesthetic.* "It's true that there's a twelve-year-old mentality in America," said Bernbach. "Every six-year-old has it."
■ *Discipline to manage.* It takes a creative person to encourage and guide other creative people and provide them with the right information. It takes creativity to be a good editor.
■ *Discipline to develop social awareness and to be responsible to the public.*[8]

Advertising Age made a similar observation in an editorial. "The essence of creativity, we submit, is working within a discipline. It's making those walls your canvas, not your cell. Advertising folks know this well. Working within the con-

A spectacular photograph by Vic Huber along with sensitive headline placement by art director John Shirley make this a memorable Acura ad. Rob Siltanen and Harold Einstein wrote the subtle copy. Agency: Ketchum, Los Angeles.

LAST YEAR, TAXPAYERS
SPENT OVER 7 BILLION ON
ROAD CONSTRUCTION.
GET YOUR MONEY'S WORTH.

Conservative estimates say that there are over two million miles of paved roads in America. In other words, over two million reasons to start thinking about the responsive 1.8-liter, four-valve-per-cylinder engine, 4-wheel double-wishbone suspension, Anti-Lock Braking System and power sunroof on the 1991 Integra GS. Which brings to mind another thought. You paid for the road. Why not enjoy it?

ACURA
PRECISION CRAFTED PERFORMANCE

The photographic art for this ad in *Restaurants & Institutions* forms a colorful and inviting frame for the headline and copy. Courtesy of Hidden Valley Ranch® Salad Dressings—FSPC, The Clorox Company. Agency: Anderson/Rothstein, Inc., San Francisco.

fines of a dull product, a duller marketing plan and a tough market, yet developing a winning ad campaign—now *that's* creative."[9]

Shirley Polykoff, president of the agency bearing her name, said, "Creativity has always been just a knack or talent for expressing a single idea or simple concept in a fresh, arresting new way—what I call 'thinking it out square,' then saying it with flair."[10]

Edward A. McCabe, copy director at Scali, McCabe, Sloves, New York, agreed that simplicity is the key. You should put your propositions forward "with such utter simplicity that people are both astonished and moved. . . ."[11]

"What I think of as creativity is an intensity of awareness of the world around you, a heightened state of consciousness, a sense of being at one with the order of things," said Rollo May, author of *The Courage to Create.*[12]

"The only truly creative being is God," observed Lois Ernst, creative director of Advertising to Women, New York. ". . . God, they say, created the world out of nothing." Mere mortals always start with *something.* Creativity as we know it, then, is "the ability to put two common things together that have never been paired before, forming a third thing by which the fusion becomes an original."[13]

Humor writer John Cleese sees creative activity taking two phases: an open and then a closed phase. In the open phase, which comes first, the creative person plays with ideas without thinking about a goal. The creative person is relaxed, expansive, and contemplative. In the closed mode, the creative person, becoming more determined, focuses on the problem.

Cleese says that the open phase is less accessible to most people. To operate in this phase, the creative person should get away from everyday distractions, allow plenty of time to try to answer "what if?" questions, be willing to make mistakes, and develop a sense of humor.[14]

Creative People: Who They Are

To John Carambat, who teaches graphic design at Louisiana State University, "It appears that talent and creativity are . . . two different things. Certainly talent and technical proficiency are required to produce great work, yet many talented people have produced facile, technically proficient pieces that were uninspired and soon forgotten." Carambat speaks of a "creative personality" and cites a number of traits belonging to creative people, traits outlined by Dr. Emanuel Hammer in his book, *Creativity, Talent and Personality* (Robert E. Krieger Publishing Co., Malabar, Florida, 1984). Among the traits are depth of feeling, instinct, detachment, and rebelliousness.[15]

Tracy Wong wrote and designed a series of ads, each showing a food product with a Surgeon General's warning and a headline, in small type, asking "Would You Still Eat It?" or ". . . Eat Them?" or ". . . Drink It?" A quiet, effective campaign for the New York Lung Association. Agency: Goldsmith/Jeffrey.

Angular surfaces in the desk, part of the Renz Collection, call for angular placement of the body type, reversed on a dark surface in this striking full-color, full-page ad for Davis Furniture Industries, Incorporated, High Point, North Carolina. The vertical row of squares picks up the African mahogany color of the desk. The ad appeared in *Interior Design Markets* magazine. "Circle 56," in small type reversed below the signature, refers to a card in the back of the magazine where readers can pick numbers to get further information about products advertised. This is part of a trade magazine's merchandising program.

Creative people are less likely than others to repress their impulses. They are less interested than others in what people think of them (so they are freer to be creative). They are not conformists, but they are not nonconformists, either. Rather, they are "independent." There are extroverts among creative people, but the tendency is toward introversion.

Creative people in advertising tend to dress casually in contrast to the people who manage the agencies, work with the clients, or perform other services.

Psychologist Kay Jamison, when doing research at UCLA, saw a link between creativity and manic-depression. In a study she conducted of British artists and writers, she found that mood disorders occurred six times more frequently among creative people than among ordinary citizens. She thinks that her study shows "pretty convincingly that there can be some very positive aspects to mood disorders, and the major one is creativity."[16]

Studying creative writers enrolled at the University of Iowa Writers' Workshop, psychiatrist Nancy Andreasen found that 80 percent had suffered some depression or mania in their lifetimes. *U.S. News & World Report,* noting her study, said, "It is possible, suggests Andreasen, that the sensitivity, openness, adventuresome nature and independent character of creative individuals in some way makes them more vulnerable to mental illness, in particular mood disorders."[17]

But Dr. Albert Rothenberg, in his *Creativity and Madness* (Johns Hopkins University Press, Baltimore, 1990), decides that creativity is a perfectly normal activity.

Creative people are not likely to be stimulated to creativity through psychological self-help books or movements. "Creativity does not emerge from a state of relaxation," said Rollo May, "but from a state of chaos. . . ."[18]

Creative people have a wide range of information on hand. This is important, for creative people essentially engage in arranging items of information into combinations. Creative people delight in complexities, and when they find them, they look for unifying principles. The more information creative people have, the more combinations they can come up with.

Designer Ivan Chermayeff saw the creative person in the field of design as "a borrower, co-ordinator, assimilator, juggler, and collector of material, knowledge, and thought from the past and present, from other designers, from technology, and from himself. His style and individuality come from the consistency of his own attitudes and approach to the expression and communication of a problem."[19]

Ron Hoff, creative director for Foote, Cone & Belding, thinks truly creative people have four qualities in common:

- *They are compulsive observers of the human condition.*
- *They enjoy building a case.* Creative people want to sway people. "There is a kind of arrogance in this desire—but it is a vital component if you want to succeed in advertising."
- *They see things differently from the way other people see things.* "Creative people have the common touch, but they express it uncommonly."
- *They want the world to see what they have done.*[20]

Creative people often become restless, looking for new challenges, moving from job to job. Many of today's important agencies were started when an employee left an older agency because it was too conservative in its approach to ad making. William Bernbach left Grey Advertising, he said, to start Doyle Dane Bernbach because Grey "didn't know how to make ads." "There is some evidence that, everything else being equal, if your agency achieves a reputation for high creativity, it will grow faster," said Paul Waddell, director of creative services at Evans Weinberg Advertising, Los Angeles.[21]

People who are creative in one area are usually creative in several. After a successful career as an illustrator, Milton Glaser turned to design—his main interest now. He continues to do illustrations for clients and causes he likes, and his designs often incorporate his own illustrations. He works in many styles. His design interests have expanded to include packages and even grocery store in-

THE CREATIVE PROCESS

teriors, exteriors, and fixtures. Glaser's interest in package design, including food-package design, stems from his interest in gourmet food. He is an accomplished chef and, with the late art director Jerome Snyder (*Scientific American*), authored a book, *The Underground Gourmet,* and a column by the same name for *New York* magazine. The "I Love New York" insignia, with a red heart in place of the word *Love,* now so widely imitated, was a Glaser idea.

After working with photographers, art directors often take up this activity themselves and do very well at it. Henry Wolfe is a case in point. His photography has appeared on magazine covers. Saul Bass went into filmmaking. Donald Spoto in *The Dark Side of Genius* (Little, Brown, 1983), a biography of Alfred Hitchcock, reported that Bass, not Hitchcock, actually directed that famous shower scene in *Psycho.* Bass had done a storyboard of the sequence, and Hitchcock was impressed enough with Bass's work that he let him take over. (Bass was listed in the film credits as a consultant.)[22]

The designer's best work may come early. According to Jerry Fields, the director of a New York placement service quoted in the last chapter, agencies like to hire the young for creative jobs because, among other reasons, "the young art director or copywriter, or for that matter, the young product, account, or ad manager . . . can take the risks involved in turning in new, exciting, innovating work." Also, "If he is shot down by his client or boss, the hell with it. He'll get a job someplace else or maybe hack around Europe for a couple of months before going to work again. But the older man can't afford to take risks with his job security because of all those obligations back in Darien. So he plays it safe and sticks to proven formula stuff that he knows worked in the past and that won't make any waves that might engulf him."[23] But Bob Gage, Doyle Dane Bernbach's first art director, thinks age has little to do with creativity. "If you keep on growing, if you know you haven't learned to do it as well as you'd like, and if you keep searching, if you remain a little unsure of yourself, you won't burn out. On the other hand, if you find a formula and stick to the formula, you can burn yourself out before you're thirty. . . ."[24]

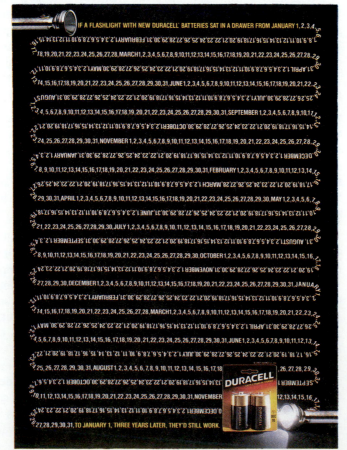

Designer Tracy Wong comes up with a dramatic way of showing how long a flashlight with new Duracell batteries can sit in a drawer (three years) and still work. This is a modern-day version of boustrophedon typography. Agency: Ogilvy & Mather, New York. Copywriter: Steve Baer.

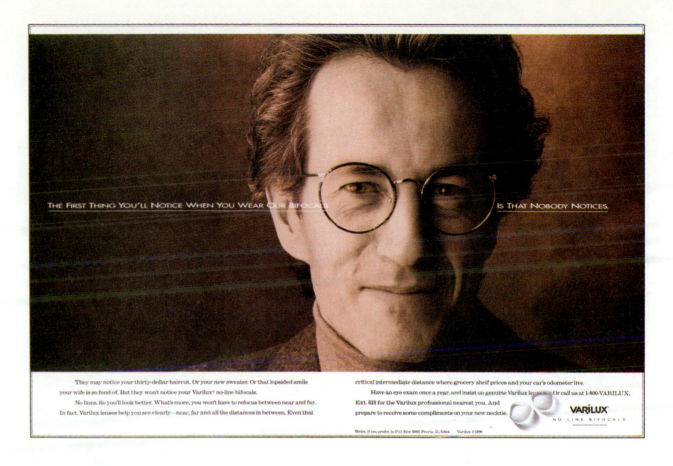

THE FIRST THING YOU'LL NOTICE WHEN YOU WEAR OUR BIFOCALS   IS THAT NOBODY NOTICES.

They may notice your thirty-dollar haircut. Or your new sweater. Or that lopsided smile your wife is so fond of. But they won't notice your Varilux® no-line bifocals.

No lines. So you'll look better. What's more, you won't have to refocus between near and far.

In fact, Varilux lenses help you see clearly—near, far and all the distances in between. Even that critical intermediate distance where grocery shelf prices and your car's odometer live.

Have an eye exam once a year, and insist on genuine Varilux lenses. Or call us at 1-800-VARILUX, Ext. 618 for the Varilux professional nearest you. And prepare to receive some compliments on your new necktie.

Write, if you prefer, to P.O. Box 3900, Peoria, IL 61614. Varilux ©1999

VARILUX
NO-LINE BIFOCALS

A clever turn of phrase and unusual placement of the caps-and-small-caps headline sets this two-page magazine ad apart from other ads selling eye glasses. Client: Varilux No-Line Bifocals. Agency: Foote, Cone & Belding, San Francisco. Art director: Keith Potter. Copywriter: Diane Moe.

The presidents of two West Coast agencies recognized as "creative" had differing ideas on how creative people should be treated. "Do not let creative people near the client," said Dave Bascom of Guild, Bascom & Bonfigli, San Francisco (now part of Dancer Fitzgerald Sample). "Most creative people would be utterly shattered and destroyed if they had to work with the client." The late Ralph Carson of Carson/Roberts, Los Angeles (now part of Ogilvy & Mather International), held a contrary view. "They should be exposed to the problems of the market." Nor did the two agree on where to find creative people. Bascom liked to draw them from the ranks of musicians, writers, and artists who had proved their creativity, and he taught them to apply their talents to the special field of advertising. Carson felt these people were too often loners; hence they were out of place in an agency where people have to work together.

But Yousuf Karsh, the portrait photographer, thinks that "The loneliness of great men is part of their ability to create. Character, like a photograph, develops in darkness."[25]

In summary:

As a creative person, you do not readily accept rules and restrictions, including rules of design. You see how far you can go with unusual typefaces and untried combinations without hurting readability.

You see patterns where, to the average viewer, no patterns exist, and take advantage of them to better organize the elements you work with.

You find beauty in mundane things. Your role is to present these things from a different vantage point.

You sense a connection between items which, at first glance, seem unconnected, and you come up with an arrangement that connects them.

You are willing to take some chances with the printer and even the client in the interest of coming up with something new. And if accidents occur, you take advantage of them. Perhaps you can improve a piece of art through imaginative cropping or even patching. If necessary, to salvage the art, you may change your design. You remain flexible.

A SNACK SO GOOD, PEOPLE EVEN EAT THE WRAPPER

It's easy to see why people go bananas over apples. A sweet Washington apple is the perfect snack food. No cholesterol. No artificial flavors. No artificial colors. ■ It's hard to find a snack lower in salt. An apple has less sodium than a stalk of celery or a carrot. Less, even, than an eight-ounce glass of ordinary tap water. ■ Unlike snacks made with processed sugar, apples satisfy your sweet tooth naturally. Forget those roller coaster highs and hunger-producing lows. The fruit sugar, or fructose, in apples triggers a slower rise in your blood sugar level. So all that apple energy sticks with you longer to help stave off hunger. ■ The next time you have a snack attack, reach for a healthy helping of Red Delicious, Golden Delicious or Granny Smith apples. ■ Nobody knows how to grow them better, skin and all, than the apple growers of Washington.

THE ORIGINAL HEALTH FOOD

WASHINGTON

Although you work best in isolation, you do not necessarily shun brainstorming sessions with others or even conventions of like-minded designers. You always look for inspiration. You can never see enough good designs, go through enough printed pieces, or experience enough visual delights.

Creative people moving in on a new account often want to put their own mark on the advertising, even though it may be working well already. And the people close to a campaign tend to tire of it long before the public does. John Mack Carter, editor of *Good Housekeeping* and one of the last of the male editors of women's magazines, has said that the advice "If it ain't broken, don't fix it" is not good enough for creative people. He offered this advice instead: "If it ain't broken, break it."

Changing a campaign, just for the sake of change, though, is a luxury creative people cannot afford. The secret of successful advertising often rests with its years of uninterrupted service.

Honoring Creativity

Those who create ads like to get a little recognition, something they are not likely to get from the general public or even from the clients. But they do get credit from fellow ad makers in the form of awards. The awards judges can't very well take into account how well the ads actually work, but they can measure the ads against standards that have grown up in the industry.

Adweek magazine estimates that the average advertising agency each year spends from $30,000 to $50,000 on entry fees to have their ads considered for the various awards. One agency spent $185,000 in a single year.

Which competitions are the best to enter? Agencies face hundreds of them.

An advertising campaign calls for a series of ads based on a single theme and designed in a way to tie the series together visually. Art director Paul Cournoyer shows how an elegant format can be adjusted from ad to ad without losing campaign continuity. Client: Washington Apple Commission. Agency: Cole & Weber, Seattle. Copywriter: Michele McKenna.

Some of the big ones are the Clio, the Ceba, the National Addy, the Advertising Club of New York, the Art Director's Club, Communication Arts, the Athena (for newspaper advertising), the Effie, Stephen E. Kelly (for magazine advertising), the One Show, the Obie (for outdoor advertising), and the International Advertising Film Festival at Cannes. One of the competitions, P.A.W. awards (for "Pets Are Wonderful"), is designed to get advertisers to use pets in a positive manner.[26]

The Clios, set up originally to honor TV commercials, by 1990 had grown to include more than 200 categories. "Awards have become a drug," observes Peter Mackey, a vice president at J. Walter Thompson. "People are addicted to these things. They are less than worthy if they don't have one."[27]

David Ogilvy thinks that awards competitions have badly hurt advertising. Creative people use these competitions to promote themselves. Once at the New York office of his agency, Ogilvy & Mather, he forbad his people to enter the competitions. Instead, he awarded $10,000 each year to the person who created the campaign that most increased a client's sales.

Developing a Style

Shortly after John F. Kennedy was assassinated, John Cogley, writing about style in politics—something Kennedy had—said that style "has something to do with taste, something to do with restraint and control, and something to do, finally, with grace and gallantry." Which is not a bad way for the designer to look at it: Style *is* a matter of taste, restraint, control, grace. (We omit *gallantry* as being peculiar to nonartistic expression.)

Dwight Macdonald, considering style from the standpoint of the writer, observed that "style requires that certain effects be given up because they are incompatible with certain others." This suggests another word to add to the list: consistency. An effective style creates and maintains a single mood. It deals with a single theme.

All of this is applicable to advertising design. A layout has style when the person who does it is a person of taste—when the designer uses restraint in the choice of elements, controlling them for just the effects the client needs. The elements are arranged so that the ad, overall, appears graceful, even when the client is a grocery chain or a discount drugstore. Each element used appears related to other elements in the ad. Nothing in the ad detracts from its theme. Nothing is used that does not advance the theme.

Of course, not every ad has to look like a perfume or quality automobile advertisement in *The New Yorker* magazine. A store with mainly *price* to sell, or variety in merchandise, must crowd its elements into the allotted space; but this can be done without doing violence to style.

Every once in a while you hear reference to a national, regional, or even a city style of graphic design. In the United States, the West is said by some to be more—what?—flamboyant than the East. More willing to take chances. You know how people are in southern California. In the late 1980s, *Time* identified an "identifiable local style" in San Francisco to the north, "sunny but sophisticated, fresh, playful, elegant."[28]

For a time, Japan seemed to many designers to be the hub of sensitive, meaningful design. In the late 1980s, London became the design mecca. Before that, Italy and the Scandinavian countries had set design trends. And who could forget the Swiss look of the 1950s and 1960s, a look still very much alive?

The truth is that any part of the country—and any country—can foster design innovation, especially in an age that offers instant international communication. Great designers, graphic or otherwise, turn up everywhere.

It is also true that New York harbors a disproportionate number of great and innovative designers, and hence, a disproportionate influence on graphic design everywhere. The reason is that the city is the capital of the publishing and broadcasting industries in the United States and the center of the advertising trade. "Madison Avenue" still stands for high-powered advertising and the design that is indigenous to it.

The Changing Face of Style

A few highly talented designers and art directors bring a beauty and excitement to advertising design it would not otherwise have. They dictate taste for a season, then step aside to make room for a younger contingent. So much momentum does each new contingent of tastemakers generate that even the contingent it replaces adopts the new styles and mannerisms. Those who never were in the vanguard follow each trend as if by rote, often late—after the tastemakers themselves, bored by it all, have moved to some new level. Each style in type or art is defended, temporarily, with the same intransigence as the last.

But in recent years the styles have become shorter-lived. Newer ones come on before the old ones can be abandoned. And the styles from earlier eras—from the turn of the century (art nouveau) and pre-World War II days (art deco)—stage their comebacks. Movements in the fine arts, like op and pop art, exert their influence.

Massimo Vignelli, president of Vignelli Associates, a design studio, saw the 1960s as a decade of discipline, with Helvetica type and grids dominating the printed page. The 1970s were a decade of "appropriateness," with more experimentation and with complexity overriding the earlier simplicity. It used to be that "less is more," but in the 1970s it was "less is a bore." The 1980s became a decade "intrigued by the pleasures of ambiguity. The fascinating possibility of conveying several interpretations, even contradictory ones, perfectly expresses the new romance with the significance of meanings, which we are now going through

Howard Paper Mills, Inc., Dayton, Ohio, expresses the right idea here about creativity. Usually it takes many starts and a lot of figuring before an idea forms itself into a great ad. Although many designers use other tools, including the computer, to develop their ideas, the pencil is still king, at least figuratively. What you see here is the front sheet of a two-page ad inserted into a design magazine to show off and sell Howard Text paper stock. Agency: Flynn/Sabatino.

An ad isn't great until you're ....here.

This is Howard Text, White, 70 Lb., Felt Finish.

with renovated passion." Ornament, for years shunned by graphic designers, came back in the 1980s.[29]

A New York *Times* writer says that "If the excesses of the booming 1980s were reflected in advertising that was opulent, slick and expensive, creative people at agencies say, the work they are producing in the constrained 1990s can be described in one word: simple." Logos grow larger and benefits get more play. The writer quotes William J. Vernick, a copywriter at N W Ayer: "Creatives are being forced to think of more creative ways of being less creative."

The argument here is that simple, basic ads best penetrate the clutter of complex ads. Moreover, they cost less to produce.[30]

But now almost every style has its proponents. The look of the 1930s and 1940s exists right next to the look of today. Almost anything goes now, sometimes at the expense of readability. All of this neutralizes to some extent the tyranny of the tastemakers in advertising. It also discourages the laying down of any rules by teachers of graphic design.

Advertising has always been more receptive to design experimentation than to copy experimentation and probably always will be. One reason is that the designer, often unlike the copywriter, works with a comparatively free hand. The designer does not have the problem the copywriter has of dealing with an area in which clients have, or believe they have, some proficiency.

THE CREATIVE PROCESS

Facing the Assignment

At the beginning of an assignment, the designer wrestles with a number of questions.

What is the purpose of the ad: to sell a product or a service or an idea? Does the advertiser want mostly to hold onto present customers or to attract new ones? Is the goal short range or long range? Must the ad do the job alone or will it be only one in a series? What is the theme? The selling points? For what audience is the ad intended? What approaches are most likely to influence this audience? What medium will be used—newspapers? Magazines? Direct mail? What are the limitations and possibilities of this medium? What printing process is involved? What paper stock? What kind of art and type will reproduce best? How much can the client spend on production? Is color available? What size is specified? What format should be used? During what time of year will the ad run? Are some elements—photographs, stock art, logo—already picked for use? Is outside help available to do drawings, take pictures, handle the pre-press activities?

Sometimes the job calls simply for an announcement of the availability of a product and a statement of its price.

At other times the job is more complicated. The designer may be asked to dispel misinformation about the product; give the product a personality that will set it apart from others that really are quite similar; suggest to the public—or publics—additional uses for the product (as Scotch tape often does); or sell non-users—purchasing agents, for instance, or retailers—on the merits of the product. Sometimes the ad means only to impress the board of directors or the stockholders that the company *is* advertising.

The advertising designer who cannot deal with intangible things, with concepts, is likely to find fewer clients in the future. Advertising deals more and more with ideas rather than with products. And there is a narrowing of audiences for ads; a greater awareness by ad people of the merits of individual publications; an insistence by clients that advertising goals be stated and advertising effectiveness be measured. The designer who keeps abreast of developments in these areas obviously is better prepared than other designers to meet the needs of clients.

Professor Ann Keding (Maxwell) of the University of Oregon teaches that an ad should evolve from a "creative blueprint." "Without it, creating advertising would be like building a house without a plan. The blueprint describes the product, targets the audience, mentions the competition, examines problems to be solved, states the ad's objective, outlines the product's features and benefits, positions the product in the minds of the target audience, decides the tone and manner of the ad, and shows just what should be said in the ad."[31]

It is one thing to come up with a great idea—and quite another to follow through on it after it's accepted. Rubin Postaer and Associates, Los Angeles, decided to explore a personality theme for the Honda Civic Hatchback (see nearby art). The art was to show a series of vanity license plates from all over the country. How to go about it?

First, agency people came up with clever names for plates, then checked the names with the Department of Motor Vehicles officers from all 50 states. If any of the names were actually in use, the agency got permission from the owner to use it. In some cases, agency people used more letters for the plates than were actually available in some states.

Then the agency hired a model maker to create the plates from plastic. Graphic artists were hired to duplicate the look of each state's plates. The resultant plates, which, in the words of copywriter Jack Fund, looked "real enough to put on the back of a car and nobody would know," were photographed and put into a dramatic two-page spread. The ad's headline read, "Instead of Trying to Give Your Car a Personality, Maybe You Should Try a Car that Already Comes with One."[32]

The words on the license plates were clever and appropriate to the states, but more importantly, the ad was one that invited reader participation by getting them to try to figure out the puzzles that many of the plates represented. for instance: "BRBDL" for "Barbie Doll" on a California plate, "YOTAXZ" for

Steamer's Seafood Cafe, Santa Cruz, uses offbeat art and copy in an ad designed to draw new patrons. Art director: Rick Tharp of Tharp Did It design studio. Copywriter: Victor Cross. Photographer: Franklin Avery.

An ad for Honda Civic Hatchback stops readers and invites them to figure out a series of vanity license plates. The ad's headline makes the point that "Instead of trying to give your car a personality, maybe you should try a car that already comes with one." The plates look real but aren't. They represent a major research and creative effort by the agency, Rubin Postaer and Associates, Los Angeles. Jack Fund was the copywriter, Larry Postaer the creative director, Keith Weinman the art director.

"Yo! Taxi!" on a New York plate, and "A4-FORT" for " 'A' for Effort" on a Montana plate.

Facing Client Stipulations

What the client wants is maximum attention and response to the ads' invitations. If the ads, however attractive, fail to bring these about, they do not count for much. Sometimes designers, intent on winning top awards at art directors' shows, forget this.

Jay Chiat, cofounder of Chiat/Day advertising agency, feels that halfway through the creative process, the client should come in. "We don't talk about techniques, only about ideas. We [the agency people] don't even try to sell. It's just a matter of telling the client, 'Here's where we stand; here's how we got where we are.' That gets the client involved—and at a point where the client can contribute and also have a sense of *ownership* in the campaign."[33]

Clients—and some advertising people and designers, too—have a great urge to unify all pieces of promotion, as if a single reader were to see all of them and in a single setting. There is some merit in this, of course; if the materials are promoted widely enough, familiarity with the firm and its program will probably be helped along by visual continuity. But the truth must be that much of this tying together of advertising pieces is nothing more than administrative tidiness, bringing great satisfaction to the perpetrators, perhaps, but having little actual effect on the sales curve.

So why, in an ad sponsored by a newspaper to get at media buyers in advertising agencies, should the designer be stuck with the Old English nameplate when the rest of the ad is in a modern typeface? Would a signature in the modern face, in place of a replica of the regular nameplate, hurt the ad's pulling power? The designer will certainly try to convince the client to drop those elements that do not fit the new design. Failing that, the designer can at least minimize them in the design arrangement or update them slightly, retaining recognition while improving the appearance. The designer Raymond Loewy (among his many successes was the orange and blue Union 76 ball) used to talk about MAYA design: the "most advanced yet acceptable" design for a client.

Visualization

In the late nineteenth-century, the few people called "visualizers" who attached themselves to fledgling advertising agencies enjoyed precious little prestige. Account people and copywriters worked up the copy, sketched a rough to show where it should go in the ad, and turned it over to the lowly visualizer, who did some lettering at the top, then carefully traced available stock art in the space left over. Visualizers usually knew a little more about typefaces than anyone in the agency, and they understood production; still, they were not much more than persons who traced things. Certainly they were not designers. The idea of *designing* an ad had not yet occurred to members of the fraternity.

As copywriters became more rushed, visualizers were allowed to sketch out the ads. The visualizers became "layout artists." As the visualizers' work increased, they asked for and got assistants, or they turned for help to freelancers in the area. They became *directors*—directors of art.

Their work took on added importance.

The earliest art directors functioned primarily as buyers, picking out paintings or drawings from submissions by artists, placing them on top of blocks of copy, and deciding on borders to fence off the ads. Appropriately, these directors worked anonymously; when the Art Directors Club of New York held its first exhibition of advertising art in 1921, the catalog named the artists who drew and painted the pictures but made no mention of the people who ordered the work, directed it, and laid out the ad in which it appeared. Not until 1934 did the club decide the director deserved a credit line on award-winning ads in the exhibition. Now, of course, the art director is recognized in the catalogs, right along with the artist or photographer, copywriter, creative director, client, and agency.

Among creative people, anything goes, but a feel for logic is important, too. A number of advertisers, wishing to show how three different qualities work to make their companies or products stand out, have resorted to the symbolism of gears, arranged like these. Many readers would notice that if they are to work, an adjustment in the placing of these gears is desperately needed.

To bring more prestige to the profession, the Art Directors Club of New York in 1971 started a Hall of Fame. Eight people were elected to the Hall of Fame in 1972, and several have been added each year since then. Some are—or were—advertising art directors, some magazine art directors, some both. Among members are M. F. Agha, Alexey Brodovitch, William Golden, Paul Rand, Cipe Pineles (the first woman member), Saul Bass, Herb Lubalin, Lou Dorfsman, Allen Hurlburt, and George Lois.

The best art directors appreciate the importance of copy in advertising, just as the best copy chiefs appreciate the importance of art and layout.

Professor Ann Keding stresses the need for the copywriter and art director to work as a team. "Ideally, teamwork means that each member of the team has as much control over the work as the other. The copywriter and art director work together to form an advertising concept or idea. The art director may articulate the headline just as often as the copywriter. And the copywriter may come up with the idea for the visual. . . ."[34]

One person—the art director or the copy chief—has to have the final say, of course (a coeditorship is never a very effective arrangement in the communications field), but it need not always be the copy chief. Some ads—some campaigns even—are more appropriately directed by art- rather than copy-oriented executives.

A few art directors *literally* write their ads. A memorable Volkswagen Bug ad, "Don't Forget the Anti-freeze!" which was "presented by Volkswagen dealers as a public service to people who don't own cars with air-cooled engines," was both designed and written by a Doyle Dane Bernbach art director, Helmut Krone.

Around the agencies you do not hear the name "visualizer" used anymore. In today's advertising, anyone working on creative aspects is a visualizer. Someone has to "visualize" the ad before it gets sketched out. The process of "visualization" is surely the most important creative phase in advertising.

Sometimes the designer—or whoever does the visualizing—can best express the idea in literal terms. Perhaps a picture of the product will do, or a picture of a satisfied user. At other times, especially when the purpose of the ad is institutional, the designer will want to express the idea symbolically. One of the famous ads of an earlier decade showed a closeup of a baby's hand holding onto the index finger of a man's hand, dramatizing effectively the "implicit faith and confidence" users place in the product featured in the ad, in this case prescription chemicals bearing the Merck label. This is a visualization so natural, so appropriate, that it has, of course, been used many times.

To dramatize the ease and swiftness by which a passenger can get to Europe,

Influenced by the op art movement, the designer of this ad from several years ago used outside edges of letters in *"Life"* for a pattern idea. "Now that we've got your attention . . ." reads the headline (not shown) ". . . Use this Coupon and get 27 weeks of *Life* for . . . ," the copy continues.

TWA showed a map with only a narrow body of water separating America and Europe. The headline said: "TWA Announces the Atlantic River."

In one of its ads, AppleCare, an extended warrantee for Macintosh computer buyers, told readers: "Think of it as an Airbag for Your Macintosh." The art showed a computer partially buried in an airbag.

At the very start—at the visualization stage—the designer wrestles with the problem of putting over a single idea. For consumer product advertising, the idea may dwell on product quality, product uniqueness, package usefulness, product availability, price, or the service that goes with the product. Taking one of these— quality, for instance—the designer considers the various ways to illustrate such a concept. The process at this stage may be all mental; perhaps the designer has not yet picked up a pencil or sat down at the computer.

Choosing art and type styles and arranging elements within the ad follow the process of visualization.

Avoiding an Advertising Look

In *Mainstreams of Modern Art,* John Canaday wrote that "The orderly sequence from one generation of painters to the next has given way to a series of abrupt dislocations to such an extent that, if we have a tradition, it is the contradictory one that each new generation is under some kind of obligation to refute and violate the ideas of the preceding one."[35] The same could be said of each new generation of advertising designers. They look constantly for new ways to break away from prevailing attitudes about how ads should look.

An ad doesn't have to *look* like an ad. "Adiness" is no virtue. The reason so many ads are look-alikes is that designers, as everyone else, are creatures of habit, prone to mimicry. With immunity to standard advertising formats well advanced among many readers, the designer should consider providing an *editorial* flavor to advertising, using the techniques the editor uses to involve readers in front-of-the-book features.

Some advertising designers play an interesting game with the media, trying to see how closely they can approximate the format—the type, the style—of the publication in which the ad is to appear without having the magazine place that line of disavowal at the top, "An Advertisement," or reject the ad outright as too close to editorial handling.

The Christian Writers Guild, a La Canada, California, organization that trains writers, sponsors an ad that contains another "ad" above its ad, but the other "ad" is obscured by what looks like a bold, scribbled note: "Hon: Look!!" accompanied by a crudely drawn arrow pointing to the real ad. It looks as though a close friend or spouse has marked the page for whoever subscribes to the magazine. It is not a large ad, but it dominates the page because of the unusual graphic treatment.

Seeing the Ad in Context

In the fifteenth century, when typefaces for printing were first designed and cut, type designers were more concerned with the looks of individual letters than the overall impressions on the page. The second wave of designers rectified this. In advertising layout, the beginning designer often is most concerned with individual elements within the ad; the veteran designer rightly sees the overall design, the composition, and the design's effect as more important, knowing that the whole of an ad is greater than the sum of its parts.

Whatever the level of creativity, a designer will be influenced by what other designers are doing, if only to be different. Furthermore, the veteran designer is more concerned with how the ad looks when it is in position than how it looks by itself, beautifully mounted and displayed for client approval. Its character may be considerably changed when seen in the marketplace. A magazine may have to change its layout when, for instance, a cigarette ad appears next to an anti-smoking article. Placement is as important in TV advertising as it is in print-medium advertising. After a scene in *Holocaust,* shown on NBC, in which Nazi victims are told that gas chambers are merely disinfecting areas, a Lysol commercial came on the screen.

The problem of juxtaposition extends to billboards. A sign outside Burnet, Texas, showing several sizes of beer bottles of a particular brand, asked, "Which Bud's for You?" A sign next to it said, "Ask God." The second sign, with its different sponsor, went on to say, "The Family That Prays Together Stays Together."

Is There a "Right" Approach?

Persons in the advertising business do not agree on the best approach to creativity. Some say the best approach is through brainstorming sessions. Brainstorming, said to have originated with Alex Osborn of Batten Barton Durstine & Osborn, brings a group of like-minded individuals together to stimulate each other into the production of ideas and solutions to problems. The group, in effect, pools its imagination. No matter how unlikely the idea may be on the surface, it gets thrown onto the table for consideration. Theoretically, no participant is embarrassed; none worries about looking foolish. Comments and reactions flow unrestricted. One idea triggers another. Random associations are encouraged. What members of the group try to do is unleash the subconscious.

But brainstorming has its detractors. Some say that such sessions *restrict* rather than stimulate thought: Participants are afraid they will embarrass themselves. Furthermore, the sessions release participants from responsibility should their ideas fail to work out after they are adopted. And it can be argued that fear of failure or an acute awareness of responsibility is a force for high-level performance. Artists no longer feeling stomach butterflies or damp palms may well wonder whether they are giving the work the attention and preparation they gave it in their earlier, more enthusiastic periods.

"Creativity, like any value, like moral or religious values, cannot be decided by a majority vote," Dr. Gregory Zilboorg told a Creativity Conference sponsored by the Art Directors Club of New York. "The worst type of sacrilege is making the artist a member of a committee." As a religious plaque says, "For God So Loved the World that He Didn't Send a Committee." Professor John E. Arnold of Stanford has said that the most daring idea a committee can adopt is the most daring idea the least daring member of that committee can tolerate.

The antibrainstormers hold that a greater volume of usable ideas comes from persons operating independently, that the production of ideas is necessarily a lonely act.

It is clear that under neither system will ideas or solutions to problems present themselves until the participants engage in activities to stimulate their imaginations. The truly creative person is the one who reads and observes and listens and searches. In advertising, as in all fields of endeavor, the best ideas seldom come from the blue. They only *seem* to; the groundwork is laid hours or days before.

William P. Lear, the late multimillionaire designer of the Learjet and inventor of some 150 patented items, thought the secret of creativity lies with the subconscious. "One of the unfortunate things about our educational system is that we do not teach our students how to avail themselves of subconscious capabilities," he said. "We don't teach them that they've got a computer, connected with the infinite, that has stored an unlimited number of relatively unimportant details which can be interrelated into the correct answer [to a problem]. You use your subconscious constantly without knowing it. It's like forgetting a name and remembering it later. What happened? You fed the information into your subconscious and then you thought of something else, but your subconscious said, 'I've got to work on this' and it came out with it. We don't teach students how to do that. We don't even tell them that they have a subconscious."

He added: "Feeding information to your subconscious is just putting the soft-

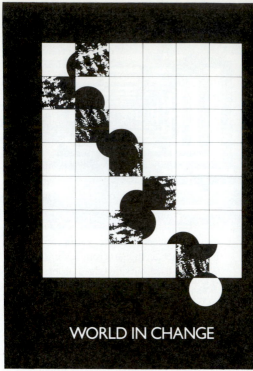

WORLD IN CHANGE

Gloria Chenoweth of the Design Council, Inc., Portland, Oregon, experiments with squares, textures, and circles to create art for a project called "WORLD IN CHANGE." The simplified globe goes through a sequence of changes in print as effectively as if the sequence were on film.

For a class project in Survey of Visual Design, Mary B. Gilbert, Corvallis, Oregon, hunted for various photographs of geometric patterns, organic textures, etc., for the left column and worked out transitions between them, using a stripple drawing technique for her in-between drawings. Her object here was to start and stop with a straight line. A good exercise in visual thinking. © Mary B. Gilbert.

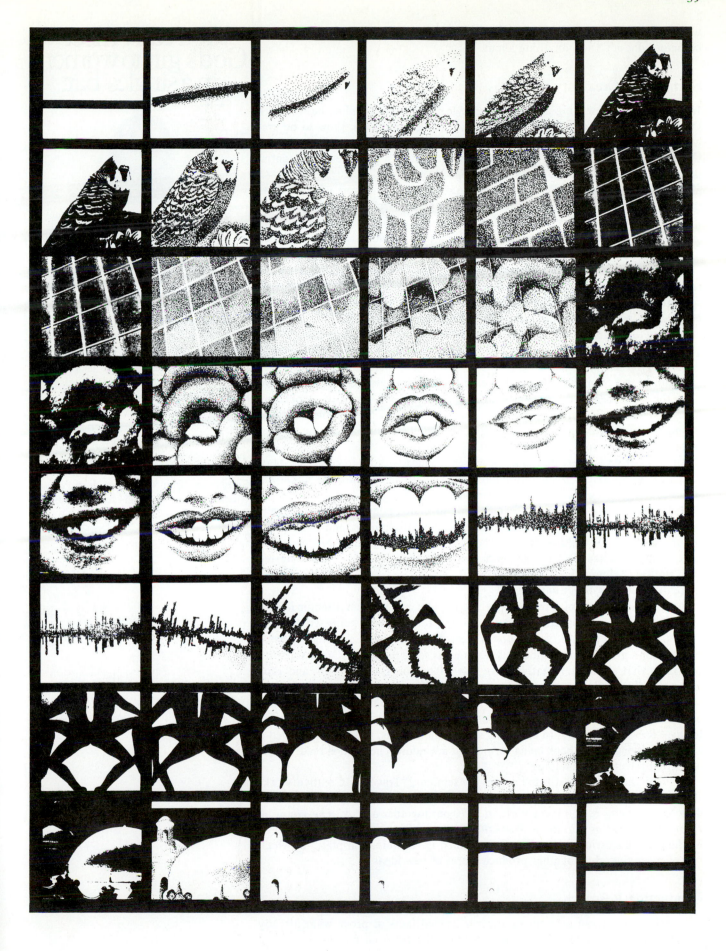

ware into a computer. But your subconscious can't work on something that your conscious doesn't know anything about."[36]

Stimulating Creativity

Imitating a 1960s writing and speaking style, Jack Roberts, when he was with Ogilvy & Mather, said, "The truth is . . . , if you gotta ask [how to be creative]—you ain't never gonna know. It's all programmed, man, all locked-up in those mysterious genes. And the very best way to obtain a high creative potential is by careful selection of your mom and pop."[37]

But whether creativity is inherited or acquired, the spring from which it flows must constantly be fed—through reading, through research, and through experimentation. And just plain observing what goes on around them helps give designers the necessary background to face assignments confidently. Designers keep aware of fashions, fads, mannerisms, trends—and it shows in their work.

Rick Levine, who created an award-winning commercial for Burlington socks showing a man dancing hard to shake a sock off his foot, got his inspiration from seeing the film *Zorba the Greek,* which showed similar dancing. The idea in the commercial was to show that the socks were made to stay up.[38]

During the course of writing *The Compleat Copywriter* (McGraw-Hill, 1966), Hanley Norins conducted a survey of advertising people, asking the question, "How do you get your ideas?"

"Almost to a man and woman, they said *through free association.* The accent is on the word *free,* and a person with imagination could start free-associating and go on forever. This may be enjoyable, but if you try to solve a problem without having a direction, a focus (i.e., a strategy), you could consume an infinite amount of time with no purpose.

"This is why you shouldn't look for a creative idea without having a strategy. The strategy gives you a starting point from which to jump into the unknown. You have something specific to free-associate *about.*"[39]

J. L. Marra, as a lecturer at Texas Tech University, pointed out that "advertising covers a wide and expansive area of various disciplines, and it is by exposure to these disciplines that advertising students benefit." Marra asked advertising students to look for analogies in creating their ads. The students started with similes ("Hot coffee is as bracing as _____ "), then moved on to more difficult, less direct analogies.[40]

As in other aspects of advertising, the computer has become a factor in creativity. A software program called IdeaFisher, for instance, helps writers find common ground between two groups of data. It can also find a variety of associations for a given theme. MindLink helps users solve problems. Other software programs that stimulate creativity are The Innovator, Decision Pad, and Idea Generator.[41]

Over the years, Young & Rubicam, one of the giants among agencies, developed a reputation for creativity. A principal in the agency, Ray Rubicam, used to say, "Resist the usual." In one of its self-promotion ads, the agency showed a cartoon drawing with a book being thrown out a window. The caption read: "Start of a great advertising campaign."

In 1987 the agency instituted a two-day seminar, "Traveling Creative Workshop," for its various offices around the world. Hadley Norins, former creative director of Young & Rubicam West, in 1990 put together a book, *The Young & Rubicam Traveling Creative Workshop,* which demonstrated the agency's methods for nurturing originality. One method is "combination play," in which two or more thoughts together produce scores of new ideas.

Conducting Research

Research is simply an attempt to uncover needed facts or prove what already may be suspected. The designer may conduct the research personally, asking questions of randomly selected persons; or, on a more scientific basis, colleagues

You can't meet God's gift to women in a singles' bar.

If the singles life sometimes leaves you feeling alone and empty, remember that God's gift to all women and men is Jesus Christ. Come join us in worship this Sunday in the Episcopal Church. **The Episcopal Church**

A series of ads—these three are representative—for the Episcopal and Lutheran Churches, prepared on a volunteer basis by Fallon McElligott, the much-honored Minneapolis agency, shows that creativity and even humor extend to advertising with a serious purpose. In an uncertain age, ads like these cause people to rethink their priorities. Art director: Dean Hanson. Copywriter: Tom McElligott. Josse Van Ghent did some of the art for the "Take Two Tablets" ad.

For fast, fast, fast relief take two tablets.

In the Lutheran Church, we believe that some of the oldest ideas are still the best. Like the regular worship of God. Come join us as we celebrate this Sunday.
The Lutheran Church

Will it take six strong men to bring you back into the church?

The Lutheran Church welcomes you no matter what condition you're in, but we'd really prefer to see you breathing. Come join us in the love, worship and fellowship of Jesus Christ this Sunday.
The Lutheran Church

who understand better than the designer the laws of sampling opinion and measuring behavior may do the job. Research does have its place in advertising. Rightly used, it is a help, not a threat, to the designer.

Many in the business think that advertising adds value to a product. People feel good buying certain brands. "Consumer research is essential to find the benefits people hope for when they buy the product and to choose the media for the advertising message," observes Martin Mayer, "but it can't tell you what value can most effectively be added to the brand. That's what the creative folk create."[42]

Landor Associates, a package-design firm, brings in potential customers and has its designers watch those customers from behind one-way glass. The designers learn things about type and color they never learned at art school. And to see how a package looks in the real world, the design firm maintains a room with stocked supermarket shelves installed.

Trace, a service of Market Facts Inc., Chicago, using microprocessors, measures viewers' reactions to TV commercials second-by-second. Viewers punch buttons on five-button, hand-held devices while commercials run. The "1" button is for a very negative reaction, the "5" for a very positive reaction.

Phase One, Beverly Hills, California, uses computers with complex software to see whether a planned commercial will say what its creators want it to say. Some 12,000 questions are asked of a typical commercial under study.

The usual copy and design research involves readers recalling details of wording and placement. Leo Bogart said that these matters are not the issue. "What really matters is whether the right idea is expressed in the right way and in the right setting."[43] And that's hard to measure.

Using the "Swipe File"

Samuel Butler, in his *Notebooks,* said: "The history of art is the history of revivals."

In Voltaire's view, originality was nothing more than judicious imitation. C. E. M. Joad thought it was little more than skill in concealing origins.

Alexander Lindey summed it up this way: "Every work of art is, in the final analysis, a compromise between tradition and revolt. It cannot be otherwise. For a composition that is wholly devoid of newness is dead; one that is wholly unconventional is incomprehensible."[44] Some artists place their faith largely in traditional solutions to their design problems. Others rely more on experimentation. However, all artists are at least partially tradition oriented and partially experiment minded.

Esquire made famous the line, "Why is this man smiling?" in its "Dubious Achievements" issues, and Volvo capitalizes on the line in this excellent two-page full-color magazine ad. This man is smiling, as the copy explains, "Because he owns a Volvo." Volvo's agency—Scali, McCabe, Sloves—helps unite a series of ads for the car by featuring the same squared-off headline face. The proportions in this ad are worth studying. The headline represents one area, a thin one; the grill represents another, a thicker one; and what is left over represents the final area, the thickest one. From top to bottom, then, you have thin, thick, and medium horizontal strips. The thick area gives designer Jim Perretti plenty of room to display the man's face, which is vital to the ad. Copywriters: Ed McCabe, Larry Cadman.

WHY IS THIS MAN SMILING?

Because he owns a Volvo. And in an age when many people are fed up with the quality of new cars, 9 out of 10 new Volvo owners are happy.

Why buy a car you'll have to grin and bear? When you can buy a car that will give you something to smile about?

VOLVO
A car you can believe in.

And all build, maintain, and use a "swipe file" of printed works that have impressed them.

Designer A copies from designer B, who copied from designer C.

"As a student at Cooper Union, I found that the best way for me to learn was to steal; to steal from the best until my ability and confidence made this nefarious activity unnecessary," admitted the late Herb Lubalin. "I think I 'borrowed' every design Paul Rand ever did. . . . And I was not alone."[45]

You could say that in graphic design there is nothing new under the studio fluorescent lamps. The novelist can only rework one of about three dozen basic plots that have been isolated in literature. Graphic designers have even fewer "plots" than novelists have.

Yet designers can bring to a basic design pattern a touch, a character, that is theirs alone.

Many of the ads that win prizes at art directors' shows owe their excellence to earlier works. Designers stimulate the creative processes through these techniques:

■ *Adaptation.* Designers lift an art truth from a work in another field. The composition of a fine painting or the appeal of a well-designed building may suggest the pattern for elements in an advertisement. And nature provides an unending source of design ideas.

■ *Addition.* An austere arrangement for, say, an institutional advertiser or for the manufacturer of a quality product may provide the basis for a more complicated ad that combines several similar elements.

■ *Subtraction.* Designers lift part of an existing ad that appeals to them and build a new ad from it. Or they note the handling of type in an ad and, ignoring the rest of the ad, put together a new arrangement appropriate to the type. Perhaps a small part of a picture begs to be lifted away and blown up— magnified—in a new ad.

■ *Modification.* Designers see an appealing ad and, for another assignment, make only slight changes in the pattern. Four pictures are made into three, for instance, but the space they occupy may stay the same. The headline is moved from the top of the ad to a place near the bottom. And so on.

■ *Exaggeration.* One designer decides to push a headline out near the edge of the ad—to nearly bleed it. Another designer likes the effect, and comes even closer in another ad to bleeding the headline *and* the copy. Or the original designer resurrects one of the flamboyant types of the 1920s—a stenciled Bodoni known as Futura Black, for instance (a misnamed type, by the way, because it has no relationship to regular Futura). The next designer increases the same face to banner-head proportions.

What the ad maker looks for, often, is a comparison. For this ad, art director Tracy Wong and copywriter Clay Williams liken the grip of a shoe to that of a fly, here beautifully portrayed by illustrator Greg Dearth. Client: Clarks of England. Agency: Goodby, Berlin & Silverstein, San Francisco.

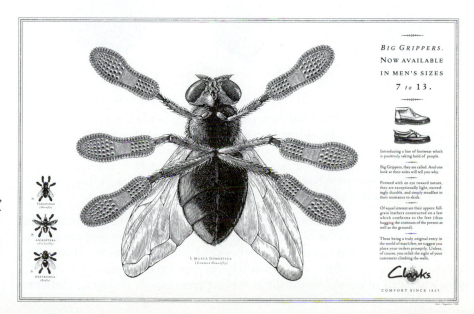

In one of its ads, Saab uses a Rorschach-like device to "test" potential car buyers. "Do You See a Practical Car or a Performance Car?" asks the ad's headline. According to the ad's copy (not shown), Saab is both. "While our version [of the Rorschach test] may not reveal your personality traits, instinctual drives, or hidden neuroses, it should reduce any anxieties you might have about buying a Saab." The idea behind the ad and the copy approach take advantage of the car's slogan: "The most intelligent car ever built." Agency: Ally & Gargano, Inc. Art director: Ron Arnold. Copywriter: Peter Levathes.

■ *Opposition.* When the trend in retail advertising in town is toward blackness and reverses, the designer comes up with an ad that features lightface type and large masses of white space. When double borders and rounded corners are in, this designer drops borders altogether and squares off the elements. When everybody is using the Swiss-inspired gothics, the designer specifies Spartan or Futura.

As a student, you should not hesitate to lean on and borrow from the work of other designers. But, obviously, as you become more at home in graphic design, you should rely less and less on the crutches of adaptation, addition, subtraction, modification, exaggeration, and opposition—at least on their conscious use. At the lower levels of consciousness the borrowing process will, of course, continue.

How do you show "high fidelity"? Maxell shows it by converting it to a high wind. The tipped lampshade and drink and blown hair and tie help establish the fact that the wind is coming with great force. And the slouched man is holding onto the chair almost in desperation. Agency: Scali, McCabe, Sloves, Inc. Designer: Lars Anderson. Copywriter: Peter Levathes.

AFTER 500 PLAYS OUR HIGH FIDELITY TAPE STILL DELIVERS HIGH FIDELITY.

If your old favorites don't sound as good as they used to, the problem could be your recording tape.

Some tapes show their age more than others. And when a tape ages prematurely, the music on it does too.

What can happen is, the oxide particles that are bound onto tape loosen and fall off, taking some of your music with them.

At Maxell, we've developed a binding process that helps to prevent this. When oxide particles are bound onto our tape, they stay put. And so does your music.

So even after a Maxell recording is 500 plays old, you'll swear it's not a play over five.

IT'S WORTH IT.

Maxell Corporation of America, 60 Oxford Drive, Moonachie, N.J. 07074

Even as a beginning designer, though, you should appropriate for your own use only *ideas* from designs you admire. To what you borrow you should add some new twist, a touch of your own. Otherwise, quite apart from the ethics of the matter, you will realize little satisfaction from your work.

It is possible to copyright an ad, and many sponsors do it now; but suits over copyright infringement are rare. What should discourage plagiarism is the healthy ego of ad people; why would they want to lean so heavily on others? Where's the fun in advertising then?

Anyway, it is the specific presentation that can be copyrighted, not the idea itself.

Letting Go

"The best ideas emerge when people loosen up and act a little crazy," observes Arthur Van Gundry, a professor of communications at the University of Oklahoma.[46]

Well-muscled creativity can carry you far afield. Gary Dahl resigned as creative director of Darien, Russell & Hill, a San Jose, California, advertising agency, when his tongue-in-cheek idea of considering rocks as pets resulted in a packaged product that became a favorite of the 1975 Christmas buying season. What Dahl did was to pack ordinary egg-shaped rocks and shredded newspapers in attractive boxes with holes to allow for "breathing."

What made the item enjoyable—and perhaps worth the $4 retail price—was the owner's manual which told of tricks you could teach your rock—tricks like rolling over and playing dead. The rolling over could best be taught on the side of a hill, the manual pointed out. As for teaching the rock to play dead: "Rocks enjoy this trick so much that often, when you're not even looking, they actually practice it on their own."

There followed the inevitable imitators and spin-offs.

After Christmas, a St. Louis company, Rock Group, promoted a Stud Rock with "instructions" on how to breed it with any other rock. The chairman of the company, Stan Leitner, admitted the idea grew out of the Pet Rock phenomenon. He realized the fad would soon be over, but he felt that there was still some time to cash in on it.

Still another firm, American Consumer, Inc., through The Crackerbarrel of Westport, Connecticut, offered a pet Baby Boulder, which, according to an ad in the *Christian Science Monitor,* was "pretrained to obey sixteen commands," such as to "play dead," "sit," "stay," and "crack nuts." "Why Settle for a Piece of *That* Rock When You Can Have our PRETRAINED Pet Baby Boulder?" asked the ad's headline (question mark added).

There was even a Pet Rock University at Glendale Heights, Illinois, that offered correspondence courses and degrees to Pet Rocks. And it was possible in California to arrange a burial at sea for your Pet Rock.

Milton Ribak, a New York PR man, published the bimonthly *Pet Rock News.*

At the tail end of the phenomenon King James Productions, Oak Park, Illinois, dreamed up a Trained Stick and sold it for $4.50. Stan Leitner, through his Rock Group, brought out an Invisible Piranha. The owner's manual listed some questions and answers about the fish. In answer to the question whether "a fish's age can be told," Leitner wrote: "Certainly. Mention it to anyone you think would be interested."

HDC Industries, Kokomo, Indiana, using the *National Observer,* "At Long Last" offered for $2.50 "the Add 'em Up Finger Machine that Helps You Count Up to Five." You stuck your fingers and thumb through the five numbered holes provided and you were ready to go. Tongue-in-Chic, Elmhurst, Illinois, offered a similar gadget.

The marketing hit of the 1983 Christmas season was the ugly, but cute-in-its-ugliness Cabbage Patch Kids doll, which had to be "adopted," not just bought. Near riots occurred at stores where the dolls, scarce because of the demand, were sold. The phenomenon was something to delight the media, which are always on the alert for Christmas stories. An editor of a newspaper reported that the doll he bought was kidnapped. He had no idea who could have taken the doll, but he knew it was not one of his reporters because, he said, there were no misspellings in the ransom note.

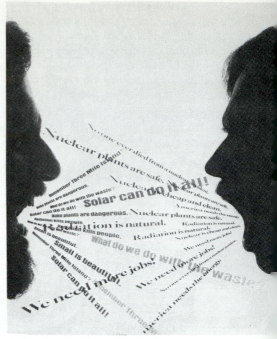

The Committee for Energy Awareness, sponsored by America's electric energy companies, took out a two-page ad in *Time* to point out that "There are two sides to the issue of nuclear power." One page consisted of the bleed photo you see here, with charges and claims coming from the mouths of the protagonists. Notice the faces chosen to represent the two sides. There is just enough stereotyping here to make the protagonists believable but not enough to cause offense. The antinuke man is, naturally, at the left, and bearded.

Facing "Designer's Block"

If, despite all your preparing and all your utilizing of the techniques for stimulating the creative process, "designer's block" happens to you, you may find these two suggestions helpful:

■ *After some preliminary work on the project, forget it for a while.* An errand run, some physical activity—or better yet, a break of several days' duration, when a deadline is not pressing—will give the subconscious and even the unconscious a chance to work on the problem. The first temporary solution to the problem is likely to look quite different when you return to it after a break.

■ *Work on more than one project at a time.* Moving from one job to another, from one activity to another, provides a change of pace that is almost as fruitful as a complete withdrawal from creative work. A solution to one problem can stimulate another solution to another problem. What can result is a kind of individual brainstorming session.

The great temptation is—procrastination.

In one of his essays Robert Benchley wrote, "I had decided to go to bed early and see how that would work, having tried everything else to catch up on my

Al Hampel came up with the concept for this intriguing public-service ad for the Muscular Dystrophy Association; Sue Gelman wrote the copy; Jon Fisher art directed. Agency: Benton & Bowles. Yousuf Karsh, as a member of MDA, contributes his photographic genius to the association each year by making camera portraits of its national poster children.

Yousuf Karsh reserves this space in his gallery of famous people for the person who discovers the cure for Muscular Dystrophy.

You can help. Send your contribution to the Muscular Dystrophy Association, 810 Seventh Avenue, New York, N.Y. 10019.

sleep." And so you might well, in the end, after taking part in a bull session, making some telephone calls, going out for coffee, plant yourself at your drawing table or computer station—having tried everything else to catch up on your assignments in Advertising Design.

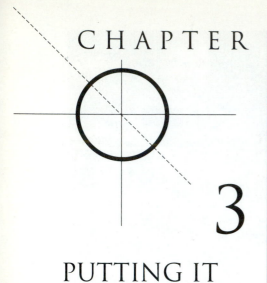

CHAPTER

3

PUTTING IT INTO WORDS

Copy and art departments once operated independently at agencies, but today they often work under a single banner. Art directors become involved in the copy, and the copywriters help visualize the ads. Allen Rosenshine, as president of Batten Barton Durstine and Osborn, considered separate copy and art departments "relics of the past."[1]

"There was a time in American advertising when the copywriters ran the show and the art people were merely 'wrists' who sketched out the writers' ideas. Today, at most agencies the two work closely together, and in the best of teams, the writer might suggest the look of the ad and the art director (or A.D.) could come up with the headline," says Wes Perrin, a founder of Borders, Perrin and Norrander.

The creative director or the "creative czar," as Perrin calls the person, supervises the work of the copywriter and art director. At some agencies, creative work comes in from outside copywriters and art directors. And, of course, most of the illustrations and photographs come in to agencies from outside.[2]

Hal Riney, founder of Hal Riney & Partners, reminds advertising people that "Art and copy aren't mutually exclusive. An art director should be something of a writer, and a writer something of an art director. I think it's simpler to visualize the ad *and* write it, although many don't agree. . . . I can't just *write* an ad. I care how it *looks* as well as what it says."[3]

"It's been easier for me as a writer since I stopped thinking in terms of words and devised a visual interpretation of the strategy first," says Larry Spector, senior copywriter at Levine, Huntley, Schmidt & Beaver. "I watch a lot of TV at night with the sound off. I judge things by how they live visually."[4]

Whether they work as team members or independently, art directors and designers need to know something about copy. "Design, no matter how brilliant, can't bring success by itself. Design is only the relation between word and picture, and you've got to have the word first," observes William Cheney, art director of *Sunset*.[5]

The Challenge of Copy

Copywriters exercise more influence on commerce than most people realize. They can even affect manufacturing processes. Jeremy Gury, copywriter for Ted Bates, said that "if you know what you want to say, [the manufacturer] can change the product so you can say it."[6]

The typical ad deals with our vanities, our insecurities, our hungers, our sex drives. If these are not problems for us, the ad makers—some of them—do their best to make them problems. The products or services the ad makers promote will, we are promised, solve our problems.

The ad creator continues to look for new ways of saying things, even for new ways to say the obvious. A startling headline helps, especially when copy explains. "Some People Commit Child Abuse Before Their Child is Even Born," says the headline for an ad sponsored by the American Cancer Society. The copy says: "According to the surgeon general, smoking by a pregnant woman may result in a child's premature birth, low birth weight and fetal injury. If that's not child abuse, then what is?"

The term *copy* originated in the early days of printing when the compositor received a manuscript with instructions to "copy it." Today, as a noun, *copy* refers to the nonvisual part of the ad: the text.

The writing of advertising copy is a demanding craft that few master. Even writers who do well in other literary endeavors do not always perform well in copywriting roles. John W. Crawford in *Advertising* divided the copywriter's job into "two coequal and commingling" parts: one "a never-ending search for ideas"; the other "a never-ending search for new and different ways to express those ideas."[7]

The advertising idea must anticipate ad placement and timing. "Houston's Hot" seemed like a good headline/slogan for a billboard showing in that city to cheer on the city's growth, but it didn't impress one visitor there on a 99-degree

You don't think you can have fun writing advertising? Consider the copy in this one-of-a-series, full-newspaper-size, rebus-format ad written by L. Baker Runyan, who gets a byline (at the top). In small type near the end, Roger Bergen, president of The Nature Company, Berkeley, California, the advertiser, says, "All my relatives are reading these ads. Is anyone else? And what do you make of this Runyan fellow, our writer? (He's not cheap.) Please drop me a line. . . ." Agency: Goodby, Berlin & Silverstein. Art director: Tracy Wong.

BY L. BAKER RUNYAN

A billion light years away, in the orange glow of two moons, a child stares into the sky and wonders about you.

You laugh. Okay. So consider another far-flung possibility. A group of beings, made mostly of water, is clinging to a whirling sphere of rock and metal that is travelling, in inky silence, around a giant ball of burning gas in a galaxy named after a candy bar. Nah. Too weird. Never happen.

Fig. 1. Can you see the bear? The horse? Anything? If not, get the Star Decoder $39.95.

AN UNSPEAKABLE ALIEN SURPRISE.

The Nature Company herewith puts forth a bold notion: stars and planets can be as awesome as anything you will discover at no-host receptions or on seventy-two channel television.

Right overhead, supernovae are exploding, dwarf stars are imploding to a mass so dense a teaspoonful weighs a ton, black holes are warping their surrounding space so that even light cannot escape. Unidentified flying objects are gathering by the millions, preparing to descend and force everyone to consume beet casserole.

As your father used to say, it is a great big world out there. The Nature Company can help you discover a chunk you might not have seen lately. It might be fun. It doesn't take a lot to find out.

Be careful out there!

First moon on the man. All-cotton T-Shirt. Adults $15.95, Kids $9.95

To receive our catalog, contact us on your communicator: 1-800-227-1114.

"IT ALL LOOKS LIKE A BLACK HOLE TO ME."

For those who occasionally mistake a streetlamp for the moon, the Star Decoder

is a frame into which you insert templates containing star maps. (*Fig. 1*) Simply hold it up and explain the night sky to your son.

("And here, son, we have Canis Minor, the little dog. A nice dog, a good dog, who somehow became a consolation…well, of course, Daddy meant to say *constellation*. Daddy was just testing you.")

As for telescopes, Galileo proved that knowing what to do with one is not a prerequisite for ownership. Upon he announced that had "ears." Everynodded and around. The identified "That's mut- here, sighting Saturn, the planet one looked "ears" were later as rings. what I meant," he tered, then went on vacation. (*Fig. 2*)

For starting out, the Meade 226 Astro-Telescope is a good choice, a serious unit (*Fig. 3*). At $199.00 it is not cheap, but it is our feeling that anyone shivering atop Mount Chutney at midnight is out for a quality experience. Or just odd.

Fig. 2. What Galileo saw

What he said he saw

"DO I HAVE TO GO OUTSIDE?"

In a spaceship going a million miles per hour, you could reach the nearest star, Alpha Centauri, in three thousand years. Better to stay at home and read.

Fig. 3. See rings on Saturn, craters on the moon, lint across town. Meade 226 Astro-Telescope $199.00. Brass $495.00

Peterson's Guide to Stars and Planets is a very good primer. Or get Coming of Age in The Milky Way. ("What really interests me is whether God had any choice in the creation of the world." —Einstein)

We have charts of the night sky, more than 40 books on stars and space (*Fig. 4*), and an inflatable star globe that is great fun, but of no assistance whatsoever.

Brass finish aluminum sundial. Batteries not included. $49.50.

JUST THIS ONCE, LEAVE WORK BEFORE DARK, OKAY?

This evening, if you'll stop by our store, we'll point out Venus in the western sky. It's the brightest spot right after sunset.

If you were standing on its surface, it would be hot, 900 degrees. And the sky would be filled with clouds of dust because there is no water. But then maybe you wouldn't need any water if you lived there. And if you were a child, maybe you'd wait for the clouds

Fig. 4. Covers the whole nine trillion yards. $49.95.

THE NATURE COMPANY

'All my relatives are reading these ads. Is anyone else? And what do you make of this Runyan fellow, our writer? (He's not cheap.) Please drop me a line: Roger Bergen, President, 750 Hearst Ave., Berkeley, CA 94710.'

Stainless-steel survival kit blocks alien rays, cuts salami. $19.95.

to clear so you could see the evening star, a beautiful star, the one full of water and oxygen, a place far too forbidding for life to exist.

Don't laugh.

Thank you.

We are scanning the horizon, waiting for your presence.

day. "Maybe the folks who came up with this gem can volunteer their sloganeering talents to other cities in need of civic pride and/or a good laugh, i.e.: 'San Francisco Is on the Move' or 'Detroit's a Riot.' "[8]

Whatever the kind of advertising, the copywriter must choose each word carefully, making sure it carries just the right meaning. Naturally the copywriter wants to use those words that put the product, service, or idea in its best possible light. Some words do a better job of selling than others. "Used" gives way to "pre-owned" for many copywriters trying to verbally upgrade second-hand cars and other merchandise. In some quarters "pre-owned" gives way to "pre-enjoyed." "This insurance available in most states" is a better way of saying "This insurance isn't available in some states." "Everyday sale price" sounds better than "regular price."

"Health and nutrition claims apparently help sell products, so about one-third of all food ads now make some such claim," observes the *University of California at Berkeley Wellness Letter*. The Federal Trade Commission, which oversees advertising, is less restrictive than the Food and Drug Administration, which oversees product labels. So what is said on labels has to be more cautiously worded than what is said in the ads. For instance, "light," "low-fat," and "fresh" carry meanings that have been clearly defined by the FDA.[9]

Researchers at Yale University drew up a list of words that aid most in the job of persuading. The words are these: *you, new, health, love, save, easy, proven, results, money, safety, discovery,* and *guarantee.* Not an inspiring list from a literary standpoint. But they are words worth considering for many kinds of advertising copy. To this list most advertisers would add *free.* Advertisers know that getting something free appeals to the rich as well as the poor. A swanky condo in Manhattan in a New York *Times* ad offered a free Rolls-Royce to people who would buy one of the units, priced at a lofty level.

Like most kinds of writing, advertising copy requires several revisions before it takes its final form. Rewriting is very much a part of the copywriter's craft. "Never be content with your first draft," Ogilvy & Mather tells its writers in its handbook *How to Write Better.* "Rewrite, with an eye toward simplifying and clarifying. Rearrange. Revise. Above all, cut."

A rewriting is best when it is delayed for a day or two or more. It is surprising how rough a piece of copy looks to a writer who allows it to cool for a time.

Often competing products possess a common characteristic, but one product

A series of ads run on consecutive right-hand pages in *The New Yorker.* These were less than full-page ads, the last one the largest, answering the questions raised in the first two ads. Boldface sans serif headlines and silhouette art tie the ads together. Client: KLM Royal Dutch Airlines. Agency: Angotti, Thomas, Hedge, Inc. Art director: Tom Thomas. Designer: Tony Angotti.

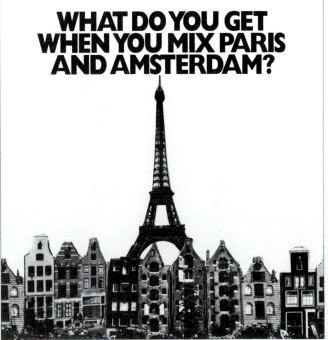

becomes better known than the others for the characteristic because it is first to speak of it.

In a sense, the copywriter operates like an explorer, staking out a claim wherever possible. Claims in recent years have become both grandiose and tongue-in-cheek. Marlboro took title to open spaces with its "Marlboro Country" concept, while United Air Lines took over the space above with its "Friendly Skies of United." A beer company claimed that "weekends were made for Michelob." No matter how you felt about it, if you happened to be young, you were a member of "The Pepsi Generation," which jumps up and down a lot. You did not just drink Dr. Pepper, you became a "Pepper."

Hanley Norins of Young & Rubicam quoted Aldous Huxley as saying, "The advertisement is one of the most interesting and difficult of modern literary forms." But Huxley did not go far enough, Norins said, for "copywriting is *the* most difficult and intense form of writing."[10] While Norins's thesis may be tinged with the hyperbole to be expected from an advertising person, he did build a strong case. In *The Compleat Copywriter* he pointed out that the copywriter should be able to handle all kinds of writing, for copy can take the form of a story, a piece of reporting, a poem, a play—any literary form. And whatever kind of literature the copywriter chooses to produce, it must be done with a limited number of words.

Not only that, the copywriter may write for an audience that does not necessarily want to read or hear what is said. If the audience is not hostile to what the copywriter says, it may at least be indifferent. Of course, the copywriter may write for a more receptive audience, too. The reader, listener, or viewer may be aware of needing the product. Or the ad may contain newsworthy information. Or the ad may deal with a product that is intrinsically interesting.

After a few years the copywriter may develop a product specialty, say in foods or automobiles, or specialize in writing for a single medium, like television or direct mail. But in the course of the job the copywriter writes for every class of reader. One ad may have to influence the youth market. Another ad, for the same product, may have to appeal to a minority group.

All of this is done without much recognition, for there are no bylines in advertising copy. The advertising copywriter remains anonymous. The only one who gains some recognition in an ad, if anyone does, is the artist who does the illustration. Under some circumstances—especially if the artist is well known—a sig-

The more cocaine you use, the more cocaine you need.

Citizens Against Cocaine Abuse

nature is allowed, even encouraged. And on rare occasions the designer's name runs somewhere in the ad in small type. (Such a line is called a "credit line.")

If you do see a byline identifying the writer, it is a form of testimonial in which a famous person praises a product, as when golfer Lee Trevino's byline appears in a Dodge ad under the headline "How I Learned to Relax and Enjoy My Drives" (a little humor there). No one really believes Trevino wrote the ad, though—any more than anyone believes a president writes his own speeches.

Art Spikol, advertising consultant and columnist for *Writer's Digest,* thinks signing ad copy might be a good idea. He says it might make copy more honest.[11]

Michael Rosen wrote and designed this starkly effective black-and-white-stripes ad with its headline/copy: "The more cocaine you use, the more cocaine you need." The ad was for Citizens Against Cocaine Abuse. Agency: Goldsmith/Jeffrey, New York.

The Research Phase

Charles Brower, retired chairman of BBD&O, says that "No one should knock research who has ever been helped by a road map."

Advertising people get involved in three kinds of research: market research about the product itself and its buyers and potential buyers; copy testing involving the advertising both before and after it is run; and research on readers, viewers, and listeners of the media carrying the advertising.

Copywriters engage in an informal kind of market research when they look for answers to questions like these: What does the product do? How does it benefit the buyer, and how will it hurt the person who does not use the product? Who is the potential buyer? Is the buyer necessarily the potential *user* of the product? What is the product made of? How well is it made? How much does it cost? Where do you find it? How does it compare with competing products?

In hunting for facts, the copywriter cannot rely solely on information provided by the client. Being close to the subject, the client may not recognize what makes the product unique. What the client considers a selling point may be only vaguely of interest to the buyer.

A sample of users of the product yields valuable information the copywriter can use in the ad. Personal experience with the product may yield even more useful information, but the copywriter should be cautious about generalizing from that.

When the facts do not yield enough unique information, bright writing becomes all the more necessary. Good copy can make even the dullest of products interesting. It can make an advantage out of what seems to be a disadvantage. Said Pall Mall, a filterless cigarette in the days when filters were being played up in many other ads: "And you can light either end." (This ad caused Malcolm Bradbury in *Punch* to envision a cigarette with filters at both ends and a slogan: "And you can't light either end.") Jos. A. Bank Clothiers, which manufactures and retails traditional clothing, said in a headline for an ad selling polo shirts without insignias: "If You'd Rather Not Be Anybody's Billboard, We Can Save You as Much as $18.50." J. C. Penney made a similar appeal with its "Plain Pockets" jeans. Goodrich took advantage of the fact that it does not have blimps by referring to itself as "the other guys."

"Ready to assemble," says the advertising for a Scandinavian furniture store. That sounds better than "KD" (for "knocked down"), which used to be the designation, but it doesn't make things any easier at home for the buyer with two left hands. One is not likely to see a line in an ad that says, "Not ready to assemble."

Williams-Sonoma, a mail-order house of San Francisco, described its Old Dutch Chocolate Bar like this: "For baking, candy making (and nibbling) its smooth texture and subtle, sweet light flavor know no equal. With any luck it will arrive already cracked, courtesy of the post office, and you can blissfully nibble on the shards. . . ."

The writer of a notice put up on a campus bulletin board understood the principle. "For Sale: Used Refrigerator," the heading said. Then: "Built like they used to build them." It was an advantageous if ungrammatical way of saying the refrigerator was old.

Whatever decision a store makes about being open on a holiday can work to its advantage. "Open 10 A.M. to 7 P.M. Christmas as a service to our customers," the ad can say. Or: "Closed Christmas so our employees can be with their families."

Sometimes an advertiser makes a virtue of big price. Farberware once showed a beautiful saucepan in full color with a $72 price tag leaning against it. "If The Price Doesn't Shock You," said the headline, "It Could Mean You're Either Very Rich or Very Serious about Cooking." The copy and some cutaway art went on to convince the person "serious about cooking" that the pan and other Farberware cookware were worth the investment.

Another tactic is to publicize a failure, but this must be done with great subtlety. *Life* used to check the list of important advertisers, and when it found one not using the magazine, it took out a two-page spread in *Advertising Age* or even a general-circulation magazine like *The New York Times Magazine* and made its pitch. For instance, one posterlike ad used reverse letters on a solid red (*Life* red) background to yell the advertiser's name on an across-the-gutter diagonal: "Calvin Klein." In smaller reverse type, it advised: "Hey Calvin Klein, you belong in LIFE!"

No doubt such advertising startles the potential advertiser and, at the same time, alerts other advertisers that *Life* is a medium worth considering. The potential advertiser also enjoys some attention from potential customers.

Another technique is to pretend that your product has a problem when the problem is really an advantage. Rent-a-Wreck used this headline in one of its ads: "Rent-a-Wreck Apologizes to All of You Who Expected to Rent a Wreck." The copy admits that the cars available are "beauties" from a few years back, fully restored on the inside.

Our cruise lines may not be known for elegant dining, but they'll take you to some beautiful islands.

Drive to the bank of the Cashie River in North Carolina, and honk the horn. And when the ferry chugs over to pick you up, you can cruise to the other side. Free. Or, you can take a ferry to faraway places with strange-sounding names like Hatteras, Ocracoke, and Rodanthe. Several of these rugged barrier islands are so remote, the people speak a foreign language: Olde English. And some are so unspoiled, you can still see the same pristine beauty that enchanted our first settlers from Wales, Scotland and England. Whether you explore 25 miles of national seashore or visit our colorful fishing villages, you'll discover this. Our cruise lines may not offer elegant dining. But they can help satisfy your appetite for adventure. **North Carolina**

For our new travel package, write North Carolina Travel, Dept 446, Raleigh, NC 27699. Or call 1-800-VISIT NC. Operator 446.

These are years of individualism, when many people are not concerned anymore about what other people think of their dress and lifestyles. This should affect the advertiser. What's "in" is not necessarily what sells, except perhaps among teenagers, a group particularly vulnerable to peer pressure.

Alvin Toffler has observed that we are becoming "demassified." The rise of special-interest groups shows this.[12]

To write effective copy, the copywriter must gather facts not only about the product but also about the potential user. Advertising copy must be slanted to a specific audience, taking into account its needs and even its background. If research can provide the information, the copywriter should know the age level, income level, occupation, gender, and geographic location of the typical user. The copywriter should know, too, if someone other than the user influences the buying decision. For instance, how strong is the secretary's influence on the boss's decision concerning equipment for the office? Maybe the ad should be directed to the secretary.

Mike Sloan, founder of Mike Sloan, Inc., a Miami agency, has his own copytesting technique. He suggests reading copy with a W. C. Fields impersonation. "If you *really* sound like W. C. Fields, no one is going to believe the copy you've written. Throw it out, and start over!"[13]

The North Carolina Division of Travel and Tourism tells of some offbeat attractions in a series of magazine ads promoting tourism, all using this format. The campaign resulted in a 26 percent increase in inquiries over the previous year. It also won a Magazine Publishers Association Kelly Award. Agency: McKinney & Silver. Art directors: Michael Winslow for the works-of-art ad and Mark Oakley for the beautiful-islands ad. Copywriter: Jan Karon.

Finding a Theme

Advertising textbooks draw a distinction between selling points and benefits. Selling points in advertising copy, they say, are points as seen from the advertiser's position. Benefits are seen from the buyer's position. In most cases it is best to develop the copy around benefits.

The buyer is interested in the product not for its intrinsic worth but for the satisfaction it brings. Will it make the buyer happier? Healthier? More comfortable? More prosperous? More secure? More popular?

Will it make the buyer feel more important?

Will it make things easier for the buyer?

If the answer is "yes" to at least one of the questions, especially if the benefit is exclusive to the brand, the copywriter has a start toward developing a theme.

Whether the ad stands by itself or becomes part of a series, it should be single-minded in its approach. It is up to the copywriter to decide which of the several advantages a product offers should get principal play in the ad. The copywriter should have in mind one primary objective for the ad. It may be to get someone to ask for a particular brand of soap; to cut out and mail a coupon; to find God—something. And everything in the ad should point to that objective.

In the beginning, a multitude of voices rang out across the wires and rumbled: "Locations!" **A**nd out of the darkness sprang forth a land filled with cities great and small. Farms and forests. River towns. Southern settings. Urban lights. Industrial sites. Shores and harbors. All heavenly. **A**nd so the producers saw Illinois and said that it was good. **T**hen the voices sought casting directors. And talent begotten in the images and likenesses of the script. And lo, casting was fruitful. And extras multiplied. **Y**et the voices coveted crews of great strength. State of the art equipment. Post-Production. And were fearful of the cost. **B**ut Illinois calmed the voices. And the producers read the bottom line and saw that it was good. Very good. **C**aterers and hotel rooms were found. And the voices made a joyful noise. **S**till they desired a covenant with those most high. And it came to pass that city and state officials were perfect angels. **T**he sea of red tape parted. **A**nd the producers looked upon all that had gone before them in Illinois, gave thanks and said: "**L**et there be "Lights! Camera! Action!" *Word has it that Illinois is a divine place to shoot. Contact Lucy Salenger, Managing Director, Illinois Film Office. Department of Commerce and Community Affairs. 310 South Michigan Avenue, Chicago, Illinois 60604. (312) 793-3600. She'll make a believer out of you.*

Illinois

An institutional ad sponsored by the Illinois Film Office to reach readers of *Variety* and *Hollywood Reporter* uses Biblical language to make the point that Illinois welcomes filmmakers. The copy ends on this note: "Word has it that Illinois is a divine place to shoot." Designer Robert Qually picked up on the slanting rays in the photograph to use bold italics for the opening words, the logo, and the caps that begin the sentences. The agency was Lee King & Partners, Inc., Chicago. Copywriter: Stephanie Ross.

The copy may make several points, but only one should stand out. The late Rosser Reeves, as head of Ted Bates & Co., came up with an acrostic for it: USP (for "Unique Selling Proposition"). Every product has one, he insisted. Once decided upon, the USP, in Reeves's view, had to be repeated in ad after ad, regardless of how much the repetition annoyed the critics. It has been reported that Reeves had the secretary at his agency answer the phone with "Good morning. Ted Bates, Ted Bates, Ted Bates." Other ad people have been less single-minded, but the one-point-per-ad idea is widely accepted.

In more recent years advertising people have talked about *positioning*— endowing a product with a personality that sets it apart from others in the minds of potential consumers. Sometimes a product is *re*positioned; Johnson's Baby Shampoo repositioned itself as a family shampoo, not merely a shampoo for babies.

A company rides a theme until its usefulness wears thin or until the times change so that the theme is no longer valid. Sometimes an old theme is revived.

What works at one time may not work at another. Goodyear ran a commercial in the early 1960s showing a woman motorist stranded with a flat tire. The theme was, "When there's no man around, Goodyear should be." Not a theme to be well received in the 1990s.

"It's not your father's Oldsmobile" and "It's not your mother's tampon" are copywriters' attempts to reach a young adult audience, playing upon this group's feeling of superiority over those who adhere to earlier preferences or old ways of doing things. But the Oldsmobile campaign may have alienated buyers who had maintained a loyalty to the car over the years.

Of course, the copywriter has to remember that advertising does not exist in a vacuum. How the competition might fight back becomes a consideration. The ad's theme should not invite a comeback. A Ford dealer in Traverse City, Michigan, once asked this question on a billboard: "This Is Ford Country. What Are You Driving?" A Plymouth dealer on another billboard came back with: "We ALL Drive PLYMOUTHS. What Country Are You From?"

After three years of success with its "We Try Harder" campaign, Avis finally felt the sting of Hertz. "For years, Avis has been telling you Hertz is No. 1," an ad for Hertz said. "Now we're going to tell you why." (Carl Ally Inc. was the agency that prepared the ad.) "A magnificent retort," one writer in *Advertising Age* said. But another writer said it was free advertising for Avis.

In their ads, some advertising people don't mind poking fun at the profession. In a radio commercial in the early 1990s, the California Table Grape Commission had little Billy telling a story to his parents before going to bed. His story concerned a little boy whose parents refused to put grapes in the lunch he took to school. He became depressed and dropped out of school and eventually (shudder) went into *advertising*. "Oh, no!" exclaimed his parents.

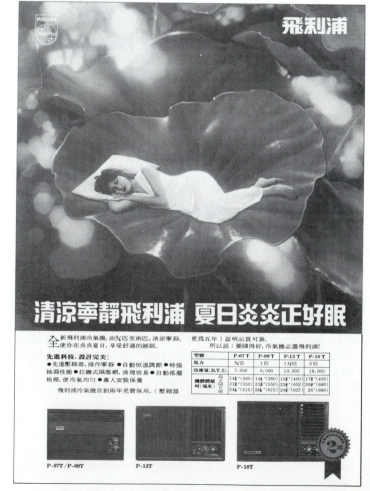

In a place like Hong Kong, an agency often must prepare two entirely different ads to put a point across. The woman-on-a-lily-pad ad, which sells Philips Air Conditioners, takes advantage of the aspect of Chinese culture that prefers poetic and visual messages to literal messages. The ad works well for the Chinese in Hong Kong. But according to Dick Pruitt, executive creative director for Ogilvy & Mather Advertising, Hong Kong, the ad does not impress the expatriates there. They expect a more direct approach. Art director: Alex Chan. Chinese copywriter: C. C. Tang. English copywriter: Paul Grezoux.

Office Pavilion, a group of office-furniture dealers tied to Herman Miller, involves the reader with powerful art by Harvey! Advertising Photography. The windowpane-check shirt of the choker provides enough contrast with the white shirt of the man being choked to show that another person is involved, and the placement of the arms creates the illusion that they belong to the reader. The cropping of the head does away with unnecessary detail. Art, headline, and copy are nicely coordinated. Agency: Rice & Rice. Art director: Nancy Rice. Designers: Nancy and Nick Rice. Copywriter: Jim Newcombe.

Is this how you'd like to get hold of your office furniture dealer?

Buying office furniture can be a frustrating experience. Especially when delivery is late, orders are incomplete, or installation is botched. And when that happens, it's not always easy to get hold of your dealer.
But Office Pavilion is a new kind of dealer.
Instead of the usual huge number of product lines, we concentrate on a small group of the very best. Starting with Herman Miller office furniture. From the Eames® lounge chair to Ethospace® interiors, Herman Miller products are known for quality and innovative design.
Our other lines include Meridian, Helikon, Novikoff, Tradex and B & B Italia. At Office Pavilion, we guarantee move-in dates in writing. And we're locally owned. So we'll be there when you need us. All of which is why you should stop into Office Pavilion.
The dealer you don't have to squeeze great service out of.
© 1987 Herman Miller, Inc. Zeeland, MI

PAVILION℠
A HERMAN MILLER DEALER

Chiat Day's series of Energizer TV commercials—the ones showing the bunny interrupting cliché ads—provide another example of the industry not taking itself entirely seriously.

Developing an Approach

In spite of all the health warnings and the growing militancy of nonsmokers wanting to breathe unfouled air, millions of Americans still smoke. A small share of this market represents staggering profits for any brand. The advertising wars here are fascinating to watch.

For one thing, radio and TV are off limits for the advertising, and the industry itself has eliminated celebrity endorsements. Magazines, newspapers, and billboards play a big role in the campaigns.

Lately the ads have directed their attention to women. Packages have been designed especially to attract this audience.

The advertising takes one of two approaches: that either the cigarettes have only moderately harmful effects (the companies don't exactly come out and say cigarettes are good for you), or that they have a new and agreeable taste. Bright, a cigarette introduced in 1983, suggested that it could actually freshen your taste.[14]

**You're afraid to drive through a neighborhood like this.
Imagine what it's like to live there.**

There are muggers in there. And rapists. And addicts. Not to mention fires, and filth, and rats. Yet people still live there.

In fact, there isn't even a problem filling those tenements. Because for many members of Cleveland minorities, it's the only housing they can get.

Prejudice built these slums. And it's keeping people in them.

The answer, the only answer, to neighborhoods like this is open housing in all communities.

To an extent, that will be reached through fair housing laws and complete enforcement of those laws.

But more importantly, open housing depends on individual action. It depends on you.

If you're a renter, or a landlord, or if you're buying or selling real estate, find out how you can help assure fair housing to every Clevelander.

Call Operation Equality at 295-1600.

You may be able to avoid that neighborhood.

But the person behind you may have to go in there. And stop.

Operation Equality, 4102 Lee Road; Joseph H. Battle, Director. An affiliate of the Urban League of Cleveland.

Cigarette smokers tend to develop brand loyalties, so any new brand—or any existing brand, for that matter—is likely to try to get people to switch. Some years ago, one brand fought back by showing various people with black eyes who apparently would rather fight than switch.

What the competition does influences the approach copywriters take in the various product categories. Anything to be different. Infinity launched its car in 1989 with ads that did not show the product. "The first time I saw them," said Stan Freberg, who has himself done some advertising soft sell, "I thought, 'That's a nice looking car—it looks a lot like rocks and trees.' "[15]

Sometimes the copywriter ties the advertising to an event in the news. If the event has favorable connotations, and the product is somehow involved, the copywriter will mention that involvement in the copy. Right after Ronald Reagan and Mikhail Gorbachev signed the treaty on intermediate nuclear forces in late 1987, the Parker pen company ran a full-page ad in the news magazines with a photograph of the signing and the headline "The Pen is Mightier than the Sword." The caption read: "The historic document is signed. The pen is a Parker."

Even if the product is not involved, a propaganda device known as the "transfer" may be used. The copy first alludes to the event, then moves gracefully to the product. The secret is to find some comparison between the event and the product. Volkswagen did it nicely for its bug in 1969 with its full-page ad showing a picture of the Apollo 11 lunar module on the moon. The headline "It's Ugly, But It Gets You There" was followed simply by the Volkswagen insignia, the circle with its *V* and *W*. There was no copy block.

An ad is effective when art, headline, and copy work together to make a single point. "The answer, the only answer, to neighborhoods like this is open housing in all communities," the copy for this ad points out. "To an extent, that will be reached through fair housing laws and complete enforcement of those laws. But more importantly, open housing depends on individual action. It depends on you. . . ." Art director and designer: Tom Gilday. Copywriter: Mike Faems. Client: Operation Equality, an affiliate of the Urban League of Cleveland. Agency: Griswold-Eshleman Co., Cleveland.

If it is hung on a news peg, copy must be written in a way to compensate for its lateness (advertising copy seldom can be as timely as news copy) and for the possibility of a change in the news.

Copywriters look for selling points where they can find them. A copywriter for Ralston Purina came up with an unusual reason for buying the company's dog food. A full-page ad in the New York *Times* showed a disgusted businessman standing on one foot, looking at the bottom of his other shoe. The headline, which had some trouble with correct grammar, read: "If More Dogs in New York Ate Purina Hi Pro, it Would Seem Like There Were Less Dogs in New York." The copy explained that "Hi Pro's high digestibility means smaller, firmer stools. The more nutrients a dog digests, the less passes through his system—and onto our sidewalks."

Advertising switches back and forth between the hard sell and the soft sell depending on the times. Bruce Roache, associate professor of advertising and public relations at the University of Alabama, sees a change occurring every fifteen years or so. "During hard economic times, the hard sell tends to be more popular," he says. "During more affluent times the creative style is more popular."[16]

The All-American Mutt Campaign, sponsored by the Massachusetts Society for the Prevention of Cruelty to Animals and the American Humane Education Society, and produced by Humphrey Browning MacDougall, Boston, won a Clio award and awards from the Advertising Club of New York, the Art Directors Club of New York, and the Advertising Club of Greater Boston. This is one in the series. The headline is inspired; the copy nicely follows through. The ad makes room at the bottom, before the summing-up headline, for an animal-shelter imprint. Copywriters for the series: Katina Mills and Veronica Nash. Photographer: David Doss.

If you can't decide between a Shepherd, a Setter or a Poodle, get them all.

Adopt a mutt at your local humane society and get everything you're looking for, all in one dog. The intelligence of a Poodle and the loyalty of a Lassie. The bark of a Shepherd and the heart of a Saint Bernard. The spots of a Dalmatian, the size of a Schnauzer, and the speed of a Greyhound. A genuine, All-American Mutt has it all.

And your animal shelter has lots of All-American Mutts waiting for you. There are genuine, All-American Alley Kittens too. Just come to:

Get the best of everything. Adopt a mutt.

Courtesy of the American Humane Education Society.

Putting Yourself in the Reader's Place

As a copywriter, you do not write primarily to fulfill or find yourself. You write to do a job for a client. To do that job, you must write with a knowledge of both the product and the target audience. You must look at the product not from the standpoint of the manufacturer or seller but from the standpoint of the user. You must put yourself in the reader's place. How best to phrase the message to convince readers that the product is for them? That is the question you must consider.

The background and needs of readers differ from publication to publication. Ideally, copy for an ad should also differ from publication to publication. A theme and style that work for the readers of *The New Yorker,* for instance, would not necessarily work for readers of *People,* or even for the readers of *New York.*

A test for copy is to read it without being able to tell whether a man or a woman wrote it. Gender should not be a factor unless, of course, the ad is designed specifically for male or female readership, going into a publication serving one or the other audience.

Gender-neutral language is necessary in most advertising. But sensitivity to demands for neutral or inclusive pronouns sometimes results in clumsy phrasing. "He or she" and "his or her" replacing the generic "he" and "his" often hurts a sentence's cadence, especially when two or three combinations appear in a single sentence. The answer to the problem in most cases is to start with a plural noun and then use "they" as the pronoun.

Involving the Reader

An organization wanting advice or financial help from someone is not above appointing that person to an advisory or governing board or committee or giving away an honorary degree. Similarly, advertisers in recent years, to fight reader apathy, have involved the reader in their advertising. "How many mistakes can you find in this picture?" a greeting card manufacturer asks in an ad headline. Find enough of them and the company will send you a free ballpoint pen—and information on how you can make money in your spare time selling cards door-to-door. "Draw me," says an ad for a correspondence school, and if your drawing is good enough (it usually is), the school will invite you to take its art lessons.

But the involvement can be much more subtle than that. The copywriter can ask rhetorical questions, leaving the obvious unsaid. "One of America's two great beers," said a brewery in San Francisco. Never mind the name of the other "great" beer. Let readers supply a name. Just so they ponder the notion and identify as "great" the one that signs the ad.

A good example of a reader-participation ad was by Del Monte showing a large, ripe tomato with the headline "If You Can See What's Wrong with This Tomato, Your Standards Are Up to Ours." It was a surprising headline, because the tomato was a beautiful specimen. A second headline, in much smaller type (so as not to give the answer away too quickly), read: "(High Shoulders Indicate a Large Stem End and Tough, Woody Core Material.)." A small inset photo at the bottom showing a Del Monte bottle of catsup and a can of tomato sauce was accompanied by the slogan "The more you know about tomatoes, the better for Del Monte." This seemed to justify the headline and at the same time praise the product.

Another example of a reader-participation ad was the one sponsored some years ago by "some citizens who think Congress made a mistake" when it killed a bill that would have given $40 million to cities and states for rat control. The ad showed a life-size rat, with a headline that read: "Cut This Out and Put It in Bed Next to Your Child."

On a less lofty level, Fort Howard Paper, to dramatize the fact that its rolls of toilet paper are larger than those of the competition, ran an industrial ad with a set of circles (to represent various roll thicknesses) and invited readers (managers of industrial concerns) to "Put a Roll of Your Tissue Here and Find Out

Copywriter Larre Johnson uses irony to make the point in this ad sponsored by the Partnership for a Drug-Free America. As a drug user, carrying an organ donor card is "the least you can do. Then no one can say you didn't do anything worthwhile with your life." Agency: Keye/Donna/Pearlstein. Art director: Rick Bell.

Part of this ad's intrigue comes from the command to save the newspaper. Why save it? Because it will work as well as a drop cloth; the copy points out that the Power Painter "is clean and easy to control." Copywriter: Ron Sackett. Art director: Dan Krumwiede. Agency: Carmichael-Lynch Advertising, Minneapolis. Client: Wagner/Spray Tech.

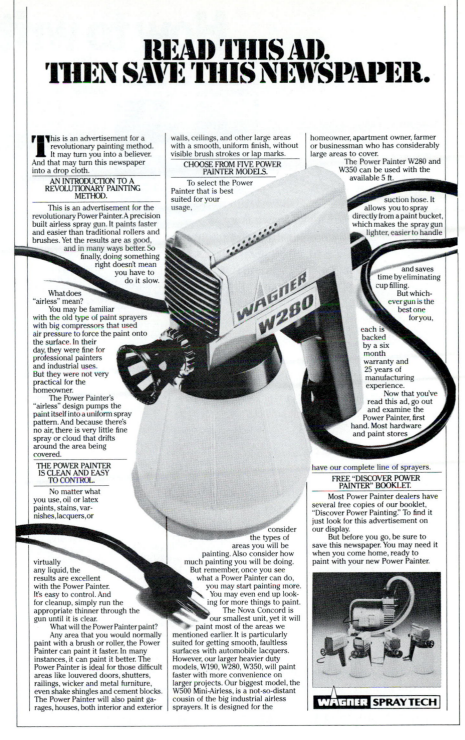

How Much Howard Can Save You in Maintenance Costs." Similarly, in a double-page full-color ad in *The New York Times Magazine,* Royal Doulton Bone China showed a place setting without a plate on the left page and a place setting with a Royal Doulton plate on the right page. The left-page headline: "Put Your China on This Page and Compare it to Ours." The right-hand page headline asked: "Honestly, Is There Any Comparison?"

Armstrong, which makes vinyl flooring, included a coupon in a *Reader's Digest* ad with the headline: "If You Can Cut This Out, You Can Install an Armstrong Floor."

Another way to involve the reader in the advertising is to use micro-

How to write clearly

By Edward T. Thompson
Editor-in-Chief, Reader's Digest

International Paper asked Edward T. Thompson to share some of what he has learned in nineteen years with Reader's Digest, a magazine famous for making complicated subjects understandable to millions of readers.

If you are afraid to write, don't be.

If you think you've got to string together big fancy words and high-flying phrases, forget it.

To write well, unless you aspire to be a professional poet or novelist, you only need to get your ideas across simply and clearly.

It's not easy. But it *is* easier than you might imagine.

There are only three basic requirements:

First, you must *want* to write clearly. And I believe you really do, if you've stayed this far with me.

Second, you must be willing to *work hard.* Thinking means work—and that's what it takes to do anything well.

Third, you must know and follow some *basic guidelines.*

If, while you're writing for clarity, some lovely, dramatic or inspired phrases or sentences come to you, fine. Put them in.

But then with cold, objective eyes and mind ask yourself: "Do they detract from clarity?" If they do, grit your teeth and cut the frills.

Follow some basic guidelines

I can't give you a complete list of "dos and don'ts" for every writing problem you'll ever face.

But I can give you some fundamental guidelines that cover the most common problems.

1. Outline what you want to say.

I know that sounds grade-schoolish. But you can't write clearly until, *before you start,* you know where you will stop.

Ironically, that's even a problem in writing an outline (i.e., knowing the ending before you begin).

So try this method:

• On 3″ x 5″ cards, write—one point to a card—all the points you need to make.

• Divide the cards into piles—one pile for each group of points *closely related* to each other. (If you were describing an automobile, you'd put all the points about mileage in one pile, all the points about safety in another, and so on.)

• Arrange your piles of points in a sequence. Which are most important and should be given first or saved for last? Which must you present before others in order to make the others understandable?

• Now, *within* each pile, do the same thing—arrange the *points* in logical, understandable order.

There you have your outline, needing only an introduction and conclusion.

This is a practical way to outline. It's also flexible. You can add, delete or change the location of points easily.

2. Start where your readers are.

How much do they know about the subject? Don't write to a level higher than your readers' knowledge of it.

CAUTION: Forget that old—and wrong—advice about writing to a 12-year-old mentality. That's insulting. But do remember that your prime purpose is to *explain* something, not prove that you're smarter than your readers.

3. Avoid jargon.

Don't use words, expressions, phrases known only to people with specific knowledge or interests.

Example: A scientist, using scientific jargon, wrote, "The biota exhibited a one hundred percent mortality response." He could have written: "All the fish died."

4. Use familiar combinations of words.

A speech writer for President Franklin D. Roosevelt wrote, "We are endeavoring to construct a more inclusive society." F.D.R. changed it to, "We're going to make a country in which no one is left out."

CAUTION: By familiar combinations of words, I do *not* mean incorrect grammar. *That* can be *un*clear. Example: John's father says he can't go out Friday. (Who can't go out? John or his father?)

5. Use "first-degree" words.

These words immediately bring an image to your mind. Other words must be "translated" through the first-degree word before you see

"Outline for clarity. Write your points on 3″ x 5″ cards—one point to a card. Then you can easily add to, or change the order of points—even delete some."

---

fragrances, or scent-in-ink encapsulation. Research does not prove that this novelty results in increased sales, but no doubt it holds the reader to the ad longer.

"Unfortunately, there are some ads that smell without scratching," observes Al Hampel, president of D'Arcy-MacManus & Masius/New York.

Writing Style

While art and design styles of other eras can serve advertisers today, copy style must be current. Rare is the advertiser who would be willing to put a sales message in the flossy, sentimental, overwritten language of advertising of the 1920s and 1930s. Take that classic ad sponsored by the New Haven Railroad in World War II, "The Kid in Upper 4." It was an appeal to civilian passengers, asking them to be patient during a time when first consideration had to be given to moving servicemen across the country. It told of the typical young soldier going to war:

"Tonight, he knows, he is leaving behind a lot of little things—and big ones.

"The taste of hamburgers and pop . . . the feel of driving a roadster over a six-lane highway . . . a dog named Shucks, or Spot, or Barnacle Bill. . . .

International Paper Company's "How to write clearly" ad, a good example of institutional advertising, contains some excellent advice for copywriters, although they are not the intended primary audience. The ad ran in *Newsweek* and similar magazines. Agency: Ogilvy & Mather. Creative director: Billings Fuess. Copywriter: Edward T. Thompson, editor-in-chief of *Reader's Digest.*

"Grit your teeth and cut the frills. That's one of the suggestions I offer here to help you write clearly. They cover the most common problems. And they're all easy to follow."

the image. Those are second/third-degree words.

First-degree words	Second/third-degree words
face	visage, countenance
stay	abide, remain, reside
book	volume, tome, publication

First-degree words are usually the most precise words, too.

6. Stick to the point.

Your outline— which was more work in the beginning—now saves you work. Because now you can ask about any sentence you write: "Does it relate to a point in the outline? If it doesn't, should I add it to the outline? If not, I'm getting off the track." Then, full steam ahead—on the main line.

7. Be as brief as possible.

Whatever you write, shortening—*condensing*—almost always makes it tighter, straighter, easier to read and understand.

Condensing, as *Reader's Digest* does it, is in large part artistry. But it involves techniques that anyone can learn and use.

• *Present your points in logical ABC order:* Here again, your outline should save you work because, if you did it right, your points already stand in logical ABC order—A makes B understandable, B makes C understandable and so on. To write in a straight line is to say something clearly in the fewest possible words.

• *Don't waste words telling people what they already know:* Notice how we edited this: "Have you ever

wondered how banks rate you as a credit risk? ~~You know, of course, that it's some combination of facts about your income, your job, and so on. But actually,~~ Many banks have a scoring system...."

• *Cut out excess evidence and unnecessary anecdotes:* Usually, one fact or example (at most, two) will support a point. More just belabor it. And while writing about some-

Writing clearly means avoiding jargon. Why didn't he just say: "All the fish died!"

thing may remind you of a good story, ask yourself: "Does it *really help* to tell the story, or does it slow me down?"

(Many people think *Reader's Digest* articles are filled with anecdotes. Actually, we use them sparingly and usually for one of two reasons: either the subject is so dry it needs some "humanity" to give it life; or the subject is so hard to grasp, it needs anecdotes to help readers understand. If the subject is both lively and easy to grasp, we move right along.)

• *Look for the most common word wasters:* windy phrases.

Windy phrases	Cut to...
at the present time	now
in the event of	if
in the majority of instances	usually

• *Look for passive verbs you can make active:* Invariably, this produces a shorter sentence. "The cherry tree *was* chopped down by George Washington." (Passive verb and nine words.) "George Washington *chopped* down the cherry tree." (Active verb and seven words.)

• *Look for positive/negative sections from which you can cut the negative:* See how we did it here: "The answer ~~does not rest with carelessness or incompetence. It lies largely in~~ is having enough people to do the job."

• Finally, to write more clearly by saying it in fewer words: when you've finished, stop.

Edward T. Thompson

"There's a lump in his throat. And maybe—a tear fills his eye. *It doesn't matter, Kid.* Nobody will see . . . it's too dark."

As copy, it would not move today's sophisticated reader.

Even "The Penalty of Leadership" ad, sponsored by Cadillac in 1915, making its point that "In every field of human endeavor, he that is first must live in the white light of publicity," seems a little smug when read today.

Guidelines for Copywriters

Copy, like layout, is too much an art to be directed by a set of rules, but the beginning copywriter may find the following guidelines helpful.

■ *Write clearly.* While flair and even cleverness have a place in advertising copy, nothing is more important than clarity. That readers understand the copy is more important than that they be impressed by its style. Use plain language and concrete terms. Use uninvolved, short, subject-predicate sentences rather than long, complicated ones. Rely occasionally on sentence fragments. (But. Sentence fragments. Can be. Overdone.)

Robert O. Bach, senior vice president, creative services, N W Ayer, made this observation: "The simple truth is that too much advertising today is too complicated in manner, and complicated in matter. Complicated in manner with devious, intricate verbal and visual conceits; by oh-see-how-clever-I-am phrases and designs. And complicated in matter by that old bugaboo—trying to say too much in one advertisement. The advertisement that's not simple in matter and not simple in manner, can evoke one of only two responses: no interest at all, or confusion. Either one costs just too much money to tolerate today."[17]

Parallel structure provides one good way to keep meaning clear. When you have several points of equal importance or you need to make comparisons, you should use the same basic phrasing for each. "Better tasting, faster acting, lasts longer" is clearer this way: "Better tasting, faster acting, longer lasting."

Do not allow sentences to carry two meanings if one of the meanings could be detrimental to your client. "We can't do enough for you" might be clear enough to most people, but the line carries the thought that "enough" is what people need and this advertiser cannot meet the need.

The Advertising Council, for the U.S. Forest Service, for years has promoted the slogan, with the help of Smokey Bear, that "Only You Can Prevent Forest Fires." As a slogan it is vague, even misleading. People who hear it are not sure what it means. Or people know it is wrong because, after all, other people can prevent forest fires, too.

"Free" has always been an attention-getting word in advertising. In this newspaper ad from the early 1930s, a power-and-light company, using plenty of copy, announces a contest to win an electric ironer.

WHAT A PERSON CAN DO IS MORE IMPORTANT THAN WHAT HE OR SHE CANNOT DO!

This headline, used in an ad sponsored by a rehabilitation facility, would flow more easily with "PEOPLE" substituted for "A PERSON" and "THEY" substituted for "HE OR SHE." Better: Use "YOU" in both places.

Jerry Della Femina, founder of Della Femina, Travisano & Partners, says: "A lot of advertising starts out with a fairly good idea. But the idea is buried inside fancy words and dumb visuals. . . . Nobody has the time to try and figure out what you're trying to say, so you need to be direct. . . ."[18]

■ *Pick your words carefully.* Within the bounds of legal restrictions, good taste, and fair play, look for words that will do the best selling job for your client. This means weighing each word carefully for all its implications. "Sugar free," for instance, is, on balance, a better term than "sugarless" because "free" has positive connotations where "less" has negative ones.

"Festival seating" is a rock concert promoter's euphemistic term for "general admission." "Installation available" means, of course, that the attractive sales price is not the whole price, unless the customer wants the muffler, or whatever, only to put on display somewhere. A rate of "$55 per night per person, double occupancy" eases the guests into a $110 room. "Some assembly required" warns the buyer of an hour or more of bruised knuckles and frustration. A car dealer saying "Not all cars sell for retail price" means, really, that "Few cars sell for retail price."

Still, flair in writing can make the difference between copy that is remembered and copy that is tossed aside. Where flair gets its best chance is in narrative copy, which comes closest to imitating what you find in a short story or in a script of the kind produced by playwrights or screenwriters.

Paco Rabanne, a cologne for men, in a two-page magazine ad shows a man in bed—he apparently is an artist, from the looks of the room—receiving a phone call. He's barely covered by a sheet. Empty glasses and a bottle rest on a tray at the foot of the bed. It is morning.

"Hello."

"You snore."

"And you steal all the covers. What time did you leave?"

And so on, with a number of double entendres of the kind to cause knowing winks and elbow jabs. She confesses that she took his bottle of Paco Rabanne with her when she left. Couldn't resist it. You get the idea that the woman is classy and well traveled; she's calling from San Francisco, of course.

". . . they're calling my flight."

She'll be back Tuesday.

It is an ad to be remembered by people who think a good-smelling cologne is the secret to a memorable night.

Another example:

Massage Pet, a roller device made for soothing back muscles, also helps the buyer make new friends, according to a tag attached to the device. (It takes a second person to roll it up and down the back.) "Let the good times roll!!!" says the tag, using more exclamation marks than necessary but, still, making its point effectively.

While the following examples happen to be headlines, the flair they exhibit is the flair body copy needs, too. Feel the rhythm. Appreciate the subtlety. Savor the word choice. See the pictures.

"All Cadillacs Are the Same," says Tinney Cadillac of Buffalo, New York, in an ad in the *Buffalo Spree*. "All Cadillac Dealers Are Not."

"We Want to Lose You as a Customer as Soon as Possible," says the Weight Loss Clinic.

"Softens the Sidewalks," says an ad for Ripple Shoes. G. H. Bass & Co. calls its shoes "Personal Transportation." "If It Hurts When You Walk Take Two of These," says a headline for an ad for Rockport Shoes. A pair of shoes is pictured.

"More Than Love Is Sweeping the Country" is the title Abbott Laboratories gives its booklet on venereal disease.

"Don't Lose Your Shape Trying to Keep It," says an ad for the Running Bra by Formfit Rogers.

"Why Lease a Car When You Can Lease a Legend?" the Porsche people ask.

"Let us Put a Vacation in Your Backyard," implores a swimming pool company.

"Pigments of the Imagination" is the way Colours by Alexander Julian describes the colors of its shirts and sweaters.

"The Lowest Price Cruise to Bermuda Is the Most Extravagant Way to Go," says Holland America, a cruise line.

"Take Me to Bed," invites Barnes & Nobel's ad for a small lamp that attaches itself to books. The light from the lamp "floods the entire page with a brilliant cool light guaranteed not to disturb anyone nearby."

"No Batteries Needed!" says William Morrow in an ad selling its children's books.

"McEnroe Swears by Them," says Nike in an ad mentioning that bad-tempered tennis player.

"We're Looking for People Who Love to Write" says the headline of an ad in *Writer's Digest* for Writers Institute, Inc., a correspondence school. That is more promising than "We're Looking for People Who Are Willing to Take Our Correspondence Course." The Institute of Children's Literature, another correspondence school (you'd never know by the name), uses a similar headline, but one that moves a little further from the real purpose of the ad: "We're Looking for People to Write Children's Books."

Using just the right words, you can impress one group of buyers without antagonizing another.

Toy manufacturers, coming out with their new boy dolls, complete with appendages, referred to them as "anatomically correct" dolls. Who could argue against something that is "anatomically correct"?

Current pressures make advertisers want to hedge in their copy. In a television commercial, Cascade showed women comparing recently washed glasses. "See the difference Cascade can make," one of them said. Notice the "can make." That is quite different from—and safer than—"makes."

■ *Write in active voice.* "You save up to 25 percent" is better than "Up to 25 percent can be saved." Textbook writers, including this one, too often lapse into passive voice to avoid attribution or to change the pace in long segments of prose. But copywriters, with their smaller segments, can avoid most passive voice. They make their copy more exciting when they do. They make it move along faster.

■ *Be concise.* As a general rule, the shorter the copy, the better—so long as it does the job. But not all advertising subjects lend themselves to short copy blocks. For a major purchase, for instance, a prospective buyer has the motivation to digest innumerable facts before making a decision. For most mail-order copy, where the prospective buyer does not have the chance to ask questions of the salesperson, copy can go on for several columns.

Even if, as for a Mercedes-Benz ad, a reader doesn't wade through long columns of copy, the impression is made that the car is good enough to merit all those words. Expensive items, especially, benefit from ads with lots of copy.

It is a simple matter to break up long columns typographically into short takes. With subheads, initial letters, small illustrations, small areas of white space, and other devices, a good art director easily can make long copy look short and inviting.

■ *Strive for easy transitions from one sentence to the next, from one paragraph to the next.* Copy should move smoothly, effortlessly. There should be no abrupt changes.

But avoid transitions that are artificial—sentence openers like "Fact is," "What's more," and "Yes." They become monotonous when used sentence after sentence.

Transitions do not always have to come at the beginnings of sentences, nor do they always have to be the obvious words of transition. The *content* of the sentence can be transition enough.

Or buy a Volkswagen.

Robert Levenson wrote the one line of copy for an ad that captured the frustration a typical driver felt during a time when gas became scarce. The value of the illustration, drawn by Charles Piccirillo, lies in its artful ambiguity. Is it a gun? No, it is only a nozzle. Still. . . . Agency: Doyle Dane Bernbach.

■ *Write vividly.* You should pick words that are vivid, precise, and memorable, putting them together so they form a picture that will imbed itself in the reader's mind. Shelton's Premium Poultry advertises that "Our Chickens Don't Do Drugs." The copy points out that the chickens are fed properly and are not injected with chemicals. Barneys, the upscale New York clothing store, announced an expansion of its "English Room" to sell more London-tailored suits. "An impressive selection at a fraction of the distance."

Fleet Glycerin Suppositories Laxative makes a compelling case for its kind of remedy over other kinds with this headline: "Oh-Oh! Where Will You Be When Your Laxative Starts Working?"

Abba Pest Control Inc. holds a "Dead Carpenter Ant Sale": $195, with a one-year guarantee.

Otto Kleppner, coauthor of a textbook for beginning courses in advertising, reprints a Hendrik Van Loon quote to illustrate how vivid writing works, even though it doesn't happen to be a piece of advertising copy. The quote, meant to describe "eternity," goes like this: "High up in the North in the land called Svithjod there stands a rock. It is one hundred miles high and one hundred miles wide. Once every thousand years a little bird comes to this rock to sharpen its beak. When this rock has been worn away, then a single day of eternity will have gone by."[19]

One of the early teachers of advertising told a story of a beggar in Central Park who, with a routine "I am blind" sign, did a disappointing business. Then he changed his sign: "It is spring—and I am blind."

You cannot deal with reality alone, a writer at McCann-Erickson has said. It would be like a man looking at a pretty woman through glasses that

Executive Life in this two-page ad admits that at one time life insurance was "a terrible buy" but makes a strong case, on a crowded right-hand page, that it is an excellent buy now, especially if it is written by this firm. A tan tint unites the two pages, and so does the placement of the two headlines. The lack of copy on the left-hand page dramatizes the fullness of the message on the right. Agency: Keye/Donna/Pearlstein. Art director: Tom Cordner. Copywriter: Paul Keye.

YOU WERE RIGHT.

(Life insurance was a terrible buy.)

NOW YOU'RE WRONG.

It wasn't anyone's fault. It wasn't a conspiracy. It wasn't Dumb Guys versus Smart or Black Hats versus White.

But the truth is that, almost a generation ago, life insurance as a savings or investment vehicle became an outdated bit of economic theory.

The social, the emotional, the near-religious arguments remained. It was a duty, an obligation. Life insurance was The Right Thing For Right Thinking People To Do.

But it was a terrible buy.

Why? What had happened? First, the typical life insurance policy—part protection and part savings—rewarded the holder with an annual interest rate on his accumulated savings of three or four or, maybe, five percent.

Not exactly a drop in the bucket, right? Right. More like a hole in the bucket. The rest of the world—even the very conservative world of banks and savings and loans—offered eight and ten and, maybe, twelve percent.

Second, the typical life insurance policy assumed that someone in his twenties was buying something to leave his family when he died in his sixties.

But he didn't die. He's still around. He's in his eighties.

Pencils and paper, everybody.

What's the difference between four percent over forty years and ten percent over sixty years?

The answer is Revolution. It wasn't that life insurance companies suddenly had to become competitive. They had always been competitive. With one another. The profound, mind-bending change was that they had to compete in the open marketplace. The whole rough and tumble financial marketplace.

A business built on Mortality and Guarantees and Emotionalism found itself cut adrift in a world of Longevity and Opportunity and Financial Sophistication.

There was one more reason: Us.

Five years ago, a company called Executive Life began offering interest-sensitive insurance policies that paid market rates on the accumulated savings in the policy.

Today, with over $1 billion in revenues and $5 billion in assets, the Executive Life Companies combine to be one of the ten largest writers of new life insurance. *Forbes* reported us as first among all life insurance and accident and health insurance companies in return on equity, return on capital and earnings per share.

We pioneered the use of current mortality tables, ones that showed how much longer you were living. (Some companies still use data from the Fifties which not only makes their clients old before their time; it makes their rates higher.)

But the principal difference between Executive Life and the rest of the industry has been the performance of its investment portfolio and the direct effect of that performance in reducing the cost of its policies.

About our policyholders. A fact and a guess.

The guess is that they are the very people who wouldn't have been caught dead owning more than a token amount of life insurance just a few years back.

The fact is that—as a group—Executive Life policyholders carry the highest average policy size in the industry.

Imitation is the sincerest form of competition.

Our representatives sell a group of evolving life insurance products, created and refined under the name Irreplaceable Life.

Today, there are a dozen companies that can sell you some pretty fair copies of the Irreplaceable Life

policies we were offering two or three years ago. But if you want our newest products, we're the only ones who have them.

Which leads to a word of caution:

There's a new piece of fine print in the insurance business.

Most of the policies like ours that are sold today are sold on "projections."

"Projections" is a formal word for "guess." More politely, a projection is an estimated rate of return. So, when you're dealing with this new language, two questions are in order: "What happens when the insurance company makes its projection?"

Because companies can only pay from earnings, it wouldn't hurt to ask any company what its rate of return has been for the last several years. (If they don't know, your state insurance department knows.)

Executive Life has earned more than its projections in five of the last five years. We have then shared our success with our policyholders who have converted those extra earnings into lower premium payments or additional coverage.

"And what happens if the company doesn't make its projections?"

You may be buying a policy that will require you to make up the difference in increased premium if your insurance company doesn't make its projected earnings. (Sort of an annual balloon payment, if you can pay it. Or less protection if you can't.)

This is a commercial.

There's one more brand new word in our business. It's called "performance." In our case, how much insurance for how much money?

Suffice to say, there's an enormous range of performance. Winners. Also-rans. Losers.

But if you'll check the Winners' list, and look at the very top, you'll find what we hope is now a familiar name.

EXECUTIVE LIFE

Net Investment Income (in millions)

$481.1
$333.5
$149.8
$57.8
$18.9

1979 1980 1981 1982 1983

Year after year, the Executive Life Companies have been among the top five in the entire insurance industry in terms of investment performance. Source: A.M. Best Company.

For more information, write or call: Executive Life Insurance Co., Dept. A, 11444 Olympic Blvd., West Los Angeles, CA 90064, (213) 312-1000, or Executive Life Insurance Co. of New York, Dept. A, 300 N. Broadway, Jericho, NY 11753, (516) 931-6400. A+ (excellent) A.M. Best-rated companies. © 1984, Executive Life.

PUTTING IT INTO WORDS

magnified the pores. "The girl you love may be 70.2 percent water, 25 percent oxygen, carbon, hydrogen, and nitrogen, and 4.8 percent mineral, but it would make a lousy love song."[20]

■ *Avoid the clichés of advertising copy.* They include such words and phrases as *at last, now, full-bodied, amazing, fast-acting, fabulous, farm-fresh, improved, giant size, quick relief, hurry, while supplies last, passing the savings on to you, it's that simple, that's what . . . is all about, the . . . designed with you in mind, don't you dare miss it!, if you like to eat—and who doesn't?, just possibly the best . . . , everything you ever wanted to know about . . . , the bottom line,* and *getting it all together.*

These days everybody running a convention arranges at least one "hands-on" session. Another tiresome expression, used widely by advertisers now, is "state of the art." "People, quality, support and technology. That's state of the art service for state of the art products," said AT&T in an ad selling its information systems.

Two other clichés in advertising: "If you spent one cent for any of these services you spent too much. . . ." and "We want to be your store [or your car maker or whatever]. . . ."

Copywriters put a lot of faith, too, in the word *creative.* They attach the word to inanimate objects as well as to people, as though inanimate objects in themselves hold the power to be creative. Conditions—even unpleasant conditions—also tend to be creative, in the minds of copywriters. A YMCA advertised classes in "Creative Unemployment."

Sometimes these words may be the best or the only way of expressing the idea. That they became clichés indicates that they did serve the advertiser well before they became shopworn. But the copywriter should search for other ways to make the point before resorting to a cliché. The reader has built up immunity to much of the language of advertising.

The clichés of advertising include nouns retrained to be self-conscious verbs and mid-length words stretched out to limousine size, like "sportcoatings" used by Southwick for its sportscoats. Ann Goodwillie of Omaha noticed a retail ad announcing a sale on handbags: "Come in and See Our Wide Variety of Stylings and Colorations." "Perhaps I will," she wrote in a letter to the editor of *Time* (whose magazine had just run an essay on English usage). "I'm sure they have large numerations of sizings and shapings. A new purse may just give me the right kind of liftation I need to carry me into the coming seasoning."

The cover says "Stock Trade Marks," and the inside pages of this booklet offer a number of them for sale. It is all deliciously tongue-in-cheek, a promotional piece for Herring Design, Houston, which turns out trademark design of a much higher order than displayed here. Although he meant the piece as a joke, Jerry Herring, the designer and writer, received a number of perfectly serious orders or inquiries about his "stock trade marks." Find a magnifying glass and read these pages carefully. The lesson is subtle and valuable.

The Star Trade Mark. Perfect for those doing movie, government or occult work. Special clearance needed to use in red.

The Crest Trade Mark. Has a quiet dignity. Especially good for new restaurants in need of a long history.

The Rainbow Trade Mark. Good for companies with a bright outlook, or a company dealing in gold futures.

The Modern Trade Mark. Can be interpreted in many ways. An ideal choice when dealing with a committee.

Despairing of colors like "grapefruit," "oatmeal," "burnt orange," and "expresso" assigned to goods advertised in a Tweed's catalog, David Greenberg, writing in *The New Republic,* said, "This sort of imaginative nomenclature from our mail-order friends has begun to grow irksome. It's one thing to get creative in the name of specificity; I mean, I can see wanting a scarf in French Vanilla instead of plain white. But Calcium? Tundra? Amish? 'Sky' no longer suffices to modify the blue of the heavens."[21]

Clichés also include words that somehow, to the copywriter, sound better than the normal words they replace. Like "plus." In advertising copy "plus" apparently means more than "and." So readers put up with sentences like this: "You get low price, plus we will. . . ."

■ *Avoid the obvious.* If a benefit is already generally known, it is a good idea to stress an additional benefit, referring to the original benefit only tangentially. Sunsweet Prune Juice did that with an ad headlined "You Bought It for One Good Reason. Now We'll Give You Four More." The copy started out with the sentence "There are lots of good reasons for drinking Sunsweet Prune Juice, besides the obvious one." Other reasons listed were for nourishment, versatility (you can enhance other dishes with the product), energy, and flavor.

Copy often contains sentences or add-ons that are there probably on the advice of attorneys. "Use only as directed." Of course. "Void where prohibited." How could it be otherwise?

Necessary lines can be written in fresh and charming ways. Gump's in San Francisco doesn't settle for "No Smoking" signs in its stores. It says instead, "Try Not to Smoke." D'Amico Cusina, a Minneapolis restaurant, covers the fact that it is not open for lunch with the line, "We don't serve lunch. It takes us all day to prepare dinner."

■ *Make comparisons.* Figures of speech can dramatize your point. Your product can be like something else; it can even *be* something else.

In a two-page ad in *Business Week,* IBM shows on the left page a huge fingerprint. On the right a headline says, "No Two Businesses Are Alike Either." The copy points out that IBM offers a wide range of computers. "There's one that can be tailored to fit your unique needs and grow as your business grows." And, "Thousands of software programs are written for IBM."

A 1991 commercial for the Chrysler LeBaron GTC convertible compared the car to Mercedes 5055L, showing three seconds on a stopwatch. Referring to a 0–60 time start, a voice said, "This is what you save with a Mercedes." When the commercial cut to a LeBaron trunk stuffed with cash, the voice said, "This is what you save with a LeBaron. Think of it as a Mercedes with an $81,000 rebate."

■ *Tailor the copy to the audience.* As a copywriter you must "guard against intellectualizing."[22] You must both put yourself in the place of your reader and understand the medium your ad will appear in. What works for one medium does not necessarily work for another. Volkswagen's "Buy Low. Sell High." ad (as an example) was designed to be run in those magazines read primarily by the affluent.

Persons other than stockholders would understand from the ad that the car does not depreciate very fast, but they would miss some of the nuances of the copy: "The day you sell your car could very well be Black Tuesday . . . our tip . . . seasoned traders . . . you don't have to make a big investment . . . sealed underneath so the bottom won't suddenly fall out of your market . . . a lot of car makers did sell us short. . . ."

Right at the start your copy should pinpoint your audience. The Sponsors of San Francisco Performing Arts Center, Inc., in an ad in "Datebook," a section of the San Francisco *Sunday Examiner & Chronicle,* used this headline to single out ordinary citizens from the wealthy: "An Appeal to the Skinny Cats of San Francisco." "The fat cats have done their part," the copy began. "Over 5800 of them have already come up with $35 million to build the new Performing Arts Center.

"But it isn't quite enough, and rather than go back to them for the last $2 million, we turn to you and all the citizens of the San Francisco Bay Area. We want you to participate. . . .

"No one, fat or skinny, gets a button, a T-shirt, a card, a membership, or a favor. All you get is a good feeling, a feeling that will last a long time. You will have the special satisfaction of contributing to the health and well-being of this city."

■ *Write for the individual.* Although what you write is reproduced for multiple readership, write as if for a single reader. Attempt to maintain through mass communication the illusion of a salesman-to-buyer relationship. Your writing should be informal, conversational, and, where appropriate, intimate. A logical way of developing a one-reader feel in copy is by writing in second person. The word *you* is deservedly commonplace in advertising copy.

Reva Korda, creative head of Ogilvy & Mather, adds three "unfashionable opinions" about copywriting to the eleven guidelines presented here:

"The faster you write the copy, the better it will be." Korda says that a copywriter given too much time tends to get "too darn smart. . . . It's so easy to lose contact with your own natural, intuitive reactions to a product and what might make another human being want to buy it."

"If you can possibly manage to get away with it, work alone." Korda thinks a lot of advertising is bad because it is created by groups or by "what sometimes looks like *mobs*." She adds, ". . . you can always tell when an ad was written by one person—it will have a very special, very personal kind of rhythm."

"Write alone, write fast, and never, never write for test scores." She concludes: *"There is no method of pretesting that can hold a candle to good old-fashioned judgment."*[23]

Naming Names

It used to be that advertisers never named competitors. If they did, it was always "Brand X." That has changed. Although the self-regulatory organizations tend to discourage "comparative advertising," the Federal Trade Commission encourages it.

For years the makers of margarines claimed for themselves the qualities of butter. The American Dairy Association fought back in its advertising, saying

National Right to Life allows an all-caps headline, separated into two takes by a compelling full-color photograph, to serve essentially as the copy for this poster-like ad. The small-type caption for the photograph says that it is of a 19-week-old "intrauterine child." "Like the bud of a flower, beautiful. But, unfortunately still a candidate for elective abortion." At least one magazine in which this ad appeared ran "An Advertisement" at the top because the magazine didn't want readers to mistake the ad for editorial matter. Photographer: Dr. Rainer Jones.

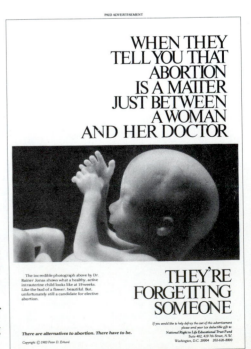

Levi Strauss & Co. used a series of classy ads like this to explain its 501® "Shrink-To-Fit®" jeans. With good humor, the ads capitalized on the fact that the product hasn't changed in 125 years. "You keep buying original Levi's 501® blue denim jeans, and we'll do our best to keep adding no improvements." The jeans have a four-button fly. "No need to go switching to something that might just be a temporary fad, like zippers." Art director: Bernie Vangrin. Copywriter: Tim Price. Illustrator: Dugald Stermer. Agency: Foote, Cone & Belding/Honig, San Francisco.

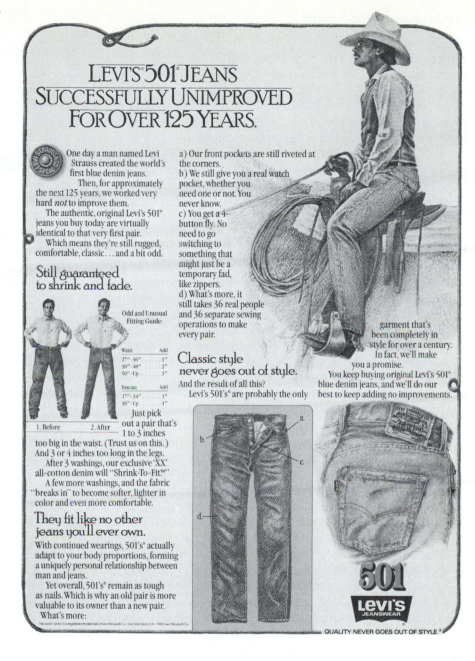

that there is nothing like the taste of real butter. Its slogan ran like this: "We'll never claim that butter tastes like margarine."

Xerox used appropriate wording in a headline to make its point against IBM. "Our New Typewriter Has More Memory Than What's Their Name's."

In promoting its fox-emblem polo shirts, J. C. Penney says, "See You Later, Alligator" referring to the better-known and more-expensive-emblem shirt by Izod.

The named product can be expected to fight back. After Scope began referring to Listerine as "medicine breath" mouthwash, Listerine in its advertising referred to Scope as a "sweet-tasting" mouthwash.

When a magazine gave Alaska Airlines high ratings in a published survey, the company took out a full-page ad in selected daily newspapers and ran a giant headline: "We Could Get Sued for Running This Ad." The copy pointed out that "This certain magazine . . . will not sponsor or endorse any service, so they won't let us mention their name. . . . So instead of telling you that we received the highest rating in almost every category, all we can do is mention that the July issue (page 462) of this certain magazine may be of interest to you. It certainly was to us."

Anthropomorphic Selling

Among famous characters copywriters and art directors have invented are Mrs. Butterworth, Mr. Whipple, Mrs. Olson, Madge (the manicurist), Rosy (who cleans up counter spills), Mr. Clean, Tony the Tiger, Morris the Cat, the Jolly Green Giant, Frank Bartles and Ed Jaymes, and Juan Valdez. Most ad watchers, especially those addicted to TV, can tie these characters to the products they sell. Naming the senators from their states—well, that would be another matter.

One of the most durable characters dreamed up by agencies to sell products is the Maytag repairman. Jesse White retired in 1989 after 21 years on the job to be succeeded by actor Gordon Jump, formerly from the TV series *WKRP in Cincinnati.* The lonely repairman with nothing to do has been so successful that when people do have trouble with their Maytag appliances and have to call for repairs, they are often angry.

To dramatize and personalize its 24-hour-a-day access to savings accounts, Far West Federal Savings uses a Mr. Moneybags character: a tight cartoon drawing of a distinguished middle-aged man in a tux with spats, carrying a couple of money bags and a Far West Savings Card. Designer: Les Hopkins. Art director: Dan Fast. Agency: Marketing Systems, Inc.

Characters who are invented or adopted to sell products don't live forever. Finally the theme and campaign have to end. IBM used a Charlie Chaplin character—the Little Tramp—to sell its computers from 1981 to 1987. An actor imitated Chaplin, of course. The campaign originated to appeal to ordinary people to interest them in personal computers. When the company introduced a new PC line and moved further into mainframe computers and other products, it felt it was time to change. Lord, Geller, Federico, Einstein, its agency, created a new campaign using the characters from the defunct M*A*S*H TV program.

A character does not necessarily have to work exclusively for one advertiser. King Features and other newspaper feature syndicates rent out their comic-strip characters to advertisers who think they can benefit from such association.

World-Wide Licensing & Merchandising Corp., New York, licenses "Mr. Magoo" as "the only sales force you need!"

For some advertisers, it is a recognizable style rather than a character that does the job. For several years one company sold insurance through the full-page, full-color efforts of cartoonist Roland B. Wilson. Always there was a character about to be badly injured if not killed. Only a companion was aware of what was happening. The potential victim was always saying: "My insurance company? New England Life, of course. Why?" One of the longest-lived campaigns of this genre involved the cartoons of *The New Yorker* cartoonist Richard Decker and the gagline/headline: "In Philadelphia, Nearly Everybody Reads the Bulletin." (Alas, the *Bulletin* is now gone.)

Sometimes the advertiser hires a well-known writer to step down from an editorial perch to produce advertising copy. For this kind of copy, a byline strikes the advertiser as appropriate. Perhaps the writer's good reputation will wear off onto the product. The same kind of thinking goes into the advertiser's request that the person who reads the news on radio or television also read the commercial, a practice journalism schools frown on.

The Testimonial

Surely many, if not most, people seeing a famous person testifying to the glories of a particular product view the episode with some skepticism. And yet the testimonials keep coming. Their real value must be that they do cause the reader or viewer to stop and pay some attention to the ad, if only momentarily.

One of the best testimonial series involved famous people who were American Express credit card holders. It was effective because it showed the famous people in everyday, down-to-earth poses. There was the Speaker of the House, Tip O'Neill, sitting barefoot in a beach chair. A two-page magazine ad, like all the ads in the series, it put the full-page, full-color photograph on the left-hand page, and the small-type, single-line combination headline and copy block on the other. The logo and familiar slogans, "Membership has its privileges" and "Don't leave home without it," were tucked away in the right, bottom corner of the second page.

"This campaign can make a very rare and special claim," said Helayne Spivak,

NA BARRYMORE
daughter of great
John Barrymore says:

"n glad that people today
ze it is as necessary to use
odorant as it is to use tooth-
e. I am enthusiastically
ed with ARRID and recom-
d it highly.

hink ARRID is a wonderful
duct. It protects dresses from
tion at the same time as it
dorizes."

Diana Barrymore

EW...a CREAM DEODORANT

which SAFELY helps

TOP *under-arm* **PERSPIRATION**

Does not irritate skin. Does not
ot dresses and men's shirts.

Prevents under-arm odor. Helps
top perspiration safely.

A pure, white, antiseptic, stainless
anishing cream.

No waiting to dry. Can be used
ght after shaving.

rrid has been awarded the
pproval Seal of the American
stitute of Laundering for being
armless to fabric. Use Arrid
gularly.

39¢ and 59¢
plus tax

MORE MEN AND WOMEN USE

ARRID

THAN ANY OTHER DEODORANT

Testimonials have always been a part of advertising. In a newspaper ad in 1945, Diana Barrymore, "daughter of great John Barrymore," appears enough an authority to observe that ". . . people today realize it is as necessary to use a deodorant as it is to use toothpaste." And the deodorant for Miss Barrymore was Arrid.

executive creative director for Young & Rubicam, New York. "It had people watching for the latest ad . . . and then looking forward to the next. That's a tribute to the Ogilvy & Mather creative team who kept it fresh and relevant."[24]

Many celebrities do commercials for more than one product. Bill Cosby has helped sell Jell-O, Coca-Cola, and Texas Instruments. Some celebrities seem ideally suited to sell certain products or services: Wilt Chamberlain, for instance, testifying to the roominess of TWA seats.[25]

Anacin used actress Patricia Neal for a time because, having recovered from a stroke, she was thought to be the ideal spokesperson for its "fight back and win against pain" campaign.

If you do not have a celebrity to endorse your product, you can crown one of your own, as a hairspray manufacturer did when it came up with Rula Lenska, the British "movie actress." Russell Baker observed in one of his columns: "Unlike the usual 'celebrity,' whom Eric Sevareid once defined as a person who is 'famous for being famous,' Rula Lenska became famous for being unknown."

Clara Peller, the tiny elderly woman in the Wendy's commercial who growled "Where's the beef?" when shown a competitor's hamburger, became an overnight celebrity in 1984. The "Where's the beef?" line was picked up and used by Walter Mondale in his race against Gary Hart for the Democratic presidential nomination. It was also parodied in cartoons and talked about in sermons. All kinds of products, including T-shirts, came out bearing the slogan.

The FTC asks that celebrities who endorse a product actually use it. For those endorsements, celebrities' fees sometimes are more handsome than fees they can earn in their own fields. Celebrities on their way up—or down—are often the most willing to give testimonials.

Stanley Hardware puts a new twist on testimonial advertising in *Corrections Today*. In an ad for its LifeSpan Institutional Hinge, the company shows a convict behind bars. The headline says, "Nine Out of Ten Inmates Prefer Our Competitor's Hinge." After explaining why its hinge is better than others, the copy says, "Now you can understand why inmates think it's a crime for prisons to use our hinges."

One problem with testimonials is that the people who make them change. In the weeks when the commercials air, the person who made the commercial might make headlines in another—and unflattering—context. The beef industry fought back against a cutback in meat consumption in the United States by launching a $30 million advertising campaign in 1987 and claimed to see a turnaround as a result. The theme was "Beef. Real food for real people." One part of the campaign featured actress Cybill Shepherd as a beef advocate, but in a magazine article that came out during the campaign she said she was avoiding red meat as part of her beauty maintenance program.[26]

The person giving the testimonial may not always be on good behavior. Or the person may die. When Jesse Owens died in 1980, Ogilvy & Mather quickly cancelled the American Express commercial featuring him, but unfortunately at least two stations did not get the word. "In the 1936 Olympics, I was the fastest man alive. But today I travel at a slower pace."

Humor in Advertising

Parting with their money, for most people, is serious business. People do not buy from clowns: That is what advertisers have believed since advertising's beginnings. Many advertisers still believe it. Perhaps they are right. But some advertisers in recent years have relaxed a bit. They have allowed their copywriters to kid the customers along.

"Humor is such a fragile thing," observes Stan Freberg, whose "Today the pits, tomorrow the wrinkles" line for Sunsweet prunes is still remembered a good two decades after it was run. "Humor in advertising is like a gun in the hands of a child. You have to know how to do it. Otherwise it can blow up on you."[27]

The famous radio comedy writing team of Dick & Bert (Dick Orkin and Bert

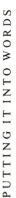

Berdis) never *made* fun of the product in their commercial; instead they *had* fun with it. "That's a big difference most copywriters fail to see," says Berdis.

"If your shoes aren't becoming to you, they should be coming to us," says an ad for Joe the Shoe Doctor.

"Perform a death-defying act," says the American Heart Association. "Have your blood pressure checked."

"Eat while the iron is hot," says the announcer for a Cream of Wheat commercial that stresses the high iron content of that cereal.

A radio station promotes a basketball game between staffers at the station and faculty members of a local middle school. A commercial sells the event. "Mark your calendar in pencil, in case we chicken out," says a fast-talking announcer. And: "Bring your cameras if you want, but please don't use them."

In *Whatever Happened to Madison Avenue?*, Martin Mayer tells about an early salesman for Stroh's who went around to bars and restaurants selling the product. He stepped into the men's rooms and put signs over the urinals that read: "Now You Can Enjoy Another Bottle of Stroh's Beer."

Some companies even bring humor to their packaging. Smartfoods, Inc., producer of popped, packaged popcorn, has carried this notice on its packages: "More than twelve billion, seven hundred ninety-four million, twenty-three thousand, six hundred and twelve kernels popped." Elsewhere on the package: "Did you know . . . archeologists have found that if you take 80,000-year-old popcorn and mix it with cement, you can make a really effective door stop."

A good deal of the humor in advertising is nothing more than punning. "There's no pain you can't Bayer," says the aspirin company.

Basin Harbor, a Vermont resort, says that "The Fun Never Sets!" there. The Nome, Alaska, Convention & Visitors Bureau advertises with the slogan "There's no place like Nome."

Sometimes it is the playfulness of the participants that gives the advertising its light touch. So successful has been Miller Lite's advertising campaign featuring good-natured ex-athletes that Penguin Books in 1984 brought out Frank Deford's *Lite Reading: The Miller Beer Commercial Scrapbook.*

Parody is another form of humor that advertisers have resorted to. From a TV commercial for a tire dealer in Florida a few years ago: "I just got a message from upstairs. We gotta sell 80,000 tires in the next month or I'm gonna die." He was parodying evangelist Oral Roberts, who, a few weeks earlier, had told his TV audience that if a certain amount of money didn't come into his organization, God would call him home.

Sometimes a company parodies its own campaign. Grey Poupon's TV commercials showing rich people in Rolls Royces stopping to borrow the product from each other generated an episode in 1991 that had one man saying yes, he did have some Grey Poupon and then driving on without handing over the jar. Another parody episode had the cars unable to adjust their parking to allow one man to borrow from the other.

Using parody to sell products or services is tempting but chancey. Ivar's, a Seattle-based seafood restaurant, latched on to the popularity of the movie, *Dances with Wolves,* in 1991 with both newspaper and TV ads. In a "Dancing with Clams" commercial, some grizzled people watch a Kevin Costner-like person cavort with a giant clam on a seaside bluff. One of the onlookers says, in Norwegian, "He has not yet learned our ways, but soon he will eat at Ivar's." (His words appear at the bottom of the screen in English.) The makers of the movie threatened to sue, and Ivar's cancelled the campaign. An Ivar's official said, "We did this for fun, and we don't want anybody mad at us."[28]

Some ads invite parody from people outside the business. Can anyone count all the parodies of the medical alert commercial that has an elderly woman crying out, "Help! I've fallen and I can't get up!"

Because unrestrained humor could hurt rather than help sales, some of the best lines never see print. A lot of the humor in advertising circulates only among those who write it. Carl Ally has said he wishes he could have Preparation H as a client. He has a slogan ready: "Up yours with ours . . . and kiss your piles goodbye."

"I sold my violin with no fiddlin' around."

"Selling my calculator was easy, as 1-2-3."

"Selling my mixer was easy-as-pie."

The Seattle *Times* uses puns in headlines for a series of ads promoting its classified section. "And no wonder!" reads the copy that follows the headlines. "500,000 people read *The Times* every day . . . more, probably, by thousands, than any other newspaper in Washington State. You can expect RESULTS—FASTER—from this great want ad value."

tuesday because of inventory m&f eugene will open at noon

meier & frank

Copywriters do not always use language precisely. What the copywriter of this ad meant to say was: ". . . M & F will not open until noon."

The Logic of Advertising

Here is Kodak in an ad telling about its grants to colleges: "No, we do not expect to sell Kodak Products on the strength of this. Buy them only because you are convinced they are good buys." That sounds reasonable enough.

"After a Point You're Not Buying any More Car. You're Just Spending More Money," says a headline for a Ford LTD ad. That makes sense.

Contrast these to Schick Super-Chromium Blades' ridiculous assertion that its blades are "so comfortable you'll actually look forward to your next shave."

In an ad for one of its upgrade models, Nissan says, "We believe some things in a luxury car should never be considered a luxury; like the safety of its occupants. Which is why the Maxima GXE offers such items as optional ABS brakes, optional driver's side airbag. . . ." If the company really believes in these things, the reader is likely to wonder, why wouldn't they be standard?

Another ad that unintentionally insults the reader or listener is the one saying that a store is conducting a sale as a thank-you for past patronage. "Because you've helped us through these hard times, we're offering you this merchandise at unheard-of prices." But readers and listeners surely didn't buy at the store to help it weather the economic storm; they bought there because the merchandise was what they wanted and the prices were right. Why can't the copywriter admit this?

And what's the value, really, of "75 years of combined experience" in a repair shop with several employees when the mechanic who works on *your* car has only two years of experience?

In a Post Oat Bran Flakes commercial, Lena Horn says that the product "keeps the brass in this Horn." The viewer is likely to wonder, in view of bran's properties, why the opposite wouldn't be the case.

A copywriter, writing a headline for a folder published by a natural gas company, comes up with "Some Secrets on How to Reduce Your Energy Costs." Why "Secrets"? Wouldn't "Tips" be a better word? Even the writer apparently has second thoughts, reusing the word in the copy block, this time putting quote marks around it. Using quote marks around a word is often an admission by a writer that a word chosen is not a good one.

Roots, the natural footwear company, has used as a slogan or headline: "Be kind to your feet. They outnumber people two to one." It is a line that at first seems clever, but when you analyze it it becomes meaningless. If kindness is to be encouraged on the basis of numbers, you might just as well preoccupy yourself with hands, eyes, ears, or breasts. And insects "outnumber people" by a margin far more impressive than two to one.

"Wake up to the sound of the surf in an unfurnished 2 bedroom Del Monte beach apartment," says an advertisement in the Monterey, California *Peninsula Herald*. The trouble here is that the writer tries to do too much in one sentence, merging the future with the present, the imaginary with the practical. One hopes that by the time the fortunate renter has taken up residence at that surfside apartment, arrangements will have been made to furnish it.

"You know," says Arnold Palmer in a Pennzoil commercial, "this old tractor and I are a lot alike. We're both still running, and we're both still using Pennzoil." Is the viewer to assume that Palmer gulps down a quart every once in a while to keep moving?

Once the ad is written, it is a good idea to read it over specifically to weed out any fallacies. That is what the copywriter for American Airlines should have done back in the early 1960s when he wrote: "Fly American's Astrojets Nonstop to California and Back for $198 Plus Tax!" *The New Yorker* picked it up for a back-of-the-book filler and added the comment one would expect from a smug and amused Easterner: "Now you're making sense." From a later ad appearing in the Los Angeles *Times:* "Non-stop Roundtrip. From $699." That doesn't leave much reason for going, unless you just happen to love flying.

Another bit of copy that found itself memorialized in a *New Yorker* filler was this from a brochure for a cosmetics company: "Now you don't have to choose between a harsh, drying lipstick that doesn't smear, and a gentle, creamy formula. Because now Hazel Bishop gives you both." Think that one over.

Robert J. Gula attacked some of the logic of advertising in his *Nonsense: How to Overcome It* (New York: Stein & Day, 1980). As for "Everything's better with Blue Bonnet on it!" Gula asked, "Ever try it on your sherbet?"

"We not only cover the news, we *uncover* it," said an ABC affiliate. "Cover" and "uncover" in most people's minds have quite opposite meanings. How can the station do both? "We don't cover the news, we *uncover* it" might have been a better slogan.

As advertisers give up on appeals to logic they turn to emotion and sentiment, the last and perhaps best refuges for the copywriter. Advertisers, like all propagandists, have always preferred emotion to logic to sell their products and ideas. One reason for moving away from reason-why copy is that such copy needs to document its claims—not always easy to do. Emotion is less subject to challenge.

Truth in Advertising

N. M. Ohrbach, the department store owner, many years ago gave this advice to Doyle Dane Bernbach, his agency: "I got a great gimmick. Let's tell the truth." McCann-Erickson, in a symbol placed on its letterhead, expressed the ideal: "Truth Well Told."

The leaders in advertising have long advised their colleagues that truth, quite apart from moral considerations, makes good business sense. "In the first place," said an ad about advertising prepared by Doyle Dane Bernbach, "you go to heaven. In the second place, Ralph Nader can't lay a glove on you. And in the third place, telling the truth is the best known way there is of moving merchandise."

Later in the ad the copy said:

"We've got a confession to make; it's got nothing to do with heaven.

"People are as smart as we are.

"That's why we tell the truth."

But the truth is hard to pin down. Is it the truth, for instance, when Twinkies tells anxious mothers: "You can't scrimp when it comes to your children"? Are Twinkies the alternative to scrimping?

Truth involves not only what's said but what's left out. Public Citizen's Health Research Group complained to the Federal Trade Commission in 1983 that Playtex tampons' advertising campaign was "dangerous and misleading" because it failed to warn women that using the highly absorbent tampon might increase the risk of toxic shock syndrome.

Some say that advertising should tell both sides of the story. TV eliminated cigarette commercials in 1971, and there were pressures in the 1980s to eliminate commercials for alcoholic beverages. The increased media attention to the tragedies of drunk driving has contributed to the pressure. *The Booze Merchants,* published by the Center for Science in the Public Interest, Washington, D.C., suggested a ban on both radio and TV alcohol advertising. Candy Lightner, founder of Mothers Against Drunk Driving, thinks beer commercials make beer drinking seem romantic and even macho. The commercials should "show what really happens," she said.[29]

What is truth to one person may not be to another. What may be understandable to adults may be misleading to children. And an occupational hazard in advertising is that copywriters, after a period of time, begin to believe what they write when once they may have been skeptical.

Another problem concerns the distinction between facts and the truth. Novelists have long functioned under the assumption that truth lies somewhere beyond fact and that you can present the truth best through fantasy.

Dunlop, maker of sports equipment, showed a photograph of John McEnroe holding a tennis racket and, stripped to the waist, looking remarkably muscular. "Max 200G Gives John More Muscle," read the headline. The body, spliced on and airbrushed in, was actually that of a body builder named Ted Martia. When a newspaper story appeared describing what had been done to the art, all kinds

Outdoor signs and billboards that are so grotesque, so poorly placed or spaced—so many miles of ugly. We've learned to live with it, even laugh about it. Until, one day, it's our oak tree they're chopping down. Our view that's being blocked.
America, the beautiful. Our America. The crisis isn't in our cities; the crisis is in our hearts. With a change of heart, we can change the picture. **AIA/American Institute of Architects**

Send this page to your local authority and ask him to support sign control laws.

One of a series of ads drawn up by The American Institute of Architects supporting housing for the poor, enforcement of air-pollution laws, control of water pollution, and sign-control laws. The series was united through picture-window photography and bold, sans serif headline typography. The call for action consisted of a last line: "Send this page to your local authority. . . ." Agency: Doremus & Co., New York.

of complaints poured into J. Walter Thompson, the agency. A creative director there, annoyed, said the ad was merely an overstatement: "Anyone that follows tennis would know instantly that the body in the ad is not John's."[30]

If advertising copy is a kind of literature, the copywriter must be free to use fantasy. But the reader must *understand* that it is fantasy. In advertising, the test may well be: What is the *intent* of the advertising? If the intent is to deceive, then, in anybody's book, the advertising is not true. To quote William Blake: "A truth that's told with bad intent/Beats all the lies you can invent."

Edward L. Bond, Jr., chairman of Young & Rubicam, told the National Industrial Conference Board: "We must ascertain and present the truth. But in the presentation of this truth, we must exercise all the imagery, imagination and artistry at our command."

"The more alike products are," said John Blumenthal, partner in Hawkins McCain & Blumenthal, New York, "the more creative advertising must be. If I want you to buy my peas versus their peas—both U.S. Government standard of identity items—give me the license to create a 'Jolly Green Giant' even though, to my knowledge, none actually exists."[31]

The Mechanics of Copy

Up until the introduction of personal computers, the copywriter typed copy on 8½ × 11 sheets of paper, double- or even triple-spacing the lines and making no attempt to type in a width to match the width of the copy as it was to appear in print. The typewriter could not duplicate the typeface to be used in the ad, either in style or size. Nor could it very easily justify the right margins. The copy turned out by the copywriter went to a professional typesetter for final setting.

Some advertising agencies and departments still use this system, but most copywriters now use computerized word processing systems. Among other advantages, copyfitting, word count, corrections, adjustments, and deliveries can be made almost instantaneously.

Scali, McCabe, Sloves, New York, was among the first of the advertising agencies to computerize its creative department. Using word processors, copywriters could call up information about a client's history, for instance, or about its personnel or marketing activities and work it into the copy. Once written, the copy went immediately to the creative director's terminal, where it was reviewed and changed, then sent back to the copywriter.

Most word processing programs include spelling checkers and thesauri. Some copywriters also depend on grammar-checker software like Correct Grammar and Sensible Grammar. Also available: software that checks the level of understanding in the copy.

Because copywriting involves mostly short takes, a copywriter using a computer can get by with a simple word processing program. But the program should be compatible with the page-layout software used by the art director.

Using a computer to write copy, the copywriter also acts as a typesetter. The decisions made at the keyboard, with adjustments by the art director, help establish the look of the ad. It is important, then, that copywriters know something about typography. For instance, a copywriter should know the difference between an apostrophe and a single quote mark, between a hyphen and a dash, between an "em" dash and an "en" dash.

Now the copywriter can put italics and boldfacing right into the first drafts of the copy. And first drafts can carry all kinds of dingbats and typographical accessories, if they are needed. (Usually they're not.)

The ad's designer, in consultation with the copywriter, can emphasize certain words or phrases in a number of ways: by putting them in all caps, boldface, italics, or color, for instance, or by underlining them. A technique inspired by what students do to their textbooks involves putting color under certain words or phrases, making them look as though someone has gone through the copy with a felt-tip marker.

Cole & Weber

COPY

CLIENT BENSON HOTEL   DATE:

TITLE

JOB NO

HEADLINE: Some of the unexpected extras you can expect
             at The Benson.

COPY: In an age of look-a-like hotel rooms and often less-
             than-helpful help, The Benson may take some getting
             used to. But it's an adjustment our guests love
             making.
                Because at The Benson, the personal attention
             they receive is every bit as lavish as their
             surroundings. Which, considering the highly-
             polished Circassian walnut paneling, the cut-glass
             chandeliers, the gleaming silver, is saying a lot.
                No wonder so many Portlanders cherish this hotel
             as something of a local landmark. And no wonder
             so many of those visiting Portland remember The
             Benson: we don't forget them.
                The Benson Hotel, Broadway & Oak. Reservations,
             228-9611.

SIG: THE BENSON:
             One of the Few Remaining Classic Hotels.
             Western International

CAPTIONS: With 24-hour room service, our guests' appetites
             can keep the kind of hours they like. We even
             guarantee drinks will be delivered within 12 minutes.

             Guests can enjoy complimentary tea in the lobby
             each afternoon. And for early risers, there's piping
             hot coffee from 5:30 a.m. to 7:30 a.m.

             Few American hotels have a concierge in their lobby,
             but The Benson does. His only job is helping guests
             feel at home.

             In each room, there's an alarm clock, electric blankets--
             even a thermometer outside the window.

Copyediting and Proofreading

William Safire, a syndicated columnist, offers annual awards—The Bloopies—to advertisers whose grammar and spelling annoy him. For instance, Safire is not happy with Campbell's Soup's headline "The Soup That Eats Like a Meal." He suggests additional possibilities to Campbell's copywriters: "The Meal That Eats Like a Soup" and "The Eats That Soup Like a Meal." He also gave an award to TWA for an ad that said that an earlier ad "contained an omission." An ad sponsored by the New York *Times* for Safire's column carried the line "Week after week he takes you behind the news for a hard look at why things sometimes turn out the way they do." Sometimes? Joseph Harriss of *Reader's Digest,* in response to the ad, noted: "The fact is, things always turn out the way they do."

Copywriters, like most writers, often fail to write with precision. "We couldn't care less" becomes "We could care less," which in reality means the opposite. Instead of allowing something to "center on," a copywriter might have it "center around," an impossibility. "All right" becomes "alright," a nonword in most dictionaries, and "a lot" becomes "alot," another nonword or a wrong spelling for "allot."

A clothing manufacturer featured this gag on one of its T-shirts: "If I said you had a beautiful body, would you promise to hold it against me?" The inclusion of "promise to" spoils the humor, such as it is. The double meaning is lost.

"Hopefully, your wardrobe will live up to it," said an ad for Targa, a fashionable pen by Sheaffer. What does the copywriter mean? That the buyer hopes it will be so? That Sheaffer hopes? That the buyer's wardrobe hopes? That the pen itself hopes? The line would be better like this: "We hope your wardrobe will live up to it." Or: "Just hope that your wardrobe will live up to it." Or maybe Sheaffer should drop the line.

Dangling construction has always been a problem for copywriters. "Originally intended for dairy cows, farmers use Bag Balm now for . . . ," a student in a

The copy and rough layout for an ad for The Benson, a quality hotel. The ad went through several later changes before it was finally approved by the client. Art director: Rick McQuiston. Copywriter: Tom Wiecks. Agency: Cole & Weber, Portland.

copywriting class wrote. The student meant, of course, that Bag Balm, not farmers, was originally intended for dairy cows.

"The reason leading roll-ons go on wet, and sticky, is because they're mostly water . . . ," said an ad for Dry Idea. It should have said, "The reason leading roll-ons go on wet, and sticky, is that. . . ." Or: "Leading roll-ons go on wet, and sticky, because. . . ."

Newspapers and other media have their full-time copyeditors and proofreaders, but advertising agencies, unfortunately, operate a little more informally. Copyreading, which, in a non-computerized operation, goes on after the copy comes out of the typewriter, and proofreading, which goes on after the copy is set in type, are conducted much of the time by the copywriter, who may be too close to the copy to catch the errors. The ad may pass through several hands on its way to publication, with nobody giving priority to such mundane activities as copyediting and proofreading.

At any rate, in a non-computerized operation, the copywriter copyedits the manuscript while writing each draft, using a pencil with soft, dark lead to make corrections. When finally satisfied with the way the copy reads, the copywriter turns it over to a typist, who puts it into shape for client inspection. In a large agency the copy may get an additional working over by a copy chief before it goes to the typesetter.

When the copy comes back from the typesetter in galley form, it is ready for proofreading. At this stage, theoretically, the copywriter looks only for deviations from the original that may have been made by the typesetter, as when "a boxing exhibition" comes out as "a boring exhibition." Making changes—even necessary changes—on galleys is ticklish business because of the chance that the typesetter may make additional mistakes in resetting lines. The copywriter, therefore, insists on seeing new proofs after any changes, to make sure the copy is at last free from errors.

The symbols used to indicate proofreading changes differ a little from those used to make copyediting changes because the typeset lines are closer together than the lines in the original manuscript. The marks must be put out in the margins rather than over or across the words to be corrected, as in copyediting.

In a computerized operation, copywriting and proofreading become the same thing, with the copywriter, using WordPerfect, Microsoft Word, or some other software program with a spell checker and thesaurus, makes corrections and reworks copy on screen.

The Headline

On a newspaper or magazine, an editor or copyeditor writes the headline or title. In advertising, the copywriter does the job. The headline, although it gets unique graphic treatment to set it apart from other elements in the ad, can be considered as part of the copy—the most important part.

Increasingly, art directors involve themselves in headline writing. Herb Lubalin said, "The most intriguing thing about advertising is writing the headline. I think more about creating an idea, writing the headline, than designing the ad."[32]

One of the attractions of *The Wall Street Journal*'s ads in *Advertising Age*— a long series featuring quotations from famous ad people—has been the cleverness of the headlines. In each case, a copywriter combines a name with a quality. For instance, in an ad featuring Jerry Della Femina, the headline reads "Very Jerry." For Jay Chiat it is "Jay's Way." For Al Hampel it is "A Hampel Sample." For Helmut Krone it is "Krone Alone." For David McCall it is "All McCall."[33]

The best approach may be to make the art and headline completely dependent upon each other. The art is meaningless without the headline. The headline doesn't make sense without the art. McComack & Dodge in an ad in *Datamation* shows a closeup of a shoestring. Curling slightly, its tip points to the headline: "You Can't Develop the World's Best Software on This." The copy points to the firm's sound financial base, "supported by Dun & Bradstreet resources," although it admits that at one time M&D faced "shoestring budgets and single package technology."

"Sex Impotency: Don't Turn Your Back on It," reads a headline on an ad for the Potency Restoration Center, Los Angeles Doctors Hospital. The accompanying art shows the heads of a couple in bed, facing away from each other.

The primary job of a headline is to arrest the reader. And, because the headline may be the only part of the copy that is read, it may have to do a selling job as well. If the message is dramatic enough, the copywriter may make one long headline out of the copy. A classic ad on air pollution prepared by Carl Ally Inc. for Citizens for Clean Air, Inc. really needed no copy block. It showed a man at the window of an apartment building overlooking an industrial complex. The headline said it all: "Tomorrow Morning When You Get Up, Take a Nice Deep Breath. It'll Make You Feel Rotten."[34] While it is best under normal circumstances for a headline to be short, there is no reason it cannot run on for several sentences.

The School of Visual Arts, New York, used one of those two-sentence, all-in-the-same-type headlines over an all-type ad: "What Our Teachers Do During the Day Is Their Own Business. Make it Yours." The implication in this ad appealing to potential night-school students was that the teachers there are professional artists.

The headline often dwells not on the product or service but on results that can be expected. Elaine Powers, a "fitness system" for women, in one ad showed a slim, well-built woman with the headline "Shapely Bodies for Sale." A coupon offered a special price on a three-month membership.

The copywriter for a TWA ad moved into Biblical language (King James version) in a headline: "In Israel, Thou Shalt Not Just Sightsee." The copy suggested that a tourist should count on enjoying the sun and beaches, as well as the "4,000 years of history" while visiting the "Miracle on the Mediterranean."

The headline can shock readers into thinking one thing with the copy soon telling them something else. "How I Get All the Men I Want," said a headline in *Advertising Age* for Times Mirror Network. With the headline was a photo of a woman. Small type told you she was a media planner. She was advising media buyers to buy space in *Popular Science, Outdoor Life, Golf,* and *Ski* to reach male readers.

"You're Wasting Your Time Reading this Newspaper," said the big-type headline in an Evelyn Wood ad. The copy explained:

"Not because it's not worth reading.

"You're wasting your time because you could be reading it three to ten times faster than you are right now.

"That's right—three to ten times faster. With better concentration, understanding, and recall."

The copy went on to make a pitch for the Evelyn Wood "reading improvement system."

A headline on a poster calling for entries in a Cleveland Society of Communicating Arts contest says: "This Year's CSCA Show Will Be Dull, Stupid, Tasteless and the Judges Will Be Hacks from Out of Town." The copy explains: "That's how it'll be if you lose."

The Nation magazine in a headline advertises "Dissatisfaction Guaranteed or Your Money Back." The copy explains: "At *The Nation,* we don't expect you to be dissatisfied with our magazine. Just what it covers." A list follows naming games PR people play, affronts to intelligence by "government spokespersons," and other practices frowned on by the magazine.

A headline for an ad in *Connoisseur* says, "Christie's. The Museum Where the Art is for Sale." It was a nice way—a not really misleading way—to upgrade the auction house from a mere gallery, where sales could be expected, to a museum.

A surprise is especially good when it traps the reader in a bias. "Don't Buy Life Insurance!" said a full-page ad in the news magazines. Great! Who wants to buy life insurance? But then, below a chunk of white space, in smaller type: "(. . . Until You Get the Facts.)." It was Northwestern Mutual Life's way of grabbing attention. "We feel confident that the more you know about life insurance, the more you'll appreciate our superiority."

A headline for an advertisement differs from a headline for a news story in that the former adheres to no set of arbitrary rules. Its letters need not be counted out to fit a given column of space. Except in small-space ads, the headline usually is written first and space is then assigned to it.

An advertising headline need not summarize the copy, as a news story headline does. Instead, it can be the first line of copy set in larger, bolder type. For instance, it can ask a question, with the answer coming in the first line of the smaller-type copy.

Like news headlines, the advertising headline often comes in two units: one in large type; one—probably with more words—in smaller type. Or the advertising headline, unlike the newspaper headline, can appear as two units of the same size type, the first unit separated from the second by a period and maybe some extra space. And where newspaper headlines omit unimportant words like *and, an, a,* and *the,* advertising headlines use them. The rhythm of the headline sentence in advertising is more important than the amount of space the headline occupies.

Advertising headlines need not contain a subject and predicate. They can be mere tags or labels. They can take any literary form. Because they come in such infinite variety, they are more like magazine article titles than newspaper headlines.

The headline's relationship to the art in an ad is crucial.

In one kind of advertising, as we have seen, neither the art nor the headline is complete without the other. Half the basic ad idea is expressed in the art, the other half in the headline. In another kind of advertising, the headline simply reiterates the art. The art says it one way, the headline another. But both say the same thing.

Either kind of advertising can be effective. What you should avoid is producing advertising in which the headline says something *different from* or *unrelated to* the art. In such a case, the two cancel out each other. They violate the rule that an ad should make but one central point. Professor Willis L. Winter, Jr., who teaches advertising at the University of Oregon, says, "The test of a headline/illustration combination is this: Does it, at a glance, convey the *essence* of the message the copywriter wishes to convey to the reader?"

Here are some classic headlines: "Do You Make These Mistakes in English?"; "They laughed When I Sat Down to the Piano . . ."; "Often a Bridesmaid But Never a Bride"; "Blow Some My Way"; "The Kid in Upper 4"; "The Penalty of Leadership"; "At 60 Miles an Hour the Loudest Noise . . . Comes from the Electric Clock." Can you identify the advertisers?

Functions of the Headline

A headline can fulfill one of these functions:

■ *It can report news about a product in the style of a newspaper headline.* When Crest came out with a second flavor for its toothpaste, it ran an ad with this headline: "Crest Is Now Only 26 Flavors Behind Howard Johnson's."

■ *It can offer advice, serving as a sort of one-sentence editorial.* "Be Good at Being Bad," said a headline for My Sin perfume.

■ *It can make a promise.* "We Don't Take Off Until Everything Is Kosher," said a headline for EL AL Israel Airlines.

■ *It can issue a command.* Zero Population Growth did it with a pun: "Stop Heir Pollution."

■ *It can arouse curiosity.* A. B. Dick did it nicely in one of its ads: "If We Tell You Something About Yourself, Promise You Won't Get Mad?"

■ *It can single out a segment of the audience.* Allen Edmonds, a high-price, high-quality shoe manufacturer, shows a closeup of a man's shoe with this headline: "For the Man Who Has Money to Spend. But None to Waste."

Clearasil singled out younger readers of women's magazines with this head-

Choice of type can have almost as much of an effect on communication as choice of words can. Here are some type choices made by art directors for words in their advertising headlines. In most cases, the entire headlines were set in these faces.

line to go with a closeup of a young woman wringing out a sponge: "Wouldn't It Be Great If You Could Just Wring Out Your Oily Skin?" followed by the blurb: "That's the whole idea behind new Clearasil medicated cleanser." Older women with the opposite problem—dry skin—could turn to some other, more appropriate, page.

To some extent headlines take the place of slogans advertisers once ran (some still run them) just below their signatures. One thing about the old slogans: They had a sense of rhythm about them. Headlines need that sense, too, especially if the advertisers mean them to be remembered and repeated. A headline should sound as though the copywriter tapped a foot while writing it. For instance, this headline for Monaco Shaver: "The Shaver That Went to the Moon."

A bit of rhyme ("Pollution Solution"—bicycle shop) and even a little alliteration ("Faith Is a Family Affair"—Institute of Life Insurance) can help make a headline remembered. But alliteration can be overdone. It works best when only a couple of words in the headline, preferably apart from each other, begin with the same letter.

Kinds of Headlines

Headlines do not fit very easily into categories, but a few categories stand out because of the frequency of their use. They include the following:

■ *The takeoff.* Some of the best headlines are variations of popular expressions, song and book titles, and even other advertising headlines.

"Ladies, Please Squeeze the Chicken," said Frank Perdue in a headline for one of his Perdue Inc. chicken ads, an obvious takeoff from a line made famous by a grocer selling toilet paper on television. "Daddy, What Did You Do in the War Against Pollution?" asked a little girl in a Keep America Beautiful ad prepared by the Advertising Council. "We're Putting Our Money Where Your Mouth Is," said a headline for an ad for General Telephone & Electronics. "From Those Wonderful Folks Who Brought You Harper's Ferry," said a headline for a new magazine called *Black Sports*—a headline takeoff on Jerry Della Femina's book title, which itself was a takeoff on an old advertising claim.

Lone Star Beer, brewed in Texas, has called itself "The Beer That Made Milwaukee Nervous."

In an ad in *Selling Sporting Goods,* the Australian Trade Commissioner used the headline "Anyone for Profit?" The tennis racket art had a big dollar sign in the strings. A subhead read: "Australian Sporting Goods Net You Sales." The headline was a takeoff on a classic line about tennis, and the subhead used a pun that related to the sport. "Sport is big time Down Under," read the copy. "That's why you'll invariably find Aussies in the winning lists somewhere. A lot of it has to do with the gear and equipment they use. . . ."

A Gillette Techmatic ad took off from another medium when it ran an ad in *Esquire* with the headline: "We Interrupt This Magazine to Bring You a Techmatic Commercial." The art consisted of a storyboard of a series of shots of a man shaving.

The Israel Government Tourist Office in a *New York* ad declared: "If You Liked the Book, You'll Love the Country."

The takeoff appears sometimes in collaboration with the pun. "When News Breaks, We Pick Up the Pieces," said a headline for an all-news radio station in New York, WINS. "What Foods These Morsels Be!" said a headline for the Knife & Fork Inn, an Atlantic City seafood restaurant. "What a Way to Glow!" said a headline for Vanity Fair Mills, Inc., in an ad for a flashy hostess robe. "Palm Springs! It's a Nice Place to Visit, But You Wouldn't Want to Leave There," said an ad for the Palm Springs Convention and Visitors Bureau.

Sometimes the takeoff is in the form of a malapropism or a spoonerism. From an earlier era: "Chevrolet—the Smartest Make You'll Ever Move!"

■ *Double meaning.* "More Goes Into a Bra Than Most Men Dream of," read the headline for an ad for *Industry Week* in *Advertising Age.* The ad told them how bras are made and concluded: "[*Industry Week* is] the new way for managers in industry to keep up on all of industry."

A dog food provides another example of a double-meaning headline. "Alpo Gives It to You Straight." The headline implies that the product contains nothing but meat and that its advertising is truthful.

Safeway Stores provides still another example with its "Try a Little Tenderness" line directing readers to its meat counters.

In one of its ads, B. Dalton, the bookseller, talked about opening "A 30,000 Story Building on West Broadway" in a West Coast city.

"We've packed all 30,000 stories into our new store on West Broadway. . . . Mystery stories. Children's stories. Reference books. Travel guides. And more. . . ."

With a double-meaning headline, it is important that both meanings have a favorable connotation. "Get the Full Saab Story" was clever in that "Saab" could be read as "sob," but is "sob story" a good term to use to sell an automobile? Another car maker's headline worked better: "Best of All . . . It's a Cadillac."

Tide employed double meaning—both meanings favorable—in "It's the Best Detergent on American Soil."

To make the point that it is both a family car and a performance car, Volkswagon's Jetta, on one of its billboards, showed itself with the headline, "Varoom for Five."

■ *The double take.* The term comes from comedy parts in the movies in which a character looks but does not see; the full impact hits him a few seconds after he turns away, and so he looks again in disbelief. Studio-type

A nice house with the headline "Nightmare"? Why? The copy clears things up by pointing out that because of insulation and heating costs and sky-high mortgages (if you can get one), ". . . the dream house has become a nightmare. Suddenly, how to keep a roof over your head has become everybody's business." This nicely designed full-page ad appearing in *The New Yorker* makes a subtle pitch both for advertisers and subscribers for *Business Week.* Agency: Robert A. Fearon Associates. Designer: Phil Gips. Copywriter: Robert A. Fearon.

greeting cards make use of the device with their two-step gags: the routine-appearing line on the cover; the surprise twist inside.

Increasingly in advertising, headlines divide into two sections, but usually the surprise section comes first, followed by the explanation. "Be the Last on Your Block," said the large-type headline for an appliance store; then, in smaller type, "to Start Supper . . . with the New Litton Minutemaster Microwave Oven."

"El Producto Flavor Is Years Behind the Competition," said a cigar ad; then, "How's That for Progress!"

"Give Him Madame Rochas Perfume. A Few Drops at a Time," said the headline in a *New Yorker* ad. The art showed a woman applying the perfume to her body.

■ *Contrast.* Sometimes the point can be best dramatized by setting up contrast within the headline. Example from a De Beers Consolidated Mines ad for diamonds: "It's the Last Thing She'd Expect. The First Thing She'd Wish For." The headline for an ad for Saga Mink read: "Life Is Too Short and Winter's Too Long to Go Without Mink."

"Good News for Bad Knees," said Converse, maker of running shoes, in the headline of one of its ads. The copy pointed to two new shoes designed to reduce the risk of knee injuries. "The Price of Looking it Up Just Went Down," said Barnes & Noble on a catalog page selling reference books.

■ *Jargon.* Regional dialect or hip language does not do much for sales. The intended audience quickly recognizes a lack of authenticity or sincerity. But a little jargon appropriate to the subject, especially if used in a lighhearted way, can add dimension to a headline.

Example: For an NBC ad announcing a five-part series called "The Search for the Nile," a copywriter, remembering a famous encounter between a reporter and an explorer-missionary, came up with this headline: "You'll Be There When Stanley Meets Livingstone, We Presume."

Slogans

Not only does an individual ad need a theme to unite each of its elements; a series of advertisements with the same sponsor—an advertising campaign—needs a theme to bring the ads together. Much of the value of advertising is cumulative.

The objectives of the advertising campaign help determine the theme, which may be expressed verbally in repeated headlines or phrasing. Or it may be expressed visually in familiar typography or art styles.

Sometimes the theme can be capsuled in a slogan. A slogan is a line of copy that appears usually at the close of the copy or with the signature or logotype, although it can serve also as the ad's headline. It differs from a headline in that it stays the same from ad to ad, and often it is in smaller type.

Nike's "Just do it" slogan nicely captures the mood of today's young people and, heavily promoted and widely used on bumper stickers, T-shirts, etc., readily associates itself with the athletic-shoe manufacturer, even when seen without the Swoosh logo.

Ex-Lax's slogan, "For regular people who sometimes aren't," serves two purposes. It helps make the buyer feel okay about using the product—we all want to be "regular"—and it suggests, if subtly, that the chronically constipated might better consult a doctor than rely on an over-the-counter cure.

Air Canada uses a good double-meaning slogan, each meaning working to its advantage: "A welcome departure." *TV Guide* also uses a good double-meaning slogan: "It's the best thing on television." "We treat you right," says Dairy Queen.

Kellogg's Corn Flakes revives interest in the product with its "Taste them again for the first time" slogan. The contradiction in the wording gives the slogan extra push.

Because it is used over and over, the slogan better be well thought out. Clairol used its "Does she or doesn't she?" slogan for fifteen years. The slogan started when coloring one's hair was considered not quite respectable.

Help stop the Salvation Army from bombing.

The Salvation Army of Rhode Island.

Please give.
Without your support
a lot of vital social programs
could disappear.

Copywriter Steve Bautista finds a connection between "Army" and "Bombing" in this effective poster for one of America's most honored charity organizations. This poster, for the Salvation Army of Rhode Island, is from HBM/Creamer, Providence. Art director: Brian Fandetti. Photography: Gene Dwiggins.

It is refreshing to find a company willing in its slogan to speak in other than euphemistic terms. *Forbes* magazine decided to play up the fact that it is a business magazine proudly devoted to the free-enterprise system. It signed off its ads with the line "Forbes: capitalist tool."

When Stimorol, a Danish-made chewing gum, made its U.S. debut in 1982, it used the slogan "At last, a chewing gum for the rich." And the opening ad in *The New Yorker* mentioned not chewing itself but "The Stimorol experience." The company was not likely to make money selling its gum only to the rich, but the slogan was enough to appeal to the curious and—according to Michael Stone, acting as Stimorol's agent in the United States (the gum has long been sold in Europe)—to the insecure as well. Stimorol has a strange taste, a stronger taste than U.S.-made gum. "If you tell people they're supposed to like it, that people with cultivated palates do, then they're more likely to respond favorably," said Stone.[35]

Cunard, a cruise-ship line, uses "Getting there is half the fun," and sometimes the variant "Life is too short to get there too fast," a dig at the more popular mode of overseas travel. Club Med, which arranges vacations, uses the slogan "The antidote for civilization," suggesting to its young patrons the getting-away-from-it-all quality of its services.

The dentists have a good slogan in their "Teeth. Ignore them and they will go away."

Rhythm and rhyme help make a slogan remembered. Texaco provides an example: "You can trust your car to the man who wears the star." Earlier, Lucky Strike cigarettes said of its product. "So round, so firm, so fully packed—so free and easy on the draw."

A Boston store provides an example of a logo that nicely combines a slogan. Above the logo it says: "It Took." Then the name of the store appears in large type: "Lechmere." Then it goes back to the smaller type for the last line: "To Give Low Prices a Good Name."

Fred Meyer, a chain of stores in the Northwest, uses the slogan "Love 'em or leave 'em" for its photo finishing department. "You either love your pictures or leave them and we will remake them or gladly refund your money. You only pay for those prints you want to keep."

The slogan need not be confined to a single sentence. The Wool Institute uses two sentences, although admittedly they are short: "Wool. It's got life."

Slogans can be protected by registering them as trademarks. The Florist Association of Greater Cleveland discovered this in 1983 when Anheuser-Busch sued for trademark infringement. The association had used "This Bud's for you" in a flower ad.

Some slogans are sufficiently well known to inspire parody. *Magazine Age* ran a "Fractured Slogan" contest and received entries like these:

"Smirnoff. . . it leaves you senseless."—Brian Hanley of Young & Rubicam.

"The Maidenform Woman . . . you never know where she'll pop out."—Rob Geiger of Durkee Foods.

"Fly the frenzied skies of United."—Karen Lane, Karen P. H. Lane Public Relations/Advertising.

Some famous slogans from the past: "It floats." "You're in good hands. . . ." "Good to the last drop." "LS/MFT." "Hasn't scratched yet." "Leave the driving to us." Some are still used. One of the most successful of the car makers' slogans was Packard's "Ask the man who owns one." It was first used in 1911, and it lasted until the car's demise after World War II.

CHAPTER

4

THE
PRINCIPLES
OF DESIGN

A layout is an arrangement of headlines, copy blocks, photographs, works of art, logotypes, borders, and other typographic devices that serves as a preview for the client and a guide for the illustrator, the lettering artist, the engraver or offset camera operator, the typesetter, and the printer. To *lay out* (two words) an ad is to engage in activity that will produce a *layout* (one word).

When principles of design are followed in doing the layout, the advertisement becomes a more than otherwise pleasing visual experience for the viewer. The advertisement then is said to be "designed," not merely "laid out." We associate the word "design," ordinarily, with the handsomest ads—those meant to stand for a period of months or years. A department store ad appearing in a newspaper might be merely "laid out"; a package or trademark almost surely would be "designed."

To paraphrase Matthew Arnold's definition of journalism, layout is design "in a hurry."

The word *advertising* used in the title of this book limits layouts to arrangements meant to help sell products, services, and ideas offered by *advertisers.* Kinds of layout activity *not* to be considered here include (1) *makeup,* the arrangement of news and editorial matter for newspapers, and (2) *editorial design,* the arrangement of fiction and nonfiction and art for book and magazine publishers. Not that *advertising layout, makeup,* and *editorial design* do not have much in common. They do. But for admirable reasons, American journalism draws a hard line between advertising and news-and-editorial; the workers in one field are segregated from the workers in the other.

Evolution of Advertising Design

The look that dominated advertising and just about every graphic arts form in the years after World War I was the Bauhaus look, with form following function. In the fourteen years of its existence, the Bauhaus in Germany moved three times, endured all kinds of criticism from both within and without, and graduated fewer than five hundred students.[1] Yet its influence was profound. Its teachers scattered to various parts of the world after the Nazis closed down the school in 1933. Several came to the United States to teach and design here. Much of what we understand about graphic design today and much of what we practice can be traced to the Bauhaus.

Despite the leftist nature of its politics, the Bauhaus brought fine arts and industry together. It recognized the needs of an industrial age.

The Bauhaus style asked for order, symmetry, and clarity in design, with grids playing an important part in the organization of material. Type lost its serifs. Heads sometimes appeared without any beginning caps. "Why should we write and print with two alphabets?" asked Herbert Bayer. "We do not speak with a capital 'A' and a small 'a'." Decorative elements simplified themselves into geometric forms. Rules and bars appeared frequently. Sometimes elements in the design appeared on the diagonal. Overall, the look was one of precision.

In the years after World War II a sort of neo-Bauhaus look was born: It was clear, crisp, and beautifully organized. We called it "Swiss" design. But by 1968 one designer had had enough: "The clean Swiss look is not the answer to every problem, no matter how much it has been embraced by designers," wrote Harvey Offenhartz. "This look is smart and extremely contemporary, but is not universally applicable as a layout solution. In its indiscriminate use as a style are the seeds of decreasing effectiveness and, therefore, eventual demise. It may well be the hallmark of the sixties, but it should never be the ultimate design style. There is no final solution in design. Searching for new expressions in communications is what good graphic design is all about."[2]

By that time a number of designers had already broken away. Their design could not have been further removed from the restrictions—and elegance—of Swiss design. The hippie culture, as much as anything else, influenced type and art styles in the ads, just as it influenced dress styles. Then, as a reaction to the reaction, there arose among some designers an interest in the near past: in the 1930s and 1940s especially. The Bauhaus sans serif typefaces, resurrected and slightly modified, replaced the Swiss gothic faces. At the same time ads became decorative and cluttered. It was all very camp to some designers, very "relevant" to others. Along with other affectations of the period there appeared again in ads the multiple stripes of yesteryear, the meandering lines, the pastel colors, the airbrushing, the cross-hatching, the swirls, the swashes and scripts, the ornate and heavy (in more ways than one) types. Just about everything was "in," including the durable Swiss look. And the juxtaposition did not matter much.

In a two-page ad in *The New York Times Magazine* in 1972, Lady Manhattan

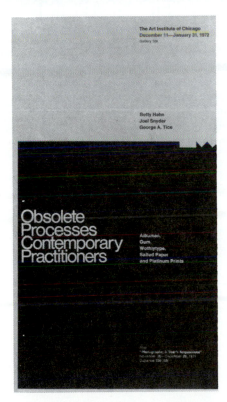

This is an example of Swiss design: highly ordered and based on a grid. Designer Michael Reid uses silver and black—camera colors—for this three-fold, all-on-one-side folder announcing a photography show at The Art Institute of Chicago. The irregular edge at the top right of the black area represents what a photographer feels for when working with cut film in the darkroom. The folder was designed to fit a no. 10 envelope, but when opened out it serves as a poster.

The shape of the Bauhaus and International Design chairs sold by Sedia, Boston, are so distinctive they can be shown in flat views, in line, in this formally balanced ad designed for *Boston Magazine*. The modern logo, with missing strokes for the *E* and *A* and a heavy black box as a dot for the capital *I*, goes at the top of this ad, serving as the ad's headline. Art director: Mittie Cuetara. Designer and copywriter: Colby Andrus.

THE MOST EXTENSIVE LINE OF BAUHAUS AND INTERNATIONAL STYLE DESIGNS, MADE OF THE FINEST MATERIALS AVAILABLE AND CONSTRUCTED TO THE SPECIFICATIONS OF THE ORIGINAL DESIGN. THESE DEFINITIVE FACSIMILES ARE OFFERED FOR UP TO 50% OF THE ORIGINAL MANUFACTURER'S PRICES.

Mailing Address: For Catalogs and Correspondences
136 West Canton Street, Boston MA 02118
Showroom: Saturdays 10 to 5 or By Appointment 617 451 2474
63 Wareham Street, Boston

showed a young woman in a blouse, tie, vest, and skirt in a variety of patterns and colors. The headline referred to "Our What-the-Hell Look." Not a bad term to describe the graphic design that seemed to prevail.

Experimentation would go on, of course. As one advertising art director put it: "For the last 1,000,000 years we have been searching for something new but it always turns out to be just another secret released by nature. We will continue searching. . . ."[3]

Ingredients of Design

The following raw materials go into the making of graphic design:

- *Line.* Lines can be straight or curved, heavy or light, smooth or rough, continuous or broken, actual or merely suggested. Two items separated in a design can cause the reader to draw, optically, a line between them. Line conveys its own mood: If horizontal, calm; if vertical, dignity; if diagonal, vitality; if curved, grace.
- *Tone.* Solid blacks or grays often fill much of the surface area in graphic design. The grays may be in the form of halftone reproductions. Tones provide contrast to lines in the design.
- *Color.* Perhaps more than any other ingredient, color affects the mood of the ad. From a production standpoint, color is an expensive ingredient. There is such a thing, though, as "black-and-white color," which is simply another way of describing "tone."
- *Texture.* When the tonal area has a discernible pattern, either even or rough, the design has texture. The paper the ad is printed on provides texture: It can be hard and smooth, hard and rough, soft and smooth, soft and rough. Texture involves the reader's sense of feel, optical or physical.
- *Shape.* Several lines placed together, a single line that bends or curves, the area of tone—all these provide shape for the design. So do the overall dimensions of the ad.
- *Direction.* Lines and the forms they make have a tendency to point, even to move. A main job of the designer is to control the direction.
- *Size.* An ad usually has elements of varying sizes. The largest elements usually have the biggest impact.

The size of the ad itself also makes a difference. Bleeding a photograph or allowing a design element to extend out of a box suggests that the message of the ad is too big to be contained. Display type can run off the page, as when it lists the good qualities of a product. The reader gets the impression that there is much more to the story. This works in commercials, too, as when an announcer recites the states where a particular automobile is the best seller. It may be that the announcer, cut off in the middle of a name, is actually at the end of the list, but the viewer-listener does not know this. What the public assumes is as important to the advertiser as what the public knows.

The Design Process

Design, like *creativity,* is a virtue word, overused and not quite understood.

Design, the noun, is more than pattern. It is more than ornament or decoration. It is structure itself and the plan behind that structure.

It is the foundation of all the arts.

Design, the verb, applies to all human activity that attempts to organize.

Elizabeth Adams Hurwitz defined the word succinctly in the title of a book: *Design: A Search for Essentials.*

Design works best "when content and form become one," Milton Glaser observed. "The sense of wholeness that implies an absolute world is the most important single quality of a work of graphic art, or, for that matter, of any creative work."[4]

An ad for Mystic Seaport museum, Mystic, Connecticut, reproduced here actual size, shows that you can crowd a lot of information, gracefully, into a small space. The thin-rule semi-box nicely holds the ad together. Created in-house. Designer: Trish LaPointe. Copywriter: Edgar Ruckle.

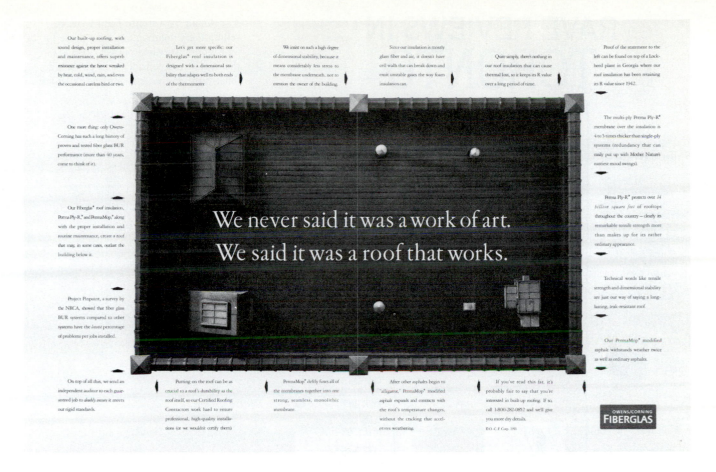

The art in the middle is a model made by Mark Burrow and photographed by Jerry Cailor. Client: Owens/Corning Fiberglas. Agency: Ogilvy & Mather. Copywriter: Dallas Itzen.

Art Director Jennifer Solow arranges paragraphs of copy to start at the upper left, move across the top of the ad, run down the right side, move across the bottom to the left, and run up the left side to the top. Short, fat arrows direct the reader.

In selecting and arranging elements, the advertising designer tries to achieve both order and beauty. The order the designer creates out of a chaos of pictures, copy blocks, headlines, and white space makes it easy for the reader to read and understand the ad. The beauty makes the reader glad to be there.

Order is the overriding consideration. It simplifies the ad, even when it must carry innumerable items, as in a department store sales announcement. Ernest Dichter, the Viennese psychologist specializing in advertising research, believes that advertising can be too ordered, leaving little for the reader to do. The designer may want to allow for some *closure*.

The order of the ad has a lot to do with its beauty. Beauty is simplicity. But beauty is also variety.

The designer's whole function, as Philip C. Beam sees it, is "to create an arrangement of visual elements in any art work which will satisfy the human need for both order and variety in a world that is profuse and confusing on the one hand, and monotonous and boring on the other."[5]

Helmut Krone, who art directed so much of Doyle Dane Bernbach's classic advertising, said that, to him, beauty and style were secondary. What he really strove for was newness. His goal was to create designs no one had seen before.

Design and Layout: The Difference

The professionals in advertising tend to draw a distinction between design and layout as nouns.

A design differs from a layout in that a design is more studied, more finished, more lasting. The person creating a design starts from the beginning, making most of the decisions about size, medium, typography, art, and so on. A design results from a truly creative effort.

A layout, on the other hand, makes use of what may already be available or what may be dictated by others. A layout involves a fitting together of elements, but a fitting together in the best possible combination and in the best possible

RAVE REVIEWS IN
TORONTO

An ad by Toronto Film Liaison selling the Canadian city as a place to film motion pictures puts cartoon art in the center and runs copy on either side, flush-right on the left side and flush-left on the right side.

order. A layout, considering the limitations, can represent a challenge every bit as invigorating as a design can.

Whether *designing* an ad or simply *doing a layout,* the ad maker follows basic principles of design, principles that, in one way or another, are applicable to all the arts.

Design Principles

What the architect's blueprint is to the potential homeowner and the builder, the designer's layout is to the advertising client and to the printer. And the skills necessary to produce a first-class advertising layout are related to the skills necessary to design an aesthetically pleasing and useful building, an appliance, even a painting.

Certain principles govern how advertising should be designed. The number of principles varies, depending upon how you phrase them. Their users may not even be conscious of them as principles. Asked to name them, many users doubtless would be at a loss, yet their designs may be highly effective, even academically appropriate. They design instinctively.

Not all persons called on to produce designs or layouts are so fortunate. They

MULTIPLE CHOICE IN TORONTO

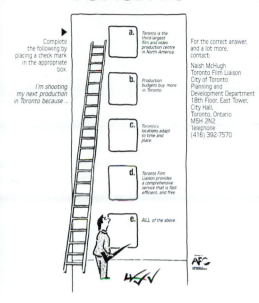

YOU *CAN* LEAVE HOME WITHOUT IT, IF YOU'RE SHOOTING IN TORONTO

The ad format is repeated in additional ads, and so is the figure in the art, although his setting changes. This helps unite the ads in the series. The ads appeared in *Millimeter,* a trade magazine for the motion picture industry.

need the help a statement of principles can bring. They can improve their designs by making a conscientious effort to apply these principles to their assignments.

The principles of design apply (1) to each element within the ad and (2) to the collection or arrangement of the elements as a whole. An understanding of the principles can help designers better manage the order and variety they bring to advertising.

The principles of design are to the layout artist what rules of grammar are to the writer. And just as the grammarians do not agree entirely on what is right and what is wrong (Can *like* ever be used as a conjunction? Can you end a sentence with a preposition?), designers do not agree wholly on what is effective and what is not.

Nor do all writers on design offer the same set of principles to follow. But the following list, from an advertising standpoint, can be considered reasonably universal and inclusive:

- *The design must be in balance.*
- *The space within the ad should be broken up into pleasing proportions.*
- *A directional pattern should be evident.*
- *A unifying force should hold the ad together.*
- *One element, or one part of the ad, should dominate all others.*

Reduced to single words, the list might read: balance, proportion, sequence, unity, and emphasis.

A well-designed ad is likely to incorporate all these principles, but it may be stronger in one than in the others.

Balance

When an ad is "in balance" it is at rest, at peace with itself. The student might well question this. Doesn't an ad need action? It does, of course, but not necessarily in its basic framework. The action comes in the liveliness of the art or photography and the copy and headlines. The design does not intrude.

The designer experiments with two kinds of balance: formal (symmetrical) and informal (asymmetrical). Under formal balance, every item that goes on one side of the ad is repeated, in size or shape, on the other. Items on an imaginary vertical center line spill over in equal portions on the left and on the right.

When does formal balance work best? The easy answer is: for institutional advertising and other serious-minded advertising. But the truth is, it can work well for any kind of advertising. One of its strengths is that it discourages trickery and gimmickry. It presents material in an easy-to-follow order. And, in contrast to informal balance, it often comes off well enough even when a rank amateur is doing the designing.

In informal balance, optical weight is still considered; but decisions affecting it are more complicated. The grown man gets on the teeter-totter with his young son: If the one moves in far enough toward the fulcrum, the other out far enough from it, their weights will be balanced.

The beginning designer should be willing to try informal balance at the very start. Formal balance is a too-easy, too-pat solution to a layout problem. And it is often inappropriate to the mood of the ad.

Laying out an ad, the designer may place one large picture on one side, probably allowing it to overlap the center line, a smaller picture on the other—out to the edge—and some type near but not on the center line. Squinting to study the ad in progress, the designer tries to determine whether or not the elements, reduced to optical weights, are balanced. Holding the ad up to a mirror to check it in "mirror-reverse" or holding it upside down helps the designer make balance decisions.

Nor should the designer forget the relationship of the top of the ad to the bottom. All units of the ad should form a composition that appears to be balanced, with the optical center of the ad, a point just above the center and slightly to the left, acting as the ad's pivot.

Tell a student that an ad has to be "in balance"—that when you draw a line down the center, from top to bottom, half of the optical "weight" of the ad must fall on one side, half on the other—and watch that student bring to class a visually effective ad with elements arranged in an upside-down L shape. Isn't *that* ad off-balance?

Well, yes and no.

The fact that an unusual amount of white space is concentrated in one part of the ad in itself provides "weight," bringing the ad into balance. For optical weight is more than a matter of size and blackness. Of course, big elements and black elements "weigh" more than little elements and gray elements. But unusual-shaped elements "weigh" more than usual-shaped elements. And color "weighs" more than black-and-white.

So an ad that at first glance appears to be out of balance may, on closer inspection, actually be in balance.

Furthermore, *placement* of the ad in the magazine can affect its balance. An ad with material running across the top and down the right side, placed on a right-hand page, will, when seen with a filled editorial page on its left, appear to be perfectly balanced.

In a few cases, a lack of balance, bringing with it an optical tension, may actually be desirable in an ad. Such an ad may intrigue a reader. Certainly it will catch the reader's attention, unless there happens to be a rash of such ads.

The point is this: Balance, as a design principle, need not—should not—straitjacket the advertising designer. More than any of the design principles, this one deserves occasional violation, even among students. Beginners are often *too* much concerned about balance. They seem to think design is *only* balance.

Proportion

When you put two or more elements together, you get proportion, whether you want it or not.

To the advertising designer, proportion is the relationship of sizes: the width of the ad to the depth; the width of an element within the ad to the depth of that element; the size of one area within an element to the size of another area within the element; the size of one element to the size of another element; the amount of space between two elements to the amount of space between one of those elements and a third element. Proportion also involves the tone of the ad: the amount of light area as opposed to the amount of dark area; the amount of color as opposed to noncolor.

Ideally these relationships vary. When they are the same—when widths equal depths, when distances between elements equal one another, when exactly half the ad is color and half noncolor—the ad becomes monotonous. This is not to say there should not be some consistency in proportion. For the sake of parallel structure, for instance, the distances between one size of subhead and the paragraphs below should all be the same.

For inspiration in matters of proportion, the designer turns to nature, where relationships are subtle. Looking at a hand, for instance, the designer sees that the distance between the top of a finger to the first knuckle is different from the distance between the first knuckle and the second. That second distance is different from the distance between the second knuckle and the third. Looking at a tree, the designer sees that the trunk does not have the same diameter as the branch. Nor is the trunk diameter *exactly twice* the branch's diameter.

As an architectural model of pleasing proportions, we have the Parthenon, said to be, in its original state, the most perfectly proportioned building in the world.

The "golden oblong,"[6] adopted by the ancient Greeks after much experimentation, remains a model of space division for the advertising designer. That ratio of width to depth boils down, roughly, to 3:2 or, better, 5:3.

To achieve pleasing proportions in an ad, then, the designer arranges spaces so that the eye does not perceive obvious mathematical relationships. In most circumstances the designer avoids dividing the ad in halves, quarters, or thirds.

Diagonal thrusts in the art lead the reader from the product to the headline, which covers that part of the art least applicable to the product. The second and smaller headline nicely ties itself to the first, making a single unit out of the type. Ordinarily you would not combine a modern roman with a slab serif, but the two work together well here. The ad appeared originally in full color. Art director: Gene Federico. Agency: Lord, Geller, Federico, Einstein. The jewelry was designed by Eugene Bertolli.

A beautiful study in proportion by designer Blanche Simkin for The Viking Press, and in the confines of small space. The ad is shown actual size. Agency: Waterman, Getz, Niedelman.

Napier* 530 Fifth Avenue, NY 10036. At fine stores everywhere.

NAPIER IS GLEAMIER.

Cuff bracelet with golden and silvery finish, $15.

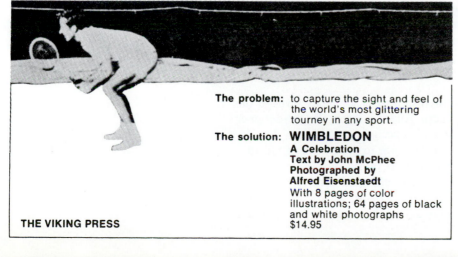

The problem: to capture the sight and feel of the world's most glittering tourney in any sport.

The solution: **WIMBLEDON**
A Celebration
Text by John McPhee
Photographed by
Alfred Eisenstaedt
With 8 pages of color illustrations; 64 pages of black and white photographs $14.95

THE VIKING PRESS

It would not be a good idea to allow the design to be half art and half everything else (headline, copy, logo, and white space). Better to divide the ad into fifths. The top three-fifths of such an ad could be devoted to art—say a large photograph. The bottom two-fifths could go to the headline, copy, logo, and white space.

All of which suggests that a square, with its four even sides, in most circumstances is not as good a design element as a rectangle, with its two different dimensions. But the square came into its own as a useful shape for some ads in the 1960s and 1970s. Some magazines have even forsaken the traditional golden oblong—the 8½″ × 11″ page—for a square format. Some advertising designers have chosen the square as the shape for annual reports and other direct-mail pieces. Designers have also shown that beautiful design is possible on the square fields of record album covers.

In some cases, designers have not only worked successfully within the square format but also have divided that square into a grid of smaller squares, and they have placed the ad's elements into position in concert with the smaller squares. They have even used square, rather than rectangular, photographs. Ads built upon a grid of squares are part of the Swiss look in graphic design.

As a general rule, however, unequal dimensions and distances make for the best—or at least the most lively—design in advertising.

Sequence

The ad *may* do its job if the reader is allowed to wander aimlessly through the items on display, stopping here, stopping there. And it may not. So the designer prefers to set up a correct order for the reader's taking in of the items. The designer leads the reader by the hand through the maze to the climax of the ad.

To control sequence, the designer can do either of these:

Place the items in the path of what would be considered normal eye movement.

Blaze new trails, marking them clearly enough so the reader will not wander off and get lost.

The sleek, good looks of the Nissan Turbo Z are enough to sell the product, this two-page magazine ad suggests. Art director Corey Stolberg, tongue-in-cheek, uses gray chalk to cross out all the "unnecessary" technical details about the car. (But of course, those details are still readable, for the ad is meant for readers of auto magazines, who take their cars seriously.) Agency: Chiat/Day/Mojo, Venice, California. Creative director: Lee Clow. Copywriter: Tom Witt. Photographer: Bob Grigg.

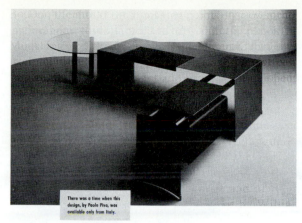

B&B Italia e Herman Miller: Una idea eccezionale!

Now, through an exclusive arrangement, the Arcada collection and other B&B Italia products are available through Herman Miller, Inc.

You can see these designs, as well as those by Mario Bellini, Paolo Nava, and Kairos, at Office Pavilions and other Herman Miller dealers throughout the United States.

For more information, call 1-800-851-1196.

B&B ITALIA

⊔ herman miller

An ad for Herman Miller uses a piece of furniture to lead the eye to the copy and logo. In this example, the furniture is kept inside a rectangular photograph. The copy appears in a color box, which overlaps the photo and is, itself, overlapped by a white band carrying the headline. Art director and designer: Stephen Frykholm. Copywriter: Nancy Green. The photo was provided by B & B Italia.

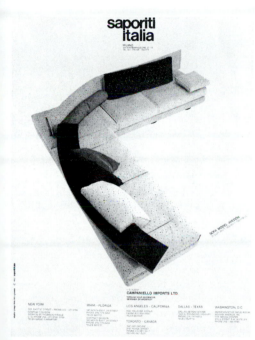

saporiti
italia

Designer Giorgio Saporiti uses a silhouetted bird's-eye view of Saporiti Italia's "Sofa Model Avedon" to lead the reader's eye from the headline/logo at the top to the listing of showrooms at the bottom of this ad, which appeared in *Architectural Digest.* Agency: Thomas Campaniello Associates, New York. Designer, art director, and copywriter: Giorgio Saporiti.

Through habit, the eye moves from left to right and from top to bottom. Realizing this, the designer can arrange the elements so they start at the upper left, move across to the upper right, down to the lower left, then across to the lower right. A Z pattern is the obvious way of controlling eye travel.

But if all ads were arranged in this way, they would be monotonous.

The eye moves naturally, too, from big elements to little elements, from black elements to lighter elements, from color to noncolor, from unusual shapes to usual shapes. Bearing this in mind, the designer actually can start eye travel *anywhere* in the ad and then direct it to the left, the right, down, even up.

Sometimes the designer controls eye travel by providing a solid or dotted line—a sort of track—along which the eye can move effortlessly. But this is too obvious. A more subtle approach is to repeat shapes and sizes; the eye recognizes the related items and moves easily from one to another—jumping across the space in between—because the territory is familiar. You could say a line—an implied line—is there to act as a track.

Or the designer can get sequence through graduation of the size of elements. The eye moves as if up or down a series of steps.

Sequence at its best involves a sort of optical rhythm. The rhythm may be staccato-like, with several even-sized elements serving to hold the reader in line.

How it looks.

How it feels.

You might think you see two trucks here, but actually there's just one. It has a massive 3.0-liter, multi-point fuel-injected V6 engine that produces 153 horsepower—more than Toyota, Mazda or any import. It also produces a staggering 180 ft/lbs of torque. Ninety percent of which is available at a low 2,000 rpm. The Nissan SE V6 King Cab 4x4. It looks like a truck. It feels like a monster.

Built for the Human Race.

To compare "How it looks" with "How it feels," Nissan perfectly lines up the two trucks on a horizontal that spans a magazine spread. This is parallel structure at work in graphic design. Agency: Chiat/Day/Mojo, Venice, California. Creative director: Lee Clow. Art director: Corey Stolberg. Copywriter: Tom Witt. Photographer: Lamb & Hall.

It may take a crescendo form, each element building in intensity. It may take a diminuendo form, the elements letting readers down easily as they move away from the ad's main thrust. Or it may be more complicated, with "long beats" and "short beats" and "pauses" arranged in no easily described pattern.

If you want to find out where the eye does *not* travel in a design, study the cigarette ads. You know that the box with the surgeon general's warning, whether it appears at the top or bottom of the ad, has been placed well away from the ad's visual thrust.

Unity

Perhaps the most important of the design principles, unity sees to it that elements within the ad tie together, that they appear to be related. Unity keeps the ad from falling apart. It is the ad's bonding agent.

Another word for unity is harmony. The designer creates harmony by selecting elements that go together and arranging them so that they "get along" with each other.

The problem of unity becomes more acute when the designer works with unusually shaped ads: ads that are long and narrow or L-shaped or ads that spill across two pages.

The elements going into the ad can best be unified when they have the same basic shape, size, texture, color, and mood. The type in a unified ad has the same character as the art.

The border. A border surrounding the ad provides one easy solution to the problem of unity. At least it keeps elements from becoming part of other ads on the page.

Sets of borders or boxes *within* the ad, provided they are alike in thickness and tone, can also help the ad's unity. The reader sees the relationship among them and so mentally ties the elements together.

White space. Wise use of white space can do wonders in unifying the ad. The secret is to keep the white space at the outside edges of the ad. Such white space plays the same role an ordinary border plays. When the designer allows white spaces to gather inside the ad, separating the units, the ad may fall apart.

The white space at the edges of the ad should take irregular shaping. It should be more than a mere band with the same thickness on all four sides. Remember the law of proportion?

The axis. To keep the elements in an ad fully related, no single device can help the designer more than an axis, real or imagined, preferably imagined. An

You'd smile too if you had to be quarantined in an Airstream.

The 1990 Airstream Motorhome

A lasting relationship since 1935.

1990 Airstream Excella

How fuel-efficient is the Airstream?

The 1990 Airstream Excella

Airstream Travel Trailers rely on nostalgia themes to tie together a series of ads attesting to the products' venerability. Using heavily leaded copy, a compressed, squared, san serif headline typeface, and duotone photographs for a faded effect, art director Mike Rylander varies placement of the elements to gain visual variety. The ads ran in trailer and motor-home magazines. Agency: Golden Opinions Ltd., New York. Copywriter: Tom Witt.

ad could well make use of two or three or more axes, running vertically and horizontally.

The axis—the line running through the ad—forms a sort of base from which elements in the ad flare outward. The edge of a picture may suggest the edge of a headline. Or the edge of a strong element within the picture may suggest the edge of the headline. Obviously, it would not be a good idea to allow elements to move *alternately* out to the left and right. That would be monotonous. Nor is it necessary to have *every* element attach to an axis. An occasional element, or even most of the elements, can run across the axis, ignoring it. But the fact that two or more elements use a common axis helps hold all elements together. A relationship is set up.

Three-point layout. The designer can also unify the ad by using a three-point layout approach. Three units (uneven number) make for better proportion than two or four units (even numbers).

Moreover, when the eye sees three different items in a given area, it tends to make a triangle of them, drawing a line to connect each point.

The ad may actually consist of more than three elements, but the elements would be organized into three basic groups. Or three intrusive pieces of art would be used, probably of unequal sizes, probably unequally separated.

Parallel structure. Showing art on the left and repeating it at the right also brings unity to an ad, even when the ad crosses the gutter in a magazine. Celanese Fortrel Polyester in a two-page ad in *The New York Times Magazine* showed a full-page figure of a man at the left in an obnoxious polyester suit, the pattern dated, lapels too wide, stitching too obvious. At the right was a full figure in a dark suit that hung nicely, the fabric looking thin and rich like fine wool. The headline read: "We're About to Change the Way You Look at Polyester."

The copy talked about the change in polyester ("Look what polyester is doing now"): ". . . people equate polyester with the artificial look of early fabrics. Well, those fabrics haven't been around for years. Advanced technology and constant developments have produced fibres that achieve the aesthetics of their natural counterparts but without sacrificing their great ease of care performance."

The use of parallel structure in the ad's design clearly dramatized the change in looks between early polyester suits and current ones. To make the comparison easy, it was necessary for the designer to keep the side-by-side figures in the same large size and to keep them at the same level on the pages.

Unity for spreads. When an ad stretches across two pages, the designer has a harder time than usual unifying the elements. Some methods for solving the problem:

■ *With eyes, a hand, a crooked elbow, let the subject on the left-hand page point to the type matter on the right-hand page.*
■ *Use the same color on the two pages, the same typeface, the same art style.*
■ *Pick up an axis from the left-hand page and use it on the right-hand page.*
■ *Allow headline type to go across the gutter to the second page, but be sure you break the headline between words, not between letters.* Or let the body copy start on one page and continue on the next, lining up the columns to form an axis. Or allow a picture to go across the gutter. Be sure you break the picture at a spot that is not crucial to its composition. Do not allow an important face, for instance, to be caught in the magazine fold, where it will become distorted. Across-the-gutter pictures in magazines work best at the center folds.
■ *As for any advertising, push the white space to the outside edges, allowing the ad elements to congregate around the gutter.*
■ *Run a border all the way around the two-page spread, as if there were no gutter there.*

J. C. Penney used this illustration in a newsletter to make the point to advertising managers at its various stores that "White space, like art, has a shape." When the art is centered, the space around it is relatively uninteresting. When the art is moved to the side and slightly cropped, the white space becomes a shape. When the art is enlarged, cropped even more, and lowered, the shape of the white space becomes dramatic.

Emphasis

Someone must make an early decision about what one item to emphasize in the ad: the art, the headline, the copy block. If the art, which *one* item of art?

With that decision made, the designer looks for ways of focusing on that item of emphasis. One way is to single it out—move it away from the clutter of other elements. Another is to change its shape, making it different from all the others. Another is to make it bigger, bolder, more colorful.

How *much* emphasis it should get is another problem. Its basic importance, the attitude of the advertiser, the class of reader to be reached—all this is taken into account. The size of the ad—the room the designer has available—makes a difference, too.

The designer must also decide where in the ad the item of emphasis should be placed. A first decision might involve the optical center of the ad. Placing the emphasized element there will assure its being seen.

The designer must keep in mind one important rule of emphasis: *All emphasis is no emphasis.* Only one item in the ad should get primary attention. No item

An example of three-point design where the visual units—the two-sentence boldface headline, the silhouette halftone, and the heavy-bordered coupon—organize into a triangle. The unjustified body copy fits into blank spaces created by the headline. The headline utilizes a sans serif with character—a face with slight differences in stroke thicknesses and with a *j* and *i* that have curved tops to accommodate the dots. Designer: Glen Ivie. Copywriter: Bill Brown. Client: Context Development Co., Florida. Agency: Denton & French.

A grid of twenty squares (top left) can stimulate thumbnails like those that follow. The first ad uses twelve of the squares for art, four for copy, and four for headline and white space. Many other combinations are possible, of course. A grid could also be constructed with a different number of squares, or with squares and rectangles, or with rectangles only. Rather than restricting design, a grid can expand its possibilities, even though it does bring order to advertising.

should upstage the chosen item. Where several items get equal billing, emphasis is canceled.

Working with many small, similar-sized items in, say, a crowded retail ad or catalog page, the designer gathers several items together in a mass, maybe even puts a border around it, and that one mass becomes the element of emphasis in the ad.

You get emphasis primarily through a contrast between what needs to be emphasized and what can be subordinated.

A sudden change in direction will give emphasis. So will a change in size, in shape, in texture, in color, in tone, in line.

Beyond the Principles

George Giusti, the widely admired illustrator, told how he put design principles to work: "By eliminating details, I achieve impact. By using fewer colors, I attain more contrast. By simplifying shapes, I make them bolder."[7]

The advertising designer follows the principles of design on each assignment either consciously or unconsciously. But it is impossible to apply these principles equally, because one may be more important than another, depending on the mood and purpose of the ad. Furthermore, the principles in some respects contradict one another. For instance, how can you have contrast if your ad is perfectly unified?

The designer tries to work as many of the principles—as much of each principle—as possible into each ad. Becoming more confident, the designer may want to deliberately violate one or more of the principles to give the ad an edge over its competitors.

Into each ad goes a bit of the designer's personality, which cannot be distilled as a "principle." Without this touch, the ad may be well designed, but it could be lifeless, sterile, dull.

The Test of a Good Layout

When you have arranged your elements into a good layout—when you have designed your ad—see whether you can remove any one of the elements without hurting the ad's balance, its proportion, its unity. If you find that your ad does not suffer from having lost an element, you might well question its basic structure.

The removing of any one element should necessitate a complete redesigning of the ad. The relationship of the elements should be that strong.

THE PRINCIPLES OF DESIGN

CHAPTER

5

LAYOUT APPROACHES

As an advertising designer, you work with several basic elements as you lay out an ad. You may decide what these elements should be, making all the plans, assigning any of the work that has to be done by others. Or you may simply put the elements together as they are handed to you.

In either case, your knowledge of the principles of design helps. You reduce the various elements to shapes—rectangles, triangles, circles, and irregular shapes—and then apply what you know of balance, proportion, sequence, unity, and emphasis.

You get enough items together so that the total elements area—the area covered by the headlines, copy, art, and logotype—adds up usually to *more than* half the area of the assigned space. (The rule of proportion suggests that an ad should not be *exactly* half message and half white space.) Then, using traditional tools or computer software, you try various arrangements of the elements. As you work, you gradually increase the detail so that the elements look like the elements they are supposed to be.

Advertising Elements

The typical ad contains these elements:

- *Headline* (or headlines). Often a headline in large type is followed by a headline, a longer headline, in smaller type. Probably the most important single element in the ad, the headline carries the theme of the ad. Seeing the headline, the reader gets everything the advertiser really has to say. Occasionally the ad is all headline, with only a signature added.

A good advertising headline brings news to the reader, gives advice, promises something, arouses curiosity, narrows the audience to people who are really interested or affected, makes a command. It does one or several of these things.

These are matters for copywriters, of course, but they are also matters for designers, even if they do not do any of the writing. In headlines particularly,

This ad in an extreme horizontal format spans two magazine pages, with space above for editorial matter. The extreme cropping emphasizes an ear and an eye, necessary for a headline that says, "Introducing television for people whose sense of hearing is as finely tuned as their sense of sight." The client: Toshiba America Consumer Products, Inc. Agency: Calet, Hirsch & Spector, Inc. Art director: Gordon Bennett. Designers: Gordon Bennett and Steve Lansberg. Copywriter: Steve Lansberg.

Introducing television for people whose sense of hearing is as finely tuned as their sense of sight.

Introducing Toshiba big screen televisions equipped with Carver Sonic Holography® Sound. So intense is the picture you'll be drawn to it. So unbelievably real is the sound you'll be immersed in it. So astonishing is the combined effect you'll be awed by it.

Your Toshiba dealer invites you to bring your skepticism and compare. At which time you can judge our superiority with your eyes closed.

In Touch with Tomorrow

TOSHIBA

Toshiba America, Inc. 82 Totowa Road, Wayne, NJ 07470

Given: a vertical and a horizontal picture and eighteen lines of copy (the shaded areas represent pictures; the ruled lines represent copy). The problem: Without changing the sizes, arrange these elements in an area about twice as big as the sum of the area of the elements to be arranged. With such limitations, is it possible to come up with more than one acceptable arrangement? The diagrams here suggest an affirmative answer. Turn them upside down and you have another set to consider.

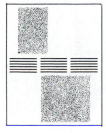

designers exercise considerable control over usage and clarity. Many headline errors can be traced to designer haste or ignorance. Designers must take care as they do lettering on the roughs; they must look for more than spacing problems when they check the proofs.

Two problem areas deserve mention: (1) the breaking up of a headline into lines or "takes," and (2) the use of punctuation.

If a headline must occupy more than one line, the lines should break at natural pauses. Consider this headline from an ad that appeared in major magazines:

**Give him
Royal Oak
Scented Lotion
and kiss small
talk goodbye.**

The lines "and kiss small" and "talk goodbye" confuse the reader. They would make more sense broken up like this:

**and kiss small talk
goodbye.**

Punctuation errors most often involve the use of the apostrophe and the question mark. With the apostrophe, it is often a matter of the copywriter or designer not knowing when it is needed. With the question mark, it is a matter of simply forgetting to draw it in. A left-out question mark can change the meaning of a sentence. Don't you agree.

■ *Copy block.* The copy block or column, in small type, amplifies the headline. It helps convince the reader. It closes the sale. The ad maker tries to keep it short, terse—but not for all ads, and certainly not for mail-order advertising.

Some advertising people don't buy the idea that pictures do more for advertising than copy does. One has written: "A picture worth a thousand words? You give me 1,000 words and I'll take the Lord's Prayer, the Twenty-Third Psalm, the Hippocratic Oath, a sonnet by Shakespeare, the Preamble to the Constitution, Lincoln's Gettysburg Address, and I'd still have enough words left over for just about all of the Boy Scout oath. And I wouldn't trade you for any picture on earth."[1]

When copy runs long, the designer breaks it up into short takes, using white space or white space with a subhead for an occasional optical oasis for the reader. The designer must not treat the copy block as though it were a neutral element occupying areas not preempted by more spectacular art elements. The designer's primary function should be to get people to read the copy block.

Too often, especially in retail advertising, the copy block is set too solid. Leading (pronounced "ledding") would make the copy more inviting. And the type should be set in the largest possible size that is appropriate to the column width.

■ *Art.* As used here, art is a panoramic term, including photographs, drawings, paintings, borders, rules, ornaments, blocks of color or gray tones, areas of white space. Furthermore, type by itself, skillfully arranged, can be considered a piece of art.

The art may merely arrest the viewer, or it may serve a higher purpose: cooperating with the headline and copy in telling the advertiser's story. "One Alternative to Flossing Daily," says a headline for a Johnson & Johnson Dental Floss ad. An accompanying photograph shows false teeth in a water glass.

The experts have not settled the half-century-old argument: What does the best job for the advertiser, a photograph or an illustration? But a comparison of advertising today with advertising of a few years ago shows that photographs seem to be winning. In most circumstances, they are less expensive, and people seem more willing to believe them. But drawings and paintings still have their place. Just as a novel can carry more truth than a piece of nonfiction, a drawing can say more than a photograph. And drawings are not put off by seasons or weather. Neither do they require models' releases.

Borders are another art element to consider. Advertisers want borders on their ads when several even-sized announcements compete with one another on a page and there is danger that readers cannot tell when one ad ends and another begins. The larger the ad or the fewer ads per page, the less need for borders. Even if they are not needed, borders are used by designers when they feel their decorative touch adds to the mood of the ad.

Borders are displayed in the printer's type-specimen book. Designers choose them as they choose types. Or they design their own.

Fine-line rules or thicker lines and bars are sometimes useful inside an ad to organize, emphasize, or segregate elements.

■ *The logotype.* Advertisers have to identify themselves. Sometimes they do it subtly, with a last line buried in the copy block. Usually they do it with a line in display-size type set apart from the body type, at the bottom of the ad. The identifying line—called a "logotype" or "logo" or (by retailers) "signature" or "sig cut"—may be accompanied by an insignia or trademark. A slogan may also be included.

Elliot Young, president of Perception Research Services, Inc., reports one of his tests showing that readers fail to see the logotype almost half the time because of its location in an ad. His advice is to "make sure the logo or product name isn't too low on the page."[2]

■ *Peripheral elements.* Some kinds of advertising require additional elements peculiar to their functions. Cigarette ad designers have this element to work with: the warning unit ordered by the federal government. Designers try to place it where it will do the least damage—away from copy and the art's center of interest.

Package designers have the Universal Product Code unit to incorporate into their designs.

All the two-page ads in a series sponsored by Round the Clock panty hose make use of this format: an arresting bleed photograph by Horst P. Horst on the left and giant all-caps roman type, each line centered, on the right. No body copy follows the headline's double-take message. Creative directors and copywriters: Gad Romann and Barry Tannenholz of Romann & Tannenholz advertising agency, New York. Art directors: Terry Whistler and Denise Desrosiers.

PANTY HOSE FOR MEN.

Bad vibes from within
and hostility from
without threaten the
collective goodwill
of a rural commune

in an explosive new novel of torment, passion,
and hope that takes up where *Alice's
Restaurant* and *Easy Rider* left off

THE MAGIC TORTOISE RANCH

A novel by
ANNETTE
KING

$5.95, now at
your bookstore

Crown

The border that holds this black-
and-white ad together and separates it
from other ads on the page is pleasantly
broken by headline and art. The ad is
shown here actual size. Illustrator:
Larry Lurin. Agency: Sussman &
Sugar.

Retail advertising appearing in newspapers needs strong price display. In
most retail ads, prices are set in type that is larger and bolder than body copy
or even headlines. Such price units can be treated as separate design elements.

Advertising in both newspapers and magazines often carries coupons,
either to present to grocers or to fill out and mail. The designer not only has to
decide on placement of these coupons but also must work on the design of the
coupon. An ad for a fashion seminar might include a coupon in the shape of a
dress pattern. The reader would have to cut out the dress along the dotted line
after filling in the blanks. Mistakes in design of a mail-in coupon are making it
too small to fill out or too inconvenient to cut out or—worst of all—printing it
in reverse letters on a black or dark-color background so that pencil or pen
markings will not show up.

One approach puts type and lines over a photograph that is strong enough
to convey an appropriate mood but weak enough not to interfere with
readability. The coupon art can duplicate a portion of the ad's main art. Or it
can be a miniature version of it.

Layout Stages

Layouts vary in quality from crude, less-than-actual-size pencil doodles to laser-
printed designs that could pass for the finished product. It is not so much the
layout artist's ability or lack of it that explains this variance as the intended use
to which the layout will be put. If it is to be used by the artist as a trial run, or
by the copywriter as a guide to the amount of space to fill, or by the illustrator
as a guide to composition in taking or drawing pictures, or by the printer as a
guide in setting type and arranging design elements, the layout can be less than
exact. If it is for the client, to help in decision making before money is spent on
production, the layout will be carried to a more finished stage.

First roughs often are more spirited than later polishings, and the designer, in
carrying the layout through the various stages, tries to hold onto any happy accidents that occur early in the process. But the designer cannot settle for a first
try; considerations involving the nature of the product or service, attitude of the
client, specifications of the medium, and the like, make the hunt for the ideal
solution to a selling problem too involved for that. Besides, later compromises
with the client certainly will force additional adjustments.

The ad in final form may be but a distant relative of the first rough layout.

Because it takes less time to doodle in miniature than in actual size, the designer usually starts out by making thumbnail sketches, or *thumbnails,* using
pencil, ballpoint pen, fine-line marker, crayon, or whatever tool may be handy.

Aetna Life & Casualty uses this
four-part, two-page format for a series
of ads, giving them a "house" look so
that readers will recognize them and
their source. This ad invites questions
about AIDS. Agency: Ammirati &
Puris. Art director: K. J. Bowen.
Copywriter: David Fowler.

At this early stage, sketching with traditional tools seems natural to most designers, but some start right out using the computer.

The thumbnail should be in proportion to the ad as it is to appear in print. Quarter-size is normal.

Even at this stage the designer thinks in terms of tones as well as outlines, suggesting halftones with areas of gray, line drawings with amoeba shapes, headlines with zigzag lines, copy with parallel lines. Dozens of sketches may precede the development of a layout in the next stage.

The second stage is the *rough layout.*

Some designers skip the thumbnail stage altogether, because they feel that whatever good effect they come up with loses too much in translation to the normal size. Their full-size layouts are as rough as thumbnails would be, maybe rougher.

An extremely crude rough layout is sometimes called a *shop rough,* meaning it is meant to serve simply as a hurried guide to the print shop. The heads may be lettered in, but type styles or weights are not approximated; instructions and descriptions are written on the outside margins. Or the compositor picks types to fit. Ads for retailers run in newspapers sometimes are produced in this way.

A *finished layout* is a rough layout carried to a stage where headings are lettered in a style and weight clear enough to make marginal descriptions unnecessary, and artwork and photographs are drawn to look much like the finished product. Copy is indicated with carefully ruled parallel lines or "greeking," if the rough is computer-generated. Spacing is close to exact.

When several people must see a layout at one time—as in department store operations when department heads and members of the newspaper advertising staff both must check prices—more than one copy of the rough layout is needed. At any rate, no retailer appearing regularly in newspapers, and certainly few direct-mail users, expect or need better than rough layouts. Even clients of advertising agencies accept layouts finished only to this level.

Sometimes a layout gets further polish. Call it a *comprehensive* or *comp.* Important clients who pay thousands of dollars for single magazine insertions understandably demand comprehensives before they okay their ads.

A comprehensive is a layout that is perfect in every detail. In a non-computerized operation, headings are hand-lettered in ink or tempera, artwork painted in acrylics or designers' colors or drawn in ink, photographs pasted into place or so carefully approximated in pastels or markers you would swear they *were* photographs. As in a computerized operation, copy may actually be set. If copy is only indicated, a ruling pen and certainly a T-square are used. Drawn and put together on illustration board, the comprehensive is matted and either covered with a flap or wrapped in cellophane.

In a computerized operation, all these activities, except for the matting, flapping, and wrapping, are accomplished in far less time, with the designer using a keyboard, mouse, electronic stylus and tablet, and scanner in place of traditional tools. And alterations, which are bound to come, can be made in seconds instead of hours.

Where comps are computer-generated, the other layout stages described here may become unnecessary. Every rough layout is a comp.

Sometimes the comp comes before rather than after the rough layout. The rough layout then merely defines some changes suggested by the client after seeing the comp.

Basic Formats

Whether you start right off on a comprehensive or try some thumbnails and rough layouts first, you will be trying to put the elements of the ad into a pleasing and useful arrangement. The number of arrangements and patterns you can come up with as a designer are almost endless, but it is possible to fit most print-medium advertisements into ten basic categories or formats, if you interpret them loosely enough. A professional designer might balk at such categorizations, saying that the art is too lively, too full of surprises to pin down so abruptly. And some other

Some designers find that, to do thumbnails and rough layouts, traditional tools still do the job in this computer age. The designer here uses a fine-line marker and a T-square to rule in some quick lines, then fills in with gray markers. His type at this early stage consists of zig-zags and straight lines. The layout takes a silhouette format, with the ad's elements crowded together to form a single visual unit framed by an irregular white frame. Time: two or three minutes.

A rough layout or comp sets the stage for the finish, but often the finish takes on a look that is quite different in the end, even though the placement of elements remains the same. This two-page ad ran sideways as a center spread in a running magazine. Art director: Tom Kelly. Copywriter: Thom Schumacher.

writer on design might come up with a different set of categories. But a set like the one that follows may help the beginner see some new possibilities for design.[3]

■ *Mondrian Layout.* Let us start with one of the most widely recognized formats: Mondrian layout, named after the Dutch painter Piet Mondrian. Involved in a lifetime affair with proportion, Mondrian, using black bars and lines and solid areas of primary color, divided his canvases into vertical and horizontal rectangles and squares.

Mondrian reworked his designs many times before he was satisfied with the sizes and relationships of each of the rectangles to be painted. He carried this concern to the decor of his studio: an out-of-place ashtray greatly disturbed him. To Mondrian, beauty was exclusively geometric. He avoided the color green because it is too close to nature. "All in all," he is quoted as saying, "nature is a damned wretched affair. I can hardly stand it."

The advertising designer, while not sharing Mondrian's intensity, nevertheless freely applies Mondrian's principles to the printed page. The designer uses rectangles filled with type or art much as Mondrian used solid blocks of color. Sometimes the designer retains the lines or bars Mondrian used to separate elements; sometimes the designer leaves them out.

Mondrian ads appear everywhere for a few months, then die out, then come back again. And no wonder the style returns to popularity: A Mondrian arrangement is an easy, logical, workable, effective way to display type and art.

The designer of Mondrian ads, like the master himself, is more interested in proportion as a design principle than in eye travel or emphasis or any of the other principles. There is nothing wrong with this. For some advertising, proportion deserves chief consideration, if for no other reason than to set the ad apart from other ads whose designers have stressed some other design principle.

The idea is to come up with a fitted set of vertical and horizontal rectangles (with perhaps a square thrown in)—all in different sizes. Lines separating the rectangles can be of even or varying widths; at their thinnest they are bolder than ordinary newspaper column rules. Sometimes the designer uses screened or color rules in combination with solid black rules.

One or two of the rectangles may be filled with halftones; others may contain copy; others may be blank.

If the ruled lines are heavy, typefaces should be bolder than normal. Sans serifs or gothics are appropriate types to use.

Mondrian layouts are used more frequently in magazines than in newspapers, because the multiplicity of lines and resulting rectangles tend to break the ad into sections that may be scattered optically when smaller ads are placed alongside, as on a newspaper page. Large reverse L-shape ads (or step ads) in newspapers sponsored by department stores or women's fashion stores, however, make use of the Mondrian principle with considerable success.

In arranging the rectangles, the designer lightly rules a series of horizontal and vertical lines, then eliminates some of them, either entirely or partially, and strengthens others, striving to leave rectangles of varying sizes and dimensions. The balance is almost always informal.

Swiss design, with its orderly approach, has some ties to Mondrian layout. But in Swiss design, lines or bars are not shown; they appear only in the mind of the designer. And the design is based often on a grid of squares instead of rectangles.

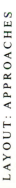

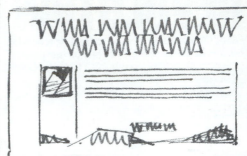

These thumbnails show some
approaches to Mondrian layout.

Rick Tharp uses a Mondrian
approach for the cover of *The Good Toy
Book* published by BRIO Scanditoy
Corporation, Milwaukee. A note inside
says: "Cover art inspired by Piet
Mondrian." A square die-cut reveals the
child's face. Jane Kimball wrote the
book, which contained "Guidelines for
Play and Toy Selection." Profits from
the sale of the book went to children's
charities. Agency: Tharp Did It.

D. Cenci's "Details, Details" ad
selling men's high-style clothing makes
use of a Mondrian design approach,
putting elements into a near-formal
balance. Agency: Severin Aviles
Associates. Art director and designer:
Anthony Aviles. Copywriters: James
Severin and Kathleen Cooney Severin.

Powerful people.

Our 50 million readers give new definition to the word "power."

In fact, if they weren't allowed to buy a single Honda Accord it would fall from being America's #1 car model—to #4. Building a brand? Don't forget the foundation.

Start with a family of 50 million. Start with The Digest.

Reader's Digest

A *Reader's Digest* two-page ad directed to media buyers in advertising agencies uses a modified version of the Mondrian approach to design. In this case, one small rectangle carrying the *Reader's Digest* logo overlaps bigger rectangles. A duotone photograph running across the gutter dominates the ad. The solid color in this ad confines itself to the "Powerful People" and "Reader's Digest" rectangles. Agency: John Emmerling. Art director: Art Gilmore. Copywriter: John Emmerling.

■ *Picture-Window Layout.* More popular than Mondrian and especially suited to magazines is the format known in the trade as "Ayer No. 1," after the agency that pioneered its use. We will call it "picture window." Doyle Dane Bernbach for Volkswagen had particular success with this format, but probably theme and copy brilliance and wit were more important than layout. The least you can say for picture-window layout is that it does not get in the way of the ad's message. No "art for art's sake" here, just generous display of picture and tight editing of copy so it will fit the small space remaining.

The designer often bleeds the picture and crops close, almost overpowering the reader. Below the picture is a one-line, centered headline; copy may be broken into two or three short columns. The logo may be worked into the last column of the copy, thereby saving some space.

To tie the picture with the copy, the designer may overprint or reverse some of the headline onto the picture. Or the designer may line up the copy with some axis within the picture. The picture is usually at the top, but nothing prevents the designer from pushing it down a bit, placing the headline and even the copy above. A smaller picture—or perhaps a line drawing for contrast—can be placed near the copy.

The nature of the picture will affect the designer's decision on placement and type style for the headline.

Leading the body copy from 2 to 6 points helps keep it from looking as if it is merely fill and also makes it more readable.

These thumbnails show some approaches to picture-window layout.

■ *Copy-Heavy Layout.* The advertiser chooses a mostly-copy format for two reasons: (1) What is to be said is too involved, too important, too unique, too dignified to be put in pictures; (2) most other ads in the medium will be picture-window or at least heavily picture-oriented, so a gray, quiet, copy-heavy approach makes a good change of pace.

Because copy-heavy advertising takes itself rather more seriously than other advertising, it usually puts its elements into formal balance. Lines of the headlines, set in roman, are centered; copy begins with a large initial letter and is broken into two or more columns. The logo is centered underneath. But a more interesting arrangement can result from less formal balance, with the ad retaining the dignity it would have in a more formal arrangement.

The designer should plan for a blurb or secondary headline as well as a main headline.

Even though the copy is voluminous, there may be room for a few quiet illustrations.

When copy is long, it must be broken somehow into easy-to-take segments. The beginning designer often makes the mistake of marking such copy to be set solid, because it is so long. But long copy, even more than short copy, should be leaded, by at least a point or two. Furthermore, the copy at logical breaks should be refreshed with subheads of one kind or another. Subheads can be flush right, flush left, or centered, in a typeface slightly larger or bolder than the body type, or in all caps. Extra space should frame such subheads.

Subheads can also be formed from the first two or three words of a paragraph, set in boldface. Extra space should be provided to separate the bold beginning from the paragraph above.

These thumbnails show some approaches to copy-heavy layout.

In the design of a copy-heavy ad doing a serious selling job, New York Life Insurance Company relies on parallel structure on facing pages to make it clear that two important points are being covered: what's in it for the reader and what's in it for the company. Agency: Chiat/Day/Mojo Inc. Art director: Susan Fitzgerald. Copywriter: Amelia Rosner.

These thumbnails show some approaches to frame layout.

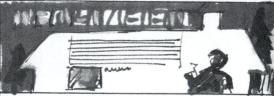

■ *Frame Layout.* A photographer can get a pleasantly composed picture by taking the shot from one of nature's nooks, with foliage and a rock formation in the foreground, dark and out of focus, framing the heart of the picture. In advertising, the designer easily frames a layout with a border, doing it sometimes with artwork that is drawn to leave room in the middle for headline and copy.

Frame layout, used more in newspaper advertising than in magazine advertising, keeps elements within bounds, preventing their being associated with some other ad on the page.

There is something cozy about frame layout.

But it does tend to decrease the optical size of the ad. Furthermore, the ad, if placed at the edge of a page, loses additional white space between the edge of the ad and the edge of the page that an unframed ad would pick up.

A variation of the frame layout is the one in which kidney-shaped artwork is spread over a large portion of the layout, creating a cul-de-sac of white in which the headline and copy are placed. Another variation is the layout using a picture—a photograph, usually—that completely covers the area. Type is either surprinted or reversed in nonpatterned or plain-toned areas.

A frame for this formally balanced ad is formed by the crab's claws reaching around the body copy. The boldness of the headline matches the boldness of the art, which has a woodcut feel. Agency: Thuemmel, Marx & Associates. Designer: Ray Dodge. Copywriter: Candace McKinley.

CHAPTER 5

The architect in question happened to be me. And the blunt answer I received led me quickly to believe that this old shoe was either very short on small talk or had a special disdain for people of my profession.

"Every roof leaks, sooner or later," I countered, hoping to incite an argument, being the young

"What I look for in a good roof," he lectured, "isn't elasticity, it's resistance to stress. *Tensile strength*, they call it."

"And believe you me when it comes to tensile strength, nothing beats an Owens-Corning roof."

"Take Perma Ply-R," for example," he explained. "When three or four plies of PPR are

"puncture-resistant, modified bitumen membrane, torch-welded for optimum adhesion."

"That's not all," he assured me.

(I had little doubt.)

"You have to think about insulation. Owens-Corning Fiberglas® Roof Insulation doesn't lose its thermal value over time like isocyanurate foams."

high water. Whatever Mother Nature dishes out."

Ironically, at that moment, Mother Nature was dishing out cats and dogs. While the roof overhead proved his argument to be literally watertight.

"Owens-Corning is the largest, most respected manufacturer in the business and roofing is their *sine qua non*."

"Why an Owens-Cor | ning roof?" asked the archite | ct naively.
"Don't care for leaks," th | e contractor said dryly.

adversarial type.

"Besides," I continued, "I thought those single plies were the new high-tech item."

Something struck a nerve. The old man rifled into his sport coat pocket.

"See this rubber band? It can stretch, yes? Given enough time and wear, it can also snap," as a piece of rubber rocketed past my forehead.

"I've been in this business for over 30 years, and I've seen a lot of roofing products come and go."

fused together with a hot asphalt like PermaMop," you get one thick, tough, monolithic membrane."

"Do you understand what that means?"

I stared at him blankly.

"I'll tell you. It means both greater dimensional stability and weather-resistance. I should know; I've been using it for 20 years."

"Yes, but...."

"Then, of course, there's Derbigum®...." he went on, cheerfully extolling the virtues of some

(Was this a contractor or chemist, I wondered?)

"In fact it can actually add to the life of the roof by minimizing blisters."

"All that, installed to the highest standards by Owens-Corning approved contractors. And backed by the strongest guaranty program in the industry."

I felt myself sinking under the weight of ice-cold logic.

"In brief, you get a roof that can withstand the elements. Come wind, come snow, come hell or

"A chemist and a Latin scholar," I mumbled under my breath.

"No, a simple contractor," he said with a twinkle.

OWENS/CORNING FIBERGLAS

If you'd like to enter in on this dialogue, call 1-800-FIBERGLAS, or send in the coupon below.

Name_____ Company_____

Address_____

City_____ State_____ Zip_____

Mail to: C.G.T. Meeks, Owens-Corning Fiberglas Corp., Fiberglas Tower, Toledo, Ohio 43659

For more data, circle No. 124 on inquiry card

In this two-page ad for Owens/Corning Fiberglas roofing, art director Mike Rylander puts a headline *inside* the columns of copy and uses illustrations of buildings to frame everything. The headline uses a form of humor called a Tom Swifty ("Don't care for leaks," the contractor said dryly). Agency: Ogilvy & Mather. Copywriter: Tom Witt.

Another frame-format ad, this one selling Avon products, is directed to a Hispanic audience. UniWorld Group, Inc., the agency, specializes in well-designed culturally relevant ads that appeal to minority groups. Art director: Bill Allen.

LAYOUT: APPROACHES

Two will be promoted.
One will be demoted.
One will move laterally.
Two will resign.
One will retire.
    One will be fired.
    That's the most predictable thing about a business. It's totally unpredictable.
And what position does that leave you in?
Needing an office system that can change as your company changes. The Morrison System by Knoll.
    Morrison is the one office system that at a moment's notice can be any office.
    It can be data processing offices for your data processors. It can be open plan offices for your administrative staff. It can be private offices, with full height movable walls for your corporate staff.
    It can be converted from private to open or from open to private, very quickly. And with our wide range of durable wood veneers, plastic laminates, fabrics and colors it can be designed to reflect your company's personality.
At Knoll, we offer everything from systems to seating and from desks to textiles. As well as the service that makes managing your office a lot easier.
    Call 1-800-633-0034 to talk with a representative or authorized dealer nearest you.
    Maybe you'll be one of those two people who get promoted next year.

How many of them will be in the same position next year?

Knoll

People apparently flying through the air ("How many of them will be in the same position next year?") form a frame for well-leaded copy selling the Morrison System by Knoll in this memorable two-page, full-color ad directed to office managers. Agency: Goldsmith/Jeffrey, New York. Art director and designer: Gary Goldsmith. Copywriter: Neal Gomberg.

A series of American Gas Association ads focuses attention on environmental and energy conservation matters. This example makes use of the frame format. The fine-line art surrounds the copy, which, visually, stands in for a radiator. The copy tells why buses and other vehicles should run on natural gas.

These thumbnails show some approaches to circus layout.

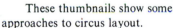

Three pages of a six-page fold-out ad bound into *Sports 'n Spokes,* a magazine for wheelchair athletes, show one advertiser's approach to circus layout. The lively design on each page helps sell a particular model of wheelchair manufactured by Invacare Corporation, Elyria, Ohio. Agency: Glazen Advertising. Art director: Dominic Russo. Copywriter: Alan Glazen.

■ *Circus Layout.* An orderly approach in design is probably more important to the editorial than to the advertising side. The reader is already interested in editorial. The purchase of the newspaper or magazine proves this. Advertising has to work harder for attention. And to set itself apart from the staid editorial material, it takes more liberty with basic design principles. It does not mind standing on its head or wearing a lampshade.

Moreover, there is something to be said for disorder in an ad. It slows down the reader, making things more difficult to take in. And in the process of working through the disorder, the reader may remember more.

We can call design of this type "circus layout." Filled with reverse blocks, oversize type, sunbursts, tilts, and assorted gimmicks, it may not win prizes in art directors' competitions, but apparently it does sell merchandise—at least a certain kind of merchandise to a certain class of customers.

Its apparent disarray (actually, under a good designer, its elements are thoughtfully arranged) is sometimes found in advertising for lofty clients. It was this kind of layout, in the capable hands of art director Otto Storch, that helped bring *McCall's* out of its "Togetherness" rut to the number-one position among women's magazines in the late 1950s.

Circus layout takes in a wide range of layout approaches and deals usually with a larger-than-average number of components.

The secret of good circus layout lies in the dedication of the designer to basic principles of design. Elements are organized into units, which in turn are organized into a unified pattern. Faced with many elements of equal weight, the designer achieves a pleasing proportion by bunching some into a particularly heavy unit, to contrast with other units in the ad.

Variety is a main concern, and the designer gets it chiefly through size, shape, and tone changes within the ad.

Retail advertisers find circus layout especially useful. Because retail ads are often directed to bargain hunters, prices played up in large sizes become an important element, ranking with headlines and art units.

One of the contributions of the underground press of the late 1960s was the attention it gave to the circus approach in graphic design. Thanks to the flexibility of the offset printing process, circus layout became the predominant format. Often self-conscious and amateurish, it nevertheless influenced the design thinking of the establishment press. In the hands of designers who knew what they were doing, it resulted in some engaging, if complicated, advertising in the 1970s.

The flexibility of desktop publishing software makes circus layout especially appealing to computer-equipped designers.

These thumbnails show some approaches to multipanel layout.

This two-page full-color magazine ad shows some of the many uses of the ordinary—correction: the *Sunkist*—lemon. The ad uses the multipanel format. Agency: Foote, Cone & Belding. Art director: Ralph Price. Creative supervisor: Jean Craig. Creative director: Jack Foster.

■ *Multipanel Layout*. Breath-purifying toothpaste, body-building iron tablets, and pimple-restricting yeasts started multipanel layout a couple of generations ago with their ads in Sunday comic sections, made to look just like the regular fare. Today this "comic strip" layout technique is more useful than ever, although it has grown a bit more sophisticated, with photos replacing the drawings, in most cases, and with conversation set in type beneath the pictures rather than ballooned within.

The designer often plans for panels of equal size, feeling that the staccato effect keeps the reader moving effortlessly through the ad. A proportional difference is achieved by keeping the block of panels larger than the area that remains to house the headline, explanatory body type, and signature.

The panels can be used to tell a story, or they can be used simply to display a series of products, pretty much in checkerboard fashion.

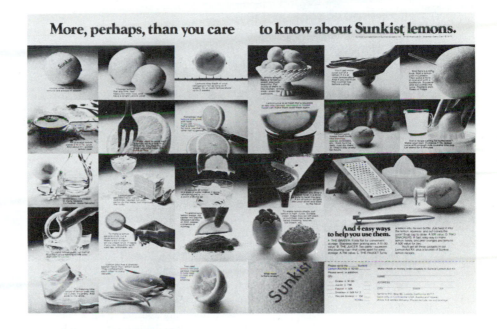

■ *Silhouette Layout*. In another kind of layout the designer arranges elements in such a way as to form one imposing and interesting silhouette. Irregular areas of white space—or blank space—form at the outside edges of the ad. Professor Hallie J. Hamilton has explained to students at Northern Illinois University that silhouette layout evolves from the unique shape created by the design of the ad, not by the shape of the elements used.

The more irregular the silhouette, the better. To test a silhouette, the designer tries to imagine the elements in the ad blacked in.

To illustrate the superiority of an irregular silhouette over a regular one, consider the ancient art of paper-cutting portraiture. The scissors artist always works from a side view, never a front view. Otherwise, no one would recognize the portrait. One portrait would look just like the next. The outline of a front view of a face is never as interesting as the outline of the side view. Silhouette layout is "side view" layout.

Just combining a silhouette photograph with some almost-touching copy will give you a silhouette ad. But you can use regular square or rectangular photographs, too. *The way they are put together*—staggered rather than stacked—gives the ad its silhouette look.

Too much white space separating elements within the silhouette destroys the unity of the ad and ruins the silhouette.

In silhouette layout many designers arrange elements so that something in the ad touches each of the ad's edges, preferably at spots unrelated to each other. This accomplishes two things: (1) It prevents the white frame from

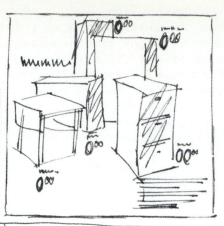

These thumbnails show some approaches to silhouette layout.

This is a full-page, full-color magazine ad for Robert Bruce apparel. The second and third words in the headline are separated to make room for the art. Each element in this ad comes close to touching another to form one massive reverse silhouette that stands out strongly against a dark background. Art director and designer: Lawrence L. Alten. Copywriters: Edmond F. Cohen and B. J. Kaplan. Agency: Alten, Cohen & Naish, Inc., Philadelphia.

turning into an even halo that could diminish, optically, the ad's size; and (2) it prevents the medium's encroaching on white space the client has paid for. Another way in a silhouette ad to guarantee that the client gets all the space purchased is for the designer to place dots at all four corners of the pasteup. Checking tear sheets of the ad and finding that both dots at the top, say, are missing, the advertiser is alerted to the possibility that the medium has taken away some of the space.

IN ADDITION TO THE 113,909 SQUARE MILES OF EXCELLENT WORKING CONDITIONS, TAKE ADVANTAGE OF THE TERRIFIC WEATHER, EXPERIENCED CREWS, TALENT AND LOWER PRODUCTION COSTS.
CALL TOLL FREE
1-800-523-6695 or 602-280-1380
ARIZONA FILM COMMISSION
3800 N. Central Ave. • Bldg D • Phoenix, Az 85012
AFC INTERNATIONAL

A less-than-full-page ad in *Millimeter,* the magazine of the motion picture and television production industries, invites filmmakers to "Shoot the World in Arizona." The design elements, including the all-caps copy block, form one irregular shape or silhouette, with white space pushed to the outside of the ad, framing it. The agency: Subia Corp. The client: Arizona Film Commission. Designer: Jim Davenport. Copywriter: Bill Kirkpatrick.

These thumbnails show some approaches to big-type layout.

■ *Big-Type Layout.* Type manufacturers, typesetting houses, printers, and periodicals all issue type-specimen sheets or books for their clients, so that the clients can look over the selection and marvel at it and pick those types that may be appropriate for a given job or use. In their largest sizes, types hold particular appeal to the artist and the designer, who derive an almost sensual pleasure through study of type's peculiar curves and corners and serifs and stroke variations. Suspecting that type beauty might also be appreciated by the lay reader, or knowing that big type commands greater attention than small type, designers sometimes turn to a type-specimen approach in their layouts. "Second coming" type pushes boldly through the ad, leading to a small amount of body copy; or the body copy itself is set in a type that is well beyond the normal 10- to 12-point sizes used in ordinary ads.

Type overpowers art in layouts like this. Art may not even be needed.

Ordinarily we associate big-type ads with hard-sell retailers; but well-designed or graceful types, used large size, perhaps screened to a percentage of black, serve image-conscious clients as well.

Some of the best big-type ads use lowercase letters rather than all caps because lower case is more interesting.

If only a few words are involved, the designer takes some liberties with readability. Lines may ride piggyback on each other; they may overlap; they may be doctored to intensify the mood of the ad.

These thumbnails show some approaches to rebus layout.

■ *Rebus Layout.* The Beef Industry Council and Beef Board ad nearby serves as a good example of rebus advertising: advertising with copy broken up into small sections by illustrations. In most rebus advertising, the illustrations—and there are often many of them—take on such importance that the copy is set to wrap around them or to be interrupted by them.

Communicators in semiprimitive societies developed rebuses to stand for difficult words or phrases. Rebuses are small, simple drawings inserted at various places in text matter, sort of as visual puns. A puzzlemaker, Sam Loyd, popularized rebuses in America in the nineteenth century. They are still used, although not widely, in word-and-picture puzzles for children.

A modified rebus is one in which an occasional word or phrase is omitted and a picture substituted. An advertiser will not make a puzzle of an ad— clarity is too important—but may want to amplify the copy by inserting a series of illustrations. They can be all the same size, for a staccato effect; or they can be in various sizes to add variety to the ad. The "copy" in some cases is nothing more than picture captions.

Good News For People Who Eat.

Beef.
Real Food For Real People.

The headline for this ad singles out an audience—or pretends to. The ad, then, meant for everybody, tells readers who are "not altogether excited about a future of organic fiber flakes" that beef is "lower in calories, leaner on fat, lighter on cholesterol than you would ever imagine." The crowded single-page ad includes some recipes for dishes using beef, as well as an illustrated table at the bottom showing beef cuts and listing calories. The sponsor is the Beef Industry Council and Beef Board. Agency: Ketchum, San Francisco. Art director: John Donaghue. Copywriter: Lynda Pearson.

This ad, using a rebus format, tells readers of *News Photographer* that Lowel-Light Manufacturing's "Four Focusable Fixtures" for cameras have a "Lust for Light." Boldface punctuation along with art pieces add visual spice to the copy. The ad was created in-house. Art director: Oleg Neishtadt. Designer and copywriter: Ross Lowell.

FOUR FOCUSABLE FIXTURES WITH A LUST FOR LIGHT

The Pro, i, Omni & DP all have remarkable performance & formidable parabolics. They're also: smoothly-floodable; intensely-spotable; super-spotable; coolly-operable; fully-tiltable; doorable, expandable, removable; diffusable; scrimable; graduatable; gelable; brellable; snootable; clampable; boomable; holdable; mountable; tape-upable; portable; affordable.

 ® Lowel-Light Manufacturing, Inc. 140 58th Street, Brooklyn, N.Y. 11220 ☎ (718) 921-0600

MY NEEDS ARE SIMPLE...A MASERATI A GOOD NIGHT'S SLEEP AND A FEW PIECES FROM SPRITZER & FUHRMANN

5 EAST 57 STREET, N.Y.C. • ARUBA • BONAIRE • CURACAO • ST. MAARTEN

A rebus ad—a small one—from *The New Yorker* does an institutional job for Spritzer & Fuhrmann, a New York jewelry store with branches in exotic places. Copywriter Dennis Webster with tongue in cheek talks about "simple" needs. John Nayduck of the John Nayduck Agency did the designing, using two weights of a modern sans serif (all caps) for the combination headline-body copy-signature. The address drops down in size.

In this newspaper ad, Palm Beach County, Florida, offers to coupon clippers (see third column) $500 worth of coupons as an incentive to visit the vacation area. Illustrations in a screened black suggest some of the things to do there. A good example of rebus advertising. Agency: Crispin & Porter Advertising. Creative director: Chuck Porter. Art director: Alex Bogusky. Copywriter: Mary McPhail.

These thumbnails show some approaches to alphabet-inspired layout.

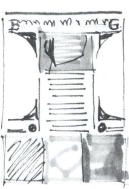

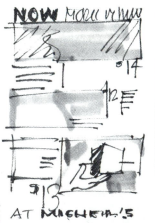

■ *Alphabet-Inspired Layout.* The beauty of letterform, established by scribes and type designers over a period of several centuries, provides one other source of inspiration for designers. The basic shape of letters, both capitals and lower case, can serve as the basic pattern for the arranging of elements within an ad.

An ad designed to approximate the shape of a letter of the alphabet—or a number, for that matter—usually is strong in both unity and eye travel, two important design qualities. The designer, however, should avoid an arrangement that too closely suggests a particular letter. The letter should serve only as the starting point. The reader ordinarily would not be conscious that the ad took off from a letter or number.

It may be helpful to consider each of the ten basic formats described here before beginning your assignment. Choosing a format, you will find innumerable variations occurring to you as you doodle. Combining two of them into a single format, you will find your explorations even more fruitful.

THE JORDACHE

JORDACHE®
Showroom: 498 7th Ave. N.Y.C. 10018
212.279.7343

LOOK

The letter *X* could be said to be the inspiration for this arrangement of headline, art, and body copy. At any rate, the two-page ad is dependent upon diagonals as a design pattern. This is one of a series, each ad showing users without tops partly for its quiet shock value and partly to show the product without other clothes distractions. Agency: Hicks & Greist, New York.

Traditional Tools to Do the Job

While the computer has become the tool of choice at many if not most colleges where graphic design is taught and at most agencies, departments, and studios where advertising is created, traditional tools still deserve some attention. Some designers continue to use traditional tools because the designers are comfortable with them, don't like the thought of change, don't like what computers produce, or can't afford the investment that a computer setup requires. Some designers move back and forth between the computer and traditional tools, convinced that each has its advantages.

In a traditional setup, you need a drawing table and a taboret to hold some of your tools and supplies. Tools and supplies include these:

■ *Layout pad.* If you plan to do a lot of tracing from a clip book or from alphabet cards, you should get a *tracing* pad—sheets of tissue-thin paper. Otherwise, a bond-paper *layout* pad will do. The bond paper should be thin enough, though, that some tracing is possible. The two most commonly used pad sizes are 14″ × 17″ and 19″ × 24″, each with fifty sheets. The instructor will probably ask that all students get the same size pad. The smaller one is big enough for most jobs and handy to carry back and forth to class (if pads cannot be stored at school); the larger one is better if you have full-page newspaper ads to do and if you cannot attach the pad high on the drawing table—if you have to let it lie against the bottom lip of the drawing table as you work.

Throw the cover sheet of the pad up and over the top of the drawing table, and there you have your exposed first sheet, ready to work on.

Using ink and black tape, Bill Shannon designs a variety of keys, one of which is to be used in a logo for a fictitious steel corporation. The lineup shows that a single abstract design concept can take an infinite number of turns. This was a project done for a class at Art Academy Cincinnati, with research help from U.S. Metalsource.

If your hands have a tendency to perspire as you work, put a sheet of paper underneath your drawing hand and keep it there as you work, moving it when necessary. Perspiration on the drawing paper not only will cause smudges but also will make areas of your paper incapable of receiving the pencil or any other medium you may be using.

To protect underneath sheets from indentations made by the pressure of your drawing instrument, cut a sheet of heavy white paper to size and slip it underneath the sheet you are working on.

You will appreciate the fact that layout-pad paper is semitransparent. Rip off the sheet you are working on when you feel you are ready to make an adjustment in the layout and slip that sheet underneath a new sheet. Move it around and trace those parts of the original rough you wish to retain.

■ *T-square*. T-squares come in 18″, 24″, 30″, 36″, 42″, and even larger sizes, in wood, in wood with transparent edges, in metal, and in plastic. Get one about the length of your layout pad's width.

The T-square must be kept true. Never use its top edge as a guide while cutting paper with a knife or razor blade. Keep the T-square hanging, T-style, from the top of the drawing table; there is less chance then that a passing student will get it hooked in a sleeve, dashing it to the floor. The top of the T must not be jarred.

In using the T-square, make sure it is pushed snugly against the left edge of the drawing table, drawing board, or layout pad. Hold it down firmly with your left hand as you rule your horizontal line.

It is possible to buy a "shifting head" T-square with one fixed head and one that adjusts to any angle. You can also buy a Rol-Ruler, which allows you to rule parallel lines at regular intervals.

■ *Triangle*. You could use both a 45-degree and a 30–60-degree triangle, but only the 30–60 is necessary. Get a 10-inch transparent one.

Like the T-square, the triangle must be protected against scratches and nicks at the edges.

The triangle, placed firmly against the T-square edge, is used to make vertical and also diagonal lines. Actually you *can* get along without one. Placing the pencil firmly against the edge of the T-square where you want the vertical line drawn, you can pull the T-square downward and the pencil with it. Some layout artists, pressed for time, do this even when a triangle is nearby. You can also rule vertical lines by hanging your T-square from the top.

■ *Pencils*. Despite the computer and all the other new tools, the pencil is still the premier tool. If you want to give it a little dignity, you can call it what

These abstractions of artists' and designers' tools appeared as art on a folder distributed by A. I. Friedman, Inc., an art supplies store.

someone in the military called it: "a portable hand-held communications inscriber."

Drawing pencils range from 6B (very black and soft) to 9H (very light and hard). This is the lineup: 6B, 5B, 4B, 3B, 2B, B, HB, F, H, 2H, 3H, 4H, 5H, 6H, 7H, 8H, 9H. You should have two or three of these in the 4B to 2H range—perhaps a 4B, a 2B, and for tracing purposes a 2H.

The harder the lead, the longer the point will hold. But you will have to press harder to make your mark, and it will be lighter.

If you want an extra-black matte finish, try Eberhard Faber's "Ebony" pencil or "Wolff's Carbon Drawing Pencil." You will also find a set of color pencils useful.

Whatever pencils you use, keep them sharp. You will want a knife or single-edge razor blade nearby to constantly whittle away the wood around the points. A sandpaper pad puts a finishing touch on a sharpened point.

It is not a good idea to combine pencil with ink in a rough layout because of the difference in the strengths of the blacks. The combination might suggest a printing job in black and gray inks, not likely for an advertisement.

■ *Erasers.* The advantage of using a pencil to do a layout is that you can correct your mistakes. You are not likely then to leave the layout the way it first unfolds just because you find it is too much trouble to change it. But you will need an eraser or two: an art gum and a Pink Pearl. You will need a kneaded eraser if you work in pastels or charcoal.

■ *Pens.* Ballpoint pens and fiber- or acrylic-tip pens are useful for drawing thumbnail sketches. They make marks that have an authority about them. They come in colors plus black; and the points are either rounded or chisel shaped (your choice).

For more advanced roughs these pens have the disadvantage of permanence. Put an experimental line down on paper with one of them and there is no turning back.

Pentel introduced a new kind of pen some years ago: a Rolling Writer, which combines the firmness of the ballpoint with the flexibility of the fiber- or acrylic-tip pen. Unlike the ballpoint, the Rolling Writer can be used upside down, in case you have funny writing and drawing habits.

Another instrument you might want to consider is a technical fountain pen, like the Rapidograph, which makes a line of uniform thickness. It can be equipped with points varying from very fine to medium thick. Unless you use your Rapidograph regularly, you may be plagued with clogging problems. A good, cheap substitute is Faber Castell's Uni-ball Micro available with fine and ultrafine points.

Unless you are doing finished drawings or very careful lettering for comprehensives, you will have little need for regular metal pen points, penholders, and india ink.

■ *Markers.* A few years ago most designers used nothing but pencils or chalks (pastels) for their rough layouts and comps. Then they turned to felt-tip markers—if not for all the elements in the layout, at least to indicate the art.

You have a choice of several shades of gray in either warm or cool tones. (If your roughs are to be reproduced, you would probably choose the warm grays, as they tend to reproduce a little better.) You also have a wide choice of colors.

Markers make transparent lines and areas that can be blended into other shades or colors. They come in fine or blunt points.

■ *Ruler.* You can get by with a discount drugstore plastic ruler. Or you might want to buy one of those plastic combination T-square rulers. But if you get into serious work, and especially if you do mechanicals, you will want a good 18- or 24-inch metal ruler calibrated in both inches and picas. Some stores carry an 18-inch C-Thru Standard Graphic Arts Ruler, in laminated vinyl, calibrated in inches, picas, and agate lines and carrying proofreader's symbols, printer's rules, percentage screens, halftone screens, copy counters, and a copyfitting system.

Illustrator Greg Dearth uses a scratchboard technique for his art in a series of two-page ads in *Footwear News*, a trade magazine. His technique, along with the unusual subject matter of the art, stopped the reader who was thumbing through the magazine. Art like this, despite its apparent tone variation, nicely takes line reproduction. "Air Cyrus" good naturedly parodies advertising by another shoe manufacturer. Client: Clarks of England. Agency: Goodby, Berlin & Silverstein. Art director: Tracy Wong. Copywriter: Clay Williams.

You can also buy a Graham Centering Rule, a transparent plastic ruler that, through colors, allows you to quickly find the center of a layout, pasteup, or piece of artwork.

■ *Chalks and crayons.* Some designers continue to use pastel color chalks. Pastels require the use of a can of fixative spray to prevent smearing.

Ordinary crayons or a set of color pencils provide the cheapest answer to the problem of indicating color on a rough layout. The beginning designer might want to start with them.

■ *Tempera.* To indicate reverse type in a solid or tone area, the designer uses a fine brush dipped in a bottle of tempera, show-card color, or designers' color. A small bottle of white would probably get the most use.

■ *Masking tape.* For use when you trace. It keeps the original from moving around. It also affixes reference material temporarily to your drawing table. And it attaches protective flaps to your comps.

■ *Glue stick.* For patching and pasting. Some designers still prefer rubber cement.

As you get into your assignments, you will find some need for a few tools you already have at home, such as a pair of scissors and a compass (the kind used

This impressive ad for The Pier, a Des Moines, Iowa, steak and seafood restaurant, is billboardlike not only in its basic shape but in the dominance of the art, boldy drawn in pen-and-ink by John Sayles, who also art directed. One of a series. Agency: Sayles Graphic Design, Inc. Copywriter: Mary Langen-Goldstein.

Loosely executed brush strokes, in three colors, suggest a staircase and amplify the small copy block that says "American crafts of the nineteen eighties have just ascended to new and exciting heights." The ad is for the American Craft Museum, New York City. Agency: Bozell, Jacobs, Kenyon & Eckhardt.

for making circles). As you become more proficient with the basic tools and materials, you may want to explore others. For instance: a pair of dividers—an instrument invaluable for making quick space comparisons and for marking equal space divisions.

You may want sheets of dry-transfer letters to make headlines on your comps look as though they are printed. And sheets of greeking to simulate body copy. And transparent color sheets to indicate flat areas of color. When you get into the designing of direct-mail pieces, you may want to work with colored paper.

Except when you design direct-mail pieces, always leave white space all the way around each layout. This provides room for handling and, if necessary, for writing instructions or explanations to the instructor, client, or printer. The ad may bleed in the medium, but it never bleeds on the layout pad.

Some Drawing Hints

Experience will tell you how hard you can push the tools—how much pressure is needed. Beginners often fail to make their marks firmly enough. You should think of most of the marks you make as representing pure black ink. The thinness of the line will vary, but the pressure will remain fairly constant.

You do not need much drawing ability to do acceptable thumbnails and rough layouts. Even to do comprehensives, you can get by with ordinary tracing, copying, and even patching. So don't apologize that you "can't even draw a straight line." What you lack in drawing ability you can make up for with your sense of design. The best drawings and illustrations, anyway, are as much designed as they are drawn and painted.

For much of your work you can get by with stick figures for people and boxes for props. You can describe these items in the margins if you feel your viewer—instructor, boss, or client—cannot make them out. But even stick figures can be endowed with size, facing, direction, mass, and tone.

You start by drawing lines, whether with pencil, pen, marker, mouse, or electronic stylus.

When you change the line's direction, you begin to define a shape. Shape is line with a second dimension. When you put the shape into perspective and add thickness, you give it form and create the illusion of a third dimension. You work with five kinds of lines: curved, spiral, meandering, zigzag, and straight.

Lines—or the *suggestion* of lines—in an advertisement in themselves contain meaning. Straight lines suggest strength, direction, opposition. Curved lines suggest grace, movement, growth. Lines convey the moods they do because they are abstractions of objects and figures that originate the moods.

You can use lines to portray the three classic shapes in art: the triangle, the rectangle (or square), and the circle. When you give each of the three classic shapes the illusion of a third dimension, you have a cone (or pyramid), a cube (or box), and a sphere (or tube) to work with—and all the elements they suggest.

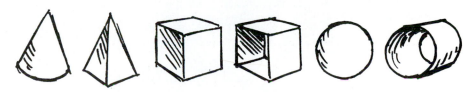

To give objects a three-dimensional feel, you turn to *perspective*. Perspective allows you to show two or three sides of an object and makes the object look more realistic. To put an object—say, a box—into perspective you must draw its parallel lines in such a way that, were the lines extended, they would meet at a common point (called the vanishing point) on the horizon. For each panel of art (drawing, painting, or photograph) in your ad you establish a horizon line that each object within the panel can relate to.

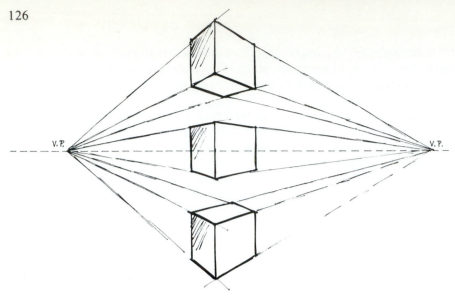

An object can be below, above, or on the horizon line. You create a "bird's-eye view" of items below the horizon line and a "worm's-eye view" of items above. In presenting an object in an ad, you must decide which view shows off the object best and most clearly informs the viewer of its properties.

When you show more than one item in a panel, your perspective problems multiply. But if you remember that you have but one horizon line to a panel, and if you establish it in your mind, you will be making a good start.

As a beginning exercise in an advertising layout class, Irene Ishikawa, using an ordinary pencil, nicely captures the feel (right) of a printed advertisement (left) by tracing it. What she produces here is really an after-the-fact comprehensive rough layout.

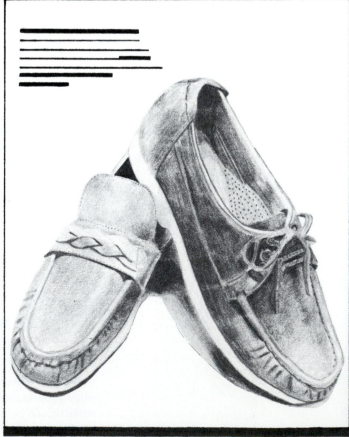

Don't feel that the vanishing points—or even the horizon line (and it is usually an imaginary line)—need to be within the panel. The closer together you put the vanishing points, by the way, the closer your viewer is to the object pictured.

Each object in your panel can have its own set of vanishing points. For instance, there are one-point and three-point perspectives as well as two-point perspective, and there are also *elevated* vanishing points (as for houses with pitched roofs), but all of this is too complicated to go into here, and a knowledge of it is not necessary to do sketches for rough layouts.

When drawing objects that are not rectangular, fit them first into rectangles

To execute this quick rough art, a Detroit *Free Press* layout artist uses gray pastel chalks and, for outlining, a marker that has almost run dry.

For this quick drawing, the artist uses a chunk of lithographic crayon. The drawing is shown actual size.

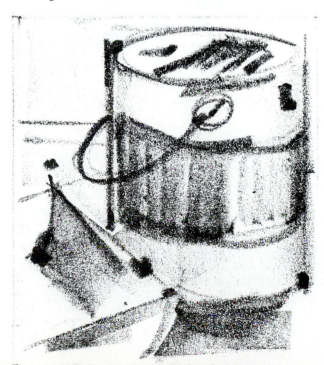

When drawing figures for quick roughs or when laying an area of gray, use an ordinary pencil boldly, applying lead from the side of the point rather than from the tip.

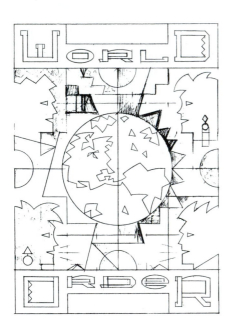

and work out the perspective. This will give you a better chance to portray the objects realistically.

Closely allied to perspective is *foreshortening,* which asks that objects close to the viewer be made to look larger than items farther back. It also asks that the part of an object closest to the viewer be made to look larger than a similar-size part that is farther back. Hence, in a front view a person's extended hand looks larger than that person's other hand held down at his side.

You can also show depth in a drawing by making objects in the background grayer or weaker than objects in the foreground. Objects in the foreground also have more detail. You can further create the illusion of distance by overlapping objects in your panel. This also helps you to create a more interesting composition.

Sometimes you may find that lines and shapes say things you do not mean them to say. Uncontrolled optical illusions may be at play. As a designer you need to understand how optical illusions affect your design.

Using conventional tools, Robert Pizzo of Studio Pizzo or Pizzo, a husband and wife design and illustration firm in Mt. Vernon, New York, demonstrates stages in the design of a "stamp" to be used in *Publish* magazine and later in a self-promotion piece. Note how the design changes and tightens between the thumbnail sketch and finished art. Although art like this could easily be computer generated, Pizzo prefers the feel of pencil, pen, paper and film, and X-acto knife.

Here is one of the better-known optical illusions, used by a number of organizations to startle or make a point. *Mad* magazine calls it the "Piouyet." Daniels, Sullivan & Dililon, Nashville, once referred to it as a "triple-shafted dual fork used in an integro-differential computer." SmokEnders, an organization that conducts seminars to help people stop smoking, once used it as a big *E* in the middle of its logotype.

■ *A horizontal line is easier to see than a vertical line.* This is because the eye moves naturally horizontally, recording what it sees easily. So a horizontal line will appear longer than its equivalent vertical line. And it will seem heavier. To compensate for this, an artist wanting a vertical to appear exactly as long and as heavy as a horizontal lengthens it slightly and makes it a bit heavier. Actually, then, the vertical is longer and heavier than the horizontal; optically they appear the same. (A good sans serif typeface that appears to be built of even strokes actually has vertical strokes slightly heavier than its horizontal strokes.)

■ *Lines or stripes running in a single direction tend to lengthen that direction.* A chubby woman understands this; she avoids dresses with horizontal stripes but keeps in her wardrobe, perhaps, a dress or two with vertical stripes. A dress with vertical stripes might not interest the tall woman.

■ *A filling-in of a shape with tone or color or with elements tends to reduce the size of the shape.* A dark room, or a cluttered room, appears smaller than an equivalent room painted a light shade or sparsely furnished.

■ *What is nearby or what surrounds a figure influences its apparent size.* This can best be shown through a diagram.

In the first example the thin lines pull back the eyes, keeping the heavy line short. In the second example the thin lines stretch the heavy line, making it appear longer than it really is. In reality, the heavy lines are of equal length.

In the examples that follow, the designer puts the optical illusion to work. The thin lines now have been converted to ad elements. Notice that in the example at the right the elements stretch the car, making it appear sleeker than the car at the left. Yet, in reality, the cars are the same length (and height).

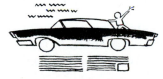 

A number of companies have used classic optical illusions as main art for their ads to make the point that readers should not jump to conclusions. "Quick, Your First Impression! A Rabbit or a Duck?" asks the Detroit *Free Press* in a media ad in *Advertising Age*. The art is a drawing from a New York Public Library collection that, seen one way, looks like a duck; seen another way, it looks like a rabbit. "Naturally," the copy block begins, "first impressions count. But, as you've probably seen from the picture above, first impressions can be deceiving. Like when you're buying the 5th largest market. . . ."

Bev Doolittle, a popular contemporary painter specializing in "camouflage art," uses optical illusions to hide her animals in their natural habitats. M. C. Escher, a Dutch artist, built a worldwide reputation for optical illusions that gave viewers several vantage points in each beautifully drawn scene.

The Computer as a Tool

The introduction of desktop publishing in 1985 with the launching of Aldus PageMaker software for the Apple Macintosh altered the way copy is handled and layouts done by most of the people who create advertising.

Those who first sang the praises of desktop publishing too readily accepted amateurish designs and typography. Professional designers and art directors looked at the new systems with suspicion. But as the 1980s came to a close, desktop publishing had firmly established itself in advertising agencies and departments, and in design studios. At the same time, many designers and illustrators began using mainframe computers, often renting time from firms with the resources to afford such equipment.

Computers range from high-end mainframe installations to electronic notebooks that users can slip into their briefcases. A minicomputer is less powerful than a mainframe computer but more powerful than a microcomputer. Most of us are familiar with microcomputers, also known as personal computers. These are the computers used in desktop publishing operations, and they continue to come out in upgraded models that operate faster and with more power. They include the IBM PC and its clones and the Apple Macintosh.

A number of software programs make desktop publishing possible. While word processing software as well as drawing and painting programs, including Aldus FreeHand, allow some ad layout, you have to turn to one of the page-layout programs to create ads with any flair or complexity. Among Mac users, PageMaker and QuarkXPress are the most popular. Graphic designers can't agree on which is best. PageMaker has the best typography and bookmaking features, some designers feel, but limits itself to one open document at a time. QuarkXPress brings more flexibility to multiple-page layouts and the rotation of elements but is harder to master. Among IBM users, Ventura Publisher software is popular.

The software originally developed for one kind of computer often becomes available in a version for the other, but what works well for one may not work as well for the other. Choosing the right equipment and programs becomes a major problem for anyone entering the computer world.

The designer who uses a computer typically adds a number of other software programs to the basic desktop program. A favorite supplemental program is Adobe Photoshop, which Robert Keding, electronic production artist for Cole & Weber, Seattle, calls "ingenious."[4] There seems to be no end to the jobs Photoshop, in the right hands, can perform. Editing and flopping pictures are among its many functions.

Improvements in computer hardware and new software keep appearing to enhance performance. Microsoft Windows changes the face of MS DOS, making IBM computers work more like Macintoshes. And software programs like Norton Desktop for Windows 2.0, Hewlett-Packard's New Wave 4.0, and XSoft's Rooms

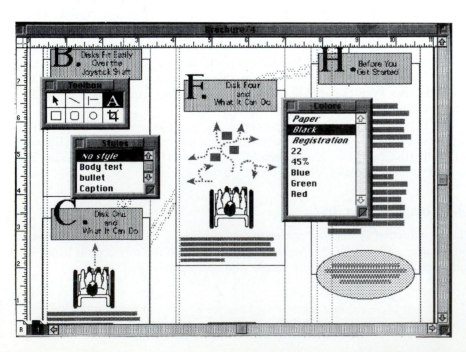

This "screen capture" shows computer-generated design in progress. Barbara Littman of Information Design Northwest creates illustrations in Adobe Illustrator and imports them into PageMaker, along with body copy, to lay out a multicolumn instructional brochure for Mobi Disk, a wheelchair training program. At this stage, the body copy shows up as gray bars.

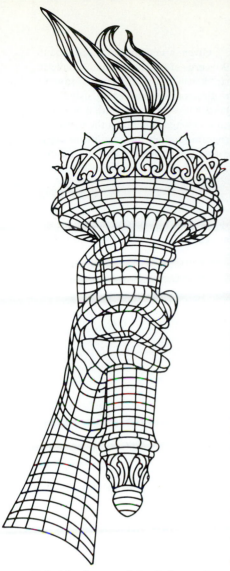

Dale Matthews and Jan Brieger of the TeleVision Corporation affixed a closeup photograph of the Statue of Liberty to a Macintosh digitizing artpad and then created this "wire mesh" three-dimensional line drawing, which was used to create a cover for *To Secure the Blessings of Liberty,* a report published by the National Commission on the Role and Future of State Colleges and Universities. Art director: Larry Smith.

for Windows make Windows easier to use. Several software programs have come along to serve specifically the people who lay out ads. The programs include Multi Ad Creator from Multi Ad Service, Inc.; AdSpeed from Digital Technology; and AdWorks from Concept Publishing Systems.

In a desktop publishing system, a laser printer with PostScript page description language produces typography and camera-ready copy in-house that is good enough for many advertisements today.

Print magazine's first Computer Art and Design Annual (1991) acknowledges "the frenzied changes that desktop graphics computers have wrought in the business of design."

"The Japanese have a saying that the more things you own, the more things own you. So it is with graphics computers. Clearly, they give designers great power. It's just as clear they exert great power over us—how we organize our businesses, what we do on a hour-to-hour basis, what kinds of work we're able to do, and how much profit we make from it."[5]

Marjorie Spiegelman, chairman of Spiegelman & Associates, a San Francisco design firm, warns fellow graphic designers not to expect magic from their computers. "Technology has its own complications, and has shown us—the hard way—its substantial limitations."

For one thing, she says, computer artwork "can't always meet the high standards set by conventional methods. . . . We've all been frustrated by the visual limitations of the pixel, and most of us have experienced at one time or another the shock of having a complex, beautiful layout rejected by the Linotronic service because of unexpected technical difficulties with the equipment or the file."

Moreover, the right computer system represents a big investment and calls for reliable technical support services. And designers must spend a lot of time keeping up with technological developments.

Spiegelman points out that not every art or design job calls for a computer. A computer may save time on some jobs, increase it on others. "No tool serves all purposes. If we become too addicted to our computers, we will become lazy, and will find ourselves adjusting design standards to suit technological limitations. An unqualified devotion to computers only limits our artistic vision, and restricts our clients' options."

Still, computers are "fantastic tools with many advantages and massive untapped potential." She adds: "As designers start to understand and work with digital information, rather than struggling to disguise computer output as traditional artwork, new forms of artistic expression will emerge."[6]

Given: a ten-word headline, about 100 words of copy, and some silhouette art. "Knock out a few roughs," says the art director. Robert Keding, using QuarkXPress software with a Macintosh and greeking available in the software program (neither the headline or copy is written yet), complies. In a matter of 20 minutes: four thumbnails, complete with a custom logo.

"I often tell people that the difference between designing electronically and designing by hand is like the difference between thinking your ideas into reality and having to chip them out of rock," says Carol Terrizzi, creative director at American Demographics, Inc., a Dow Jones company, and convert to computers after initial skepticism. "Any graphic designer . . . can imagine the difference between endless hand-drawn tissues and lightning fast electronic alterations in resolving a page-design problem."[7]

Want a full-size version of one of the roughs? A click or two, and here it is.

By 1991 computer artists and designers had formed their own organization, the International Design by Electronics Association, 244 E. 58th St., New York, NY 10022, with chapters in several cities.

Page-layout software allows the designer to bring together textmatter from word processing programs and art from drawing and painting programs and arrange them in an ad. Copy and art can easily be resized to better fit assigned space. Scores of different arrangements can be tried and previewed on screen before a decision is made. And when the client, seeing the printout, suggests changes, they can be made effortlessly, with the stroke of a key or the click of a mouse.

Page-layout software also allows quick construction of boxes, shadows, tint blocks, and other devices. (That these devices are so readily available make them overused in some advertisements, especially in those done for newspaper ads and direct-mail pieces.)

When copy is still to be written, the designer, using page-layout software, can call up some greeking. Computer-generated greeking consists of real type not meant to be read. It can be quickly set in the desired style, size, and measurement; it is used for placement only. PageMaker offers greeking under the heading "Lorem ipsum," the first two "words" that are set in that software's greeking option.

You can create thumbnails quicker with an ordinary pencil than you can on a computer. And you can make faster line drawings with pen or brush and ink. But with tools like these, you can't create the endless variations you can using a computer. Many designers make first sketches in traditional ways, then scan them into the computer to manipulate them.

FFXCV BNE RTY OPIY DGFH KJL OIO UIQTE RTYERUBN MTUI.

Ffxcv bne rty opiy, dgfh kll oio uiqte, rtyerubn mtui io gfh jklasdf rtweerw. Asfe rpuif dgfh kjlo uiqt, rtyerub mtui io gfh jklasdflk jiouy rtwerw. Qnbv ccx zjug, yurts gtyr dg kjlo uiqte, rtyerubn mtui io gfh jkl rtw. Qnbv ccx zjugh, yurts daf gtyru io kjh gas dfxcv bne rty opiy, dgfm po io kjlo uiqte, rtyeru bn tu tofi io gfh jk rtweerw. Auti kats foh t fdgviu yr tqwer dasf rpuif adthn shesid to doito it notw. Murdf gtyru ifau io kjhgas dcv e rty opiy, da kjlo moluiqte, rtye ru mtu io gfasd. Gasf rpuif dgfh lonr uiqte, rtyerubn mtui Io gfh jklasd rer.

Dbliasf rpuif dgfh kjlo uiqte, rtyerub mtui umti gfdgviu yr tqwer dasf rpu mif dgfh kjlo uiqte, dgfh kjlo iqte rtyerubn.

Kgfh kjlo uiqte, rtye irub mtui io gf jklasdf rtweer. Lnbav ccx zj, yu rtsdf gtyruu io kjhgas dfxcvne rty.

Lorem Ipsum

CHAPTER

6

PRODUCTION

What goes on after the creative phase and before the ad is printed for mass distribution or sent to a publication is the *production* phase. This is the time for *pre-press* activity. With the advent of computers, production has taken on greater in-house importance. Where once most of the details of production were left to outside printing firms and typesetting houses, today most of the work is done by "creatives" right there at the agency or department or studio.

In some ways, this is a blessing. Now "creatives" can really control how an ad will look. And they don't have to wait to have things done.

In other ways, this is a curse. It means a lot of extra work for the people who create the advertising. And it means a big investment in equipment, which rapidly becomes obsolete.

With new waves of equipment and software coming along with increasing frequency, designers find it necessary to involve themselves in continuing education. Fortunately, a score of excellent computer magazines, some narrowing in on design and production activities, help designers keep up. Every new software program is reviewed in these magazines, and, if not reviewed, touted in the ads. Considering all the changes, Pauline Ores, editor in chief of *Desktop Communications,* wonders "why everyone is so driven to move on to the next wave when they haven't got the original stuff working yet. There's the rub: once you start relying on computers, you're married for better or worse, as it becomes next to impossible to divorce yourself from the technology you've steeped your business in."[1]

If you use a Macintosh and have trouble getting it to do what you want it to do, despite its heralded user friendliness, you will find the books by Robin Williams helpful, especially *The Little Mac Book* (Peachpit Press, Berkeley, California, 1990).

What Production Entails

Production is the process whereby the idea for an ad becomes a reality. It is what happens to the ad after the copy has been written and the ad designed. A lot can go wrong.

James Craig recognized the problem when he dedicated his *Production for the Graphic Designer,* "to every graphic designer whose printed piece did not quite measure up to his expectations!" In the Introduction he said, "The designer should know enough about production to understand: (1) what the possibilities are in terms of typesetting, printing, paper, etc., (2) what factors to consider when choosing between systems, methods, processes, etc., and (3) how to *communicate* specifications to the people responsible for translating the designer's ideas into a printed piece."[2] Some aspects of production have changed dramatically since Craig wrote his book—putting more demands on designers but also expanding the possibilities for innovation.

Production includes the setting of the type, the making of the plates, and the printing and binding. It also includes the pasteup of the elements that go into the ad. Sometimes this is left to the printer, but increasingly it is done by the designer or an assistant called a *pasteup artist.*

In a self-promotion booklet, Impression Graphics, a Mesquite, Texas printing firm, uses silhouette art to span a gutter and unite pages in the center spread. The illustration with the T-square shows the stripping of halftone negatives on a flat in preparation to making a plate. Design by Douglas May Design.

Coast Engraving Companies, San Jose, uses a pen and double-take art in an ad directed to art directors and advertising agency people to remind them of one of their several production services. The stripping, of course, involves negatives for printing plates. Designer and art director: Rick Tharp of Tharp Did It design studio, Los Gatos. Copywriters: Tharp and Roy Parvin. Photographer: Franklin Avery.

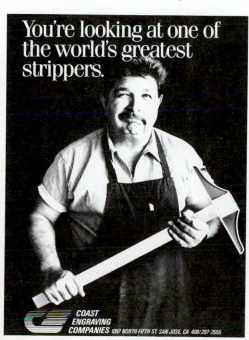

You're looking at one of the world's greatest strippers.

COAST ENGRAVING COMPANIES 1097 NORTH FIFTH ST. SAN JOSE, CA 408/297-2555

Chapter 5 discussed the three stages an advertising design can go through: the thumbnail, the rough layout, and the comprehensive. The pasteup is actually a fourth stage in the process. It is also called *the mechanical* or *camera-ready copy.* What is produced at this stage is exactly what will show up in the final printing.

A person just starting out in advertising, especially with an advertising agency, may be assigned to the production department to take care of the many details involved and to see what happens to an ad when it leaves the creative department.

A knowledge of production is especially important in direct-mail advertising, where every detail of design, typography, art, paper, and printing must be worked out. Ads going into newspapers and magazines require fewer production decisions, because the printing process, for instance, has already been determined, and paper choice has already been made. But many production problems must be solved there, too.

Pasteup

In traditional production, the layout artist, after waxing or applying rubber cement to the back of a reproduction proof from a typesetting house, positions it on the layout sheet, and then lays down areas of red or black to show where the art goes. Someone who works for the printing house strips in the art, photographed separately, onto the negatives or flats, which are used to make the plates. In electronic production involving the computer, the person at the workstation guides the work through typesetting, art instigation and placement, ad or page design, and production of hard copy for the camera. In some operations now, the process extends to film-making or, avoiding film, right through to plate-making.

Art directors are paid to come up with concepts and to design or supervise the design. And so, at many agencies, *production artists* do the pasteups. But production artists are more than mere pasteup artists. Some do a little art directing themselves. Many spec type. They form what is known at some agencies as "the studio," at others "the bullpen." They work closely with art directors, especially now that computers are here.

Robert Keding, electronic production artist at Cole & Weber, Seattle, where 90 percent of production is Macintosh-generated, says that a person needs some traditional board work before engaging in electronic pasteup. "I would much rather have a traditional layout artist to train than a person who just knows computers."[3]

Interestingly, electronic pasteup has adopted much of the language of traditional pasteup. The designer with a computer uses "clip art," a "clipboard," a "scrapbook," "leading," and any number of other items we associate with the older system. There is no paste in electronic "pasteup," yet "pasteup" is what it is.[4]

Even though the pasteup is more important than the comprehensive, it is not so easy to read or so attractive. The pasteup artist is concerned only with what the camera can and cannot record, and works accordingly. A finished pasteup is photographed directly; the negative obtained is used to make the printing plate.

Doing a pasteup is a tedious and exacting job, even when a computer is used. What is put into place in the ad stays there, as is. A line of type pasted down just a fraction of an inch away from where it belongs will call attention to itself when the printing is done. Fingerprints, smudges, too-heavy guidelines—all hang on until they find their ill-won places on the printed sheet.

If you draw the job of doing the pasteup, you'll do it actual size—or you'll do it larger, to take a reduction. Increasing the size at the platemaking stage would accentuate any imperfections in the type you use.

Sometimes all or part of the rough layout is so successful from an artistic standpoint that it is incorporated into the pasteup.

If the size of the ad must be determined, you will want to refer to the appropriate *Standard Rate & Data Service* publication or to the rate card of the medium in which the ad will appear. Periodicals sell their space in standard-size units. If the ad is for a newspaper, you will do the ad in a size that is a multiple of a column inch (1 column wide by 1" deep). If the ad is for a magazine, you will do it in column-inch multiples or perhaps in a quarter-, half-, or full-page size. The medium may have some special restriction you will have to know about. Most newspapers, for instance, will not accept an ad that is wider in number of columns than it is deep in inches—an ad, say, that is 8-col. × 1". But a 1-col. × 22" ad may be okay. Some papers restrict the use of reverses (white set inside black blocks) and typefaces that are the same as typefaces used in the editorial section.

Assuming that no color is involved, all line material—type proofs and drawings—to be run actual size is put on the same master sheet. Line art that has to be reduced or enlarged is simply noted on the sheet and turned in as separate pieces to be photographed in another operation and stripped into place on the negative flats by the people at the printing firm. In electronic pasteup, sizing is done at the computer terminal.

Photographs can be pasted into place, actual size, but in the platemaking process they will have to be shot separately from the pasteup itself. It is better to submit the photographs as separate units.

When colors are involved, you may have to provide thin plastic or acetate

The trouble with the first ad is that the reader is not sure where to start the copy. Right after the three dots? Or over at the left? Both the headline and art lead to the second column. But logic tells you to start with the first column. A little rearrangement (the ad at right) solves the problem. The new ad also makes more interesting use of white space, brings the columns together to make a unit of them, and brings art and headline together, too. The vertical line, which serves no purpose, is eliminated. So are the dots, which are a design cliché. None of the type has to be reset in the new ad; nor is the art cropped any differently.

The second two pages of a three-page magazine ad show how easy it is to change Radius' Pivot monitor screen from vertical to horizontal display. Agency: Goodby, Berlin & Silverstein. Art director: Tracy Wong. Copywriter: David Fowler.

overlays, with separate art for each color. This calls for register marks (tiny crosses) on the original and the overlays so that the printer can correctly line up the negatives and plates. In electronic pasteup, color separation can be done at the computer terminal.

For simple two-color jobs, you can mark on a tissue overlay those pieces that are to run in color. The printer then shoots the original pasteup twice, once for the black and once for the color.

The camera will pick up smudges, scratches, and dents as well as the pasteup image. It is necessary, then, to protect the finished pasteup with a flap of paper hooked to swing out from the top. The pieces of art that are to be photographed separately should be flapped, too.

If the client must see the pasteup, show a photocopy of it rather than the real thing. This will protect the original from smudges and markings and fall-offs. The less handling the better.

At many agencies and design studios, all aspects of production are computerized now. A campaign of ads running in several publications can be sent there by modem, where software will develop the ads for printing, taking into account each publication's special requirements.

Scitex Corp., Crossfield, and Linotype-Hell Co., among others, have developed useful microcomputer pre-press equipment. Light Source offers Ofoto, a scanning software that automatically crops and sizes black and white photographs and line art. ElseWare offers CheckList 2.0, a program that collects and lists type fonts, art, and style decisions for an ad going to a publication.[5]

A software program called Image & Likeness creates a camera-ready ad in about a fourth of the time it would take using traditional production techniques.

Some electronic pasteup jobs require equipment the ad makers can't possibly afford. For these jobs, the ad makers have to go outside, to places like these:

■ *Type houses.* True, most of the type may be set in-house, but sometimes more sophisticated typesetting equipment is needed.

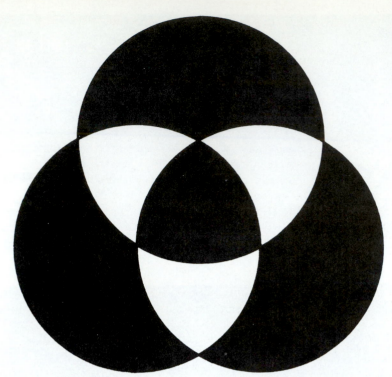

This keyline drawing was used as art for the three color circles reproduced in chapter 9. That the circles are not completely filled in allows the printer, with some handwork, to make three different negatives from one piece of art.

■ *Color-separation houses*. Color can be generated on microcomputers in-house and separations made, but quality process color requires specialization.

■ *Service bureaus*. These places "output" your computer files on high-end equipment, giving you camera-ready copy with more fidelity than what is available from laser printers. A service bureau would have a Linotronic, for instance, that could get up to 3,600 dpi instead of the usual 300.

But finding a service bureau that can handle any graphic arts challenge is not easy to do. "Most service bureaus specialize," says computer artist and designer Gary Olsen. "One will be strong in four-color process and not know a thing about making color transparencies or slides. Another will have a top-of-the-line, high resolution imagesetter and not know how to produce much more than film positives."[6]

Working with service bureaus makes your operation vulnerable to computer viruses. A bureau that doesn't screen disks coming in can spell trouble for any number of patrons. You should run your own disks through an anti-virus program when you get them back or invest in a good virus detection program for your system.

The camera-ready copy or mechanicals that result from all this pre-press activity eventually go onto printing presses; in-house, if the job is small enough with a modest press run, but usually outside, to printing plants or to publications that are picked to run the ads.

Typesetting Systems

Printers call the setting of type "composing" and the type itself "composition." They work with two basic kinds of composition: *hot type* and *cold type*.

Somewhere in the manufacturing process, the type we call hot type makes use of molten metal poured into molds, or mats (matrices), as type is cast.

The first method of setting type—hand setting—dates back more than five hundred years to Johannes Gutenberg, who perfected it. To set such already-manufactured pieces of type—called foundry type—the printer or compositor picks up each letter or symbol one by one and places it in a composing stick, which may be adjusted for the line length desired.

A pasteup artist demonstrates how to use transfer letters. The next letter to be "set" here is *E*. In the top picture, the artist lifts the sheet of letters to the mechanical. Second, he positions the *E*. Third, using a blunt stylus, he rubs the letter from the top so it will transfer from below onto the mechanical. Fourth, using the flat end of the stylus and the backing sheet of the transfer letters, he smooths down the letter. (Photos courtesy of Chartpak.)

The second method of setting type (we are still dealing with hot type) is by linecasting machines. You know it as Linotype composition; but Linotype is a trade name and, technically, should not be used as the generic name for this process. At least one other brand name is involved here: Intertype.

Printers call this process for setting type the "linecasting system" because the product of the Linotype or Intertype machine is a line of type cast as one unit on a metal slug. Such composition is cast line by line; the lines, or slugs, are gathered in a tray or galley and then "proofed" for client inspection. (Proofing of all hot-type composition involves making a first printing from the type on long, narrow sheets of paper on a proof press that is usually hand-operated.)

In machine composition, what is assembled are not pieces of type but the mats (molds) of the individual letters and symbols from which the lines are cast. The type is then manufactured right on the scene from molten lead.

Essentially, the Linotype and the Intertype machines have four basic sections: the magazine, which houses the mats; the keyboard, which releases the mats from the magazine and causes them to assemble in lines; the casting mechanism, which does the manufacturing; and the distribution system, which, in Rube Goldberg-like style, causes each mat to return to its compartment in the magazine.

Linecasting machine composition is used for small sizes of type—for columns of copy; but it can also produce type as large as half an inch high. The linecasting machine can be activated with tapes typed by typists, thus doing away with the high-salaried operators.

The third method of setting hot type involves the Ludlow process. Ludlow composition is in one way related to the foundry operation, in another way to linecasting composition. The letters assembled in Ludlow are assembled by hand. But they are not individual pieces of type; they are matrices, or mats, from which the type will be cast in lines, or slugs.

The Ludlow mats are kept in cases or drawers, as type is kept for the foundry operation. After the mats are assembled in the compositor's stick, they are put into the casting device and the line of type emerges almost at once. Like type in the foundry operation, the mats have to be redistributed by hand for further use. Ludlow, its slugs T-shaped, is useful for setting large-size types, especially types for headlines in newspaper ads.

The fourth method of setting hot type involves the Monotype process, an English invention. Monotype consists of two machines, one with a keyboard to punch a tape or ribbon, the other with a casting mechanism that receives the tape and automatically casts type from each matrix case. The final product is more like the product of the foundry operation than Linotype setting in that individual pieces of type are produced.

The Monotype system makes possible careful fitting of type and easy corrections and is especially useful in tabular and scientific work.

Each of these hot-type composition systems was developed for letterpress printing. But they can be used for offset printing, too. What is needed there is a reproduction proof, made on a special press, to be used in a pasteup.

The coming of offset lithography has virtually eliminated hot-type systems. Most typesetting is done now with cold-type systems.

"Cold-type composition," as a term, sometimes gets confused with "photo composition." The first term is the broad heading; the second term is a form of cold-type composition.

You can count six different methods of cold-type composition. The first three produce mostly large-size letters.

■ *Hand lettering.* In the hands of a professional, hand lettering surpasses types for beauty and effectiveness. In the hands of an amateur, nothing could be worse aesthetically.
■ *Hand setting of letters printed on sheets.* Two kinds are common: cut-and-press-on letters, and the more popular dry-transfer letters. The press-on letters (they are a little hard to find now) come on sheets that are lightly waxed on one side for adhesive purposes. The user cuts the letters out with a knife or razor blade and presses them into place one by one on the pasteup. Transfer

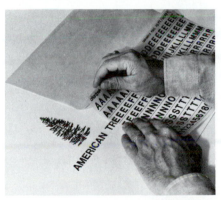
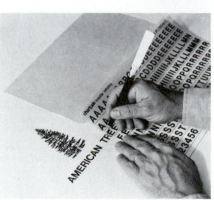
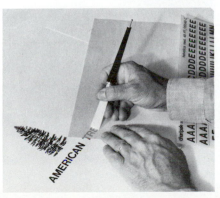

letters are printed on the underside of their transparent carrying sheets, their faces rather than their backs against the sheets. The user moves the whole sheet until a letter is in the right place and then literally rubs it off the back of the sheet onto the pasteup.

Both kinds of letters come in countless varieties and sizes from several manufacturers, and in opaque white as well as black inks. Prestype, which claims to have invented dry-transfer letters, offers some alphabets in opaque colors: red, yellow, blue, and gold.

To use these letters correctly, you have to understand letterform and spacing. Beginners often space the letters unevenly and too generously. And beginners have trouble lining up lowercase letters that have ascenders or descenders. The *g,* because of its two loops, often ends up out of alignment. Beginners also fail to realize that some letters are designed so that their angles and rounds extend above and below the guidelines.

■ *Photolettering.* Machines from several manufacturers make use of negatives of complete alphabets that are dialed or otherwise put into proper position for light to shine through the desired letter onto sensitized paper. Such machines release strips of paper which carry photographically produced headlines.

■ *Strike-on composition.* This kind of composition can be produced on anything ranging from the lowly portable typewriter to a sophisticated tape-operated machine with proportional spacing (letters of various widths). If a typewriter is used, it should be an electric or electronic one. For crisp impression of letters, it should also be equipped with a use-once carbon ribbon.

■ *Phototypesetting.* In the early 1950s linecasting machines were made available in versions equipped with individual negatives in place of the familiar mats. When the operator hit the keyboard keys, the negatives moved into position and, line-by-line, allowed light through to sensitized galley paper. Here we had columns of type produced photographically—type as good as though it were produced by conventional hot type machines.

Newer phototypesetting machines operate photoelectronically. They use master disks or grids containing all necessary characters in negative form. Even more sophisticated phototypesetting machines make use of cathode ray tubes. In the process, pictures of type characters on the tube are projected onto photographic paper.

Cold type is designed primarily for offset printing; its product is meant to be photographed. But now the printer can use phototypesetting negatives to make exposures directly onto plates, thus bypassing the photographing of prints.

■ *Computer composition.* Today most advertising type of the cold-type variety is set by computerized electronic systems involving keyboard entry devices, computers, and output devices. Digital information originated by the first of these components is stored by the second and manipulated by the third. The verbal output is in the form of printed pages that are the equivalent of reproduction proofs.

The typesetting process starts when an operator punches a keyboard and the video display terminal (VDT), a cathode ray tube that looks like a TV screen, shows what is being typed or has been typed. The material typed can be stored and called up later for editing and correcting.

The computer to which the VDT is attached can be programmed to spell and hyphenate correctly and to make other decisions in connection with the typesetting.

In computer typesetting, hyphenation should always be checked, because

Can you read this headline? Foundry type, the original "hot type," was set upside down in the stick, the top line at the bottom. Otherwise the setting would have been from right to left. This illustration was used in an ad sponsored by Lederle Laboratories of Pearl River, New York, and is shown here by permission.

How type used to be set. Mergenthaler's "Elektron" tape-operated Linotype linecasting machine set fifteen standard newspaper lines a minute. The machine could also be operated manually. The magazines of matrices were at the upper right, the keyboard below, the casting mechanism at the left. The matrices went up and across the back for redistribution to the magazines.

no program handles the complicated rules of hyphenation perfectly. For instance, you will want to watch out for "hyphen ladders," when several lines in a row end up with hyphens.

Often the design calls for wrapping the copy around silhouette art. Computers have made this procedure easier than in the past. In PageMaker, for instance, you establish "handles" in several places to outline the art and then allow the text to flow automatically up to the outline these handles define.

A major contribution of desktop publishing has been to bring computer composition in-house.

Working with Type 1 font software from Adobe, an industry standard, you can use a variety of computers and print typefaces at any resolution on all PostScript and non-PostScript printers: dot matrix, inkjet, and laser. With Type 1 font, you have access to more than 12,000 typefaces from more than 30 vendors.

Adobe Type Manager, another Adobe software product, eliminates jagged type on the computer screen and on the printed page. What you see on the screen is what you get on the page. The type comes in "outline fonts." Outline fonts are stored as mathematical formulas, in contrast to bitmapped fonts, which are stored as patterns. Outline fonts can be scaled to any size and otherwise manipulated. That the type begins as outline letters makes possible smooth rather than jagged curves in display sizes. The output devices can range from 144 dots-per-inch dot matrix printers to 300 dpi laser printers and monochrome, gray-scale, and color displays of any resolution.

In some offices, the ad maker keyboards the type on a personal computer and, using a telephone modem, sends copy to a type house. This cuts typesetting costs by as much as one-third. Of course, as Ronald Labuz puts it, you have to "believe that all the extra work you're now doing doesn't cost you anything."[7]

Some of the newer typesetting systems don't offer the quality earlier systems offered. The people who run the machines may not be as well schooled. "Computers Can't Recognize a Bad Setting," Line & Tone Typographix Corp., a New York type house, says in the headline of one of its ads to the trade. "Unfortunately, Neither Can Some of the People Who Run Them." The theme of the ad is that this house employs typographers with demanding design standards. And, with "state-of-the-art computers," the house claims it can deliver "typositor quality settings from headline to coupon copy."

This is the claim many of the modern type houses make, but some art directors turn to the more traditional systems for jobs they really care about. Real type houses in 1988 began running a Hermann Zapf-designed "Q"

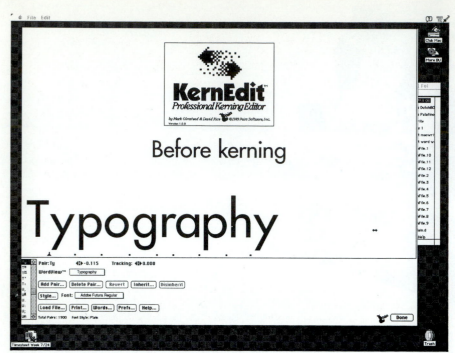

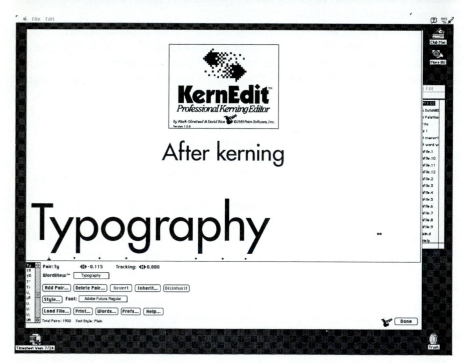

A "screen capture" shows how KernEdit software, in this case imported into QuarkXPress 3.1, can be used to improve the spacing in display type, in this case Adobe Futura Regular. Note that in the kerned type, the "y" has been moved to the left to find a place partially under the crossbar of the "T." All the spacing in this word has been adjusted to achieve optical rather than mechanical spacing. (Demonstration by Robert Keding.)

symbol (the "Q" is for "quality") on their reproduction proofs or prints to mark the product. For many jobs, though, computer setting and the accompanying short cuts produce perfectly suitable textmatter and headlines.

Reproducing Art

Paintings. Wash drawings. Pen and ink sketches. Cartoons. Scratchboard drawings. Photographs. Computer-generated drawings and paintings. The list of kinds of art the advertising designer works with is a long one. But from the printer's standpoint, the list boils down to two items: line drawings and halftones.

Put another way, the printer can reproduce art in one of two ways.

Artwork done in black ink on white paper in lines and solid areas of black calls for *line reproduction.* In making the plate, the printer (more correctly, the engraver or offset camera-operator) takes a picture of the art, using high-contrast film. The operator uses the film then to expose a sensitized plate, as a photographer in a darkroom exposes a sensitized sheet of paper.

For letterpress printing, the plate goes through the etching process, by which parts that are not to print are, in effect, eaten away and parts that are to print are left standing. This is photoengraving. For offset lithography, a different kind of a plate—thinner, for one thing—is used; it does not have to be etched. The term *photoengraving* does not apply.

Artists and printers work constantly to devise ways of adding tone to line drawings to give them the effect of halftones or more pattern and texture. The original system for adding tone to line drawings was developed by Benjamin Day in the nineteenth century. Still in use today, it involves the affixing of a pattern in certain areas of either the negative or the plate by the printer or engraver. The artist directs placement by shading in those areas with a light-blue pencil or watercolor tone (the engraver's camera does not pick up the light blue). More recent developments allow the artist to place the tone directly onto the drawing. There are several methods: the use of sheets of transparent paper or plastic on which a pattern is printed; the use of drawing paper with built-in patterns that can be brought out with chemicals or pencils; and the use of sheets from which shading patterns can be rubbed off onto the original artwork. Desktop publishing systems offer a number of patterns that can be applied to the art by moving the cursor to an icon and clicking the mouse.

The tone, of course, is an optical illusion; it is formed by closely placed black dots or lines that merge into middle values as the eye recedes from them. Under a magnifying glass, they show up for what they are: line art, ready for camera.

Line art can be patched, scratched, and retouched; the printer has no trouble keeping resulting shadows and slight differences in tone from registering on the

This kind of drawing, strong, rough, done with a brush on a rough-textured paper, calls for line reproduction. Part of an ad sponsored by *Printing Production* magazine; used by permission.

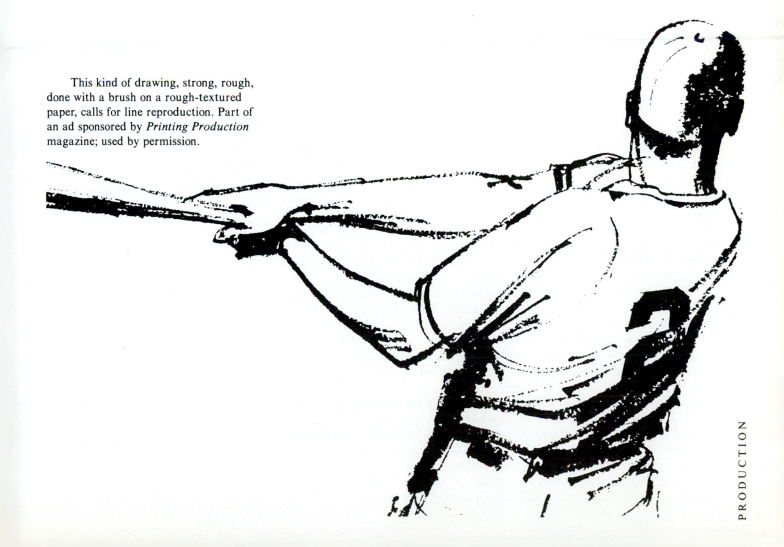

PRODUCTION

plate. Often line art is reduced to remove slight imperfections in the drawing. If reproduction proofs of type are to be used, they would be shot as line art.

A designer wanting to use a photograph or piece of artwork that has a continuous tone moving subtly up and down the tonal value scale (a wash drawing, fine pencil drawing, or painting) will ordinarily order *halftone reproduction*. ("Halftone" is not a very good term, because many tones are involved: light, middle, and dark. It is more than a matter of having tones that are halfway between white and black. But "halftone" is the term we are stuck with.)

Photographs with a good tonal range give you the best reproduction. With the new technology, glossy prints are no longer necessary, and in some cases they are actually less useful than matte-finish or luster-finish prints. The luster-finish print is less subject to cracks and scratches, and it is easier to retouch.

To hold onto the many tones of the original, the engraver (or offset camera operator) inserts a screen between the lens and the film. The standard screen is a two-ply piece of glass; one ply has opaque lines cut in one direction, the other has lines cut perpendicular to the first lines, forming a cross-hatching. The resulting small squares act as individual lenses, breaking up the light into dots of various sizes, depending upon how much is reflected from the subject being photographed.

From then on the negative is used as the negative for a line reproduction is used.

A halftone, then, has small dots over the entire area of the print, even if some of the area is meant to be white. With special handling, the printer's camera operator can work some blank areas—pure white—into the artwork where it is needed. Such halftones are called "highlight" or "dropout" halftones.

A line drawing like this sometimes can better show detail and texture than a photograph can, especially if the art has to be reproduced under less-than-ideal circumstances. This is Sedia's Confort Club 221 (*Confort* rather than *Comfort*). Designer and artist: Mittie Cuetara. Art director: Colby Andrus.

Gilbert Paper Company used this computer-generated art in a direct-mail piece to advertise its New-Tech correspondence paper made for electronic printing systems. Jim Pollock created the art using a Macintosh 512K-E computer and FullPaint. Pollock started out with his own photograph, scanning it with ThunderScan. "On the original photo only part of the water was visible, so I had to create some of the water by hand. I did spend a considerable amount of time manipulating the image after it was scanned."

© 1986 Jim Pollock 86.8.6.6

This computer-generated art did not start as a photograph. Pollock drew the scene using a mouse.

©1986 Jim Pollock 86.5.2.3

The author's quick sketch of eager shoppers, done with a Uni-Ball Micro (.2mm point) pen, is shown here actual size. Any sustantial reduction would weaken the lines, causing some of them to drop out in the reproduction.

ROY PAUL

Whatever system of printing is used, where continuous-tone artwork must be reproduced, screening is necessary. Printers do not print ordinarily in shades of gray. They print in black. The effect of gray must be achieved through optical illusion. Stepping back from a halftone printed in a publication, you see it as tones of gray, from light to dark. Looking at it closely (perhaps with a magnifying glass), you see the dots—and nothing but black ink. Pinpoint dots cover and define the lighter areas, larger dots the darker areas.

For pictures in color, separate plates and printings must be made for each color used. Through judicious use of the plates for black, yellow, red, and blue inks, the printer is able to achieve the illusion of full color. If the color picture is a halftone, each of the plates will be made up of dots.

As artists and printers work to make line art look like halftone art, they also work to make halftone art look like line art. Eastman Kodak Company in 1953 introduced the Tone-Line process by which continuous-tone art—photographs, primarily—is changed into line art with unusual texture. Several different textures are available. A photograph thus converted is ready for line reproduction. Looking at the reproduction, the reader might conclude it was a drawing of some kind.

A similar effect can be had simply by ordering line reproduction for a continuous-tone original. What happens is this: The tones darker than 50 percent fill in as solids; the tones lighter than 50 percent drop out altogether. It is as though an artist had drawn a picture using no lines, only shadows.

A lot of art going into ads now is computer-scanned. Once on the screen, the art can be adjusted in a number of ways and fitted into a layout. Two kinds of scanners are available: *bi-level scanners,* which convert the art to bitmaps, and *gray-scale scanners,* which convert the art to a scale of "grays." (The grays are simulated, of course.) Gray-scale scanners, using something called Tagged Image File Format (TIFF), produce higher quality halftones.

Scanner quality varies greatly, and so do prices. A drum scanner works best, but flat-bed scanners are coming close to matching what drum scanners can do.

Paper Stock

All graphic designers consider paper in their planning. Some types reproduce well only on smooth stocks; other types seem designed for rough stocks. Halftones, depending on their screens, need certain papers in order to show up well. The designer always makes adjustments to fit the paper used by the medium carrying the ad—except in direct mail. Here, as a representative of the "publisher," the designer can choose paper stock to fit the design. Faced with hundreds of different papers from scores of manufacturers, and aware that paper represents from one-quarter to one-half the cost of the job, the designer of direct mail quickly becomes something of a paper expert.

Paper, priced by the pound, is sold in rolls or in reams of 500 sheets. If the sheet size is 24″ × 36″ and 500 such sheets weigh 70 pounds, it will be designated: 24 × 36—70. The last number indicates the thickness of the paper. A "70-pound" sheet is thicker than a "60-pound" sheet in its class (more about classes in a minute). But a 60-pound sheet in one class might be thicker than a 70-pound sheet in another class. Likewise, 70-pound book paper is much thinner than 70-pound cover stock because the basic size for cover stock on which ream weight is based is smaller.

The classes of paper used in printing are these:

- *Newsprint.* Used almost exclusively by newspapers.
- *Book stock.* This is an important class. We break it down into:
  Antique. Soft, bulky, rough. The *texts,* used in fine printing, have some rag content. The *vellums* are smoother. Often off-white or cream-colored.
- *Offset.* Smooth, uncoated. Usually seen in harsh white.
  Gravure. Absorbent, to take the large amount of ink applied in rotogravure printing.

English finish. Clay-content paper, smooth but not glossy and without much bulk. Used extensively by major magazines.

Super. Clay-content paper that is polished (although English-finish paper is sometimes polished, too). The clay acts as a starch.

Coated. Coating substance is attached to the surface, not built in. The paper then is supercalendered, resulting in high gloss.

Bible paper. Tissue-thin but opaque.

■ *Writing stock.* It comes in flat varieties (calendered to smooth finish), bonds (crisp, permanent, sometimes with rag content), and ledger (with good folding properties because it is made from long-fiber pulp).

■ *Cover stock.* Heavier paper than book paper, but with many of the same qualities and in the same varieties.

■ *Cardboards.* Sheets are bonded to one another, like plywood veneers. This class includes the Bristols and coated blanks, usually with smooth, English finishes.

Advertisers wishing to be considered friendly to the environment use recycled paper when they can. Such paper requires designer compromises. The paper often has a gray rather than a pure white look, and it does not offer the printing fidelity that, say, coated papers offer. Designers specifying recycled papers often avoid type with fine serifs and use line rather than halftone art.

Printers

In his *How'd They Design and Print That?*, Wayne Robinson catalogues 60 printing or print processes. "Although each process has its limitations, which are frequently the subject of irate discussions between designers and printers, each process has its potential, which the many printers I have spoken to often believe to be unfulfilled by designers, simply because they are not always aware of all that the industry has to offer."[8]

The term "printer" is one to cause confusion in this computer age. Traditionally, it has been used to refer to the person or firm, divorced from the ad maker (or journalist), responsible for making copies for mass distribution. Today it is used, too, to mean the output device that turns out hard copy for the computer. This device is good for single copies only or very short press runs. In advertising, what comes from this kind of printer should be regarded as "camera-ready copy." It usually goes to a commercial printing house, either directly or through a publication selected to run the ad.

The hard copy or proofs from computer-generated ads can come from daisy wheel, dot-matrix, or laser printers, but, except for some in-house use, daisy-wheel and dot-matrix output is not good enough for advertising production. Only laser printers have enough fidelity and flexibility to print out ads for commercial use.

With their 300 dpi resolutions, laser printers produce camera-ready copy good enough for many direct-mail jobs. But ads meant for magazine insertion must come from better equipment, say an outside Linotronic. Linotronic output can

This printed halftone is blown up to show the relationship of dot size to tonal scale. A print like this can be used as-is for an unusual effect, as designer Doug Lynch used this one on his jacket design for *New Deal Mosaic,* a book published by University of Oregon Books.

A silhouette halftone of the Model A. The original print was improved through airbrushing.

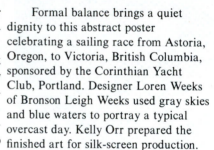

take the form of a positive or a negative. In some cases it is a good idea to order a negative. This saves a step in the platemaking process and insures better halftone fidelity.

Apple's LaserWriter and Hewlett-Packard's LaserJet are the two prominent laser printers. Both now come with PostScript page description language, widely used in desktop publishing operations. For best results, use paper that is recommended by the manufacturer of your equipment.

If you go to color printing, you have other kinds of printers to consider: inkjet printers, thermal transfer printers, and film recorders, all very expensive to own. ". . . in-house color printing hasn't reached the point at which it's worth the investment to *most* people," Professor Tom Bivins observed in 1990. "However, if it's like the rest of the computer industry, it won't be long before it's cost effective and aesthetically satisfying."[9]

Formal balance brings a quiet dignity to this abstract poster celebrating a sailing race from Astoria, Oregon, to Victoria, British Columbia, sponsored by the Corinthian Yacht Club, Portland. Designer Loren Weeks of Bronson Leigh Weeks used gray skies and blue waters to portray a typical overcast day. Kelly Orr prepared the finished art for silk-screen production.

Printing Processes

Besides knowing something about the printers used to produce camera-ready copy, designers need to know something about commercial printing processes used to make copies of ads for mass distribution. What kind of printing a newspaper or magazine uses determines to some extent what a designer does to design, lay out, and paste up an ad. And when handling a direct-mail piece, the designer has to *pick out* a printing process, taking into account both quality and price. Whatever the ad, the designer works closely with the printer to make the job go smoothly.

One reason for checking with a printer before beginning a design job is to determine the ink flow for the piece. If, for instance, a booklet has a number of color photos, it might be necessary to arrange them so that the printer can adjust the inking to better maintain their quality.

You should plan your pasteup, as well as the design itself, so that you do not ask the impossible of the printer. "When you design a piece that requires a 'perfect' anything in the production sequence, you are paving the way for disappointment," observed Norman Sanders, president of Sanders Printing Corporation, New York. "This is especially true when the design requires perfection in the final trimming."[10] For instance, you would not line up a series of small geometric shapes right next to the edge of a page.

By far the most popular printing process—for direct-mail pieces as well as for newspapers and magazines—is *offset lithography*. Even a small town is likely to have several printing houses with offset presses.

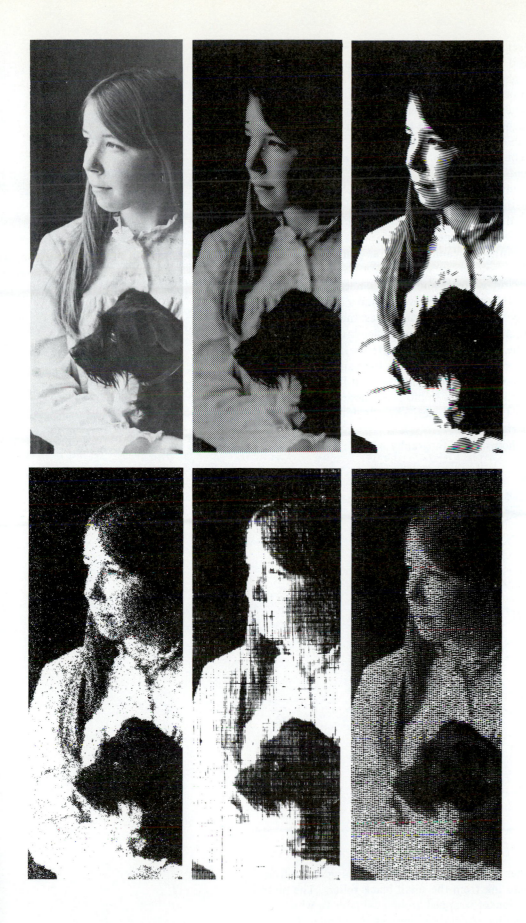

A photograph shown first as a
regular halftone and then as halftones
made from other than dot screens.
(Photo by the author.)

This book was printed by offset lithography.

No other process for short and medium pressruns, and even long pressruns, can so inexpensively reproduce photographs and artwork and so evenly lay on large areas of color. No other process can use as copy blocks the product of so many different typesetting machines. Even typewriter "composition" can be used. Graphic designers like offset because (1) it is more flexible than other processes, offering unlimited design possibilities, and (2) the designer can do all the makeready work, bypassing the composing room. The designer can exercise exact control over placement of elements.

Offset lithography, as a printing process, is based on an art form: stone lithography. In offset lithography, the printing impression is made from the plate to an intermediary rubber-covered roller, then to the paper. The impression, in other words, is "offset" on the way to the paper.

The image on the plate is smooth; you cannot feel it as you rub your hand over it. How, then, can it print?

Chemistry provides the answer: oil or grease and water do not mix. The image is grease-based; in the printing, both a water with glycerin and an ink are applied to the plate. The water stays away from the impression areas; the ink stays away from the damp or watered areas and sticks to the impression areas.

In regular stone lithography, the artist draws on a flat plate with a grease-base crayon; the artist applies the water and ink, then places the paper down on the plate. What results is an impression in mirror-reverse; a head facing right, for instance, would be facing left in the printing. In offset lithography, the "wrong facing" takes place on the rubber-covered cylinder; when the impression is then made on the paper, the facing is right again.

The following diagram shows how offset lithography works.

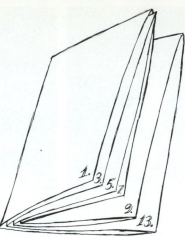

A folded-down sixteen-page signature ready for trimming at the top, right, and bottom.

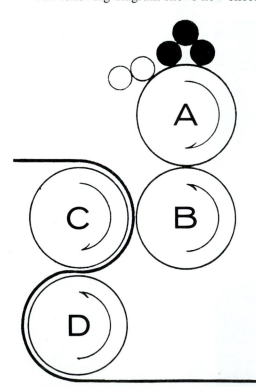

The plate wraps around cylinder A and picks up the dampening agent from the small rollers at the top left and ink from the small black rollers. The plate transfers its image to the rubber blanket wrapped around cylinder B, which re-transfers to the sheet of paper coming around the impression cylinder, C. The sheet-transfer cylinder, D, delivers the paper from the press.

To make a plate for the press, somebody has to make a pasteup. Line artwork and reproduction proofs of type are pasted in position exactly as they are to appear in the final printed version of the job. Photographs and other continuous-tone art

You are looking at the *reproduction* of a *photograph* of a *mat* of a *line drawing* offered by Crown Zellerbach to grocers wanting to feature a picture of Tuf 'n Ready Towels in newspaper ads (when the newspapers were letterpress). The newspaper backshop would use the mat to make a casting in metal. The words "Tuf 'n Ready" and "Towels," the outlines, and the screened tones below "Towels" were recessed in the mat to receive the molten metal.

are usually submitted separately to the camera operator, who photographs them through a screen and then "strips" the negatives into position with the line negatives. If original line artwork is oversize (or undersize) it is shot separately and reduced (or enlarged) to the correct size and stripped into place. The composites of stripped-in negatives—they are called "flats"—are then used to make the plates.

Because everything on the pasteup page has to be photographed anyway, you can use all the line artwork you want (provided it is done to size) for no extra cost.

Offset lithography makes desktop publishing ideal for ad making.

In *letterpress printing,* a *raised surface* makes the impression. The material that will do the printing (it usually is unyielding, tough metal) is "type high" (something slightly under an inch); anything not meant to print must be less than "type high."

Letterpress can make immediate use of type set by hand or machine. No photographing is necessary. Many advertising people and printers agree that all-type jobs of quality call for letterpress printing.

But letterpress, with its sharpness and harshness of impression, does an excellent job of printing pictures, too. No process is better for line drawings. And halftones, provided the screen is fine enough and the paper smooth enough, are at their best in letterpress impression. They should be square or rectangular, however. The hard edges of letterpress have a tendency to "fill in" on vignettes and highlight halftones.

The cost-conscious designer should understand that, good as pictures can look in letterpress, they do cost more in this process than in offset lithography.

The printer if not the designer regards letterpress as the flexible process. Last-minute changes can be made easily, even to the point of stopping the presses. More readily than other printers, the letterpress printer makes proofs available at any stage for checking by the designer and client.

For long runs in letterpress and for all runs on letterpress rotary presses (not all letterpress presses are rotary), the printer makes mats (molds) of the pages, from which durable plates are cast. Plates used for rotary presses have to be rounded to fit the cylinder. For short runs (a few thousand) on nonrotary presses, the printer uses the type and engravings as provided.

In *gravure printing,* everything that is to print is incised on the printing plate, making tiny wells of varying depths. That includes the type. The ink is deposited in these wells (excess ink is wiped from the plate by the "doctor blade") and moves from them to the paper in the printing.

Everything that is to print, then, has been screened. You do not notice the screen because it is 150-line or finer; and the small dots are further minimized as the ink is sucked out of the wells and onto the slightly absorbent paper. The type, though, even to the naked eye, is often fuzzy. Obviously, this is no process for reproducing column after column of type.

It is an ideal process, however, for reproducing photographs or any continuous-tone art. The gradations of tone in gravure, thanks to the fine screen, are almost as complete as in the continuous-tone original.

Gravure is called "rotogravure" when the presses take paper on rolls rather than in sheets. Rotogravure is reserved for extra-long pressruns—runs in the millions. The setting up of the original plates, whether for sheetfed gravure or rotogravure, is costly.

In *stencil printing,* there is no plate to hold and transfer ink. Instead, the ink passes through a cloth, called a "stencil."

In silk-screen printing, the cloth is stretched over a frame, and areas that are not to print are covered with a frisket made of paper or some similar material. The ink is literally pushed through onto waiting paper below; it hangs up in areas that are covered. Silk-screen printing is useful for posters with small pressruns. Transit-advertising cards often are silk-screened. Recent developments make possible the printing of coarse-screen halftones.

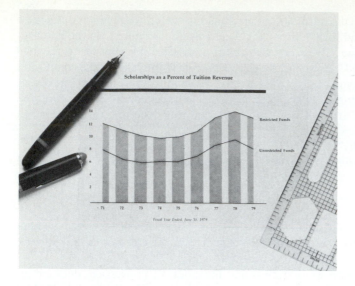

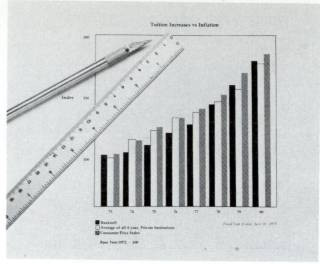

In-House Printing and Duplicating

An increasing number of advertisers are doing their own multiple-copy printing.

As in commercial printing, in-plant printing makes wider use of offset than any other printing process, but a number of substitute printing processes are available.

Duplicating machines, all needing some kind of stencil or master from which to print, can be used for letters and uncomplicated leaflets and folders. These machines include the following:

- *Mimeograph.* In mimeographing, a form of stencil printing, a cloth comes covered with a layer of wax. When you type or draw on the stencil, in effect you push to one side some of the wax and expose the cloth, which is porous; it then allows ink to pass through. It is possible to reproduce halftones, which can be scratched onto stencils in dot form electronically.
- *Spirit duplicator.* Typing or drawing with an ordinary hard pencil or ballpoint pen makes the master, which is the reverse side of the work sheet. In operation, moistened paper comes in contact with the carbon, picking up some of the carbon for the impression.
- *Multilith.* This baby offset machine prints with either a flexible metal or a paper plate. A pasteup must be photographed to make the metal plate; you can draw and type directly onto the paper plate.
- *Multigraph.* This is a baby letterpress process, with type, looking like typewriter type, set by hand and slipped into grooves on a drum, which is covered with an inked ribbon to make impressions. Once popular, the process is now infrequently used.
- *Automatic typewriter.* An activating device on the typewriter is controlled by a perforated tape (the master). A secretary types in the name, address, and salutation; then the machines type automatically, shutting off for a name insertion occasionally, if desired.

Then there are the office copiers or photocopiers. They have an advantage over duplicators in that anyone can operate them.

The first of them—by the Xerox Corporation—went on the market in 1960. Suddenly carbon paper and stencils were unnecessary in some offices.

At one time it was not economical to use a copying machine to make more than a dozen copies of an original. If several hundred copies were involved, the job called for a duplicating machine. But copiers have their per-copy cost set low enough now that for many jobs it is a toss-up as to which process is more economical. And the copiers are getting more sophisticated. Some print on both sides at once. Some reproduce color. Some collate.

To dress up this line graph and bar chart used in an annual report of Bucknell University, Newton Art/Advertising, Selingsgrove, Pennsylvania, added traditional chart-making tools—the tools themselves—to the art and pasteups, then photographed the result. Each photo was run as a regular black-and-white halftone. The tools shown include a technical fountain pen, a template, an X-acto knife, and a ruler.

The reproduction doesn't show it, but the trolley car punches out from this thick-paper reproduction and folds into a three-dimensional toy. The restaurant has a real car like this inside, and patrons can be seated in it. This printed unit is distributed free to kids and others who want it. Designer: Byron Ferris.

Copiers can also aid in the rough-layout stage of design. Students find that they can reduce full-color reproductions from magazines to black-and-white prints when their instructors have specified "no color." They can also copy, if crudely, three-dimensional objects. If they want the printing to be on a color stock and they've done their roughs on white paper, they can use tinted paper to make copies on a copier.

Special Effects in Advertising

Among production and post-printing tricks and devices available to ad makers are these:

■ *Varnishing.* A booklet cover, for instance, gets a coating of a special varnish to make it glossier and more durable.

■ *Pop-ups.* The advertiser with money to spend can use a technique popular with the publishers of some children's books.

■ *Fragrances.* An inch-long scratch-and-sniff strip made by 3-M Company contains some 50,000,000 microscopic plastic bubbles impregnated with just about any aroma you can think of. The bubbles burst when a fingernail runs across the strip. A strip on a can of shaving foam, for instance, means that a potential customer can scratch and then decide if the fragrance is desirable. Northern Illinois Gas Company used scratch-and-sniff strips on a direct-mail piece to help customers recognize the smell that accompanies a gas leak. 3-M has worked out a system with leading magazine printers so that the magazine itself can handle production. The fragrance can be applied directly to the ad as part of the printing. A natural for advertising sponsored by perfume manufacturers. Rolls-Royce ran an ad in *Architectural Digest* that carried the smell of a leather interior.

■ *Die-cutting.* Provided the paper stock is heavy enough, the designer can ask for the "printing" of holes or cutouts of various shapes. These should be

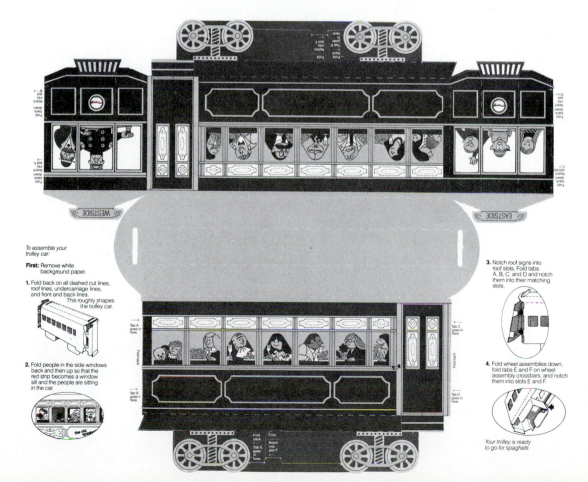

PRODUCTION

kept well away from the edges so they will not weaken the printed piece and cause it to tear. The designer can get the effect of a die-cut by asking the printer simply to cut one end of the piece on the diagonal. No special plates are required for this.

■ *Embossing.* This is achieved through use of a relief die (below) and an engraved die (above). The resulting insignia or design can be blind (without ink) or printed. If printed, the ink is applied before the embossing. Embossing can add the look and feel of luxury to letterheads, annual reports, and brochures.

■ *Automatic numbering.* For letterpress jobs, the printer can lock up with type and engravings a little mechanical device that prints numbers and changes automatically to a higher number with each impression.

■ *Perforating.* For pages or coupons that are to be torn from mailers, the printer can "print" a higher-than-type-high dotted knife edge wherever the designer wants it. Like die-cutting, perforating requires a special pressrun.

Some ads are accompanied by bound-in records or carry little recording devices that start playing when a page is opened.

In 1987 Toyota included 3-D viewfinders with four-page ads in *Time, People,* and *Cosmopolitan.*

Special-effects advertising should have a theme that capitalizes on the effects. A full-page 3-D ad for Galleria Orlando, a new shopping center in Florida, in *Shopping Centers Today,* an oversize trade journal, included a bound-in pair of 3-D glasses, with one red and one blue plastic lens, and an invitation to "Be the Focus of Attention at Galleria." The ad itself was the typical misregistered scramble when not looked at through the glasses. The focus made possible by the glasses exposed the message, which extolled the virtues of locating a store at the center.

Don't be misled by David Ogilvy's satire on the agony of designers in selecting just the right face: "Once upon a time I was riding on the top of a Fifth Avenue bus," he wrote, "when I heard a . . . housewife say to another, 'Molly, my dear, I would have bought that new brand of toilet soap if only they hadn't set the body copy in ten-point Garamond.' "[1]

Ogilvy himself takes his typography seriously: Do not use type "self-consciously"; do not print it in reverse or over a tint block; do not use more than one face in a headline; do not use sans serifs for body type; do not go wider than forty characters; break up long columns with subheadings; indent at the beginnings of paragraphs—these are among his famous twenty "precepts for the production of a good layout."

Typography, which involves both the design and the use of type, has intrigued people for centuries. People whose livelihoods depend upon a knowledge of typography develop strong preferences for certain typefaces and then change their minds as new typefaces are introduced. Book publishers put out a surprising number of books each year celebrating the history of typography, displaying some of the thousands of faces available, or offering advice on how to use them.

Where Our Letters Came From

To appreciate the uses and abuses of type, a designer should know something about how type came into being. The Egyptians first worked out an alphabet, but theirs was a mixed affair: partly alphabet and partly picture writing. The Phoenician, businessmen-traders on the east shore of the Mediterranean Sea, borrowed from the Egyptians and developed an alphabet that had trade rather than literary purposes. It was made up of what we today call consonants. The literary-minded Greeks, adding vowels, improved the Phoenician alphabet (and gave the alphabet its name), and the Romans modified the Greek alphabet. Scholars count some two hundred alphabets, fifty of them in use today. Our own alphabet of twenty-six letters, derived from the Roman alphabet, is the world's most widely used.

The history of letterform is largely the history of writing tools. The nature and shape of the writing instrument affected the character, the flow of the letters. The reeds, either sharpened to a point to make a pen or frayed at the end to make a brush, gave character to Egyptian writing on papyrus; the stylus used on wax tablets helped shape the rather angular Greek alphabet. Putting important Roman inscriptions on columns of stone affected roman letters (but differently from what one would suppose; the letters were apparently drawn first with an instrument that made thick and thin lines).

Letters of the alphabet were first drawn or written and only lately in world history cut and punched in metal. The tool used in most writing hands was the broad-nibbed pen. Turned at a slight angle, with the angle kept constant, the pen made its thick and thin markings on the writing surface—markings that became the inspiration for our roman typefaces.

The Greek alphabet, completed by the sixth century B.C., was an alphabet without serifs (serifs are tiny cross strokes at the terminals of main strokes). By

A ligature brings two letters together to make a single unit of them, in this case dropping the dot over the "i." To facilitate better letter spacing, especially in body-copy sizes, many typefaces come with ligatures.

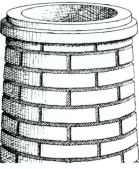
the time typefaces were cut for printing, some twenty centuries later, serifs had been added to the alphabet. One explanation of the coming of serifs is this: When letters were carved in the columns of Rome, the up-and-down strokes, straight as they were, seemed to bulge in the center. An optical illusion, to be sure, but maddening, nevertheless. So the lapidary artists swelled the ends of the strokes slightly to compensate for this. The swellings evolved into serifs.

The copy you are reading has serifs.

It was not until 1816, when type cutting was well established, that the idea of a serifless type occurred to the type designers and punch cutters. The design of letters had come full circle.

Sans serif types, popular for a time, then forgotten, came back strong in 1916, when Edward Johnston designed a beautifully balanced version for the London Underground Railway, and then in the 1920s, when a group of typographers and artists at the Bauhaus in Germany began giving their attention to type design, which in Germany and elsewhere had degenerated as an art. Widely acclaimed then, the types coming out of the Bauhaus were probably too impersonal, too much stripped down (an overreaction to decoration that had perverted so many of the faces at the turn of the century). But at least one of the faces—Futura— is still highly regarded by many typographers.

Meanwhile, in England, Eric Gill developed a sans serif with a personality. There was the slightest hint in the Gill face of variety in the thickness of the strokes. Some said his sans serif had some of the character of the Trajan caps.

In the 1950s European type designers brought out several new sans serifs that differed from earlier sans serifs in that vertical and horizontal strokes varied slightly in thickness, the rounds of the letters were slightly squared, and the terminals were cut on a constant horizontal. We refer to these sans serifs—there

Four more ads in the American Gas Association campaign (see Chaper 5) show ways copy can form art without hurting readability. Reproduced by permission.

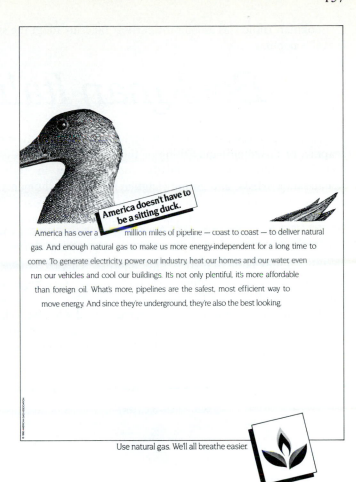

are several of them—as "Swiss gothics." Three of the best known are Helvetica, Univers, and Folio. So popular did they become that they nearly eclipsed the earlier sans serifs. But a reaction set in among some designers, and in the 1970s Futura, Spartan, Kabel, and others of the earlier sans serifs were back to compete with the Swiss gothics.

At the beginning of the sixteenth century, Aldus Manutius of Venice cut a new type called "Cancelleresca" or "Chancery," a face we have come to know as italic. A roman face that slanted slightly, it earned wide popularity because it not only was a beautiful face, it also saved space. Italic letters can be designed narrower than upright letters without impairing their readability.

Most typefaces today come in both upright and slanted—or italic—versions. The slanted version differs considerably in character from its upright relative; italic's job, after all, is to provide emphasis within a block of copy. But the sans serif faces and at least one roman face—W. A. Dwiggins's Electra—come with italics (sometimes called "obliques") patterned on the upright letters of the face, the listing to the right being the only difference. (Electra also comes with a more normal cursive italic.)

This line is set in italics.

Some roman italics come with a special set of capital letters—and lowercase letters, too—called "swash caps" or "swash letters." Terminal lines on these letters curve gracefully and maybe a little self-consciously beyond their ordinary boundaries. Out of favor for a time, swash caps enjoyed a revival among graphic designers when the first edition of this book was published. It was in the 1960s that the swash feature extended to some lowercase letters as well. By 1970 type designers had even come up with swash letters for some sans serifs. Swashes seemed to be everywhere.

Bookman Italic was among the earliest faces to adopt the swash treatment. It is still a popular face.

Bookman Italic

From Gutenberg's day until the eighteenth century, type designs were calligraphic, or based on handwriting of the period. Two styles of handwriting predominated: humanistic (rounded), found mostly in Italy and favored by Renaissance artists, and gothic (angular). From the humanistic hand came the types we today know as roman; from the gothic hand came the types we today know as black letter or text—or "Old English," although the hand belongs to Germany and the Low Countries. The blackness of the gothic hand—and the letters based on it—struck the Italians as crude; hence the term of derision, "gothic," a nickname that stuck until another "vulgar" type came along, this one without serifs. Today "gothic" no longer refers to Old English but instead to the modern form of sans serif type.

The eighteenth century saw the appearance of what we today call the modern roman faces: faces with a more precise look, with greater contrast in main strokes, the serifs thin and flat, looking as though they were tacked on as an afterthought.

The Carolyn Davis Story

Swash caps and even swash lowercase letters made a comeback in the 1960s and found continued wide acceptance afterwards, especially for book titles and magazine advertising. Swashes seem best suited to heavy roman letters like Bookman, but they are also available in other roman and even sans serif typefaces. This example is from a direct-mail piece published by *Reader's Digest* to promote a monthly signed advertising column.

Thermador® uses a headline typeface that captures the character of the main illustration for this ad. (Compare the flair of the "v" with the lines of the lobster.) The heavily leaded, narrow-measure body copy, interrupted by silhouette art, invites readership. Agency: Ketchum, L. A. Art Director: Dennis Lim. Copywriter: Sam Avery. Photographer: Carin Krasner.

UNIVERS Univers 45

UNIVERS Univers 46

UNIVERS Univers 47

UNIVERS Univers 48

UNIVERS Univers 55

UNIVERS Univers 56

UNIVERS Univers 57

UNIVERS Univers 58

UNIVERS Univers 63

UNIVERS Univers 65

UNIVERS Univers 66

UNIVERS Univers 67

UNIVERS Univers 68

UNIVERS Univers 75

UNIVERS Univers 76

A Swiss-designed sans serif (or gothic), Univers comes in twenty varieties of weights and widths, each ranging in size from 6 to 48 points. The designer of the face, Adrian Frutiger, found it necessary and logical to give each series a number rather than a name like "medium" or "ultra" or "condensed." Here you see some—not all—of the variety in the 18-point size. Studying this chart you can see that odd-numbered faces are roman, even-numbered italic. In each group of ten numbers, the faces become more condensed as the numbers increase. And at each jump of ten, they become bolder.

Bodoni, the most famous of these, remains a respected and much-used face today in fine book text matter and (in bolder versions) newspaper headlines as well. Modern roman faces marked a departure from the practice of patterning types from handwriting and lettering. These were letters designed specifically for the printing process. The mark of mechanization, of industry, was upon them.

And then came the avalanche of new faces in the nineteenth century: the fat faces, the antiques and Egyptians, the sans serifs. They came to answer a need for boldness and blackness, for advertisers especially, who needed attention-getting types.

The English, in the main, designed them. Fat faces were wide versions of romans, bearing the blackness of the early gothics. Egyptian types were composed of strokes of uniform thickness, and at their terminals lay unbracketed, slablike serifs. Sans serif types—first cut by William Caslon IV—had strokes of uniform thickness; serifs were missing. Caslon called his letters "Egyptian," too (things Egyptian were "in" at the time), but the term did not stick. "Sans serif" did—and then an old standby, "gothic," and later "grotesque" (descriptive term!) served as names, and still do.

The Point System

We must concern ourselves not only with type style but also with type size.

The typographer has a unique system for measuring types. The key word is "point." There are 72 points to the inch; a half-inch is 36 points; a quarter-inch, 18 points.

"Pica" is particularly useful as a unit of measurement. Worth 12 points, it divides an inch into handy units of six. Points are used mainly to measure type sizes, picas to measure column and picture widths and depths. A column of copy 3 inches wide would be, using printers' terminology, 18 picas wide. The designer finds it easier to work in pica units than in sixteenths. Picas and half-picas provide 12 units to the inch. Twelve is more dividable than 16.

Types vary in size—in the heights of their capitals—from 5½ points to 72 points; and, in some styles, they go even larger, and even smaller. The letters never are quite as high as their point size. The measurement is taken from the slug on which the type is cast; there has to be a little room left over for the descending strokes that go below the base line.

Standard sizes are, for body types, 5½, 6, 7, 8, 9, 10, 11, and 12; for display types, 14, 18, 24, 30, 36, 42, 48, 60, and 72. These sizes all used to have proper names: agate (5½) and pica (12) remain useful.

You may be surprised as you compare faces in the same point size. They will

Careful editing and visual emphasis make the important words in series of quotations stand out and read like a headline. Client: Royal Viking Line. Agency: Goodby, Berlin & Silverstein. Art director: Tracy Wong. Copywriter: David Fowler.

not appear to be in the same size. One may have a small x-height, the other a large x-height; the baselines may even be on different levels, making for differences in the length of the descenders. Some faces come in what is called "titling" form: That is, only in caps, with the caps occupying nearly all of the available letter height. Such caps would be considerably larger than ordinary caps in the same point size.

A single face, in its various sizes—certainly in its various weights—changes character. For instance, as the size of the type gets smaller, the counter area increases in proportion to the size of the letter. Otherwise, in the very small sizes, it might be so small heavy inking would fill it in.

Some faces are designed to be wider than others. When you want to pad your copy block, you might well choose such a type—a much better practice than adding unnecessary words. Baskerville is a wider-than-average typeface. Some faces—the extended faces—carry width to an extreme. Others—the condensed faces—carry it to the other extreme.

Categories of Type

We can classify types broadly into four basic categories (sometimes called "races"):

■ *Romans.* Roman letters make use of both thick and thin strokes, which bring some variety to the letters. Hooked on at the terminal points of the strokes are the serifs. It is possible to put the romans into three subcategories: old style, modern, and transitional. In the old-style romans the difference between the thick strokes and the thin strokes is not great, and the serifs seem to merge into the main strokes; they are triangular in shape, sometimes somewhat cupped.

The thickest part of the strokes in the rounds of the letters—as in *C, G,* and *O*—fall at points that are on a diagonal. The axis of the old-style romans, in other words, is tipped—as it happens, to the left.

Often the old-style romans have a hand-cut look about them; slight imperfections add to their charm. The left top serif on the *T* may slant in one direction, the right top serif may be just slightly off that angle. There is a subtlety to these letters that other letters do not have.

The letters are based on early roman letters, especially those carved in that majestic column in Rome honoring the Emperor Trajan. Many typographers consider them even today the most beautiful of all our letters—and the most readable.

Two of many families that fall under the old-style roman heading are Caslon and Garamond.[2]

In modern romans the difference between the thick strokes and the thin

ABCDEFGHIJKL
MNOPQRSTUV
WXYZ
abcdefghijklmnopq
rstuvwxyz
1234567890

In the opinion of many art directors, one of the most beautiful roman faces ever designed was Baskerville, shown here in an 18-point size. Baskerville is used mostly as body type.

These representative display or headline faces are broken down into series. Some of these faces come in body-type sizes, too. Each of the italic faces is available in an upright version. Most of the faces are available in other weights. Ultra Bodoni italic is a modern roman. Optima is a sans serif, but one that looks a little like a roman because of its classic design. Can you put each of the others in its proper "race"?

Ultra Bodoni Italic Optima **BROADWAY** *Garamond Italic* **Lydian**

Stymie Light **Eurostile Bold Extended** *Palatino Italic* **P. T. Barnun**

Franklin Gothic Condensed **Franklin Gothic Wide** *Kaufmann Script* **Brush**

Century Schoolbook *Century Schoolbook Italic* **Spartan Black** *Mistral*

BALLOON EXTRABOLD Caslon No. 540 **Caslon Bold Condensed** Engravers Old English

COPPERPLATE GOTHIC HEAVY *Commercial Script* Cheltenham Medium

ABCDEFGHIJK LMNOPQRSTU VWXYZ
abcdefghijklmno pqrstuvwxyz
1234567890

One of the most useful of the new-wave, Swiss-inspired gothics is Helvetica, shown here in an 18-point size, medium weight.

strokes is more pronounced, and the serifs are stiff and straight. The thickest parts of the rounds are on a horizontal line. Not quite as readable as the old-style letters, they still are useful and actually preferred by some typographers.

They look best on slick paper.

The best known of the modern romans is Bodoni, which comes in a great variety of sizes, weights, even styles. Today's Bodonis are somewhat removed in character from the original Bodoni types.

Some of the roman types just do not fit in the two main subcategories. They have some of the old-style character, some of the modern. That beautiful face called Baskerville is lighter than the usual old style, but less mechanical than the modern. Ditto Times Roman, a form of which you are now reading. We call such romans "transitional."

Art directors love the standard old-style, modern, and transitional romans—the Caslons, the Garamonds, the Bodonis, the Baskervilles, the Times Romans—but occasionally they look for a more relaxed roman, one with an oddity of character. Such a face is ITC (for International Typeface Corporation) Souvenir, a face widely used by advertisers in the 1970s and 1980s. The example below shows you some of the face's characteristics: the bowed look of the *v,* for instance, and the unfinished lower loop of the *g.*

ITC Souvenir Light

■ *Sans serifs.* These are faces with strokes of even thickness. No serifs terminate the lines. Without the horizontalizing offered by serifs, the eye, some typographers say, has trouble getting from letter to letter. Readability is impaired. And the even thickness of the strokes makes for monotony.

But some of the sans serifs are designed to overcome this. If readability is a problem with sans serifs, it is basically a problem brought about by uniqueness. We are not used to columns set in sans serif types. Perhaps in the future sans serifs will be seen more often in body types. And we will find them every bit as readable as the romans.

Right now sans serifs appeal to almost everyone as headline faces.

Sans serif faces come in three distinct varieties: the Bauhaus-inspired sans serifs with their T-square, triangle, and compass look, like Futura and Spartan; the Swiss-inspired gothics and the grotesques with their less geometric, more sophisticated look, like Helvetica and Univers; and the types that have the thicks and thins of romans but not the serifs, like the beautiful Optima, the not-so-beautiful Radiant, and the funky Broadway type.

■ *Slab serifs.* Call them "square serifs" if you like. These letters have much of the character of the sans serifs (some students of type put them with the sans serifs), but they *do* have serifs, rather strong ones, in strokes that match the main strokes of the letters in thickness. In the past these letters have been known as "antiques" and "Egyptians." Some of the family names reflect the Egyptian influences: Cairo, Karnak, Stymie, Memphis. Another family name reflects the buildinglike quality of the letters: Girder.

Most slab serifs are quite unreadable in large doses of body copy. But for special kinds of advertising, slab serifs make good headlines. When the serifs are bracketed (when they merge gradually into the main strokes), and when some difference in stroke thickness is evident, as in the Clarendon faces, the type has considerably more grace and beauty than otherwise. Some type scholars put the Clarendons in a category by themselves, because from both a historical and a design standpoint, they have little in common with the basic slab serifs. Others class the Clarendons with the romans.

■ *Miscellaneous.* You may have seen other lists of faces that give Old English, Latins, scripts, even italics, separate headings. It is best for our purpose to combine all these under one heading, keeping them with the ornamental families that do not seem to fit any other category: faces like P. T. Barnum (with oversize serifs), Dom Casual (looks as if it were done with a

There are many pleasures to be found at Lakeshore Resort & Yacht Club in Hot Springs.

Along with the beautiful view of Lake Hamilton, you'll enjoy the convenience of having the beach and boat slips right in your front yard...guaranteed good fun for all water-sports! Our two bedroom villas feature complete kitchens plus all the amenities you expect from a first class resort. An indoor pool, whirlpool/hot tub, restaurant and tennis courts are located on site. Also available nearby are golfing, raquetball and horseback riding facilities.

So, when you're ready for that perfect getaway, call Lakeshore Resort & Yacht Club for our special rates. We'll make sure you have a great time.

Lakeshore Resort & Yacht Club

Highway 270 West, Hot Springs, Arkansas • 501-767-8408
Located adjacent to Sheraton Lakeshore Resort

Lakeshore Resort & Yacht Club, Hot Springs, Arkansas, puts its headline and copy block in reverse in a place where it acts as a backdrop for the club itself. A slab serif typeface like this is ideal for reversing. A mortise carries the abstract logo. Agency: Woods Brothers.

brush), Umbra (shadow letters), Balloon (looks as if a cartoonist did it), Cooper Black (a grocery handbill type that made something of a comeback in the 1960s), Peignot (with its French look), and other types with only occasional uses.

Old English, sometimes called "text," sometimes "black letter," sometimes (wrongly now) "gothic" has little value to advertisers. A lumber company manager might think it a dandy type for his letterhead, but the designer who understands typography will soon talk him out of it. If the company must have "dignity" in its printing, it will get it more easily with an old-style roman. Even a church will find old-style romans more fitting, and certainly more readable.

The *Latin letters* are characterized by oversize triangular serifs. The letters of some Latin families are wider than normal letters.

The *scripts* have never been very successful as types. One word describes most of them: phony. They are supposed to look like handwriting. Trouble is, they have little of the grace, none of the irregularity of handwriting. When a handwritten look is needed, the designer should turn to a lettering person or a calligrapher. National advertisers make little use of script types these days. But local advertisers who cannot afford original art do use them. Old standbys are the Brush and Kaufmann families.

One thing the designer soon learns when working with a script or Old English face: Never order it in all caps. In the Brush letters that follow, "TEACHING" is almost unreadable.

TEACHING JOB FOR YOU?

When script letters do not join, they should be called *cursive,* but the assigned family names in the cursives and scripts ignore the distinction. Some students have trouble distinguishing between cursives and roman italics, even though cursives seldom have the grace of italics.

Italics, from a historical standpoint, could be considered a separate type category, as could "Old English," but in the case of the italics, the slanting feature had been applied to all the other races—we have roman italic, sans serif italic, and so on. So the designer today thinks of italics as a *form* of any of the main categories.

The categories to stick with for most ads are the romans, the sans serifs, and, to a limited extent, the slab serifs—and their italics. The other categories contain too many faces that are affected, too cute, unreadable. Type should not upstage the message.

Once in a while one of the decorative faces gets rediscovered by an eager young designer, who uses it. A few others use it. And until everyone jumps on the bandwagon and spoils the party, the type is hot for a while. But it soon crawls back into its hole.

With so many different cars on the market, each looking for an image, some art directors turn to unique and exclusive typefaces for advertising headlines. At Scali McCabe Sloves in the early 1970s, art director John Danza studied established Swedish and German typefaces for inspiration for a special face for Volvo. The squared sans serif capitals with rounded corners he came up with have come to be associated with Volvo, helping the reader quickly sort out Volvo ads from ads sponsored by other car makers.

Families, Series, and Fonts

Fitting into the several categories are the many "families" of types. The families are divided into series, and the series are divided into fonts. Modern roman, for instance, would be a category, Bodoni would be a family in that category, Ultra

1234567890
1234567890

Some typefaces, especially those falling into the old-style roman category, offer two kinds of numbers: one regular, the other with some small units and units with descending strokes that dip below the baseline. These are numbers found in Caledonia, a face designed by W. A. Dwiggins for Linotype.

A piece of art forms one of the letters for this ad for the Swiss National Tourist Office, Zurich, Switzerland. To emphasize height, the designer uses a condensed version of a typeface much like Cooper Black. The copy inside the map of Switzerland extends the theme: "There's a mountain of wonderful reasons why so many experienced travelers in Europe vacation in Switzerland."

g g g g g g g g gg

This selection of lowercase *gs* shows some of the variations of that letter found in both roman and sans serif families.

Bodoni would be a series within that family (it is a fat letter with unusual stroke contrast), and 24-point Ultra Bodoni would be a font in that series.

A typeface family often gets its name from the person who designed the face. Caslon came from William Caslon, an English engraver. Baskerville came from John Baskerville, an English writing master. Bodoni came from Giambattista Bodoni, an Italian printer. People like these are now called type designers. They may be responsible for a number of faces, not just faces that bear their names, and they are likely to design typefaces fulltime.

Type Designers

A few type designers in England at the turn of the century—William Morris among them—revolted against the garish faces then so popular and brought out revivals of the earlier faces of Nicolas Jenson, Aldus Manutius, and others of the fifteenth-century Venetian school. Morris, the medievalist, interested in a heavy-textured type page, also designed an "Old English" that was readable—unusual for such a face.

No other day makes you feel this way.

THRILL

At Sea World you're not a spectator who sits passively by and watches the entertainment. In fact, you're not really a spectator at all.

TOUCH

Because at our park you become involved, you interact.

Whether it's at the Shamu® Killer Whale Show, where you experience the incredible thrill that comes from seeing 5000 lb. killer whales catapult through the air. (And, of course, the wetness you feel if you're one of those splashed when the whales land.) Or the very different feeling you have—the infectious giggling and laughter—that comes from seeing the outrageous new Pirate Water Ski Show, Sea World Animal Secret Show or hilarious Sea Lion and Otter Show.

There's also the total sense of awe and fascination at the Shark Encounter™—the result of staring face to face with one of nature's most feared

creatures. As well as the incredible warmth and closeness you feel when touching and hugging and feeding and petting our animals.

Which brings up something else about a day at Sea World. At our park you won't find signs that say "Please don't feed the animals." We actually encourage you to feed and pet our animals. We have a dolphin feeding pool where you can do just that. And the Baby Shamu Celebration where, if you're lucky enough to be selected, you can hug a killer whale, maybe even kiss one.

GIGGLE These aren't the kinds of things you can do at most parks. They're the kinds of things you can only do at one park.

Sea World. Where no other day makes you feel this way.

Sea World
ORLANDO

GASP

Boldface sans serif words, with art standing in for some of the letters, take the reader on a ride through the copy for a Sea World of Florida, Inc., ad. Agency: DDB-Needham, Los Angeles. Art director: Bob Kuperman. Copywriter: John Stein.

TYPOGRAPHY

Among type designers in America, Thomas Maitland Cleland, Daniel B. Updike, Bruce Rogers, Frederic W. Goudy, William A. Dwiggins, and Will Bradley stand out. Cleland styled *Fortune* magazine and later the experimental newspaper of the 1940s, *PM*. Updike became the nation's foremost typographic historian. Rogers became famous for the Bibles he designed and for several typefaces, primarily Centaur. Goudy designed several faces, including an old-style roman that bears his name. Dwiggins designed fine books for Alfred A. Knopf and designed several faces for Linotype, including Caledonia, the face used for the first edition of this book. Bradley designed faces for the American Type Founders.

Hermann Zapf stands out as a contemporary type designer. Among the many faces he has designed are Palatino, Optima, and Melior, examples of which you see here. The faces come in a variety of weights, of course, and, like most faces, their true beauty comes through better in the regular rather than the bolder versions. But advertisers tend to prefer bold weights, at least for their headlines.

Newer Zapf faces include Zapf Book, Zapf Chancery, and Zapf International, all developed for the International Typeface Corporation.

Zapf believes that type designers should not adapt classic designs to the present but should, instead, come up with new designs appropriate to today's printing technology. "We should show our respect for the typography of the past by not using it as a cheap source of ideas."[3]

Type designer Ed Benguiat says he and others in the business design type by looking at people. Type changes as fashion changes. "When skirts got short, something had to happen to the ascenders and descenders of the typeface."[4]

Tom Carnase was involved in the designing of logos for *New York* and *Esquire* and L'eggs pantyhose. But he is best known for the typefaces he has designed: more than fifty of them, including Avant Garde Gothic, which he created in collaboration with the late Herb Lubalin. Lubalin greatly influenced the course of graphic design in this country until his death in 1981. He designed a number of other typefaces, including Serif Gothic and Lubalin Graph. He was a founder of *U&lc.,* a lively magazine of typography, and the International Typeface Corporation.

Today's type designers must create faces that fit computer-generated letterforms. Their letters must accept the digitizing required. Zapf has found that his Optima, for instance, does not take to digitized storage.[5]

One of the most respected of the modern type-designing firms is International Typeface Corporation. One of its many faces, available from a number of suppliers, is ITC Benguiat, shown here in a medium weight. Another roman, it is a face with a good deal of character. Some might classify it as an eccentric face. Note the pulled-out look at the bottom of the *C;* the small, triangular upper loop on the *B;* and the cramped, squatty look of the *g.*

Palatino Semi-Bold
Optima Semi-Bold
Melior Semi-Bold

These are three of the many typefaces designed by Hermann Zapf. Of course, they come in various weights and sizes.

ITC Benguiat

International Typeface Corporation licenses its hundreds of faces to manufacturers of all kinds of typesetting equipment and press-on and dry-transfer type sheets and to software companies.

Letterform artists, calligraphers, and others who love typefaces can design new typefaces and submit them to International Typeface Corporation for consideration. Its review board makes decisions based on the beauty, uniqueness, and practicality of the face. The company wants typefaces that work both for display and text settings and in both uprights and italics in several weights. Designers earn flat fees plus royalties on sales.[6]

The Variety of Faces

The typical printer's type-specimen book displays a bewildering number of faces. But with two or three standard faces in all their various sizes and weights, the designer often has all that's needed.

When asked to design a good book typeface, Edward Johnston replied: "There is one already." The implication was that one good face was enough.

Kurt Weidemann, the German typographer, has said that "three thousand typefaces are no progress, but a declaration of bankruptcy. To communicate a message effectively, ten typefaces and ten times ten ways of typographic arrangement are more than enough."

"Most graphics today are like explosions of garbage through the stratosphere," observes George Lois, chairman and creative director of Lois Pitts Gershon Pon/GGK, New York. "It's like MTV with images of type blowing up all over the place. Everything's a mess. . . ."

"A lot of people are thoroughly abusing typefaces today," adds Jeff Level, type-research director at Monotype Inc.[7]

Helmut Krone of Doyle Dane Bernbach says, "I'm not looking for obscure typefaces. You need to have a damn good reason not to use Helvetica, Goudy or Times Roman."

"It's not the choice of typeface as much as the way you use it," adds George Lois. "If you know what you're doing you can just use Franklin Gothic and Helvetica for the rest of your life and each campaign will look different."[8]

See the variety you can get in a single font—a single face in a single size:

ALL CAPS
SMALL CAPS
CAPS AND SMALL CAPS
Caps and Lower Case
all lower case
ALL CAPS ITALICS
Caps and Lowercase Italics
all lowercase italics

Then, staying in the same face and size, but adding boldface, you get eight more varieties. Many faces come not only in regular and bold but also in several other weights, from extra light to ultra bold. Further, you can get some faces in expanded (wide) and condensed (narrow) versions.

Finally, you can l e t t e r s p a c e.

Multiply these by the hundreds of *different* typefaces, then by the several sizes in each face, and you get some idea of the great variety of typefaces available.

Still, the type-design houses keep introducing new faces.

Much can be said in defense of them, even though their design violates much of what many of us learned from earlier typographers and type designers. True, these new faces—many of them—*are* eccentric. In place, line after line, they present a pattern that is busy. Yet, in small takes the faces can be lively and useful. They *are* a change of pace. And in short headlines they are readable enough and so full of character as to nicely amplify what the words themselves are saying.

Although some type-design houses have been pressing for it for years, typefaces do not enjoy copyright protection. Hence new faces, once introduced, are soon duplicated by other houses that give the faces different but similar names. Paladium, for instance, is almost a dead ringer for the classical, calligraphic Palatino. Oracle duplicates the handsome, serifless roman Optima. Helios has the modern look of Helvetica. Century Textbook looks like Century Schoolbook, California looks like Caledonia, English Times and Press Roman look like Times Roman.

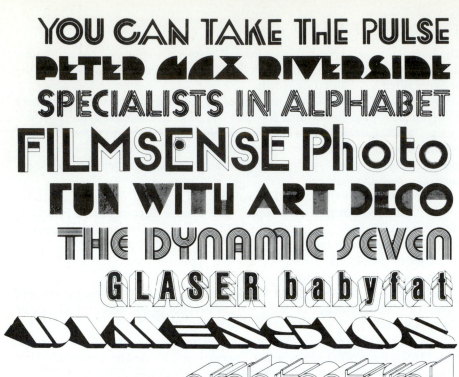

YOU CAN TAKE THE PULSE

PETER MAX RIVERSIDE

SPECIALISTS IN ALPHABET

FILMSENSE Photo

FUN WITH ART DECO

THE DYNAMIC SEVEN

GLASER babyfat

DIMENSION

architectural

THREE DIMENSIONAL magic gives

Seymour Chwast ArtTone

THE FAT'S IN THE

GRUMPY'S LARGE

JURY YOKES LIQUOR CZAR

PHOTO PSYCHEDELITYPE

TOO MUCH TENSION

CHWAST BLIMP

WHAT DIRECTION

I: COMPUTER MAGNETIC

PAPERCLIPS TO KEEP your message

Double Header Sunday

HOBO OUTLINE gives greater

This lineup shows a few of the thousands of novelty display typefaces created by Photo-Lettering, Inc., New York. The names of these faces:

- Mierop Inline
- Peter Max Riverside Drive
- Neon
- Glaser Filmsense
- Bifur Graphic
- Prisma Bauhaus
- Glaser Babyfat Outline
- Cenotaph
- Delacroce Beta #1
- Allen Sculpture
- Chwast Art Tone
- Obese
- Bordanaro Grumpy Open
- Rosenblum Razzamataz
- Jefferson Aeroplane
- Tenison
- Chwast Blimp
- Calypso
- Magnetic Ink
- Julino Paperclip
- Benquiat Chrisma Contour
- Hobo Outline

Type Preferences

Graphic designers using the faces often develop strong preferences for one over the others. Their preferences change as times change and new faces become available. That everyone else uses a face can be a discouraging factor. Helvetica, possibly the most popular sans serif face ever designed, has recently come in for some criticism.

Peter Rauch, art director of *Money,* says he would "never specify Helvetica outside the borders of Switzerland." He contends that roman faces are more believable than sans serif faces. They are also "more humanistic." For a poster announcing the availability of International Typeface Corporation's version of Garamond at Typographics, a typesetting firm, Jack Summerford featured a big "Helvetica"—set, of course, in Garamond.

The choice of a typeface should depend not on a designer's personal preference but instead on the appropriateness of the type to the ad's message and readers. Typefaces do carry moods. A mood can be important in the choice of a face for an ad's headline.

Some art directors are too busy keeping up with changes in design thinking and technological advances to keep up with changes in typography. That's why an increasing number of art directors and their agencies rely on the help and advice of people rather new to the business: type directors.[9]

Type Moods

Type can be graceful, powerful, quiet, loud, beautiful, ugly, old fashioned, modern, simple, decorative. The roman faces suggest a classic mood, the sans serifs a contemporary mood, but this should not prevent your using Baskerville for young professionals or Futura for retirees. And if you want a mood to be obvious, you can turn to one of the offbeat faces.

For instance, Hobo, designed in 1910, has an art nouveau feel. Not a graceful face, it still would be an appropriate face to go with art from that period.

Hobo

One of Photo-Lettering's recent faces is Moore Digital Upright, shown below. If you were looking for a headline face to sell digital clocks, this might be the one to use.

DIGITAL

And if you want to suggest that something is changing to better fit its environment, you could turn to Photo-Lettering's Allen Chameleon.

CHAMELEON

Many of the one-of-a-kind typefaces Photo-Lettering Inc. has offered to advertising art directors over the years have been converted to PostScript by Adobe Systems, Inc. and TrueType formats by Alphabets & Images, Inc., which means they are now available for the Mac and PC.

When you decide to run a headline in color ink, you choose a typeface a little larger, a little fatter than you would choose for black ink. This will compensate for the lack of darkness. When you decide to run a headline in reverse, you choose a face that does not have small, weak serifs. The sans serifs are best for reversing. Bodoni among the romans would be a poor choice.

Six 36-point alphabets illustrating main type categories: (left page) old-style roman, transitional roman, modern roman; (right page) sans serif, slab serif, miscellaneous. Families represented: Garamond, Times Roman, Bodoni; News Gothic, Clarendon, Cooper Black. Notice that some 36-point faces look bigger than others (because of differences in boldness and in x-heights). Notice the differences in alphabet widths. Clarendon, classed here as slab serif, has some of the characteristics of a modern roman; Cooper Black (the grocery store type), classed here as miscellaneous, has some characteristics of old-style roman.

ABCDEFGHIJKLMNOPQRSTUVWXY
abcdefghijklmnopqrstuvwxyz
$1234567890 .,-:;!?"'&

ABCDEFGHIJKLMNOPQRST
VWXYZ
abcdefghijklmnopqrstuvwxyz
$1234567890 .,-:;!?"'&

ABCDEFGHIJKLMNOPQRSTUVWXY
abcdefghijklmnopqrstuvwxyz
$1234567890 .,-:;!?"'&

ABCDEFGHIJKLMNOPQRSTUVWXYZ
abcdefghijklmnopqrstuvwxyz
$1234567890 .,-:;!?"&

ABCDEFGHIJKLMNOPQ
RSTUVWXYZ
abcdefghijklmnopqrstuvw
xyz
$1234567890 .,-:;!?'""&

ABCDEFGHIJKLMNOPQRS
TUVWXYZ
abcdefghijklmnopqrstuv
wxyz
$1234567890 .,-:;!?"&

On Mixing Types

Ideally, you would stick to the same type family for any one job, getting your variety through changes in both size and blackness, and by turning to condensed and expanded versions and to italics. But often a single face is not versatile enough. Or the printer does not have a full range in any one family. And so you mix types.

The mixing of one *body* face with another *headline* face is not so vital a matter as the mixing of one *headline* face with another *headline* face.

For most ads you should confine your mixing to two faces—or three, at the most. Four or more faces in headlines create a hodgepodge.

You should be less concerned with historical factors—types designed at the same period do not necessarily go together—than with the character of the letters. Caslon and Bodoni faces, for instance, both designed in the eighteenth century, do not go together; one is an old-style roman, the other a modern roman. Common sense tells you that an old-style and a modern type do not go together. This is true especially for the romans.

Sans serifs are another matter. A good sans serif can be used with almost any other type. In mixing, it is considered a neutral type. Types that should not be mixed with sans serif are the slab serifs (they are too much like the sans serifs in basic structure) or Old English (which should be combined only with romans).

To lay down a set of rules on type mixing is impossible. Type mixing is so much a matter of taste. And in the right hands, almost any combination, for certain effects, is workable.

Perhaps this rule will help: The types you mix should be either very similar or very dissimilar. If one of the types is almost-but-not-quite like the other type, the reader will sense that something is amiss.

The Case for Readability

It should not be necessary to argue for so obvious an ideal as readability. But the new crop of student designers each year continues to insist on making headline letters and copy blocks "different"—understandable in light of the hush that comes over teachers in the elementary and secondary schools as their young charges engage in their acts of creativity.

The typical student has to learn that, when working with type, being different is seldom a virtue.

The reader has no time to learn a new alphabet or variation; familiar type design and arrangement do the best jobs for advertisers.

What is the reader used to?

- *Capitals and lower case, not all capitals.*
- *Letters reading from left to right, not up and down.*
- *Lines of type running horizontally, not on a diagonal.*
- *Letters and words with even spacing.*

So, as a designer, you are well advised to avoid all-cap headlines, headlines with letters arranged stepladder fashion, tilted display lines, and peculiar spacing. Make it easy for the reader. Do not let the type upstage the advertiser's message.

Professor David A. Wesson of Marquette University's College of Journalism questions some of the arguments that roman faces are more readable than sans serif faces. "Because differences are slight . . . the decision to use a face will remain largely aesthetic and situational."

He says that "if there is an edge for romans, it may be that the added strokes to many letters may assist readability by providing additional information—in the classic Information Theory sense—to ambiguous letter combinations. A case in point is the word 'Illinois,' which, set in a monotonal sans serif, is a real eye-stopper."

He cites Univers as a nonambiguous sans serif because it mimics the thick and thin strokes of the roman faces, adding information that makes it close to roman in readability. Optima, less subtle in its thick and thin strokes, is another example. Even so, Wesson advises romans for long columns of body copy.[10]

Menagerie Mime Theatre

Typography is a subtle art. The headline accompanying the nicely framed line-conversion art at the left suffers somewhat from poor optical spacing between lines. There seems to be more space between "Menagerie" and "Mime" than between "Mime" and "Theatre." The handling at the right shows one way of solving the problem. In the new handling note the diagonal axis formed by the *i, i,* and *t.*

Norwegian Caribbean Lines uses tight-fitting all caps for the headline over a two-page magazine ad—and all caps for the body copy, too. But the body copy is heavily leaded to keep it readable. The copy partially wraps around the clever headline. Agency: McKinney and Silver. Art director: Larry Bennett. Copywriter: Steve Bassett. Photographer: Randy Miller.

Menagerie Mime Theatre

Body Copy

The size of the typeface affects the width of the column. The bigger the face, the wider the column can be. Some designers believe the copy block should be about as wide as an alphabet-and-a-half—thirty-nine characters—of lowercase letters. When they want copy to spread over a wider area, they break it into two or more columns.

The copy in this book is set in columns twice as wide as they should be, according to the thirty-nine-characters rule, but the numerous subheads and art pieces and the generous gutter margins help overcome readability problems. A two-column-per-page format would complicate the handling of art in the book.

Your copy block or column can take these forms:

■ *Fully justified.* Left and right edges are perpendicular. Stated differently, the copy is flush left, flush right. This is the normal way of setting copy.

■ *Flush left, ragged right.* The right edge is ragged as on a manuscript produced by a typist. This is seldom used in long blocks. But actually, because we are accustomed to typewriter copy, and because ragged right means more uniform word spacing, such copy possibly is easier to read than justified copy. A few newspapers are experimenting with such composition for their news columns. And many book publishers are using it for art books. Specialty magazines, including company magazines, seem to prefer it. And, to suggest warmth and informality, annual reports increasingly are using it.

Flush left, ragged right setting results in less hyphenation at ends of lines as well as more even spacing between words. If you do not mind an extra-ragged looking right edge on your copy block, you can order a flush-left setting that eliminates all hyphenation.

■ *Flush right, ragged left.* In this kind of setting, the left edge rather than the right edge is ragged. Now this is a different matter. The eye has to hunt its

place after each line, and the reader is slowed. But in short takes, flush right, ragged left typography can be effective, as for a fashion advertisement. Use it sparingly.

■ *Ragged left and right.* This setting is better for multiline headlines than for copy. Sometimes it works for small sections of body type. The silhouette the copy makes certainly has character. Sometimes the silhouette takes a recognizable shape—geographic, facial, or whatever. It is easy to be too cute with this form of typography.

■ *Each line centered.* In short takes, this setting works well enough, especially if the ad needs a classical or formal look. Such setting, though, is a novelty.

If copy is long it is sectioned into paragraphs. Paragraph beginnings should be noted with indentations and extra spacing—or both. Some designers forego both indentations and extra spacing, leaving each new paragraph marked only by space that may occur at the end of the last line of the preceding paragraph. Other designers run the copy as one long take, letting dingbats mark where paragraphs begin.

An initial letter—the first letter of the first paragraph writ large—enables the reader to make the adjustment from the large headline type to the small body type, but some designers consider initials as dated. If you use initials, you have several kinds to consider: initials rising higher than the other letters in the first line, or sticking out at the left, or buried in the block. The remainder of the first word can be set in caps or small caps to further ease the reader into the copy block.

How ever the type is set and in whatever style and size, it should always be leaded by at least a couple of points. A little space between lines adds greatly to readability.

Display Type

The rules for typography—the rules for readability—break down a bit when you get to display types, especially when you have only a few words to contend with. In display types, you can crowd, tip, fit in and under, screen down—and still not hurt readability much.

Almost anything goes. The Lady Carpenter Institute of Building & Home Improvement Inc., New York, used this headline on an ad for "creative survival classes."

Swissair ended the headline for an ad with the word *sleep* and, to dramatize it, laid the letters on their backs. The period after the words makes the arrangement obvious.

Some typographic tricks are best performed by a lettering artist or a pasteup artist using reproduction proofs. Others can be done on the computer. The computer can change one dimension of type (expanding or condensing the type) while holding another dimension. It can slant the letters either to the left or right, put them in perspective, put them in an arc or circle, convert them to outline letters, twist them, or otherwise distort them. The equipment can do the same thing with artwork. Obviously the designer should use such tricks sparingly.

If this copy seems more obscure than some of the other copy in this book, it is because it is not copy at all but greeking, a dry-transfer material used on finished layouts and comps (but not mechanicals) to simulate copy. You would rub it onto your layout in the same way you would rub on dry-transfer letters. Greeking is also available in page-layout software for computers.

The Nature Company for one of its ads starts copy in a display size, then, line by line, moves down to normal size. This style of typography eliminates the need for a headline and encourages readers to keep reading. Agency: Goodby, Berlin & Silverstein. Art director: Tracy Wong. Copywriter: David Fowler.

Corner Audio, a high-fi store in Portland, uses highly-leaded body type to superimpose one column of boldface type over two columns of regular-weight type. It is an unusual but still readable handling of type, helped by a color block under the column of boldface type. Designer Michael Satterwhite puts the Corner Audio logo in a corner, of course. This is the cover of a 5½ × 8½ folder designed for customers and potential customers.

When you want a headline with more than one line, avoid arranging the lines—squeezing and expanding them—to fit a geometric shape. This is an old-time newspaper headline practice that, unfortunately, has been brought back by computer users. Certainly "inverted pyramids" and flush-left–flush-right headlines have little to recommend them to advertising designers.

You should avoid changing type as you move from line to line in a single headline. You want your headline to appear as a unit.

Calligraphy

Hand-drawn letters and handwriting do a job for advertisers that machine- and even computer-set type can never do. For headlines on institutional ads, formal ads, and ads with headlines displayed more prominently than usual, designers turn to the calligrapher rather than the typographer.

"Calligraphy" means, simply, "elegant handwriting." Calligraphic letters combine a certain freedom with a certain order. For some jobs they stand separately, as type does; for others, they merge into each other in a sort of advanced stage of penmanship.

The father of modern calligraphy is Ludovico Degli Arrighi, a sixteenth-century scribe, whose *La Operina,* perhaps the world's first handwriting manual, still merits scrutiny. His particular style—there are a number of styles—became known as "chancery cursive." His tool was the broad-nib pen. His slightly slanting strokes were quick, sometimes connected, sometimes not. The style is neither re-

Wo der Geist des Herrn ist, da ist Freiheit.

where the spirit of the Lord is, there is liberty.

PAUL/SECOND CORINTHIANS 3:17

strictive nor precise. Some of the beauty of chancery cursive lies in the imperfections of the strokes.

Since World War II we have seen a renaissance in the use of chancery cursive—or "italic handwriting," as some call it.

Punctuation in Display Type

"Don't worry too much about punctuation. We know an editor who agonized so much over a colon that he got colitis and ended up with a semicolon," wrote Alden S. Wood in *Reporting,* a defunct magazine for industrial editors. But *someone* has to worry about punctuation. Nowhere is correct punctuation more important than in display type, where errors are so harsh, so noticeable. Designers, in their haste, often are responsible for them.

Allen Q. Wong, professor of art at Oregon State University, demonstrates the beauty of calligraphy in this two-language inscription. He skillfully combines three different letterforms into a single unifying design. Part of the beauty of the piece of art (and that's what it is) comes from the dry-brush texture in the Old English letterform. Note the condensed nature of the Old English and the closeness of its fit.

For certain kinds of headlines, a set typeface cannot give you the flair and personality that hand lettering gives. Marilyn Holsinger, graphic designer, calligrapher, and art professor, demonstrates with this quickly drawn script, done with brush-and-ink. This is a first try. Often lettering artists like Holsinger redo some of the letters several times for just the right effect, then patch the letters together. The camera ignores the patching. For this word, Holsinger would redo the *c* to make it as heavy as the other letters, and, to stress the informality of this lettering, she would bounce the letters a bit. Right now they line up too severely, she feels.

October

Elizabethan Lyrics FROM THE ORIGINAL TEXTS *chosen, edited and arranged* BY Norman Ault

This book jacket was designed in 1949 by Oscar Ogg for William Sloan Associates, the publisher. The beautiful calligraphy is not only appropriate but also timeless. In the original, the large lettering is black, the smaller lettering and border red, the decorations green.

Misused quotation marks can be more a problem than omitted ones. Consider this headline for an ad for Scott Tissues:

**Don't let this
"SO-CALLED BARGAIN"
fool you!**

The writer meant, of course, SO-CALLED "BARGAIN," with the quote marks only around bargain. The people who are fooled by so-called "bargains" do not go around calling them "so-called bargains"; they call them, simply, "bargains." The "so-called" is the copywriter's editorializing; as a matter of fact, when quote marks are used with "bargain," editorializing is already accomplished; the "so-called" is not even needed.

To save space, newspaper headline writers use single rather than double quote marks in headlines, but advertisers need not follow this practice. (No problem for the British: They wisely use single quote marks throughout, except, of course, when they have a quote within a quote.)

Newspaper headline writers never use periods in headlines, but advertisers often do. Using periods, you are able to show two complete sentences in a headline. You do not have to go to a new typeface for the second sentence. You are able to present two parallel thoughts. You are able to deliver a one-two punch.

Maybe you will use a little white space to separate the two sentences, and maybe not.

Sometimes you need two pieces of punctuation after a line, because no one piece will do the job. Some typefaces provide interrobangs—question marks merged with exclamation marks—but readers are not used to them. When you have a combination question-exclamation, you are better off doing what the *Christian Science Monitor* did in this heading for a subscription renewal notice: Use both a question mark and an exclamation mark.

Ordinarily you would avoid exclamation marks—they are an admission you could not bring enough excitement to the headline through legitimate design innovations. Nor should you rely on that much-overused device the ellipsis (a series of dots at the end of a headline), unless it is necessary to carry the reader across a page or panel to a connecting headline.

Word Emphasis

It is easy to fall into the trap of emphasizing a word in the headline by making it bigger or by setting it in another face. Designers who do this are unsure of themselves. They are like writers who overuse exclamation marks or italics.

Ordinarily a headline does not need internal graphic change of pace. When it does need it, the change of pace should involve a single word or phrase. If two different sections of the headline get the treatment, the two will cancel each other out.

In the following headline, Lady Madonna Maternity Boutique, New York, emphasized "PRETTY" by giving it its own line, but the real reason for the second line is to make the headline clear. If "PRETTY" had stayed up there with the other words, the headline would not have worked very well.

WE MAKE PREGNANT PRETTY

Spacing

Spacing becomes a prime consideration in composition. You could say that spacing is more important than type style or size.

The designer, not the printer or typesetter, must make most spacing decisions. The rule of good proportion comes up again; the designer tries to provide unequal space divisions between sections of typography (the space between the headline and the start of the copy will be different from the space between the end of the copy and the logotype), but not, of course, within a section, such as between lines within a block of body copy or lines within a headline. And if several copy blocks are preceded by same-size headlines, the space between the headline and the block of copy in each case would be the same. Consistency here is more important than variety.

Type is designed by the manufacturer so that the space between letters is constant. This is all right for smaller sizes, but in display sizes the equal spacing becomes unequal *optically*. The space between two As (AA), for instance, appears larger than the space between two Ms (MM). Advertising designers can see to it that some adjustment is made by the typesetter; in the layout, too, they will compensate for the spacing irregularity.

The beginning advertising designer soon tries the trick of adding uniform spaces between letters—letterspacing. It is best to avoid letterspacing because it inhibits readability. A more durable trend among designers is to take space away, to crowd the letters somewhat, especially in the sans serifs and gothics.

And it will take beginning designers a while to catch on to the fact that the spacing between *words* in type is really less than they think (about the width of an average-width lowercase letter). Too much space between words detracts from the unity of the headline and makes it hard to read.

Almost any type in its smaller, body sizes is made more readable, however, if a little extra spacing is provided between *lines*. Type can be leaded automatically as it is set or afterwards. Leading, of course, increases the depth of the copy block. It is possible to lead too much. This is the test for a copy block: Squint and look at it. If it appears as a rectangle of gray, fine. If it appears as a series of horizontal stripes, you have too much leading; if it appears as a solid, cramped pattern, you have too little. A good rule of thumb: For advertising copy, always lead two points.

Indicating Type on the Layout

When using a computer to do a layout, you ordinarily manipulate real type, setting it as you go. When using traditional tools, you create the illusion of type.

If you don't use printed greeking, you show body-copy type simply by ruling a set of lines, one line for each line of type in the correct column width. Or you rule a set of double lines. The sets represent the x-height of the letters. Some designers like to show body copy on roughs as spiral-like lines. (See nearby illustration.)

WHEN SPORTS NEWS IS HOT, CALL A HOT REPORTER.

When you have a multiline headline, each line centered, it is a good idea to arrange words so that each line takes a different length; and the lengths should not grow progressively wider or narrower. Irregular lengths like these make for a more pleasing silhouette. Pacific Northwest Bell, in this all-caps headline for an ad promoting its Sportsphone, uses tight spacing not only between letters and words but also between lines. If each line carried more words, tight spacing like this might result in decreased readability.

How long has it been since you said, "Let me speak to someone in charge," and she said, "Speaking"?

Because punctuation does not have the weight of regular letters, many designers leave it outside any axis they set up in arranging lines in a headline. See how it works in this flush-left headline for a Research Information Center ad.

Four ways of indicating body copy on a rough layout using traditional tools. Body-copy indication should be line for line.

Indicating display type—headlines—takes a little more work.

Here is one way to do the job: Scribble the headline quickly at first on an odd-size sheet, trying to take up as much room as you know it will take up in type. Check the sheet with an alphabet of about the right face and size and decide on guidelines.

On another sheet, rule three guidelines for every line in the headline: a line for the top and for the bottom of the capitals and a line for the top of the x-height. You skip some space before ruling the next set; that skipped space is the interlinear channel. It can be a little bit less than the x-height if the type is to be set solid, or it can be considerably more if the type is leaded. But you must leave at least enough space for descending lowercase strokes. The x-height is usually a little more than half the cap-height space; but this depends, of course, upon the design of the face.

Rule your guidelines with a finely sharpened pencil. Rule them dark enough so you can see them without hunting for them but light enough so the reviewer of your work will not be conscious of them.

You might want to rule a series of vertical lines to help keep your letters perfectly upright—or a series of slightly diagonal lines for italics. The beginning designer tends to make italics slant too much. The slant is minimal.

Now you are ready to begin lettering. You can draw the letters freehand, or, using the alphabet sheet under your semi-transparent drawing sheet, trace them, moving the alphabet sheet back and forth as needed. Fill in the strokes where needed to give the headline its weight. Use pencil; and do not be afraid to erase when you need to. Too often students who find lettering a tedious job get caught up in a wrong size and refuse to make an adjustment because they have already invested too much time on the original.

Use a 2B or a 4B pencil for large display letters; something a little harder—as hard as an HB—for smaller letters. Hard-lead pencils hold their point better; and you need a sharp point for small letters.

Here are the six basic strokes and some rough lettering made with them. For roman letters, use a chisel-point pencil for the basic strokes, then go back and, with a sharp-point pencil, draw the serifs. Making sans serif letters with single strokes is a little more difficult; you must constantly change the pencil angle. As you move to more finished roughs, you will want to use the outline and fill-in method, drawing letters freehand or tracing them. Letters for the last two lines here were traced from 60-point Caslon and Futura Demibold alphabets.

You should not attempt to letter sizes any smaller then 14 points. Twelve points and below can be considered body type.

Even for rough layouts, try to imitate real letters. Do not make up your own alphabets. Put serifs where they belong. When lettering sans serif headlines, some students put serifs on the capital *I*. This is usually wrong. Typewriter typefaces may use serifs to give width to the *I*, and license-plate letters use serifs to help the police distinguish between *l* and *I*, but few sans serif typefaces come with serifs on any of the letters.

In lettering large-size types you should be concerned more about optical spacing than mechanical spacing. Allowances have to be made when parallel strokes fall next to each other and also when diagonal strokes running in opposite directions fall next to each other. Furthermore, certain letters should extend slightly over top and below bottom guidelines—the top of the *A,* for instance, and both the top and bottom of the *O.* Triangles and rounds of letters, in other words, should extend slightly beyond the guidelines.

When aligning headlines vertically—when lines are flush left—you make some allowance for optical illusion. The left leg of the *A,* for instance, can protrude slightly from the vertical alignment of lines. Some designers like to let quote marks fall outside the vertical alignment, feeling that the true edge of the line begins with the letters themselves.

When you get away from tracing the letters—when you draw them free-hand—watch particularly the relationship of the stroke width to the height of the letters. And watch the width of each letter—widths vary a great deal from letter to letter and from face to face. (One notable exception is Century Schoolbook, with its near sameness in letter width—a little like the type on the typewriter.)

Watch, too, the counters (enclosed spaces in lowercase letters). It is too easy for the amateur to increase or decrease counter space, greatly altering the character of the letter.

In lettering italics, notice that italic caps are very much like the upright caps, only sloped, while lowercase italics are quite different from lowercase uprights.

To understand where the thick and thin strokes fall in roman letters, you should try this exercise: Using a chisel-point pencil or, better, a Speedball pen in the "C" series, sketch out an alphabet of both capital and lowercase letters, first with the pen held at an angle, for old-style roman letters, then with the point held straight up, for modern roman letters. Remember, the angle is held constant, regardless of the stroke. (You may have to relax the angle somewhat when you make your *M, N, U,* and *Z.*)

The standard height of the capitals can be from five to ten times the width of the broad pen stroke (the boldness of the typeface would determine this).

When you have drawn the two roman alphabets in both upper and lower case,

A quick way of indicating a reverse is to scribble your "letters" in first, using *M*s and *W*s, then scrub strokes up to and around them.

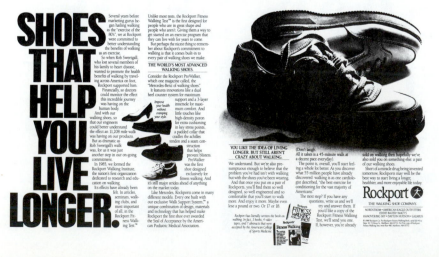

In a two-page magazine ad, Rockport, The Walking Shoe Company, breaks up a long block of copy by (1) arranging it into five unjustified columns, (2) varying the column lengths, (3) using subheads, (4) wrapping the copy around pieces of art, and (5) fitting the six-line, one-word-per-line headline into the left margin of the first column.

AN ENDLESS STREAM OF THE FRESHEST FISH

Conveniently located at the Brookline Village stop
on the MBTA Green line. Valet parking.
Open Monday thru Saturday 11 a.m. to 11 p.m.,
Sundays 12 noon till 10 p.m.

2 Brookline Place • Brookline, Massachusetts 02147 • (617) 232-8887

An ad for Skipjack's Seafood Emporium, Brookline, Massachusetts, lets a stylized fish swim through an "endless stream" of fish names, set in a screened sans serif type to contrast with the solid-black lines of the fish. The restaurant's slogan is "An endless stream of the *freshest* fish." Art director: Charlotte Bogardus. Designer: Warren Freedenfeld. Agency: Bogardus, Lowell & Pyle. Copywriter: Charlotte Bogardus.

try a sans serif alphabet. This time, you will have to change the pen angle with each stroke, twisting the wrist to give each stroke the full width of the point.

In doing these exercises, be sure your pencil or pen rests firmly on the paper before you begin each stroke. Otherwise you will get only part of the instrument's point width.

The exercises will not make a lettering artist out of you, but they will help develop in you a better appreciation of typography, even if you avoid a drawing board or table and do all your design work at a computer terminal.

Playing with Type

A little type playfulness goes a long way. Most graphic designers avoid it, feeling that readability, not trickery or even variety, is the key to good typography. But sometimes the trickery is useful.

When the Bellevue Art Museum in Washington put on a "Wearable Art" exhibit, designer Anne Traver created a direct-mail piece that used letters for the word "Art" that had fold-back tabs on them, like the tabs on clothes for paper dolls.

Playing with type takes place mostly in logos, headlines, titles, and other display settings and usually involves sans serifs rather than romans. All caps lend themselves to unusual treatment more readily than lowercase letters do. That's because lowercase letters are more complicated.

The experiments can be as simple as using outline letters and filling them in with something appropriate.

Some designers like to invent oddball alphabets, not for commercial use, necessarily, but to amuse themselves. Jeanine Holly, a freelance copywriter and sometimes artist, is one of these. She is the typophile who discovered that Campbell's Condensed Alphabet Soup has only seventeen letters. She wrote: "Several evenings ago, whilst entertaining myself with my favorite book, *The Design of Advertising,* I noted a few [typeface] omissions, which your postperson and I humbly bring to your attention. . . ."

Three of Holly's faces follow:

One is Gara-baldie. Its tie to Garamond is not pronounced. But if you are after a virile look in an advertising headline . . .

Another face is Noose Gothic, not to be confused with News Gothic. The new face might fit an ad with a Wild West theme. Unfortunately, the example submitted does not show the treatment Holly has in mind for such hard-to-hang letters as *I, J, L,* and *U.*

Still another face is Five O'Clock Shadow Xtra Heavy. Too bad the face was not available to newspapers and magazines during the Nixon presidency.[11]

Dover Publications, New York, offers art directors *Fantastic Alphabets,* twenty-four ready-to-use faces created by Jean Larcher, a good-humored French artist and designer. The example you see here is Crayon (French for "Pencil"), a face you might want to consider for the headline for an ad for office supplies.

Letters have long held a fascination for many people in advertising and related businesses. In a playful mood, Joshua Faigen of Downtown Type, Pittsburgh, worked up a "menu" of "type dinners." (All dinners included alphabet soup.) Among entrées:

Crunchy Caslon Cakes .... 12½ picas
Delectibly kerned and served on a bed of tender boiled semicolons.
Stymie Stew .... 8 picas
Delicious diphthongs and dot-leaders in a rich, justified broth.
Helvetica Cutlets with Asterisks .... 15½ picas
We'll gladly substitute Century Schoolbook Steaks for those who prefer serifs.

Robert Keding shows a block of body type set in Adobe Times Roman before kerning (above) and after kerning (below). He uses a software program here called KernEdit.

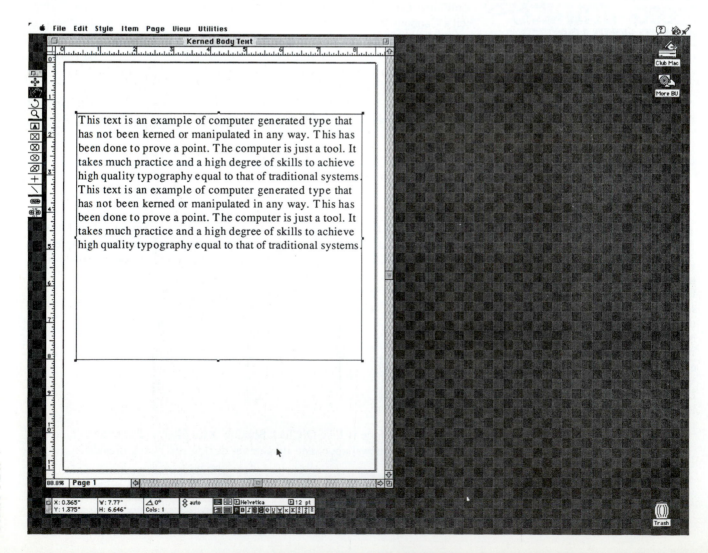

Typography and Technology

One of the results of the computer revolution has been a decline in typographic excellence. The hardware and software of desktop publishing got the blame at first, but as technology improved and new programs came along, many of the early problems disappeared. For instance, in the new programs, designers could get better spacing and truer hyphenation.

The typesetting problems we still have involve the people—some of them—who operate the equipment. They know computers, all right, but they do not know typography. They can't help calling up all the tricks, using all the faces. Old-school typographers have called computer typesetting, especially in display sizes, "ransom-note typography."

"What we really need," says Howard Fenton, a member of the board of directors of the New York Professional PostScript Users Group, "is a dialogue box [on the screen] that says, 'A serious error has occurred. The document is okay but cannot be printed because it is typographically offensive!' "[12]

Typical mistakes made by computer people without a typographic background include:

- *Choosing oddball typefaces that discourage readability.*
- *Using too many different typefaces per advertisement.*
- *Manipulating typefaces on screen to squeeze them together, spread them out, make them take on shadows and other affectations, or make them fit into unusual shapes.*

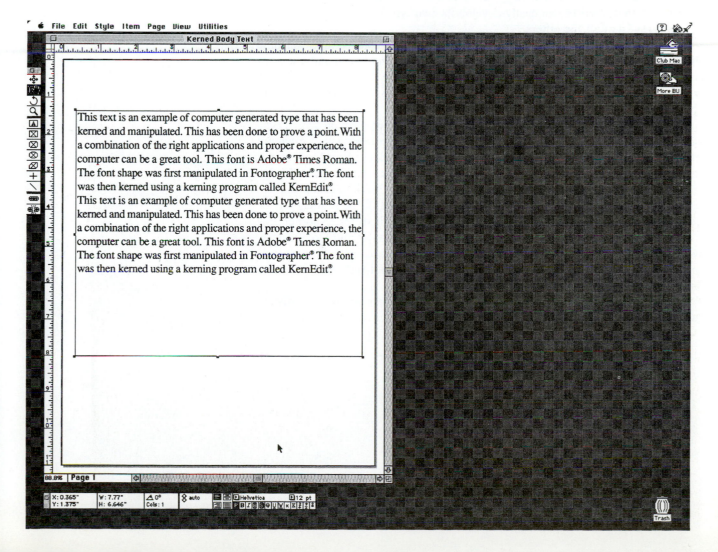

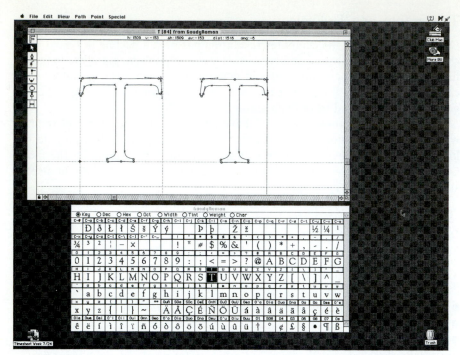

In another demonstration, Robert Keding shows how to use Fontographer software to adjust a letter set in Adobe Goudy Roman, shortening the cross stroke to make the letter better fit a combination of letters in a headline. He could have altered the letter in Adobe Illustrator or Aldus Freehand, but it would no longer be type; it would be artwork. In Fontographer, the altered face is saved as part of a font to be used in other software programs.

But for people who know both typography and the computer, the possibilities are endless. Recent software makes possible, even in a desktop operation, the adjustment and redesign of existing faces and also the design of new faces. This means that an advertiser can easily develop its own typeface to help distinguish its messages from all the others.

Type-managing software like FontStudio and Fontographer allows welcome adjustments in settings, making existing typefaces more functional and more appropriate to a given campaign. Using such software, the designer "colors" the type: kerning it, creating ligatures, changing stroke lengths, tightening or opening up the spacing.

One typography software program, Adobe TypeManager, gives on-screen type better definition so that designers can be more precise in redrawing and respacing letters. Another program, KernEdit, refines PostScript fonts to alter the spacing, and it does this permanently so that the refined type can be used in other software programs. QuarkXPress can do this, too, but only for a QuarkXPress job.

More of the computer typefaces now are coming with all the refinements of traditional fonts, including alternative characters and ligatures. Another improvement in computer typography concerns the availability of multiple masters, which means that a bigger or smaller version of a typeface has been redrawn, not simply enlarged or reduced. The concept one-font-for-all-sizes does not make for good typography.

In the right hands, computer-generated typography can be almost indistinguishable from traditional typography.

Creating an ad, you often plan the art before all else. What art you decide upon determines the content of the headline, the style of the type, the placement of the headline, what the body copy says, and perhaps the size and shape of the ad.

In deciding an ad "picture first," you hunt for an existing picture and build your ad around it. Or, better, you conceive a picture and then make arrangements to have it made.

Whether the art provides the ad's pivot or simply emphasizes a point made by the copy, its nature is crucial to the ad's effectiveness.

The illustration should have an obvious tie to the headline. And the headline should have an obvious tie to the copy. A single theme should unite all three.

Often the best way to express an advertising idea is through visual analogy. The VW ad shown in this chapter sees a connection between a gas pump nozzle and a gun. Another ad example elsewhere in this book sees an ink blot as an automobile. A mountain in another ad becomes the letter *A*. A lowercase *g* in a logotype becomes a pair of scissors.

Most designers find it easier to present tangibles rather than intangibles. They can think of ways to show the product itself, the product in use, the procedure for using the product, a benefit resulting from use of the product, and the harm that comes from not using the product; but how can they show, in a picture, "Sincerity"? "Integrity"? "Economy"?

Symbolism may be the answer. For instance, to illustrate stress you can show an executive type (cropped, maybe, so a face doesn't have to show) sitting at a desk after having snapped a pencil in two (each hand holding half of the pencil). If you don't want to show a snapped pencil, you can show one that's been chewed on.

It is a mistake sometimes to exaggerate a condition to make a point. It may be better to understate. Gravity Guiding System, a product to control sagging

CHAPTER

8

ART

What IBM wanted to show in this ad prepared by Ogilvy, Benson & Mather (now Ogilvy & Mather) was speed! The accompanying copy discussed the rapidity with which the company's computer systems worked, especially the one employed at the scene of the 1964 Olympics competition at Tokyo.

bodies, in a magazine ad with the headline "Your Chest Doesn't Belong on Your Stomach," shows a man with a bulging stomach. But the stomach is barely bulging. The picture of an excessively bulging stomach might cause a reader to think: "I'm not that bad. This product is not for me." A slightly bulging stomach, on the other hand, would tend to make the reader think: "Gee. Mine is worse than that. If that one is bad, I'd better do something about mine."

The Logic of Art

As an art director, you must be careful that you do not settle for a scene or camera angle just because it is convenient. Solarcaine antiseptic spray, in an ad headlined "The Sunday Sunburn," showed a family coming home from the beach obviously suffering from sunburn. As a bird's-eye view into an open convertible, the art showed clearly the suffering of the parents and the two children. But the reader might well have asked, "Why not put the top up to make some shade?"

Columbia Record & Tape Club under the headline "Imagine . . . One Boring Day When You Have Nothing to Do . . . 11 Great Tapes *or* Records Arrive in the Mail . . ." showed a photograph of a mailman at the door holding the records—and they were unwrapped so that all the covers showed. As if we do not have enough trouble these days with the Postal Service without putting up with nosey mail carriers opening our packages for us.

This illustration accompanied a headline that said: "Is Small-Town America Really Disappearing? Not if 59,360 of Us Can Help It." The point of the ad, an institutional one, was to show that International Telephone and Telegraph Corporation was interested in small towns; a large percentage of its employees lived and worked in them. To get the effect of a small town "disappearing," art director Laurance Waxberg first had a black-and-white print made from a 35mm color transparency, had the print airbrushed around the edges, and then had a line conversion made of the art (with a circular-line screen). Photographer: Ward Allen Howe. Agency: Needham, Harper & Steers.

Photographic art effectively and humorously makes the point in this ad. Copy other than the headline would have been superfluous. Agency: DDB Needham Worldwide. Art director: Garrett Jewett. Copywriter: James Walsh. Courtesy of The National Federation of Coffee Growers of Colombia.

Colombian coffee is now being served in the starboard lounge.

The richest coffee in the world."

Of course, artistic license sometimes take precedence over logic in the art of advertising. In the record-club case, the headline spoke of an arrival. Maybe the unwrapped delivery better made the point than a wrapped delivery or a scene showing the recipient (should it have been a man or woman? and how old?) sitting in the living room admiring the albums.

To make the point quickly and clearly, the art may combine elements that ordinarily don't go together, as when a store selling electric adjusting beds shows people sleeping or relaxing on bare mattresses. The store—and the manufacturer supplying the art—are more eager to show the thickness of the mattress and its texture and ticking than to show a more realistic scene.

The Value of Vagueness

Sometimes the client needs art that can be read in more than one way, with detail minimized or even hidden.

An example is the retailer conducting a clearance of women's coats. The clearance involves various styles. The retailer does not want the customer coming in looking specifically for a coat that is pictured. In this situation an illustrator can overlap a group of coats, showing them at angles that do not highlight the cut of the collar or the slant of the pockets. The illustration can avoid showing coats in their entirety. It can overlap figures and allow accessories to obscure some of the details of the coats.

In a two-page ad, IBM solves the ethnic-representation problem—and the male-female equality problem, too—by substituting baby booties for babies

Money Isn't The Only Thing You Can Save With This $5 Offer.

The INTERPLAK

George Washington would have given his wooden teeth for today's INTERPLAK® Home Plaque Removal Instrument. Because it cleans teeth nearly plaque free every time you brush, reducing gingivitis and improving the health of your gums. The INTERPLAK instrument has been accepted by the American Dental Association and, in fact, is the brand most recommended by dental professionals.

$5 Refund

We're so sure you'll see an improvement in the health of your teeth and gums, we'll even give you a $5 refund when you purchase any INTERPLAK instrument. But don't take our word for it. Use the money towards your next visit to the dentist and see what he says.

To receive the refund, just clip this coupon and fill in the information requested below and mail it with the following proof of purchase requirements: the original sales receipt, with the purchase price of your INTERPLAK instrument circled, plus the UPC code which you'll find on the bottom of the package.

This offer is valid on all INTERPLAK instrument models, only in the continental U.S., and is not redeemable in retail stores. Void where prohibited by law. Only one offer per household. Allow eight to ten weeks for redemption. All items must be sent in one envelope and be postmarked no later than March 31, 1991.

George Washington Offer, P.O. Box 5200-C, Plainville, Connecticut 06038.

Name: _____

Address: _____

City/State: _____ Zip: _____

Phone: _____

BAUSCH & LOMB ORAL CARE DIVISION **INTERPLAK®** HOME PLAQUE REMOVAL INSTRUMENT

Using parody art, Interplak, a Baush & Lomb product, surprises magazine readers with a section of a dollar bill showing the first president badly in need of his teeth. "Money Isn't The Only Thing You Can Save with This $5 Offer," says the headline. "George Washington would have given his wooden teeth for today's INTERPLAK Home Plaque Removal Instrument," the copy begins. The coupon offers a $5 refund on a purchase. The Agency: Fitzgerald & Company. Art director: Sheila Rogers. Designer: Steve Spetz. Copywriter: James Paddock.

themselves. One pair is blue, one pink. "Guess Which One Will Grow Up to Be the Engineer," intones the headline. The point of the ad, of course, is that the girl baby these days has as good a chance as the boy baby. Some militant feminists might still object to the stereotyping colors, blue and pink, but applaud the intent of the ad.

When the Advertising Council came up with a raised-hand "Fair Campaign Pledge" symbol for the Fair Campaign Practices Committee, feminists complained that the boxlike hand was too masculine looking, and the Council redesigned it, slimming it and making the fingers longer. It became a hand that could belong to either sex.

In one of its ads, New Balance, a running shoe, showed only the ankles and shoes of a runner (why face the problem of deciding whether to show a man or woman runner and deciding what ethnic group the runner is to belong to?). The art was a painting rather than a photograph to show fists jutting up from the pavement to pound at the soles of the shoes. The headline read: "When You Hit the Road, Does the Road Hit Back?" The shoes in this art were generic; detailed

How to illustrate the headline, "Over-Regulation Could Cost You the Shirt Off Your Back"? The National Cotton Council, Memphis, used this nicely staged photograph. The unlikely combination of formal dress with bare arms and chests gives the photograph its impact. It occupied most of the space in full-page ads appearing in the *Atlantic, Dun's Review,* and similar magazines. "You might never get to wear cotton again," the copy began. "Not if the government has its way. Because federal regulations are demanding that the air in cotton processing plants be cleaner than is technologically possible. . . ." The copy ended on this note: "We, in the cotton industry, think it's time to get more reason into regulation. For more information. . . ." Agency: Ward Archer & Associates.

New Balances were shown below along with copy saying, at the end, that if you buy this brand "You'll hit your stride. Without getting hit back."

Pictures and the Truth

Chapter 3 touched on the ethical problems faced by the copywriter wrestling with word choices to sell the client's products. The art director working with pictures faces similar ethical problems, and in some respects they are more subtle and more persistent.

Because pictures can communicate more readily than words, they can also lie more effectively. And their lies are the more insidious because people tend to believe pictures where they would distrust words.

Picture lies seem more blatant in mail order than in other kinds of advertising. In their enthusiasm for their objective, the art director and the illustrator for a

mail-order ad sometimes show the product with more glamour, more gloss than it actually has. The proof is in the customer's unwrapping.

More than ethics is involved in using pictures that lie either directly or indirectly. Increasingly it is a matter of legality. Advertisers who use deceptive pictures are finding themselves challenged by consumers and consumer groups. Retailers with art only closely resembling merchandise for sale are careful to include the line "Similar to Illustration."

A series of ads selling surety bonding by USF&G Insurance go back into history to make their points. This one uses a painting by Michelangelo supplied by Bettmann Archive. Agency: VanSant Dugdale Advertising, Baltimore. Creative director: Glen Bentley. Art director and designer: Ed McGrady. Copywriter: Bruce Jacobs.

What to Watch for in Art

Photograph or drawing or painting, the picture you choose to use is subject to the same principles of design the ad itself is. The good advertising picture is the well-designed picture. Composition of the picture is much more important than the medium the artist uses.

Sometimes the designer purposely plans a picture with a composition defect: too much neutral foreground or background. But the designer has a purpose: to use this area for surprinting or reversing some type. With tone all around, the ad holds together remarkably well.

Always important is the size of the art. Obviously, the larger a photograph or illustration, the more impact it will have.

Sometimes important is scale within the picture. If you want to show size, you will have to include in your picture something the reader can use to measure your primary subject, something to compare it with. A picture of rolling hills and a picture of something under a microscope can look the same in photography.

To show the breadth of its membership, American Express in one of its two-page magazine ads showed a photograph of Wilt Chamberlain and Willie Shoemaker, dressed in white suits to look alike; but, of course, Shoemaker came up only to Chamberlain's waist. The only type on the page opposite the full-page photo, aside from the logo, was: "Wilt Chamberlain. Cardmember since 1976. Willie Shoemaker, Cardmember since 1966."

Most line art is submitted to the printer larger than it will appear in print. But try this sometime: Ask your artist to do the drawing much smaller than it is to appear. When it is blown up by the camera, it will look massive, crude, and quite imposing. Or encourage your artist to use a make-shift tool, like a match-stick dipped in ink and drawn across a sheet of blotter paper.

You should collect as many examples of renderings as you can and refer to them as you work on the picture phase of your advertisement.

Information Graphics

Statistics, locations, and directions fail to excite the average reader. So ad makers change them to pieces of art. We call such pieces "information graphics." Computers are especially suited to producing them, and so we see them in all kinds of ads now.

Lehndorff, one of the nation's largest owners of shopping centers, uses a full-color optical illusion in an ad in *Shopping Centers Today,* an oversize trade journal. The art illustrates the ad's concept that "Vision is never bounded by the obvious." Agency: Sibley Peteete. Art director and designer: Rex Peteete. Copywriter: John Heikenfeld.

They tend to take five basic forms: charts, bar charts, pie charts, maps, and diagrams. In their most elementary forms, line and bar charts are called graphs. But most advertisers like to dress them up, making charts of them—or pictograms, as they are sometimes called. And, with good art direction, ordinary flat maps take on dimension or put themselves into perspective. They also become abstract and even decorative. Diagrams move away from mere boxes and arrows to become elaborate drawings.

Line charts show trends over a given time period. The line or lines zigzag from left to right to show at a glance whether amounts are increasing or decreasing. (Another simple way to dress up a line chart is to superimpose it over a photograph that illustrates in some way what is being measured.)

Bar charts can involve horizontal bars as well as vertical bars and, for that matter, diagonal bars. Vertical-bar charts are sometimes called column charts.

A pie chart works best in situations where you want to show percentages rather than number of units. The circle representing the pie can be tilted and given thickness, with the slices carrying different colors to make them stand out, and even lifted slightly away from the remainder of the pie. An artist can convert the circle into any number of round objects besides a pie: a coin, for instance, or the top of a barrel.

Diagrams range from flow charts and organization charts to technical drawings showing how things are made or how they operate. Such art calls for tight drawing styles rather than loose renderings.

You can crowd a lot of information into art—more than what you can crowd into paragraphs occupying the same amount of space. At the same time, you can make the information more interesting than with words alone. Of course, the art can't work by itself. It needs some well-chosen words of explanation.

Bayleton Fungicide uses bar charts (sometimes called column charts when the bars are upright) in one of its ads directed to wheat growers to report on tests on the effectiveness of the product. The bars are converted to wheat stalks to make the charts more appealing. Large decorative art on the left-hand page sets the style for the other art pieces. Client: Mobay Corporation. Agency: Valentine-Radford, Inc., Kansas City, Missouri. Art director: Gary Custer. Designer: Ed Linblof. Copywriter: David Schuttey.

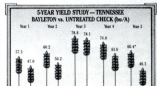

An ordinary pie chart becomes a cookie picture chart in this two-page ad sponsored by *Business Week* to appeal to media buyers. The "Top Mana gement" of the headline becomes "Top Management" as the headline crosses the gutter in bound magazines where the ad is run. Agency: Edwin Bird Wilson, Inc., New York. Associate creative director: Robert Lapkin. Copywriter: Jerry Silverman. © 1987 McGraw Hill, Inc.

Computer Art

At first, computer art was used to illustrate ads dealing with high-tech clients and computers themselves, and for copy dealing with statistics. Here was a way, finally, of turning out accurate charts and graphs effortlessly. Harvard Graphics software for IBM and IBM-compatible computers, was the leading program in this vein and is still widely used.

But computer art quickly took on larger dimensions as traditional artists and people with a fine-arts background, suspicious at first of the new medium, moved in to explore its possibilities.

With all its graphics capabilities, Macintosh is the computer of choice for most artists. MacPaint and MacDraw were early software programs establishing Macintosh as an art medium. They are still used, but many other programs have come along, some considerably more sophisticated.

Adobe Illustrator and Aldus FreeHand software programs, used to produce object-oriented drawings, offer a number of features that MacDraw doesn't offer, which means they are more difficult to use. SuperPaint, another illustration pro-

This "screen capture" shows one stage in the design of a transparency for an overhead projector. The transparency, in full color, of course, is to be used at a conference by Scudder Research Associates. Artist/designer Barbara Littman manipulates or redraws clip art imported or scanned into Aldus FreeHand to get her effects.

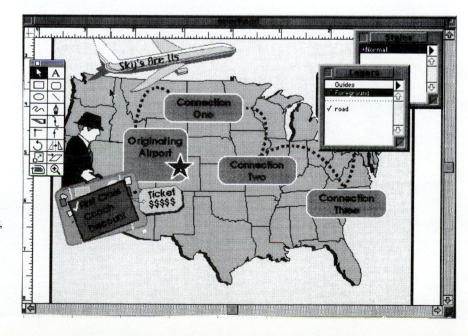

In a media ad in *Advertising Age,* *Forbes* magazine, which likes to call itself a "Capitalist Tool," used this worm's-eye-view photograph to illustrate the headline, "The Action Doesn't Begin Until the Quarterback Calls the Play." "The men who call the plays are the men who start the action," the ad copy begins. "In boardrooms just as on gridirons. So if your advertising hasn't been getting the yardage you want, it may not be reaching the executives who are in charge of the ballgame." The copy goes on to discuss *Forbes* readers and their prominence in the business world. "More officers in the headquarters of the 500 largest industrial companies read FORBES regularly than any other magazine." Jon Foraste is the photographer. Art director: Robert Fearon. Agency: Doremus & Co.

American Telephone and Telegraph Company uses a full-page photograph of a crowded city street, shot from a high building, to dramatize the fact that "Right now, nearly half your salesmen's time is spent just getting to appointments." The solution, says a two-page ad in magazines read by businessmen: a new AT&T program called "Phone Power," whose purpose is to train salesmen in the art of selling by telephone. Agency: N W Ayer & Son, Inc.

gram, combines the bit-mapped graphics of MacPaint with the object-oriented graphics of MacDraw.

Paint software is pixel-based. Draw software is object-based.

Paint software utilizes pixels that form a bitmap. The artist alters each in-place pixel to form or alter a picture. We associate paint software with continuous-tone art and halftones.

Draw software creates and manipulates objects. The artist creates, changes, moves, and groups the objects to make a picture. We associate draw software with line drawings.

The computer has an advantage over other drawing and painting tools. It makes users think differently, and this may result in an elimination of some of the visual clichés in advertising. Of course, computer art, overused, has itself become something of a cliché, but between the geometric hard-line look and the airbrush look, there is plenty of room for innovation. One important feature of computer art is that, once created, it can be viewed from various angles until one angle comes along that seems to best display what's being shown.

Creating art on a computer allows instant changes and easy storage. A collection of computer-generated art on disk becomes a kind of clip-art service. Called-up art can be reused repeatedly, each time with adjustments to customize it.

Some computer artists become so proficient with the tool that they develop their own software and even market it.[1] Recognizing the role the computer now plays in generating art for commerce, PennWell Publishing Company in 1992 introduced a quarterly magazine, *Computer Artist.*

Graphic artist and designer David Foster especially likes the challenge of the computer, which he refers to as "an electronic blackboard." "But I don't consider it high tech. It's low tech alongside the human brain." He adds: "The computer will sink you if you don't understand design."

Foster does not try to do "computer art." He simply makes the best use he can of the medium, taking advantage of what it can do.

To produce a series of Oregon landscapes and scenes of small towns in the state, Foster has converted a van to a traveling computer studio, making it possible to create his images through open doors *on location.* He powers his PC with a RV battery-converter system providing 120 volts (AC) for about 14 hours. He rigged his system to recharge itself while traveling to the next site. He uses an electronic pen and tablet with a pioneer software painting program called Dr.

ART

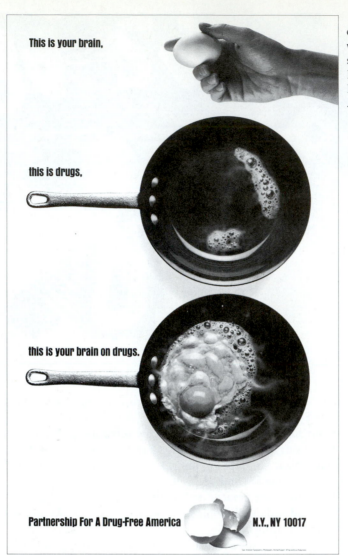

This is your brain,

this is drugs,

this is your brain on drugs.

Partnership For A Drug-Free America   N.Y., NY 10017

Art director Scot Fletcher uses a closeup demonstration and a bird's-eye view to make the point in this ad sponsored by the Partnership for a Drug-Free America. Agency: Keye/Donna/Pearlstein. Copywriter: Larre Johnson.

Halo. "A true freehand drawing program," Foster calls it. The program gives him a modest 256 colors to use, with 16 on board at any one time. (Some graphic computers can work with 16 million hue, saturation, and value variations.)

Foster prefers Dr. Halo to more recent software programs. "The simpler the tool, the better," he says. More recent software has too many built-in effects for his purpose. He would rather work out his own effects for a particular image.

When he returns to his home studio, he converts the PC disk to a Macintosh disk, using Adobe Photoshop software, and on his large-screen Radius color monitor, he refines his work with Electronic Arts Studio 32 software on his Mac IIci. He prints from a Hewlett-Packard PaintWriter XL.[2] (See his work in Chapter 9.)

Art Styles

The history of art records many movements in which groups of artists rebelled against current practices. The Postimpressionists rebelled against the objectivity and the "moment in time" nature of the Impressionists. The Expressionists brought emotion and strong personal responses into painting. The Fauves ("wild beasts"), who came along at the beginning of this century (see the work of Henri Matisse, André Derain, Maurice de Vlaminck, and Raoull Dufy), produced hectic but decorative canvases with vigorous color and broad, free strokes.

The following list of currently used art styles is offered to alert you to the existence of one or two you may not be aware of or have forgotten. It deals more

New York Life Insurance Company uses silhouetted bird's-eye-view art to show several of its agents taking part in a seminar. "The way we see it, there's always more to learn." Agency: Chait/Day/Mojo Inc. Art director: Cabel Harris. Copywriter: Jamie Barrett.

To emphasize the fact that the blondes, brunettes, and redheads who read *TV Guide* were younger than the women who read the general-circulation magazines (you will find "fewer heads tinged with silver among *TV Guide* readers"), the art director, for an ad meant to reach advertising media buyers, used this photo with its unusual vantage point. That women in this ad were classified by hair color made concentrating on the hair by photographer Harold Krieger entirely reasonable.

If there's one thing we've learned at New York Life, it's that we still have a lot to learn.

At New York Life, we know the financial world doesn't stand still.

That's why our life insurance agents are required to continue their education throughout their careers. Even if they've been in the business 20 years. And even if they're wildly successful.

The way we see it, there's always more to learn. Whether it's the latest tax laws and insurance products, or the current banking and investment trends.

So we conduct seminars and study groups on an ongoing basis. In fact, we spend about $150,000 on an agent's education in the first 3½ years alone.

Surprised? Well, as we like to say here at New York Life, you learn something new every day.

NEW YORK LIFE

The Company You Keep.

Joel Shapiro, CLU, ChFC,
New York Life agent for 31 years

Sol Silverman, CLU,
New York Life agent for 30 years

Bernard Klazmer, CLU,
New York Life agent for 36 years

Steve Blake, CLU, ChFC,
New York Life agent for 29 years

with illustration than photography, because illustration is easier to categorize. It does not pretend to be exhaustive. Some styles simply defy categorization. Please understand, too, that it is impossible for a list like this to avoid overlapping.

■ *Tight art*. Art that is smooth, polished, precise. It is carefully executed. There are no imperfections, but the artist may distort certain art truths, such as perspective. At worst, the art may seem painfully contrived. Often it has a flat, patterned quality. Much computer art qualifies as tight art.

Using a stick dipped in ink on rough-textured paper and drawing in a loose style, Charles Politz creates a series of caricature-like portraits for the covers of oversize folders honoring famous women, two of whom are shown here. The folders were used by Emanuel Hospital & Health Center, Portland, as invitations to office staff luncheons.

Joan of Arc

Eleanor Roosevelt

With pen shading of fine lines and cross-hatching, line art can give the effect of tone. Union Pacific Railroad used this art for an institutional newspaper ad telling readers that the line is "a vital link in speeding . . . perishables to distant markets. . . . These fruits are delivered to consumers in 'Orchard Fresh' condition."

Mexicana Airlines uses bold, stylized, almost abstract art in this newspaper ad to show that exotic cities in Mexico are "just a few steps away." The horizontal look of the ad is achieved through the art, the stretched-out two-line headline, the wide subheadline, and the four shallow columns of type. All of which matches the horizontal logo drawn in unique all caps. Art director: John Coll. Designers: John Scott MacDaniels and John Coll. MacDaniels also wrote the copy. Agency: Dailey & Associates, San Francisco.

Mazatlan & Puerto Vallarta are just a few steps away.

Beginning April 29, Mexicana Airlines offers Northwest vacationers headed for Mexico the only nonstops from San Francisco to the beaches of Mazatlan, and on to Puerto Vallarta. Daily.

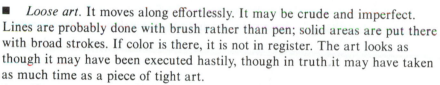

Now you can get the flavor of Mexico on the way to Mexico. The minute you board Mexicana Airlines in San Francisco. On the first and only nonstops from the Bay Area to Mazatlan.

On the way, you'll get the great one-class service Mexicana's famous for: complimentary French champagne and wine, continental entrees, and the warm hospitality of Mexico.

And besides, as long as you have to stop somewhere between the Northwest and Mazatlan, San Francisco is the nicest place to do it.

So fly to San Francisco. Then fly non-stop to Mazatlan on Mexicana. From the great Northwest, it's the best way going.

■ *Loose art.* It moves along effortlessly. It may be crude and imperfect. Lines are probably done with brush rather than pen; solid areas are put there with broad strokes. If color is there, it is not in register. The art looks as though it may have been executed hastily, though in truth it may have taken as much time as a piece of tight art.

■ *Abstract art.* Simplified art, reduced to fundamental forms. If it has meaning, the meaning is subtle. It may carry different meanings to different viewers. The viewer's reaction to it is likely to be more emotional than intellectual, although it is defended and presumably appreciated more by intellectuals than nonintellectuals. Its opposite is realistic art.

■ *Realistic art.* Also called representational art. Highly detailed, it leaves little to the imagination. It shows all the pores. It comes in a number of forms: sentimental-realistic (as in the early Norman Rockwell paintings), starkly realistic (to shock or disgust), surrealistic (to intrigue). There are many degrees of realism, including the recent superrealism that magnifies to the point of distortion.

■ *Cartoon art.* Art that exaggerates or amuses. Cartoons can be executed in any medium, including oils, but they are most often produced in pen-and-ink or in washes (black watercolor). Comic-strip artists and gag cartoonists who have built reputations on the news-editorial side of publications are often enlisted to do cartoons for advertisers. We could come up with a list-within-a-list of cartoon styles.

■ *Painterly art.* Art that makes no attempt to hide its technique. The brush strokes are there for all to see and appreciate. The appreciation is likely to come from other artists rather than the general public. In watercolor paintings, the painting is done on smooth paper not meant to take the medium, causing a sort of water-on-oilcloth look. In line art, the rough pencil lines under the inked lines are not removed. This category would also include the kind of sketches done for rough layouts or comps and deemed good enough to use as finished art.

■ *Calligraphic art.* Line drawings executed in carefully controlled thick and thin lines.

■ *Shadow art.* Bold drawings with areas expressed by shadows, not outlines. Some edges are not defined. Milton Caniff provided an example of the style in the *Steve Canyon* cartoon strip.

The photoengraver or offset camera operator has almost put the shadow artist out of business. The camera operator can get a strong shadow effect by handling a photograph as though it were a piece of line art, photographing it without a screen, and dropping all the middle tones.

ART

■ *Silhouette art.* The artist reduces figures, faces, or props to solid, usually black, shapes. Silhouettes are in reality filled-in outlines that stand out against a light or white background, but the light and dark can be reversed.

A photograph of a figure or object with the background opaqued out would qualify as a silhouette.

■ *Op art.* Geometric art that capitalizes on optical illusions. It causes eye vibrations. It is a good attention getter, but its message is limited. It was popular for a time in the 1960s, but it is used only rarely now.

■ *Pop art.* Another has-been, although vestiges of it appear in some of the "now" art. It created quite a stir in the 1960s both as a fine arts movement and as a style for advertising illustration. Essentially it is an application of the comic-strip style (adventure strip division) to the higher arts. Lots of blown-up Ben Day pattern. Balloons with conversation in them are big in pop art. It professes to see beauty in the mundane and banal. Or is it critical of them? Pop art is part of the "camp" picture.

■ *Psychedelic art.* Art said to be inspired by the drug culture. Containing swirls of improbable colors, it is decorative and contorted, a precursor of funky art.

■ *Art nouveau.* Art made from sinuous, graceful, decorative, curving lines in the manner of Aubrey Beardsley. Sometimes the lines are combined with areas of solid black or color. Pattern is important.

Art nouveau appeared originally in the late 1800s in the architecture of a building erected in Brussels. Beardsley was not the only artist to embrace art nouveau. Edvard Munch, the pessimistic Norweigian painter and lithographer,

This is not an ad from the 1930s. It is an ad from the 1970s, showing how a style can be revived to do a selling job forty years after it dies out. The style is art deco, alive in the 1990s. The medium used for the illustration is airbrush. Client: TWTF Restaurant Group. Agency: Warwick, Welsh & Miller. Art director: Ken Barre. Illustrator: Peter Palombi. Copywriter: Bob Skollar.

Pop art helps sell newspaper readers on sending out for pizza. "There will be times when the most important bit of knowledge you possess is that fact that Rocky Rococo® delivers," says the copy. Agency: Frankenberry, Laughlin & Constanble, Milwaukee, Wisconsin. Art director: Mary Mentzer. Copywriter: Patrick Pritchard. The drawing, with its strong tonal pattern, is by Matt Jumbo, Hansen Graphics.

Does your hotel have a hard time saying goodbye?

Not us. Just drop your key at the desk and be on your way. No tears. We'll bill you later.

And, if you need extra attention, or extra privacy, you've got it.

Come to the Dupont Plaza. We're right on Dupont Circle. Near the embassies, near the Phillips Collection and Georgetown. Near all the Washington you came to see.

If you'd like a little extra Washington the next time you come to town, come to the Dupont Plaza.

In this *New York Times Magazine* ad, the Dupont Plaza hotel in Washington, D.C., uses a *New Yorker* cartoonist, Robert Weber, to illustrate the point that people at other hotels have trouble checking out. At the Dupont Plaza you "Just drop your key at the desk" and you are "on your way. No tears. We'll bill you later." The various types of people in this other hotel's checkout line are worth studying. The cartoon approach is an ideal one to use in this kind of a presentation. Art director: Len Zimmelman. Copywriter: Carolanne Ely. Agency: Keye/Donna/Pearlstein.

used it, for instance, in his *The Cry* (1893), and so did Paul Gauguin in his paintings.

■ *Art deco*. The look of the 1920s and 1930s has recently been revived. It offers set of lines or stripes, rounded corners, geometric shapes, pastel colors, and rainbow motifs. The "deco" stands for "decoration." It is related to "camp" art.

Much of the work that comes out of the influential and prestigious Push Pin Studios in New York is art deco. A leading art deco illustrator (although the term does not adequately cover his versatility) is Milton Glaser. His widely imitated style is flat, decorative; everything is done in consistent and persistent outline, even the shadows. Design seems more important than draftsmanship.

■ *"Camp" art*. It is so bad, corny, or low brow that it is good. It takes on charm of its own. Rather than fight popular culture, it embraces it. It finds beauty in ugliness. It is part of the nostalgia kick we seem to be on. In an extreme form, it is "high camp."

■ *"Funky" art*. Inspired by the underground press and underground comic books (comix), funky art is characterized by much detail, rendered in fine line and cross-hatching or, at the opposite extreme, airbrushing. A leading figure in the movement is Robert Cumb, a cartoonist.

Funky art is often vulgar, eclectic, and amateurish. Its practitioners say its lack of slickness attests to its "honesty."

■ *The montage*. A set of separate sketches are drawn or put together in a single unit. Or a set of photographs can be used. The pieces can butt up against each other, they can merge into each other, or they can overlap. Techniques involved in producing the various pieces can be the same or they can be wildly dissimilar. When the resulting art moves from the representational to the abstract, it is usually called a "collage."

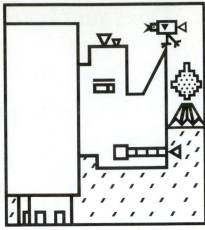

Ron Hansen does illustrations in several styles. Inspired by computer art but not using a computer, he developed this straight-line technique to use for illustrations for a series of children's books and posters published by Purple Turtle Books Inc., Seattle, a firm he founded. His only tools are a Rapidograph and a ruling pen.

Doug Knutson used cloth and thread to create this illustration for *JD Journal,* a company magazine published by Deere & Company, Moline, Illinois, for employees and dealers. The unusual medium was appropriate to a cover story on "Strengthening the Rural Fabric." Tom Sizemore art directed.

Commercial Art vs. Fine Art

Commercial art smarts under unfair attacks by purists. The line these attackers like to draw between commercial and fine art looks very thin as you study closely the fine paintings and drawings that go into many advertisements.

"In this day and age," said Tomi Ungerer, a painter and widely admired offbeat cartoonist for advertisers, "it's ridiculous to make any differentiation between commercial and fine art. But if it has to be made, I would put myself on the side of commercial art. Fine art has no function in society any longer. It lacks social meaning and is limited to museums and rich collectors. Stylistically, it is further limited. . . ."[3]

Perhaps Ungerer overstated it. But this much is certain: The challenge commercial artists face as they set out to create an agreed-upon effect is every bit as great as the challenge easel artists face as they pick up paints and brushes and wonder what wonderful accidents will happen to the canvas this time.

"If art directors are the backbone of the ad world, then illustrators are the muscle," *Adweek* observes in announcing a Society of Illustrators annual exhibition.[4]

While copywriters and designers work anonymously in advertising, artists and photographers often get some kind of credit mention. Artists sign their drawings or paintings; photographers get 6-point credit lines. The advertiser and agency welcome artists' signatures if the artists are well known. A name like "Schulz,"

The horizontal look in advertising design. Art director Scot Fletcher uses vignette art to tie the two parts of this ad together. The ad occupied the bottom halves of two magazine pages. Client: California Department of Commerce Office of Tourism. Agency: Keye/Donna/Pearlstein. Copywriter: Larre Johns.

for instance, on *Peanuts* characters selling Metropolitan Life is a real plus. "Get Met. It Pays." Get Schulz. He pays, too.

Art directors can refer to *The Creative Black Book,* a two-volume directory published by National Register Publishing Company, Wilmette, Illinois, for names of artists and suppliers available on a freelance or job basis. (NRPC also publishes *The Standard Directory of Advertising Agencies* and *The Standard Directory of International Advertisers and Advertising Agencies,* invaluable reference books issued periodically. People in advertising agencies know these books as the "Red Books.")

Stock Art

When clients cannot afford original art or when it is not available, they have access to the work of the clip-art services. Clip art, consisting of drawings of every imaginable product and situation, comes on slick paper stock ready to cut out and paste into place, or on disks for computer operations.

Dynamic Graphics, Inc., Peoria, Illinois, offers its art in both proof and disc form, which it separates into Traditional Clipper and Electronic Clipper. Electronic Clipper art is available for either the Mac or PC. The subscriber gets monthly sets of illustrations.

Another well-established service, Volk Clip Art, Washington, Illinois, offers art in compact booklets that can fit in or through computer scanners. It also offers art on disks.

T/Maker of Mountain View, California calls its electronic clip art software ClickArt. An example of specialized computer clip art comes from 3-G Graphics, which offers, among other collections, "People I," a set of drawings of ethnic men and women in various occupations and livelihoods.

One of the best sources of stock art for advertising is Dover Publications, New York, with its Pictorial Archives series of books. The art in these books is in the public domain. Here are some pieces from *Chinese Cut-Paper Designs,* selected by Theodore Menten, published by Dover in 1975.

A R T

All kinds of drawing and rendering techniques are used by these services. All kinds of subjects are treated. Lots of the art comes as prescreened halftones (shot with a 120-line screen). You paste this art down directly onto the mechanical, and the printer treats it as though it were line art (which it is). You can also find prescreened separations for four-color art.

To at least one user, clip art and its computer version is "like Muzak—pleasant, but not meant to be particularly thought-provoking. Instead, it's designed to be versatile and widely applicable."[5]

Stock drawings are also available from a number of sources that have gathered together art in the public domain (no longer protected by copyright) and made it available in books that can be used as clip books. The only cost is the cost of the books themselves, which is minimal. A designer with a talent for drawing can add to or subtract from these drawings and combine them to make new drawings. Dover Publications, New York, is probably the biggest source. Its "Pictorial Archives Catalogue" lists scores of books, including the two-volume *Handbook of Early Advertising Art* and *293 Renaissance Woodcuts for Artists and Illustrators*. Art Direction Book Company, New York, offers a series of four looseleaf *Ron Yablon Graphic Archives* books.

Stock photographs and old prints are available on a one-time-use basis from dozens of organizations, located principally in New York. R. R. Bowker Company lists these organizations in each year's issue of *Literary Market Place*. The annual *Writer's Market* carries a list, too. Charges for stock photographs are based on size of the advertiser and use to which the picture is put. A disadvantage, as with all stock art, is that other advertisers may use the same illustration.

The Coming of Photography

It was the talk of Paris in 1839. Louis Jacques Mandé Daguerre had found a way to record and fix an image on a silver plate. An early application to advertising can be found in an 1853 New York *Daily Tribune* ad, signed by a hatter, offering to every hat purchaser a free daguerrotype that, placed in the hat liner, would be "a great convenience in indicating one's own hat."[6]

What was to revolutionize advertising was the application of the principle of photography to the art of engraving. No more woodcuts or handcuttings on steel. In 1880 the New York *Graphic* ran its first crude halftone. Advertisers were quick to appropriate the new picture-reproduction process.

To come later was the use of the photograph itself to advertise. The drawn or painted illustration now reproduced through the marvel of photochemistry remained king until well into the twentieth century.

The development of the 35mm camera in 1925 made picture taking, anywhere, easy and informal. And in the twenties the Bauhaus in Germany began its experiments with abstract photography. Then came color in the 1930s.

Photography gradually moved in on advertising. As it became more realistic, painters and illustrators, beaten at their own game, veered in an opposite direction. Nowadays, with photographers doing abstractions and signing their work, no wonder the poor advertising illustrators feel frustrated!

Photography's Advantages

The big advantage of photography, of course, lies in its *believability*. The camera can lie as much as—more than—words, but the consumer will not believe that.

Speed provides a further advantage. A photographer in a single day can deliver to the advertising designer a couple of dozen shots in contact form; the client can pick a favorite and have an 8″ × 10″ glossy print in a matter of hours.

Then there is the *flexibility* of pictures. They can be cropped to any size or shape and retouched with brush or airbrush or otherwise doctored to create a desired effect.

Some advertising photographers prefer the Hasselblad to 35 mm cameras because its large, square format allows the user to produce large vertical or hori-

Two samples from Dynamic Graphics' "Clipper" Service show part of the range of styles available.

zontal pictures in addition to square ones. This gives the art director more choices from single shots.

Finally, *price* must be considered. Although a good photographer might charge anywhere from $100 to $3,000 or more for an assignment, some photographers come cheaper; and for routine jobs, when you compare the rates for photographs with rates for artwork, artwork often suffers.

Some photographers need a lot of guidance; others are more creative. But you should have an idea in mind before you turn to any photographer.

Lou Dorfsman, creative director at CBS, says that if, as art director, you cannot explain your idea over the phone to your photographer, your idea is not thought out well enough. You are not ready for photography.

It is not necessary to appear on location passing out suggestions. "Allow photographers the opportunity to use their talented eyes, their good taste, their design and color sense as well as their technical skills," said David Deutsch, president of David Deutsch Associates, New York.

And do not stop there, Deutsch advises. Be willing to accept the ideas photographers offer. One of Deutsch's most successful ads for a client, Oneida stainless and giftware, showed a just-hatched chick alongside a spoon and bowl of eggs. The chick was the idea of photographer George Ratkai.[7]

Art directors look everywhere for the right photographers, who often come to advertising assignments from editorial work. To cite one example: The Leo Burnett agency hired French fashion photographer Gilles Bensione to work on the New Virginia Slims Ultra Lights account. Bensione had taken many of the exciting photographs found in *Elle* magazine.

Some of the best photographs move away from dazzling color, settling instead for subtle, subdued, or monochromatic colors. The most sophisticated ads sometimes go back to black-and-white photography, now remote enough to stand out from the competition.

If captions are used, they should appear near enough to their pictures so the reader will see at once the connection. They appear most often in italic or in type smaller or bolder than the body type. The caption ordinarily goes below the picture, but it can go at the top, side, even inside a hollowed-out box (called a mortise), as a surprint (black type over a gray area), or as a reverse (white type in a gray or black area). But in most ads, the headline and the copy do whatever picture describing is necessary; a caption is not needed. If a picture has to be explained, it probably is not pulling its fair share of the advertising load.

Dency Kane took this photograph of architectural detail of Alwyn Court, New York, for use in a newspaper ad for the Petrossian Restaurant ("Paris Is in the Air"), housed in the building. The building's facade, widely celebrated, is ornamented with neo-French Renaissance detailing. The agency: Warren/Kramer. Kane is a fine-arts photographer who occasionally accepts an advertising assignment. © 1989.

Models

An illustration has an advantage over a photograph in that the illustrator or advertising agency does not need a model's release. When a photograph is used and it shows clearly a real person, that person's permission must be solicited before

"Has the toast of Chicago had too much marmalade?" asked a Chicago *Sun-Times*/Chicago *Daily News* full-page ad in the advertising trade press when both papers were still alive. "Sad about that old star. She used to be such a paper doll. Now she puffs a lot. Performs mostly for older audiences— who remember her when. Times have changed. You've got to see the new talent in town. The Sun Times and Daily News combination." The media buyers for agencies, readers of the ad, understood full well the *Sun-Times/ Daily News* was making a case against the competition, a Chicago institution called the Chicago *Tribune*.

Robert Reynolds arranges the photographs on one side of a two-fold folder (the right panel is narrower than the other two) to direct eye travel from one to another. He also arranges them to form a single visual mass. This brings order to the design. To bring variety to the spread, he crops for various sizes and for verticals as well as horizontals. The client: Melvin Mark Brokerage Company.

the photograph is published. A release does not have to be secured if the photograph is to be used for news purposes, but permission is always required in advertising. Without it, the agency or client faces the possibility of a suit for invasion of privacy. And the permission must spell out the specific use to which the photo will be put.

An agency in a small town learned this the hard way. One picture of a woman taken for a store catering to "queen size" women turned out to be just what the agency wanted for a reducing-academy client. The woman, looking well fed, was trying to get into a pair of pants. The ad carried the headline, " 'I Must Lose Weight.' " The model promptly sued the agency, charging that such publication damaged her reputation and caused her embarrassment and humiliation.

You can bet that the toast-of-Chicago dancer shown in this chapter had the uses of her picture spelled out to her before the paper went ahead with its ad. The *Hustler* man, shown in a later chapter, knew what was going on, too.

Advertising agencies have their own forms for model releases. The photographer takes the responsibility for having them signed. Standard model release forms are also available from camera stores. A fee for the model, real or token, is involved.

When an agency buys a photograph from a photographer, it usually buys one-time rights. Prices vary, but generally photographers expect to get more for advertising photography than for editorial photography. Photographers base their rates on time spent on the jobs, uses to be made of the photos, and their own reputations.

Some observers criticize advertising for underrepresenting blacks. But there are problems showing blacks and other groups in correct proportion to their numbers in the general population. The various advertisers and their agencies can't very well get together and choose models in concert. John E. O'Toole, president of the American Association of Advertising Agencies, points out that because most ads are designed for placement in a number of publications, ad makers tend to choose "the model that reflects the majority of their constituency, which for most consumer products is white."[8]

A number of companies use disabled persons as models in their ads. For instance, in a TV commercial, Kmart shows a person in a wheelchair moving down the store aisle selecting merchandise. Advertising executives feel that the use of such models not only is socially responsible but also good business, considering

Photographer Barry O'Rourke used a special lens to dramatize the perspective, and he shot from a worm's-eye angle to make these books look like massive Greek columns. Cropping at the sides and bottom added to the illusion. The art was part of a "Let These 3 Wise Men Into Your Home" ad of The Classics Club, Roslyn, N.Y. Agency: Schwab, Beatty & Porter.

the fact that the population in the United States includes an estimated 43,000,000 disabled persons.

Esprit, the San Francisco-based sportswear manufacturer, bucked tradition in the 1980s when it featured real people—employees and their friends—instead of professional models. Company owners "almost reinvented credibility, and for a while their naive fashion models became role models for a generation of young people for whom shopping was a wholesome form of entertainment."[9]

Amateurism in Art

An advantage photography has over illustration is that in photography amateurism is harder to detect. We have cameras now that are virtually foolproof. Not that everything they produce is art. It still takes a great artist to be a great photographer. But from the standpoint of clarity and polish, you are more likely to get a useable piece of art from an amateur photographer than from an amateur illustrator.

One of the unfortunate aftermaths of the creative revolution of the 1960s was the feeling, still somewhat prevalent, that anybody can do it. We have long suffered retailers appearing on the TV screen doing their own extolling of the "preowned" cars or other merchandise they are selling. Now we have clients doing their own artwork. Rock stars design and letter their own cassette or CD covers. The anti-intellectualism of the 1960s and 1970s has made an impact on graphic arts just as it has on the political, educational, and publishing establishments.

We can thank the underground press for a lot of this. The impact it has made on advertising typography and art is considerable. Not all the influence has been bad. Much of the art has been refreshing. But "funky" art is good only when it is executed by persons of talent. Amateurism is still amateurism. It is almost a sure bet that an art style that looks easy is actually very difficult to emulate.

Small, local advertisers without access to professional or stock art should explore the many possibilities of art-free advertising before settling for work prepared by amateurs.

Editing Pictures

This is the day of magnified detail. Designers prefer photographs cropped close. They eliminate detail that does not contribute to the ad's message. Failing to get exactly what they want from the photographer, designers doctor photographs—crop, retouch, or otherwise alter them.

The Hyatt hotel chain, for art in a 1991 campaign, featured doctored Polaroid shots made by Los Angeles photographer Michael Going. Using tools to manipulate the dyes while the shots were developing, Going was able to create shots that looked like impressionist paintings. Artists had been doing this for some time, although a change in the film by Polaroid in the 1980s made the process more difficult.

Pictures, like copy, can be edited.

Not liking its direction, a designer can decide to "flop" a picture (if the head is facing to the right, have it face left) simply by marking it "flop" in instructions to the printer. (The printer has merely to turn the negative over from its usual position when making the plate.) But the designer, before requesting this, should make sure the subject does not have a part in his hair (which would come out on the wrong side), or is not wearing a double-breasted suit (the buttons would be on the wrong side), or is not standing in front of a sign (the letters would be backward). The designer should turn the picture over and look at it through a light table or up against a window to check such details.

But saying that editing of pictures is possible is not saying that editing is always or even frequently necessary.

Sometimes a piece of *line* art needs retouching. Maybe it is a piece that has already been reproduced; you want to reprint it in an ad, and you do not have access to the original. Part of the reproduction is faint. Some of the lines must be strengthened. But the piece is small, leaving you little room to maneuver in. The thing to do is to make a blowup copy, do your touching up on that, and then have the printer reduce it to the right size.

Or you can scan the art and change it on a computer screen.

Electronic photography—computer digitizing—has taken the place of hand retouching in improving photographs for advertising. Quantel Graphic Paintbox, Scitex, Pixar, and Sun systems, among other computer programs, can completely alter photographs, merge them, and tell visual stories far different from what original photographs tell. ". . . if 'the camera doesn't lie' was always a fallacy, it's now both easier to change the essence of photographs and harder to detect the process," a *Newsweek* writer observes.[10]

Desktop publishing makes digital retouching and doctoring of photographs available to everyone.

Cropping

Sometimes you can give a photograph more impact by "cropping" it—trimming away some of the detail. Perhaps you feel you can improve its composition. Perhaps you feel you can make it clearer.

Sometimes you would crop part of a figure out of a photograph to focus attention on an item of apparel. To sell a dress, for instance, you do not want the reader to squander attention on shoes, or the hairdo. When the art is a drawing rather than a photograph, the illustrator can render the garment in detail and tone, and permit the remainder of the drawing to fade or to appear in rough, weak outline.

In changing the dimensions of a picture you must settle arbitrarily on three different measurements, then figure out what the fourth will be. The four measurements are the width and depth of the original art and the width and depth of the art in its printed version.

You may start by picking a width and depth on the original. Then you will decide on either the width or the depth of the printed version. It can be anything you want. The part of the original area you want, let us say, is 25 picas by 33

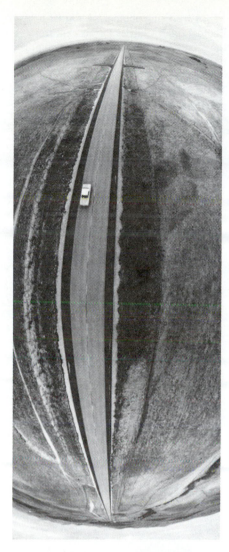

Hertz used this art to dramatize its "pay-nothing-per-mile" rates for persons who want to do long-distance driving. Put together from two separate photographs and retouched at the center where the photographs meet, the art said "distance" in a most unusual way. Agency: Carl Ally Inc. © Hertz System, Inc., 1972.

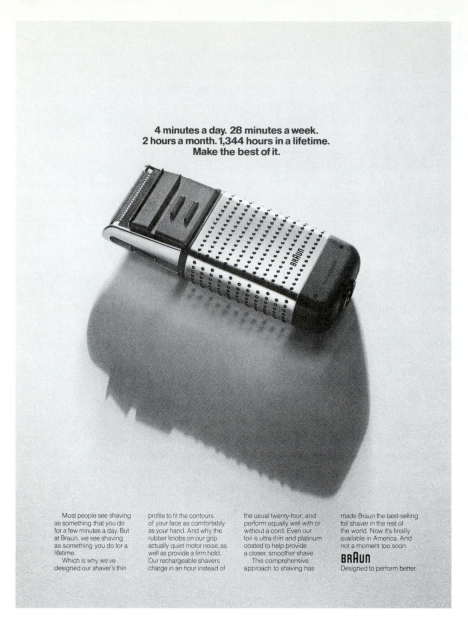

4 minutes a day. 28 minutes a week.
2 hours a month. 1,344 hours in a lifetime.
Make the best of it.

Most people see shaving as something that you do for a few minutes a day. But at Braun, we see shaving as something you do for a lifetime.
Which is why we've designed our shaver's thin

profile to fit the contours of your face as comfortably as your hand. And why the rubber knobs on our grip actually quiet motor noise, as well as provide a firm hold. Our rechargeable shavers charge in an hour instead of

the usual twenty-four; and perform equally well with or without a cord. Even our foil is ultra-thin and platinum coated to help provide a closer, smoother shave.
This comprehensive approach to shaving has

made Braun the best-selling foil shaver in the rest of the world. Now it's finally available in America. And not a moment too soon.

BRAUN
Designed to perform better.

Advertising photography at its best. Photographer Charles Purvis captures the product in a neutral setting, defining its handsome design through skillful lighting that casts an interesting shadow. The copy is excellent, too, making the point that shaving is something you do for a lifetime. Agency: Lowe Marschalk. Art director and designer: Marty Weiss. Copywriter: Ken Sandbank.

picas. The printed width you want is 16 picas. Now, what will the printed depth be?

25 is to 33 as 16 is to x.

You can figure it mathematically; you can use a specially made slide rule or a "wheel" (a circular proportional scale calibrated in numbers that could represent picas or inches or anything you choose); you can use the diagonal method.

Your answer will be 21 picas. Your printed picture will be 16×21 picas.

To figure dimension change when working with silhouette art, you will have to enclose the silhouette in a tight-fitting rectangle.

Here is another problem you might face. You have a space for a picture that measures, say, 18 by 50 picas, a deep vertical. Your original is a regular $8'' \times 10''$ glossy photograph. The original picture is horizontal. You are going to have to take as much of the depth of that picture as possible. About the most depth you can take from a picture like that is 46 picas. So that is your third dimension. Now, how much width can you take from that original so that area will, in this case, *blow up* to fit the allotted space?

Figure that x is to 46 (the original area) as 18 is to 50 (the printed area). (Your equation is always "original width is to original depth as printed width is to printed depth.") So x equals 16½ picas.

Some designers like to work with square originals because it is easier to move

An interior mortise with centered lines of copy, set in italics, finds a place where it doesn't do much damage to a beautifully composed photograph. A heavy black-line box makes the mortise stand out, inviting readership. A public-service ad for U.S. Savings Bonds.

NOW, THE MAIN STREET OF THE AMERICAN DREAM HAS A PASSING LANE

We share a dream,
the American Dream, and a
remarkable number of us take advantage
of U.S. Savings Bonds to reach it.
Bonds are the Main Street of
the American Dream.
Now, we've added a passing lane.
The interest you earn on your
U.S. Savings Bonds
can be tax free for qualified individuals
when used for college tuition.
For complete details write:
U.S. Savings Bonds
Box MNE, Washington, DC 20226

INVEST IN BONDS FOR EDUCATION

U.S. SAVINGS BONDS
THE GREAT AMERICAN INVESTMENT

to either a vertical or a horizontal from a square than it is to move from a horizontal to a vertical.

Arranging and Handling Pictures

Back in the 1920s and 1930s, some designers thought it chic to tear the edges of photographs, order them in vignette forms, put them in montages, round their corners, put straight-line or decorative borders around them, or otherwise mutilate them. Although these methods of displaying art enjoy short revivals, they die out again, and designers let the art itself, not its accessories, do the talking.

For most advertising, it is a good rule to present pictures honestly and simply, without quirks, and in a size that can be easily read. So far as a photograph is concerned, nothing serves it quite so well as an ordinary rectangle.

At times its effect can be intensified by exaggerating the rectangle into a severe horizontal or vertical. The late Allen Hurlburt, an editorial art director (of the old *Look*), was a prime mover here. His magazine beautifully displayed deep vertical and wide horizontal photographs along with the more traditional rectangles and squares. But they were seldom tipped in at angles, nor were their edges tampered with.

Look was often able to pick up a subject, a line, or a direction from inside one photograph and match it with a visual thrust in a nearby photograph, thereby unifying a page or spread. Advertising designers do that, too. They also try to relate edges of pictures. They set up an imaginary axis—or several of them—within an ad and use them to line up pieces of art or copy.

When an ad calls for a bleed picture, you should plan for enough extra picture area at the bleed so that when the paper is trimmed, the composition of the picture will not suffer.

With several pictures in the same ad, you might want to butt one edge against the other. Or you may want to arrange the pictures so that, from a distance, they blend into a single irregular shape. You would seldom run a headline across the face of a picture, and you would never run the headline partly over the picture, partly over the white space. The headline's background should be even-textured.

As always, you would arrange the pictures so they "point" into the ad, not away from it. Using several pictures, you would try hard to make one picture lead into the other. And one of the pictures should always overshadow the others. Either that, or the mass of several pictures should overshadow other elements in the ad.

Pictures must be protected from the ravages of wear and harsh treatment so they will be at their best when they finally are put up in front of the printer's camera.

If it is a photograph, you must not write on its back, unless you use a soft grease crayon. Nor can you attach a note to the picture with a paper clip. Any kind of an indentation will pick up a shadow, which will reproduce in the final printing. Crop marks, made with a grease crayon, must be put out in the margins. Ordinarily four are enough: two at the bottom showing width extremities, two at the right side showing depth.

You don't want to get fingerprints on the photograph. You should handle it as you would handle a stereo record or CD.

No photograph should be folded or rolled.

To use a proportion wheel, you turn the inside disk, which represents the size of the original art, to where an original measurement lines up with a printed measurement (outside disk). Let's say your original is 17″ × 20″ (width first) and you want the width of the printed art to be 7″. As this portion of a wheel shows, 17″ (below on the wheel) is to 7½″ (above) as 20″ is to 8⅞″. Proportion wheels are available from a number of sources, including Vip Engineering Services, Stanfordville, N.Y., and most have a built-in "percentage of original size" indicator. In the example used here, the percentage is just short of 45.

Indicating Art on Your Layout

As a nonartist student taking a course in advertising design, you may stand back in awe at that part of the work that requires some drawing. But the instructor does not expect fine draftsmanship. After all, it is not a "Freehand Drawing" or "Drawing and Sketching" course. What the layout needs is simply the *feel* of the planned-for art. The details of the art are not important.

If you use traditional tools instead of a computer to do rough layouts, you should learn to work in broad strokes.

If the drawing is supposed to be in line, a sharp pencil should be used, or a fine-line marker. Where blacks are desired, the areas should be blackened in. They should not be *grayed* in.

For halftones, a blunter pencil, a chisel-point pencil, a lithographic stick, a piece of charcoal or charcoal pencil, a set of gray pastel chalks, a set of gray markers, gray watercolor or opaque paints—any of these can be used to do the job. Then make your drawing on top of the tone. Or you may want to paste down a piece of gray bond or construction paper in the size of the halftone and draw on that. Or you can leave the gray paper as is.

Tone is what is important. Squinting at the drawing or viewing it from a distance, the onlooker should get the general idea of technique and medium and subject matter.

A good way of making the ad stand out from the layout paper without drawing a border around it is to rub a tone up to its edges. Taking a squared sheet of paper, place it up against the border, from inside the ad, then, picking up some lead rubbings from the sandpaper pad, rub a tone across the edge of the overlaid sheet and onto the layout proper. Pulling the overlay sheet away, you will have a crisp edge in gray that feathers out away from the ad.

The diagonal method of changing a picture size on your layout involves putting a transparent sheet over the art (represented here by the heavy box) and, being careful not to press into the art, drawing a vertical line at its left edge and a horizontal line at its bottom and a diagonal line from the left bottom corner to the right top corner and beyond. Measure off the width you want along that bottom line and send up a new vertical. You can create a size for a narrow version of the art (say at *A*) or a wider version (at *B*). Either will be in correct proportion to the original.

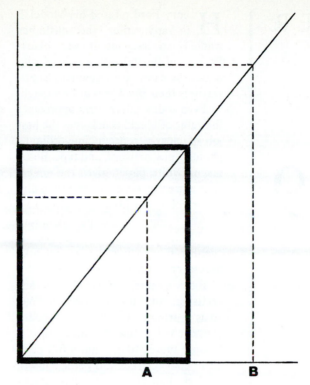

Depending upon how finished your ad roughs are, you will want to prepare them for viewing by someone: instructor, client, printer, overseer, or just an admirer. In a classroom situation, the instructor may want the layouts kept attached in the layout pad. In this case, you will merely keep them unsmudged; and you will print a description of the assignment at some spot, say at the bottom, away from the ad proper. Otherwise, you can rubber-cement the layout to a heavier sheet and flap it with a protective cover. Or you can cut a cardboard frame for it. Or you can cover it with cellophane after first cementing it to a stiff backing board.

The technique for preparing the work for presentation or viewing can be an art in itself.

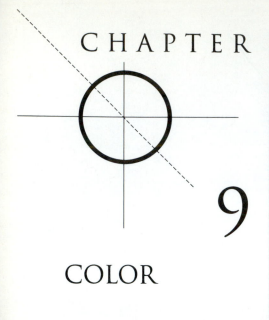

CHAPTER

9

COLOR

Henry Ford offered his Model T in any color the customer wanted, so long as it was black. Printers of the day operated basically under the same arrangement. To advertisers then, black was quite enough.

Even today advertisers appreciate the value of black. Black does the best job of clearly reproducing ordinary photographs, artwork, and type. Black ink on white paper gives the advertiser a greater range of tone than any single color on white.

And using a single ink—it should be black—to reproduce an ad is cheaper than using the several inks necessary to create color.

Black by itself has its place in advertising, but if luring readers to your ad is a primary concern, you should consider color, too. A Starch INRA Hooper survey found that a full-page ad in color attracts 50 percent more readers than the same ad in black-and-white. Better than black alone, color represents with high fidelity the product, its setting, and the people using it. It creates the right atmosphere, the right mood for the ad. It can emphasize easily what needs to be emphasized.

"Black-and-white is for budgets," Eastman Kodak Company said in an ad in *Advertising Age*. "Color is for results." It is the Kodak company's contention that "many products are bought for function, but are sold on appearances. Such as fine tools. To show them in black-and-white can indicate ho-hum work. Color can say pride and craftsmanship."

Food and fashion advertising, especially, benefit from full color. "But the acid test involves the product or situation which is essentially colorless," says the booklet *Color Is for Results* published by Eastman. "The budget-minded advertiser can show a glass of milk, a tuxedo, or a ski slope in black-and-white and get away with it. But if he uses four-color printing. . . ." What followed was a series of "white"-product ads showing that white carries some beautiful built-in colors. You have to look hard for colors in four-color printing of white. But colors are there.

". . . [White] carries with it a reflection not only of other colors, but of texture and tone variation that needs the warmth of four-color reproduction": Phil Gleeson, director of advertising for Paris Accessories for Men. "The interplay of metallic highlights, shadows, and reflections is too subtle to be captured in black-and-white": S. G. Force, vice-president of marketing, Hardware Division, Emhart Corporation.

Full color in a consumer magazine costs the advertiser about a third more than black-and-white. But where advertisers have checked effectiveness of full color, as in a split run, results from the color version of the ad have run as high as fifteen times better than those for the black-and-white version.

There are other reasons for using color. College athletic departments use full color for the tickets they sell to football games—partly to make them appear to be worth the $20 or more they cost the patron, but mostly to discourage outsiders from duplicating the tickets and selling them.

Color is a main ingredient in package design. Color identifies. People look for a red box or a green bottle or a yellow tube. Ask a student what book was used in a course in Principles of Advertising last year, and chances are you will hear

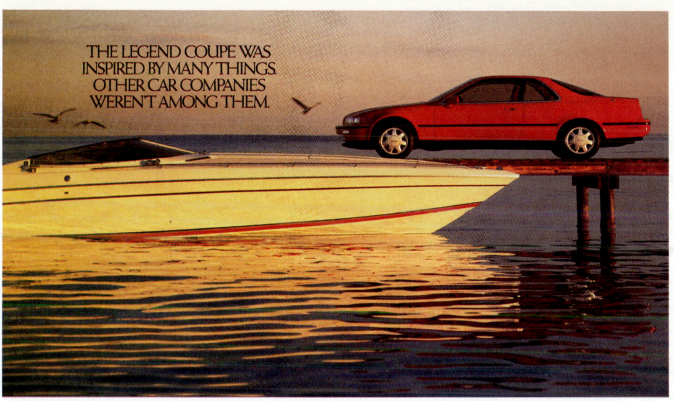

THE LEGEND COUPE WAS INSPIRED BY MANY THINGS. OTHER CAR COMPANIES WEREN'T AMONG THEM.

The Scarab® high-speed racing boat. The Beechcraft Starship® aircraft. The French TGV supertrain. Each is considered to be among the world's most beautiful designs. Each is known for its power, its aerodynamic shape and its ability to combine elements of styling and performance. Elements reflected in the complete redesigning of the 1991 Acura Legend Coupe. An automobile with a 3.2-liter, 24-valve, V-6 engine that now offers 25% more power. A responsive independent double-wishbone suspension that enhances handling and road feel. Driver's side and available passenger's side air bags. And a more luxurious, more ergonomic cabin. With features like these, the real question may no longer be how much the Legend Coupe was inspired by other designs, but how much other designs will be inspired by the Legend Coupe. Call 1-800-TO-ACURA for the dealer nearest you.

Ⓐ **ACURA** PRECISION CRAFTED PERFORMANCE

Photographer Joe Baraban colorfully combines the lines of a boat with the lines of a car to give this Acura ad its impact. Agency: Ketchum, L. A. Art director: Jillian Stern. Copywriter: Bryan Behar.

"a red one" or "one with a brown cover." Faber Birren has observed that where people in tests are exposed to various shapes in various colors, they recall the colors more readily than the forms.

Time and *National Geographic,* among the magazines, gain recognition through persistent use of color borders on their covers: *Time* with red, *National Geographic* with yellow. Think of all the products or companies that incorporate color in their names: Green Giant, Blue Bonnet, Blue Ice, Yellow Cab, Red Zinger among them. In most cases the packages show the colors.

Some ads build their themes around the color used. For a two-page spread in a *New York Times* special travel magazine, *Life* went with a single color: maroon. The bold color covered both pages, with only a floating bottle on the left page and a small amount of copy on the right page, both of them reversed in the color. The bottle had a note in it, as though someone marooned on an island was summoning help. The ad, directed to media buyers in advertising agencies, compared *Life* to *Travel & Leisure.* "Has *Travel & Leisure* Been Marooned?" read the headline. "Not really," the copy began. "But though no one's leaving them behind, the latest Simmons shows that *Life* has made impressive gains." *Life* was selling itself to advertisers wanting to reach travelers and others with high incomes.

If extroverts dominate your audience, you would be more likely to use color than otherwise. Hermann Rorschach, the Swiss psychiatrist, found the cheerful person more responsive to color, the melancholy person more responsive to shape. (In any circumstance, the color lover is more easily influenced than the person who is not much interested in color. The person interested more in shape than in color tends to be introverted and pedantic while exercising strong control over impulses.)

When depending on shape alone—no color—the designer forces the respondent to do more of the work, to *participate* in the ad. Color allows the reader to be more passive. Color comes to the reader. It follows that to weed out lukewarm prospects, an advertiser might want to avoid color.

COLOR

D. FOSTER 90   *HALSEY, ORE.*

But, in general, color these days is almost mandatory in advertising. On long-run ads especially, where so much is invested, the additional cost for color in proportion to the complete cost for the job is minimal in most media. Even in newspaper advertising, color has taken hold.

Through open doors in his computer-equipped van, David Foster, using an electronic stylus and tablet with Dr. Halo software, captures the feel of Halsey, a small town in western Oregon.

What Color Can Do

In a *New Yorker* cartoon, Robert Weber shows a clerk in a men's wear store trying to sell a shirt to a customer. The clerk says, "It comes in five important colors."

People attach remarkable—even healing—qualities to color.

The Impressionist painters helped us develop a love of color and an appreciation of what it can do. No longer do ad makers shy away from unusual com-

A black-and-white version of
Foster's computer painting of Halsey.

FOSTER 90 SUMPTER,OR

In another on-location computer painting, Foster shows a rusty, abandoned car emerging from a melting snow bank at Sumpter, Oregon. These paintings are examples of how integrated computer software can provide color definition and dimension in art.

binations of colors. Ad people try all kinds of colors and combinations, using them for their psychological and emotional possibilities. Advertisers pay attention to the cultural and social application of colors as they create their ads for various groups.

". . . the real value of color is intellectual, not decorative," designer Jan White writes. "It must not be used to dazzle, but to enlighten." He adds: "Whatever 'color creativity' you can muster should be used to impose logic on the content and to enhance the reader's grasp of the message. . . ."

He adds that color can point the reader to special information, create relationships among elements, establish identity, and enliven the message. Using lots of color isn't useful. It is just gaudy. Readers don't want gaudiness; they want guidance."[1]

Sometimes an advertiser picks a color for its shock value rather than for its appropriateness. Poster colors tend to be primary colors: bright, even fluorescent, and generously applied. Sophisticated advertisers tend to use more subtle colors. Often a color ad, even though printed in four (or full) colors, has the look of a single color, with the other colors severely restricted to create a near monochrome. An RCA album featuring The Judds in 1984 showed the mother-daughter duo in what appeared to be shades of violet only, but the printing was actually in full color. This is not a new idea. Pablo Picasso created monochrome paintings during his blue and rose periods.

The mid-1980s saw a trend toward muted, pastel colors. One writer traced the trend to an architect, Michael Graves, who had created a stir with his unor-

Some
products
ask you to
swallow
a lot.

Not
K·Tab® 10mEq

POTASSIUM CHLORIDE
EXTENDED-RELEASE
TABLETS, USP

Abbott Pharmaceuticals, Inc.
North Chicago, IL 60064

6013764

It took full color to provide the right contrast and realism for the white elephant shown in Martin Marietta's two-page magazine ad: "Computer Simulation is Making White Elephants Extinct." That's money the white elephant is eating. Agency: VanSant Dugdale. Art director: Don Schramek. Copywriter: Susan Turner.

thodox buildings with chalky facades. Bloomingdale's in New York commissioned Graves to design one of its shopping bags: "a lovely pastel bag featuring a light blue column with delicate yellow curls," as *Art Direction* put it.[2]

Many advertisers rely on advice and findings of the Color Association of the United States. For instance, they have learned to put bright-colored letters on white packages because such colors suggest strength and purity. Soft-drink manufacturers use white on cans to suggest that the product is low in calories.

Color preference often stems from public events. A rush to golds, browns, and earth tones followed the 1978 King Tutankhamen traveling exhibit. When times are bad, grays seem to be preferred. When times get better, colors become more lively. The love of change also influences the choice of color. Faber Birren, a color researcher, figures an "in" color has a life of about three years.[3]

Kids' exposure to video games, television, and bright, bold colors caused Crayola in 1990 to retire some of its standard colors from its 64-crayon boxes and substitute trendier ones. Among the casualties: blue gray, lemon yellow, orange red, orange yellow, and raw umber. Among the newcomers: dandelion, fuchsia, jungle green, teal blue, and wild strawberry. Crayola introduced a 96-crayon box in 1993 with 16 new colors and invited users to send in names for them.

A magazine called *Colour* made its debut in 1991. A controlled circulation magazine, it went out to 77,000 people in the communications business who work with color. The magazine accepted black-and-white ads (". . . as a creative tool, [color] will never go away"), but the cost of the space was the same as for color ads.[4]

COMPUTER SIMULATION IS MAKING WHITE ELEPHANTS EXTINCT.

It starts innocently enough. Someone gets an idea. A decision is made. And before anyone realizes it, thousands of dollars and innumerable hours have been spent on a system that may not work as intended.

That's how white elephants are born. And why Martin Marietta uses computer simulation to help avoid them. With the aid of some of the world's most power-ful computers, telecommunications and computer software, we're able to put designs to the test while they're still ideas.

The advantages are obvious. We can fine-tune an information network or predict the behavior of a spacecraft all before a penny is spent on design and development. Computer simulation even helps us train users in advance so that they're up to speed by the time a system is ready.

At Martin Marietta, we apply the same creative intelligence to information management that we bring to other systems and products in communications, space, defense electronics, energy and materials.

Because a bad idea can end up costing a lot more than peanuts.

MASTERMINDING TOMORROW'S TECHNOLOGIES *MARTIN MARIETTA*

6801 ROCKLEDGE DRIVE, BETHESDA, MARYLAND 20817

COLOR

Dimensions of Color

You can think of color in terms of both light and pigment. The color is in the light, as Sir Isaac Newton proved in 1667 when he subjected light to a prism. But it takes pigment to show it. All items in nature and on paper that have "color" really have pigments that soak up some of light's color waves while reflecting others. What is reflected is the color you see. The skin of a banana, for instance, soaks up all waves but yellow.

Inks used in printing are made, basically, of pigment concentrates derived from plants, animals, and minerals. Printers can use these as they come from tube or jar or mix them for additional colors.

Like any of nature's wonders, color has its three dimensions: the "width" is the *hue,* the "depth" is the *value,* the "thickness" is the *intensity.*

The hue is the name of the color: red, blue, or whatever.

Value has to do with the lightness of the hue. The lighter the hue, the greater its value. Adding white—lightness—to the hue, you get a *tint;* adding black—darkness—you get a *shade.*

Intensity has to do with the brightness of the color. High-intensity colors are bright colors. A color that has faded through exposure to the elements—maroon is particularly vulnerable—is said to have lost its intensity or "chroma," another word for intensity.

An object shown in a bright color looks larger than the same object shown in a dark color. The bright color radiates—draws the eye outward, expands the object. So if size is what you are selling, you would show a bright-color version of your merchandise.

Any hue can be high-value or low-value, and any can be high-intensity or low-intensity. A hue with high value (light yellow) can still have low intensity (it can be grayed down).

When you realize there is more to color than hue, you can see why colors that ordinarily you would not put together (green and blue? red and brown?) *do* go together very well, provided you choose the right values and intensities. You can combine *any* colors (as nature does) if you give them some thought. Even a green and a pink.

Convince yourself that there is no such thing as an ugly color. There are only wrong combinations. Or the right color in the wrong setting.

Let us say your school colors are green and yellow and you are asked to use them on a direct-mail piece. If you choose a middle kelly green and put it next to canary yellow, you may well be disappointed. But darken and gray the green (lower its value and its intensity) and push the yellow to an umber or an ocher or a beige, and you may change your mind.

White or black or the gray they make in mixing have value—gray can range from light to dark—and you could say they have hue, but they have no intensity.

Of the three dimensions of color, value is the most important. Otherwise, black-and-white advertising would be *infinitely* inferior to color advertising. And that just is not so.

The importance of value can be seen in most of the illustrations in this book. Many of them appeared originally in color. They show up as well as they do in black and white because of the values of the colors used. The hues and intensities make little difference. Color-blind people[5] get along in life as well as they do because the values of colors are different enough to establish solid contrasts.

So when using color in advertising, give plenty of attention to the values of the colors you choose.

Primary and Secondary Colors

Scientists have cataloged any number of primary colors on the spectrum, but to an artist or designer, there are three: red, yellow, and blue.[6] These colors or variations of them, along with black, when printed on white paper, are capable of producing the whole range of color needed in advertising.

Any two primary colors mixed in equal amounts make a *secondary* color. Sec-

Milton Glaser (note the signature) did the illustration for this "Earth's First Soft Drink" Perrier ad. That the bottle seems to be bursting forth from the earth helps the copy line make its point that the product is "Not manufactured, but created by the earth when it was new." The green of the bottle matches the green of the earth to tie the two together. The merging-colors background nicely sets off the art and the reversed and surprinted type lines. Agency: Waring & La Rosa, Inc., New York. Art director and copywriter: Joe La Rosa.

Magically slim. Small, sleek and
very beautiful. Quartz, in 14 karat gold.
The 5½ Ligne, by Movado.

MOVADO
Swiss watchcraft at its most bewitching

It is almost impossible to get away from this ad, your eye moving from the Movado watch up the hand, down through the cat, and onto the watch again, ready to read the small amount of copy. A truly beautiful piece of work designed by Vincent J. Schifano, using a photograph by Barry Seidman. Copywriter: Carol Corwen. Agency: Tolson & Company Advertising, New York.

ondary colors are violet[7] (red and blue), green (blue and yellow), and orange (yellow and red).

The primary and secondary colors make up what are known as "standard colors."

Additional mixing of the standards provides any number of other colors, including the so-called earth colors—the browns—and colors subtle and subdued. The S. D. Scott Printing Co., Inc., New York, has published a *Process Color Guide* that shows five thousand colors that can be made by mixing the three primary colors and black. To pick the right colors for printers, many art directors rely on the Pantone Color Matching System. Information is available from Pantone, Inc., 55 Knickerbocker Road, Moonachie, New Jersey 07074.

You can sharpen your appreciation of color by studying covers of *The New Yorker*. You may not always like the art, you may miss the irony or the nuance, but you will see, each time, a subtle combination of colors that can only be described as satisfying. Watch especially for the covers painted by Gretchen Dow Simpson.[8]

The Color Wheel

To help students understand color, teachers introduce a color wheel containing six standard colors—yellow, green, blue, violet, red, and orange—and six colors in between them.

The closer colors are on the wheel the more harmonious they are. Colors opposite each other on the wheel have nothing in common; different as they are, they "complement" each other. Mixed together, they turn a neutral gray.

Staring at one color for a while, then moving away and looking at a white sheet, you see a hint of its complement. And when one color is featured in a sunlit setting, its shadow will show evidence of the complement.

When you use more than one color in a job, you may want color harmony. You will use mostly colors adjacent on the color wheel then. But if you want color contrast, you will use colors widely separated on the wheel.

Designers do not shrink from combining harmonious *and* complementary colors in a single job. Nor do they avoid always the mixing of warm and cool colors. But colors should be *mostly* harmonious or *mostly* complementary; similarly, they should be *mostly* cool or *mostly* warm.

This color wheel shows the common hues. Colors close to each other on the wheel are harmonious. Colors opposite each other are complementary.

Appropriate Colors

Color is an area in design (along with type) that can be researched. Falstaff Brewing Company, for instance, through studies made by Lee Research, St. Louis, found that reds, oranges, and yellows worked best for its products in its direct mail, point-of-purchase, and packaging programs.

People develop—maybe they are born with—individual preferences in color. An R. H. Bruskin Associates survey found that, among adults, blue is the favorite color—and by a wide margin: red was the second-favorite color; green was third. Other studies show that men like blues, women reds. The Fred Feucht Design Group, Pleasantville, New York, says that people who like purple have deep mystical feelings, seek new experiences, like to ski, and tend to pay for things with cash. "One quarter of college women say purple is their favorite color," the firm reports. "But only nine percent of college men pick purple, and many actively reject the color."[9]

For ads meant to be read by one or the other sex, you might capitalize on information like this. But you must not indulge yourself, from a color standpoint, by playing your favorite just because it is your favorite. For instance, while you may prefer subdued colors, you should remember that in an ad directed toward teenagers, harsher, brighter colors might be a better choice.

Not only should you have an awareness of color preferences among various publics; you should know the moods certain colors create. Take the matter of warmth and coolness in colors. Certain products, certain services deserve a cool setting, others a warm setting. Cool colors are the greens and blues. Warms are the reds and yellows. A blue with some red in it—a blue tending toward the violet—would be less cool than a blue without any red. Even neutral colors—grays—can be either warm or cool, depending on the mixture of pigment.

Warm colors cheer readers, stimulate them; cool colors calm them, make them feel rested. When a color is too cool, it becomes depressing. When it is too warm, it is too stimulating.

Warm colors seem to advance—move out from the sheet. Yellow is the most advancing color of all. Cool colors recede. When you want a hand jutting out from a poster in an "Uncle Sam Needs You" pose, you will see to it that the hand gets painted in warm tones, the area around it in cool tones. Working warm colors in at the edges of the ad you will, in effect, give it a border and unify it.

A single hue, though basically warm *or* cool, comes in *both* warm and cool versions. For instance: red, a warm color, when blued a bit becomes cooler than normal.

Consider how reference to color has entered the language to help it cover mood and attitude: *green* with envy, true *blue, yellow* in battle, *red*-faced, *purple* prose, *white* knuckles, *black* mood.

Nobody knows how all these references to colors got started, but some of them seem logical enough. When some people are embarrassed, their faces *do* turn red. When you hold onto a steering wheel too hard, you *do* stop the flow of blood to your knuckles.

It is certainly true that some colors stimulate people more than others. Knute Rockne, former football coach at Notre Dame, had his team's dressing room painted red, the visitors' dressing room blue, because he was convinced the red would keep his team fired up. Blue, he thought, would relax the visitors, causing them to let their guard down.

Interior decorators know that warm colors tend to make rooms smaller, while cool colors make them larger. It has even been suggested that rooms where temperatures must be kept low *feel* warmer to people if the rooms are decorated in warm colors like browns, oranges, and reds.

Symbolism of Color

Colors not only carry moods; they also carry symbolism. The symbolism and the mood may be related, but a good bit of the symbolism results from mere usage. Interestingly, a single color may say opposite things.

In working out details for a Schmid Brothers campaign to sell its fine giftware, art director Harry Kirker of Marvin & Leonard Advertising Company, Boston, decided to show, through full-color photography, a contrast of textures. "Each piece is delicate," he said, "and we wanted to put it against something rough." Kirker hired Phil Marco, New York, as his photographer. Each of the photographs used in the series, including this one, took about three hours to produce, not counting preparation. Kirker and Marco looked long for models—men on the street—with just the right hands to provide the contrasts. For this photo, Marco used a glazier who had been installing windows in a nearby building. A mixture of fine clay and water was rubbed on the glazier's hands before the photograph was taken.

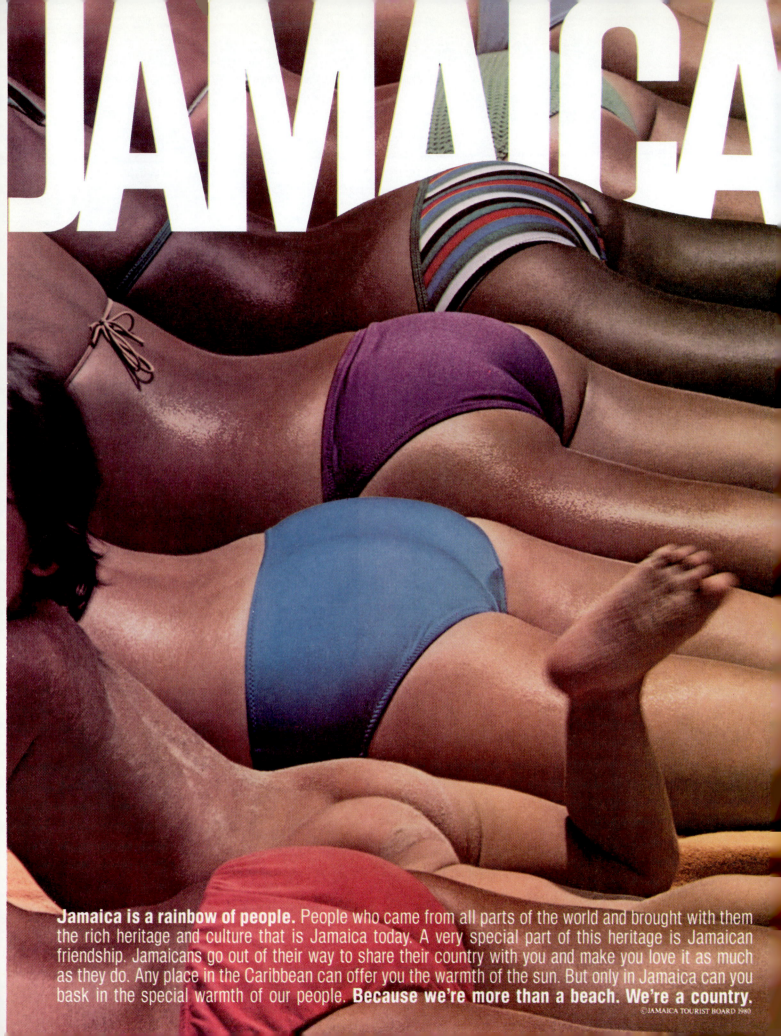

JAMAICA

Jamaica is a rainbow of people. People who came from all parts of the world and brought with them the rich heritage and culture that is Jamaica today. A very special part of this heritage is Jamaican friendship. Jamaicans go out of their way to share their country with you and make you love it as much as they do. Any place in the Caribbean can offer you the warmth of the sun. But only in Jamaica can you bask in the special warmth of our people. **Because we're more than a beach. We're a country.**

Full color helps this strong, beautiful ad make the point that "Jamaica is a rainbow of people." The one-word headline is set in a typeface large enough to appear in reverse letters in a patterned area of the photograph and to even bleed at the top. Note how the headline settles down in back of one of the bodies, as a logo for a magazine might do. The ad has a kind of magazine cover look. Arlene K. Hoffman, president of Hoffman Mann Inc., New York, designed the ad. Robert Freson took the photograph.

For instance, *yellow* is a sacred color in the Orient and in Europe, especially as it approximates the color gold. In the West it can mean treachery or a lack of courage.

We associate yellow with madness. It is, after all, the color van Gogh was at home with.

With a small amount of green, yellow becomes especially unpleasant to most people.

Popular in America in the 1890s, when it said "elegance," yellow later lost favor. But if the color you use must be luminous, what better choice (sticking with standard inks) than yellow!

It is the warning color.

Red symbolizes passion. Some say it raises the blood pressure, speeds the pulse. The American Automobile Association is convinced that people who drive red cars cause more accidents than people who drive cars painted other colors. Red-car drivers appear to have a more carefree spirit.

But red is also a color appropriate to the religious. It is zealous.

Red also suggests happiness.

Orange represents knowledge and civilization. And it is the color of warmth, energy, force, and gaiety.

Violet, combining blue (spirituality) with red (courage), is the logical color for royalty. It also stands for loneliness.

More on the blue side, violet stands for depression.

Blue, a cool, passive color, stands for both aloofness (the blue blood) and fidelity (true blue). It also stands for sobriety and fear. It suggests sky, water, ice. It says "transparent."

Green, the most restful of colors, says "fresh." It is a fruitful color. But it can also convey a feeling of guilt, disease, and even terror.

White is for purity, of course, and truth. In some Oriental countries, white is used for mourning.

Black symbolizes depression, sorrow, gloom, death. Yet it carries with it a degree of sensuality and even elegance.

But perhaps we pay too much attention to these attributes. Humorist Fran Lebowitz says that "Blue is supposed to indicate serenity because it is the supposed color of water, which is supposedly a calm and restful element. In dealing with champions of this hue one could do worse than remember that water is also the favorite environment of sharks and the cause, nine times out of ten, of death by drowning."[10]

The Unusual in Color

Do not be afraid to move away from ordinary use of color. For instance, try overlapping colors, letting a new color form in the area of overlap. The transparent ink will do this for you automatically. For dramatic treatment of a short headline, you can allow a large letter in one color to overlap a large letter in a second color.

Or run part—only part—of an illustration in color, the rest in black-and-white. Or run a tint block behind the part you want emphasized.

Or use color blocks alternately with black-and-white blocks, placing items and prices in each block.

Or run artwork in a medium-to-light color as a pattern or decorative element, leaving the type, in black, in full command.

Or underneath a copy block run some art in a weak color, not so it will be seen clearly but so it will provide atmosphere for the ad. An old device, admittedly, but one that can be dusted off and used occasionally.

Or use off-register color. The color plate is prepared without much regard for how it fits, so that one color will spill over into another's area. The resultant art has a refreshing looseness.

Or have the art for the color plate prepared with a crayon after the fashion of the elementary school artist. The primitive look has a charm all its own.

These three color balls show how additional colors are made in printing when one primary color is printed over another.

Or run only one tiny spot of color in the ad, but in a bright ink. You could, for instance, design your ad so all type is reversed in a black block. Then you would choose one of the reversed lines or words and fill it with color.

Or run a line reproduction of a photograph over a solid color block. You will be surprised at the strength, the power of such treatment.

Or surround your color areas with bold, black lines and boxes.

Or try fluorescent or metallic inks and papers made from offbeat materials and in nondescribable colors.

The Production of Color

When you settle for black-and-white, you get a one-color printing job. Adding a color, say blue, you get a two-color job. Blue would be called, then, a "second color."

You can get two-color, three-color, four-color printing—or more. *Look* magazine, before it died, made noise about offering advertisers a fifth color: white. That does not sound like much, but when you compare a pure white ink with the off-white you have in most magazine paper stock, you see that a little added white might be worth the extra expense. Some auto manufacturers, when they introduce their new models, buy a fifth color in the magazines. The fifth color often is silver.

But for most ads, four colors will give you all the color range you need: Besides the primary colors, you get green, orange, brown, purple, and the others. Primary colors are either printed side by side, and the reader's eye mixes them, or, transparent, they are printed on top of each other and so change in the printing.

The graphic designer works basically with two kinds of color in printing: *process* and *spot* (or *flat*).

In process color work (four-color) the photoengraver or camera operator, using filters, separates the primary colors in the color original (color transparency, color print, or painting) and records the separation on film. In this case, the primary colors are yellow, magenta, and cyan blue. The resultant negatives help produce positive prints, which are rephotographed, through a screen, to make new negatives. The new now-screened negatives help make plates—one for each primary and for black. The combination of colors provides a full-color effect. "Full color" is possible with just three plates (omitting the black), but such short cutting produces inferior reproductions.

Solid yellow in the area illuminating the burglar helps this ad make its point on home security. Client: Arkansas Power & Light Co., Little Rock. Agency: Cranford, Johnson, Robinson Associates. Art director: Debbie Strobel. Designer: Jim Johnson. Cartoonist: Jim Johnson. Copywriter: Craig Smith.

The author's black-and-white photograph of Alice Chan at work on a layout is shown (1) in black-and-white, (2) in duotone, (3) in black on a tint block, and (4) as posterized art.

In spot color, an artist can separate the colors for the printer, offering artwork for each color on its own sheet. This can be done by making the principal part of the drawing, usually the black part, on a sheet of drawing paper or a piece of illustration board, then making a drawing of each of the other main colors on a sheet of frosted acetate, which is fastened over the original. Even though the overlays are for other colors, the artist works in black or red, colors that will be picked up easily by the camera. When the plates are ready, the printer will use the correct inks.

In making the overlay for the printer, the artist puts down a series of "register marks" to help the printer line up the plates in printing.

If the colors are rather simply used with no overlapping, the artist can make a single drawing—called a "keyline drawing." On a tracing paper overlay—a guide to the printer—the artist marks with color pencils where the color is to go. The printer simply makes more than one copy of the line negative—three if the job is three-color—and then paints out on each negative the part that is not to print.

While advertisers like color in their ads to make the product realistic or the package recognizable, there are problems. For instance, it is difficult to match exactly a color on a package with a color in a periodical. Different inks are used. And color on one kind of stock—on the carton—looks different when it is printed on magazine stock or newsprint.

Where you place the color in designing a direct-mail piece can make a difference in the quality of the color, especially if it involves both process and spot color pieces. Check with your printer at the design stage to determine the most advantageous placement.

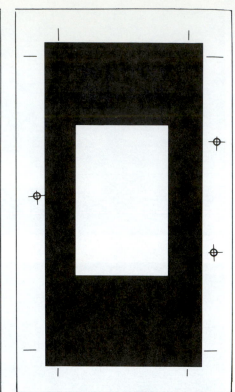

For the mechanical for the two-color folder shown above and at the right, the designer had to prepare the original art (in black) and three overlays: one for the outside color (a tint of black plus yellow), one for the pure yellow inside the sun, and one for the tint of black in the clouds. Client: Midgley's Glass. Art studio: Rubick & Funk.

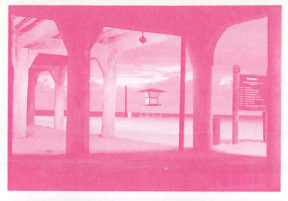

Tom Rubick's photograph of the pier at Huntington Beach, California, is shown here separated into four colors for printing. The full-color reproduction results from combining the four plates made from the separations.

Color and Computers

The color that shows up in the printed version of an ad is several times removed from first sketches. The tools used for thumbnails and rough layouts may differ from those used for comprehensives. And the printer's inks differ in color from the color in artists' and designers' tools, although manufacturers make efforts to coordinate the colors. Often the color in printed ads becomes a disappointment to designers—or at least a surprise. Keeping in touch with the printing firm and checking proofs become important parts of art directors' jobs.

Of course the computer has taken its place in the color world.

Counting all the hues, tints, and shades, you can call up nearly 17,000,000 colors at a computer station. At least that's the claim made by computer manufacturers. But, asks Alyce Kaprow, a computer graphics consultant, "How many colors can the eye actually see at any one time? How many colors do we actually need at any one time? How many colors can be displayed on the screen simultaneously?"

Kaprow points out that when working with computer color an artist must consider the output device. "Most low- to medium-cost printers can't faithfully reproduce color on screen. What is full-color, sometimes thousands and thousands of individual pixel colors, is only approximated with tabletop printers."[11]

Soften the look of security.

Black-and-white photography would have told about the shape and workings of this hardware, but it took full color to bring out its beauty and to capture the attention of persons making important decisions about building design and construction. With the right photographer on the job, there is color to be found in every object, no matter how gray it may appear to the uninitiated. Client: Russwin. Agency: Horton, Church & Goff, Rhode Island. Art director: Bob Saabye. Copywriter: Ted Albert. Photographer: Clint Clemens.

Desktop computers can be used today not only to create ads in color but also to make the color separations necessary in platemaking.

Cutting the Cost of Color

Whenever you use color in advertising you can count on an earlier deadline—to take care of color separations, additional presswork, and the like—and more expense. For a short-run job, the expense and trouble may not be worth it.

As a designer, you have a number of ways of keeping color costs down. For instance, when you would like to use color photography but cannot afford it, you might consider one of three possible handlings of black-and-white photographs which, although more expensive than regular handlings, still keep the budget manageable.

One is the *duotone*. In this case, a single photograph submitted to the printer is used to make two negatives (the screen is turned slightly for the second) and two plates. One plate prints a color, the other prints black. (In some advertising, where high quality is needed, one plate prints black, the other a gray.) With a duotone you get the feel of color while holding onto the strength, the tone variation, offered by black.

Another handling is the *halftone over a tint*. The student may not be able to tell this from a duotone, but the trained observer sees a big difference. The color under the halftone remains constant; the picture has less depth, but there is a satisfying, a restful quality there that you cannot get any other way. It is like printing in black on a pastel stock, but with pure white at the edges of the picture.

A third handling involves a *silhouette halftone in a field of color*. The color goes only up to the edge of the black-ink silhouette, so the halftone itself is printed on the white paper stock. A special piece of artwork has to be made for the color plate.

All three of these require two printings. You would use any one of them when you plan to use a second color anyway.

You might also try "posterizing" the colors. You will get "full color" without resorting to process color. And you will get an unusual effect.

Here is how it works:

Submitting a regular photograph to the printer, ask for two, three, or four line negatives (depending upon how many colors you want), each negative getting more exposure than the one before. One negative, for instance, might pick up all tone 80 percent and above, another all tone 60 percent and above, another all tone 30 percent and above. Use the negative that picked up the most tone—30 percent and above—for the *lightest* color—yellow. Use the one next in line for red. Use the third for blue.

The colors are printed on top of one another (the lightest color being printed first) so that one color does not obscure the others.

And now consider the ways of getting color without paying anything for it:

■ *Use tints of a single color*. In black—or in any color—you can use Ben Day-like blocks of various strengths. The same inking, the same presswork takes care of it all. The tints range from 10 percent of the solid tone up to 90 percent of the solid tone. Taking one of them, say 60 percent, you can ask for it in any of several screens, from 50- to 133-line and beyond. In other words, a single tint is available in various degrees of coarseness.

To get a tint of the second color, you shouldn't go darker than a 70 percent screen. Higher-percentage screens result in a closing up of the dots. Nor should you often go finer than a 100-line screen. Finer screens (120-line, 133-line, 150-line) need a lot of attention in printing, and the stock should be smooth, preferably coated.

Printing a tint block over another color, you get a brand new color—a third color. A tint of black over yellow will give you a green. The same tint over red will give you a maroon.

■ *Print in a colored ink, skipping the black*. This will work only if the color you choose is dark, near a black. Otherwise your halftones will be washed out.

COLOR

faded. And your type will be hard to read. You can print the color on a stock other than white, say dark green on gray.

- *Print in black, but on a colored stock.*
- *Confine your color to one side of the sheet—or one side of the signature, if a booklet is involved.* You will get a second color on fewer pages but at a lower printing cost.
- *Rely on "black-and-white color."* This simply means combining generous blocks of blacks with ruled rectangles and Ben Day tints; putting reverses in some of the blocks, surprints in others; using a variety of types. The effect is circusy, perhaps a little cheap; but the job will be "colorful."

Choosing a Second Color

An advertiser talking about color in a magazine—especially in general-circulation magazine—means, usually, *full* color. Talking about color in news-papers or direct mail, the advertiser means, usually, black plus one color—a second color.

As an imaginative designer, you can do a lot with a second color. You can almost create the illusion of a full-color job, and at a considerable savings over full-color costs. All in one ad you can run black on white, color on white, white surrounded by color, white surrounded by black, and color surrounded by black. Screening the color to a tint or tints and using further surprints and reverses and tints of black over the color, you can get even more variety.

So the second color to choose, usually, would be in the medium range—light enough to contrast with the black areas, dark enough to contrast with the white of the paper. Red is especially useful.

Medium greens and blues are good. Yellow is poor. If yellow is the second color, it should be used in large blocks with no reverses; it should not be used by itself to print the type.

EVERY FALL, NORTH CAROLINA HAS A COLORING CONTEST.

Each fall, our heartland forests and mountain ranges compete in glorious displays of color. Yet, the color isn't just in our leaves. You'll find it in yellow-slickered fishermen casting in the emerald surf. In the pastel prism of Rainbow Falls. In jars of golden honey and blueberry jam on a roadside stand. In quilts hand-stitched in vibrant hues. And in lively Cherokee festivals and county fairs. So, come to North Carolina this fall. And enjoy a contest that makes everyone a winner. Just send in the coupon to receive our colorful, free travel package.

Name _____
Address _____
City _____ State _____ Zip _____

North Carolina
North Carolina Travel, Dept. 707, Raleigh, NC 27699. Or call 1-800-VISIT NC. Operator 707, weekdays 9 a.m.-5 p.m.

This small-space ad talking about color in North Carolina doesn't itself need color to put its point across. "Coloring Contest" in the headline refers to the fact that "Each fall, our heartland forests and mountain ranges compete in glorious displays of color." The copy points to other color in the state, inviting readers to "enjoy a contest that makes everyone a winner." The client is the North Carolina Division of Travel and Tourism. Agency: McKinney & Silver.

The party begins.

I can drive when I drink.

2 drinks later.

I can drive when I drink

After 4 drinks.

I can drive when I drink.

After 5 drinks.

I can drink when I drive

7 drinks in all.

I can drive when I drink

The more you drink, the more coordination you lose. That's a fact, plain and simple.
It's also a fact that 12 ounces of beer, 5 ounces of wine and 1¼ ounces of spirits all have the same alcohol content. And consumed in excess, all can affect you. Still, people drink too much and then go out and expect to handle a car.
When you drink too much, you can't handle a car. You can't even handle a pen.

The House of Seagram

For reprints please write Advertising Dept. PR-85.
The House of Seagram.
375 Park Ave., N.Y., N.Y. 10152.
© 1986 The House of Seagram, N.Y.

Joseph E. Seagram & Sons, Inc., has been running this institutional ad for many years. This version is only slightly different from earlier versions. The ad is another example of simple use of a second color. All of this went on a single sheet, with the handwriting separated out by the platemaker for blue inking. Blue represents handwriting better than black does. Agency: Warwick Advertising.

Max Seabaugh did the pop art, appropriate to the story line, for this ad for Radius, a computer monitor that shows colors exactly as they are to print out. No surprises. Rob Bagot wrote the third-person, past-tense, narrative copy. Agency: Goodby, Berlin & Silverstein. Art director: Tracy Wong.

At least for direct mail, no two-color combination works better than red and black. One group of tests over a fourteen-year period showed red and black out-pulled every other combination. Writing to circulation directors of magazines, Eliot Schein, president of Schein/Blattstein Advertising, said, "If the graphics people you use are getting tired of red and black, it would be better to change graphics people rather than to allow them to change your colors."[12]

That is a pretty black-and-white observation, and obviously there are some clients—and some audiences—who deserve different color combinations in two-color printings. But at least you should give some initial consideration to red and black.

It is not a good idea to cover the *entire* area of the ad with the color. When you do that, you throw away your white. Actually you are back to a one-color job again: black on a colored stock.

Indicating Color on Your Layout

With a computer, you can call up colors on screen and print them as proofs. You can also make the separations necessary to make negatives to make the plates. But assuming you need to indicate color using traditional tools, proceed like this: Pick from among color pencils, crayons, pastel sticks, color felt markers, color ink, colored paper, tempera paint, designers' colors, and watercolors. Because it is impossible with these tools to depict exactly the color you have in mind, as a guide to the printer, submit with the layout a color swatch clipped from some other printing or a code number from an ink-specimen book.

The ideal tool is the marker, available in a generous variety of colors and in blunt and fine tips. If you cannot afford all the colors you need to do a layout, you can come close by applying available colors over each other on the layout.

If you use a color pencil, use it "side fashion" to cover large areas.

Crayon or pastel sticks are useful for covering large areas, too. Break off a less-than-one-inch chunk and scrub on the color, like this:

In covering large areas, work in broad sweeps. Do not be concerned about filling in perfectly to every edge. What you want is a basic tone. In some cases you may be able to use pieces of colored paper.

You may find it necessary to use more than one tool to indicate a single color: something blunt for the solid areas, something fine for the lettering. It is not always easy to match the colors. One of the advantages of markers is that blunt and fine tips are color-coordinated.

To show type in reverse you can either outline the letters and fill in around them or lay down a solid area of color and do your letters in white paint. If you use pastels for the solid areas, you will have to apply a fixative before you paint the letters.

Keep the principles of design in mind as you work. Proportion is particularly important. Do not allow your ad to become half black and white in area, half color. Either let color dominate, or use it for accent purposes. A spot of color in two or three places in the ad will give you more color impact than color scattered indiscriminately throughout.

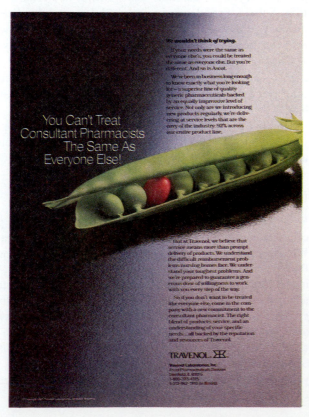

To dramatize a headline, Travenol Laboratories, Inc. (Baxter Healthcare Corporation) uses red—the only red in a full-color ad, which appeared in *The Consultant Pharmacist*—to make a consultant pharmacist pea stand out from other peas in a pod. Agency: Noble Arnold. Designer: John Perkins.

CHAPTER 9

10

NEWSPAPER ADVERTISING

With reports showing that most people get their news these days from television and radio, newspapers appear to be a dying medium. Numbers are down, and, worse, young people—people advertisers most want to reach—are less likely to read newspapers than older people. Yet, nearly 1,600 dailies continue to serve readers in the United States, with a total circulation of more than 60,300,000. More than 100 dailies operate in Canada with a total circulation of more than 5,000,000.[1] You can double or even triple the figures when you consider pass-along readership. (Circulation figures are always smaller than readership figures.)

About 875 of the dailies publish Sunday issues. Add to these figures the several thousand weekly and semi-weekly papers and the hundreds of ethnic, religious, and college and university papers and you get a still-vital advertising medium. In fact, newspapers rank right up there with television in the total amount of money spent on media by advertisers. Yes, newspapers continue to represent a major showcase for advertising, a place where many people not only get their start in this creative business, but also spend entire careers.

Of course, newspapers feel the competition from other media, especially from direct marketing, including direct-mail and specialty publications. As a result, newspapers of the 1990s are developing computer data bases of information about readers so that advertisers can better target them.

Here's one way this worked for the Spokane, Washington *Spokesman-Review*: The paper pulled the names of 7,000 dog owners from its list of subscribers and sent them a letter about a promotion for a local pet shop. The letter asked readers to watch for an ad in the paper that would give them a discount on any purchase and a dollar off a photograph that would be taken of dog owner and dog. The shop owner estimated that the letter and ad brought between 200 and 300 new customers to the store in addition to many old ones.[2]

Although evening newspapers outnumber morning newspapers, the switch is to morning publication, partly to better serve local advertisers. Most of the big papers are morning papers.

Advertising accounts for close to two-thirds of the contents of daily and Sunday newspapers. What is left is called the "news hole," and into that go news, editorials, and features of various kinds.

What a newspaper charges for various size ads is covered on a rate card made available to all advertisers. Some cards list rates; others also celebrate the region served and push the papers as ideal vehicles for reaching buyers. *The Siuslaw News,* a weekly in Florence, Oregon, with a circulation of a little more than 6,000, talks about the makeup of the people there. ". . . a diverse cross section. . . . Many of the local residents are direct descendants of early settlers of Florence and its environs. . . . The stability of the economy is enhanced by a flourishing retirement community."

Many papers offer special rates to non-commercial advertisers. The *News* charges non-profit groups and clubs $4.40 per column inch instead of the base rate of $5.25 if paid in advance. The *News-Times,* up the coast at Newport (circulation about 11,000), offers a $4 rate to local non-profit and civic groups instead of a $6.36 base rate if the advertising will "aid or otherwise assist a worthwhile local cause."[3]

One of *Standard Rate & Data Service*'s regularly issued publications covers newspapers and their rates and requirements.

Like other media, newspapers do some policing of ads, refusing to accept those that violate rules set up by management. Part of the screening comes from the threat of lawsuits. Under fair housing laws, newspapers can be successfully sued for real or implied discrimination in the wording of housing ads. Terms to be scrutinized include "exclusive area," "good family neighborhood," "near churches," and even "ocean view." (The latter might offend blind people.) Even the pictures in ads can cause problems. The courts could conclude that a picture of only whites in a housing ad could mean "whites only." The Washington *Post* tells advertisers that one-fourth of the people shown in real estate ads appearing in the paper must belong to minority groups.[4]

Like magazines and other media, newspapers tend to build specialized audiences. This was especially true when many of the cities supported competing newspapers. One paper may have been for the better educated, for instance, while another served the working class. When, years ago, the sensationalist New York *Post* was trying to increase its circulation to match that of the *Times,* the *Post*'s advertising director went to Bloomingdale's to sell the store some space. Bloomingdale's told the director that the *Times'* readers were *its* customers. "Your readers are our shoplifters."[5]

Newspapers in the United States are a medium serving local or regional audiences. Two exceptions are *The Wall Street Journal* and *The Christian Science Monitor.* The category of national dailies expanded in late 1982 when *USA Today* appeared. Unlike the other two, *USA Today* is designed for the average reader rather than for the businessperson or the intellectual.

The product of computers and satellite transmission, *USA Today* draws on writing from its own staff and the staffs of Gannett's chain of local dailies. With its mostly short news items, the paper is marked by flashy graphics and excellent full-color-printing. It directs itself especially to the television generation. It is no accident of design that the dispensers placed everywhere to sell copies of the paper look like TV sets on pedestals. One of its ads directed to media buyers shows one of these dispensers with rabbit ears. "The People Who Grew Up on TV . . . Have Helped Us Grow Into No. 1!" says the ad's headline.

Unlike other print media, newspapers generally maintain their own printing plants. The weeklies, to keep their presses busy, often do job printing on days when there are no issues.

The Appeal to Advertisers

Like other publications, newspapers strive to keep their images up. Aware that some critics think it is superficial, *USA Today* used front cover space on *Editor & Publisher* (the magazine carries ads there) to say that "if *USA Today* is lightweight, call it Boom-Boom Mancini!" The ad quoted an *Adweek* writer to say that the features are written to be understood, that people quote from them at cocktail parties, that the sports section is "a sports fan's dream," and that the lively and colorful graphics in the paper inspire better graphics in other papers. "Like the championship boxer, [*USA Today*] 'packs a wallop'—for readers and advertisers."[6]

Some image-making campaigns for newspapers are designed to attract subscribers, others to attract advertisers. The campaigns to attract advertisers are the more persistent. Such advertising sells the community as one that is receptive to brand-name as well as local advertising. It sells the paper as a vital force in the community, respected for its news and editorial coverage. It also tells of its advantages over other media, including competing newspapers.

The bigger dailies have been upgrading their locally edited magazine sections to woo local advertisers who lean toward the city and regional magazines and magazines with regional editions. To give advertisers better production, newspapers sometimes print these sections at rotogravure plants away from their home

These are two of a series of full-page newspaper ads sponsored by the *News-Sentinel* of Fort Wayne, Indiana, to gain reader appreciation for the paper's various sections. Body copy placement varied from ad to ad, but the large headline and gridded background held the series together. The pictured reader was always dressed appropriately. Agency: Bonsib, Inc.

PGE (Portland General Electric), a utilities company, shows how good design can make an almost impossible shape work for an ad. These one-column-wide by full-newspaper-deep public service ads stress safety as it relates to powerlines. The art is all in line for good newspaper production. The headline for the rattlesnake ad reads: "Unfortunately, downed powerlines don't come with a built-in warning system." Agency: Borders, Perrin & Norrander. Art director: Terry Schneider. Copywriter: Greg Eiden.

The headline for the hole-in-the-earth ad reads: "Dig down about eighteen inches and what you find may shock you."

The headline for the tree ad reads, "See how easy it is to spot a powerline when you're pruning a tree?" The point, of course, was to show that it *isn't* easy. The copy block says, "Powerlines love to hide behind tree limbs. . . ."

Unfortunately, downed powerlines don't come with a built-in warning system.

It's impossible to tell if a downed powerline is hot, or not. If you see one, don't touch. But do call 911 and ask for assistance.

Portland General Electric

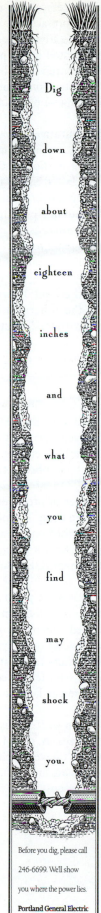

Dig down about eighteen inches and what you find may shock you.

Before you dig, please call 246-6699. We'll show you where the power lies.

Portland General Electric

See how easy it is to spot a powerline when you're pruning a tree?

Powerlines love to hide behind tree limbs. Don't set yourself up for a shocking surprise. If there are powerlines near or in your trees, call 644-6707 for advice before you prune.

Portland General Electric

bases. Or they make use of "heatset" offset presses that offer better quality printing than that available from regular offset presses.

Many of the larger dailies offer advertisers the advantage of regional editions to reach people nearest the stores or most interested in the products or services.

Sometimes a local advertiser takes an ad prepared for it by one paper and re-uses it in another. People in the newspaper industry don't worry much about this and, in fact, may send PMTs (camera-ready copies) of the ad to other newspapers as a service to the advertiser.

Many newspapers employ publishers' representatives (reps) to sell advertising space to national advertisers. To aid advertising agencies in the preparation of this advertising, which represents only a small portion of the total amount of advertising in newspapers, the industry in the United States in 1984 adopted the Standard Advertising Unit (SAU), a modular system of measurement. Canadian newspapers adopted a similar system, the Canadian Newspaper Unit (CNU), in 1985. In their billing for space sent to national advertisers, newspapers now use a Standard Advertising Invoice (SAI). You can get information about these standards from Newspaper Advertising Bureau, 1180 Avenue of the Americas, New York, New York 10036.

American Newspaper Publishers Association and Newspaper Advertising Bureau decided to merge in 1992, becoming the American Newspaper Association, to "more efficiently and effectively deal with the industry's daunting problems."[7]

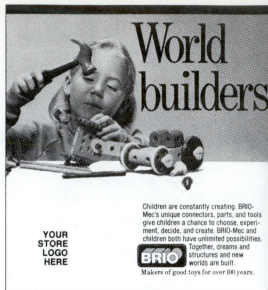

Brio, a toy maker, makes this ad available to local stores for newspaper insertion. Art directors: Rick Tharp and Thom Marchionna of Tharp Did It design studio. Copywriter: Jane Krejci. Photographer: Franklin Avery.

National Advertising

Two kinds of advertising get into the newspapers: national and local.

National ads for newspapers, prepared by advertising agencies, are much like magazine ads. Local ads, prepared by local advertisers, local agencies, or by the newspapers' advertising departments, are something else again. This chapter is concerned mostly with these ads.[8] But first, some observations about national advertising.

National advertising arrives at the newspaper in proof, or plate form, ready for insertion. The creative work has already been done. The newspaper does little more than make sure the advertising gets published on the appointed date.

For the national advertiser, the newspaper offers a chance to go into detail about advertising first placed on TV or in the magazines. But the newspaper ad can introduce products as well.

Like all media, newspapers suffer from as well as profit from trends in advertising. An advertiser—or a class of advertisers—will become disillusioned with one basic medium and move to another. Mercedes-Benz for a time discontinued its newspaper advertising in favor of spot advertising on television because of the "irresponsibility" of some newspapers. The company felt that it was getting poor reproduction. And some papers would not even send tear sheets. Another reason given by the company was that the price of the car kept it out of the reach of most newspaper readers.

At one time newspaper ads were measured in agate lines (14 to the column inch), but now columns and inches mark the sizes. A 1 × 1 ad would be an ad one column wide by 1 inch deep, an ad that can't have much impact. A 2 × 10 ad would be a two-column-wide by 10-inch-deep ad, an ad that would do a better job for the advertiser but that would, of course, cost more in space charges. A 2 × 10 ad would be billed as 20 inches.

A national ad for WD-40 going into newspapers wipes out part of a headline to dramatize the product's cleaning capacity. The list of what can be cleaned bleeds at the bottom to suggest that the list is too long to fit into the ad. A second color—yellow—on the can helps duplicate its true look. Readers will be able to spot the product on store shelves. Agency: Phillips-Ramsey, Inc., San Diego.

Amway uses vertical alignments for the elements in this large newspaper ad but puts everything on a slant for a sense of urgency. The logo and the horizon line in the photo of the yacht are the only horizontal elements, and they are there to provide a bit of contrast, and change of pace. Amway is unable to show all one million of the distributors mentioned in the headline, of course, but the cropped crowd-scene photograph helps make the point. Designer: Ward Veldman. Agency: Stevens Inc. of Grand Rapids, Michigan.

For best reproduction quality, the Newspaper Advertising Bureau asks agencies and others preparing ads for newspapers to:

- *Create art that doesn't have to take a big reduction.*
- *Use an 85-line screen for halftones. (Some large-circulation offset papers prefer a 65-line screen.)*
- *Avoid using black-and-white prints from color transparencies (even though some newspapers shoot all their news photos in color and run some in black-and-white).*
- *Avoid textured paper for photographic prints.*
- *Use sans serif typefaces for any reverse type.*

Local Advertising

Local advertising breaks down into two categories: classified and display. Classified advertising makes little use of design. For most newspapers it is nothing more than column after column of small-type listings.

Display advertising, on the other hand, *does* require designing, and often it is the newspaper that does the job.

The newspaper medium has the advantage, important to designers as well as copywriters, of serving readers who are actually hunting for ads. It also gives designers a giant format to work with.

Retail stores are the big users of display advertising in newspapers. A few stores take out full-page newspaper ads, especially at holiday time, to polish their images, but primarily the stores take out ads, large or small, to sell merchandise,

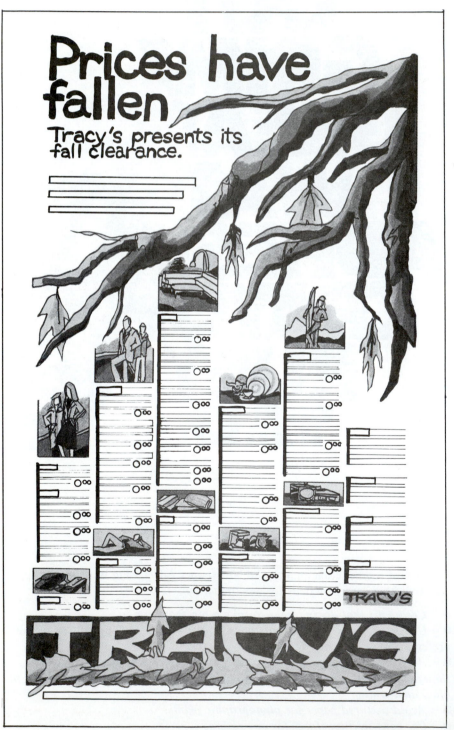

As a student, Tracy Wong used nylon-tip and felt-tip markers to produce this rough layout for a full-page ad announcing that "Prices Have Fallen" at the fictitious Tracy's department store. In this ad, the sale items are like leaves falling from the tree, but the gimmick is kept well within bounds. Note the pileup of leaves around the logo at the bottom.

To reach tire buyers, 4-Day Tire Stores in Southern California use mostly copy in their unusual and persuasive full-page newspaper ads. The name and logo play up the fact that the stores are "Open only during the 43 most efficient selling hours. Developing maximum sales with 1-shift overhead helps us cut tire prices." Agency: Lansdale, Carr & Baum. Designer: Marv Rubin.

and often merchandise that has been marked down. Stores constantly search for new ways to say "sale" and new excuses to conduct one. A sale becomes a "celebration" (or a "sell-a-bration"), a "riot," or, if the store has class, an "event." And the reason for the sale turns out to be that somebody goofed and ordered too many of the items, a new shipment is coming in, the tax season is at hand, a holiday is ahead, the store manager is out of town and the assistant manager has run amok, or it just happens to be the end of the month.

A New York grocery chain, D'Agostino, during the one hundredth birthday celebration of the Brooklyn Bridge, offered "50 cheers for the Brooklyn Bridge"— fifty sale items in a New York *Times* full-page ad. The bridge was "twice the age of D'Agostino, yet she makes us feel so young!" said the opening copy. This store's slogan is "If there's not one near you . . . move!"

NEWSPAPER ADVERTISING

THE **NEW** COLORFORMS' PLAY IT UP!   SWITCH ON THE **BRIGHTS** & IGNITE THE NIGHT. IT'S THE PARTY OF THE YEAR!

The Newspaper Advertising Bureau says retail advertising should clearly identify the store and narrow in on potential customers, make one element in the ad stand out from the others, leave out any unessential elements, organize elements as the store itself is organized, and stress benefits of shopping at that particular store.

Sometimes retail advertising does more. The ads for Swensen's Market, Twin Falls, Idaho, contain short editorials written by the store's owner, Jerry Swensen. Some are humorous, some argumentative and even controversial. Subject matter varies. One editorial criticized Evel Knievel's daredevil jump over Idaho's Snake River Canyon. Swensen tries to tie his comments to what's being advertised. He ran his anti-Knievel editorial in an ad selling bologna. He says he produces his unusual ads to make them stand out from the big ads sponsored by chain groceries.

Even when it's for a department store, the advertising may narrow in on a specific audience. Bloomingdale's went after young buyers and apartment dwellers who could shop only on Saturdays with a "Saturday's Generation" series of newspaper advertisement in Saturday morning papers. This resulted in a special "Saturday's Generation" shop within the store featuring contemporary furniture, molded-plastic goods, and play clothes.

That the advertising department of a store must satisfy the various merchandise department heads and buyers does complicate things. The job becomes even more complicated when departments within a store are franchise operations.

Then there is the matter of co-op money. When a manufacturer offers to pay for part of the cost of the advertising, the store advertising usually has to incorporate certain items into the ad and run them at agreed-upon sizes.

A&S (for Abraham and Straus), a Brooklyn-based store, gets bold, exciting design from Richard Martino and sprightly copy from Shen Henricks to sell bright, colorful dresses. You can imagine how big this type was when you consider that the ad ran across two newspaper pages. Note the placement of the exclamation mark.

The designer of a retail ad can show price in various ways. The dollar sign can be the same size as the numbers—or smaller. Making the cents smaller than the dollars tends to lessen the price visually. When the price is in dollars only, what is the reason for including zeroes after the period?

$25.00

$34.50

$24⁷⁵

$1199

$609

$953

Robin Rickabaugh designed this unusual restaurant ad and did the calligraphy. Marilyn Musick wrote the copy. The studio responsible for the design is Rickabaugh Design, Portland.

Arlan Koehler, creative director for Norman, Craig & Kummel, New York, described the "Seven Deadly C's of Retail Newspaper Ads." They are *color,* poorly used; *co-op* money that forces a store to bend its image to fit the manufacturer; *contracts* with the media that lure retailers into running ads when they have nothing to say; *consistency,* whereby a store's style does not change with the times; *cuteness* that produces such empty phrasing as "Where quality and economy walk hand in hand"; *competition* that prompts stores to copy each other; and *cost* that causes a store to settle for less than the best advertising and most qualified advertising personnel.[9]

Most department stores, discount stores, chain drugstores, grocery stores, furniture stores, and building supply stores produce omnibus ads, with many items pictured and described. The better stores engage occasionally in one-item advertising, and when that happens the ads look more like magazine ads. One-item ads often dwell on quality, but sometimes they feature low price.

It is vital that a store develop a graphic style that will immediately identify the store for regular customers. Perhaps the store will always use the same typeface for its headlines and the same style of art for its illustrations. It will surely develop a logo or sig cut that has a character of its own. Ohrbach's changed its logo to include an exclamation mark after the "Oh" and in front of the "rbach's." The "Oh!" helped lend excitement to all the ads.

Because telling readers where to buy is a chief function of retail advertising, the logo or signature should show up large in the ad and maybe in more than one place. The address, hours of business, and phone number should be included. Realizing that people have trouble remembering numbers, some advertisers study their phone numbers on the dial and discover combinations of letters that spell out appropriate words. Low Q, Box 937, Sag Harbor, N.Y. 11963 for a fee offers a computer printout of "up to 2,187 letter combinations inherent in your . . . phone number."

Hog Wild!, a Boston store that sells, among other items, an Oinkolator alarm that attaches to a refrigerator to sing out "Oink! Oink! Oink!" when you open the door, uses this phone number: 523-PIGS.

Are word phone numbers overused? Allan Provost, Longan-Provost, Advertising, Miami, thinks so. Responding to United Air Express's 800–PACKAGE number, he said he could dial 722–5243 much faster. "Phone numbers like . . . [PACKAGE] are too much 8768253."[10]

You don't have to be a musician to appreciate this.

A Chopin waltz played for the first time since a traumatic injury to one hand. Not a flawless performance, mind you, but the most satisfying one of the pianist's career.

It's a performance that could never have taken place without some remarkable advances in the field of reconstructive surgery.

Today, physicians around the world are perfecting surgical techniques that would have seemed like science fiction a generation ago.

Many of those techniques were developed right here in our corner of the globe. At Norfolk General Hospital and Eastern Virginia Medical School (EVMS).

This innovative work began more than 25 years ago when two talented specialists, a urologist and a plastic surgeon, teamed up to devise a new way to repair hypospadias, a genital deformity affecting one in 350 baby boys.

Then, a few years later, other physicians at Norfolk General applied those techniques to mending the uretha—the tube that carries urine from the bladder—when it's damaged by injury or disease.

Since then, our hospital has encouraged collaboration among specialists in every field. In reconstructive surgery that teamwork has turned up a treasure of practical, reproducible results.

A good example is the use of myocutaneous flaps. Developed by surgeons working at Norfolk General, myocutaneous flaps are thick pieces of skin with underlying muscle and the vessels necessary to continue blood supply.

What makes them so valuable? These flaps can be moved successfully from one part of the body to another. And in their transplanted location, they look and work like the original, displaced tissue.

The applications of this technique are virtually limitless.

Myocutaneous flaps have been used to replace severely burned tissue. They've also been used with remarkable success in urogenital reconstruction. They've even been used to construct new breasts after mastectomies.

The vacularized nerve graft was another exciting breakthrough. This revolutionary technique, pioneered at EVMS's Microsurgical Research Center in 1981, enables physicians to replace damaged

nerves with new ones.

The beneficiaries of these innovations are numberless.

Patients with facial paralysis can now undergo a surgical procedure in which nerves are grafted and muscles reinervated. So the face performs its special magic of smiling once again.

Using high-powered microscopes, surgeons can reattach severed fingers, hands, arms and legs.

When critically injured patients, victims of car wrecks and industrial accidents, are rushed to Norfolk General, specialists here don't stop at saving lives. They save the patient's appearance as well. Now it's even possible to build a new penis that looks, feels and functions normally.

The influence of reconstructive surgery at our hospital extends far beyond Hampton Roads. Patients come to us from other nations, other continents, when there is literally no one else in the world to turn to.

And every year physicians from around the world visit Norfolk General to observe and learn about reconstructive surgery. They hear lectures and read articles and books written by the leading specialists in the field.

When they return home, our visitors take with them new knowledge and skills they'll put to good use in the hospitals where they work. That way, patients who never see or hear about Norfolk General Hospital can live happier, more active lives because of the work that goes on here.

The ingenious collaborative effort that has produced so many heartening results continues today.

And the promise of the future has never been brighter.

In one area, researchers at EVMS's Microsurgical Research Center are investigating substances that will speed up the healing of reattached nerves.

On another frontier, urologists and plastic surgeons are now researching new processes that could permit near normal bladder function in paraplegic patients.

And that's just the beginning.

For more information about reconstructive surgery or any of the 41 specialities at Norfolk General Hospital, call our Health Information Center at 628-3408. We'll be glad to fill you in.

It's the least we can do for an encore.

One Of These Hands Is A Work Of Art.

NORFOLK GENERAL HOSPITAL

An arresting idea celebrating reconstructive surgery is beautifully presented in this much noticed full-page newspaper ad for Norfolk General Hospital, Norfolk, Virginia. The hospital has received many requests for reprints. Agency: Lawler Ballard Advertising. Art director: Don Harbor. Designer: Jeff France. Copywriter: Ken Hines.

A full-color, full-page newspaper ad, designed as a sampler, sells Lloyd Center, Portland, as a place to go Christmas shopping. Designer: Joe Erceg. Illustrator: Art Farm.

The Emerald People's Utility District uses a horizontal newspaper ad to invite readers to stop by its county fair booth for "a little light conversation." Tom Kelly did the happy light bulbs and designed the ad. Copywriter: Craig Copeland. Agency: Cappelli/Miles/Wiltz/Avery/Kelly, Ltd., Eugene, Oregon.

NEWSPAPER ADVERTISING

Who Does the Ads?

Much of the retail advertising appearing in newspapers originates not with advertising agencies but with the newspapers running the ads. The typical medium- and big-city newspaper offers advertisers most of the services an advertising agency offers, including marketing advice. With what its marketing research staff uncovers, a newspaper may know more about a local advertiser's potential customers than the advertiser knows. This information, along with information provided by the advertiser, helps the newspaper prepare advertising for the advertiser's approval and use.

At many, if not most newspapers today, this advertising is Macintosh-generated. Advertising salespeople meet with local advertisers and then confer with people in the papers' creative service departments, where the ads are created. In some cases, ads are created first, on speculation; then salespeople try to interest advertisers in buying the necessary space to run them. At smaller papers, the salespeople may also be the people who create the ads.

A few local advertisers are big enough to maintain their own advertising departments to prepare advertising.

At the Eugene, Oregon *Register-Guard,* a 75,000-circulation daily, the four or five persons in the creative service department can both write and design ads, although they tend to specialize. "We try to assign each job to the person most suited to complete the job in the most expeditious, timely, and creative manner possible," says Dan Villani, lead artist (actually the creative director). The department employs a part-time photographer in addition to the artists, designers, and writers. Of course, the staffers in this department, as in all newspaper departments of this kind, are completely separated from the staffers in the news/ editorial department.

Juster's, a quality men's store in Minneapolis, decided to let its customers try writing ads, and so conducted a contest that drew 148 entries. The winning ad was published, along with copy (extreme right) describing the contest and naming other winners. Bruce Bildstein wrote the prize-winning copy. Designer: Joe Duffy. Agency: Duffy, Bringgold, Knutson & Oberprillers, Inc.

Dan Villani, lead artist in the creative service department of the *Register-Guard,* works at his computer station to create a house ad. To change the detail in his art, he will move the image to the 21-inch gray-scale screen at the right. Villani prefers a roller-ball mouse to one that is moved on a pad. (Photo by Steve Baker.)

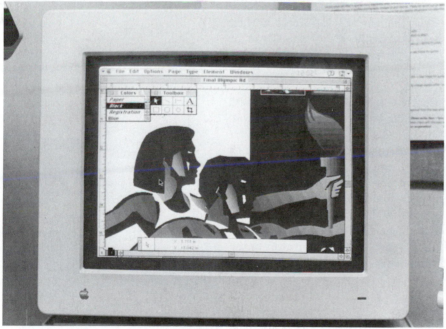

An up-close look at the art. Using Aldus FreeHand, Villani has drawn a woman in the background to match the style of the foreground figure, which he imported into Aldus PageMaker from clip art. (Photo by Steve Baker.)

Copywriting, typesetting, layout, clip art, and some custom art go to the advertiser without charge. Most custom art and photography costs extra. The paper likes to scan art from Print Media Services and Metro Creative Graphics to import it into Aldus Illustrator and Photoshop software programs, where it is cropped, redrawn, refitted, and manipulated. "We rework the scanned art so it isn't just 'plunked' into an ad," Villani says.

The creative service department at this newspaper, and other newspapers, has to scramble to keep up with all the technological changes taking place in the business. Paul Burke, retail advertising manager for the paper, sees "massive changes coming" the production of retail ads.

What this paper's creative service department turns out are comps that you can't tell from camera-ready copy. Clients increasingly expect to check ads that are close to a finished state. (After any changes, the comps go to the newspaper's production department where, because of an agreement with the union, they are redone as true camera-ready copy matching closely the comps.)

NEWSPAPER ADVERTISING

STREET *of* NATURAL CHOICE
All Natural Gas Homes

PageMaker is the basic software in the creative service department because it is the one the staffers started with; changing over to, say, QuarkXPress, would be, in the words of Villani, "rather counter-productive. I try to add programs that will enhance our design capabilities and build on what the staff has already learned. In other words, if a program is getting the job done and everyone is comfortable with it, I try not to mess with it. I would, however, make a change if the benefits outweighed the time it would take to get everyone up to speed again. In this sense, PageMaker is not necessarily the best program on the market, but, for us, it meets our needs. And with new updates on the horizon, who knows what we'll be using in the future?"

An artist and designer with experience at the board, Villani found layouts harder to do at first on a computer, but now he wouldn't go back, although some staffers in the still do some board work. Even though everyone works a Mac, Villani likes to hire people "with a broad base of experience and expertise in all facets of advertising design." To him, "the perfect graphic artist would have computer experience along with a background in the more traditional aspects of the visual arts."[11]

Service to advertisers works a little differently at the semi-weekly Springfield *News* (circulation 11,200) in the adjoining, smaller city of Springfield, Oregon. The three-person display advertising staff there calls on potential local advertisers to sell space and create rough ads while making the call. The finished work is done by people in the composing room. "But I see the time coming when our people will be calling on potential advertisers with computers to create finished ads on the spot," says retail advertising manager Tom Chastain.[12]

By far the biggest part of this paper's business is the job printing. The *News* prints a number of other newspapers as well as direct-mail pieces for advertisers. Chastain sometimes sells printing as well as newspaper space. A truism in the business: The smaller the paper, the more versatile the staffer is expected to be.

Those Special Sections

Both daily and weekly newspapers make it a practice to publish special sections, usually in tabloid size, to take clusters of ads built around the subject. The Springfield *News* does about 20 of these a year. One of the *News'* special sections, "Gold Mine," is a collection of coupons that comes out monthly, and, in addition to serving as an insert in the paper, it serves as a delivered publication to non-subscribers.

The daily Sacramento *Bee* puts out about 60 special sections a year, some broadsheet and some tabloid. Among the subjects: spring fashion, home improvement, and skiing. For several years the paper brought out a section that invited school students—up to 20,000 of them—to design ads for specific advertisers. Advertisers picked out the ones they want to run, and a panel of judges picked by the paper decided on grand-prize winners.[13]

Special sections represent one area in newspaper journalism in which editorial and advertising departments sometimes work together. Feature material on the theme helps separate the ads. Some newspapers take their features from outside organizations. The features come camera- or scanner-ready. These are called "advertorial packages."

Organizations like Champion Spark Plug Co. and National Home Improvement Council provide newspapers with free advertorial packages.

This logo for a Northwest Natural Gas Company newspaper campaign promoting new homes using natural gas started as a quick sketch by Carol O'Shea at a drawing board. She turned it over to Dan Villani at a Macintosh. Deciding not to scan it, Villani used a roller-ball mouse and Adobe Illustrator to redraw it and set and place the type. Time at the Macintosh: 35 minutes. Later, an advertising agency made some minor adjustments in the style of the houses. (Courtesy the Eugene, Oregon *Register-Guard*.)

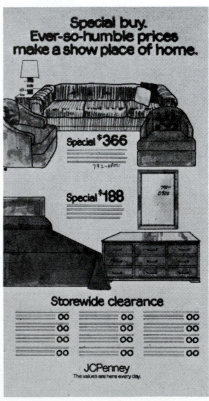

Here is a rough layout for a J. C. Penney ad. Note that the three-line headline is all in one type size. There are no typographic tricks. The headline, captions, and art combine to make one massive unit.

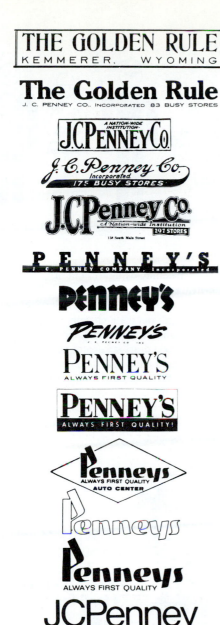

Here are some—but not all—of the changes in the J. C. Penney logo since 1902, when the store was known as The Golden Rule. The version shown at the bottom represents not only a change in typeface but also a change from Penneys back to J. C. Penney. The three initials, without periods, come close to touching, making a sort of ligature. The typeface (Helvetica) is also used for ad headlines.

Increasingly, advertisers are preparing their own newspaper sections, in tabloid form, to be inserted into copies after they come off the presses.

The reliance on preprinted tabloids makes early deadlines for advertisers a necessity, and this means that stores have a harder time stocking the items advertised. This is especially true of branch stores, whose advertising is prepared out of town. Hence, in many newspapers, you find small-space disclaimer ads in the regular sections of the paper, pointing out that certain items did not arrive on time. Such ads often contain corrections, too, to merchandise descriptions and sometimes to prices listed. A Sears, Roebuck & Co. executive has suggested that newspapers carry a single "retraction page" to cover all the errors in all the inserts for a single day.

Illustrations vs. Photographs

When display advertising began, in the last century, the illustrator was king. Then along came photography, and the illustrator lost out in the scramble for believability, which the photographer, with so little effort, seemed able to deliver. But photography never did dominate retail advertising as it did advertising in the magazines. The retail advertiser found that, in newspapers, line or wash drawings worked best. They were easier to reproduce.

With the change by most newspapers to offset and the resultant improvement in the reproduction of photographs, retailers turned more and more to photography. Some stores, to get away from the pack, switched back.

An artist at Saks Fifth Avenue said, "You can really fake it with a drawing. With a photo there's no way to help a bad outfit." A B. Altman artist pointed out that "A woman can more closely associate with the way she would look in a sketch. In a photo, she sees another woman's face."[14]

Another advantage of illustration over photography in newspaper advertising is that, typically, it costs about a third of what photography, including model's fees and retouching, would cost. This does not mean that in the major markets art comes cheap. Some artists charge more than $300 per figure.

Such prices are beyond the reach of retailers in the smaller cities, of course, but does this mean these retailers have to settle for art of inferior quality? Not necessarily. The art schools turn out hundreds of eager young illustrators each year, and most of them will have trouble locating in the major markets. Illustration can come cheap.

The Art Services

Newspapers and their retail-advertising accounts can always use the art services, which are convenient, economical sources of ready-made illustrations. An art service consists of a proof book of illustrations, issued periodically, along with mats of each of the illustrations for the few letterpress papers still published. A mat is a thick-paper mold into which the stereotyper pours molten metal, thus duplicating the original engraving from which the mat was made.

Editor & Publisher International Year Book 1992 lists about three dozen firms in its "Newspaper Art and Mat Services Directory." Some of these firms supply art and ready-made ads for local advertisers, some for newspapers. A number of the firms offer several programs.

Metro Creative Graphics, Inc., New York, offers newspapers close to 30 different services, including its long-established Metro Newspaper Service, Metro's Spanish and French Special Supplements, Classified Dynamics (for classified advertising pages), LaserArt (art on disks for PageMaker, QuarkXpress, and Ready,Set,Go! for the Macintosh), and ImageBase (for the Mac or IBM and its compatibles.)

Funeral Advisory Counsel, Oklahoma City, offers some 1,300 "totally different powerful ads" for exclusive use by funeral homes in their communities.

Retail Reporting Bureau, a division of Milton B. Conhaim, Inc., New York, among other services offers *Retail Ad Week* for study. *Retail Ad Week* is a reg-

ular reprinting of department and specialty store advertising culled from United States and Canadian newspapers.

Retailers have their own supply of art and ready-made ads from the home office, from specialized mat services, or from manufacturers.

Most newspapers get two or more copies of each art-service book, one to file, the others to cut up and use. All the art can be computer scanned, of course. For rough layouts, the designer can trace or clip the art and paste it into place. The printing and paper stock are of a quality that allows the art to be used in finished pasteups, too.

Artists can get more out of art services than nonartists can. Artists see any number of possibilities for combining pieces or parts of pieces to make new art. In the hands of artists, stock art almost becomes exclusive art.

But nonartists can get a lot out of the services, too. Deciding which pieces are appropriate is more of an editing than an artistic exercise. And some art pieces come in parts separated with thin white lines. They are designed to be cut apart and refitted.

Some of the art each month comes as color separations. And much of the black-and-white art separates easily enough into two parts for two-color printing. A given piece of art also comes in several sizes.

A problem can arise when art from several sources is combined in a single ad. The various pieces of art may be executed in different, incompatible styles. Or one piece of art may come in the wrong size; it may have to be reduced or enlarged. If the art is a halftone, this will affect the dot pattern. The ad may appear with one item in a coarse screen and with other items in a regular screen.

For ads carrying listings unrelieved by illustrations, borders become the only decorative element. "Newspapers can't seem to get enough of them," observed Hazel L. Kraus of Metro. The art services always includes a number of borders in each new proof book.

Borders may surround the ad or fence off certain of its sections or simply appear and reappear in places in the ad to provide continuity or typographic relief.

The border may be made up of tiny illustrations taken from the art service and run in a line. It can build atmosphere for the ad: a lineup of holly leaves for Christmas, for instance, or a set of stars between two flowing stripes for the Fourth of July. But it should be in character with the headline face.

Some advertisers develop borders of their own and use them ad after ad to tie their series together.

A warning about borders: They make ads look smaller than they would look without borders. Furthermore, when the border is too imposing, it acts as an optical fence, discouraging entry. Some advertisers solve this by running borders on only two of four sides—usually at the top and bottom.

Constructing his figures out of geometric shapes for a highly stylized, flat, abstract look, a Print Media Service artist manages to create enough variations (above) to give the advertising designer a good cross-section of people to work into an ad that is to appeal to everybody. But suppose you do not want a horizontal lineup. You cut the figures apart, make prints of varying sizes, and overlap them, as in the PMS-prepared ad below. Same art, different effect.

You Work Hard for Your Money. It's Time Your Money Worked Hard for You.

Money in a Citizen's savings account earns the highest interest rate allowed by law, compounded daily. That's a hard-working savings account! Start yours today.

CITIZENS' BANK
204 Central Avenue
Mon-Thurs 9 a m 5 p m Fri 9 a m 7 p m

You can also take part of the
regular lineup and reverse the figures
into a black block.

United Syndicated Artwork
demonstrates how one piece of stock art
(upper left) can be cropped to create
new pieces.

Color in Newspapers

"Has *USA Today* ushered in the era of the four-color daily newspaper?" asked
a writer in *Editor & Publisher,* who then answered his own question: "Quite
possibly so."[15]

Newspapers have been criticized for using color as a graphic device rather
than a communication tool. Richard Curtis, managing editor of *USA Today,* says
that "if color can't be done properly with quality, then it should not be used." To
some editors, "properly" means confining color—full color—to food and fashion
sections and soft news. There is some feeling that full color gives glamor to photographs of killings and other tragedies. Black-and-white-handling, they feel,
works better here.[16]

It could be argued that papers using little color on the news and editorial side
provide a more receptive background for color in advertising. The advertising
stands out more. Probably the first firm to use color in a newspaper was Mandel
Brothers, Chicago, adding red to the black in a full-page ad. That was in 1903.

For some years color in newspaper advertising remained a rarity. Now it is common—even in small and medium-size papers.

And restrictions on its use have died.

It used to be that an advertiser, to get newspaper color, would have to agree to run the ad at a spot where it was convenient for the printer to apply color. Now the advertiser enjoys ROP (run-of-paper) color.

A "major technical breakthrough in the reproduction of ROP newspaper color" was announced by the American Newspaper Publishers Association in 1971 with the introduction of a color line-conversion process for "a richer, cleaner, poster-like reproduction at lower cost."[17] The Nashville *Banner* and *Tennessean* pioneered its use.

Offset presses and color scanners have greatly improved the quality of newspaper color.

The advertiser also has access to color for advertising in the Sunday comics section. Some comics sections are printed by the newspapers that run them, some by organizations removed from the papers. Sunday comic strips may look like the result of process color work, but the color is strictly flat or spot. Four plates are made—yellow, red, blue, and black—and all are in line. The tone is accomplished with Ben Days and juxtaposition of dots.

As in magazines, color in newspaper advertising raises the cost of the space to the advertiser. The more colors, the higher the space cost, naturally. And in some cases the advertiser has to buy a given amount of space—say more than half a page—before being able to buy color for the ad. Some newspapers charge a flat additional fee for color, no matter how big the ad. Using color means observing a deadline hours earlier than the regular deadline.

Although a Milwaukee *Journal* study has shown that full-page, full-color newspaper ads get up to 60 percent more readership than similar ads in black-and-white, a full-page ad or a well-designed smaller ad does not get quite the lift from color that a poorly designed ad gets, because the big and good ads do not need color as much. Color becomes a crutch to some designers.

Roughing in the Ad

The typical local newspaper ad contains (1) a feature illustration, larger than any other in the ad; (2) a related headline; (3) a blurb or supplemental headline, longer than the first and in smaller type, that takes off logically from where the main headline leaves off; (4) a main copy block, short, amplifying the headline; (5) additional illustrations with their own headlines and copy blocks; and (6) the store name (logotype) shown at least once, perhaps twice. Prices are usually played prominently, in bold or display types, inside or alongside the copy blocks. Borders are optional.

For an extra-large ad covering a wide range of items, you should plan on one main unit, a couple of secondary units, a few smaller—spot—units, and a listing. Each of the units can have its own illustration, the size often but not necessarily decreasing with the size of the unit.

It is best even for a multimerchandise store to concentrate, in a single ad, on one class of merchandise or on one department. If a hodgepodge is ordered, you should organize it at least into logical sections, with garden supplies in one place, auto supplies in another, and so on. Of course, one item should dominate. It would be an item specially priced or new to the store. You would have a good reason for playing it up.

Like any ad, a retail ad needs a theme. That the store has launched a sale may not be enough of a theme. The reader likes to have a reason. "Good Riddance," says a headline over a sale ad sponsored by Director's, a furniture store. Perhaps that is reason enough.

You do not have to force the theme. You do not have to mention it several times in the ad. But you should include a short block of copy after the headline to elaborate on the theme. The reader may not bother with it. But it is there, just in case.

To make your product or products look inexpensive, use heavy borders and

A newspaper ad for The Old Spaghetti Factory's opening at Charlotte, North Carolina, uses public-domain art and imaginative typography to suggest antique furnishings and a long history. Byron Ferris, who designed the ad, assembled two 1895 James Montgomery Flagg drawings for the illustration.

A page from a Multi-Ad Services brochure shows how its Multi-Ad Creator software allows a layout artist to quickly try any number of ad arrangements before settling on one that works visually.

boxes, reverse blocks, large illustrations, graphic gimmicks—and *crowd* your ad. To do the opposite—to stress quality rather than price—lighten the typeface, use white space liberally. Choose roman for your headlines.

Do not bother with thumbnails when doing newspaper ads. Using traditional tools or your computer, start with an actual-size ad, roughing in quickly the areas you plan to cover with illustration and type. Be concerned at first with sizes and relationships of areas, not with the looks and placement of the illustrations. With areas roughly established, look for illustrations in the clip-art book. If you are using a pencil or marker, slide your layout sheet around over the illustrations until you find good placement for them, then trace them quickly. Do not be afraid to leave out parts of the illustrations. Use only what you need. That is one way of proceeding.

Another is to look for the illustrations first. What you find will determine the arrangement areas. Make quick tracings, then place them under your working sheet. You can rough in the headlines and establish unit areas while you retrace your drawings, moving from one to the other and back again. Work loosely, changing as you go, erasing, even throwing away a working sheet halfway along (you have not invested much time on it) and starting fresh. It is just a matter of retracing your tracings. Save those parts of the ad that look promising. When

you have things pretty much as you want them, go back over your working sheet, tracing and marking more firmly than before.

If your client can afford original art—or if you cannot find what you want among the stock art files—the making of the ad rough becomes a more demanding job. You create the ad much as you would an ad for a national magazine. You are then less the layout artist, more the designer.

What is being sold in an ad should influence its size and shape. The test is not so much how the ad looks in rough or even proof form. The test lies in how it looks on the page in competition with other ads. It is not a bad idea to place the proof on a page with other ads to see how well it stands out.

Not only do newspapers offer advertisers deep verticals and wide horizontals; some of them offer L-, reverse L-, and T-shapes. Many newspapers have experimented with FlexForm, a system pioneered by the Peoria, Illinois *Journal Star,* in which the advertiser can design an ad in *any* shape, zigzagging among news columns on a page for up to 65 percent of the space.

Odd shapes require extra designer attention. What you do to unify the ad is particulary important. You can use art that curves naturally into each area of the ad. Or you can use borders or illustrations that repeat themselves. On the other hand, you can divide the space into rectangles and treat each rectangle as a near-separate ad, repeating the logo each time.

Retailers like the idea of ads-within-ads, even in regular-shaped ads. The advantage of this format is that the readers are able to pick out and stay with sections that particularly interest them.

Small-space ads offer an even greater challenge to the designer. What can you possibly do in a 1-col. × 1″ ad? With reverses, borders, type in two or three sizes, and compact illustrations, you can do quite a bit.

Using art in small-space ads, you should crop even closer than usual, using just a hint of the scene or product you want to exhibit. The reader, seeing this art, has a tendency to complete the drawing mentally, in effect increasing the dimensions of your ad.

Told to design an ad of so many column inches, you can take up space either vertically or horizontally. "Around 60 column inches," for instance, would make an ad 3 columns by 20 inches, 4 columns by 15 inches, 5 columns by 12 inches, 6 columns by 10 inches, 7 columns by 8 inches, or 8 columns by 7 inches.

A series of 6¼″ × 10″ newspaper ads for The Salvation Army of Greater New York, prepared *pro bono* by Brouillard Communications, a division of J. Walter Thompson, uses silhouetted photographs and surprise headlines to lure readers into the copy, which modernizes the organization's image. Renn Cavanaugh art directed; Ted Speck wrote the copy.

Some designers convince themselves that several small ads get better exposure than one large ad. Not only does the ad reach readers on several pages; it is sure to get placed at the top of the pyramid in each case. Other designers argue that one large ad has greater total impact than several smaller ads.

Many retail advertisers are convinced that right-page placement is better than left-page placement and that ads high on the page get better readership than ads low on the page. Further, they insist that their ads be placed next to regular reading matter.

Newspapers often arrange the ads in a half-pyramid, with the low point at the left; small ads go at the top, larger ads at the bottom of the pyramid. Under this system, every ad has a fighting chance of getting next to editorial and news columns. No ads are "buried."

Ad Director, an expensive software program offered by Managing Editor Software, allows a newspaper layout artist to dummy all the ads for an issue, putting ads in place, pointing out competitive ads that are next to each other, gathering categories of ads on special pages, and performing a number of other functions.

CHAPTER

11

MAGAZINE ADVERTISING

Although ads—classified ads, anyway—appeared in newspapers from the very start in this country, and newspapers appeared before magazines, the advertising industry really got its start with magazines. When well-printed, semipermanent magazines—weeklies and monthlies—came on the scene in the nineteenth century, manufacturers had the national audiences they were looking for.

The proliferation of magazines created the need for advertising agencies to keep track of numbers and to broker space. It was only natural that these agencies eventually would produce the advertising going into the periodicals.

In deciding which magazines to buy space in, advertising agencies largely determine which magazines will survive, which will fail.

Magazines continually adjust their editorial formulas to hold onto and build audiences. When the record industry began its decline in 1979, *Rolling Stone,* which had been a bible to rock 'n' roll enthusiasts, began to make changes—to reposition itself in the market. New advertisers had to be recruited. Many nonrecord advertisers saw the audience as too narrow. Other advertisers were not impressed by the newsprint stock. So *Rolling Stone* began running more political articles and other articles likely to appeal to a slightly older audience. And it went to a slicker stock.

In a late 1980s campaign to media buyers, *Rolling Stone* ran a series of ads showing "Perception" of the magazine on the left and "Reality" on the right. The "Perception" side showed, for instance, a half a dozen coins, as though readers of the magazine had little to spend. "Reality" for this one ad showed a pile of credit cards, with an American Express card on top. A copy block below the "Reality" art said that "One and a half million Rolling Stone readers are card carrying capitalists."

Any major trend, any switch in attitudes among Americans gives rise to a whole new collection of magazines.

James K. Glassman, publisher of *The New Republic,* contemplated the new-magazine phenomenon in a column in his magazine. Maybe the magazine had

(Opposite Page)

Foot-Joy takes advantage of the availability of L-shaped space from *Golf* by allowing the product shown to take the same shape. Agency: HBM Creamer.

A horizontal, across-the-spread ad in a trade publication, *Valve Magazine,* uses same-size contrasting halftones and all-caps headlines and caps-and-small-caps body copy to make a point about Norris/O'Bannon valves. "Hot" here has two meanings. Choosing the wrong valve "could leave you pretty steamed." Agency: Phillips & Johnson Advertising. Art director: Mick Thurber. Copywriter: Meg Renolds.

CHOOSE THE WRONG BRAND, AND THE DIFFERENCE BETWEEN NORRIS/O'BANNON'S HIGH PRESSURE, HIGH TEMPERATURE, FIRE SAFE VALVES AND OTHER COMPANIES' VALVES COULD LEAVE YOU PRETTY STEAMED. BECAUSE NORRIS/O'BANNON'S HIGH PERFORMANCE VALVES HAVE FEATURES NO OTHER VALVES HAVE. LIKE A PRIMARY PTFE SEAT WITH A SECONDARY METAL SEAT OF ICONEL 625, SO THE VALVE WILL MAINTAIN ITS SEAL DURING PARTIAL OR COMPLETE DESTRUCTION OF THE PTFE SEAL.

THEN THERE'S OUR WIDE CHOICES OF VALVES AND TRIM MATERIALS, AVAILABLE IN A VARIETY OF SIZES TO FIT PRACTICALLY ANY NEED. AND, NORRIS/O'BANNON'S EXCLUSIVE *3-YEAR LIMITED WARRANTY*. CALL OR WRITE FOR MORE INFORMATION ABOUT NORRIS/O'BANNON VALVES. THEN THE NEXT TIME YOU NEED A VALVE, GIVE ALL THE OTHERS A COLD SHOULDER. CHOOSE NORRIS/O'BANNON VALVES. AND GET 'EM WHILE THEY'RE HOT.

P.O. BOX 2070 TULSA, OK 74101-2070 918/446-2610 TELEX 4630037 DOV RUI FAX 918/446-6941.

NORRIS/O'BANNON

missed the boat on new magazines, he wrote. In a frivolous mood, he wondered if the magazine should launch a sister publication: *New Republic World: The Magazine for New Republic Readers.*[1]

Magazines are for the elite. This is reflected not only in the messages and the ads but also in their design.

Well-designed ads need well-designed settings. Hence, magazines put a great emphasis on how they look. Their art directors constantly change formats in an attempt to stay contemporary. A critic of magazines, Daniel Harris, reviewing some recent books about them in *The Nation,* refers to "the visual wealth and intellectual bankruptcy of a field whose innovations in the long run have proved to be more pictorial than literary."[2]

Consumer Magazines

Professor Theodore Peterson of the Department of Journalism, University of Illinois, traces the modern magazine to 1893 and the cutting of the price of *Munsey's* to a mere dime. It was Frank Munsey's way of rescuing his failing magazine—to build a large circulation to offer to advertisers, who would pay his costs and give him his profits. "It was a daring, revolutionary move, and it worked. . . . [Munsey] outlined the basic pattern that magazine publishers have traced ever since."[3]

Munsey's magazine and others like it appealed to the broad middle class, a good target for the emerging brand-name advertisers.

When television came onto the scene after World War II and threatened magazines—and the other media—with its ability to deliver mass audiences to advertisers, magazines decided to join the numbers game in earnest. They tried to prove that they could deliver audiences of the kind TV could. Never mind how the magazines got their subscribers; just marvel at how many signed up. And never mind how much loss each subscriber represented; advertising revenue would make up the difference between what it cost to produce the magazine and what the subscriber was asked to pay.

Well, it turned out that you could not beat television when it came to delivering large numbers of persons to advertisers, and when a magazine was able to point to a large audience, not many people were aboard because they really wanted to be. This meant they were not very good prospects for the advertisers.

When *Woman's Home Companion, Collier's,* and the original *Saturday Evening Post, Look,* and *Life* died, it was not because they did not have large audiences—each of the magazines had a circulation in the millions; it was because their audiences were unfocused. Agencies were not impressed with the buying potential of these audiences. The magazines died because they could not get enough advertising.

To stay alive, magazines began to specialize. Each magazine brought together

BEST THING NEXT TO YOUR FOOT-JOY SHOES.

Be sure you're wearing Foot-Joy Xtra Cushion golf socks that stay up securely and cushion your feet comfortably every step of every round. They're knitted of Hi-Bulk Orlon® acrylic and stretch nylon, come in just about every color and you'll find them wherever you buy your Foot-Joy shoes.

Foot-Joy, Inc. Brockton, MA 02403

© 1985 Foot-Joy, Inc.

a group—a class—of readers who had much in common, who shared an enthusiasm for a way of living or a point of view. And the magazines began to let the reader pay for more of the costs of producing magazines. Previously what the reader paid was only token; advertisers covered most of the costs.

A magazine with a broad base enters into a specialty when it provides advertisers with only a portion of its audience, if that is what the advertiser wants. That portion can be geographic or demographic. The advertiser pays less for an ad, then, and reaches only one section of the country, say, or one class of reader: business people, for instance, or educators.

Specialized Magazines

Advertisers who want exposure in magazines face a choice of about 17,000, most of them focused in on special audiences. It is hard to think of an interest or activity not represented by a magazine. Boat lovers, for instance, have *Sail, Cruising World, Yachting, Boating, Motor-Boating and Sailing,* and *Sea* to turn to.

Ethnic groups are served by a number of magazines. Among magazines published primarily for blacks are *Ebony, Jet, Essence, Black Enterprise, Black Scholar, The Black Collegian,* and *Black Teen.*

Like general-circulation magazines, specialized magazines thrive mainly on advertising revenue. An exception would be the opinion magazines—*National Review, The New Republic, The Nation, The Progressive,* and the like—whose editorial policies are too controversial and circulation figures too minuscule to appeal much to advertisers. For these magazines, subscription rates—or endowments—must cover most of the costs. Only an occasional book publisher seems willing to invest advertising dollars here.

Another category of specialized magazines carrying little or no advertising are the company magazines, sometimes called house organs. They contain no advertising because they are published to do a public relations job for the publisher, not to make money. In a sense, a company magazine is nothing but one big institutional advertisement.

People sometimes confuse company magazines with trade journals, which do contain advertising, and plenty of it. Thumbing through a typical trade journal, fat with advertising directed to executives in the trades and professions, you get the impression that the magazines exist solely to carry advertising. As a matter of fact, the advertising—for new products and equipment needed in industry—may interest readers more than the editorial matter, which in some trade journals is nothing more than puffery for the products and equipment advertised. Some trade journals do not charge for subscriptions, but they carefully control circulation to reach only those persons qualified to receive the magazine.

A magazine that is narrowed in on a special interest tends to play a cheerleading role. But not always. Some of the trade magazines have run highly critical articles about aspects of the industries they cover.

National advertisers make the most use of magazines, but local advertisers make some use of magazines, too. National magazines offer their regional editions to such advertisers. With an eye on magazines' regional editions, newspapers establish locally edited magazine sections. City magazines, set up partly to compete with the newspapers, represent another segment of the magazine industry.

Weekly magazines like *Business Week, Forbes,* and *People* lead all magazines in yearly totals of pages of advertising. Among monthlies, women's magazines are big. So are computer magazines.

Statistics on Magazines

Overall statistics on magazines as an advertising medium are a little hard to pin down because magazines appear in so many formats and frequencies, serving so many different audiences, and fulfilling such a variety of purposes. Some exist primarily to make money, some to spread ideas, some to serve members of an organization, and some to do a public relations job.

No. *Come on.* **No.** *Please.* **No.** *What's wrong?* **Nothing.** *Then come on.* **No.** *It'll be great.* **No.** *I know you want to.* **No I don't.** *Yes, you do.* **No.** *Well, I do.* **Please stop it.** *I know you'll like it.* **No.** *Come on.* **I said no.** *Do you love me?* **I don't know.** *I love you.* **Please don't.** *Why not?* **I just don't want to.** *I bought you dinner, didn't I?* **Please stop.** *Come on, just this once.* **No.** *But I need it.* **Don't.** *Come on.* **No.** *Please.* **No.** *What's wrong?* **Nothing.** *Then come on.* **No.** *It'll be great.* **Please stop.** *I know you need it too.* **Don't.** *Come on.* **I said no.** *But I love you.* **Stop.** *I gotta have it.* **I don't want to.** *Why not?* **I just don't.** *Are you frigid?* **No.** *You gotta loosen up.* **Don't.** *It'll be good.* **No it won't.** *Please.* **Don't.** *But I need it.* **No.** *I need it bad.* **Stop it.** *I know you want to.* **No.** **Don't.** *Come on.* **No.** *Please.* **No.** *What's wrong?* **Nothing.** *Then come on.* **No.** *It'll be great.* **Stop.** *Come on.* **No.** *I really need it.* **Stop.** *You have to.* **Stop.** *No, you stop.* **No.** *Take your clothes off.* **No.** *Shut up and do it.* **Now.**

WHEN THE MAN OF YOUR DREAMS BECOMES YOUR WORST NIGHTMARE. ... people couldn't ignore. In fact, it ignited a national debate. It's the kind of thing TIME ... level by addressing issues that touch their lives. Now, can your clients really afford to ... Date rape is one of those cover stories that over 24 million ... does. Stories that engage the reader on a more personal ... miss out on reader involvement and numbers like that?

A running conversation takes up most of the space in this two-page ad designed to illustrate "When the Man of Your Dreams Becomes Your Worst Nightmare." *Time* magazine, the sponsor, tells media buyers reading the advertising trade press that a date rape cover story ignited a national debate. "It's the kind of thing *Time* does." Agency: Fallon McElligott, Minneapolis. Art director: Bob Brihn. Copywriter: Phil Hanft.

Harvest Restaurant, Cambridge, Massachusetts, uses one deep column in *Boston Magazine* to quote George Bernard Shaw in small type reversed in a black area at the top: "There is no love sincerer than the love of food." The art, by Guarnaccia, shows a man with a sensuous-looking pear. Patrick Bowe art directed and wrote copy for this handsome ad with its generous solid black and pure white areas. Agency: Altman & Manley.

Advertising Age in its annual listing of media groups and their shares of advertising dollars spent, makes separate categories of "magazines" (weeklies, monthlies, women's), "farm publications," and "business publications."

Serving as clearinghouses of information about magazines as advertising media are the Magazine Publishers Association, 575 Lexington Ave., New York, N.Y. 10022 (general magazines) and the Association of Business Publishers, 205 E. 42nd St., New York, N.Y. 10017 (trade journals). In Canada information is available from the Magazine Association of Canada, 1240 Bay St., Suite 300, Toronto, Ontario M5R 2A7.

Magazines are almost impossible to count. There are well over 1,000 general-circulation or consumer magazines, most of them available on the newsstands, and around 2,000 trade, technical, and professional journals, few of them on newsstands. Almost all of these carry advertising. In addition there are well over 10,000 company magazines.

A few consumer magazines have circulations in the millions, but most, because of their specialized nature, stay under 1,000,000, and in many cases well under 1,000,000.

An advertising agency, in evaluating its magazine buy, is careful to distinguish between circulation figures and readership. Typically, a magazine claims two or three times more readers than subscribers and newsstand buyers. Only the subscribers and newsstand buyers can be accurately measured, though—through the Audit Bureau of Circulations.

Not all magazines can fairly claim that readership exceeds circulation. "A magazine distributed only to members of an association or institute may have fewer readers than its circulation because not all members will spend time reading something they receive as part of a membership," wrote Norman Hart in *Industrial Advertising and Publicity*. "Furthermore they probably do not bother to take it to the office and circulate it. Against this, many publications exist which can fairly claim a readership of eight or more people per copy."[4]

If a high percentage of a magazine's circulation comes from newsstand sales,

MAGAZINE ADVERTISING

advertising agencies are likely to be impressed. Newsstand sales are a good indication of reader interest. Newsstand buyers read their magazines right away. They do not leave them lying around, their pages unturned.

Magazines have learned that advertising agencies are interested not only in numbers but also in quality. They are interested in the editorial content of the magazines and in their design. Agencies want the right climate for their advertisements. This is why magazines occasionally, if not frequently, redesign themselves. They do it largely to impress advertising agencies.

The New Yorker is unusual among consumer magazines in that it is not designed in the ordinary sense. No one, not even an admirer of Baskerville body type and that unique display face designed by a cartoonist, opens up the magazine and goes into ecstasy about the graphics. And yet advertising agencies greatly appreciate the magazine's looks. In *The New Yorker* it is the beauty of the advertising that provides the visual treat. That and the gag cartoons, an art form *The New Yorker* practically invented. What a marvelous showcase for full-color, full-page advertisements! Nothing to detract the browser from the advertisers' messages on each slick-paper page. *The New Yorker* has even rejected advertising that is not well designed.

With a change in editors in 1992, *The New Yorker* began running more editorial art and color and showed signs, in an increasingly competitive market, of becoming just another slick magazine.

Many of the art directors on magazines moved to their jobs from similar positions at advertising agencies. In some cases, art directors design magazines and advertising simultaneously, especially if they are attached to design studios serving various clients.

Magazines try to keep the editorial and advertising sides in their organizations separated, but on small magazines carrying advertising, the magazine art direc-

A two-page ad in *M&C: Meetings & Conventions,* a trade magazine, combines silhouette art with rectangular art to promote The Broadmoor, Colorado Springs, Colorado, as a place to hold a convention. The art at the bottom is something of a visual oxymoron, combining an oversize plate of food with a mountain range to startle the viewer. Agency: Erickson Comm. Designer: Arthur Taylor.

A two-sentence headline and well-leaded copy tell the story for Valvcon, which, in this prize-winning no-nonsense ad in *Valve Magazine,* asks readers to "Include us in your next installation." Agency: Collage Advertising, Nashua, New Hampshire. Art director: Carol Richards. Copywriter: Dan Richards.

tors sometimes design the ads for those advertisers not big enough to hire an advertising agency. Dugald Stermer did some ads for *Ramparts* when he art directed that magazine. *D.A.C. News,* a magazine published by the Detroit Athletic Club, runs house ads to tell potential advertisers that it will write and design their ads at no charge, except, of course, for printer's composition fees. Space rates decrease with frequency of ad placement.

Magazines, unlike newspapers, ordinarily do not have their own presses. Using desktop-publishing setups, many take care of pre-press activities in house, but they farm out the actual printing.

Restrictions on Magazine Advertising

Magazines have worked out clearly defined guidelines of what their advertising departments will accept. Several magazines, *The New Yorker* and *Saturday Review* among them, said no to cigarette advertisers after the surgeon general's report. The old *Saturday Evening Post* up until its last decade would not accept liquor advertising. *Ms.* said no to anything smacking of sexism. *Reader's Digest* for its first three decades would not accept *any* advertising.

Modern Maturity, which avoids showing images of its over-50 readers as anything but active and upbeat, rejects some 35 percent of the ads submitted because the ads don't uphold the image. Only about 20 percent of the ad space can be devoted to incontinence pads, laxatives, and similar products, and the themes of the ads must deal with the effects of using these products, not the symptoms that call for them.

The magazine attracts advertisers because of its giant circulation (more than 22,000,000 subscribers in 1991) and the buying power of its older readers.

Some magazines—*Good Housekeeping, Parents,* and *Weight Watchers*—offer seals of approval for advertising appearing on their pages. Many magazines insist on testing products before accepting the advertising. *Prevention* magazine claims it spends many hours each month screening companies for reputability and financial responsibility, checking advertising copy and examining products and services submitted for advertising.

Sometimes a magazine accepts an ad reluctantly—and then runs an editorial disavowing it. *Commonweal* did this for a book, *Living with Sex: The Student's Dilemma,* which the editors felt contained "a number of moral judgments and recommendations . . . difficult, and in some cases impossible perhaps, to reconcile with Catholic teaching."[5]

In a note above its "Personal" classified-advertisement department, where men and women seek out each other's companionship, *National Review* has said this: "NR extends maximum freedom in this column, but NR's maximum freedom may be another man's straightjacket. NR reserves the right to reject any copy deemed unsuitable."

Not that all this watchdogging is peculiar to the magazine medium. But magazines, because of their tendency to cater to select audiences, set up a greater variety of restrictions than other media do and in many cases adhere to them more rigidly.

Serving the Advertiser

In their attempt to win and hold advertisers, magazines court media buyers in agencies through personal contact, direct-mail advertising, and ads in the advertising trade press. A magazine's typical sales pitch contains information on the buying power and habits of the audience the magazine can deliver. Often the magazine is able to cite a price advantage.

But how can the media buyer compare advertising rates of magazines with different circulation figures? Of course, a magazine with a large circulation will charge more per page than a magazine with a smaller circulation. But how *much* more is reasonable? Is a $13,000 black-and-white page in a magazine with a 1,400,000 circulation about right when you compare it to a $40,000 black-and-

This full-page, full-color consumer-magazine ad is designed to show some "neat ways" to organize items in the kitchen using Rubbermaid products. No white lines or bars separate the twelve panels. Except for the copyright line, all type is reversed. Designer: Michael Feldman. Copywriter: Walter Burek. Agency: Ketchum MacLeod & Grove, Pittsburgh. Used with permission of and © by Rubbermaid Incorporated.

If an ad too closely approximates editorial style of design, a magazine may label it "Advertisement," as the *Columbia Journalism Review* does in this ad for The National Right to Work Legal Defense Foundation. Two editorial touches: (1) the use of an initial letter to bridge the gap between headline and copy start, and (2) the use of column rules, which in this case, are interrupted by silhouette art. The logo is kept in the same type as the body copy to make the ad look less like an ad. Agency: Lee Edwards & Associates.

white page in a magazine with a 2,500,000 circulation? To help the media buyer make decisions, magazines compute their CPMs. A CPM represents the cost to reach one thousand subscribers and newsstand buyers with a full-page black-and-white ad. Magazine CPMs range from a dollar or two to fifty dollars or more. A small, specialized magazine is likely to have a higher CPM than a large, general-circulation magazine has. CPMs are not quite as useful as they once were because, in their attempt to fight TV statistics, some magazines are figuring in pass-along readerships. This causes some confusion.

Most magazines base their page rates on the "live-copy area": the trim size of the page minus a border of white all around. If an advertiser wants the ad to bleed off the page, there is often an extra charge of from 10 to 20 percent. Advertisers feel that the extra charge is not justified now that most magazines are printed by offset or gravure. In the days of letterpress, bleed ads did cause extra trouble for magazines. Advertisers like to bleed their ads because, some feel, the ads look more contemporary. More important, bleeds on 8½″ × 11″ pages mean about 25 percent more space.

Any number of loosely knit organizations exist to make it easier—and cheaper—for an advertiser to appear in several different magazines. For instance, in 1976 *Atlas, Columbia Journalism Review, Commentary, Foreign Affairs, National Review, The New Republic,* and *The New York Review of Books* formed The Leadership Network, a group of unrelated magazines edited for affluent intellectuals. The network could claim a combined circulation of 550,000. The divergent editorial policies, ranging from far left to far right, meant little audience duplication. Putting the same ad in all seven magazines, the advertiser could save 20 percent from what was needed when approaching each magazine separately. That same year *The Progressive, Change, Environment,* and *Bulletin of the Atomic Scientists* announced a similar alliance.

To help advertisers get additional mileage out of their ads, many magazines offer special marketing services, such as reprints wrapped in the magazines' covers and "As Advertised in _____ " display cards. Magazines also send out calendars showing special issues planned so that advertising can be tied to editorial content. Once when *Newsweek* decided to run a major article on "Showdown Over Smoking," it notified its cigarette advertisers, and all pulled out of the issue. They were back the next week.

Magazine Formats

Magazines come in a variety of formats, from pocket-size (*Reader's Digest*) to near-tabloid size (*Advertising Age*). Most magazines come in an 8½″ × 11″ size—or something close to that.

Magazines in a similar field tend to adopt the same page size so that an advertiser, producing an ad for one, can use the same ad for the others. But often an ad has to be designed so that it can be enlarged or reduced to fit magazines with different page sizes. Sometimes the ad will appear as a one-pager in one magazine, a two-pager in another. The designer's job is to take the original and redesign it, holding onto the same elements but resizing and perhaps reshaping.

A two-page ad poses a problem for the designer, who has to figure out ways to overcome the gutter that tends to keep the two pages separate. A two-page spread in a side-stitched magazine (like *Esquire*) is more difficult to manage than a two-page spread in a saddle-stitched magazine (like *Playboy*).

Some magazines accept inserts of a size different from the magazine proper. Some offer gatefolds—covers that open out to three or more pages. Some magazines accept advertising designed in an irregular shape, place it in the middle of a page, and fit editorial material around it.

The message may dictate the space. When Arco in 1987 guaranteed that its gasoline would clean fuel injectors, it took out a gatefold ad in the news magazines (three pages), with the first page carrying only this headline: "Presenting the Biggest Guarantee in Gasoline History." The ad had to be big. The formally designed guarantee on the inside two pages spanned the pages, posterlike.

The appropriate volume in the *Standard Rate & Date Service* series gives you all the information you need about a given magazine. A listing tells you, among other things, what the space rates are, what editions (geographic or demographic) are available, whether the magazine offers split runs (to test the relative effectiveness of two different ads), whether the magazine accepts ads that bleed off the page, and what the mechanical requirements are. Another *SRDS* volume that will prove useful is *Print Media Production Data,* which brings production information together from several *SRDS* publications.

In considering a magazine's rate card and the information in *SRDS,* the agency creative department will have to decide, for instance, whether bleeding the ad is worth an extra 15 percent charge and whether specifying position in the magazine is worth *that* extra charge. (Advertisers seem to feel that being up front in a magazine and on a right-hand page gives them better readership.)

The most expensive page, because it is a page likely to be seen often, is the back cover. So revered is this page that a magazine would rather plant the address stickers over front-cover art than over any part of the back cover. A few magazines—*Editor & Publisher* is one—sell space on their front covers.

Up until the mid- to late-1970s you could stand out in a magazine if you used full color. Since then, most of the ads in magazines have appeared in full color. Advertisers have looked for new ways to stand out, and magazine publishers—

A well-designed small-space magazine ad with plenty of art. It says a lot, and most of what it says is hand lettered.

some of them—think they have the answer: Try checkerboard, staircase, or other offbeat sizes and shapes.

A checkerboard ad occupies the top half of a left-hand page and the bottom half of a right-hand page—or the top-left quarter and bottom right-hand quarter of a single page or succession of pages. A staircase ad takes one full column and then flattens out and spreads across two or three more columns. Another approach is for the ad to start on one page and finish on the other, with room for editorial matter on both pages.

Other ways to get unusual impact in magazine advertising are to buy the three- or four-page spreads offered by cover gatefolds, to buy a succession of magazine pages, to use a fifth color like silver, and to pay for inserts of various kinds. You can also buy a scattering of space in magazines, allowing a series of ads to build momentum in a single issue.

Advertorials—ads that look like editorial matter—have become more popular in magazines as advertisers look for new ways to lure readers into their copy.

Magazines use ads in *Advertising Age* and other industry trade journals to tout their superiority as media buys. *Modern Maturity* in one ad claims that it reaches almost half of the over-50 population. *Popular Photography* talks about an environment for ads that is "picture perfect." *Smithsonian* says that it "captivates 2,000,000 subscribers each month." *PC World* claims that it is "the one magazine . . . [that sellers of PCs] prefer over any other." *Advertising Age* itself, in a house ad, names many television networks, newsmagazines, business magazines, and big newspapers and asks: "Why do all these news sources get their news from *Advertising Age?* Because it's the first word in marketing. The authority. Always has been, and always will be.

"To advertise in the foremost marketing publication in the world, call. . . ."[6]

Advantages of Magazines

The big advantage magazines have over other media—an advantage shared by direct mail—is that magazines can really pinpoint an audience. A principal job of the designer of a magazine ad is to understand the interest group and command its attention.

Magazines have other advantages. With some exceptions, they tend to devote less of their total space to advertising than newspapers do. One study of fifty-two leading magazines showed a 51–49 ratio of advertising to editorial.

Magazines like to compare themselves to TV for advertising clutter, claiming that viewers are growing increasingly intolerant of the amount of broadcast time given over to commercials. The Magazine Publishers Association especially likes to cite the medium's advantages over television, which gets a much bigger share of the advertiser's dollar. True, commercials take up only a fraction of TV time, but you cannot escape them quite as easily as you can escape the ads in magazines.

Readers find magazine advertising less irritating. A majority of readers, Opinion Research Corporation finds, prefer magazines with advertising to magazines without.[7] And magazines can claim that some readers want the advertising as much as they want editorial content.

An ad in a magazine has longer life than an ad on TV and even in a newspaper. The reader can refer to it later. And copy can be longer. Using an 8½″ × 11″ (full-page) all-copy magazine ad sponsored by the Magazine Publishers Association, Al Hampel, then director of creative services for Benton & Bowles, demonstrated the fact that, as his headline phrased it, "It Would Take Eighteen 30-Second TV Commercials to Tell You What's on This Page."

In spite of the magazine industry's jealousy over TV, the advertising in magazines often ties itself to TV advertising. One reason is for the advertising to provide arguments in detail based on a theme only barely touched on by the commercial. The magazine ad puts the original ad in perspective. Or the magazine ad capitalizes on a popular TV commercial by simply restating its theme, giving it a little more mileage. The most memorable frame in the commercial is frozen for print. The magazine ad becomes reminder advertising.

Introducing Dakin Huggables. So soft, they're an entirely different animal.

These aren't your typical stuffed animals. Their designs are a little simpler. A little more classic. They aren't called Huggables, however, for nothing. Take a look at the plush. Or better yet, touch it. Then, consider the stuffing. We've spent years doing exactly that. Resulting in some of the softest toys around. Give them a squeeze, we think you'll agree. Huggables even have one feature you won't find on any other soft line: the Dakin name. That means more variety. With over fifty different animals, we'd need more than ten ads like this to show them all. From pigs to penguins, there's a Dakin Huggable for everyone. It means you'll pay less for a name brand. It also means you'll get the personalized service Dakin is famous for. As well as extended terms with low minimum orders. So call your Dakin representative now. The line is soft. But its sales won't be.

When Jell-O used real housewives on television to demonstrate how easy it was to prepare a new gelatin dessert, the announcer, at the end of each commercial, referred the viewer to the women's magazines, where, in ads, the recipe could be found.

Occasionally a magazine ad shows the TV commercial in storyboard or photoboard form. The most important frames form into a "multipanel" ad (a kind of ad described in chapter 5).

The big advantage that magazines hold over newspapers as an advertising medium centers on production. Both offset lithography and gravure are used for magazines. Sometimes a single magazine uses both processes. Paper quality in magazines allows for crisper impressions, less show-through, finer screening for halftones, and better color fidelity.

Nine associations covering media, advertising agencies, and production firms got together in 1976 to set color standards for advertising placed in publications printed on web offset presses. The new standards, updating a 1964 letterpress set and a 1966 business publications set, were spelled out in a fourteen-page booklet, now available from the American Association of Advertising Agencies, the Associated Business Press, and the Magazine Publishers Association. The standards were designed to assure advertisers the same color in magazines that they see and okay on progressive proofs.

Using *GR: Gift Reporter* Magazine, Dakin introduces to merchants a new line of stuffed animals: Huggables™. "With over fifty different animals, we'd need more than ten ads like this to show them all." After advising merchants to "call your representative now," the ad ends on this note: "The line is soft. But its sales won't be."

The Challenge of Magazine Ad Design

Because the space it occupies is expensive, because it is meant to be seen several times, and because it is produced by highly creative people in advertising agencies, a magazine ad often represents the best in current design thinking. Design quality remains at a rather consistent level in consumer magazines. In trade and professional journals it rises to high levels—and sinks to low. Because trade-journal ads often deal with technical matters, most creative people prefer to work on ads for consumer magazines, where the imagination often is allowed greater play.

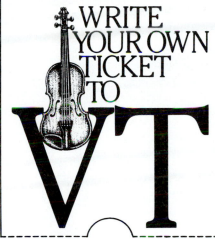

But, in view of the numerous trade magazines published, much of the creative activity must center on ads done for the less familiar magazines.

Magazine ads, unlike newspaper ads, seldom make use of borders. The magazines' smaller pages give dominance to each ad. There is less need to fence out competing ads.

Often a coupon is involved. If it is a coupon to be filled out and mailed in, chances are it will contain a key: an agency-assigned "Dept." number, different for each magazine, that allows the agency or advertiser to measure the pulling power of one magazine against the other or one ad against the other. The designer should avoid tone in the area where the key number is to go. Otherwise a small rectangle will have to be cut out to accommodate changes in the number, and the number each time will stand out awkwardly.

If an ad is to bleed, the designer must remember to bleed only the art, not the headline or copy. Where bleeding is to occur, the final pasteup will carry art that extends slightly beyond the trim edge.

A magazine may set up any number of regulations as to what a designer can do. For instance, it may not be willing to let the designer adopt an editorial format that makes the ad look like part of the magazine itself. It may insist that the designer avoid using the magazine's headline or title face and body face. But, in general, the creative potential in magazine advertising design is boundless.

A ticketlike box encloses a small-space ad that carries the headline "Write Your Own Ticket to VT." The entire ad is a coupon, which, when filled out, will bring a vacation-planning ticket to the reader. To emphasize the fact that Vermont is more than beautiful scenery, the ad shows a violin. "Wherever you want to go in Vermont, you'll find lots of offerings in the arts. . . ." Designer: William Clark. Copywriter: Bruce Patteson. Agency: Kenyon & Eckhardt.

For a one-column by 2½" ad in the *Los Angeles Times Magazine,* The Pet Dept uses its cat-and-dog logo and a rounded-corner box to keep other ads from intruding. The strong, stylized logo nicely integrates the two animals with a line drawn between them that they both share. Irwin Rickel designed the small-space ad, shown here actual size.

CHAPTER

12

BROADCAST ADVERTISING

A generation raised on television finds it difficult to imagine people planning their evenings so as not to miss the latest episode of "Amos 'n' Andy," "Fibber McGee and Molly," or one of the other popular radio programs of the 1930s or 1940s. The members of that earlier generation gathered in front of their radio sets and actually watched the dials as they listened to the words and music. What pictures they saw had to be pictures in their heads. In those days the commercials as well as the programs did their job without benefit of visual stimulation.

When TV came along after World War II, advertising agencies used techniques they understood: They simply made more radio commercials, adding pictures as one adds frosting on a cake. A lot of experimentation had to go on before TV commercials could attain the degree of sophistication and integration they now have.

Television not only added a visual dimension to commercials; it also added motion. When color came along later, television as an advertising medium was complete.

Ad makers in agencies who made the switch from radio and the print media to television discovered staggering staging possibilities, although the first TV commercials were not much more than radio commercials with announcers shown on the screen. The first experimental commercials were the ones that used simple animation.

Like most forms of advertising, TV commercials have gone through phases. The 1960s saw a creative explosion, with all kinds of techniques tried, some at the expense of the message. In the 1970s commercial makers depended more on research. Creativity seemed to move to Europe, where some of the best commercials were being made. In the early 1980s TV commercials relied largely on "new wave" graphics. What was shown was impressive but cold. As the decade unfolded, the commercials seemed to take on a new warmth. They were people-oriented rather than machine-oriented.[1] There was also a preoccupation with special effects.

Many—too many—commercials in the 1980s made use of technographics, which changed items into different forms or made them fly or perform other tricks. "Bloodless commercials," Piet Verbeck of Ogilvy & Mather Partners called them, "from a society with a crush on computers." He added: "Technographic images can only augment the story. They cannot tell it. . . . The eye is drawn to them. But not the mind."

Verbeck thought that technographics *did* work when a human emotion was involved or realism added. He cited a Jell-O commercial in which a package becomes a shimmering pool and an ITT commercial in which a small town becomes a large city.[2]

Some commercials are unusual enough to catch the attention not only of consumers but also of comedians. Beginning in late 1989, Energizer ran commercials in which a pink drum-beating bunny interrupted other "commercials" for other sponsors by running across the screen to show that the battery that propelled him lasted longer than other batteries. Jay Leno reported the death of the Energizer Bunny when it tried to march through a home pregnancy test commercial.

This photoboard for "Shady Acres," a 30-second TV commercial for Pepsi, uses a mixup theme that has Pepsi going to the old folks, Coke to a fraternity house, with unexpected results. Agency: BBDO, New York. Chief creative director: Phil Dusenberry, with art handled by Don Schneider, copy by Jonathan Mandell.

BBDO

Batten, Barton, Durstine & Osborn, Inc.

Client: PEPSI-COLA COMPANY

Product: BRAND PEPSI

Title: "SHADY ACRES"

Time: 30 SECONDS

Comml. No: PEPX 7193 (STEREO)
PEPX 7173 (MONO)

(MUSIC STARTS)

WOMAN IN FLORAL SHIRT: "Rock and Roll is o.k. but I prefer rap."

(MUSIC CONTINUES)

GUY WITH HAT AND SUNGLASSES: "Awesome!"

FIRST GUY: "Wait a second, Shady Acres was supposed to get the Coke and the frat house was supposed to get the Pepsi."

SECOND GUY: "Coke, Pepsi, what's the difference?!"

(MUSIC STARTS)
GUY WITH RED CARDIGAN: "I-24."

(MUSIC CONTINUES)

GUY WITH HAT AND SUNGLASSES: "This is radical!"

Thomas Sowell, the newspaper columnist, observes: "The longest and most boring commercials are those on non-commercial television during pledge drives. Where is the battery-powered rabbit when we need him?"[3]

The Federal Communications Commission no longer limits the time that commercial stations can give to commercials. Infomercials are one result. Infomercials are those after-hours programs that are pure advertising, programs that sell betterment courses, get-rich-quick schemes, and cleaning products.

Time describes infomercials as "program-size commercials that are disguised as real shows." Often a has-been actor acts as host. "Not since the legendary Veg-O-Matic ('It slices! It dices!') has TV advertising been so gloriously tacky," *Time* reports.[4]

Filmmaking vs. Commercial Making

The same kinds of talents that go into the making of motion pictures go into the making of TV commercials. But there are some important differences.

In the first place, commercials are short, usually no longer than thirty seconds. So the director can show only a few details. Mood becomes all important. The director must establish it instantly. And every action counts.

Second, the screen size is much smaller than theater screen size. This calls for more closeups. The commercial, then, achieves a sense of intimacy.

Third, commercials on television, because they evolved from radio, depend more on audio impressions than theater films do. The idea for a commercial usually comes from a copywriter's script; the art director does the storyboard, with its visual impressions, later. Some of the time the TV viewer may not be watching the screen at all, just listening.

Fourth, commercials tend to intrude while theater films serve an audience that has paid to see them. Commercials must work to get the viewer's attention. They must dazzle. No wonder they sometimes appear to be more elaborate, more compelling than the programs themselves.

Fifth, commercials run again and again. The people who make them must try, somehow, to take the sting out of the redundancy.

Sixth, commercials direct themselves to selected audiences. The media buyers in agencies, then, in the time slots and stations they buy, play a big role in making commercials successful.[5]

Considering the Audience

To be effective, TV commercials must overcome two major handicaps. Both have to do with the audience. One concerns the hostility members of the audience harbor for this kind of advertising. Commercials intrude on their entertainment.

Creators of TV commercials must contend not only with viewers who zap commercials in progress but also with viewers who zip past them when watching programs they've recorded on their videocassette recorders. ". . . only 6 percent of adult viewers of recorded programs claim that they never zip through commercials. One-third claim that they always do," an *Adweek* writer reports.

The really bad news is that the people most likely to zip through commercials are the young, well-educated viewers in the higher income brackets, the very people most of the advertisers want to reach.[6]

The other problem concerns the welter of commercials seen each day by the typical viewer. In the average home, a TV set sends out programs—and commercials—for just about seven hours a day. While this statistic does not identify who watches what and for how long, it does suggest that, with present practices of stacking commercials, the typical viewer sees scores of them every day. They parade before the viewer in rapid succession, in no particular order, each with the same degree of urgency.

Under such circumstances, how much of what's seen can the viewer possibly retain? Not much—or at least not much *accurately*. One survey found that about 25 percent of commercials are attributed by viewers to competitors rather than to actual sponsors.

This photoboard shows what happens in a playful Ray Charles TV commercial in which someone tries to push a soft drink other than Diet Pepsi onto the popular blind entertainer. ". . . All right now, who's the wise guy?!" Charles demands. Agency: BBDO, New York. Chief creative director: Phil Dusenberry. Art director: David Harner. Copywriters: Al Merrin and David Johnson.

BBDO

Batten, Barton, Durstine & Osborn, Inc.

Client: PEPSI-COLA COMPANY		Time: :30 SECONDS
Product: DIET PEPSI	Title: "RAY CHARLES"	Comml. No: PEDX-4683 (MONO)

(PIANO RIFF) Ray Charles: "You know when you got it right, you got it right."

Ray Charles: "Whether you're talking about this,"

(PIANO RIFF)

Ray Charles: "or whether you're talking about . . .

the one and only diet cola that does it for Ray, Diet Pepsi."

Ray Charles: "You know, nothin' tastes as good to me as Diet Pepsi."

Ray Charles: "Hmm - All right now, who's the wise guy?!"

AVO: Diet Pepsi with 100% NutraSweet

Ray Charles: "Now, that's the Right One baby!"
Super: Diet Pepsi. The Right One.

Ideally, then, a TV commercial makes restitution for the irritation it causes: It entertains the viewer. At the same time, it does something out of the ordinary to gain attention. And it makes sure that the viewer correctly associates the message with the specific product.

MMM Carpets in California has run snide comments in type at the bottom of the screen, comments that have little or nothing to do with the routine hard sell going on in the commercial. This is a daring practice, perhaps even questionable; but it does show that the firm wants to somehow relieve the tedium of commercials that might have to be seen again and again.

"Remember," says Professor Ann Keding, "people like television commercials when they are good ones. When done well, they can be tiny jewels of enjoyment and viewers will look forward to watching them again. This is the aim of creative television advertising."

Keding's prescription for a good 30-second TV commercial: no more than 90 words, the product as hero, instant client recognition—all with entertainment value.[7]

Advertisers Who Use TV

Manufacturers of food products, grooming aids, cleaning agents, home remedies, appliances, and automobiles continue to rely heavily on TV as an advertising medium, but some previously print-oriented advertisers are moving into TV, too, especially at the local level.

Among the department stores turning to TV is J. C. Penney, whose no-nonsense, one-item-per-spot commercials reflect the clean, crisp design thinking evident in its newspaper ads. The store's New York headquarters has advised local store advertising managers to concentrate spots in one program rather than scatter them over several days. The store believes it can get more impact that way.

Even magazines use TV to sell their product. *People* and the three news magazines often use spots to call attention to features in current issues. *The New Yorker* uses TV now, something it would never have done in its glory years. The *National Enquirer* uses TV to congratulate its readers for having "enquiring minds." *The Wall Street Journal* uses TV to line up new subscribers.

Book publishers, too, show an interest in TV advertising—for both their hardback and paperback editions. Peter Ognibene, who has written many TV commercials, explains why: "TV's potential for hardcover books is so enormous that titles selling 30,000 to 150,000 copies could, with TV advertising behind them, sell as much as ten times that number. And for paperback publishers the opportunities are equally dramatic."[8]

While many advertisers develop media mixes, some advertisers do it all on TV. Their products seem eminently suited to use by TV viewers.

When advertisers have moved away from TV and back to print, it has been for reasons of cost and clutter. The most frequently heard complaint these days is that stations crowd too many commercials together at program or station breaks. The switch by advertisers from thirty-second to shorter commercials explains some of the crowding.

The Idea Is to Sell

In his *Hi and Lois* comic strip, Dik Brown in one episode has a kid talking about how funny a TV commercial is. A man interrupts to ask what the commercial is selling. The kid looks puzzled. "Selling?"

Too often the idea of selling gets lost in the attempt to be entertaining. Whatever techniques are used to involve the reader must lead, and quickly, to a pitch. Many ad people think that the pitch should come on right away.

And whatever is said must be repeated, not only within the ad but from ad to ad. Typically in a series, the related stories all lead to the same conclusion. The detergent *does* clean better, the margarine *does* taste like butter, the car *does* go farther on a tankful of gas.

A 30-second soft-sell Acura commercial produced by Shelley Predovich takes the viewer on a pleasant ride. Agency: Ketcham, L. A. Art director: Mark Erwin. Copywriter: Sam Avery.

ACURA
PRECISION CRAFTED PERFORMANCE

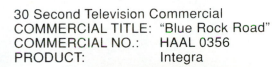

(MUSIC THROUGHOUT)

COBURN: At Acura,

we've discovered that when we go the extra mile,

so do

the people who drive our cars.

The 1991

Acura Integra.

AT&T

CLIENT: AT&T CORPORATE   AGENCY: UNIWORLD GROUP   TITLE:"BEHIND THE SCENES"
                                                                                    :30

ROLLINS: To put on a successful theatrical production,

it takes a lot of skilled and talented people.

It's the same with providing quality communications service.

HOWARD ROLLINS FOR AT&T

At AT&T there are thousands of people working to make our services the best in the industry.

In phones, long distance,

business systems and computers.

When it comes to serving you better,

AT&T people are a tough act to follow.

AT&T
The right choice.

ANNCR: Whether it's telephones, ...long distance services, information systems or computers... AT&T. The right choice.

Like other advertisements, TV commercials can build images as well as sell products. To sell their new light beers, breweries were careful to show he-men calling for it in commercials. The companies did not want the beer burdened with an effeminate image, figuring the bulk of the buyers were men and that, further, women drinkers would not be turned off by a manly image.

And like other advertisements, TV commercials can address themselves to specific audiences in time slots when the best prospects can be reached. Consider how TV was used to sell 800,000 copies of a long-playing record by Roger Whittaker, a middle-aged British singer of sweet ballads (". . . the man who has thrilled millions around the world now brings his exciting music and pleasing manner to American audiences"). Tee Vee Records filmed Whittaker before a large and receptive Canadian audience and spliced the footage into the commercial to prove that he could draw an audience. The company also filmed Whittaker talking with great sincerity—the nice guy image. The commercial ran over and over again on selected stations in the United States. Tee Vee Records explained its success with the observation that people who bought the record are the kind who are ill at ease in a record store, with its heavy beat and its smoking paraphernalia.[9]

Many advertisers use their commercials to make the point that their products have *two* redeeming values. A mint has both taste and breath-sweetening qualities. A toothpaste has both fluoride and breath-sweetening qualities. A toilet paper has both softness and color. A beer has good taste and is less filling. In each case two silly people argue about the qualities, each adamant about one quality, each blind to the other. The beleaguered viewer gets the point.

Emotion and Sentiment in Commercials

AT&T's "Reach out and touch someone" campaign, which started in 1979, prompted a rush by other advertisers to sentiment and emotion as selling tools in the 1980s. "Many advertisers have turned to sentiment because they've run out of compelling appeals to logic," a *Wall Street Journal* writer observed; ". . . for the increasing number of products that don't differ markedly from their competitors, new arguments are hard to find."[10]

Advertising agencies have found that sentimental or emotional commercials need to be seen several times before they register on viewers. Commercials based on logic score better on first-time-seen tests.

Japanese commercials, especially, rely on emotion. The population density in Japan means less need for verbalizing, more need for intuition. For instance, body language means more there.

The Japanese don't want reasons. Any fast talking or hard or persuasive sell turns off the viewer. Repetition is not a problem, because the viewer feels that if a commercial is popular, the product must be selling well.[11]

Commercials and other ads created originally for one country do not often translate effectively into ads for other countries. The ads for foreign audiences need different themes, different words, different design. When a Swedish ad for Electrolux vacuum cleaners was translated into English and run in a Korean magazine, it read: "Nothing sucks like Electrolux."

Kinds of TV Commercials

Advertisers use commercials in three ways: as *network advertisements,* shown on national shows; as *spot advertisements,* prepared nationally and shipped to various stations for local showings; and as *local advertisements,* prepared locally and shown locally. In each case the advertisement is called a "commercial" or a "spot."

Commercials tend to fall into these categories:

■ *The narrative.* Like a feature-length motion picture, this kind of commercial has a plot. Typically the story introduces a problem, then shows how the use of a particular product solves the problem.

The story can be told in live-action photography or in animation. Often a

AT&T uses Howard Rollins to sell the idea of quality communications service, as this photoboard shows. Agency: UniWorld Group, Inc., New York. Art director: Bill Allen. Copywriter: Len Dia.

little exaggeration, a little humor moves the story along. IBM, to sell one of its sophisticated typewriters, showed a typist with several arms doing several things at her desk while her typewriter was automatically centering, underlining, and so on. At the end of the commercial a man came up with several gloves and asked: "Are these your gloves?"

Federal Express in one of its humorous commercials portrayed the Postal Service, its competitor, as run by lazy, incompetent people. The angered Postal Service demanded that the commercial be taken off the air. *New York* magazine, noting this, offered the Postal Service its "If the Shoe Fits Wear It" Award.

■ *The slice-of-life*. Advertisers in a less enlightened age referred to it as "the two broads in the kitchen" commercial. More believable, theoretically, than a story, this commercial does not have a traditional hero or heroine. Instead it features people who are very, very ordinary—people who could well live next door to the viewer.

While the story commercial leans heavily on fiction techniques, the slice-of-life commercial creates the impression that it is a piece of nonfiction. Viewers are supposed to have a sort of "Ain't it the truth!" reaction to the commercial.

Slice-of-life commercials often show an ordinary person burdened by some everyday problem—bad breath, cavities, constipation, clothes that do not come clean—only to be advised by some other ordinary person who has the word about a miracle product.

In slice-of-life commercials people like to pull the bill of someone's cap down over his forehead, or they like to wink. Another favorite device is to have ordinary people in commercials singing off-key. Apparently agencies and advertisers feel that we can listen to commercials like this without losing our lunches.

Closely allied to slice-of-life commercials are "continuing character" commercials that feature a presumably believable character who seems to spend his every waking moment praising a certain product: a soft toilet tissue, a tasty coffee, an altered coffee that does not cause jangled nerves.

One of the most talked-about series of commercials in the late 1980s involved a couple of Hal Riney's folksy types who appeared to be the owners of a small, struggling company trying to make it in the wine-cooler market. Bartles & Jaymes was really part of the giant Gallo wine operation, but the low-key, soft-sell, almost pathetic commercials had many people believing that if they purchased that brand they'd be helping a couple of good ol' boys battle the big-city competition.

The two characters were not professional actors. They appeared usually on a front porch, one doing all the talking. One of the commercials had the quiet one making a chart showing all the foods that go well with the product. Apparently only two didn't make the list: an obscure vegetable and candy corn.

■ *The testimonial*. Famous people—or unknowns—caught by a candid camera tell what they like about a product and urge, directly or indirectly, others to try it. These people are not acting a part; they are believers—or so it appears. Viewers are supposed to react like this: "If it's good enough for her, it's good enough for me."

BBDO had some fun in a 1990 commercial when it showed an unsuccessful attempt to fool Ray Charles into drinking Diet Coke instead of Diet Pepsi, but not before checking the idea with an association for the blind to make sure it wouldn't offend.

The testimonial can also be used to *unsell* a product or do an institutional job. One of the most moving TV commercials ever made had William Talman, the TV actor, in a starring role some six weeks before he died of lung cancer. He was a cigarette smoker. He knew he was dying, but he wanted to expend what energy he had to dissuade others from smoking.

In the commercial, which was produced by the American Cancer Society, the Talman family was shown in various settings, then Talman was shown with

A photoboard for Toro snow throwers shows how the machine can overcome the problems left by the city's snowplow. The thirty-second commercial ends on the note, "The only challenge left . . . getting out of the driveway . . . to go buy one." The last frame leaves time for a dealer tag. Agency: Campbell-Mithun Advertising, Minneapolis. Art director: George Halvorson. Copywriter: Terry Bremer.

CM
CAMPBELL-MITHUN ADVERTISING

222 SOUTH NINTH STREET
MINNEAPOLIS-MINNESOTA 55402
612-347-1000

CLIENT: THE TORO COMPANY
PRODUCT: Snowthrowers
CODE NO./TITLE: XTNS8602 "Driveway/Power Shift"
JOB NO.: TOSNOM7008 DATE: June, 1987 LENGTH: :25/:05

1. (MUSIC AND SFX UP AND UNDER)

2. Until now,...

3. ...plowing through...

4. ...what the snowplow...

5. ...left behind... (SFX: BOINK!)

6. ...was one of winter's toughest challenges.

7. Now Toro introduces the exclusive Power Shift snowthrower.

8. (MAN SHIFTS LEVER) The Power Shift...

9. ...automatically puts more weight on the front...

10. ...for a more powerful bite...

11. ...on winter's toughest snow. The new Toro Power Shift.

12. The only challenge left...

13. ...getting out of the driveway...

14. ...to go buy one.

15. (DEALER TAG)

fellow actor Raymond Burr, and then Talman was shown in a closeup. "You know," he said, "I didn't really mind losing those courtroom battles [on TV]. But I'm in a battle right now I don't want to lose at all because, if I lose it, it means losing my wife and those kids you just met.

"I've got lung cancer.

"So take some advice about smoking and losing from someone who's been doing both for years. If you haven't smoked, don't start. If you do smoke, quit. Don't be a loser."

■ *The announcer commercial.* Many commercials make use of an announcer who makes comments while a story unfolds. But some commercials are simpler than that. They show *only* an announcer, a no-nonsense type, often, who looks straight into the camera, telling viewers why they should try a product or order a service. If the announcer is well known, the commercial takes on some of the qualities of a testimonial.

The announcer commercial has less flair than the testimonial, and the viewer understands that a professional pitchman is on the screen, however sincere the pitchman may appear to be.

The announcer commercial, like the testimonial, is relatively inexpensive to produce.

Sometimes the owner of a business is its best spokesperson in ads. Dave Thomas in the early 1990s starred in Wendy's TV and radio commercials that gave the company a homey image and increased volume, which had been in a slide. His agency, Backer Spielvoge/Bates Worldwide, pressed him into service after he made a spirited talk to staff members questioning their knowledge of his business.[12]

Among the most successful of the company-head commercials have been those for Chrysler starring Lee Iacocca. Some say that advertising made a folk hero out of the man. Certainly his frequent appearances on TV helped sell his autobiography. There was even some talk before the 1988 elections that he should run for president.

His commercials fostered the sincerest form of flattery. "If Lee Iacocca were here," said the owner of a local pizza parlor in a commercial, "I'm sure he would say, 'If you can find a better pizza, buy it!' "

■ *The demonstration.* The best way to sell some products is to show how they are made, how they compare with others, or how they are used. A demonstration commercial may call for rather elaborate graphics and casting. Or it may show just the product and one announcer to do the demonstration.

Television is remarkably suited to this kind of selling—better suited, even, than face-to-face contact. In television, the camera can move in close to focus on detail, then move out again to give an overall view. And live action can be combined with drawings and diagrams.

An effective commercial of this genre was created by Doyle Dane Bernbach for Heinz. It started by focusing on two bottles. One was labeled, simply, "Catsup" (the word has two spellings). The other was "Heinz Ketchup." The audio went like this: "Announcing the first televised/ketchup race./On the right . . . the world's leading ketchup . . . /on the left . . . /a well-known challenger./On your mark . . . /Get set. . . ." Then there were several frames showing the bottles turned upside down. Catsup poured out of the challenger, but it barely oozed out of the Heinz bottle. Then: "Heinz loses./Heinz is too thick . . . /too rich . . . /to win a ketchup race." It worked because it had an element of surprise in it. It pretended to show the product in an unfavorable light, but of course the viewer was not to be fooled.

Sprint ends its TV commercials with a pin dropping to suggest fidelity of sound. After the symbol was well established, the company offered this number for placing orders for the service: 1–800–PIN–DROP.

One of the most persistent users of the demonstration technique has been

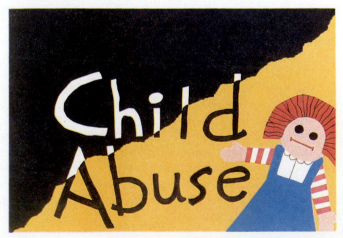

Chris Pontrelli uses a childlike style—a combination of paper cutting and drawing—to create art for slides and a video presentation on child abuse. What you see here is an opening frame. The presentation also included photographs. Client: Emergency Medical Planning, Inc., which produces first-aid and medical training programs in all media.

A promotional piece—a photoboard—showing enough stills from Blitz-Weinhard's prize-winning TV commercial to give you a good idea of how it went. The Oregon beer company played to the suspicions that Oregonians feel for their fast-living, resource-consuming neighbors to the south. Oregonians do not want any more immigrants. Some Oregon cars carry the bumper sticker: "Don't Californicate Oregon."

Polaroid. The demonstration is a natural for this advertiser. During its first years, Polaroid was sure enough of its product to do its demonstrations live.

■ *The song-and-dance.* In this kind of commercial, the advertiser tries to get the gaiety and flavor of a musical extravaganza into a thirty-seconds-or-less format.

Radio long ago proved the value of songs to sell products. The person living in the 1930s and 1940s found it almost impossible to escape the advertising jingles of the period or to keep from humming them. Coca-Cola showed that in the 1970s a jingle can still work. Its "Buy the World a Coke" commercial even fostered a pop record. Other advertisers have enjoyed similar success. "We've Only Just Begun," made popular by The Carpenters, was originally part of a series of commercials for Crocker Bank, San Francisco, when that bank was trying to appeal to youthful patrons.

But the full-fledged TV song-and-dance commercial we saw in the 1960s is a bit rare now because of the expense involved.

■ *The special-effects commercial.* The television commercial producer has access to all kinds of equipment and skills to bring about special effects. Camera tricks include unusual angles, fades, frozen action, and interruption in

Vern: Hey Earl, how come we're takin' this whole load of beer up to Orygone? Don't they have enough beer in Orygone?
Earl: Oh it ain't that Vern . . . I think it's. . .

probly that we got too much beer in Cali . . . Uh – oh . . .

Inspector: Well now, where you fellas goin' with all that beer?
Vern: . . . ah, here . . . Orygone!
Inspector: Now, you know this is where . . .

we brew Blitz-Weinhard . . . And you know it's brewed entirely natural, without any artificial ingredients . . . Is yours?
Earl: Uh - uh.

Vern: Uh - uh.

Inspector: Well then, why would you fellas be bringin' a whole load of that beer up here to Oregon?

Vern: Earl here says it's probly cause we got too much beer in California!

Announcer: There's no better beer, than the beer from here.
Vern: Earl . . . wanna try Idaho?

time so doors can close by themselves and people or props can change position, disappear, or appear as if by magic. Goldsholl Associates of Chicago, one of the leading studios for special effects, often uses the "stop-motion" technique, in which the object is moved slightly by hand before each frame is shot. A technique for filming a drawing in progress is to show the drawing first, erase a bit before each frame is shot, and then show the film backward. Nytol uses a modest special effect when it films two of its tablets upright, the Ns showing, then allows them to roll slightly to the left so that the Ns become Zs, appropriate letters for a product that brings sleep to the user.

Toppling dominoes became a popular special effect for commercials for a while. Someone pushes off the lead domino and down they go, one after the other, some thirty of them each second, spelling out a name or leading the viewer to some final visual treat or message. A Penn State student, Bob Speca, made a fine living for himself setting up dominoes for advertisers and then toppling them as a camera recorded the effect. National Bank of Dallas, Northern California Savings Bank, Purolator Air Freight, and other advertisers signed him up at fees ranging from $1,000 to $3,000.

A famous special-effects commercial from a few seasons back was the one showing a man floating down from the sky and into the driver's seat of a Hertz rental car. Others from the era included washing machines zooming up to ten-foot heights, hands reaching out of washing machines with boxes of detergent, and white knights spreading cleanliness as they rode past the camera.[13]

Jingles

Nothing brings life to a TV commercial more readily or makes it better remembered than a jingle.

A lot of advertising jingles originate in Nashville with its country and western music heritage. The city's music unions have more than 5,000 members. Not only do C & W stars step in to record jingles; they often go out in tours sponsored by companies like GMC Trucks and Miller Beer.

Some jingle writers—like Barry Manilow—move on to write popular songs. Joe Brooks, with jingles to his credit written for Pepsi-Cola, Dr. Pepper, Pan Am, American Airlines, and other advertisers, wrote the Academy Award winner "You Light Up My Life."

Unlike regular songs, jingles are not covered by ASCAP or BMI, so jingle writers ordinarily do not earn royalties. They get a one-time fee for each jingle, a fee that for a national advertiser ranges from $5,000 to $10,000. The singers, though, get residuals, and often earn much more than the writers. No wonder some of the writers try to do their own singing.

An advantage of the jingle in TV advertising is that it can easily move to radio, tying a campaign together.

Some Technical Aspects

Commercials come mainly in sixty-, thirty-, twenty-, and ten-second lengths. Most are thirty seconds long. In the mid-1980s, fifteen-second commercials began to catch on. Many were directed to younger viewers with short attention spans. But of course their real appeal was to advertisers who needed to cut time costs. Some thought that fifteen-second commercials would become the standard in the industry.

A short-length commercial is often merely a pruned version of a longer one. Such a commercial is called a "lift."

Local commercials as a rule are longer than network commercials because the time costs less. They may also *seem* longer because they are so often poorly done. "Have you noticed how classy auto commercials are? And how classless auto dealer commercials are?" asks Frank J. Romano, editor of *Type World.*[14]

There are three ways to present commercials.

■ *Film.* Film is the most versatile medium for commercials and also the most expensive to produce.[15] The film can be made in a studio or, for greater realism, on location. Films made on location cost more than films made in a studio.

An advertiser who cannot afford on-location shooting buys stock film and combines it with studio film.

The size of the film—it's in color, of course—is almost always 35mm. But some commercials are done in 16mm because 16mm film, made with easily maneuvered equipment, provides more realism or a "news" feel. And 16mm films are less polished, which can be an advantage.

But agencies doing commercials that need high visual appeal, as for food and travel accounts, feel that 35mm filming is worth the extra cost.

■ *Tape*. The big advantage of videotape is that it requires no processing. The production team can preview the takes immediately, then make new takes when necessary. The new equipment permits frame-by-frame editing and offers many special effects.

But film is still better for on-location shots and animation. And copies of commercials in film form are less expensive than copies in tape form.

■ *Live action*. You see it in some locally produced commercials; but live action, like tape, is only infrequently used these days for commercials. In the early days of television, it was just about the only way of showing them. Those were the days when, to the embarrassment of advertisers, the appliance door did not open or the dog balked when placed in front of a plate of dog food.

Since late-night talk shows and network news shows are taped earlier in the day, what appears to be a live lead-in is itself taped.

For local commercials, live action often takes the form of a succession of slides or a few flipped hand-lettered signs or an on-camera announcer talking about a product.

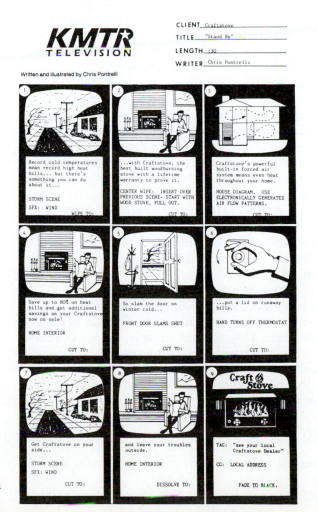

Like local newspapers, local TV stations offer creative services to advertisers who don't have their own advertising agencies or departments. Chris Pontrelli of KMTR-TV did the writing and art for this storyboard for a wood-stove manufacturer.

Apple Computer in 1992 introduced QuickTime, a software program that allows Macintosh users to manipulate video, animation, and sound. Looking back at how the Macintosh revolutionized print media ads in the 1980s, Louise Vondran, senior vice president at Ogilvy & Mather, New York, said that the Mac in the 1990s could make changes just as radical in how agencies make commercials.[16]

Animation

On-location expenses, sound-stage rentals, large crews, equipment, casting, sudden changes in weather—all these send costs for live-action film commercials soaring. And the fact that commercials are shorter than in the past cuts down on creative possibilities. Howard Sutton, a partner in Tanner/Sutton Studio, New York, producer of animated commercials, makes a case for animation: "Animation has always had certain advantages over the live-action medium, and these advantages seem to be increasing. . . . Animation works very well in compressed formats, and the proliferation of new techniques and art materials offers a great deal of creative freedom. It's no accident that animated commercials display so much more originality than live-action commercials."[17]

". . . the possibilities are endless," says Zander's Animation Parlour in an ad in *Art Direction*. "We have the power to defy all laws of science and rationality by making cups and saucers sing and dance, by making the common cold a living, breathing character, by giving man the strength to literally support the weight of the world on his shoulders."

With so much clutter on TV, a commercial has to stand out, and animation is one sure way to get attention.

Animation often makes use of animals. Kellogg for years has relied on "Tony the Tiger" to put its message across. Another tiger has seen a lot of service with Esso. But animation in advertising involves more than cute cartoon figures. It can bring to life the product itself (showing it in use or being demonstrated), the package it comes in, or the product name or company logo. In animation, these elements swell and twist and change marvelously right before the viewer's eyes.

An estimated 5 percent of TV commercials involve animation.

For story, song-and-dance, and special-effects commercials, animation can beat live-action film on price. To keep costs down, animators sometimes produce commercials without synchronizing lip movement with body action, without elaborate backgrounds, and with rough, scratchy color rather than the tight, registered color we have come to associate with Walt Disney productions.

Some film commercials combine both live human action and animation, a technique Disney introduced in his feature-length movies in the 1930s. And some animation involves puppets rather than cartoon drawings.

One different approach to commercial production is a form of animation called Claymation developed by Will Vinton's studio in Portland, Oregon. California Raisins' "Heard It through the Grapevine" spot became one of the most popular ones of the 1987 season. Earlier the Vinton studio had won an Oscar for a Claymation film called "Closed Mondays."

You cannot assume that animation is only for the young. It can serve as the ideal medium for explaining complicated or scientific processes to adults as well as children. An enzyme detergent for one of its ads used animation to portray dirt as locks attached to cloth fibers. Then enzymes came on as keys to unlock the locks. And some public-service advertisers find that animation provides the necessary light touch to enhance otherwise dull material. But animation does not rank high in credibility. For that reason agencies tend to use it mostly in advertising for products purchased on impulse.

Planning the Commercial

Every detail in a TV commercial has to be just right. Every nuance must be carefully planned.

No literary or entertainment device is overlooked. For example, Taster's Choice

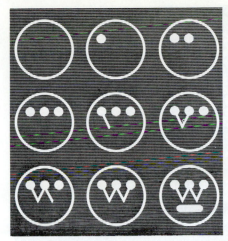

This is how Westinghouse made use of its circle-*W* trademark for TV animation. (Used by permission.)

Coffee used sequential commercials to sell its instant brand in the early 1990s. A serious woman borrows coffee from a knowing neighbor, a male, for her dinner party, and in a later commercial when she returns a jar, she and the neighbor exchange looks and comments that suggest a later meeting. Real soap opera stuff.

A former agency employee tells of the care that goes into the "pour" shots in beer commercials. "How the beer looks going down the glass; whether the glass is completely clean and suggests ice-cold beer; how the bubbles look; whether the head on the beer is big enough, but not too big. . . . I remember one pour shot which took 124 takes before the beer looked exactly right."[18] Mort Levin, former copywriter on the Ford account, tells of steps taken to make car commercials effective. If any other cars are in the scene, they are older models of the car being sold, not competitors' cars (unless the ad is a comparison ad). Sound tracks of closing doors are improved with added bass. Station wagon tailgates are closed by youngsters to demonstrate how easily they work. To show a car coming to a stop, crews shoot it backing, then run the film forward. That way there's no bobbing up and down at the end.

A commercial becomes "an effort to harness attitudes, biases, tastes, lifestyles. It seems absurd to ascribe so much to so short a device as a commercial," mused Jeff Greenfield, the writer and political consultant. "But when thousands of dollars go into the planning of every second of what we see and hear, that effort becomes a lot less ludicrous, and a lot more feasible.

"For the most remarkable fact about [TV] advertising is that it *works*. Call it offensive, puerile, insulting to the intelligence, barbarous, intrusive, antihumanistic, but the damn thing moves the goods."[19]

Many commercials are planned so that if the volume is turned down too low, the viewer will get the message just by looking. Where explanation is needed, type is superimposed over picture. At the same time, the audio is explicit enough so that the message is not lost on the viewer who has ducked into the kitchen to refill a glass or put together a quick snack to get through the next program.

An attempt is often made to relate the commercial to ads in other media. This contributes to the cumulative value of the advertising. Stills from the commercial may be adapted to magazine, national newspaper, outdoor, and P-O-P (point-of-purchase) advertising.

A thirty-second commercial can handle a maximum of sixty spoken words—two words per second. But it should not be the goal of the writer-designer to completely fill the time with words, or even music. It is sometimes effective to show some of the action in pantomime. A little silence is as useful in television advertising as white space is in print advertising.

A commercial can consist of one scene, with all the action taking place in front of a fixed camera. Or there can be changes of scene—several of them. Six seconds per scene is considered about right. This means no more than five scenes for a thirty-second commercial.

After working out an idea for a TV commercial, the creator types out a script to indicate audio and video action. The next step is the storyboard, which consists of a series of sketches showing the scenes as visualized by the commercial's creator. Not all the action is shown, of course—only enough so that the sponsor, before putting money into production, can get an idea of what the commercial will look like and what it will say.

The Storyboard

At one time Hollywood made its motion pictures through improvisation, the director working from rough notes. With the coming of complicated—and expensive-to-produce—films, the studios insisted on carefully worked out scripts, with scenes, props, and sound effects described in detail and every camera movement plotted. When animation became popular, the script took on added importance; it could save hundreds of expensive drawings. The few rough sketches that became a necessary part of the animation script were pinned up on a board for review, and the term "storyboard" was born.

The art form was a natural for the TV commercial when it came along.

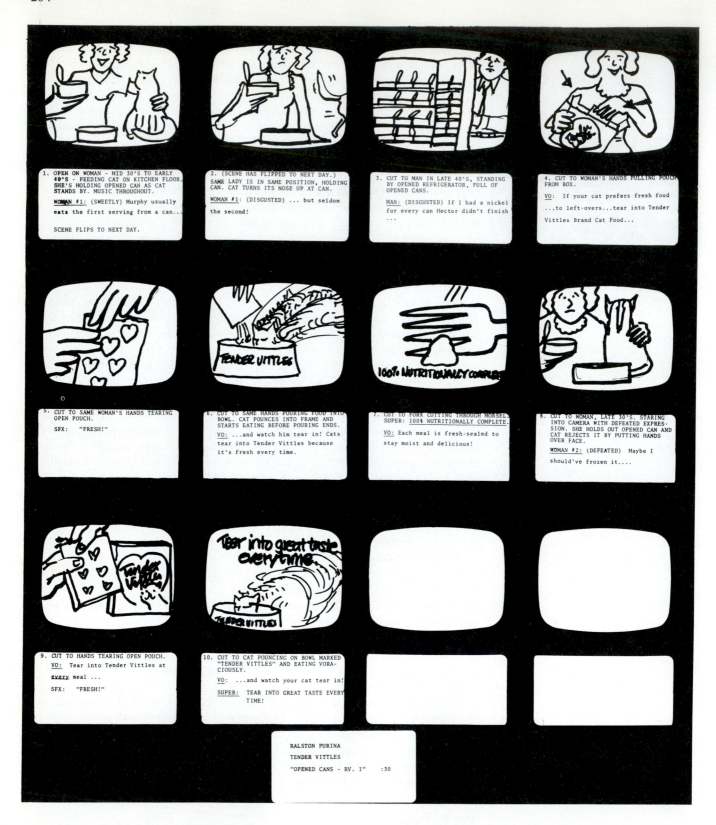

The storyboard for a TV commercial consists of sets of two frames, the top frame in each set representing a regular TV screen, the bottom frame carrying (1) a description of what the screen shows and (2) the words being spoken, on camera or off, by an announcer or an actor. The number of sets of frames, as shown on the storyboard, varies from commercial to commercial and is not necessarily dictated by the length of the commercial.

A storyboard may go through more than one stage, just as a rough layout for the print media does.

The first stage involves very rough sketches of panels with descriptions and

(MUSIC UNDER)
WOMAN 1: (SWEETLY) Murphy usually eats the first serving from a can. . .

(DISGUSTED). . .but seldom the second.

MAN: (DISGUSTED) If I had a nickel for every can Hector didn't finish. . .

VO: If your cat prefers fresh food to left-overs, tear into Tender Vittles Brand cat food. . .

SINGER: "FRESH"

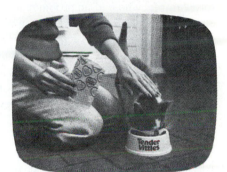

VO:. . .and watch him tear in. Cat's love Tender Vittles, it's fresh every time.

Each meal sealed to stay moist and delicious.

WOMAN 2: (DEFEATED) No? Maybe I should've frozen it.

VO: Tear into Tender Vittles at every meal. . .
SINGER: "FRESH"

VO:. . .and watch your cat tear in.

The rough storyboard at the left was the start of a Tender Vittles commercial, shown at the right as a photoboard. A photoboard is created by lifting key outtakes of a finished commercial. Agency: Wells, Rich, Greene, Inc. Art director: Bill Mullen. Copywriter: Jim Aaby. (Reproduced with permission of Ralston Purina Company.)

dialogue scribbled in below. At this rough stage, the agency's creative supervisor, the account rep, and someone who knows a lot about TV production go over the storyboard with the copywriter and art director. When the problems have been resolved, the storyboard goes to the art department for a new, more careful rendering. This is the *comprehensive*.

Then the client takes a look. The comp may have to be reworked to incorporate client suggestions or directives. When it is finally ready, duplicate copies are made for the producer, director, camera operator and others involved in production.

The presentation to the client includes the look and feel of the unit used to display the storyboard. The presentation can be on a flat board with a simple flap hanging from above, protecting the artwork from smears. But it can be more elaborate than that. It can be a unit that folds out like an accordion, with one set of frames per panel. It can be a spiral- or plastic-bound book. It can be a filmstrip or even a motion picture like the final.

The script, which accompanies the storyboard, is typed on regular 8½″ × 11″ paper, two columns per page. The column on the left describes the video scenes; the column on the right carries the words spoken by the announcer and actors. This audio material is broken into paragraphs, according to scenes.

". . . Rules for writing copy for this . . . ad medium didn't necessarily carry over from other media," wrote Roger D. Rice, president of the Television Bureau of Advertising, looking back on TV's beginnings. "Top-notch print copywriters, for example, who had no problem adapting to radio, often were stumped by TV's combination of pictures and spoken words. Ad agencies went everywhere looking for new people, hiring such unlikely candidates as recruits from drama schools and unpublished playwrights to build their TV copy departments."[20]

Sometimes one person comes up with the concept, writes the commercial, and designs it. But as in advertising for other media, in most cases the commercial evolves from the creative efforts of several persons.

Designing the Storyboard

Among points to keep in mind as you design a storyboard are these:

■ *Relate the video with the audio.* Do not say one thing while you show another. Some agencies feel they must change slightly the spoken word from the words superimposed over the picture, a practice not unlike using a wrong font in a paragraph of otherwise well-printed copy. "He's reading it wrong," is the viewer's reaction.

■ *Let the video carry the weight.* The copy must be secondary in this medium. And among the frames, one frame should stand out as a key frame.

■ *Superimpose type over some of the scenes.* You cannot treat pictures quite so reverently in this medium as in some others. Superimpositions are necessary to take care of the person who turns the volume down at commercial time. They also reinforce what is being shown or said.

■ *Explore fully your camera possibilities.* For long commercials allow for changes in both distance and angle.

■ *Don't expect too much of your viewer.* Keep the cast of characters small, the number of scenes minimal. Of course, there are occasions when the creator of a commercial wants to impress the viewer with numbers or variety, crowding many rapidly changing scenes into the commercial.

■ *Use mostly closeups.* Avoid unnecessary detail. Consider this as "coarse-screen" advertising. The horizontal lines that form the picture on the screen are too heavy, too far apart to hold detail that is fragile or far away.

■ *Put the same careful design thinking into each frame that you would put into designing each print-medium ad.* Each frame must be fully designed.

As a storyboard designer, you become artist, director, camera operator—all in one. Words that may be added simply reinforce what the pictures under your direction have to say.

Bear in mind that the pictures you draw in storyboard frames will be strictly from your imagination. The art is not yet available. The sets will be built, cast selected, shooting done after the storyboard is approved. So, more than many other layout jobs, the storyboard calls for truly creative effort.

No matter how carefully you plan the action, you should expect many differences between the storyboard and the actual commercial.

The final commercial—the film—will consist of many, many frames; the storyboard will consist of only a few—from a half-dozen to three dozen, depending upon the length of the commercial and the number of scenes, camera changes, and action changes.

A concentration on closeups shows facial expressions in this sixty-second spot for United California Bank. This was one of a series starring Sandy Duncan. Agency: Doyle Dane Bernbach, Los Angeles.

VIDEO: Man leaves Sandy's window as Mrs. Grossman approaches.

SANDY: Hello, Mrs. Grossman. How are you today?

MRS. GROSSMAN: Oh my feet are just killing me. I want to make a $100 deposit and then I want to go home and lie down.

SANDY: (not too distinct) I know. Every day about this time my feet...

MRS. GROSSMAN: Oh, my money ...it's gone! I had a $100 bill!

SANDY: Where do you remember having the money last?

MRS. GROSSMAN: I remember, I was in a department store and I was buying pajamas for my grandson. That's him right there.

SANDY: Now you bought the pajamas...

MRS. GROSSMAN: Yes. They have little blue bunnies on them.

SANDY: Did you break the $100 bill to pay?

MRS. GROSSMAN: Oh no, I always charge it.

SANDY: Then you left the department store?

MRS. GROSSMAN: Yes, but I sat down because my feet were killing me.

SANDY: Did you take off your shoes?

MRS. GROSSMAN: Ooooh! (laugh) Sandy, you should be a detective. (laugh)

The best tellers in town.
Or your money back.

ANNOUNCER: United California Bank has the best tellers in town. Or your money back.

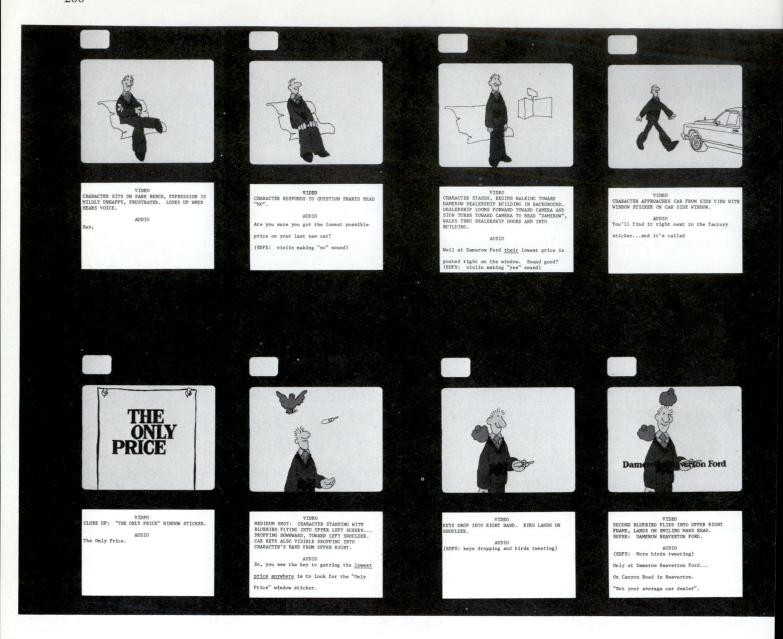

What you present for client approval on a storyboard are *representative* frames: a picture for each scene or action and for each major change of camera position.

You do your designing and drawing in the top frame of each set. The ratio of width to depth is 4:3. A convenient work size is 4″ × 3″. Because the frame represents a TV screen, some designers like to round all four corners.

Working within the frame, you should try to approximate halftone rather than line art. Keep your action—the important details—in the "safety area"—an area slightly smaller than the picture-tube area. Do this to preclude any chance that a part of the message will be missed by the viewer whose set might need some adjusting.

Directly under the "TV screen" frame, separated by a half-inch margin, is the description-and-words frame. Its size is 4″ × 2½″. You can type in the words—or print them in cartoonlike lettering.

A 1″ margin separates each set of frames.

If you do not want to draw boxes for your storyboards, you can buy a Tomkin Telepad with its perforated segments containing video and descriptive boxes surrounded by a gray area. You can also buy black storyboard masks with cutout areas to match the white areas on Tomkin Telepads.

The storyboard precedes the making of a commercial. After the commercial

This is the original storyboard for a thirty-second commercial for a car agency. The nondescript fellow who emerges has become a sort of symbol for customers of Damerow-Beaverton Ford, which advertises "the only price," a no-dickering discount on its cars. The beauty of this character, a sort of grown-up Charlie Brown, is that almost anybody can identify with him. As in most original storyboards produced by agencies (in this case, Swearingen Advertising Agency, Portland), a box below each panel carries first, the description (labeled "VIDEO") and second, the words and sound effects (labeled "AUDIO"). Copywriter Dan Cox developed the ad; Robin Atherly did the animation and developed the character.

To execute this extreme closeup for a storyboard, the author uses nylon- and felt-tip markers.

is made, its sponsor may produce a *photoboard* from some of its frames. The photoboard serves as a record and as a promotional piece.

Elements to Work with

You can use live actors, animation, puppets, a combination of live actors and animation, superimposition of type over pictures, stop motion, or a split screen with two different actions going on at the same time. And, less expensive, you can use still photos (preferably dull or matte finish) and art pieces. These can be flipped during reading. Or the camera can move from one to the other.

As storyboard designer, you should appreciate costs involved in the building of sets. If you can show your subject in a less expensive setting, do so. Often you can simply hint at the setting, letting a part of a prop do the job. Camera angle can help suggest detail not really there. Crowd scenes can be simulated with noise offstage.

You have long shots, medium shots, medium closeups, closeups, and extreme closeups to consider.

You can zoom in suddenly from a long shot into a closeup, or you can move gradually through the stages.

Keep the subject facing in the same direction through the camera's moving in and out during a scene; otherwise, the viewer will lose continuity and may think a new actor has come on.

Sequence is your most important design consideration. A single frame does not stand by itself. This is "advertising in a series." With occasional exceptions, one picture should flow into another. Transitions are important.

Transitional devices used to change scenes are "opticals." These include (1) *cuts* (the change is abrupt), (2) *dissolves* (one scene fades out as another fades in), and (3) *wipes* (one scene is pushed off while another is pushed on, vertically, horizontally, diagonally, and through geometric shapes).

Producing the Commercial

Commercials are complicated enough to produce that they require the services of an outside organization specializing in their filming or taping. The agency takes the work through the storyboard stage; then the production house takes over, working at the agency's direction.

The agency may send out copies of the storyboard to several film production houses for bids. Production houses tend to develop reputations for excellence in certain areas, as in animation, humor, special effects, photographic excellence, use of animals, slice-of-life approaches, and so on. Reputation as well as price determines who gets the job.

The production house, once selected, lines up the actors and announcer, finds the costumes, designs the sets, arranges the props, and fixes the lighting. It also picks a director, editor, cameraman, and (to arrange titles and captions shown with the film) a typographer.

The production house may also make the decisions about music. One question to be settled: Will the music be written and performed especially for the commercial, or will it be taken from a bank of music and musical effects?

A commercial may be filmed or taped in one long session. Or the work may be done in several sessions taking weeks and sometimes months. The producer may end up with separate tapes or films—one of the announcer, one of the music, one of the sound effects, several of the actors in their performances. It is the tape or film editor's job to get it all together.

The director is interested primarily in the shooting of the commercial.

Typically an agency submits copies of the storyboard to several directors who then bid on the job. The director who gets the job then makes a "shoot board," which helps plan the actual filming. The storyboard does not really indicate staging, lighting, lenses, lengths of shots, camera angles, and so on. These are matters for the director to decide. The director also does the casting, making sure these days to get an acceptable mix of personalities and ethnic types. But the director works always in consultation with the copywriter and art director. Changes occur all through the filming.

A director like Joe Sedelmaier departs from the script and storyboard to put his own stamp on the commercial. The Federal Express fast-talking man was a Sedelmaier commercial. So was Wendy's "Where's the Beef?" commercial. Sedelmaier is responsible for "surreal thirty-second dissertations on the fears of daily life . . . by far, the strongest advertisements on television," as an *Esquire* writer put it.[21]

The director is not involved in the editing—the final stage—when sound mixing and voiceovers take place.[22]

And what does the creator of the commercial do when the director and editor take over? About what the novelist does when the book is made into a picture: observes and advises, nothing more.

Of course there are some people in the advertising business versatile enough,

This durable thirty-second Doyle Dane Bernbach-created commercial so impressed Quaker Oats Company officials when they first saw it that they put it on the air (in 1972) without pretesting. Sales for the previously slow-selling Life cereal increased dramatically. The three kids in the commercial are brothers in real life, too.

1ST BOY: What's this stuff?
2ND BOY: Some cereal. Supposed to be good for you.

1ST BOY: D'you try it?
2ND BOY: I'm not gonna' try it, you try it.

1ST BOY: I'm not gonna' try it.

2ND BOY: Let's get Mikey!
1ST BOY: Yeah!

2ND BOY: He won't eat it. He hates everything.

2ND BOY: He likes it!

Hey Mikey!
ANNCR: (VO) When you bring Life home, don't tell the kids it's one of those

nutritional cereals you've been trying to get them to eat. You're the only one who has to know.

experimental enough to put together the complete package. In nearly every advertising center there are art directors who dabble in copy and photography as well as design and who have created artful commercials for small clients or non-profit organizations. Under these conditions it is possible to produce a commercial for not much more than a few thousand dollars. But for a commercial produced in the more conventional manner the cost goes much higher than that.

Restless and often seeking further challenges, some art directors move over to directing commercials. "A lot of ADs are in love with the apparent glamour of directing, but their ideas are often based on watching bad directors work," observes John Danza, who left the Scali McCabe Sloves advertising agency in 1980 to direct commercials. "Bad directing makes it look easy, so an art director thinks, 'I can do *that*.' " But Danza advises art directors to ask themselves if they have anything new to contribute before making the jump. They shouldn't do it just to escape art directing at an agency. "It's a very competitive world out there."[23]

Costs

To produce a commercial costs more, in some cases, than it costs to produce the situation comedy it interrupts. What sends production costs skyrocketing are special effects, exotic settings, and elaborate musical numbers.

But the costs of producing the commercial in most cases represent only a small part of the total cost of television advertising. There is also the matter of network and station costs. Time for a single 30-second spot can run to hundreds of thousands of dollars. For a 30-second network spot on Super Bowl XXVI, an advertiser had to pay more than $800,000.

You can't control network or cable costs, but there are many ways to keep production costs down. You can save money, for instance, by confining the shooting to one location and using daylight instead of artificial night lighting and avoiding on-camera sound.

The commercial can be planned using stock footage—that is, film from commercial film libraries that cover every imaginable subject. And concentrating on closeups allows a producer to eliminate some of the costs of staging, setting, props, and extra actors.

Using a process called Introvision, TV commercial makers can recreate hard-to-get-to or no-longer-available scenes from still photographs and put their action into these settings.

Union scales for on- or off-camera performers are high enough that adding one or two can increase greatly the cost of running the commercial. The performers earn a fee each time the commercial runs on a network. In the words of Arthur Bellaire, a TV creative director, "As soon as the commercial hits the air, the talent payment meter starts ticking." For local spots, performers get a single fee for each thirteen-week period.

"It has never been proved that the greater the production budget, the greater the commercial's pulling power," Bellaire has pointed out. "More often the reverse is true. I have seen more commercials ruined by money because that money is so often thrown in desperately to try to bolster a weak idea, while a sound idea needs surprisingly little dressing up."[24]

Because it involves so large a total investment, the TV commercial for a major account, like other forms of advertising, is subject to scientifically conducted tests to determine effectiveness. The commercial can be tested before live audiences in special theaters run for the purpose, or it can be tested in actual use, with adjustments in the commercial being made for later showings. One way researchers test a commercial in actual use is to call a sample of TV viewers the next day to see what they remember of it.

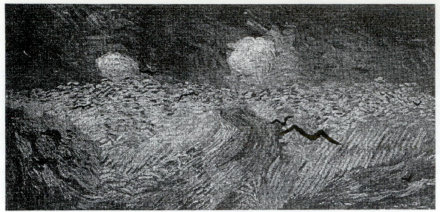

To create a sequence for a potential television commercial, Chris Lindberg, animator and graphic artist with X/Factory, a film and production firm, uses Adobe Illustrator, Photoshop, and Director software on a print of a painting by Van Gogh. At Lindberg's direction, the birds in the painting suddenly become alive and fly around in the scene before flying off into the distance. The frame shown is representative of the midflight frames. Of course, the animation is in full color.

Researchers using tools developed by social scientists can determine the answers to such questions as these:

- *What kinds of persons see the commercial?*
- *Do they understand it?*
- *Do they remember it?*
- *Does it alter their opinion of the product?*
- *Will they buy the product?*

While the ultimate goal is to sell the product, service, or idea, the commercial may take as its *immediate* goal the job of simply making the viewer *aware* of what is advertised or providing information about it. It may be the kind of advertising that accepts as its *only* goal, immediate and ultimate, the building of a reputation.

Restrictions on Commercials

The restrictions advertisers face from government as well as media groups multiply as the advertiser moves from print to broadcast, because broadcast media, unlike other media, operate under government license. And public pressure against real or imagined advertising abuses focuses on the electronics media, especially television.

The advertiser finds restrictions more intense at the network than at the local-station level. An agency can never be sure of what will be accepted for airing and what will not.

The continuity-clearance departments of networks make sure that commercials no longer put glass balls into bowls of soup to make the soup appear to have more diced vegetables than it really has. Nor can commercials put white smocks on actors to make them appear as doctors.

For fear it would offend stutterers, CBS and NBC in 1976 refused to broadcast a dog food commercial featuring someone who stuttered. The network officials apparently did not recognize the stutterer, Mel Tillis, a highly regarded country-and-western singer, who threatened to file a discrimination complaint with the FCC. "If this isn't discrimination, I don't know what is," he said.

An airline commercial that did not meet network standards a few years ago showed a well-endowed woman leaning into the camera saying: "Now I have two big 747s flying to Atlanta."

The clients themselves are careful about placement of TV advertising. Abbott Laboratories (Selsun Blue, Tronolane, Murine eye drops and ear drops) has set up formal guidelines. It avoids "programs portraying the unlawful or inappropriate use of drugs, excessive or unnecessary violence, or treatment of sex that is judged to be in poor taste." The company studies advance reviews of programs and employs an independent firm "to screen and audit all network programs carrying the company's commercials prior to telecast."[25]

Writing the Television Commercial

Writing commercials is more a job for a playwright than for an ordinary prose writer.

The challenge is to overcome viewer annoyance over program intrusion and commercial clutter. The writer can respond by making the commercial either so vociferous it can't be avoided or so interesting or entertaining it can't be ignored. Unfortunately, doing the former is easier than doing the latter. Every community, it seems, must put up with announcers shouting into echo chambers or interrupting themselves after the first couple of sentences with: "Hi. I'm _____ ."

As a writer of a television commercial, make your first rough draft a series of quick thumbnail sketches of frames. Think *pictures first.*

The script that you turn over to the person preparing the storyboard would be a sheet of paper divided into descriptions of the scenes at left, labeled "Video," and dialogue and descriptions of sounds at the right, labeled "Audio." Because in most cases you have but thirty seconds to fill, usually a single sheet will do. Still, the words are important. You have only about sixty of them to work with in a thirty-second commercial. Each one counts. Even so, you allow some redundancy. You should not be afraid to repeat words or to restate what you stated at the beginning.

The first few seconds are essential. Your lead must immediately enlist the viewer's attention. You do not have time to build to a climax. So you deliver it right away.

Write in a conversational tone if an announcer is speaking. Use brief pieces of dialogue if your commercial is a play.

If you write a series of commercials, make them related. Repeat your theme. Do not attempt to develop more than one theme in a campaign. Strive merely for variations to drive home your single point.

If any advertising writing asks for single-mindedness, it is television writing. You have time for so few words, and what you write must fit perfectly the pictures you show. Although it is an oversimplification to say so, writing a television commercial is like writing a picture caption. Your "caption" can do no more than create a single impression about your product or service.

"Writing copy for television can be demanding and nerve-wracking, but it is never dull," say textbook writers W. Keith Hafer and Gordon E. White. "There is always excitement to every television venture because it is, after all, advertising and show business combined."[26]

Designing the Radio Commercial

Including a section on radio advertising in a book about design may strike some readers as odd. What is there to say about radio-commercial design other than that you should not include a coupon?

If you accept the broad definition of "design" offered in the introduction, you will see that design *is* involved in the production of radio commercials. For instance, pauses in radio are the areas of white space in print-medium ads. The various advertising-art-and-design-show annuals are beginning to reproduce the scripts of outstanding radio commercials along with storyboards, posters, trademarks, direct-mail pieces, and print-medium ads.

The industry, advertising itself as a medium for advertisers, uses the slogan, "You saw it on the radio."

People tended to write off radio when TV came along in the late 1940s, and radio did suffer from lack of interest for a number of years. But radio came back. By the end of the 1970s it was an important advertising medium. Advertisers turned to it when TV became overcrowded with commercials and too expensive.

Radio has found a new place for itself as a local as opposed to a network medium. It has found a big audience especially among morning people and, of course, among car drivers. It has also found an audience among people who can't sleep at night. It has adapted itself to specific groups of people, forming audiences advertisers can really appreciate. Stations focus on rock-oriented people, country-music fans, classical-music lovers, news-hungry types, talkers, ethnic groups, and others. FM radio, especially, appeals to specific audiences.

As in any kind of advertising, in radio advertising you strive to make a single point. You resist the urge to crowd too much into the few seconds allotted to you. Forcing the announcer to speak too rapidly is like using too-small type in a print-medium ad. But sometimes you would want to use a machine-gun delivery of product benefits. A thirty-second radio spot can get in about seventy words. The client's name should be mentioned at least twice.

Writing radio copy is not simply a matter of editing copy written for print. Writing for the ear rather than for the eye imposes restrictions on word choice, sentence length, and sentence construction. The best advice for the radio writer is to write in a conversational tone, using short, declarative sentences and to pay more attention than usual to sentence cadence.

You have to keep numbers—and prices—to a minimum. A retailer must be content to feature one—and certainly no more than three—items per spot.

Much of what you have to say can be said with sound effects. A common practice is to insert sound effects after each sentence. What the copywriter does here is much like what a designer does in a rebus ad. (See chapter 5.)

You don't have to say that spring has arrived. You can arrange to have the listener hear birds chirping.

You have an inexhaustible variety of sounds, songs, and voices to draw upon. The commercial can consist of straight talk from an announcer, with or without background sound; it can be a song; it can be an exchange of conversation, an interview, a play.

Perhaps more than any other form of advertising, radio commercials depend upon humor to get their points across. The trick is to use humor that wears well, for the commercial is likely to be heard again and again. Understatement does the job for many advertisers. Parody works for others. One example of parody comes from The Bon Marche, a Northwest department store.

> ANNOUNCER: And now, "Book Review Weekly."
> REVIEWER: Yeah, Yeah. I read some classics this week. My reviews: *Moby Dick*—slow. *War and Peace*—long. And finally, *The Bon Marche Coupon Sale Book*—couldn't put it down. This is sensational stuff! Spine-tingling store-wide savings on every page! Plus, *The Bon Marche Coupon Sale Book,* now available in paperback, has a great feature you don't find in many other books: [Sound of paper being torn] tear-out pages. Huh? Oh, and the ending's great! Thirty percent off—aw. I don't want to spoil it for you.
> ANNOUNCER: The coupon sale is going on now—at The Bon Marche.

With only a few seconds to play with, the copywriter had to make the "reviews" brief, and he had to limit the number of books. Two real books—and then the important book, so far as this commercial is concerned. The only sound effect is the mid-commercial sound of paper being torn. Two different voices keep the commercial, short as it is, from being boring. The humor is gentle enough to allow the commercial to be aired many times in a short space of time without annoying the listener.

Radio humor often involves a switch on an old joke. You remember the story of the man telling his psychologist what each ink blot reminds him of. So far as he is concerned, each blot is a nude woman. The doctor finally says: "You have a problem." The patient demurs. "Doctor, *you* have the problem. *You're* showing all the naked women." A tire company in a commercial has a man telling his doctor that each blot reminds him of "Schmunks' Tire Company, with all those people standing around smiling—with a car up on a rack, with the owner standing nearby smiling." Finally the doctor says, "You have a problem." The patient answers: "You have the problem. You're showing me all of those pictures of Schmunks' tires."

Ann Keding's copy for a radio spot selling membership in the Mid Valley Athletic Club, Reseda, California, depends on the sound effects of breathing to make its point. Agency: Hamilton Advertising, Inc., Los Angeles.

Hamilton Advertising, Inc.	2029 Century Park East Los Angeles, California 90067 Telephone: (213)552-3517 **Copy**

Date: 10/21

Client: MID VALLEY ATHLETIC CLUB
Description: :60 RADIO SPOT
Job Number: LONE RUNNER

VO: Man panting, struggling for breath.

SFX UNDER: One set of footsteps plodding along. (Footsteps start heavy and lighten up to sound energetic by the end of the spot. Likewise, man's breathlessness decreases as spot moves to the end, where he's breathing believably winded... like a runner in shape.)

ANNCR: (READ GRAVELLY.) Listen to this man.

PAUSE:

Listen closely. Because he won't be breathing like this for long.

PAUSE:

(READ MORE OPTIMISTICALLY.) He's just joined Mid Valley Athletic Club. And he's started a training program that's going to help him breathe a little easier.

In fact, the same amount of time it will take him to get his breathing to sound like this...

PAUSE: (BREATHING IS LIGHTER, MORE NORMAL AND FOOTSTEPS ARE LIGHTER.) is all the time you have to join Mid Valley before our rates go up.

SFX. DOWN AND OUT.

LIVE ANNCR: Join Mid Valley Athletic Club before November 8th and get next year's membership at this year's rate. For more information call 705-6500. Or come by. We're located at 18420 Hart in Reseda.

While the celebrated radio commercials seem to depend upon humor to put their points across, the advertising can be serious, too—even moving. In one of its commercials, Rose Hills Memorial Park in Southern California started out with an epitaph written by Mark Twain for his daughter, who died at 24:

> Warm summer sun, shine kindly here;
> Warm summer wind, blow softly here;
> Green sod above, lie light, lie light—
> Good-night, dear heart, good-night, good-night.

Then an announcer came on to say:

"When a loved one passes on, a funeral with dignity and simplicity in a setting of great, natural beauty is the most poignant way for those on both sides of life to say goodbye.

"We're Rose Hills.

"A place to remember."

Niel Klein, Greg Koorhan, and Alan Lawrence of Klein/Richardson, Beverly Hills, worked on this commercial.

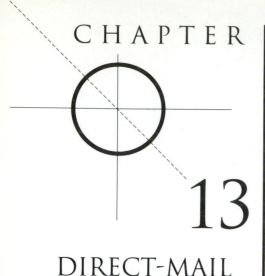

CHAPTER

13

DIRECT-MAIL ADVERTISING

Direct mail is the universal medium, produced by a vast army of writers and artists, from the most hopeless amateurs to the most polished professionals, and used by every conceivable kind of advertiser. Mail-order businesses rank among the biggest users of direct-mail advertising, and so do magazines, a competing medium that finds direct mail the ideal way to get renewals and new subscriptions. Retailers and small businesses find direct mail useful, as do book clubs, publishers, insurance companies, pharmaceutical companies, and religious and fund-raising organizations.[1]

Direct mail not only accounts for most third-class mail; it also accounts for a healthy chunk of first-class mail.

Everyone gets in on the act, and that accounts for a general low level of design. Direct mail shares with retail advertising the stigma of tasteless, amateurish layout; yet, as in retail advertising, exquisite arrangements often emerge from the mass. In fact, some of the best design in advertising today comes in direct-mail form.

Some of the recent upgrading in direct-mail design can be traced to advertising agency interest in the medium. Such advertising usually is not commissionable; but with the development of the straight-fee concept among agencies, J. Walter Thompson Co., Ogilvy & Mather, Young & Rubicam, and McCann-Erickson, among others, have spent considerable sums of their clients' money with this medium.

In spite of rising paper and postal costs, direct mail is still a relatively inexpensive way of reaching a selected audience. Interest in direct mail accelerated in the 1980s with the introduction of desktop publishing, ideally suited to the medium. Direct mail has become particularly important to people running for office. It can explain things in great detail and in the most partisan of terms. Richard Parker, a direct-mail consultant to Democrats (and an activist from the 1960s), looks upon the medium as today's "underground press."[2]

Like other advertisers, direct-mail advertisers try to get their readers involved. These advertisers include order cards with punchouts and invite readers to pick one or the other—a "Yes" or a "No"—and attach it somewhere, or slip it into a slot, to register reaction.

The magazine people, working to gain new subscribers or hold on to those whose subscriptions are expiring, have developed direct mail to a high art. To get renewals, magazines and other periodicals send out a series of mailings, each more urgent than the last. For a sixth letter in a series, *The University of California at Berkeley Wellness Letter* had the circulation director saying, "I'm concerned about the matter enough to have considered even phoning you. But I decided that, as important as *Wellness* is, it does not justify interrupting you while you're relaxing. (We believe greatly in the benefit of relaxation.)"

The letter asked the disinclined subscriber to end the impasse by returning a checked yes-or-no card in an envelope that was provided. Then, picking up on the earlier relaxation theme, the circulation director said, "It only takes a moment and then, one way or another (although admittedly more one way than another), I'll be able to relax too."

The Direct Mail/Marketing Association, Inc., 6 East 43rd St., New York, N.Y. 10017 represents persons and organizations producing direct-mail adver-

(ISLER & CO.)
Certified Public Accountants

Trust is a very big word, particularly when it involves someone else's finances. At Isler, we think we earn that trust by how we do business. If you're a new young business, you may need us to help you set up your own internal accounting system or inventory controls. If you're a large business, you may need help with corporate restructuring, multi-state operations or international financial and tax planning. Whatever your needs, whatever your business, you can trust us to help you meet your goals.

We accomplish that in a number of very concrete ways. First, we take our job seriously. Making mistakes, overlooking deadlines, miscalculating figures can be costly and time consuming. Our dedication to detail is your guarantee that the work will be done right, be done carefully, be done on time. That is why bankers, credit managers, and bonding companies have come to depend on us, because they know our figures are reliable. Plus—there are no surprises. We keep you informed at all times through our newsletters, meetings, and visits to your business. And we return calls promptly.

Second, we have developed a unique system that is built to benefit our clients while establishing long-term relationships. Each accountant is carefully trained to be well-grounded and knowledgeable in a variety of areas, so that problems can be solved quickly and directly. Our staff is also continually involved in classes and seminars, so that they're always abreast of modifications and innovations. We then back these people up with specialists in such fields as tax law and computer systems. Each client benefits by working with the same person, an individual bright and responsive enough to change as your company changes. They will be there year after year to encourage and support you in achieving your business and personal goals.

That's what we mean when we say you have to earn someone's trust. You see, clients want to know, want to be absolutely confident that they can trust you with the financial side of their business and not look back.

"I trust the people at Isler, both the partners and the staff. They keep me out of trouble by making sure our financial statements are accurate and our record keeping up-to-date. But the really nice thing is—they're working to help us succeed. It makes me feel safe to know someone is looking out for our business."

CEO
Automotive Services Group

You Can
Trust
Us To
Be There
When You
Need Us.

Accountants conferring with clients—that's what you would expect to see in photographs run in a brochure published by an accounting firm. A brochure published by Isler & Co. takes a different approach. A series of spreads uses action photographs of the firm's clients on left-hand pages and explanatory copy on right-hand pages. The caption in each case consists of client testimony. For the spread shown here, Isler & Co.'s client is Automotive Services Group. The headline, "You Can Trust Us to Be There When You Need Us," ties things together. Designer and photographer: Robert Reynolds.

tising. Among its various services is a library of portfolios showing direct-mail campaigns. Its library also maintains files of direct-mail pieces that illustrate the many forms that are possible. DM/MA members pay round-trip postage to make use of the library services. Nonmembers may visit the library at the association's New York headquarters.

Sensitive to public criticism of "junk mail," the association also maintains a Mail Preference Service (a nice, positive name, that) to remove names from mailing lists. More people want on than off, it turns out.

A measure of the growing importance of direct mail—or direct marketing—could be seen in the launching in 1991 of a *Journal of Direct Marketing*. The publisher is John Wiley & Sons, New York.

Direct Mail Advantages

Some writers prefer the term "direct advertising" or "direct marketing" to "direct-mail advertising," because the field is so broad and not all of the ads go through the mail. Some of them are picked up at counters or passed out in the streets. But this book will use the still-popular term "direct-mail advertising."

Direct-mail advertising is advertising in which advertisers act as their own publishers by (1) producing their own "publications" rather than renting space in existing ones, (2) selecting their prospects, and (3) sending copies of their publications directly to prospects. As a medium of advertising, it is used by mail-order (or direct-marketing) advertisers, but not exclusively by them. *Any* kind of advertiser can use direct mail.

"Maximizing direct mail success depends first upon the lists you use, second upon the offers you make and third upon the copy and graphics you create," says Bob Stone, a direct marketing consultant.[3]

Direct mail claims four advantages over other media.

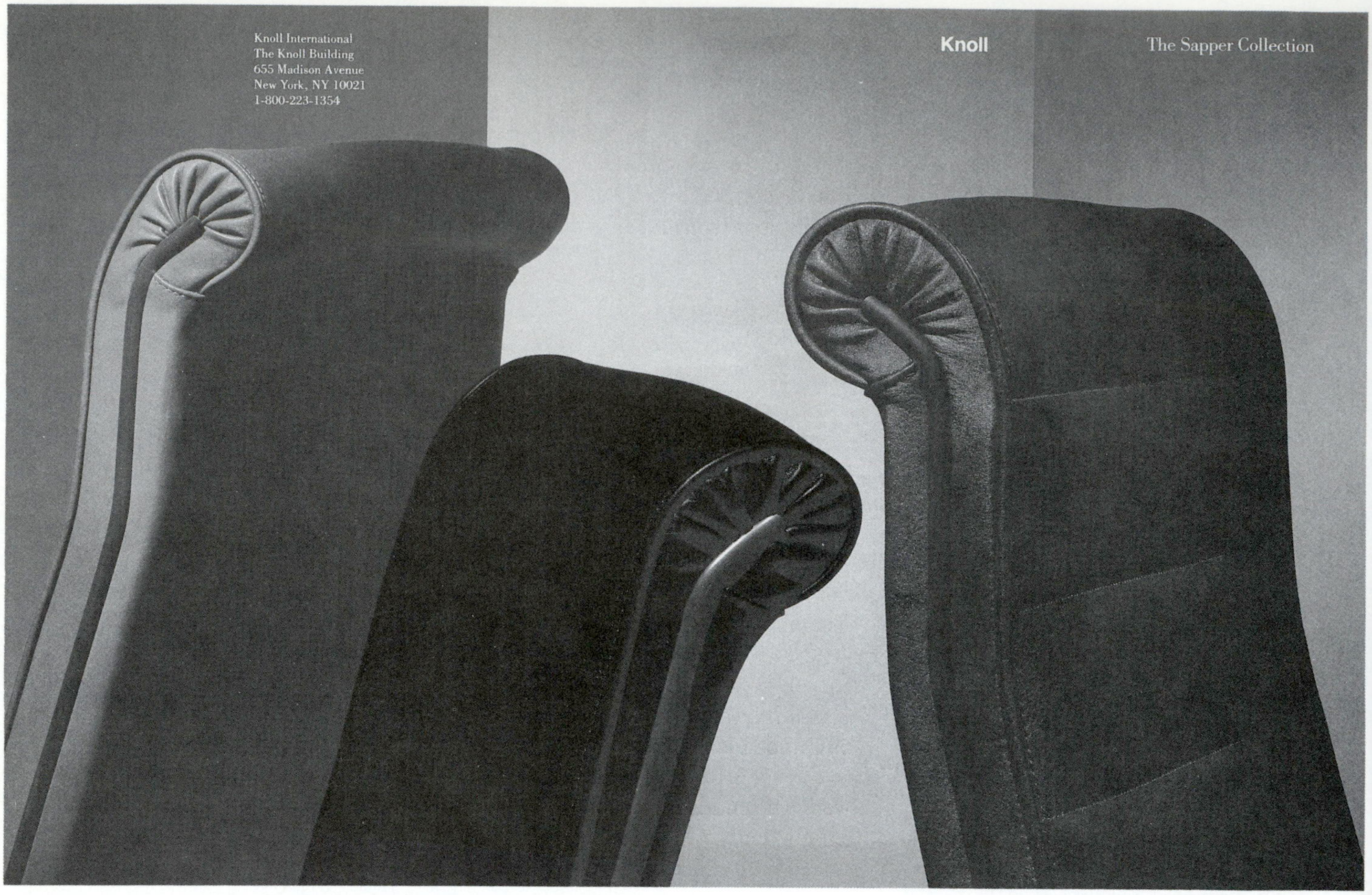

Knoll International
The Knoll Building
655 Madison Avenue
New York, NY 10021
1-800-223-1354

Knoll   The Sapper Collection

■ *It is selective*. An advertiser can rent or build a mailing list covering the most specialized kind of audience. The advertiser times the material to reach a specialized audience when it is most likely to respond.

Ralph Ginzburg published a string of magazines primarily to build lists for direct-mail advertisers. He practically gave away publications like *Moneysworth* and *American Business*. Subscribers' names went on dozens of mailing lists. One of Ginzburg's folders sent to mailing-list brokers described *American Business* subscribers as inherently "scissors-wielding, checkbook-armed, incurably addicted mail-order buyers."[4]

■ *It is personal*. The contents can be made to look like a regular letter. Personalized computer-produced letters that several times in the text show recipients' names and locations have become a major form of direct mail.

A plain wrapper or envelope without an elaborate return address can help maintain privacy.

■ *It is flexible*. Format possibilities are limited only by the imagination of the designer and, to be realistic, the budget of the advertiser. To promote a supermarket sweepstakes sponsored by Coast Central Credit Union, Eureka, California, Kathleen Gordon-Burke designed an envelope that was really a folded-down kraft-paper sack. It carried several direct-mail pieces giving details. A poster was designed to resemble a large paper bag, complete with band saw cutting at the top.

All production choices belong to the advertiser. Time-Life Television, to sell a series of "Wild, Wild World of Animals" books, was able, in one of its direct-mail enclosures, to point out to conservation-minded potential customers that "this stationary is made with recycled fibres and recycled water."

■ *It is self-contained*. A direct mailing may contain everything needed to

The back of the chairs in Knoll's Sapper Collection have enough flair and character to form strong wraparound art for the covers of a brochure advertising the chairs. Brochure design by Knoll Graphics. Art directors: Harold Matossian and Alison Choat. Designer: Alison Choat. Copywriter: Neal Gomberg.

No restaurant gets the reviews we get.

Yes, we're grateful for the smiles and thanks we get from folks who come to eat with us. No, we're not glad they keep coming back for more. But until somebody solves that problem, we're going to have to keep on feeding the homeless. Last year, we served more than 500,000 meals to the hungry in the New York City area. More than 100,000 to the homeless through the mobile feeding program alone. Impressive figures. But equally impressive is the number of meals we managed to squeeze out of every dollar. The fact is, we can feed a lot of people for the price of one restaurant meal. Or even just the tip. So don't think of us simply as some do-gooders with a food truck. Think of us as a well-run, cost-efficient restaurant whose best customers happen to be homeless.

A spread from an annual report of The Salvation Army of Greater New York, one of several in a series of similar spreads, makes the point, in heavily leaded copy, that "No restaurant gets the reviews we get." The copy begins: "Yes, we're grateful for the smiles and thanks we get from folks who come to eat with us. . . ." The copy ends with ". . . Think of us as a well-run, cost-efficient restaurant whose best customers happen to be homeless." The agency: Brouillard Communications. Art director: Renn Cavanaugh. Copywriter: Ted Speck.

complete a sale. It may contain, in addition to the advertising literature, an order blank, a pencil to mark it or a cutout of some kind to fit into a "Yes" slot, and a no-postage-necessary envelope to carry the order blank to the seller. Omaha Steaks International, which sells expensive steaks packed in dry ice, found that the use of miniature steak tokens, which had to be punched out and slipped into a slot, increased replies 25 percent.

The pieces in a multiunit direct mailing are not necessarily design coordinated. There is some value in letting the recipient be overwhelmed by the variety of materials inside the envelope. The mailing becomes a kind of surprise package.

A direct mailing to sell a Time-Life Books series typically comes in an oversize envelope and consists of a four-page letter/folder that appears to be typed; a well-printed, full-color broadside; an oversize postage-paid order card; and an "afterthought" note assuring potential buyers that the free-trial offer is for real ("I'm always surprised when people don't take us up on our 15-day free-trial invitation"). In the case of a series of books on home repair and improvement, the afterthought note was "typed" on a ruled yellow tablet sheet.

The success of direct-mail advertising depends upon the mailing lists used. Some organizations maintain their own lists. Some rent from others or buy or rent lists from brokers. American Business Lists, Inc., Omaha, compiles its lists from Yellow Pages directories. "There's no better source for prospects than the Yellow Pages. Virtually every legitimate business is listed in the Yellow Pages." This broker in 1988 had compiled a database of more than 14 million business names and numbers, available on lists, cards, mailing labels, tape, and diskettes.

Examples of prospects: 1,114 concrete block and brick manufacturers, 3,831 meat-packing plants, 11,168 typesetting houses, 3,153 Ace Hardware stores.

Direct Mail and the Designing Process

Like the newspaper reporter gathering facts for a story, the direct-mail advertising designer seeks answers to who-what-where-when-why-how questions.

Who is the piece going to? Teachers or business people (to name two broad audiences) might want to file or post it. This would influence size and format.

Young people and middle-aged people (to name two broader audiences) may require different art and design approaches.

What is the piece trying to accomplish? If it pleads for funds for a non-profit organization, would it be wise to use full color on glossy stock?

Where will it be received? If at an office, the designer's job may be to somehow convince a secretary to get it to the boss. A mailing piece going to the home may

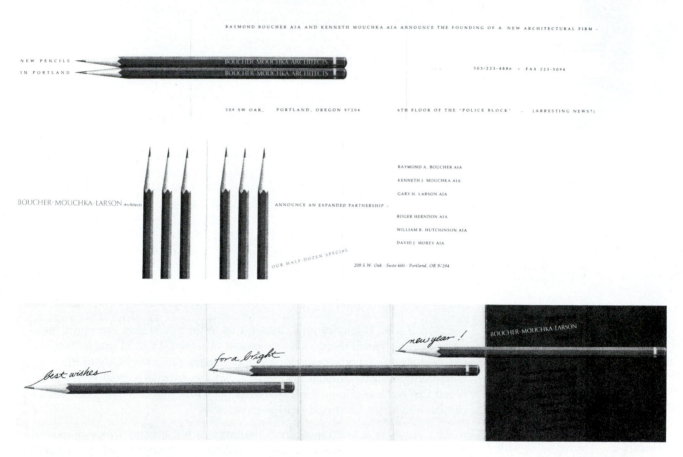

When Boucher-Mouchka Architects formed a new firm in Portland, Oregon, Byron Ferris designed a folder with a new-pencils-in-town theme for the announcement. He continued the theme when, as the firm expanded, he designed additional folders. He also used the pencils theme for a Christmas card when he showed tree ornaments attached to pencil shaving curls.

need a more elaborate envelope, as publishers of classy mail-order books have demonstrated.

When should it be mailed? What other influences are likely to be at work on the recipient at that time?

Why should the recipient be interested? The designer's job is to show why—early in the letter or folder or maybe on the envelope itself.

In direct mail, the advertising must do it all. Ads placed in periodicals and on the air bask in editorial splendor supplied by others: sprightly features, intriguing photos, hilarious cartoons, high adventure, foot-stomping music. The reader or viewer has already had some satisfaction. The direct-mail piece, by contrast, must start from scratch. It gets help from no one. It makes it on its own.

As the designer of a direct-mail piece, your primary assignment is to get the piece picked up, opened out, and read.

As a designer of direct-mail pieces, you may find it easier at the early stages to use traditional tools rather than a computer. You begin not by drawing thumbnail sketches but by folding and cutting paper. An ordinary two- or three-fold folder may do; an unusual-shaped folder, with varying panel sizes, might be better. Experimentation will tell. A knowledge of paper sizes will help you settle on a form that will cut economically from standard stock with a minimum of waste and when properly folded fit a standard-size envelope.

The first rough will be actual size, with art and copy indicated crudely and without benefit of T-square or triangle. At this stage, the kind of paper is not important, although you will probably use something other than paper from your layout pad, which may be too thin and transparent for folding and for sketching on both sides.

For the comprehensive, to be shown to the client, you will use the actual stock set aside for the printing, or, if it is not immediately available or not suitable as a drawing surface, a good bond, construction, or drawing paper. The comprehensive is not mounted for the client, who will want to hold it to see how big it is, how it folds, how the panels "read."

The Tribune Company Syndicate sent out "The Newspaper Game" to newspaper editors to promote its *Broom-Hilda* comic strip by Russell Myers. The game, a 36″ × 24″ poster-playing board and a separate sheet of cards and rules, carries a lot of inside jokes and asides that editors can appreciate. For instance: "All people who can legitimately refer to Katherine Graham as Kay are banned from the game. . . ." From the game board: "Subject of obit calls with a correction. Go back to square one." © 1983 Tribune Company Syndicate, Inc. (The syndicate adopted a new name in 1984: Tribune Media Services.)

To facilitate use of your T-square and triangle and your drawing and coloring tools, you should indicate copy and art and letter your headings on flat surfaces, before they are folded. This will mean doing some panels out of their normal order.

You may find it easier to do one side on one sheet of paper, the other side on another sheet, and then paste them together.

If you use pencil or chalks, you will have to use a fixative when you are finished; the comprehensive doubtless will get a good deal of handling.

The designer often plans direct mail as a campaign of related pieces to be mailed at stated intervals over a period of several weeks. A single mailing may consist of an outside envelope, a letter, a folder, an order card or reply form, and a business-reply envelope. For these the designer must make decisions involving form, format, paper stock, and printing process.

Letters

The forms of direct-mail advertising are limited only by the inventiveness of the designer. They range from single sheets of paper to three-dimensional objects. To many advertisers, the best form of direct-mail advertising is still the ordinary letter, although it may have to be one that is duplicated instead of hand-typed. It is duplicated in most cases to closely resemble the look of a real letter.

So designers arrange for electronically typed-in names in the middle of the copy and "handwritten" notes and underlines that accompany typed letters. Regular postage stamps rather than postage-meter printings seem to work better, too. Rumor had it that by the late 1970s the industry had available a machine that pastes stamps on envelopes—slightly askew.[5]

Willamette Egg Farms

31348 SOUTH HIGHWAY 170, CANBY, OREGON 97013 503-651-2152

Willamette Egg Farms puts an egg, embossed and printed in an opaque white, at the bottom of an all-tan letterhead. Designer: Tom Kelly.

Not only is the illustration appropriate for this letterhead for a child-care center (Pine Valley Child Care Inc., Wichita), but so is the "type," which is hand lettered in a style similar to what a child would produce. In its original form, the letterhead comes in two colors: The wagon and handle are red; the legs and type are black. The same illustration/design appears on the envelope, but in a smaller size. Designer and illustrator: Jim Cox of Jim Cox & Associates.

If signatures must be printed, Eliot Schein, president of Schein/Blattstein Advertising, suggested printing in blue-black ink to better approximate a real signature. He also stressed the importance of a postscript. "Take full advantage of this device to reiterate your basic selling message, emphasize a benefit, drive home a no-risk guarantee. It also provides the necessary transition to the order form and helps close the sale."[6]

So far as many designers are concerned, the *letterhead* is what counts on a letter. Designer Elinor Selame, who has designed countless letterheads, offers this advice: Never start with a blank piece of paper. Instead, have a letter typed, with preferred margins set. This gives you a sort of grid to work against.[7]

Elements to be arranged always include the company name and address, often a phone number and fax, and occasionally a cable address, a description of the company, a slogan, a trademark, some art, and a list of officers. The simpler the letterhead, though, the better. Organizations that insist on listing their officers soon find that when an officer dies or retires or advances, the entire stock of letterheads goes out of date.

Types for most letterheads should be kept small. The name of the firm should be larger than the address or any other element in the design.

A number of firms have moved to colored stock for their letterheads. The color has to be light enough for the type to be read easily.

Designing a letterhead is often one part of a total design job, where letterhead, envelopes, business cards and forms, and other units are brought together. Unifying these pieces calls attention to the company as one that is run in an orderly fashion. Such a design program also saves costs because the same typefaces and art pieces are used and the printing is coordinated.

The envelope need not carry all the elements carried on the letterhead. In working on the envelope, the designer should consult postal authorities to determine how much of the envelope's surface can be used.

The design of the envelope often plays a vital role in getting the reader inside. The design may incorporate a headline, as on *Psychology Today's* often-cited "Do You Close the Bathroom Door Even When You're the Only One at Home?" envelope. The type and design on the envelope often plays down or omits the name of the advertiser.

Bill Jayme, who, with his partner Haikki Ratalahti, created the *Psychology*

A letterhead for Bolliger Hampton & Tarlow, attorneys at law, uses a law book-spine motif. The name is stamped in gold foil on a maroon panel for a leather look. Business cards, labels, and other company pieces carry this same look. Agency: Bronson Leigh Weeks.

Herb Dungey uses this handsome card in his business—and hobby—of restoring and repairing Model A's. Designer Jane Dungey/Spangler uses an appropriate old-style roman typeface and gray ink on a gray textured stock. Her cropped Model A is big enough to give the card visual impact.

Today envelope, says that an envelope carrying direct-mail is "the cover of the magazine . . . the sleeve on the record album . . . the dust jacket on the book . . . the display window that lures you into the store. . . . I would estimate that about a third of the time my partner and I spend creating a mailing package goes into conceptualizing the outer envelope."[8]

To get the reader to open an envelope, some advertisers resort to questionable practices, such as simulating the hand-stamping of "Urgent—Return Reply Requested" or making the envelope look as though it comes from a government agency by using tan paper and Copperplate Gothic typefaces. A siding company, apparently fearing the words "Vinyl Siding" might turn readers off, recently sent out a mailing in a greeting-card-size envelope. In the upper left-hand corner: "An Invitation to Our Neighbors. Photos Enclosed—Do Not Bend." The "photos" turned out to be "before" and "after" *printed cards* showing halftones.

Every once in a while you have to update the design of your stationery. Fashions in type change. Design attitudes change. The company wants to keep up. This is not to say that a period piece—art that smacks of the past—has no place in business stationery. It may be that an old, established look is exactly what is needed.

Those firms wanting the finest in letterheads turn to engraving—real engraving. This process allows for what one creator of business stationery calls "the most brilliant results of all the graphic arts processes."[9] But most letterheads are produced by offset lithography.

Thermography—or imitation engraving—is another process for producing letterheads. Like engraving, it makes possible a raised surface on the paper. It works best on delicate or lightface types.

Some firms like blind embossing, another process. It creates a raised surface that is not printed. The blind embossing involves, usually, a symbol of some kind or maybe the name of the company, if it is set bold enough. Small type, like the address and phone number, would appear as regular printing.

Another process, foil-stamping or gold-leaf stamping, adds foil to the printing surface, giving it a rich, shiny look.

Some of the most inventive graphic design can be seen in the letterheads of graphic designers themselves. When the Gilbert Paper Company, Menasha, Wisconsin, introduced its 25 percent cotton Gilbert Writing Bond, it produced some letterheads designed by name designers. Saul Bass, grumbling that "what this world doesn't need is another Saul Bass letterhead," nevertheless came up with one that showed his appropriate and charming trademark, a bassfish with the head of a man (Saul Bass) produced as blind embossing.

Heidi and Robin Rickabaugh are a wife-husband design team who have managed a design that works as a personal letterhead for each partner. The name and address of the firm is printed in the center of the left margin on both sides of the sheet. On one side, the name "Heidi" stands out (above the printing) in blind embossing. On the other, the name "Robin" stands out (below the printing).

Tri-met, Portland's bus system, uses small folders to announce its schedules. Each cover has its own color and symbol, all part of a nicely coordinated system. The solid-color area is framed in each case by a white border. Note the abstract nature of the art.

Cards and Leaflets

Self-mailers (postcards) or inserts to accompany other direct-mail advertising (reply cards) are a form of direct-mail advertising often relegated to standardized or last-minute treatment. They should be handled as if they were small-space ads, which they are; principles of design should apply as they do for any ad.

Like a card, a leaflet is a single sheet, but of lighter weight paper. It can be larger. It can be printed on both sides. It is used usually as an insert for envelopes or packages. It seldom gets enough design attention.

A leaflet is sometimes referred to as a "stuffer."

Folders

A folder is a sheet folded at least once but more commonly two or three times. The folds make for "panels"; each new fold adds two more panels, one for each side of the sheet. So a two-fold folder has six panels, three on one side of the sheet, three on the other. A three-fold folder has eight panels.

The folding is arranged, usually, so that the panels are equal in size. Each panel may be complete in itself in what it says; or the panels may combine to make one large spread when they are opened out.

In a well-designed folder, the message reveals itself logically, in steps, as the panels are opened. The panels can be folded in any number of ways. For instance, the piece can open and close like an accordion. The panels in an accordion-fold are folded outward and inward, alternately.

A more serviceable arrangement is the one in which the panels all fold in the same direction. This is called a "roll-over" fold. The folder unravels as it is opened, as an ordinary folded business letter does. In designing such a folder, it is necessary to establish for the reader where the front cover (panel 1) is and where the back cover is. In most cases, the designer gives the front cover the display, leaving the back cover blank or nearly blank.

Panel 1's main job is to lure the reader inside. But, where possible, it should also give some hint of what the advertising is about. The sponsor's name ordinarily does not belong on panel 1.

A folder can have vertical or horizontal panels—or square panels, for that matter. It can be designed as a self-mailer or to fit an envelope.

Colorful bars on a slant along with other geometric shapes give this folder interior a liveliness designed to convert readers, from blue-collar workers to sports enthusiasts (see art), to bus riders. The headings inside the slanted bars tick off reasons for riding the bus. Agency: Cappelli/Miles/Wiltz/Avery/Kelly, Ltd. Art director: Tom Kelly. Copywriter: Craig Copeland.

DIRECT-MAIL ADVERTISING

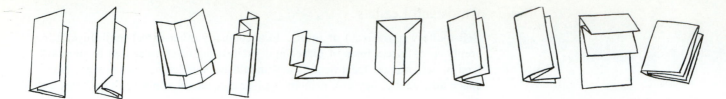

Often an organization puts out a series of direct-mail pieces, using a consistent design approach to unite them. The possibilities for innovations for folders, both in copy and design, are endless. You should file away the many folders that come to you, then study them for ideas.

Broadsides and Tabloids

A broadside is a large sheet of paper (17″ × 22″ is a standard size) folded down to a convenient mailing size. In some cases, as the recipient opens out the broadside, the message builds in intensity until all panels on one side are exposed. Then

These are some common forms of folders. The folded-down size determines the envelope size needed. Some of these pieces can be used as self-mailers, in which case a staple or paper seal may be used to keep them from opening in the mail. Self-mailers need all or part of the panel for addressing purposes. The designer should clear the design with the post office before printing. The accordion folds (fourth and fifth from left) and the gatefold (sixth from left) call for a heavier-than-normal paper stock. For the French fold at the extreme right, popular with producers of inexpensive Christmas cards, a single printing impression will take care of the front and back covers and the inside two-panel spread.

A setting worthy of the occasion.

o restore the Recital Room to its legendary splendor, we summoned the mastercraftsmen. The magnificent stained glass windows, rich oak paneling and the glorious pipe organ have all been beautifully restored.

For smaller meetings and receptions, three charming rooms—The Rousseau Room accommodates 20; the Corot Room, 40; The Millet Room accommodates 80 and can subdivide into two areas.

thought about what you'd really like in a hotel.

In touch with the times.

omething as simple as complimentary coffee and a croissant in the morning in your room. Something as splendid as pot au feu in a restaurant reminiscent of Monet's Dining Room in Giverny. Something as rejuvenating as a day just for yourself in The Spa. This is the new Barbizon.

We've preserved a wonderful landmark and transformed it into a hotel where you'll feel very much at home.

In touch with you.

Detail by detail, we've planned the new Barbizon for you. Intimate guest rooms in subtle pastels. Fresh flowers every day. The morning paper delivered to your room. A concierge, with a computer at his fingertips, to put you in touch with the city's lively arts and entertainment. And we've installed the most advanced security available.

Let the senses rejoice!

The best of New York.

ixty-Third and Lexington. Here you are in the midst of one of New York's most fashionable neighborhoods. All around you is New York: celebrated theaters, restaurants, boutiques and galleries.

The Barbizon puts you temptingly close to Bloomingdale's and your favorite Madison Avenue shops. Close to the auction houses, the Museum of Modern Art and the Metropolitan.

Bring your walking shoes, because we're just a short stroll from Central Park. And convenient to a number of universities, research institutes and medical centers as well as the Decoration and Design Building.

Enjoy the best of New York all around you.

Cuisine Bourgeoise in Monet's Dining Room.

Cuisine as celebration.

e've called our charming little European bar Cafe Barbizon. Blissful for a light breakfast, cold lunch or a late supper. Nibble a pastry over perfect espresso. Or join us for an aperitif any time.

La Maree is a joyous celebration of Cuisine Naturelle. Delicious. Healthful. And beautifully prepared. The best of the sea's own bounty for lunch and dinner. And a breakfast menu that's an inspiration for morning meetings, in a setting that's aglow with sunlight from skylights above.

Monet was as much a master of Cuisine Bourgeoise as he was a master of impressionism. In Monet's Dining Room we've created the atmosphere of his country house in Giverny. Taste the hearty, generous cuisine, so typical of the hospitality of the French countryside.

The Spa. Health. Fitness and Beauty.

ow did we create the quintessential spa? By consulting some of the most respected and innovative names in fitness, health and beauty. They've joined us to offer you the best facilities of any hotel in the city.

Dive into a large refreshing pool. Exercise to music in two aerobic exercise rooms. Work out on our impeccably equipped exercise circuit. Unwind in rock steam rooms. Swiss showers. Swedish and Shiatsu massage. Herbal wraps. The Spa is complete with its own skin and body care salon and hair grooming salon. and Cuisine Santé menu. Guests may enjoy all the Spa activities as a complete daily program or a la carte.

Refresh your body and soul in The Spa.

Meet for a marvelous breakfast in La Maree.

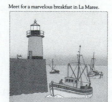

Comfort and Style.

o suit the way we live now, we've opted for comfort and style over opulence. The charming guest rooms and suites with their refreshingly residential flavor will make you feel very much at home.

The carpeting is a soft, rosy terra cotta. Prints by some of our favorite French artists adorn the walls. Even the bedspreads are uniquely Barbizon—a delicate pattern based on traditional provincial designs. There is, of course, HBO in all guest rooms. We've captured some of New York's loveliest views from many of our rooms and suites for you.

Bathrooms are handsomely tiled in warm beiges, complete with makeup lights, magnifying mirrors, wonderful soaps and shampoos and massage showerheads—so you'll feel and look your best.

You see here both sides of a three-fold, eight-panel folder, "We thought about what you'd really like in a hotel," designed by Milton Glaser for the Barbizon Hotel, New York. The illustrator was Guy Billout. The cover and some of the inside panels use three-dimensional initial letters made from parts of the building. The colors are muted and subtle, and they pick up on colors used in the hotel's interior, which also was designed by Glaser.

The inside spread of a two-fold, six-panel folder for Norwegian Cruise Line uses highly stylized silhouette art to dramatize various kinds of entertainment cruises that are available. Agency: McKinney & Silver. Creative director: John Russo. Art directors: Harry Hartofelis and Kathy Jerrett. Copywriter: Tony Burke. Illustrator: Robert Pizzo.

the full shock or impact is realized. The least used, perhaps, of the direct-mail forms, the broadside fits best a freewheeling, hard-sell client, but a sophisticated client every once in a while, as a change of pace, resorts to the broadside with considerable success.

With a broadside the danger exists that the reader will miss the message on one side. The piece should be designed to encourage the reader to open it all the way. For one of its broadsides, the DeVry Institute of Technology solved the problem by arranging the folds so that the inside panel-spread was slightly smaller than the outside spread. At the bottom of the inside spread was this notation: "Lift Here."

A tabloid is a half-size newspaper used, for instance, as a sales catalog by retailers. The regular rules for retail advertising layout apply.

Booklets and Pamphlets

Byron Ferris' cover for a broadside (an appropriate format, considering the subject) promoting an exhibit of early circus posters at The American Advertising Museum, Portland, uses an array of typefaces reminiscent of 19th Century circus advertising.

Synonymity links these terms, but "pamphlet," suggesting political propaganda, belongs mainly to the layman. We will use "booklet." To qualify as a booklet, a direct-mail piece carries eight or more bound pages either saddle stitched (as for *The New Yorker*) or side stapled or sewn (as for *Ladies' Home Journal*). Some booklets with a limited number of pages get by with saddle gluing, a cheaper method of binding.

The printer produces booklet pages in *signatures,* a signature being a set of pages printed on a single, large sheet that, after being printed, gets folded down to page size and trimmed. (See the illustration in chapter 6.) For saddle-stitched booklets, signatures are cradled inside one another; for side-stitched booklets, they are placed side by side.

Signatures come in multiples of four, eight, sixteen, thirty-two, and occasionally sixty-four—depending on the size of the press and the paper stock. A sixteen-page booklet could evolve from a single signature—or from two eight-page signatures.

A knowledge of signatures enables you to better plan your double-page spreads and color. Consider color for a moment. Each side of a signature needs a separate impression or printing. One impression takes care of half the pages. These pages are not in numerical order. If, say, on page 2 of a sixteen-page signature you want to use a second color, you might just as well use the same color on pages 3, 6, 7, 10, 11, 14, and 15, but if you want to run the same color on page 4, it will mean an additional printing impression, adding considerably to the cost of the job. In booklet design, planning the signature precedes any other layout step.

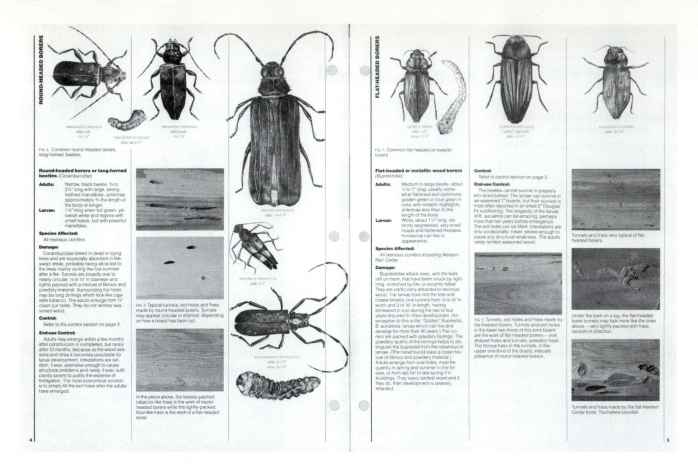

In arranging the pages, you should decide on standard margins for the running copy block and see that they remain constant. This is one way to achieve unity for the book. The margin next to the fold, or gutter, is narrowest; the margin increases a bit at the top and more at the outside edge. It is largest at the bottom.

You should consider each double-page spread as a single unit. If art is used, you make one item stand out on each two pages. You join pages together by running pictures or headings across the gutter or by repeating design elements on both pages. Of course a consistency in body type and headings also unifies the pages.

Booklets come in a great variety of shapes and sizes, but the roughly 4″ × 8½″ size that fits into a regular no. 10 business envelope remains a favorite. This unique vertical poses a problem for the designer. The single page is too narrow for many design treatments.

You should consider two kinds of covers: self-covers and separate covers. Page 1 of the first signature acts as the self-cover. The client wanting a separate cover orders an additional four-page signature, often on a different, heavier paper stock, that is wrapped around the booklet's regular signatures.

Typical booklet jobs include annual reports, employee handbooks, instruction manuals, company histories, and speech reprints.

Catalogs

Catalogs, part of the booklet family, have gained in popularity as the mail-order business has boomed. There are several reasons for the success of mail-order catalogs. In many families both husband and wife are working, so a leisurely afternoon of shopping is out of the question. It becomes easier to shop from catalogs. In many cases you can call in your order on a toll-free 800 number. You can pay by charge card. If you send in an order form, you do not even have to fill in your name. You simply peel off the address label that brought the catalog to you and restick the label to the order form.

A spread, one of several in "Insects in Western Wood," an 8½ × 11 booklet, shows insects, drawn in correct proportion to each other, that attack or infest softwood lumber. Photographs of wood samples, in full color, show kinds of damage that can be caused by these insects. To control detail, illustrator John Lewis used sharp pencils to draw the insects. Van Waters & Rogers, Inc., did the photographs of the various woods. Western Wood Products Association published the booklet. Robert Reynolds did the designing.

(Opposite Page)

These four pages from *A Small Treasury of Swedish Food,* a booklet published by SMR, the Swedish Dairy Association, and The Swedish Farmer's Meat Marketing Association, Stockholm, show how a designer can get variety within a grid. In each case, the heading is centered over the middle column, and the sink—the space between the top of the page and the "live copy" area—remains the same. But the size and shape of the cartoon art vary, and so then does the amount of body copy. Art director: Anders Gäfvert. Designer: Olle Malmberg. Copywriter: Loulou Lindborg. Agency: Ted Bates AB.

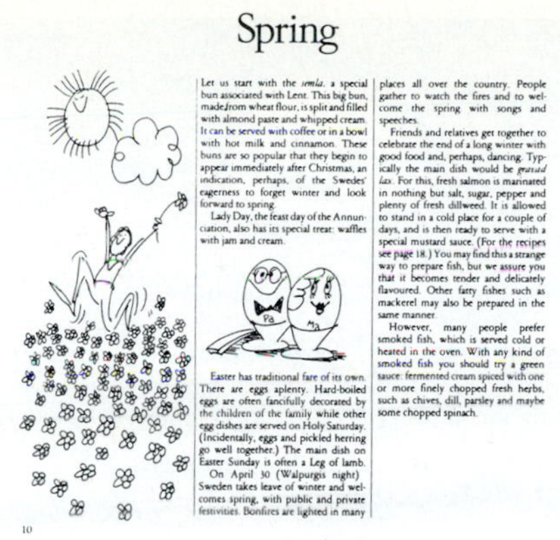

Spring

Let us start with the *semla*, a special bun associated with Lent. This big bun, made from wheat flour, is split and filled with almond paste and whipped cream. It can be served with coffee or in a bowl with hot milk and cinnamon. These buns are so popular that they begin to appear immediately after Christmas, an indication, perhaps, of the Swedes' eagerness to forget winter and look forward to spring.

Lady Day, the feast day of the Annunciation, also has its special treat: waffles with jam and cream.

Easter has traditional fare of its own. There are eggs aplenty. Hard-boiled eggs are often fancifully decorated by the children of the family while other egg dishes are served on Holy Saturday. (Incidentally, eggs and pickled herring go well together.) The main dish on Easter Sunday is often a Leg of lamb.

On April 30 (Walpurgis night) Sweden takes leave of winter and welcomes spring, with public and private festivities. Bonfires are lighted in many places all over the country. People gather to watch the fires and to welcome the spring with songs and speeches.

Friends and relatives get together to celebrate the end of a long winter with good food and, perhaps, dancing. Typically the main dish would be *gravad lax*. For this, fresh salmon is marinated in nothing but salt, sugar, pepper and plenty of fresh dillweed. It is allowed to stand in a cold place for a couple of days, and is then ready to serve with a special mustard sauce. (For the recipes see page 18.) You may find this a strange way to prepare fish, but we assure you that it becomes tender and delicately flavoured. Other fatty fishes such as mackerel may also be prepared in the same manner.

However, many people prefer smoked fish, which is served cold or heated in the oven. With any kind of smoked fish you should try a green sauce: fermented cream spiced with one or more finely chopped fresh herbs, such as chives, dill, parsley and maybe some chopped spinach.

10

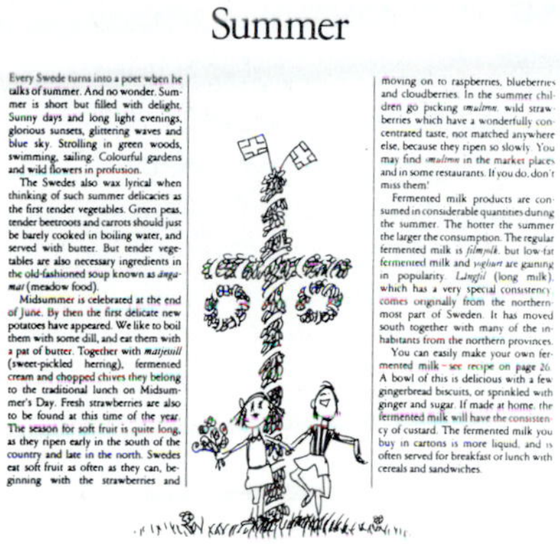

Summer

Every Swede turns into a poet when he talks of summer. And no wonder. Summer is short but filled with delight. Sunny days and long light evenings, glorious sunsets, glittering waves and blue sky. Strolling in green woods, swimming, sailing. Colourful gardens and wild flowers in profusion.

The Swedes also wax lyrical when thinking of such summer delicacies as the first tender vegetables. Green peas, tender beetroots and carrots should just be barely cooked in boiling water, and served with butter. But tender vegetables are also necessary ingredients in the old-fashioned soup known as *ängamat* (meadow food).

Midsummer is celebrated at the end of June. By then the first delicate new potatoes have appeared. We like to boil them with some dill, and eat them with a pat of butter. Together with *matjessill* (sweet-pickled herring), fermented cream and chopped chives they belong to the traditional lunch on Midsummer's Day. Fresh strawberries are also to be found at this time of the year. The season for soft fruit is quite long, as they ripen early in the south of the country and late in the north. Swedes eat soft fruit as often as they can, beginning with the strawberries and moving on to raspberries, blueberries and cloudberries. In the summer children go picking *smultron*, wild strawberries which have a wonderfully concentrated taste, not matched anywhere else, because they ripen so slowly. You may find *smultron* in the market places and in some restaurants. If you do, don't miss them!

Fermented milk products are consumed in considerable quantities during the summer. The hotter the summer the larger the consumption. The regular fermented milk is *filmjölk*, but low-fat fermented milk and *yoghurt* are gaining in popularity. *Långfil* (long milk), which has a very special consistency, comes originally from the northernmost part of Sweden. It has moved south together with many of the inhabitants from the northern provinces.

You can easily make your own fermented milk – see recipe on page 26. A bowl of this is delicious with a few gingerbread biscuits, or sprinkled with ginger and sugar. If made at home, the fermented milk will have the consistency of custard. The fermented milk you buy in cartons is more liquid, and is often served for breakfast or lunch with cereals and sandwiches.

11

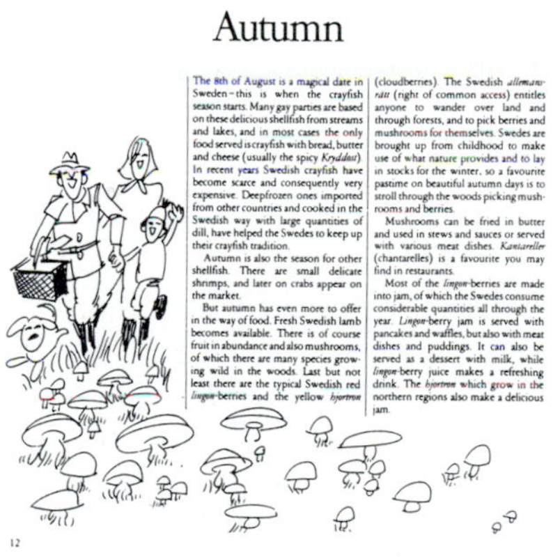

Autumn

The 8th of August is a magical date in Sweden – this is when the crayfish season starts. Many gay parties are based on these delicious shellfish from streams and lakes, and in most cases the only food served is crayfish with bread, butter and cheese (usually the spicy *Kryddost*). In recent years Swedish crayfish have become scarce and consequently very expensive. Deepfrozen ones imported from other countries and cooked in the Swedish way with large quantities of dill, have helped the Swedes to keep up their crayfish tradition.

Autumn is also the season for other shellfish. There are small delicate shrimps, and later on crabs appear on the market.

But autumn has even more to offer in the way of food. Fresh Swedish lamb becomes available. There is of course fruit in abundance and also mushrooms, of which there are many species growing wild in the woods. Last but not least there are the typical Swedish red *lingon*-berries and the yellow *hjortron* (cloudberries). The Swedish *allemansrätt* (right of common access) entitles anyone to wander over land and through forests, and to pick berries and mushrooms for themselves. Swedes are brought up from childhood to make use of what nature provides and to lay in stocks for the winter, so a favourite pastime on beautiful autumn days is to stroll through the woods picking mushrooms and berries.

Mushrooms can be fried in butter and used in stews and sauces or served with various meat dishes. *Kantareller* (chantarelles) is a favourite you may find in restaurants.

Most of the *lingon*-berries are made into jam, of which the Swedes consume considerable quantities all through the year. *Lingon*-berry jam is served with pancakes and waffles, but also with meat dishes and puddings. It can also be served as a dessert with milk, while *lingon*-berry juice makes a refreshing drink. The *hjortron* which grow in the northern regions also make a delicious jam.

12

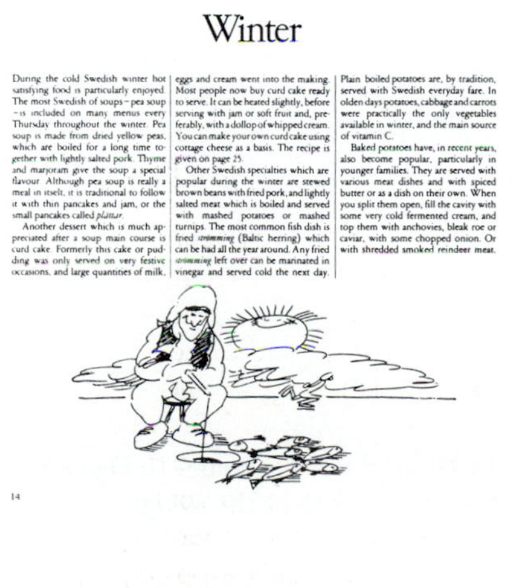

Winter

During the cold Swedish winter hot satisfying food is particularly enjoyed. The most Swedish of soups – pea soup – is included on many menus every Thursday throughout the winter. Pea soup is made from dried yellow peas, which are boiled for a long time together with lightly salted pork. Thyme and marjoram give the soup a special flavour. Although pea soup is really a meal in itself, it is traditional to follow it with thin pancakes and jam, or the small pancakes called *plättar*.

Another dessert which is much appreciated after a soup main course is curd cake. Formerly this cake or pudding was only served on very festive occasions, and large quantities of milk, eggs and cream went into the making. Most people now buy curd cake ready to serve. It can be heated slightly, before serving with jam or soft fruit and, preferably, with a dollop of whipped cream. You can make your own curd cake using cottage cheese as a basis. The recipe is given on page 25.

Other Swedish specialties which are popular during the winter are stewed brown beans with fried pork, and lightly salted meat which is boiled and served with mashed potatoes or mashed turnips. The most common fish dish is fried *strömming* (Baltic herring) which can be had all the year around. Any fried *strömming* left over can be marinated in vinegar and served cold the next day.

Plain boiled potatoes are, by tradition, served with Swedish everyday fare. In olden days potatoes, cabbage and carrots were practically the only vegetables available in winter, and the main source of vitamin C.

Baked potatoes have, in recent years, also become popular, particularly in younger families. They are served with various meat dishes and with spiced butter or as a dish on their own. When you split them open, fill the cavity with some very cold fermented cream, and top them with anchovies, bleak roe or caviar, with some chopped onion. Or with shredded smoked reindeer meat.

14

The Direct Mail/Marketing Association maintains a Mail Order Action Line that deals with complaints when a customer gets the run-around from a company. But most mail-order houses take returns without questioning them and offer refunds.

Selling by mail is attractive to a retailer because costs are lower. *Advertising Age* says that the profit margin is 6 percent on sales compared to the regular retailer's 3.5 percent profit.

The first catalogs came out in the late nineteenth century. People thumbed through them, and rethumbed, and bought. The catalogs became known as "wish books." Many of the current catalogs sell luxury products or novelties. Catalogs are important in industrial, professional, and trade selling as well as consumer selling.

The name and address of a person making a purchase by mail gets on all kinds of catalog lists. How long the catalogs continue to come depends on buying frequency and company patience. Catalogs are expensive to produce and send. Some companies charge for catalogs to discourage mere browsing.

Neiman Marcus calls its year-end catalog of luxury items a "Christmas Book" and gives it a sturdy side binding. The catalog often gets media attention for its extravagant "his and hers" matching gifts. In 1991 they were squared-back LTV Hummers, in civilian dress, which were made famous in Operation Desert Storm.

For many companies, a recognizable catalog style evolves, and each succeeding issue draws on that style. A buyer or prospective buyer looks forward to the next catalog in a series.

A catalog need not be elaborate, especially if it is meant to sell inexpensive products. The Vermont Country Store, Weston, Vermont, puts out a nationally distributed digest-size catalog on newsprint, without any color.

Archie McPhee, a Seattle firm calling itself "Outfitters of Popular Culture," publishes a hodgepodge of a catalog with scattered silhouetted art and tipped copy blocks. ". . . The [rubber] chicken's back," one copy block announces. "Quite simply, this one's the best there is. . . . Not the cheap Far East knockoff, but a rubber chicken in the classic tradition of Europe. You may only buy one rubber chicken in your life . . . why not the best?"

The nationally known Lynchburg Hardware & General Store, Lynchburg, Tennessee, runs folksy, first-person copy blocks under or next to the items being sold through its full-color catalogs. The copy for Jack Daniel Large Rugs says, "I know we call them rugs, but I've got mine framed. I just couldn't imagine wiping my boots on Mr. Jack's face." A note under the copy for the Gallagher "Doc Watson" Guitars built by Don Gallagher ("Don doesn't trust many folks with his guitars") says: "P.S. Just for you, Don, we spelled Gallagher right this year."

The catalog carries the slogan, "All goods worth price charged."

With its unusual style of illustrations and interesting copy, Banana Republic's small-format catalog has a loyal following. Well-known travelers who wear the company's clothing offer testimonials throughout the catalog, and a box on the back cover announces a toll-free number for the "climate desk," which gives travel tips and weather information from all over.

Banana Republic first promoted its No-Horse Shirt in its catalog as an Un-Alligator Shirt—a putdown of the trend toward logos on shirt fronts. Later, the company sold the shirt as a No-Polo Shirt. Attorneys for Polo were "not amused," according to catalog copy. "We debated *re*-naming it the No-Lawsuit Shirt, but thought that might leave a few of you scratching your heads at the joke. So we'll stick to the facts: no horse. And no monkey business: just 100% two-ply cotton piqué knit with horn buttons and a pleasing selection of low-key colors. And that's no bull."

With catalogs like those published by Banana Republic and Lands' End looking more and more like magazines and with some of them selling at racks in bookstores, *Step-by-Step Graphics* in a headline wonders if they shouldn't be called magalogs. Or maybe catazines.

Lands' End lets the friendliness of its catalog extend to the literature accompanying the mailing of its merchandise. From a folder on returns: "If you've lost your packing slip (tsk, tsk), just give us your name and address, along with the date you placed your order."

The J. Peterman Company, Lexington, Kentucky, which sells clothing and accessories, puts out a series of informal 5¼″ × 10½″ catalogs called "Owner's Manuals," written in first person and illustrated with full-color drawings rather than photographs.

"People want things that are hard to find. Things that have romance, but a factual romance, about them," J. Peterman himself writes in an introduction.

"I had this proven to me all over again when people actually stopped me in the street (in New York, in Tokyo, in London) to ask me where I got the *coat* I was wearing.

"So many people tried to buy my coat off my back that I've started a small company to make them available. It seems like everybody (well, not *everybody*) has always wanted a classic horseman's duster but never knew exactly where to get one.

"I ran a little ad in the New Yorker and the Wall Street Journal and in a few months sold this wonderful coat in cities all over the country and to celebrities and to a mysterious gentleman in Japan who ordered *two thousand* of them. . . ."[10]

Garry Trudeau, the comic-strip artist who courts controversy with his strip, but who remains aloof from interviewers, decided to commercialize his characters in 1991 with a catalog issued by The Great Doonesbury Sellout of Sausalito, California. But the venture differed from others in that all the creator's royalties and a portion of the company's revenues went to selected social movements and organizations. The pages contained scattered quotes from critics of the strip, calculated to bring guffaws from the strip's fans. Trudeau himself wrote the copy.

For a watch featuring the face of the character Duke: "Sooner or later, someone will design a watch that measures quality time, that elusive commodity that children, charmingly, often confuse with quantity time. Until then. . . ."

For a Duke A-2 Aviator Classic bomber jacket: "What is it about the clothing of guys who drop bombs for a living that fires the imagination? . . ."

Aware of the fact that one in twelve people in the United States has a disability, Nordstrom, the classy Seattle-based store chain, issued a Christmas catalog in 1991 that featured some models in wheelchairs and a young model with Down's syndrome. Observers applauded the move as public spirited and good business practice as well.

Using shirts, ties, and a giant button, art director Mike Cammuso creates a "landscape" as cover art for a Lands' End special catalog: *Buttondowns and Beyond*.

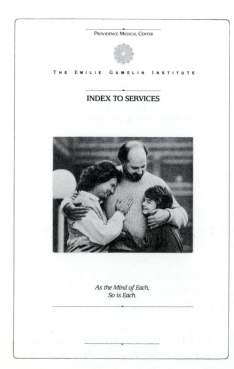

The front of one sheet and the back of another show some of the design detail worked out by Robin Rickabaugh for a prospectus for The Emile Gamelin Institute of the Providence Medical Center.

Principles of booklet design and retail advertising design, already discussed, apply to catalog design. The advertiser determines the order of presentation in a catalog but the designer plays a role here, too. Bob Stone, a direct marketing consultant, advises catalog makers to put "proved winners" on front pages and, for a higher response rate, to issue 32-page rather than 24-page publications.[11]

Some of the catalogs accept ads from outside—from magazines, for instance, looking for new subscribers.

Leichtung, a Cleveland firm selling tools by mail, does not set its prices in type in its full-color catalog. It has an artist draw the prices—and prints them in red ink. This makes them look like sale prices.

In its catalog, Wally Frank Ltd., a Middle Village, New York, tobacconist, keeps its information about cigars in front, its information about pipes and pipe tobacco in back. The latter material is printed upside down. To read this material you turn the catalog around so that the back cover becomes the front cover.

Hilary House Publishers, Inc. puts out a yearbook, *DMMP: The Direct Marketing Market Place,* that lists printing services, artists and copywriters, catalog houses, advertising and sales promotion agencies, and other people and organizations connected to the mail-order business. A trade magazine, *Catalog Age,* serves the industry. In 1987, Edward Palder brought out *The Catalog of Catalogs* (Woodbine House), a 423-page book with 8,000 listings arranged by products sold.

Company Magazines

A company magazine is a publication issued on a regular basis for public relations and institutional advertising purposes. It is known in some circles as a "house organ."

Sometimes the "magazine" takes the form of a newspaper tabloid with un-

Designers of company magazine spreads, like designers of two-page magazine advertisements, look for ways of uniting the pages. They do this often by running art across the gutter. *Access* magazine, designed by Bryan Peterson of Peterson & Company, Dallas, uses both rectangular and silhouette art to unite the pages here. This is a carryover spread for an article entitled "Rx for Strategic Success." *Access* is published by Northern Telecom Inc., Richardson, Texas.

NOT AN EXPENSE, BUT AN ASSET

The electronic switching system at Hospital Services is only one example of how Johnson & Johnson is using Private Branch Exchange (PBX) and other telecommunications systems. Since Johnson & Johnson Baby Products installed its first Meridian SL-1 nearly 10 years ago, the company has used telecommunications systems to meet not only telecommunications goals, but also business goals. In fact, during the past three years, Johnson & Johnson has installed 25 digital telephone systems in locations throughout the United States.

Johnson & Johnson has followed an aggressive approach to the installation of PBX systems because of the benefits these systems provide—reduced costs, increased functions and greater flexibility—to a fast-growing, highly decentralized company. (Johnson & Johnson consists of 165 companies marketing health care products in 153 countries.)

PBX applications at Johnson & Johnson run the gamut from the highly sophisticated automated call distribution system used by Hospital Services to the increased efficiency provided by telephones with one-button access to features such as Call Forward and Conference Call.

"We view communications as a business asset that can help provide a competitive advantage," says Hank Schoening, director of corporate telecommunications for Johnson & Johnson. "If you're going to be competitive today, you must

bring your customers and your suppliers closer to you. You've got to be more effective and more efficient. You must control costs. You can't let diverse geographic locations and differences in time zones deter you. The right approach to communications can help meet those goals."

Johnson & Johnson created an internal communications consulting group under Schoening's direction in 1983 to assist Johnson & Johnson companies in evaluating telecommunications options in a deregulated communications environment. Nick Kaltneckar, manager of voice communication, manages this group of consultants. Based at Johnson & Johnson's Management Information Center in Raritan, New Jersey, this group plays two key roles. First, it evaluates new telecommunications products and services. (The group is currently reviewing Northern Telecom's LANSTAR PC local area network and Meridian Mail voice messaging.) Second, it serves as a resource to Johnson & Johnson companies in determining how telecommunications systems can support business objectives.

A key element in Johnson & Johnson's approach to telecommunications has been a multivendor approach to systems selection. Specific business needs of Johnson & Johnson companies are carefully evaluated and system selection is based on the vendor with the best solution. Northern Telecom is one of three primary vendors. Its open architecture allows

telecommunications components from different vendors to work together in a wide array of applications.

"The ways in which Johnson & Johnson companies use digital telephone systems vary from company to company," Schoening says. "That's one of the advantages of our approach—each company can pick and choose applications that meet its needs."

SHARED RESOURCES, INCREASED FUNCTIONS

Johnson & Johnson has taken its communications strategy in central New Jersey a step beyond individual PBX systems. In the Raritan and New Brunswick areas, Johnson & Johnson has used Meridian SL-INT and SL-IXT PBX systems to create wide area networks that serve 16 Johnson & Johnson companies located in the area.

The first of these networks, based in the company's Management Information Center in Raritan, connects five Johnson & Johnson locations representing 4,500 telephones. The second network, scheduled to begin operation before year-end, will be located at corporate headquarters in New Brunswick and will connect six locations also representing about 4,500 telephones.

"Our objectives in creating these networks are to assure the lowest possible cost for long-distance service and to provide centralized attendant service for Johnson & Johnson companies," Schoening says. "There are substantial advantages in this approach, both from a cost and a function standpoint."

Kaltneckar explains that long-distance calls from Johnson & Johnson companies on the networks are routed through network nodes or hubs where the least expensive routing is selected electronically. Nodes are also responsible for the management of long-distance service, assuring cost-effective response to changes in tariffs as well as an adequate number of trunk lines. Network hubs provide detailed cost reports to individual Johnson & Johnson companies on long-distance calling.

Centralized attendants or operators located at the network hubs answer calls to main office numbers for each of the Johnson & Johnson companies on the network, forwarding calls as needed.

"Six operators with our centralized attendant service can meet the needs of 16 Johnson & Johnson companies in central New Jersey," Schoening says. "If we didn't have a centralized attendant service, we would need more than 20 operators."

Although networks created in central New Jersey illustrate benefits resulting from shared resources, the secret to success in Johnson & Johnson's use of telecommunications has been in increased available functions. Another advantage has been the high degree of flexibility that individual companies enjoy in selecting functions most important to their business.

A good example of this approach is Ortho Pharmaceutical Corporation,

10

bound pages. People in the business of putting out a publication of this kind may refer to it as a "magapaper," for it uses the same kind of paper stock a magazine uses but looks like a newspaper, with several columns of copy on each page, starting with page 1.

If the publication has but a few 8½″ × 11″ pages, it may go to still another format: the newsletter. Among formats, the newsletter is the least expensive to produce, and it is ideally suited to desktop publishing using the simplest software. Elaine Floyd, who has developed more than 50 newsletters for organizations, has published a book that shows advertisers how to use this medium.[12] And designer Polly Pattison has published a booklet of money-saving tips for newsletter production.[13]

Some newsletters—and some magazines, too—are produced nationally for local imprinting. Under such an arrangement, a doctor, dentist, or clinic, say, without incurring all the original costs of production, can send out a quarterly slick-paper publication to patients as part of a public relations program.[14]

The laying out of a company magazine, no matter what format it takes, is more a job for an editorial designer than an advertising designer, but the basic principles of design still apply.

Unlike other forms of advertising, company magazines tend to give bylines to writers and credit lines to photographers. Editors of company magazines draw a distinction between a photograph taken for journalistic reasons and one taken for illustrative reasons. The former gets a "Photograph by . . ." credit line, the latter a "Photo illustration by . . ." credit line. Not a bad distinction.

Photographs in company magazines require captions; photo illustrations do not.

The cover and back page of a colorful four-page newsletter, *Arts & Letters,* carries a general-interest article on flying and a shorter piece, surrounded by giant quote marks, about a printing firm, Barton Press, Inc., which, along with Photostats Unlimited and Klein Coleman Corp., a design firm, publishes the promotional newsletter. Art directors: Joseph Coleman and Leslie Klein.

CHAPTER 13

A spread from *Pacific,* a company magazine published quarterly by Pacific Telesis Group, San Francisco, uses a big-type, wide-measure opening, then moves down to more normal body copy to discuss the problem of foreign competition faced by U.S. business and the need for research and development. The article, by Thom Elkjer, continues after this spread, which is dominated by a Max Seabaugh illustration with an art deco look. "Win back our turf" is a term used in the article's introduction. Studio: Michael Mabry Design. Art director: Michael Mabry. Designers: Michael Mabry and Renee Holsen.

COMPETITION: THE IMPERATIVE FOR R&D

Folio, Magazine Design & Production, and *Communication World* cover the problems of publishing magazines, including the problem of designing them. *Communication World* specializes in company magazines.

Annual Reports

A booklet issued once a year to report to stockholders on the financial condition of their company is an annual report. The Securities and Exchange Commission makes annual reports mandatory for companies owned by stockholders. The content of corporate annual reports is to some extent dictated by the commission. Certain features must be included.

"When the Securities and Exchange Commission (SEC) was formed in 1934, the accompanying securities laws required public companies to file certain financial data and other information about their operations with the SEC so it would be available to investers," points out Elizabeth Howard, an expert on annual reports. "What they didn't require was embellished prose, slick four-color photographs and fluorescent pie charts and graphs. There are no legal requirements for a company to publish this type of annual report."[15]

Nearly 10,000 U.S. companies that are publicly held issue annual reports to shareholders and financial analysts.

In the years since 1934, companies have dressed up their reports, to make them more appealing visually, but they have rarely changed the general content. The typical annual report contained—still contains—a letter from the president, some company history, statistics, a financial statement, sales records, production information, and material on company policies and personnel. This is accompanied, usually, by decorative materials and photographs of plant facilities. In the past few years annual reports, like all advertising, have featured members of minority groups in some of their photographs and references to ecology in the copy.

Some annual reports carry features similar to what company magazines would carry. For one of its annual reports the Parker Pen Co. featured a review of its advertising over the years and included many illustrations.

Increasingly, annual reports appear in several languages to reflect corporations' global interests. The designer attempts to come up with a format that will accommodate the several languages.

Like advertisements, annual reports sometimes use gimmicks to be noticed. Reebok International for its 1990 annual report included a pullout poster of a man wearing nothing but Reebok running shoes. Although the black and white photograph used a back view and shadows to minimize the impact, one expert on annual reports called the poster "infantile exhibitionism." A company official, defending the photo, said it was part of Reebok's effort to promote a "fun" image.[16]

After becoming a publically-held company in 1991, Marvel Entertainment Group issued a quarterly report that took the form of a comic book (although a four-pager) that showed its Spider-Man and Incredible Hulk characters talking to each other about how successful the period had been.

Annual reports are important enough in some companies that executives begin working on them six months before they are published. A company may publish two versions, one for shareholders and a simplified version for employees. Some companies also put out quarterly reports or summary annual reports. The latter are designed to give stockholders information at a glance.

The designer of an annual report must keep in mind the purpose of the publication: to give investors and potential investors information to help them make intelligent decisions. In addition, the company expects the publication to build the company's image.

Some annual reports revolve around themes. Reference to the themes appears on most if not all of the pages. The themes evolve from subject matter or design approach.

Nonprofit organizations issue annual reports, too. Their efforts are not guided by Securities and Exchange Commission directives, but they have their boards of directors to answer to.

Annual reports are produced usually under the direction of public relations directors or chief financial officers rather than advertising directors. Outside design firms usually handle the graphics.

IBM, with design by Paul Rand, in the 1950s introduced the idea of impressive graphics for annual reports. Litton Industries, with design by Robert Miles Runyan, was another leader. In the 1960s annual reports went "super-glossy," according to Richard A. Lewis, president of Corporate Annual Reports, Inc. They were filled with "elaborately stated concepts and expensive, irrelevant graphics."

Lewis saw the turning point for annual reports occurring in 1969, when the stock market plummeted "and a series of forces were put into play that have altered the content and form of the modern annual report significantly."[17] No more three-printing-processes reports (as General Dynamics produced) or stained-glass covers (as Litton Industries produced).

Pressruns for annual reports go into the tens of thousands—sometimes two or three times the number needed to reach stockholders. The extra copies serve promotional and educational purposes.

For some annual reports, the production and printing costs amount to $5 or more per copy. Yet, "Most companies, I believe, have accepted the fact that the annual report is one of the least expensive forms of corporate communications," Lewis wrote. The cost of an annual report, he observed, "roughly equals one to three spreads of color advertising in *Business Week*. Considering the variety of audiences and the complexity of the message that the annual report must deal with, the cost is really quite reasonable."

More so than in other areas, the designer of an annual report has to deal with paper choices. Paper manufacturers offer a bewildering selection of stocks for annual reports. In the environment-conscious 1990s, designers paid more attention to recycled and recyclable paper. "Then some used . . . soy-based inks," reported Dan Danbom, director of communication planning for Public Service Co. of Colorado, Denver. He added, tongue in cheek: "Then some used . . . vegetarian, ozone-friendly printers who operate their solar-powered plants only in places that have outlawed business dealings with totalitarian regimes that contribute to deforestation when they are not netting dolphins."[18]

As in other forms of advertising, the computer has become an important tool in the creation of annual reports. NovaCare, Inc., when stuck with a collection of snapshots to include in its 1990 annual report, found that it could avoid an amateurish look by converting them to low-resolution imagery (blurring them) through use of Photoshop software from Adobe Systems. One observer saw the prints as "impressionist 'paintings' with subtle computer noise."[19]

This cover for a PacificCorp annual report features an Oregon oak tree, which, according to a caption inside, symbolizes the "solid roots that provide stability for the company's three major businesses, as well as support for continued branching out in newer areas of opportunity." Designer and art director: Robin Rickabaugh.

Trained to use traditional design tools, Letha Wulf turns to the Macintosh and QuarkXpress software to design an employees' annual report for First Interstate Bank. The report carries a series of portraits of employees along with short biographies. To bring some variety to her bold pages, Wulf uses different typefaces in display sizes for the names. Robert Reynolds took the pictures.

Brochures

A brochure is an *elaborate* booklet, with a cover, often oversize, that may be cut from parchment or an exotic cloth- or leatherlike stock, and inside pages cut from coated or from deckle-edge antique stock. While an ordinary booklet costs the client as little as a dime or two a copy, the brochure costs several dollars per copy.

The brochure format fits important prospectuses or sales presentations. Some annual reports are elaborate enough to be considered brochures.

Ways to Cut Costs

The problem often is not how to dress up a direct-mail piece but how to keep its costs down.

Line art made from routine photographs, one ink printed on a colored stock for a two-color effect, stock art and stock photos—these are some ways of getting special effects economically.

The designer may find it possible to use one of the company's advertisements designed for other media. A magazine ad, introduced with appropriate type and art on the cover, could be used intact in the center spread of panels. Or the ad could be cut apart and spread over panels on both sides of the mailer.

Paper Direct, Lyndhurst, New Jersey, and Queblo Images, Brentwood, New York, offer a number of papers with printed designs, in colors, that can accommodate the advertiser's design, saving the cost of multiple-color printing.

Like all advertising, direct mail finds its greatest costs not in production but in *distribution.* More than any other single item, postage bleeds the advertiser; in response, the designer chooses the thinnest and lightest paper consistent with the needs of the job, limits the number of items in the mailing, cuts down on their size, decreases frequency of mailing, goes third class rather than first, and engages in a never-ending effort to update the mailing list to prevent wasted circulation.

The problem of double mailings is always there. Because it may cost more to eliminate the duplication then to simply send extra copies, advertisers try to cover themselves with notes like this: "Please excuse us if you have already received a copy of this mailer. If you have, why don't you pass this copy along to a friend?" A burial organization included this disclaimer on a direct-mail piece: "We sincerely regret if this letter should reach any home where there is illness or sorrow, as this certainly was not intended."[20]

CHAPTER 14

POSTERS AND DISPLAYS

Aside from word-of-mouth advertising, until the fifteenth century the poster and the sign served as the only media through which advertisers could reach their customers. With the coming of printing from movable type, handbills became popular; they were posters made portable. Then with Alois Senefelder's remarkable 1798 discovery of lithography, in Germany, posters took on new life. Drawings could be reproduced as easily as type. Drawings were what posters needed.

Two unlikely figures—widely separated in time, geography, and inclinations—emerge as fathers of modern postermaking. One was the American showman P. T. Barnum, who used sensational sketches to lure people into his shows. The other was the artist Henri de Toulouse-Lautrec, who brought feeling and design to the medium. There is today a little of the Barnum, a little of the Lautrec in the posters dotting our highways and decorating our walls.

One of the unique outdoor poster campaigns was conducted by a maker of shaving cream. The year was 1925. Gas stations and other local establishments for years had drummed up trade by putting signs along the nation's highways. Perhaps, thought Allan Odell, the family business could step up sales by using the same medium. He could put up sets of signs. Five in a set.

They would not have to be big. A short line on each sign would do. At first he tried the hard-sell approach. Sales began to increase at once. But that did not satisfy Odell. Motorists see these signs, he told himself, at remote spots on the highway, perhaps after hours of monotonous driving. Wouldn't they appreciate a touch of rhyme?

It was not long before the catchy Burma-Shave signs—some ironic, some cynical, some absurd, but all of them funny—caught the fancy of nearly everyone, including those ordinarily critical of advertising. Alexander Woollcott said it was as difficult to read just one of those sign sets as it was to eat just one salted peanut.

An example:

**IF YOU DON'T KNOW
WHOSE SIGNS THESE ARE
YOU HAVEN'T DRIVEN
VERY FAR
Burma-Shave**

They lived as a one-company advertising medium for thirty-five years. And then, when cars traveled too fast for their drivers or riders to take in the more than a dozen words painted in rather small letters, the company phased out its roadside advertising.

Posters and the Ecology

Perhaps a growing criticism of advertising that got in the way of highway scenery had something to do with Burma-Shave's decision, too. And with major political candidates announcing they would not use billboards, no wonder the industry grew edgy.

The American Association of Libraries produced this full-color poster during World War I to encourage citizens to donate books to U.S. troops.

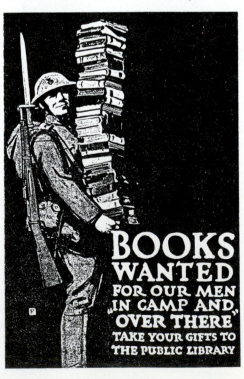

Radio station KFBK, Sacramento, put up a series of billboards to promote the controversial talk-show host Rush Limbaugh of the Excellence in Broadcasting network. This poster uses art to suggest that some who saw the message reacted violently: smashed tomatoes, a tossed egg, bullet holes, and even the hint of arson at the far left. Another poster in the series, showing a hand reaching toward a push-button car radio, asked: "Wouldn't You Like to Punch Rush Limbaugh?" The agency: Mering & Associates. Creative director: David Mering. Art director: Brian Burch. Copywriter: Dean Chance.

By late 1965 the criticism from ecologists and others resulted in Congress passing President Lyndon Johnson's—and Ladybird Johnson's—Highway Beautification Act, authorizing a federal-state campaign to landscape major highways, screen or remove junkyards, and push billboards back far enough so they would not interfere with the view. During debate, Senator Warren Magnuson (Democrat, Washington) pointed out that on Route 99 just south of Seattle, Mount Rainier was obscured by a Rainier Beer billboard that showed—a picture of Mount Rainier. The bill warned that lack of compliance in any of the states could result in withholding 10 percent of federal highway funds to those states. Signs on roads not part of the federal-aid highway system were not affected by the law. Nor were signs in commercial and industrial areas. In the form in which it passed, the bill had the support of major segments of the outdoor advertising industry. And one firm, the Stoner System, Des Moines, while the bill was being discussed, had some fun with the junkyards provision. It put up a board reading: "Help Beautify Junkyards. THROW SOMETHING LOVELY AWAY TODAY."

Signs came down in places, but *Newsweek* observed in 1979 that "the program is widely considered a failure, and may soon be abolished." A total of 88,000 signs had been removed by 1979, but 208,000 others remained.

Enforcement of the act had been left to the states, and not all complied. Missouri and New Jersey, to name two states, had done nothing. Georgia had erected 573 new nonconforming signs.[1]

The industry showed signs of recovery in the 1980s as advertisers turned back to outdoor signs—probably the cheapest of the mass media.

More outdoor boards were to come down in the 1990s in compliance with the 1965 Act.

Commenting on pending bills in Congress to further limit billboard construction in the environment-conscious 1990s, an editorial in *American Advertising*, the American Advertising Federation magazine, said, "One needn't be a fan of billboards to admit that they aren't exactly a threat to the biosphere. Last time I checked, no billboard had ever spilled oil, leaked toxic waste, or spewed carcinogens into the atmosphere. Billboards don't pump raw sewage into streams and rivers, catch dolphins in their nets, or slaughter elephants for ivory.

"There are serious environmental problems staring us in the face. Billboards aren't one of them. Well known environmental organizations like the Sierra Club, Greenpeace, and Ducks Unlimited all use outdoor advertising."[2]

concerts

SEPT 16 · 8PM
Seth Austen
Aul Vielle que pourra
Ray & Cilla Fisher
Garnet Rogers

SEPT 17 · 4PM
Norman Kennedy with
Elizabeth Stewart
and Sheila Stewart
The Psaltery
Melusine
Yank Rachel with
Paul Geremia

SEPT 17 · 8PM
Kallet, Epstein & Cicone
Joe Cormier
John Jackson
Robbie O'Connell,
Jimmy Keane,
Eileen Ivers &
Seamus Egan

SEPT 18 · 4PM
Danny Carnahan &
Robin Petrie
Hedy West
Tony Cuffe
Swallowtail
Laurie Riley &
Michael MacBean

CONCERT HOSTS
Mike Raminoff · Martha Burns
Lorraine Lee · Chuck Wentworth

seventeenth
southeastern
massachusetts
university
rain or shine
folk music
festival · 1988

FREE

WORKSHOPS

DANCING

CRAFTS FAIR

CHILDREN'S AREA

& PARKING

SMU
Eisteddfod

telephone
(508) 999 · 8166

North Dartmouth
massachusetts 02747

workshops

with Full Concert
Performers Plus
Neil Atkinson &
Doug Bliss
The Beans
Peter Bellamy
Saul Broudy
Bubblefic
Howie Bursen
Joli Gonsalves
Louis Killen
Little City String Band
Linda Morley
Roaring Jelly
Gail Roberts
Sparky Rucker
Heather Wood
Royston Wood
Mike Zeeto

tickets

Full Event $30
Fri & Sat 8pm $10 each
Sun 4pm $10
Sat 4 pm $4
Children under 12
half price
Discounts for SMU
students, personnel
& senior citizens
at box office with ID
Mail Order Full Event
received before sept 10 · $26

Professor Howard Glasser of the Department of Design, Southeastern Massachusetts University, North Dartmouth, a noted calligrapher, designed this poster for a folk music festival. Of course, everything here is handwritten or hand-printed. A beautiful example not only of calligraphy but also of formal balance and sensitive spacing and placement. Note how Glasser repeats a small portion of the opening art in the third column.

The Poster as Art

What has bothered the critics has not been the quality of art so much as the intrusion on the landscape. In fact, the art for national outdoor advertising placed by agencies has improved over the years. For one thing, agencies no longer recrop and boil down existing print media ads for outdoors. Outdoor design is not derivative. If anything, the directness and simplicity of outdoor advertising have influenced the look of all other advertising.

As in other areas of graphic arts, Push Pin Studios, New York, with the work of Milton Glaser and Seymour Chwast, set many of the standards in poster design.

A good deal of the excitement in poster design is to be found in the small-size posters that serve both as advertising and avant-garde room hangings. In their homes, apartments, and dorm rooms people display colorful posters promoting travel, concerts, and sports events. People become collectors.

Perhaps the poster with the most impact in the 1960s was one advertising a Jefferson Airplane rock concert in San Francisco. Eager fans removed the posters as rapidly as promoters could put them up. New ones were printed and sold.

Rock music concerts inspired a wave of wild posters. Today the posters are collector's items, some of them worth hundreds of dollars. Paul D. Gruskkin, who shows 2,000 of them in his hefty book, *The Art of Rock: Posters from Presley to Punk,* says that "Graphic art is still associated with rock 'n' roll; there seems to be some inextricable link between the two."[3] Rock posters featured freakish colors, irreverent design, and often hard-to-read type, but in their way they communicated effectively with their readers and concertgoers.

In the 1960s and afterwards, various enterprises produced and sold nonadvertising posters of every description, many of them political, some of them sick, some of them erotic, some of them psychedelic, some of them pretty and sentimental. And to take advantage of the wave of nostalgia sweeping the country,

Joseph Kowal uses an art deco style to design and paint this promotional poster for Marc Advertising, "The Shop That Gets People to Shop."

publishers reprinted posters from the turn of the century, from World War I days, from the 1920s, 1930s, and 1940s.

Spring Mills, Inc., Fort Mill, South Carolina, dug up a couple of its risqué Springmaid sheets ads from the 1940s and 1960s and made them available to nostalgia buffs for $5 the set.

America and other countries had gone through an earlier period with the poster as art—at the end of the nineteenth century, when painters and printmakers became interested. Hayward and Blanche Cirker called this period "The Golden Age of the Poster."[4] Among artists and designers participating then were Aubrey Beardsley, who did posters for theaters and publishers; Will Bradley, art director of *Collier's, Good Housekeeping,* and other magazines; Edward Penfield, art director for *Harper's Magazine* and other magazines; Maxfield Parrish, book and magazine illustrator; and, of course, Toulouse-Lautrec.

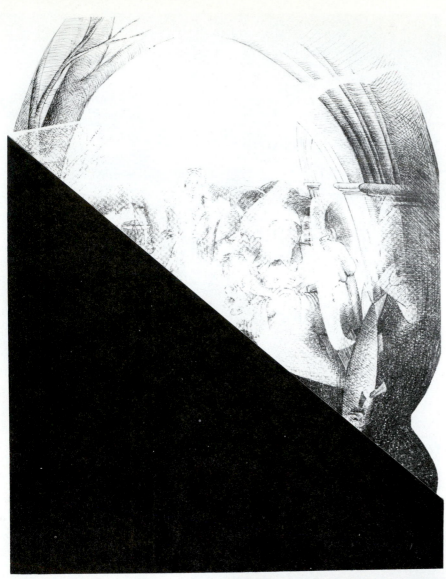

This eye-stopping art was included in a poster for *Squanto,* a play described by its author, Jim Magnuson, as "an epic of the American past replete with pilgrims, Shakespeare, Caliban, Spanish nuns, the ghost of Elizabeth I, and the host of the first Thanksgiving." It was artist Chris Ragus's job to capture all this, which he did by drawing a montage that impresses the viewer at first as merely a portrait. The play was produced at Princeton.

Campus Voice, a 42″ × 47″ "magazine" published to hang on school hall walls, accommodated this lively Snickers poster designed by Robert Pizzo of Studio Pizzo or Pizzo. Agency: Backer Spielvogel Bates. Art director: Fran Sheff-Mauer.

Outdoor Advertising

You can design a poster in any size or shape, of course. It can go up on a bulletin board, in a store window, on a wall outside—wherever the advertiser can get permission to display it.

The term "outdoor advertising" is reserved for standard-size posters or panels—known as "billboards." The billboard industry—or, to use a term more acceptable

It started out as a routine assignment: Come up with a safety poster to encourage workers at Pacific Power & Light's plants to protect their hearing. Larry Oakner and Warren Eakins of Pihas, Schmidt, Westerdahl Company, a Portland, Oregon, advertising agency, came up with the concept shown here: the hands of someone who had lost the ability to hear spelling out the message. Help came from Tom Stewart, who did the photographs; Marsh & McLennan, the insurance safety underwriter; and Mary Ruhl, who gave advice on American Sign Language.

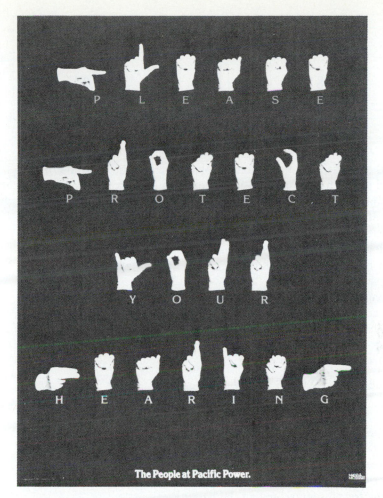

The People at Pacific Power.

to it, the *outdoor advertising* industry—counts several hundred operators of standard outdoor advertising facilities who pay rent to thousands of property owners for the space occupied by structures erected to display posters.

But standardized outdoor advertising accounts for only a small percentage of the signs and other displays set out along the highways and in the cities. The Outdoor Advertising Association of America, Inc., and the Institute of Outdoor Advertising naturally are sensitive to criticism of outdoor advertising that lumps the standardized posters with less tasteful, nonstandardized roadside posters and signs over which they have no jurisdiction. The Institute of Outdoor Advertising offers Obie Awards each year to the most effective billboards.

The outdoor advertising industry makes a distinction between billboards and "on-premises" signs that identify various businesses and appear on their buildings and properties. Real outdoor advertising is subject to local, state, and federal laws regulating size and placement. Local ordinances also regulate "on-premises" signs.

Outdoor advertising is sometimes referred to now as "out-of-home" advertising. The change has come about because of the posters seen, for instance, inside subway stations and airports. The new term could also be used to include painted walls, point-of-purchase advertising, signs and logos on trucks, and transit advertising.

The medium lends itself best to reminder advertising to supplement advertising in other media. But some advertisers use the medium almost exclusively, and some campaigns are kicked off with outdoor advertising. It is a medium for both national and local advertising.

Close to half of the outdoor billboards in this country advertise tobacco products and beverages. Car manufacturers and dealers and food companies are also big users of outdoor advertising. National advertisers who use outdoor advertising use it in geographic areas with people especially receptive to the products.

POSTERS AND DISPLAYS

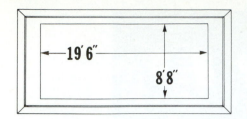 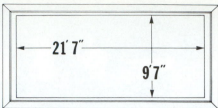 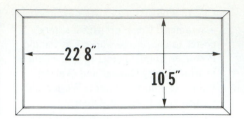

The national advertising is not designed solely to reach the consumer. Some of it is designed to reach retailers as well, to get them to stock the product. The retailers presumably not only see the promotion but also feel the demand.

Like other national advertising, outdoor advertising can be localized. And, of course, many outdoor signs are locally produced for local audiences. Local billboard advertising is likely to be institutional, with a single point to make. The look is likely to be simple and uncluttered, a look appropriate to all billboards, no matter who sponsors them.

Sunkist, a long-time national user of outdoor advertising, sometimes puts the names of local grocery stores in its signs. For instance, it has adjusted its "You have our word on it" slogan to read "Vons has our word on it." A Vons store might be just up the street.

This diagram shows how the three standard poster sizes—24-sheet, 30-sheet, and bleed—fit on a standard panel. (Courtesy the Institute of Outdoor Advertising.)

Size and Placement

Standardized posters come in these sizes and styles:

■ *The panel poster.* The client can choose the 24-sheet poster, with a copy size of 19′6″ wide by 8′8″ deep; the 30-sheet poster, with a copy size of 21′7″ × 9′7″ (25 percent more display area); or the bleed poster, with a copy size of 22′8″ × 10′5″ (40 percent more display area). The plant operator makes no additional charge for posters occupying the larger areas.

A standard panel designed some years ago by Raymond Loewy to display both 24- and 30-sheet posters, and now bleed posters, measures 24′6″ × 12′3″ at the outside edges. About half of the panels used for standard posters are of the Loewy type. The frame is gray. Inside the frame is a white border or mat (for 24- and 30-sheet posters). Obviously the 30-sheet poster has a narrower white mat than the 24-sheet poster has. The white mat assists in squaring up the sheets and centering the completed poster on the panel.

On a painted bulletin with an extension, Kemps New York Vanilla Ice Cream, a division of Marigold Foods, emphasizes "New York" by showing a cow marked with representative graffiti found on subways and buildings in that city. Agency: Martin Williams Advertising, Minneapolis. Art director: Mark Haumerson. Copywriter: John Jarvis.

The industry in the 1980s began replacing standard boards with boards rising from a single pole.

The terms "24-sheet" and "30-sheet" are misleading. They date to the time when it actually took that many sheets of printed material to fill the board. Now, with larger presses available, the standard panel can be covered with as few as ten sheets. But the terms persist.

■ *The painted bulletin.* Painted bulletins used to come in a variety of sizes, but now the 48′ × 14′ is pretty much standard. And many "painted" bulletins are no longer painted; like regular poster panels, they are printed and posted. The advertiser can buy one such bulletin (in which case it probably *will* be painted) or several. Large, colorful, always lighted, sometimes three-dimensional or with a section extending beyond the set dimensions, with or without a frame, the painted bulletin offers the designer great flexibility in design techniques and construction.

One innovation is to use three-sided vertical panels that can be turned continuously to reveal, alternately, three different pictures.

In 1980 Western Insecticide, Spokane, put up a painted bulletin that dramatized in an unusual way the fact that termites were a problem people should worry about. The sign said, "There Are No Termites in Spokane." Each week for four months the company broke off pieces of the sign, so that at the end it was almost "eaten" away.

■ *The electric spectacular.* It is a huge, complicated, painted display, permanent or near-permanent, making use of moving parts and unusual lighting effects. Perhaps the most famous of the "spectaculars" was the huge Camel sign that blew smoke rings over Times Square for twenty-four years before becoming a victim of progress early in 1966. The R. J. Reynolds Tobacco Company paid a rental fee of nearly $10,000 a month to show various war, TV, and athletic heroes, bigger than life, using the product.

A new outdoor "spectacular" came into being in 1976 in which electronics and computer technology combined to activate thousands of tiny lights. The effect was akin to an animated scoreboard at a sports event. It was possible to program one of these "spectaculars" so that an early morning message could address drivers on their way to work, a midday message could address shoppers heading for supermarkets, and an evening message could address people going out on the town. The developers were Ackerley Communications, Seattle, and American Sign & Indicator Corp., Spokane. (American Sign is known for its on-premises time-and-temperature signs used by banks and savings and loan associations.)

This painted bulletin with a space extension (the thumb sticking up over the top) uses five fingers and a thumb to say, "6 nonstops a day. . . ." The captain's stripes say "airlines." Agency: Chiat/Day Advertising. Art director: Jerry Box. Copywriter: Roger Livingston.

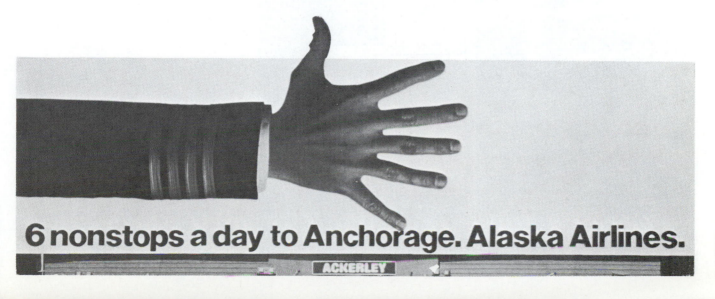

6 nonstops a day to Anchorage. Alaska Airlines.

ACKERLEY

In the early 1980s giant, air-filled, three-dimensional billboards began appearing along the highways. The parts that protrude toward viewers are air bags made of vinyl-coated nylon. An electric fan keeps them puffed up. What protrudes can be, say, a huge beer bottle or a plane.

Solar-activated parts can move on a billboard as the sun moves during the day. Reflective discs vibrate as the sun shines on them. Art can be backlighted. Fiber optics (light-transmitting glass fibers) can illuminate the art.[5]

Panels are scientifically located to give complete coverage of the market. An advertiser buying standard poster coverage buys a "showing." A 100-showing in a city means that enough boards are contracted for so that by the end of a month everyone in town probably will have seen the ad at least once and probably many times. An outdoor advertising company has a number of 100-showings available in its city. Lesser showings are also available, and so are showings more intensive than 100-showings. Or a single panel can be rented.

"Circulation" of outdoor advertising includes number of passing pedestrians as well as number of passing automobiles. Traffic Audit Bureau, Inc., has provided the statistics to advertisers and agencies since 1933.

Outdoor Advertising Production

It takes about two months to put a poster design into production and get it up on boards.

The outdoor advertising "plant operator" can take a job from the beginning, writing and designing the billboard, printing or painting it, putting it up and maintaining it. Or it may be a matter of taking a layout and producing the poster to order. Or it may be a matter of taking already-printed sheets from an advertising agency or printer and seeing that they get the proper display.

When fewer than half a dozen posters are needed, they will probably be hand-painted, even in regular 24- or 30-sheet sizes. An order up to one hundred would call for silk-screen printing. One for more than one hundred would call for offset lithography.

Artwork for hand-printed or silk-screened posters is often "posterized." That is, the gradations in tone are reduced to two or three or four. The tones up close look "patterned," with one quitting abruptly where the other comes on. There are no blends. Just flat colors. Such crisp treatment need not detract from the beauty of the artwork. It is, in fact, quite suited to poster visibility.

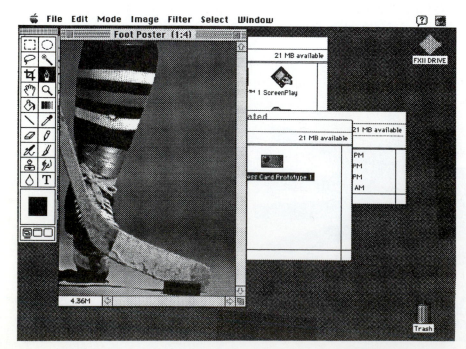

For a poster for a hockey team, Mark Dixon, production manager for X/Factory, scans his own photograph, calls it up on a Macintosh screen, and uses Photoshop software to fine-tune the colors. Placement of type created in another program is still to come. You see here several windows on the screen desktop. The program's tool box appears at the left.

Bring Your Class To Our School.

The Seattle Aquarium. It's Always Fresh.

A colorful car card, using stylized cartoon art bleeding at the top, left, and right, invites schoolchildren and teacher bus riders to plan a trip to the Seattle Aquarium. The ad plays on the versatile word *school*. For design unity, the main and secondary headlines use the same bold roman typeface, but in two sizes. The two headline units are centered. Agency: Tycer Fulz Bellack/Davis, Seattle. Designer and art director: Rayne Beaudoin. Illustrator: Gary Jacobsen. Copywriter: Jeff Tuininga.

A billboard for the Palm Springs Convention and Visitors Bureau moves in so close that all you see is part of a diving board, the bottom of a pair of legs, and a pleasant sky—enough to say this is a place to vacation. The art nicely illustrates the "Bounce" in the headline. A later version of this poster art uses the headline, "Better Board Meetings." An advantage of the cropping is that the diver can be either a man or a woman. Art directors: Newell Nesheim and Darryl Shimazu. Photographer: Walter Swarthout. Copywriter: Elaine Cossman. Agency: Gumpertz/Bentley/Fried, Los Angeles.

The outdoor advertising industry is now using "computer painting," a process by which artwork and transparencies are reproduced to billboard size without the need for color separations. A computer center can transmit coded graphics to all parts of the country.

B. Roland McElroy, president of the Outdoor Advertising Association of America, in 1991 predicted that ". . . designers will be able to create sales messages with a few strokes of an 'electronic brush' and by executing a series of computer commands, have the image appear on billboards throughout the country."

He said that billboards of the future "will more closely resemble a TV picture tube than the painted or vinyl surface of today's billboards. And, of course, the message may be changed as often as deemed necessary."[6]

The Poster Idea

If it is true for advertising in general, it is all the more true for this kind of advertising: A single theme is all you can develop. A single point made is all you can hope for.

Here are some possible approaches:

- *Make a claim, outright or implied.*
- *Offer some news, like the price of a nationally advertised product.*
- *Remind the reader to. . . .*
- *Suggest something different to the reader.*
- *Make a comparison.* Show your product in association with something already admired.

You can do any of these by jarring the reader, by paraphrasing, by using offbeat humor, through human interest, maybe even through symbolism.

There is plenty of room for creativity. In a powerful ad poster prepared by Fallon McElligott, Minneapolis, for *Reader's Digest,* Stevie Wonder with dark glasses is shown saying, "Before I'll Ride with a Drunk, I'll Drive Myself."

Like other advertising media, posters sometimes employ parody to put their points across. The Badvertising Institute, Deer Island, Maine, has circulated a poster to schools that makes fun of Merit cigarettes and that brand's packaging by showing a coffin with the headline, "New Crush-Proof Box."

North Dakota had some fun with promotional billboards within the state a few years ago. "Isn't this the flattest place you've ever seen?" one of them asked. A billboard just outside Minnesota read: "You are now entering Minnesota. Why?"

Sometimes an individual contracts for a billboard to impress a spouse or sweetheart with a personal message or just to pull a gag. When Seattle, Washington, was going through a depression because of a slowdown at Boeing, some individuals bought space and said, in effect: "Will the Last Person to Leave Please Turn Off the Lights."

In 1991 Mark Heckman, an activist graphic designer, put up a billboard on a tollway outside of Chicago to advertise the Afro Country Club, "Where Only the Ball is White." The art showed a smug black golfer holding up a white golf-ball. Vandals quickly defaced the poster and it was removed, but not before Heckman's point was made, through the ensuing publicity, that racism was alive in the area. There was no Afro Country Club; Heckman was simply making a statement about the exclusion of black golfers from some clubs in the country.

Heckman designed another billboard in 1991 that caused a fuss, this time among Catholic leaders in Grand Rapids, Michigan. The poster, sponsored by radio station WLAV-FM, showed the Pope wearing headphones listening to the station's rock music. The headline: "Father Knows Best." Heckman defended the poster, a bit lamely, by saying that the Pope probably *would* listen to that station if he were in Grand Rapids.

Tom Kelly did three different comps for an opera poster before the sponsors saw what they wanted: the third one.

Doing the Rough Layout or Comp

To design a standard poster, start out with thumbnails done in a 2¼: 1 proportion. When you come up with one that looks promising, you work up a rough layout or a comp. At this stage you can work in either a 13½″ × 6″ or an 18″ × 8″ size. The finished art for a printed poster is usually done in a larger size, though not, of course, in actual size.

For painted bulletins the proportions would be roughly 3½: 1. A good comp size would be 26″ × 8″.

The shape is fixed: a horizontal—an *extreme* horizontal if the poster is a painted bulletin. That may limit some things you can do. For instance, you may find it difficult to show a tall building or a full figure standing erect. But the horizontal shape has its advantages. You have an easy time moving the reader from left to right, across the ad. Sequence is no problem.

Outdoor advertising is a medium seen from close up but also from blocks away, at an angle or head-on, in all kinds of weather, under natural light and artificial light, in congested and noncongested areas. The design must do its job under all these conditions.

One designer has described his job as that of "creating a visual scandal." To shock the reader is a necessary function of the billboard. Another designer has described his art as "art of omission." "In poster communication, you can say more by saying less."

You sometimes have trouble at the comp stage seeing the ad in its actual size and in place. Can you be sure your elements are large enough to see? William Miller, art director of General Outdoor Advertising Co., suggested that the designer step back a distance equal to seventeen times the width of the comp and see if it can be read.

The design of a good billboard is very much like the design of any other advertisement. The same basic principles apply. But you should remember that a billboard differs from other forms of advertising in these two important respects:

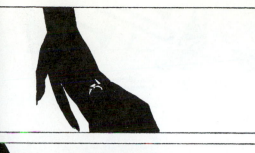

The silhouette the artwork makes can mean a great difference in visibility in outdoor advertising.

The audience sees the advertisement while on the move; and the audience sees the advertisement from a distance. It follows that, more than other forms of advertising, the billboard has to be arresting. It also follows that it must be simple, strong, and clear.

Rules for Designing Billboards

Here are some rules for designing billboards, based in part on advice offered by the Institute of Outdoor Advertising.[7]

■ *Confine the number of elements in the ad to three or, if possible, two or even one.* If you use three elements, they will probably be a photograph or painting of the product either on display or in use, a headline, and some background.

If you show background, keep it uncluttered. And give consideration to the overall silhouette formed by your placement of elements.

■ *Keep the number of words to a minimum of three, four, or five—certainly no more than nine or ten.* The Institute of Outdoor Advertising points out that the poster idea must register within six seconds.

■ *Make sure the illustration is big enough.* It is not always necessary to show the product in its entirety. You can move in close, cropping if necessary.

Sometimes you may find that art alone is enough. A bottle of Coke lying in some ice or snow may be all the selling necessary in a summer showing.

The art will almost surely be in full color. To show the product off to advantage, it may be desirable to foreshorten it, exaggerate its perspective, or, to fit the space, show it from a worm's-eye view.

■ *Make sure the art says what the headline says.*

■ *Make sure the type is big and thick enough.* Use a sturdy face in at least a medium and probably bold or ultrabold weight. Consider sans serifs. Legibility is perhaps more important than readability in outdoor advertising.

Beginning designers invariably make the mistake of using letters that are either too spindly or too small in relation to the available space. Or they put them in a color that does not contrast sufficiently with the background.

■ *Organize the elements so they work together as a single unit.*

■ *Use color boldly, in broad strokes.* Cover large areas with flat color. For most jobs choose bright primary colors rather than pastel shades. And choose colors to achieve the greatest possible contrast. Few posters these days go up without color. Black-and-white or full color, the cost for a showing is the same.

■ *Make sure the product is clearly identified.*

Rolling Billboards

The sides and backs of trucks provide additional advertising space, and many companies give truck posters special consideration these days. "Rolling Billboards," they're called.

An American Trucking Association Foundation study showed that an over-the-road tractor-trailer makes 10.1 million visual impressions a year during daylight hours, and a local delivery vehicle makes 16 million impressions. The ATA found that trucks with visual designs are seen by the public as less threatening than trucks without them. When made with reflective materials, the signs can also contribute to safety by making trucks more visible.

That a truck moves rapidly along the highway means that the design should be especially simple, bold, and colorful.

Truck graphic designs range from mere logos, identifying the truck owner, to posters and paintings in a wide range of colors. Brunckhorst's Boar's Head Brand Provisions, a firm supplying hams and specialties to delicatessens and grocery stores, had its trucks hand-painted with a simple logo design that incorporates some 23-karet gold-leaf lettering.

Many fleet truck managers prefer decals to painting. Decals last longer and are easier to repair.[8]

Lowen Sales Corp., Hutchinson, Kansas, is one of several firms specializing in the design and installation of big-truck signs. Modagraphics Inc., a firm based in Illinois, arranges for other firms to rent space on truck trailers. The program allows a trucking company to earn up to $7,000 a year per truck. The truck can carry its own identification at the rear.

Transit Advertising

Yet another medium available to advertisers is transit advertising: car cards shown either on the inside or outside of moving vehicles. People associated with this medium have claimed, "This sign is 26 miles long."

Inside transit advertising directs itself to a captive audience. It is read by persons who are more often than not bored by their ride. They read the transit ad with a kind of go-ahead-see-if-you-can-amuse-me attitude. That may be a disadvantage. On the other hand, the reader in many cases is riding to the stores. That may be an advantage.

An inside transit ad is shaped much like a spread in a magazine. It is a spread that does not have to be held to read. But it cannot merely duplicate a two-page ad in a magazine. It needs some of the impact of the poster. It can contain a pad of coupons or order blanks, allowing any number of viewers to respond.

The outside transit ad is even more a poster—a poster that moves. It is the reader who often is stationary. In that sense, it is traditional outdoor advertising in reverse. But like any poster, it must say what it says quickly, simply.

The Transit Advertising Association has standardized the sizes of both inside and outside car cards. On the inside the cards may measure 14″, 21″, 28″, 42″, and 84″ wide by 11″ deep. The 28″ × 11″ size is the most common.

The cards are printed by the advertiser and shipped flat for placement by the medium. When the advertiser buys a *full service,* its card is shown on every vehicle operated by the transportation company. Half and quarter services are also available. The service remains in effect for thirty days, as does a *showing* for outdoor advertising.

Outside car cards, also called "traveling displays," measure 27″, 36″, or 44″ by 21″ deep. A 12′ × 2′ size is also available in some markets.

One advantage of inside-the-car transit advertising is measurement of audience exposure. The fare box is "an auditing system that ranks with the best," as *Advertising Age* has put it. Exposure to outside car cards is almost impossible to measure.

Transit advertising also includes posters and displays in bus, train, and subway stations and in airports.

This kind of advertising is particularly effective when it takes advantage of the setting, as in subway advertising that reads: "If you ate Diet Mazola there'd be more room in this car" and "Let the owners of RCA color TVs get off first. They have a better reason to rush home."

Perhaps the biggest user of transit advertising has been the William Wrigley Jr. Company. Other important users include alcoholic beverage, food, tobacco, and pharmaceutical companies.

Transit advertising faces some special restrictions in that ads appear in or on

National Screenprinters, Inc., Auburn, Alabama, uses a small-space black-and-white ad in *Refrigerated Transporter* magazine to advertise its services to the trucking industry and to companies owning trucks. To appeal to the widest possible audience in this specialized field, the company uses generic, abstract art here. Agency: Ellis Harper. Art director, designer, and copywriter: Dee Dee Harper.

A car card on Mini buses in San Francisco, using a variation of a bumper sticker slogan that became popular in the late 1980s, promotes a radio station. Art director: Rick Tharp of the Tharp Did It design studio. Copywriter: James Smith.

Childlike lettering helps create the illusion that a puppy wishes he could grow up to be a cat so he could enjoy Spillers Choosy cat food. One of a series of 4-sheet and superlite-format posters displayed at roadside bus stops and supermarkets in Great Britain. Agency: Bartle Bogle Hegarty. Art director: John Gorse. Copywriter: Nick Worthington. Photographer: Tony Evans.

publicly owned vehicles. The Freedom from Religion Foundation, Madison, Wisconsin, objected to Knights of Columbus advertising, arguing that religious advertising on buses was a violation of the separation of church and state. The foundation followed its objection—fighting fire with fire, as it explained—by placing anti-Bible ads in eighty Madison buses.

Bumper Stickers

Bumper stickers—or "bumper snickers," as Paul Harvey calls them—are the individual motorist's answer to transit advertising.

Bumper stickers date to at least the Eisenhower-Stevenson presidential race in 1952. Since then they have advertised all kinds of causes, but the most memorable of the stickers are simply playful. People express their biases and sense of humor through them. One sticker inspires another. Some stickers that were around in the past decade:

> **I've got something money can't buy—poverty.**
> **I'm not as think as you stoned I am.**
> **If you don't like the way I drive, stay off the sidewalk.**
> **Support higher education. Hug a professor.**
> **I brake for tailgaters.**

Related to bumper stickers are license frames that tell the world where people buy their cars; or, if purchased in the stores, tell what happiness is; or brag about certain worker types being better lovers; or assure us that the drivers of the cars would rather be skiing or performing other sporting acts.

Each of these—stickers and frames—require deft design to crowd a word or two and possibly some decorative element into a small and distorted shape.

Point-of-Purchase Advertising

The advertisers' one last chance to accost the potential customer is at the point of purchase. Almost everyone who makes products for sale at the retail level uses the medium. Point-of-purchase advertising has come into increasing favor among advertisers since the advent of self-service stores; P-O-P materials do the job salesmen once did.

The Point-of-Purchase Advertising Institute, Inc. calls P-O-P advertising a "mover and shaker." It consummates sales in the store aisle "where money, shopper and product all come together."[9] "As unbelievable as it may sound, in some retail outlets on-the-spot decisions made *inside* the store account for almost two-thirds of all sales."[10]

The 1990s saw the introduction of VideOcart, a system of advertising that puts computer screens on grocery carts. The manufacturer claims the device makes possible a 33 percent average sales increase for brand-name products using the service—and without price promotion.

The stores themselves produce P-O-P advertising when they have signs lettered or printed to call attention to their sales, point directions, mark departments, or urge compliance. There is room even here for innovation. A store in New York put a quiet, neat sign in its window: "Cheer Up. Mark Cross is Having a Sale!" Crouch & Fitzgerald, another New York luggage store, showed this sign dealing with its hours: "Never on Sunday." A Goodrich tire store had some fun with this enigmatic sign in its window: "If It's in Stock, We Have It."

Making the most use of point-of-purchase advertising are the automotive, beverage, food, household goods, personal accessories, and personal products industries. Point-of-purchase advertising serves either as a reminder to buyers, when a product is heavily advertised in another medium, or as a stimulus to impulse buying.

Point-of-purchase advertising dates to the signs used by early tradespeople to identify their various shops. In those days, because people were illiterate, signs featured symbols rather than words. Today we have returned to symbols for many of our signs, especially for our road signs, not because people are illiterate, but because they travel more widely and run into language barriers. Symbols are a universal language. Besides, they can be read more rapidly than words.

One of the most popular store markers of the 1800s was the cigar-store Indian. He stood as a symbol for tobacco shops because it was the Indian who introduced tobacco to the colonists. For their signs, other businesses used larger-than-life mockups of their products: watches, spectacles, keys, boots. The red-and-white barber pole, still seen, managed to bridge the gap between this century and last.

Neon signs made their debut in the 1920s.

Signs continue to be used both outside and inside stores as well as in store windows. They are one form of point-of-purchase advertising. Another form is

A free-standing, three-dimensional sign, designed by Charles Politz, directs potential customers to Marty Zell & Associates, Ltd., a fifth-floor jeweler in downtown Portland, Oregon. The calligraphy and use of type, along with the design of the unit, suggest quality merchandise. Photograph by Alan Hicks.

These four 18″ × 24″ posters can stand alone or fit together to form a mural for store display. Notice that the fourth poster fits onto the first so that the mural can run continuously. Art director: Rick Tharp. Designers: Tharp and Thom Marchionna. Client: BRIO Scanditoy.

the product itself. Another is the container the product comes in. Still another is the carton the containers come in. Sometimes the carton both transports the product and, lid propped up to reveal an advertising message, sells it when it is in the store.

P-O-P comes in an infinite variety of forms. Here are some of them:

Banners	Posters
Bar and fountain units	Racks
Cash register units	Shelf units
Clocks	Signs
Counter units	Sound
Dealer loaders	Store fixtures
Department markers	Tags and labels
Floor stands	Testers
On-product units	Wall units
Overheads	Window displays

P-O-P units can be made temporary or permanent. They can be located inside or outside the stores, lighted, given motion, and treated in other ways.

To design a P-O-P unit, you should know something about the total advertising program, so that you can design it to fit; you should know what the competitors are using in the way of P-O-P; you should know where the unit or units will be used.

Production in P-O-P involves the designing of materials and the supervision of their manufacture.

It all starts with a few rough sketches. A "blank model" follows. A "blank model" is a rough mockup, showing what the unit will look like—in three dimensions, if it is that kind of P-O-P. If the unit is to hold the product as well as advertise it, the designer will need some engineering ability.

When the client approves the "blank model," the designer does a "mechanical" for use by the printer and manufacturer.

The technical nature of P-O-P materials calls for help from special P-O-P production houses. In fact, advertising agencies have little to do with this advertising medium. Because the work is not commissionable, the house designing and producing P-O-P advertising usually deals directly with the advertiser. Harvey Offenhartz in *Point-of-Purchase Design* recommends the establishment of point-of-purchase agencies that would specialize in this kind of advertising.

This P-O-P poster (16″ × 24″) was designed by Bernhardt Fudyma Design Group for Penguin. This one is in black and a second color: maroon. The poster advertises a Chinese-shapes game by demonstrating what can be done with the pieces. An Indian chief tells a Chinese person that "You don't have to be Chinese to like TANGRAM." The line is a takeoff on a famous early slogan for a bread advertised in New York. "You don't have to be Jewish to. . . ."

You don't have to be Chinese to like TANGRAM.

NGRAM: The ancient Chinese shapes game from Penguin

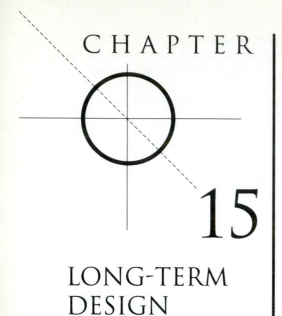

CHAPTER

15

LONG-TERM DESIGN

An impossible deadline may proscribe a designer's producing an ad with any real flair, but never mind—after it has had its few days in the magazines and newspapers, the campaign is over and another one launched. The ad quietly recedes from consciousness, perhaps not even to yellow as a clipping in the files. Nothing to recall the designer's folly.

But one day someone will ask the designer to design a trademark or other item equally enduring. Years later the trademark will haunt the designer from billboard, check, letterhead, package; the logotype from ads forever inside the paper; the book jacket from counters in bookstores and bookshelves in homes; the record cover from bins in record stores and discount drugstores as well; the package from grocers' shelves.

When design is long-term, the designer comes to grips as never before with the principles of typography, spacing, art and color choices, and symbolism. Long-term design requires the services of the most experienced graphic designers, increasingly these days aided by the computer. For some jobs, an industrial designer becomes involved.

Trademarks

Used in commerce well before the time of Christ, trademarks developed to serve two divergent needs. One was the artisan's need for adulation. Just as painters signed each canvas, potters or other skilled artisans developed individual marks that singled their products out from others for a competitive advantage. The other need was for identification so that medieval authorities could trace a product to its maker—to punish the artisan if it was inferior or to keep alien products off the market. To the artisan, the trademark was a desirable or undesirable adjunct of trade, depending upon the circumstances. The who's-responsible-for this? cloud has now largely dissipated, of course; the trademark today is a badge worn proudly.

Printers' marks. The most discussed and honored of the early trademarks are the marks used by printers of incunabula. Originating with Johann Fust and Peter Schöffer, successors to Johannes Gutenberg, the printer's mark from the start was subject to pirating, unprotected as it was by copyright or patent laws. Fust's and Schöffer's obscure-in-meaning but unique insignia on the *Psalterium Latinum,* published at Mainz in 1457, was picked up and used surreptitiously by one printer in 1490 and by some twenty others in the years that followed. Aldus Manutius, the printer-publisher-typographer-scholar of Venice, had a pirating problem with his anchor-and-dolphin symbol, although he acquired some protection from local authorities. This did not stop the counterfeiters outside Italy. Everyone, it seemed, wanted to cash in on the prestige of his Aldine Press. The design was to turn up centuries later as the trademark for that giant American publisher Doubleday & Company, Inc.

The most popular of the early printers' marks was the orb-and-cross, used in various forms until the middle of the sixteenth century, when more elaborate marks came into vogue. The orb-and-cross was a circle with a double-bar cross rising from out of it, suggesting the earth—and faith. (You will find a form of the orb-and-cross surviving on the Nabisco packages of the National Biscuit Company.)

A trademark for the USA film Festival cleverly spells out the USA initials with rolled film. The symbol has the feel of the flag as well. Agency: The Richards Group. Art director and designer: Jack Summerford, Summerford Design, Inc.

OREGON**EYE**ASSOCIATES
SM

Tom Kelly's beautifully simple service mark for Oregon Eye Associates, with its pattern of dots, suggests a lens or pupil.

The post-orb-and-cross period was marked by trademarks "so cluttered with ornament that they could be mistaken for book illustrations . . . trapped in a decorative jungle teeming with allegorical elements, mottos and allusive sentences," one art historian has remarked.[1] The first trademark registered in the United States (in the 1800s for a paint company) was that kind of monstrosity. The design of trademarks from then on could go nowhere but up.

Watermarks. Pioneered by eighth-century Chinese, developed by twelfth-century Arabs, used extensively by fifteenth-century German and Italian printers, paper, a substitute for parchment, made printing on a mass scale possible. Like their fellow artisans, paper makers wanted to put their mark on their product. Quite by accident they found a way to do this. In the papermaking process, pulp sifts over a wire screen. Somehow a bent piece of wire fell on one of these screens, and as the pulp was pressed against the screen to remove excess water, the imprint, an imperfection in texture, was made. Today watermarks add prestige to some papers, particularly the better-quality rag-content bonds.

Coats of arms. The love of medieval rulers for pomp and pageantry ushered in an era of heraldry. Artists of the Dark Ages kept themselves busy designing coats of arms and crests. "We find in heraldry an unlimited sphere of expression throughout an epoch of more than 1,000 years," wrote Ernst Lehner, an admirer of this ancient art.[2]

Heraldry flourished in the twelfth century to help warriors distinguish between friend and foe. Because suits of armor all look pretty much alike, battle leaders designed crests to identify their own soldiers. The marks appealed to civilians, too, and "coats of arms" became popular with all aristocrats. Today the College of Arms, London, decides which English families are entitled to display coats, but no such agency attempts to police heraldry addicts in America.

Cattle brands. Trademarks have some relationship to cattle brands, which date from the medieval custom of putting family marks on everything a family owned. The early-arriving Spaniards first branded cattle on this continent.

Hobo marks. Over the years hoboes developed a special sign-on-fence language as an aid to their fellow travelers. A drawing of a cat, for instance, meant that "a kind lady lives here." A cross meant that "religious talk gets a free meal."

Present-day trademarks. The Industrial Revolution and the introduction of packaging and brand-name advertising stimulated business's use of identification marks in the nineteenth century. The same old pride in the product of one's hands or one's machines was there, but, more important, the mark was needed to assist customers in picking out a widely advertised product from a shelf crowded with competitors' products. The mark as well as the product was advertised; and, if it was well designed, the mark itself on the package did a point-of-purchase advertising job.

Here is how a few modern trademarks evolved.

In London in the 1800s a curio dealer started selling shell-covered boxes to the tourists. As his business prospered, he took on new products: jewels, mainly, and trinkets of various kinds. Eventually he went international, adding barreled kerosene to his offerings, then oil. Because of the early specialty, the dealer adopted a drawing of a shell as an identification mark for his company—and it stuck. It became one of the world's best-known trademarks, despite the fact that buyers would not ordinarily associate a seashell with gasoline.

Another well-known trademark is the Prudential Rock of Gibraltar. The Rock achieved fame as impregnable to sieges when in 1779–1783 the Spaniards failed and failed again to recapture it from the British. It was not until 1896 that the insurance company adopted the Rock as its symbol. But the Rock was still a legend even then. "To associate this known strength with a great financial institution was a happy stroke of advertising skill," one student of trademarks observed. "It is perhaps one of the most effective trademarks ever conceived, as the picture tells the story better than words."[3] Recently, Prudential changed its Rock from representational to abstract art.

Simon & Schuster, the book publisher, patterned its trademark in 1924 after "The Sower," a painting by Jean Frâncôis Millet in 1849. The sower represented a source of knowledge, sowing seeds of inspiration with the printed word. Car-

PURE VIRGIN WOOL

This symbol-only trademark is helped along by some words below. The Wool Bureau, Inc., authorizes its use in ads promoting products made of wool rather than synthetics.

toonists like Charles Addams and Walt Kelly, in their books for Simon & Schuster, did their own versions for the title pages. "The Sower" on the title page of Jerry Della Femina's book on advertising is shown carrying a briefcase.

Similarly, Alfred A. Knopf has shown various versions of its borzoi, and Random House has shown various versions of its house drawing.

The term *trademark* needs to be further refined.

Ordinary trademarks are any name, symbol, or visual device—or combination of these—used by manufacturers to identify their product or products and distinguish them from other products. A mark used by an organization offering a service (an insurance company, for instance, or an appliance repair company) is called a *service mark*. A mark used by a nonprofit organization is called an *insignia, seal,* or *emblem*. A mark used by a trade association (like the American Plywood Association, for instance) that is interested in promoting a certain kind of product rather than the product of a particular manufacturer is called a *collective mark*. A mark used by a testing company to show that a certain product is of a particular quality is called a *certification mark* (the *Good Housekeeping* "seal of approval" is an example). A rendering in type or hand lettering of the name of the sponsor of an advertisement, with or without trademark, is called a *logotype* or *logo*[4] or *signature*.

These various kinds of marks differ not so much in design as in use.

It is easy to confuse *trademark* with *trade name*. A trade name is simply the name of the product or organization; it *may* be in the form of a trademark, or it may be only a word or words to be spoken or printed, like "Liquid Wrench" (a penetrant that loosens rusted bolts and nuts). As graphic designers, we are concerned with the trade name only insofar as it is lettered, arranged, and illustrated.

These are things trademarks do for their owners:

■ *Indicate the origin of the product.* Presumably the manufacturer is proud to claim responsibility.

■ *Guarantee quality consistency.* The trademark tells the prospective buyer that the product is the same as an earlier unit bought and presumably enjoyed.

■ *Serve as an advertisement.* Simple enough to catch attention, complete enough to tell a story, persuasive enough to move the viewer to action, the trademark is an advertisement in miniature.

The same trademark, though not necessarily in a standard size or rendering, can be used on company stationery, invoices and statements, purchase orders, labels, checks, and all advertising. It can also be used on the product itself and its package and on company trucks and buildings. Because it is so widely used and for so many years, the trademark is a matter of no small concern to a company. It would be reasonable to spend months on its design and testing.

What happens to a trademark can't always be imagined or controlled. For close to a hundred years Procter & Gamble Co. has put a small moon-and-stars symbol—an innocuous symbol—on its packages. In the 1980s some groups and individuals decided the symbol carried an evil connotation and so published pamphlets and organized boycotts against P & G products. The company handled as many as 12,000 calls a month from people who had questions about the symbol. It was no laughing matter to P & G, which found it necessary to file libel suits against some of the activists. In 1991 Procter & Gamble redesigned the logo, simplifying it and eliminating curly hairs on the man-in-the-moon's beard that some thought looked like the number 666, which, in the Book of Revelation, is linked to Satan.[5]

Symbolism

Trademarks range from the literal to the symbolic. The more symbolic, the more successful. Obviously, when a design is to be looked at again and again, it has a better chance for long life if viewers do not get tired of it. Symbols wear better than words in trademarks. They also say more.

Long before people learned to write, they created symbols as a means of communicating. To warn, to guide, to announce—they built cairns, marked trees,

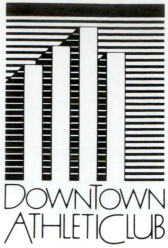

Tom Kelly's symbol for the Downtown Athletic Club, Eugene, Oregon, wonderfully merges downtown buildings with a vertical-bar chart, suggesting the club's appeal to business people. An unusual sans serif type, interestingly spaced, completes the unit.

The flying pig symbol for RFI, a firm offering product review and design consulting, stands for "the flight of inspiration but with wallowing in the mud of reality built in," to use the words of its designer, Byron Ferris, a principal in the firm and a man known to occasionally put his tongue in his cheek.

WOMEN'S
RESOURCE
CENTER

Tom Kelly's symbol for the Women's Resource Center, McKenzie-Willamette Hospital, combines an abstract Laura Ashley pattern with graceful swans, also abstract. The type is a classic roman.

For Artemis, a text and cover paper manufactured by Mohawk Paper Mills, Inc., Cohoes, New York, Leverett Peters designed this attractive insignia. You are looking not at a circle but at a simple ring of *A*s based on a typeface called Optima.

tied knots, piled sticks, and scratched drawings on whatever flat surfaces were available to them. People could represent the sun, they found, with a simple circle, the moon with an arc. At first their drawings were literal, then abstract. The circle became a symbol for warmth and life, the arc a symbol for mystery.

Designers are free to use long-recognized symbols or to establish ones of their own. Designers know that a symbol can convey two different—even opposite—meanings. "Symbols seem to be neutral," designer George Nelson told a conference of the Art Directors Club of New York. "Symbols look to me like a kind of fly paper, to which various associations get stuck. Then the symbol gets to be a real symbol."[6]

The 1970s saw the gradual shift on U.S. highways to symbol rather than word signs, part of an international program to make highway signs quickly understood by everyone, with no language barriers. An arrow pointing left with a diagonal line through it, for instance, means "No left turn." Such signs had earlier been used widely in Europe.

Some of the most common symbols in general use are these:[7]

anchor   hope. This Christian symbol dates to the Apostle Paul, who wrote: "Which hope we have as an anchor of the soul, both sure and steadfast . . ." (Hebrews 6:19, King James version).

circle   eternity (a circle has no end).

cross   Is there a better-known symbol in all the Western world? The vertical stroke originally represented the oneness of God; the horizontal stroke, earth, on which everything moves on the same plane. Combine the two strokes and you have God and earth in harmony.

crown   honor or glory.

dagger   death. A biologist uses a dagger to say "obscure species."

fish   Christ. The initial letters of "Jesus Christ, God's Son, Saviour" in Greek spell the Greek word for *fish*.

heart   affection or love.

lion   strength, courage, majesty.

olive branch   peace.

owl   wisdom.

palm   victory.

pine cone   fertility.

rose   beauty.

scythe or sickle   death.

serpent   evil.

skull   death.

star   supremacy. If six-sided, the Jewish faith.

sun   deity.

swastika   revival and prosperity. *Swastika* is a Sanscrit word meaning "well-being." For American Indians it represented the sun and infinity. Because of Hitler, it took on sinister implications.

umbrella   protection. A latter-day symbol, like many others, it is a paradox. An insurance company thinks enough of it to run it in red in all its advertising, but to cartoonists of the twenties it stood for prohibition, and to cartoonists of the thirties and later, because of Neville Chamberlain, who carried one, it has stood for appeasement.

What's in a Name?

Before the symbol or trademark comes the name. Choosing it can be one of advertising's most important, most creative exercises. The company will be stuck with its name for a long time. Its advertising theme will revolve around it.

The late 1980s saw a rash of name changes among America's corporations to accommodate the various mergers and business expansions. Some of the changes simply reflected a name restlessness and a felt need to reflect a high-tech age. Other changes attempted to shake off bad images.

Anspach Grossman Portugal Inc., a consulting firm, works with organizations in name-change programs. The Salinon Corporation, Dallas, offers ad people a computer software program, Namer by Salinon, that "creates names based on the images and meanings you desire."

Changes often put unwieldy names into shorter versions. Sometimes proper names run together but beginning capitals remain. American Credit Telephone became CardTel.

Sometimes the name is picked for its sound. Picture-takers still ponder the question: What prompted George Eastman way back in 1888 to call his company Kodak? One explanation is the name resulted from Eastman's strange affinity for the letter *K* and his preoccupation with sound effects. The word works like the click of a camera.

The "PAWS" stands for Progressive Animal Welfare Society. Artist-designer Ron Hansen saw the *W* as a paw print.

You have to stay away from real-people names or even names that are associated with real people. A portable toilet manufacturer thought it had the ideal name for its product: Here's Johnny. But Johnny Carson sued and, rightly, won his case against the manufacturer. Most people surely would associate such a name with the introduction to the then host of the "Tonight Show."

Oink Inc., a small firm in Albuquerque, New Mexico, ran into problems with its Lardashe jeans for large women when Jordache complained that the name might be confused with its name. But a court in 1987 found that the parody name could continue. The firm had considered some other names before settling on Lardashe. Calvin Swine and Vidal Sowsoon were two of them.[8]

A name can make all the difference in a product's sale. Take cockroach traps, which are nothing more than glue on paper. A Japanese firm came up with the name Gokiburi Hoy-Hoy ("Hey, hey, cockroaches, come over to my house") for its trap and captured a big part of the market in Japan, where the pests are a real problem. Black Flag in America then introduced Roach Motel, a cigarette-package-size box with the slogan, "Roaches check in, but they don't check out." Sales were impressive. "Saturday Night Live" parodied Roach Motel with a segment on Roach Brothel: "Roaches make out, but they don't get out."[9]

Another pest killer calls itself Snail Jail. A car wax calls itself Rain Dance. A household cleaner calls itself Janitor in a Drum and shows up in an appropriate drum container. An animation company in New York calls itself The Ink Tank. A correction fluid calls itself Boo Boo Goo.

Fashion Conspiracy sells new styles to young women at discount prices. Beyond Conception sells maternity clothes. A store for large women calls itself Renoir's Lady. Olga makes a bra it calls Secret Hug. It is "an embrace of Lycra lace that softly stretches to fit you in beautiful comfort."

Sometimes the cleverness in a name is for insiders only. A used-car dealer calls itself Somewhere West of Laramie, the title of a classic ad that only an advertising major would recognize. Some products take on names that segregate buyers. Probably not many adults like stepping up to a candy counter and asking for a Hershey's Whatchamacallit, a bar that advertises itself in magazines like *Sports Illustrated for Kids*.

Some names turn out to be clauses or sentences. Love My Carpet is a carpet cleaner. I Can't Believe It's Not Butter! is a margarine. Some names cause a double take: Courtesy Auto Wreckers, in San Francisco.

That so many names of service companies begin with *A* is no accident. Everybody scrambles to be first in Yellow Pages listings. Ace, Acme, and Ajax are so common that cartoonists use them freely, knowing that they cannot be sued.

Some names make enemies among customers and consumer groups. The year 1978 saw the introduction by Yves Saint Laurent of $100-an-ounce Opium perfume to America's affluent, after a year of success in France. And what is such a choice of name if not a celebration of drug taking? Does not the manufacturer or its agency have some kind of responsibility to the public to refrain from glamorizing that kind of activity? The American Coalition Against Opium and Drug Abuse formally objected to the name in 1979 as an insult to Chinese people, but the product was still being pushed years later. A headline bragged: "Never Has a Perfume Evoked Such Emotion."

And what about names picked with no thought of expansion? Surely Frigi-

For his logo for Dolphin Press, artist-designer Ron Hansen fills in a *D* to make room for a graceful, playful dolphin.

VICKI GRIFFITHS

Ron Hansen takes two letters from this name set in a classic roman and gives them swashes to give the logo grace and make it stand out.

daire for its stoves, Hotpoint and Whirlpool for their refrigerators, and Toastmaster for its power tools have had second thoughts about their choice of names.

"Is it my imagination, or are car names getting stupider?" asks Jacob Weisberg in *The New Republic*. "Two that amuse me especially are the Ford Probe, which I imagine on its way to a congressional hearing on auto safety, and the Honda Prelude, which sounds like it ought to be driven by Wordsworth or J. S. Bach. . . . But my favorite . . . is the Daihatsu Charade. What happens when it collides with a [Mitsubishi] Mirage is for the insurance company to determine."[10]

The computer has helped many corporations come up with names that are easy to remember, that don't conflict with existing names, and that don't carry undesirable meanings in other countries or in other languages. Some trade names come from parts of several names. Dyazide, a drug for high blood pressure, comes from "diuretic," a term for something that reduces fluid in the body, and "hydrochlorothiazide," one of the drug's ingredients.

Martin Mayer in *Whatever Happened to Madison Avenue?* reports that E. J. Korvette, the discount operation, took its name from Eight Jewish Korean War Veterans who founded it. Gatorade took its name from the Gators' football team at the University of Florida, where research led to the development of the beverage.

Sometimes something happens or events change to make a carefully-thought-out name inappropriate. When "gay" became a synonym for "homosexual," a Northwest men's store decided to change from The Gay Blade to simply The Blade. Ayds, an "appetite suppressant candy," faced a crisis when AIDS (Acquired Immune Deficiency Syndrome) cropped up as a serious disease in the United States. AID Insurance Co., Des Moines, Iowa, decided in 1985 to change its name because of the unpleasant association the all-caps word then had.

Designing the Trademark

It was a school child responding to a $5 prize contest in 1916 in Suffolk, Virginia, who, inspired by one of Palmer Cox's Brownies, designed the monocled, high-hatted Mr. Peanuts. At one time trademark design could be left to people entering contests. Today too much rests on the design to entrust it to anyone but an experienced designer. Even back then Planters' Peanuts hired a commercial artist to revise the child's entry.

From a design standpoint, a trademark must be:

- *original,*
- *legible,*
- *stimulating,*
- *appropriate to the product,*
- *easy to remember.*

The trademark can take these forms:

- *symbol,*
- *type (or lettering),*
- *a combination of the two.*

Symbol-only marks. Symbol-only marks come in varying degrees of subtlety, from portraits or drawings of the founder or a deceased U.S. president (living presidents and deceased presidents with living widows are taboo) to stripes of color. No living person can be portrayed without that person's consent, of course; and if the mark is to be registered, a depiction of the flag or a drawing that is "immoral" would not be permitted.

Animals stand near the front of the symbol line. Some of the best known are Mobil Oil Company's put-to-pasture but still-remembered flying red horse (designed by Jim Nash, who also did the smiling Quaker for Quaker Oats); Mack Truck's bulldog; Greyhound's greyhound; Hartford's stag; and MGM's lion.

An English bull terrier, Spuds MacKenzie, became a popular symbol or mascot

Old Rugged Cross Press, a new religious book publisher in Alpharetta, Georgia, uses this well-designed logo in various sizes in all its advertising. Art director: Andy Daley. Design by Image Concept.

LONG-TERM DESIGN

in the late 1980s for Anheuser-Busch, appearing in TV commercials and on T-shirts, and creating something of a stir because, some charged, the dog encouraged beer drinking among the young.

The symbol-only trademark is the ultimate in design, but it is the hardest to attach successfully to a product. Nike has done well with its Swoosh, but only with massive promotion. For almost everyone, a red cross means only one organization; that eye symbol on television (designed by the late William Golding) is seen often enough that there is little danger of its being associated with any network other than CBS. But not all products or organizations lend themselves to trademarks so abstract.

Type-only marks. The typeface or lettering trademark can involve made-up words (like "Kodak") or dictionary words, personal names, or geographic names. Initials can take the form of monograms and are easiest to handle when the letters involved are those with symmetrical round or triangular shapes—the *O*s, *V*s, *W*s, and *M*s, particularly. Volkswagen shows the possibilities with its sans serif *V* over a *W*.

Among the many fine examples of work shown in *Ideas on Design* (Faber and Faber, London and Boston, 1986) are type-only marks like the ones on this page. The logos and all the other examples in the book, which covers all kinds of graphic design, are the work of designers in the London, New York, and San Francisco studios of Pentagram, one of the world's premier design organizations.

What you see here proves that subtle manipulation of letters and even punctuation can bring memorable and durable results. You don't need to add drawings or photographs.

The *S* with its merging directions, is for the Scottish Trade Centre, an organization that brings manufacturers and buyers together. The thick and thin strokes, reminiscent of the old Scotch Roman typeface, add character to the letter, and the arrowheads, a cliché in the hands of a less sophisticated designer, serve as interior serifs. The slant of the stroke beginning along with the back edges of the arrowheads forms a diagonal axis. Designers: David Hillman and Sarah Pine.

The pattern of black boxes, forming a *T* when some of them are tipped, serves as a symbol for Tactics, a brand of men's toiletries from Shiseido of Japan. To Pentagram's designers, "Tactics" suggested a game; hence the checkerboard. Designers: Mervyn Kurlansky and Lora Starling.

The "Eva" symbol is for a printer with that name. Again, we encounter a cliché: starting a proper name with a lowercase letter. But the cliché works here because it sets the stage for using the same *e* in mirror reverse as a stand-in for

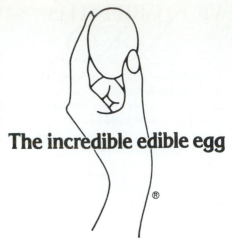

The incredible edible egg

The logo used by the American Egg Board, done in line for easy reproduction in any size, features a slogan that crosses through the art without detracting from the art or hurting the type's readability. Used by permission.

Pentagram, one of the world's most respected design studios, does all kinds of design, including logos. These particular examples show that letters alone—and even punctuation marks—can do the job. Details in the accompanying text matter.

The logo for M&M Stables, Murray, Kentucky, run in reverse, like this, or in colors on a white background, features abstract initials and a graceful, abstract horse, created by Joe Rigsby with an economy of uniform-thickness, unconnected lines.

a at the end. Pentagram calls this design "economic use of typography." The two *e*'s nicely sandwich the *v*, and extra-tight spacing gives the symbol a modern touch. The typeface has the feel of Times Roman, a beautiful typeface in display size as well as in body-copy size, the size we more often see it in. Notice how high-waisted the *e* is. Designer: Alan Fletcher.

"Napoli" is for a poster for the Napoli '99 Foundation, established to create awareness of the city's problems and to enlist help in restoring cultural monuments and social pride. The handsome classic roman letters in all caps, letters we associate with old Italy, are themselves deteriorating. The challenge here was to chop away at the letters just enough to establish the mood but not enough to destroy the elegance or ruin readability. Designer: John McConnell.

The final example is perhaps the most inventive. It appeared on a calendar produced by Face Photosetting. "This was the year of the punctuation mark." Designer: John McConnell.

Combination marks. Combinations of symbols and lettering are the most serviceable and most-often-used trademarks. The layout artist using an already designed trademark as an element to arrange can make a "combination" mark out of a "symbol-only" mark by putting another element—the name set in type—next to the trademark.

Of whatever kind, the mark can fit into a circle, oval, triangle, square, rectangle, diamond, or shield, but often such shapes become intrusive. Some of the best marks form their own silhouette.

Because a trademark might appear in various sizes, the designer should use stroke thicknesses that can take both enlargement and reduction.

The designer picks a typeface for the trademark not so much for the face itself but for how the letters needed will lend themselves to the design. That the name has letters with descenders—letters like *g* and *y*—can influence the choice. "A word with no descenders tends to look more stable. . . . That little descender is a costly thing, too. It takes up more newspaper space [in ads], for example," says Joe Selame of Selame Design, Newton Lower Falls, Massachusetts.[11]

To keep a trademark from becoming dated too soon, you should avoid the following:

- *Unusual typefaces that happen to be popular at the moment.* Scripts, for instance, fail to pass the test of time. Romans and well-designed sans serifs are best.
- *Pictures of people in modern dress.* The width of the lapel, the length of the dress, the hairstyle—after a few years these will have to be changed if the mark is to do its job. Period costume is something else again; if the company feels it is appropriate to its product now, it likely will be appropriate in the future.
- *Background props that would date the trademark: automobiles, appliances, and the like.* Keeping the mark simple would automatically take care of this.

Legal Considerations

Hawaiian Airlines combines highly stylized thematic art with unusual type, hand drawn, for its logo.

The Lanham Act of 1946 (known as the Trade-mark Act), which went into effect in 1947, provides the legal basis on the federal level for registering of trademarks and seeking redress when trademark rights are violated.

The U.S. Patent Office houses registration papers on some three-quarters of a million trademarks, and state agencies have records on many others. Additional thousands appear on packages and in advertising without benefit of registration.

A small ® placed inconspicuously on the mark shows that it has been registered. To be registered, the trademark cannot appropriate a common word like "Fresh" or "Big" or "Good," put a graphic fence around it, and expect to keep trespassers away. Before adopting a new trademark, the company will want to check it with its lawyers to make sure it conforms with both federal and state regulations. At the national level, someone will have to check both the Principal

Register and the Supplemental Register in the U.S. Patent Office to make sure no other organization is using the mark in substantially the same form.

A well-known trademark occasionally finds itself used by another advertiser, not always to its advantage. To announce an increase in its audience for its news program, Channel 7 in New York, a non-CBS station, ran a full-page ad in *New York* showing the CBS eye slightly closed with a big tear dripping from it. The ad said, "Some of the . . . [new viewers] must have come from Channel 2 [a CBS station]." *Penthouse,* the magazine challenging *Playboy,* has run an altered version of the *Playboy* bunny in some of its ads directed to media buyers.

The legal implications of using—or even *mis*using—another firm's trademark are not always clear. The designer should do some checking with a lawyer first.

Parker Bros. in the 1980s found that "Monopoly" was too common a name to tie up for a game when a U.S. circuit court of appeals decided that "Anti-Monopoly," a game by another company, was not a trademark infringement.

It is possible to do such a thorough job promoting a trademark (and trade name) that the name becomes generic and falls into public domain, as aspirin did. Companies now know that the best way to protect identity is to use the proper name as an adjective: Bayer Aspirin, for instance, and DuPont Cellophane, and to insist on capitalization of the full name in editorial and news columns as well as in all company advertising. Coca-Cola (or Coke) is one of several firms campaigning almost monotonously, but understandably, to get editors and writers to use uppercase when mentioning the product.

It is also possible to lose control of a trademark (and name) by making it descriptive rather than merely suggestive. If some of today's trademarks seem descriptive, it is because they were well established before laws became stringent.

The owner of a trademark ordinarily can hold a name only for one kind of product. As a name, Cadillac is attached to products other than the high-priced automobile, possibly to the chagrin of General Motors. There is *Life* magazine and there was a cigarette with the unlikely same name. Then came Life cereal.

Any kind of description makes for what the lawyers call a "weak" trademark, and a "weak" trademark, to be protected, is likely to involve its owner in litigation. A picture of the product makes for a "weak" trademark, too; other makers of the product can hardly be forced to refrain from picturing their products in their trademarks if they feel such picturing is desirable.

For protection against pilfering, owners of marks used in interstate and international business register their marks with the U.S. Patent Office. Some firms doing only intrastate business register their marks with an appropriate state agency. But the designer looking to other trademarks for "inspiration" should remember that even if the mark is not registered, the courts are likely to decide for the original owner in any suit over ownership.

Above: William Korbus's *N* symbol for the Nebraska Educational Television Network—a symbol that preceded NBC's *N* symbol, much to the embarrassment of NBC. Below: The educational network's new symbol, adopted after NBC made an out-of-court settlement for the *N.* Art director: William Korbus. Designer: Michael Buettner.

Corporate Identity Programs

Big companies feel compelled to establish "corporate identity" programs. More than just the trademark is involved. The typical program modernizes and standardizes all corporation design—business stationery, advertising, packaging, building and vehicle colors and signs, uniforms, and other units. For some companies, elaborate books are prepared, giving instructions to various branch plants and offices on how and where to use the new symbols and typography. Not only do companies change these; they sometimes adopt new names, being burdened with names inadequate or inappropriate to fields into which they have expanded.

Much of the design work appears to be beyond the scope of the firms' advertising agencies. These are jobs for "image consultants" like Lippincott & Margulies, Inc., and Unimark Corp. for Design & Marketing.

One of the most interesting corporate redesign cases involved a TV network and an educational station. In 1975 NBC decided to retire its peacock trademark, which, after seventeen years, had lost its significance. When it was adopted, TV color was a novelty. The magazine [*More*] announced that the bird with the brilliant plumage that unfolded at the start of each color program would be

Ron Hansen's symbol for a series of Purple Turtle Books called "Animal Squares" puts four animals into abstraction and into squares.

"relegated to the corporate trademark limbo now inhabited by Little Nipper, listening for 'His Master's Voice'—the symbol of NBC's parent company RCA."

Lippincott & Margulies stepped forward to work out a new design, taking a year or so to research and produce it. The firm settled on the single letter *N,* causing *U&lc.,* a typography publication, to speculate with some amusement: "Did extensive research studies show that the letters 'BC' are outdated since they refer to a period over one thousand nine hundred and seventy-six years ago?" NBC explained that the single-letter design helped separate NBC from the other two television networks. And *N,* besides being the first letter in the corporate initials, was also the only one neither of the other networks had.[12]

This was no ordinary *N.* It was an *N* built from two trapezoids, one red, one blue—an *N* solid enough to allow photography and art effects to evolve inside. The only trouble with it was that another organization, the Nebraska Educational Television Network, had one just like it, except for the color.

Since the big organization must spend hundreds of thousands of dollars in fees and printing costs to switch to a new logo, NBC was, understandably, nervous about the matter after the duplication was called to its attention. There was no question that the Nebraska network's *N* had been put into use before NBC unveiled its version. It was not a matter of plagiarism. No one charged that. The duplication was accidental. Two widely separated designers independently arrived at a logical design solution. Even by checking state and federal registers of trademarks a designer cannot be sure that a new mark—or something close to it—is not in use somewhere.

NBC, after its huge investment of time and money, had no choice but to arrange an out-of-court settlement with the Nebraska Educational Television Network: $55,000 in cash and $500,000 worth of new and used television equipment.

The press, which delights in reporting TV embarrassments, had a field day with this story. It had the right ingredient: Tiny educational network gets the better of giant corporation. But what caught the reporters' interest most, perhaps, was the disparity between what the educational network paid for its logo (an estimated $100) and what NBC paid (an estimated $750,000).

It was not a fair comparison, though. NBC executives told *Advertising Age* that comparing the educational network's costs to NBC's costs was like comparing apples to oranges. NBC paid for "a whole corporate identification program." Such a program includes elaborate instructions, with layouts and grids, showing exactly how and where the insignia is to be used on stationery, trucks, building walls, and so on. The company gets what Margulies of Lippincott & Margulies calls a "system," not just a logo or trademark.

The cash settlement to the Nebraska Educational Television Network would, among other things, finance the designing of a new logo. A story going around Nebraska had it that Bill Korbus, the NETN staff artist who designed the original N, was asked what kind of a new design he would come up with, and he answered: "I was thinking of a sort of eye symbol. . . ."

In 1986, NBC dropped the *N* logo, which had been modified to include a stylized version of the peacock, to go to a flat, abstract peacock with six feathers instead of eleven. Chermayeff & Geismar Associates created the new design.

Stephen Wm. Snider designed this logo, which effectively converts a letter into an object.

Designer Fred Caravetta of Caravetta, Allen, Kimbrough designs his own letters here, with swashes turning into waves, to act as a logo for Norwegian Caribbean Lines.

Logotypes

The logotype is the type or lettering, carried usually at the bottom of the ad, that names the sponsor. Sometimes it incorporates a trademark or insignia into its design. It is in retail advertising where logotypes get the most use. The retailer refers to the logotype as the "signature" or "sig cut."

The principles of design applying to trademarks also apply to logotypes. Yet most logotypes for retailers look as though they were designed not by designers but by show-card writers. The scripts so preferred by fashion houses and some department stores are tight and angular rather than loose and graceful. The gothics of the discount houses and appliance stores are fat and foolish; and to make matters worse, they are tilted, arched, put into perspective, buried in dots and stars and sunbursts and lines of type.

That each logotype has a specific audience to reach and that in many cases the audience is the bargain-basement crowd suspicious of white space and Garamond cannot be denied. One cannot insist that all logotypes look as if they came off the Trajan column of ancient Rome. One can suggest, however, that well-designed, standard types in their normal settings can do anything typographic experiments by tasteless amateurs can do, and without tiring and offending the reader. Ideally, logotypes should be hand lettered by qualified lettering artists who understand letterform; but a perfectly acceptable logotype can be put together by a designer using a computer.

Elements that may be included are the store name, kind of store, address, phone number, hours, and slogan. The big store needs no address in the logotype; the name alone may be the logotype.

In national ads, as opposed to retail ads, a logotype is usually smaller and more subtle. It is also referred to, usually, as a "logo" rather than a "logotype." "Logo" has grown in meaning in recent years to include all kinds of symbols, art pieces, and designs. Magazine nameplates are "logos."

Helmut Krone, art director at Doyle Dane Bernbach, does not like logos in ads, especially national or brand-name ads. "[A logo] . . . says 'I'm an ad. Please turn the page.'" How does he keep clients from insisting that he include a logo? "There's a way of keeping the bottom of the page so clean and effective that they can't—they don't dare—put a logo in." But he always carefully works the name into the ad so that the reader will know what brand to buy or what store to visit.[13]

Trademark and Logo Redesign

"Corporate heraldry," *Time* called it, and noted an increase in it due partly to reorganizations, mergers, and name changes. One of the most important of the logo designers and redesigners is Lippincott & Margulies, which has created several thousand logos for such companies as Xerox, RCA, and Uniroyal.

"Big business graphics probably is the only art form in our time that is both uncompromisingly modern and genuinely popular," a writer in *Time* has noted.[14]

It is natural that a trademark should change after years of use. Sometimes the change is gradual. But more often, the trademark change is sudden, because companies get used to their trademarks and do not notice they have become completely outdated. Then it dawns on them.

Not everyone likes what is happening to America's trademarks. One dissenting voice comes from Barbara Knight, a collector of old trademarks. She

Max's, a Westport, Connecticut, art-supplies store, uses a logo that crosses drawing and painting tools to form an "X." Designer: James Williams.

The John Deere trademark has changed gradually from clutter in 1876, when it first appeared, to simplicity, keeping up with the times.

A nameplate or flag for a publication of the Oregon Research Institute develops from the use of both Aldus FreeHand and Adobe Illustrator. The illustration was scanned and then redrawn (electronically traced) in PostScript to better define the detail in the silhouette. This "screen capture" does not reflect the clarity of the eventual printing. Art director and designer: Barbara Littman of Information Design Northwest.

thinks the trend toward modernizing and even dropping familiar trademarks is robbing the country of a folk art. The old marks, she says in an article written for the American Institute of Graphic Arts, were often "picked up from paintings, comic strips, encyclopedias, children's sketches. Some were concepts; some commissioned or designed; but most just happened, and many companies don't know quite how. Their records don't contain such information."[15]

Writing in *New York,* Tom Wolfe, after his experience as a judge in an American Institute of Graphic Arts awards competition, pondered why abstract logos or trademarks, even though they did not identify as well as, say, Coca-Cola's script or the Alfred A. Knopf borzoi, were popular with corporate executives. He concluded it was because "the conversion of a total-design abstract logo formation somehow makes it possible for the head of the corporation to tell himself: 'I'm modern, up to date, with it, a man of the future. I've *streamlined* this old baby.' Why else would they have their companies pour $30,000, $50,000, $100,000 into the concoction of symbols that any student at Pratt could and would gladly give him for $125 plus a couple of lunches at the Trattoria, or even the Zum Zum? The answer: if the fee doesn't run into five figures, he doesn't feel streamlined. Logos are strictly a vanity industry, and all who enter the field should be merciless cynics if they wish to guarantee satisfaction."[16]

Saul Bass echoed Wolfe's sentiments. Symbols have become sterile, he said. They are cold. They are too abstract. "I can't think of any corporation that can't use some expression of responsiveness to human needs, and to the society in which it exists."[17]

Despite any great effort on the designer's part to produce a memorable trademark, two conditions beyond design determine the effectiveness of that mark.

One is the extent of its use. A trademark is not effective or valuable unless it is used widely. A poorly designed trademark fully exploited is more effective than a beautifully designed trademark only half exploited. The main goal of the trademark, after all, is to be recognized.

The other factor is the character of the company behind the mark.

Book Jackets

A book jacket's function is primarily to advertise the product and only secondarily to protect it from sun and dust. But so conditioned have book buyers become to this form of advertising that when a jacket is missing or torn, the value of the

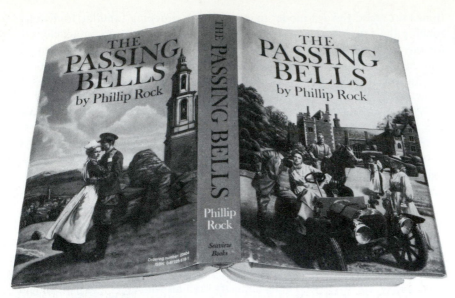

The back cover of a book jacket usually carries a photograph of the author and an author's blurb. But this Seaview Books back cover repeats the front cover title and author's name and gives the reader a new piece of bleed-all-around art. What happened was this: The publisher could not decide which Rowena Morrill painting it liked best, so it used both of them. "We decided to let the booksellers choose which side to display," said advertising director Morrie Goldfischer.

book plummets. The bookseller has to mark down the price and throw the book on the clearance table. In the college bookstore the "text" edition of a book may differ from a more expensive "trade" edition only in that it is without a jacket.

What is there about the jacket that makes it so valuable? Mainly information—about the book's contents and about the author; but also *design*. And pattern, beauty, color. It is less costly to provide all this on a paper jacket than on a cloth cover.

A bonus value of a good jacket was pointed out by a panel of book reviewers at the Trade Book Clinic of the American Institute of Graphic Arts. These people agreed that the design of the book—and this would include the jacket—helps the book-review editor decide whether or not to review the book.

A book jacket designer tries to make five panels—the front, the back, the spine, and two inside flaps—into a unified whole that (1) captures the spirit of the book and (2) convinces the browser to buy. The two inside flaps are the least important panels. Some designers do not even deal with them. They are left to the publisher to make a last-minute sales pitch in a long copy block. Ideally, the flaps would be designed with the covers and spine to make a unified whole.

The most important single panel may well be the spine. Aside from a few best sellers, most books in the stores are stacked or stand front-to-back, on shelf after shelf, so that only their spines show. A readable spine may be a book's only chance.

From a design standpoint, there is not much you can do in a space that is half an inch to an inch deep. So you settle for good, clean, colorful, heavy type. You study books on the shelf and try to come up with a combination of type and color that will stand out.

The spine contains three elements: title, author, and publisher (and perhaps the publisher's trademark). For thin books, the type must run sideways; sideways type is more readable on the shelf when it starts at the bottom and runs to the top, but most publishers seem to prefer that the type start at the top. It is not a good idea to be different here, because then the customer would be forced into a contortion to read your particular title. For thicker books, the type can be arranged in normal left-to-right fashion, but in short takes. A condensed type often is required. Word separation is allowed. No matter how the type is arranged on the spine, only last names for the author and publisher need to be used.

Of course, the front cover will get major attention from the designer. For important books, the front cover will be crucial; even for lesser books, once the spine has captured attention, the front cover will take over to develop interest. If a book is to be advertised, the front cover of the jacket is what will be pictured. This means that the colors and tones and sizes must be chosen so that when the jacket is reduced in size for the ad and limited to black-and-white reproduction, the important elements will be readable.

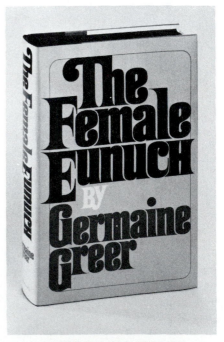

S. Neil Fujita's beautifully drawn and arranged letters are art enough for this book jacket. The book title is in black; the author's name is in purple; the "By" is reversed in a gold background. The book was published by McGraw-Hill Book Company.

The front cover and spine of a paperback book usually work as a poster, with the back cover being reserved for copy. As "packages," paperback book covers (or back covers) have to put up with universal product codes, which often strike a discordant note. Matt Teppler art directed this handsome cover; Martha Sedgwick did the design. Avon Books was the publisher.

The publisher will decide what to feature most prominently on the cover—the title or the author's name. If the author has a wide following, the name may call for the largest type—and it may be the largest element—on the cover. If the name is placed above the title, the word "By" is omitted.

Artwork takes a secondary role to type on book jackets. In this regard, book jackets differ from most other forms of print advertising. But the type, carefully chosen or drawn, ingeniously spaced and prominently displayed, *becomes* art for the book jacket. Usually two colors are used. Only the subsidy publishers—the "vanity publishers"—seem willing to settle for a single color on the jacket these days. And that is to keep their hapless authors, who must pay the publishing costs, from being overwhelmed by the charges.

Elements that must be included on the front cover are the book's title and the author's full name. Elements that might be added include some identification of the author; the title of another of the author's works; a blurb or some description of the book; some art. *The Dictionary of Jargon* by Jonathan Green used a drawing of an ear encased in a question mark (the two are similarly shaped when the ear is on a head facing to the left) on its jacket. It was a good symbol to suggest that the book demystifies occupational slang.

The cover of *The Bronx Zoo* by Sparky Lyle, ace relief pitcher, and Peter Golenbock, showed a baseball with a mustache on it. The symbol nicely represented Lyle, whose story the book told.

The more clutter, the less appeal the cover will have to the sophisticated buyer; and here is a field where customers have a greater degree of sophistication than usual. Of course, some books are not meant for sophisticates; as in all graphic design, the artist will slant the work to the audience.

The back cover is usually reserved for information about the author, perhaps with a picture; or for information on other books offered by the publisher; or for quotes from reviewers who had something good—and promotable—to say about the book. Room must be reserved here for a bar code. It is not necessary that the front cover, spine, and back cover be a wraparound; that is, an art device is not needed to hold all three panels together. Unity can be achieved through judicious use of type and repetition of color.

The inside front flap carries the name of the book again (but in smaller type), a copy block describing the book, and the price (in the upper right or lower right corner so it can be clipped off by gift buyers). The inside back flap carries a continuation of the book description and, if it is not carried on the back cover, a rundown on the author. The publisher's name runs on either the inside front or the back flap. If color is used, it is available for the flaps without extra charge (the flaps are printed on the same run with the covers), but it is not a good idea to use it lavishly here; you do not want to diminish your cover impact.

The layout should be done actual size, without margins, in the manner of direct-mail roughs (see chapter 13). The front cover panels are the same size as the book itself; the flaps are usually a little more than half the width of the cover, except for oversize books, for which the flaps are proportionately smaller. The size of the spine panel cannot be determined until a dummy copy of the book is bound; but at the beginning layout stage it can be estimated. For final production, of course, sizes have to be exact; to be off as little as an eighth of an inch could make the spine unreadable or cause some of the cover to disappear into the flap.

Ink color and paper stock are problems to consider at an early stage. A light-colored jacket makes a book look larger than it is; a dark jacket or a jacket with a border around the front cover makes the book look smaller. Books on display in sunny windows end up with faded jackets, particularly if the colors used are pale blues, pale pinks, and mauves. Smooth paper is best for jackets, because rough paper, with its "valleys" that trap dirt, becomes soiled more easily; books put up with an unconscionable amount of pawing during their normal two-year life span in the bookstores. If a coated paper is used, the stock should be polished on only one side; otherwise, the jacket will be slippery against the book. And the grain of the paper should run down the spine, not across it.

The front cover of the jacket is always slightly larger than the page size, to fit the cover board, which, of course, overhangs the pages.

Despite the rules, there is still room for experimentation for uniqueness. Alexander King's first popular book, *Mine Enemy Grows Older,* came with two jackets, both designed by Ben Feder Inc. The outside jacket, featuring a full-color painting of a hideous character, King, played a viola that looked shockingly like the back of a nude woman, carried this note: "If this jacket (the author painted it) is too strong for you, take it off. There's a conservative jacket for conservative people underneath." The underneath jacket was of a more standard design: all type, centered, with no illustration.

Nancy Etheridge, art director at E. P. Dutton, designed a jacket for Edward Topol's novel, *Red Snow,* that was so unusual she took out a patent for it. It involved a transparent polyvinyl chloride pocket filled with white stage snow of the kind found in glass balls with Christmas scenes. When the jacket was moved, the book buyer got the impression of snowflakes falling.

Some graphic designers specialize in book jackets, doing them on a freelance basis.

He's not known to the general public (who looks at the credit lines on a book jacket?), but among his fellow designers Paul Bacon has earned applause for his covers and jackets of some 4,000 books, including Robin Cook's *Coma,* E. L. Doctorow's *Ragtime,* and Henry Kissinger's *White House Years.* What makes Bacon popular with book publishers' art directors is his versatility (he draws, he designs, he does lettering when he doesn't find the right typeface) and his thorough reading of a book to find appropriate symbolism.

The book jacket he did for Ira Levin's *Compulsion* brought him first fame among book designers.[18]

Most artists and designers take a lot of direction in this field, but some veterans, like Paul Bacon, are given a free hand. Some handle the type or hand lettering as well as the art.

Designing covers for paperbacks—mass paperbacks and the more expensive trade paperbacks—is much like designing jackets for hardbound books. Mass paperbacks, especially, put great emphasis on cover art. The art, according to Len Leone, former art director for Bantam Books, has to be "spectacular."[19] It may take a series of comps and several meetings between the art director and artist before the job is finished.

Trina Robbins uses an airbrush to create her art for the jacket of her book, *Catswalk: The Growing of Girl,* published by Celestial Arts, Berkeley. The lettering was done using Ventura Publisher software. Designer: Ken Scott.

A poster advertising Trina Robbins' book, for use in bookstores, shows the jacket art in its original state, as a single piece. The poster shows two pieces from inside the book, too. Poster designer: Hal Hershey.

Album Covers

"The letters CD are not only an abbreviation for Compact Disc. They also stand for the Certain Death of the twelve-inch album cover," observes *Rolling Stone,* which, in 1991, devoted a special issue to "The 100 Greatest Album Covers of All Time." "With the forced retirement of the long-playing vinyl record has come the end of a dynamic era in rock art, in which the marketing needs of the record industry and the renegade aesthetics of rock 'n' roll came together in a remarkable, often spectacular visual marriage that was part collision, part collusion."

Admitting that album cover design was already an art before the Beatles and the Rolling Stones, especially for jazz albums, the magazine argues that it took rock 'n' roll to take design decisions away from "the suits" and give it to the performing artists.

While a case could be made against the amateur in graphic design, the reader of that issue could find some remarkable examples among the 100 covers reproduced. The Number 1 design, chosen by the magazine, was the art used for the Beatles' 1967 *Sgt. Pepper's Lonely Hearts Club Band* album. A complicated collage of various characters in a head-on pose, hand tinted, it was the work of Peter Blake, a photographer of London rock society. "Blake's design has since become one of the most parodied images in rock history," the magazine points out.

Another cover to make *Rolling Stone's* "Top Ten" was the one for *Blind Faith* (1969, before the lunar landing) showing Bob Seidemann's photograph of a young nude holding a space ship to symbolize "the fruit of the tree of life" and "the fruit of the tree of knowledge." ". . . Within months . . . Seidemann's . . . cover was a collector's item." Another "Top Ten" album (for *The Velvet Underground,* 1967) featured an Andy Warhol banana on the cover which, in the original, could be peeled to change color from yellow to pink.

The art created for these albums is worth a great deal of money today. The original ribald cartoon art of Robt. Crumb that was used for Big Brother & the Holding Company's *Cheap Thrills* album (1968) recently brought $21,000 at a Sotheby's auction.[20]

Many of the old album covers utilized gimmicks of one kind or another. Some included additional compartments, folded into portrait stands, took on other than square shapes, used exotic paper stock, carried mirrors or other paste-ons as well as poster inserts. Alice Cooper's *School's Out* album yielded a record wrapped in something approximating a woman's undergarment. The Rolling Stones' *Sticky Fingers* album had a real zipper built into the cover, over an Andy Warhol photograph of a pair of pants. A clever idea, but the zipper handle pressed against the records and caused some damage. DJs getting advanced copies complained. Jacket designer Craig Braun told Dugald Stermer: "Then I got one of my best ideas: Unzip so that the handle would fall over the label. Nobody cares about scratched labels. I wish I had filmed the scene: hundreds of ladies . . . unzipping millions of flies."[21]

The gimmick is not dead, even in a CD age. When it sent out copies of Ice-T's controversial *Body Count* albums to radio stations, Time Warner enclosed them in miniature body bags, an extra outrage to those who objected to the lyrics of one of the songs, "Cop Killer," which contained, among other offensive lines, "Die, Pig, Die!" According to *Time,* Time Warner explained away the bags by saying that they were "in keeping with the theme of the album, which includes cuts warning about the dangers of drug use and gang warfare."[22]

Elements to be arranged in designing an album cover include a picture of the performer, title of the album, and whatever additional art may be called for. The new, smaller formats seriously affect the design. There is less playing with type and more emphasis placed on photographs. The design has to be bolder and simpler.

The small space also causes retailers a problem when they prepare their newspaper ads: CD album covers don't allow adequate display of songs included. Often the covers must be redesigned for this use, squeezing the art to allow necessary listing of songs. The design for record packaging involves many compromises.

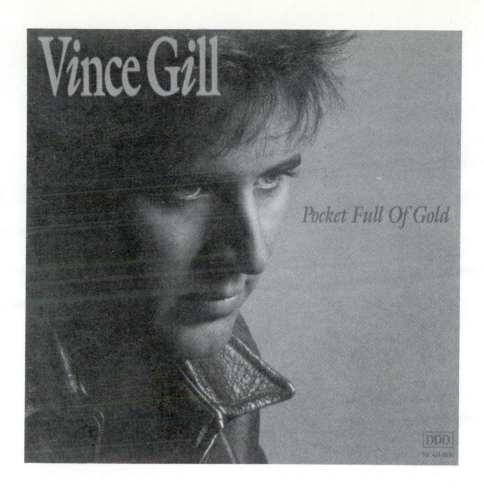

Pocket Full Of Gold

MCA Records makes a slight adjustment in cropping and type placement in the design of its *Vince Gill: Pocket Full of Gold* album design to create both the CD booklet and the long box housing the disc. Note the unusual combination of upright and italic letters in the "Vince Gill." Art direction and design by Katherine DeVault; photography by McGuire. © 1991 MCA Inc. Used with permission.

Like other advertisers and packagers, record companies, especially with budget releases, figure out ways to cut album costs. For its *Original Chess Masters* series of re-releases on CDs, MCA Records produced regular 5¾″ × 12½″ boxes with only logos and generic information imprinted. Die cut squares on the fronts and backs allowed potential readers to see and read the album cover and the back cover with its song listings.

Packages

Not many remember the cracker-barrel days when foods like flour, sugar, and coffee were sold in bulk. Yet, packaging is a rather recent phenomenon in the United States. The idea of individual units, wrapped for protection and convenience of handling, gained momentum only in the late part of the last century.

One early packager was a St. Paul, Minnesota, grocer who, in looking for a name for an expensive blended syrup he was about to market, thought of his boyhood hero, Abraham Lincoln. "Lincoln" as a name might not be appropriate, but "Log Cabin," almost synonymous with "Lincoln," would work, and with that name, why not shape the can as a log cabin? Another pioneer was the National Biscuit Company, which took its crackers out of the barrel and put them into rather remarkable packages with inner wax-paper wrappings. To dramatize the fact that such wrappers kept the product uniquely dry, the biscuit company adopted as a package symbol a little boy dressed in oilskins.

Among other things, packages extend the life of products, cut shipping costs, and eliminate the need for sales people. Dr. Ernest Dichter, president of the Institute of Motivational Research, thinks that people frequently buy the product for the package itself, rather than for its contents. He refers to the package as "the silent salesman."

With the on-shelf tampering of Extra-Strength Tylenol capsules in 1982, the safety and security of packages became an important consideration. The Food and Drug Administration ordered nonprescription drug companies to make their bottles tamper resistant.

And there is this to consider: The item may not even get on the retailer's shelves unless it is attractively packaged. For pet food can labels, this means using pictures of healthy animals rather than pictures of the product itself. This follows loosely the familiar advice to ad makers to sell the sizzle instead of the steak.

The art on a package makes a big difference in sales. One company producing canned pet food put pictures of more fetching animals on labels for flavors that weren't selling as well as other flavors.

Milton Glaser, who did designing for Grand Union supermarkets, says designing packaging for generic products represented a special challenge. Generic products are supposed to come in simple, unadorned packages. ". . . it is very important to signal that no costs are involved." Yet the company Glaser was working for wanted *its* generic products to look better than generic products at other stores.[23]

Companies have tried to outdo each other in a rush to make their packages useful, handsome, and unique. But ecologists have attacked the concept of convenience packaging. Some companies have cut back on packages-within-packages, and they have come up with packages that eventually will self-destruct or deteriorate. Some packages carry a circular-arrow insignia sponsored by the American Paper Institute to signify the use of recycled paperboard. In the stores, especially in college towns, clerks are asking customers whether they want purchases placed in paper or plastic sacks, or if they want sacks at all.

That packages are wasteful of our resources is one of the most persistent criticisms. Some plastic wrappings are actually harmful to health, it is also charged. And the product often does not live up to the promises of the package design. Even the nature of the design—its "commercialism"—irks some buyers. One of the facial tissue companies has put its name and advertising on a wrapper that can be removed and discarded once the product is in the home. That way there

Inspired by the art of the 1930s, Robert Pizzo designed these bags used to carry percussion musical instruments. The client, Rhythm Tech, manufactures musical instruments as well as bags to carry them. Richard Taninbaum and Robert Linett own the company. "They basically handed me four blank bags and said 'Go nuts!' " Pizzo reports. John O'Donnell took the photograph.

In a departure from its usual mailings to doctors, the Texas Pharmacal Co., San Antonio, sent dermatologists samples of Meted® Shampoo and Texacort® Scalp Lotion in a box with graphics showing the intended use for the products. Designer: Ralph Grigg. Agency: Sudler & Hennessey. (Photograph courtesy Texas Pharmacal Company.)

The well-designed Flush A Brush puts its product in a well-designed 30° × 60° triangular box with strong graphics to make it stand out on store shelves. (Photo by the author.)

is no commercializing in the bedroom or bathroom. And Chiffon has advertised: "Each colorful box . . . gives you more than one color. The top, sides and end panels are different shades of blue, green, pink, yellow, and orange. Which means you can match the decor of your bathroom—no matter what your basic colors happen to be."

Package designers face all kinds of criticism and pressure. One of the never-ending introductions of new breakfast cereals ran into a snag in 1987 when General Mills introduced Count Chocula chocolate-flavored frosted cereal. The package designer decided to duplicate a Count Dracula movie poster from the early 1930s. Unfortunately, Count Dracula had a Star of David on his chest. Some read the art as anti-Semitic, and so the package art had to be changed, although the company decided not to remove existing boxes from store shelves.

The production of the package may add considerably to the cost of the product. It is estimated that packaging represents about a third of the price of cosmetics, for instance. A single package design may cost $25,000. It takes many comps and package mockups before a client registers its approval. The Schechter Group created more than 150 designs for Diet Coke before one was chosen.

Once accepted, a package design does not last as long as it did in years past. Companies feel that they have to change their designs often to keep up with the competition.

The big stores frequently change the design on their shopping bags, a form of packaging. The design may change from season to season. Bloomingdale's has half a dozen different shopping bags available at any given time. The bags vary from department to department. The New York-based store pioneered in the design of bags that omit the store name. Fashion-conscious buyers still could easily recognize the store behind the design. ". . . the once-ignored shopping bag had been fully recognized for what it was—a form of portable graphic art which, carried incessantly by customers and by those who wished to appear as customers of a particular establishment, resulted in millions of dollars' worth of free advertising."[24]

Most stores charge for their shopping bags to discourage unreasonable requests for them and to help cover, if not fully cover, their costs.

Neiman-Marcus has come out with designer trash bags: red plastic bags bearing the store's script logo. Following the 1987 Christmas season, *Time* reported that the bags caused some problems in some parts of the country because, in garbage circles, red bags symbolize hospital waste and are meant to be handled with special care.

N-M planned to continue marketing the bags but in other colors.

The problems of packaging call for decisions involving the following:

■ *Kind of material for the vessel containing the product.* Legal considerations may be a factor. Is the container sanitary? Will it keep the product safe? Materials available include glass, plastic, metal, and paper. A new packaging technique—aseptics—became popular in the 1980s. Aseptics produce boxes made from thin layers of polyethylene, foil, and paper. The boxes hold liquids and keep them fresh for months without refrigeration. Some come with straws attached. Unfortunately, aseptics can't hold carbonated beverages because pressure from the gas breaks the container.

■ *Shape and size of the vessel.* Sometimes it can provide a service after the product is consumed. Processed-cheese containers, for instance, become drinking glasses.

■ *Nature of the device for opening and closing the vessel.* Sometimes the convenience of such a device makes a difference in how well the product sells.

■ *Design of the label.* The label can become complicated, what with all the legal and marketing requirements these days.

■ *Shape and design of the package that may house the vessel.* How well will the package ship and stack?

■ *Design of the package enclosure* (if one is needed). Many manufacturers include a folder or tag with their merchandise that, among other things, congratulates the purchaser. "You have just purchased a garment which is a compliment to your taste and judgment," says a tag for London Fog outerwear. Presumably this gives the purchaser some additional satisfaction.

■ *Design and construction of the carton to ship the packages.*

Package design can originate at the company that manufactures the product, at the company's advertising agency, at the place where packages are manufactured, or at a design studio.

A design firm specializing in packages avoids working for competing products. Often its job is to redesign an existing package, holding onto at least something of the original so as not to lose loyal users of the product.

The challenge is to go far enough to make the package compelling but not so far as to make the buyer uneasy. A detergent box, for example, needs to catch the eye but "it can't be *too* bold, go *too* far," said J. Mac Cato of Cato Johnson Inc., New York design firm. "You can't hype the customer. She'll resent it, be offended, turn off. The important thing is that the package wants to be basically likable."[25]

Walter P. Margulies, a principal in Lippincott & Margulies, points out that a good package must both create a mood and do a selling job. This is particularly true for highly competitive products—for household cleaners, for instance, which number more than one hundred. Margulies has high praise for Janitor in a Drum's plastic replica of an industrial drum, calling it "brilliant imagery suggesting factory-style strength and reliability. . . ."

Fractal Design Painter software for computer artists comes packaged in a paint can, and Fractal Design Sketcher software—a grayscale paint program—comes with a spiral-bound instruction manual that looks and feels like a sketch pad you'd buy at an art-supply store.

A number of firms specialize in package design, but advertising agencies design packages, too. Certainly they like to be consulted. Advertising agencies like to become involved in package design not so much for the mechanics of how the package works but for its appearance. "We are creative people," said Robert Taylor, group creative director for J. Walter Thompson Co., "and there are times when we can contribute good ideas to a receptive client. We like to be consulted—not because we want things our way, but because it will help us do a better job advertising the finished product."[26]

As a design problem, a package is unique in that it is three-dimensional. The designer is concerned with the package's ability to sell from any one of its six sides (assuming it is a box rather than a cylinder). Each side must be complete in itself, although the main identification and display are reserved for the side most likely to face out from the dealer's shelf.

Before beginning your design project, you should study a lineup of every competing package in order to determine how to make your package stand out. Package designers can use a Lightspeed Design System to "place" a design on store shelves, surrounded by other products, to test color and impact. Big-city studios and agencies unable to afford systems like this can rent time on systems in "access studios."

Because the package must appeal to the customer, cater to the display practices of the dealer, and conform to the facilities and needs of the manufacturer, you must sacrifice some desirable features in order to achieve others.

The package should be designed to be easily recognized in reproductions in ads as well as in competition with other packages on the shelf. The customer should be able to walk right to it and pick it out. On one of the panels there must be included a set of basic instructions for the product's use, even though a leaflet is included inside.

Perhaps the best-looking packages can be found in the ethical drug business, the same business that produces the handsome direct-mail advertising addressed to doctors. Other good-looking packages can be found in the cosmetics and technical and electronics industries. The worst packages, so far as looks are concerned, come from among those produced by food processors and other consumer-goods companies. But these packages can be handsome, too.

One of the important package-design firms, Landor Associates of San Fran-

Which came first: the product or the egg? L'eggs assures us it was the product. The packaging concept, the design of the package, and the name were the inspiration of Roger Ferriter of Lubalin, Smith, & Carnase, Inc., a design firm. The idea was to create packaging as well as a product that would stand out from the more than 600 brands then on the market. The egg is said to be nature's most perfect package. The L'eggs version, made of plastic from an injection-molding process, gives the hosiery protection from rough handling and moisture. Shown here is a "boutique," a P-O-P unit that both advertises and sells the product.

Two Neiman-Marcus shopping bags, the one on the left in light olive, orange, black, and white; the one on the right in brown and white. A store with Neiman-Marcus's image is sure enough of itself to confine the store name to a small spot on the sides of the bags. (Photo by the author.)

cisco, is responsible for the design of an estimated 30 percent of the packages in frozen food compartments of grocery stores. The red slash on Sara Lee boxes came from the firm, as well as the star on Armour meats.

"Each design [coming from Landor] is a combination of art and psychology, based partly on instinct, partly on research. The design of the package isn't just a way of grabbing the customer's eye as he wheels his cart down the aisle at the supermarket. It may also be a wordless, instantaneous way of telling the customer something about the product. In Landor's trade, that's called positioning the product," wrote a San Francisco *Chronicle* reporter.[27]

Landor Associates tries to bring an informality to its packages to get away from a large-corporation feel. It puts little floral arrangements on bottles and jars. It produces abstractions of birds. If initials are used, they tend to look like personal monograms. Every firm, every product has a personality, the design firm feels. It is up to the designer to find it and dramatize it.

It is possible, though, to overdesign a package. A too-arty look for a tool package, for instance, could hurt sales.

Going after the look of nostalgia is popular among package designers because such a look suggests the past, better times, and lasting quality.

How the sides can be coordinated can best be determined by studying other packages. Some boxes use a wraparound design, each of the four main sides carrying a quarter of the basic design. Correctly fitting four boxes together on the shelves, the dealer can build a sort of poster of them.

Some manufacturers with a varied line of products want a design relationship among their packages; others feel that each product represents a unique problem in packaging, and design unity is not important, or that unity can be maintained by simply repeating the company identification mark.

Color in package design may be the single most important factor. People who have bought a product previously go back to the store to look for a green box or a red can or a bottle with a yellow label.

Primary colors appeal to the less sophisticated, pastels or muted colors to the more sophisticated customers. This consideration must be tempered with a consideration of the appropriateness of color to the product. As a package designer, you would rely on available information about psychological reaction to color. White, for instance, suggests purity; silver or gold suggests richness. The brand

To design this two-color wine label, Tom Rubick picked a classic roman italic in all caps and put the lines on a slant so that they would form a vertical axis. He also allowed the second big *C* to drop below its base line so that the words *Crystal* and *Creek* could fit closely together. A thick rule and two thin ones provide the only art for this elegantly simple design. Chris Berner codesigned and did the mechanical for Rubick & Funk Graphic Communications.

that first uses a color puts a claim on it. But it is easy for a newcomer brand to use a similar color and cash in on the goodwill the color has built. Don E. Forest, a partner in Harte Yamashita & Forest, a Los Angeles design firm, says that designers should also be influenced by what colors the competition is using. Where most breakfast-food packages use white, yellow, and other light colors, a deep brown box may be the best bet for a new product in that category.[28]

Philip Morris introduced a new brand of cigarette in 1983, Players, and put it in a classy black box. The company took something of a risk in going after young, professional smokers with that kind of a box. Black as a package color is considered by many as too somber. But the unusual box was designed to become something of a status symbol.[29]

Specialty Advertising

Specialty advertising employs useful articles of merchandise as a medium. The ad—it may be no more than a logo—goes onto the article, to serve as a constant reminder to the user. The advertiser usually delivers the article to the potential customer at no charge. Circulation must be carefully controlled, of course, because the cost per unit can be high.

The Specialty Advertising Association International, Irving, Texas, traces the birth of that kind of advertising to an Ohio printer, Jasper Meek, who put the name of a shoe store on a tote bag for books. The tote bag as an advertising medium remains popular, especially with makers of cosmetics.

The association estimates that there are more than 15,000 different kinds of items used as advertising specialties, including ballpoint pens, T-shirts, keytags, matchbooks, and calendars. Some 6,000 manufacturing and distributing firms comprise the industry.

As a category, specialty advertising expands easily enough to include direct-mail advertising, especially when the direct-mail format is unusual enough to stay around on the recipient's desk or shelf for a while. A firm that wants to involve the recipient might send out an advertising message as a simple jigsaw puzzle, for instance. The several big pieces of heavy cardboard pour out of an envelope, and the curious recipient puts them together, if only once.

To help Emanuel Hospital and Health Center promote its Life Flight helicopter service, Byron Ferris designed this model that can be punched out from a cardboard sheet carrying instructions for assembly. Directed mostly to kids, the instructions, which Joan Campf and Ferris wrote, end on a happy note: "Hooray—Your Life Flight helicopter model is done! Have a great time saving people."

Here is Ferris's Air Rescue helicopter fully assembled.

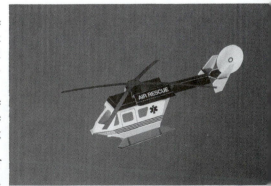

You see here one-half of the menu for Eli McFly's Restaurants, Cupertino, California. The menu opens out into a pyramid, which sits nicely on the tables. All in one color (purple) on a tan stock. Rick Tharp of Tharp Did It design studio was the designer.

This is the cover of a 4¼″ × 5½″ four-page tag for Castle Mfg., a Corvallis, Oregon, furniture maker. The printing is in gold on a dark blue stock. Designer: Deborah Kadas. Agency: Attenzione!

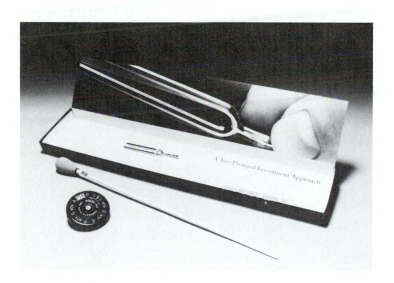

Fourth Investment Advisors, Tulsa, Oklahoma, used a series of three mailings to get in touch with 150 financial executives responsible for investing substantial money funds. The campaign was built on the theme, "Well Orchestrated Investments." The mailing, followed up by personal calls, included an orchestra conductor's baton, a pitch pipe, and this tuning fork. The tuning fork called attention to "a two-pronged investment approach." (Photo courtesy of Specialty Advertising Association International.)

The designer has to be something of a package designer and even inventor. Pop-ups, as found in some children's books, prove popular with some advertisers and specialty-advertising designers.

People who produce specialty advertising items find a number of magazines to stimulate their thinking, including *Specialty Advertising Business, Zip Target Marketing, Potentials in Marketing, Premium/Incentives Business, Direct Marketing, DM News,* and *Catalog Age.*

The CPM (cost per thousand readers) runs high in this medium, but the targeting is precise and the items distributed, even though useful, are themselves usually inexpensive to produce.

An advertising specialty differs from a premium in that the recipient buys nothing, sends in no coupon, does nothing to earn the item. And a premium usually carries no advertising message.

The most expensive of the advertising specialties are called "executive gifts," and whatever messages they carry are only dimly seen. A watch, for instance, might carry a small logo on its face.

LONG-TERM DESIGN

Whatever the carrier, there is not much room for design. Sometimes the big and only decision is where, exactly, to put the logo.

Dr. Willis L. Winter, professor of advertising at the University of Oregon, sees specialty advertising as the most flexible of all advertising media and perhaps the one best able to target an audience. With a high cost per thousand because of the worth of the product, which acts as the medium, specialty advertising boosts a high recall. The ad is seen over and over again as the product is used.

Professor Winter puts his highest grades on products that are appropriate to the sponsor. A heating firm, for instance, offers a thermometer that carries a printed message. A printing or typesetting firm offers a pica ruler. A bank offers a ballpoint pen to write checks with.

Yellow Pages Advertising

Because a Yellow Pages ad stays put for a full year or more, we can consider such advertising as part of the long-term picture. Many of the ads come in display sizes—and with art.

The term *Yellow Pages* and the walking-fingers trademark are no longer protected by patent or copyright in the United States. This has greatly confused directory users, who can't tell the original directories from the upstarts. And advertisers must decide which of the several directories in their areas they should appear in.

Some 7,000 directories, including Yellow Pages directories, serve various businesses and customers in the United States.

The use of yellow paper for directories began in Cheyenne, Wyoming, in 1883 when a printer ran out of white paper. The breakup of AT&T in 1984 resulted in the proliferation not only of telephone companies but also of Yellow Pages directories. Some of the new directories specialize. For instance, some serve older people, some children, some minority groups, some Christians.

And so the directories have become more aggressive in their appeals to both advertisers and directory users. Because the ads are local, newspapers, especially, feel the competition.

Advertisers wanting to convey timely information, including prices, turn to newspapers and other media, says Professor Alan D. Fletcher of Louisiana State University. Advertisers wanting to convey excitement turn to television. Yellow Pages advertising is designed to *complement* other advertising, "bringing what the industry refers to as *directional* advertising to the media mix."[30]

Yellow Pages Update, a quarterly published by the American Association of Yellow Pages Publishers, points out that Yellow Pages are not meant to create awareness and demand, as other media do, but to direct consumers to a business when they are ready to buy. "Yellow pages should not replace radio, TV, or newspaper advertising but should be considered an important part of the overall media mix. . . ."[31]

Yellow Pages advertising has been regarded by some advertisers as a necessary evil, and little attention has been paid to the design of the display boxes that appear with the listings. But lately, with the proliferation of directories, these ads have been getting more attention from advertisers and their art directors.

Because Yellow Pages directories categorize ads, the ad you would design for this medium does not need to identify the kind of business your client is engaged in. But the ad does need to stress features that set your client apart from the competition. It can do this with the headline.

The ad should prominently display a name, phone number, and address. Often it would include some art and a limited amount of body copy.

A second color can make a Yellow Pages ad stand out, even in a small size.

One Yellow Pages company, Ameritech, has produced directories with "white knockouts"—ads on a white background surrounded by the yellow of other ads on the pages. "White knockouts" go for the two-color rate. The directories are printed on white paper; the yellow, which is screened, is a second color. The "white knockout" ads can carry additional color at additional prices.

Yellow Pages advertising, despite its confined space, can take on a classy look, too. Deborah Kadas designed this all-centered ad for Ron Federspiel, D.D.S., Corvallis, Oregon. Copywriter: Linda Ahlers. Agency: Attenzione! (The exclamation mark is part of the agency title.)

To produce Yellow Pages display ads, Volt Information Sciences, Inc., Blue Bell, Pennsylvania, markets a RAD-GRAF workstation that generates type out-lining, drop shadowing, type and art rotating, screening, and other effects and the quick printing of ads in low resolution on plain paper. The program offers 6,000 pieces of art appropriate to Yellow Pages and 3,200 trademarks and logos.

LONG-TERM DESIGN

CHAPTER

16

CAREERS

"Advertising is a craft executed by people who aspire to be artists, but assessed by those who aspire to be scientists. I cannot imagine any human relationship more perfectly designed to produce total mayhem." That's the assessment of his craft made by John Ward of B & B Dorland, Great Britain, as reported by Martin Mayer.[1] Yet, the field continues to intrigue young people contemplating careers. Advertising courses remain among the most popular offerings in journalism schools and departments. Advertising designs are what students do in many of the art schools.

A career in advertising becomes a continuing educational adventure. Always reading, always observing, the ad maker keeps up with what's going on all over the world, not only in business and fashion but also in politics, science, art, and every other field. The ad maker is nothing if not well rounded.

The people who create advertising form an elite group that tends to become alienated from the people who see, watch, or read what's placed in the media. Research helps define the audience, but ad makers need to get closer to those who are to be reached. For instance, taking a job as a copywriter for the advertising department of a retail establishment, the ad maker may be asked to spend some time on the floor selling merchandise.

What to Expect

Although graduation may be a year or two away, it is not too early to consider getting your "book" ready. What follows applies mainly to job hunting by designers, but much of it is applicable to copywriters as well.

Unless you are applying for work with a small agency, do not pose as a person who can do it all. If you want to be an art director, show mostly design. If you want to be a copywriter, show mostly copy. But feel free to make the point that you offer *some* versatility. Most important, make sure the agency or studio—or store or newspaper—sees that you are interested in selling, not just in impressing people with your talent.

Your goal is to work full time as an art director or on your own as a freelancer. As the candidate for an art director's job, you may have to work at first in the production department or in the bullpen doing traditional or electronic pasteups. "In most first jobs, people start out doing strictly production work, gradually progress into doing comprehensive layouts for art directors and eventually start . . . [taking on] jobs of their own . . . ," says Don Harbor, associate creative director of Lawler Ballard Advertising, Norfolk, Virginia.[2]

From art director you could expect to go to a creative director's spot or eventually a vice-president's or president's position. Formerly, only writers or businesspeople moved into those positions, but the art director's role in advertising is seen as being much more important today. And more is required of the art director.

Some art directors and designers are primarily idea people. They *plan* design and art pieces but assign the finished work to artists with steady hands, a mastery of the tools, and an eye for detail. Many designers do comps of ads but assign the finished work to pasteup artists. Some don't even do comps.

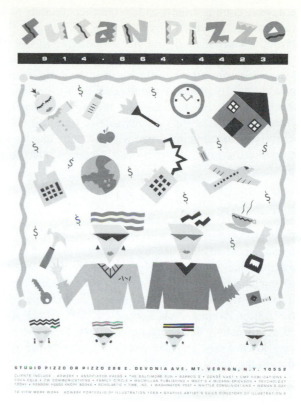

Using X-acto knives to cut various shapes out of solid and textured sheets, Robert Pizzo and Susan Pizzo of Studio Pizzo or Pizzo, Mt. Vernon, New York, show off their related styles to potential clients in self-promotion mailers. (You saw the steps involved in producing one of these art pieces in an earlier chapter.) Each artist has done work for major companies, listed at the bottom of the pieces.

"I don't think . . . that graphic designers are stepchildren in the industry anymore," says Leatrice Eisman, executive director of the Pantone Color Institute and editor of *Color News,* a quarterly newsletter. "I don't think that they can take a backseat to the 'lofty' designers in fashion, interiors, or architecture. I think that graphic design has been raised to a level so that graphic designers are on an equal plane with other creative professionals."

She adds: "I look to a future with large, multi-faceted, multi-disciplined design firms working on a wide variety of projects from print to interior to architectural design and beyond."[3]

The Importance of Ideas

Don Harbor says that a portfolio of logos, letterheads, and similar pieces "is about as likely to impress . . . [an agency art director] as slides of your last vacation. The art director appreciates good design but wants more to see ideas."

"Advertising is about ideas or, as we call them, concepts," he adds. "The art director wants to know how the job applicant thinks. What is the applicant's problem-solving ability?"[4]

Tracy Wong, formerly an art director with several major agencies and now creative director with Livingston & Co., Seattle, makes a similar observation. "Great design and art direction mean absolutely nothing in the face of an ad without an idea—a mistake commonly made in both print and TV."

Wong has found that print advertising is often more difficult to do than TV advertising. This is because in print "you have approximately two to three seconds to capture someone's attention. You don't have the safety net of a brilliant director or extravagant production. . . . I would venture to say that the greatest creative minds and the hottest agencies built their reputations on print, which is something I've seen a lot of students and young art directors lose sight of."

Wong talks sadly of the mergers of the smaller, highly creative, idea-rich agencies like Doyle Dane Bernbach into the new mega-agencies. He thinks the best work these days is coming from London and recommends to students the study of the British annual, *Design & Art Direction.*

Wong earned a journalism degree before studying at the Art Center College of Design in Pasadena. He credits journalism school classes, in addition to art school classes, with preparing him for his graphic design career. His training in writing, he says, "really made all the difference in the world."[5]

Wong thinks that "having an account management background has helped immensely, too, in realizing the strategy side of the business." Such experience, he says, helps art directors empathize with account management people, "who often have conflicting interests with creatives as to what work should be presented or produced."[6]

Where the Jobs Are

It is a good idea to keep in touch with your professors who, in turn, keep in touch with employers. Local ad clubs are also useful for making contacts. Help-wanted ads in magazines like *Advertising Age* and *Adweek* offer good leads for design and copywriting jobs, but professional experience is usually expected. Help-wanted ads in local newspapers offer other possibilities. So do employment agencies. Jerry Fields, 515 Madison Avenue, New York, New York 10022, specializes in placing experienced art directors, designers, copywriters, and others who create ads.

Narrowing in on a city, you can check out advertising agencies and art and design studios in the Yellow Pages. The *Standard Directory of Advertising Agencies* lists agencies nationwide.

Chris Parker, an advertising art director in San Jose, California, took out a full-page ad in the tabloid arts and entertainment section of *The Oregonian,* Portland, in 1992, paying about $1,200 to get the attention of Wieden & Kennedy, the hot agency that numbers Nike among its clients. The ad ran in the city editions of the section. He took this unusual step to get an interview and show his portfolio because, he said, he wanted to move to Portland and work for the agency he considered the best in the country.

You can find jobs in advertising with any of the following groups:

- *Advertising agencies.*
- *The media, including, especially, newspapers and broadcast stations.* They prepare ads for clients who don't have their own advertising departments or agencies.
- *Advertisers, even when they have agencies.* Some of what they produce, especially direct mail, may be prepared in-house.
- *Art and design studios.* As specialists, they work with both agencies and clients.

   Design studios are not all the same. Some have a corporate-image orientation, specializing in logos, annual reports, packaging and other projects related to marketing. Others have more of an interest in pure design.
- *Book publishers.* Although books themselves need *editorial* rather than advertising design, their jackets, if the books are hardbound, and covers, if they're paperbound, need advertising design. Jackets and covers are really posters.

   Because they issue so many books—some 45,000 different titles a year—book publishers depend especially on freelance designers. Each book needs is own feel on the jacket or cover. A staff designer is likely to repeat designs. New ideas need to come from outside.

   Book publishers—there are several hundred of them—are not all headquartered in New York. Some can even be found in small cities.
- *Printers.* As part of their services, some printers, at a price, offer design, illustrations, and even copy to clients who can't easily get these elsewhere. These services apply mostly to direct-mail advertising.

There are many other possibilities, including corporations, trade organizations, nonprofit groups, and government agencies. Everybody has something to sell, and everybody publishes or buys time or space.

Through its choice and handling of type, Metzdorf Advertising Agency, Houston, dramatizes its need for secretarial help. Art director, designer, and copywriter: Lyle Metzdorf.

There's nothing fancy here. Nothing to stir the hearts of judges at an art directors awards competition. But, despite what the headline says, this is not a lousy ad. It is a simple, direct invitation designed to single out promising job hunters scanning the several pages of help wanted ads in *Advertising Age.* The ad worked. It drew sixty responses for the sponsor, the Townsend Agency, Ltd., now located at Rosemont, Illinois. Art director and designer: Adriane DiMeo. Copywriter: Laurel Johnson.

Helmut Krone, an art director who became a big name at Doyle Dane Bernbach (and executive vice-president), says, "Kids today spend half their lives agonizing over their first move, first job. It doesn't matter; it's how you tackle your work. Stop worrying so much and do *something.*"[7]

Jack Summerford, Dallas designer, started out as a layout artist for a department store, "laying out newspaper ads day in and day out. I learned how to use a pencil and how to work fast." Then he worked for an advertising agency, doing tighter layouts and designs as well as mechanicals. His next step was to start his own design studio.[8]

The average design professional makes close to $50,000 a year, an American Institute of Graphic Arts survey showed in 1981. Earnings ranged from $21,900 for salaried junior designers to $54,000 for designers serving as creative directors. Owners of large design firms averaged a lot more. Freelancers earned an average of $37,400.

The survey also found that women made less than men, partly because women are slightly younger on the average with fewer years of experience. About 52 percent of designers are women.[9]

Internships

It has become increasingly important in recent years for students to work as summer interns on publications or with agencies or advertising departments before they graduate. Such work not only helps students make important contacts; it also gives them something to put in their résumés. While it is unlikely that an intern working with an art director would create designs right away for major clients, there may be opportunities to do some layouts and pasteups. Just seeing how an agency or studio works is worthwhile.

The nature of the work makes graphic design internships less available than, say, copywriting and production internships. But when graphic design internships are not available through their schools, aggressive and talented students often are able to arrange them on their own.

Knowing Production

A first job for many in advertising is in the production department, where ads, after they are designed, are readied for the printer or the medium to which they are to be sent. Time spent in production will help you become a better—more useful—designer.

"I feel that a thorough knowledge of production is fundamental to any design or art direction job," says Don Harbor. "Without this knowledge, the art director, out of sheer ignorance, either underdesigns or overdesigns every job. [Art directors without a production background] . . . either create a design of such complexity that literally it can't be produced, or at least not for the budget and time constraints available, or they produce something far less impressive than they might have done had they understood more about what could be accomplished within their means."[10]

A familiarity with production terminology can help you communicate with the printer. The printer's "It can't be done"s will be fewer when it is clear that you understand production. And you will no longer make impossible printing requests.

Production experience will help you take advantage of the economies each printing process offers. You will learn to design an advertisement "to fit." When you can't work directly with the printer, as for an ad going into a national magazine, you will consult the appropriate *Standard Rate & Data Service* volume covering that medium and see at once what the mechanical requirements are for the medium. Without an understanding of production, you will not even be able to *read SRDS.*

Production experience will help you prepare materials so they will reproduce at their best. Knowing, for instance, that the halftone process picks up all tones,

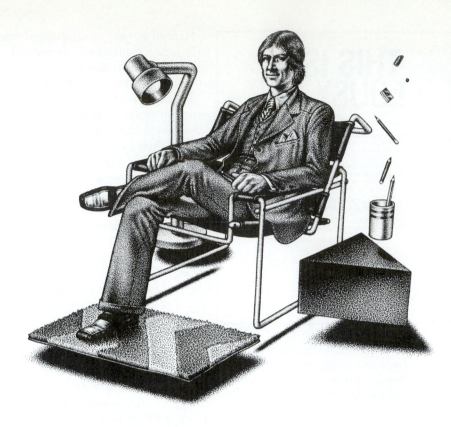

you will avoid making any marks on photographs, even on the back, for fear they might be picked up as shadows and reproduced as lines or blotches.

Appreciating the fact that a printer can hardly be expected to *improve* the quality of a photograph in printing (the printer's camera operator, after all, copies a copy from a negative), you will insist that the starting photograph have enough quality to hold up in copying.

With production experience, you will know what kinds of types show up best in the various processes. With production experience, you will be infinitely better prepared to handle assignments in direct-mail advertising. You will make much better use of color in your work.

Knowing Computers

When the economy falters, designers must learn to work with less. To keep costs down, they must work faster. "Graphic designers are working in a world that's whirling ever more rapidly. We have to learn to move at that speed."

Which means learning to work with a computer. "The computer is going to give us time. . . . I can take a computer and teach it all the facts and figures that I know, and then let it run for 20 minutes by itself. In 20 minutes it will do what would take me hours." And "I might forget something—that's how most of the mistakes in this business are made. The computer doesn't forget."[11]

That was David Strong, head of a Seattle-based design studio, speaking way back in 1982. Within a few years, most studios and agencies had the message.

Gary Cunningham, director of print services at Avrett, Free & Ginsberg, says that computerization gives his agency "total control and greatly accelerates the speed at which we can produce ads."

Smaller advertising agencies embraced computer technology more enthusiastically than larger agencies. "Large agencies don't want to upset the apple cart, but the smaller ones are doing it for them," said Mike Antebi, president of Blue Chip Group, a computer consulting group.[12]

Computers allow agencies not only to show ad ideas to clients in an almost finished state but also to quickly set budgets, bill clients, and pick media. But agency people complain that software programs aren't really tailored to agency

In a whimsical booklet, *How to Be a Successful Designer,* the Neenah Paper Divison of Kimberly-Clark Corporation showed drawings of typical art directors, among them this one, called "Continental Urbane." He's sitting in a Marcel Breuer chair. A tongue-in-cheek caption said: "Empty desk suggests that design is generated by magic and genius, not work, because nothing so mundane [as a layout] ever passes over it." Illustrator Alex Murawski achieved the stipple effect by laboriously putting in each dot with a Rapidograph pen. Creative concept: Sebstad & Lutrey, Chicago. Art director: Tim Lutrey. Copywriter: Brad Sebstad.

Asako Matsumoto of Japan, at the conclusion of her advertising studies in the United States, prepares a series of speculative ads for United Airlines to sell readers on travel to her home country. This ad says, "Turn the pages of 1,000 years of history at 490 MPH." The slogan reads, "Make the past and the future UNITED." The "screen capture" shows Matsumoto's collection of art pieces from various sources and includes a video camera shot of real leaves. Her small blocks of copy in this "Fit in window" view appear as gray bars. Software for the project includes Photoshop and PageMaker.

use, especially in media buying. Many agencies find it necessary to write their own programs. Yet, few agencies employ computer specialists. They rely largely on consultants.[13]

In the creative areas of advertising, designers are finding the computer eminently useful. With desktop publishing systems and all the available software, advertising designers find they can do a lot more than before. They can create art, store it, call it up in seconds; what they don't have on screen or in storage, they can scan. They can set body and display type easily, adjust its spacing, and, in seconds, change sizes and settings. Using layout software, they can bring all the elements of an ad together in any number of arrangements, and almost instantly make any adjustments they or their clients want. Doing electronic pasteups, they can avoid all the old tools and supplies a designer used to contend with. At their desktop stations, they can produce the camera-ready copy or film or even plates needed in the final printing. They can produce the necessary color separations. They can also produce the animation for commercials.

These are powerful, relatively new capabilities designers have, and anyone entering the business must know how to exercise them. These days, it would be unthinkable to venture into the graphic design field without knowing computers. Look at any of the graphic-designer-help-wanted ads in *Advertising Age* and similar trade magazines and try to find one that don't include a line like this: "Ability to use the computer essential." Usually the computer specified is the Macintosh.[14] Many of the ads even spell out a specific page-layout software program the job applicant must know.

Of course, the job applicant must understand principles of design in order to use the computer effectively.

Preparing the Résumé

A good résumé acts more like a teaser than an encyclopedia. There should be enough there to intrigue the reader but not enough to make an interview unnecessary. The point of a résumé is to get an interview, not a job.

A versatile advertising person should prepare several résumés, each one stressing a single strength or interest, although there should be a hint there of versatility, too. The best résumés are those created especially for the organization being contacted.

Wes Perrin, an advertising agency founder, admits résumés are important but

The 1812 Overture on a cassette deck.

And on a laser deck.

The greatest dynamic range in stereo.

Sony Laser Sound. Live music has met its match.

says that the importance may be overrated. ". . . entry jobs at most agencies are much more a factor of opportunistic timing than résumé chutzpah. These agencies, even the superstar ones, cannot afford to build a bench of untried rookies. Consequently, they hire only when pressed to the wall because of (a) growth of existing accounts or (b) acquisition of new business."[15]

Jim deYong, whose copywriting successes propelled him into top agency jobs and ownerships in southern California, got his first jobs with unusual letters and résumés and has, himself, been swayed by what young job hunters have sent him. He feels that noncreative openings in agencies may call for serious, even stilted résumés of the kind advocated by headhunters but that creative openings deserve creative approaches.

"Advertising is a business based on promotion," he says, "and the most important thing you have to promote is you."[16] Now a principal in deYong Ginsberg Weisman Bailey, Irvine, California, deYong got an early job in advertising by sending manikin arms to a few choice agencies. Attached to the arms was the note: "I'd give my right arm to write copy for you."

Maxine Paetro, who hires creative people at Foote, Cone & Belding, told of an offbeat résumé that carried a drawing of a man holding a portfolio. The headline said: "This Is an Ad for a Product That Isn't Working." The body copy gave the man's name and said that he was looking for his first job. She thought it "effective." But other offbeat résumés have struck her as offensive. One came shaped like a pizza placed with pieces of *real* pizza in a pizza box. It said something about "A Slice of Life."

Said Paetro: "A tasteful, simple résumé—one that can be scanned quickly, written on, and easily filed, is the best. . . . From where . . . [the job hunter is] sitting, it's mighty tough to judge what's going to be mind-sticking good and

Tracy Wong's ad for Sony Laser Sound, done as an Art Center College of Design assignment, uses weapons to make the point that *The 1812 Overture* would have a much greater range on a laser deck than on a cassette deck. This full-color comp is the kind of a piece that could be included in a portfolio.

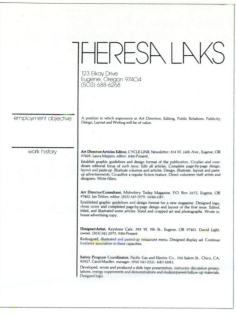

By the time of her college graduation, Theresa Laks had enough experience to take up two pages of a résumé. But she used generous doses of white space to give her entries plenty of display. She played a bit with the first letter of her name to draw a vertical bar to introduce a unifying force and set up some good proportions. The name and bars (vertical and horizontal) were in a second color.

what's going to be dumb, tacky, or trite. (I've seen about four hundred 'Wanted' poster résumés, for instance.)"**17**

A thin line separates something memorable in résumés from something embarrassing. If you have an unusual idea but think you might not be able to bring it off, you might be better advised, even when applying for a creative job, to play it straight.

It's best to keep your résumé to a single page, but take more space if you need it. Coming from a designer, your résumé should look better than most others. It can be neatly typed and photocopied, but increasingly job seekers are having résumés printed. A printed résumé offers a chance for quiet, confident design, based on a grid, perhaps using a few thin-ruled lines.

Parallel structure is particularly important. Make sure each heading uses the same grammatical form and that each entry under each heading starts off in the same way. The usual headings are "Personal Details" (optional), "Education," "Work Experience," and "References." You might also want to include "Honors and Awards" after "Work Experience." If you're a "preowned car" person rather than a "used-car" person, you might want to change "Work Experience" to "Professional Experience."

Under "Work Experience" include some details about clients and assignments. Leave out nondesign or nonadvertising jobs, or bunch them in a single unit. If you are short on "Work Experience," you could expand the "Education" section to include a description of courses taken in advertising and design and assignments completed.

With your résumé should go a cover letter introducing it and elaborating on it, if appropriate. Here is where you can show off your writing style. Valerie Shaw in the Los Angeles *Times* told of a copywriter who got an interview with an agency by typing his letter on graph paper and drawing a wavy red line between the typed lines, in the manner of an electrocardiogram. Whenever he mentioned the agency in the letter, he changed the line to fast ups and down to simulate excitement.

In your cover letter you can spend one paragraph stating your goals and another explaining why you want to work for the organization. End the letter with a call for some kind of action. Or announce that you will telephone for an interview. Your letter should show off a well-designed letterhead.

Your stationery deserves careful planning. Designer Michael Satterwhite uses a satelite logo on his letterhead and starts off his address with "Global Headquarters." *In House Graphics* in 1990 noted one art director's tongue-in-cheek business card that listed all the jobs he performed: designer, editor, pasteup artist, production manager, etc. The card, a gatefold with a panel devoted to each function, was 24″ long.

Preparing a Portfolio

The beginning designer's chief selling tool is the portfolio. It can be a big zippered case, an attaché case, or a hardboard folder that ties at the top, right, and bottom. The usual size is 14″ × 17″, big enough to show most pieces and small enough to fit under the arm conveniently and open out gracefully on the table of the hiring art director.

You should include about a dozen examples of your work in your book or portfolio. A creative director won't have time to look at much more than that. Show only your very best work. Don't show work that didn't turn out right and try to explain away the mistakes.

Limit the number of classroom assignments you show. If you have no published work, pick out products or services you are familiar with and do some ads on speculation. Perhaps you will want to do a whole campaign involving more than one medium. Unless you have a lot of self-confidence, stay away from ads featuring the clients of the agency you're pitching. The people at the agency will

Student Kathy Rotramel, her future address up in the air at graduation, designs her first business card without an address or phone number but with a real string attached to create the illusion of a tag, part of the stencil-letter motif she's chosen. The design provides for a later address/phone number imprint.

know far more about their clients than you will, and they will be quick to spot weaknesses in your strategy.

How should you arrange your work in your portfolio? "First, pick out the three best pieces in order, first, second, and third," says Martha Metzdorf, a partner in The Arts Counsel, Inc., New York, which represents graphic artists. "Open your portfolio with piece number one, close your book with number two, and use piece number three [somewhere] in the middle."[18]

Potential employees want you to have a great book, "but they also expect you to articulate the thinking behind your book, to be able to fit into their established group without making waves and stirring up office politics, and to be enthusiastic," Metzdorf says. She reports that above all an employer looks for intelligence. "The bottom line here is that hand skills don't replace brains."[19]

The portfolio should be rearranged for each showing to fit the needs of the potential client or employee. Often the presentation involves the showing of transparencies or the playing of a video cassette.

You should be prepared to leave your book or portfolio behind for further study. And you should consider preparing a printed self-promotion folder, brochure, or booklet either for leaving behind or for opening a door for an interview. This piece could show various examples of your work, or it could take one piece and show its progression through the various steps, from conception to production and printing.

A résumé by a student, Serene Chew, is boxed and organized to fit a single page.

The Job Interview

In *The Big Time: How Success Really Works in 14 Top Business Careers* (New York: Congdon & Weed, 1983), Glenn Kaplan tells of an advertising copywriter who always wore pinstripe suits when meeting with his client. Once when he was wearing blue jeans at the agency he was called into an emergency meeting with the client, who was apparently pleased with the man's informal dress. "It's good to see you looking like that," the client said. "We were beginning to wonder if you were really creative."

It makes an interesting story, but the truth of the matter is that what a creative person wears in an agency setting does not make much difference to anybody. The ideas for an ad and its execution are what count.

But setting out to find a job, you will want to pay serious attention to what you wear, maybe for the first time in your life.

Art directors tend to dress more informally, even more wildly, than other advertising people, but for a job seeker to come in as a caricature is a mistake. It is better to err on the side of conservative dress. Let the work shown carry the excitement.

Being on time for the interview is important, not only because it shows respect for the hiring art director but also because it establishes the fact that the job applicant is devoted to deadlines. The art director will ask most of the questions; when the questions slow down, the applicant should make an effort to leave. The art director in all probability will want to get back to the drawing board. A half-

Esprit (ĕ-sprē'), *n.* 1. Spirit, vivacity, sprightly wit. 2. Spirited group of artists, designers and writers offering fresh and professional creative services to clients throughout the Pacific Northwest. 3. Producers of clever, innovative advertisements, brochures, annual reports, etc.

Esprit de corps (ĕ-sprē' də kôr'). A devotion and common bond of enthusiasm you will develop when you work with Esprit Design on your next creative project.

David Schwantes, launching his new Esprit Design & Creative Services, Inc., at Walla Walla, Washington, sent out this unique announcement card to agencies and printers in the area. His definitions were cleverly tailored to promote the three-person organization.

hour is plenty of time to spend at a first interview. Perhaps you will want to leave a printed piece for the art director's file.

Follow up your interview with a warm but crisp thank-you letter. If you don't hear from the art director for several weeks, you can send a brief, polite letter of inquiry, maybe including a just-off-the-press sample of your work.

Making the Transition

If you thought your design or graphics professor was making too many demands on your time while you were in school, you'll soften your attitude toward school when you are on the outside. There you'll have several jobs going at once, all due yesterday, and right in the middle of one job a client will come in with an entirely new set of instructions.

Designer James Craig has pointed out that "in school, the instructor will accept whatever you do and grade you accordingly. In business, the job is either accepted or it is not. The client is not going to grade your efforts."[20]

What this boils down to is this: that you should be prepared for a different reception on the outside from what you had in school.

The World of Freelancing

As a graphic designer in advertising, you have a choice of working on the staff of an organization or as a freelancer. A staff job offers regular paychecks and a certain amount of security; freelancing offers more excitement but also more frustration.

As a freelancer, you need a lot of self-discipline, a high degree of self-confidence, and an ability to sell yourself and your work. You need to be able to put yourself in the place of a client or potential client, see and appreciate the design needs, and produce the kind of work that brings the desired results. You need to be able to set prices and keep books.

A freelancer can charge more for a piece of work in advertising than for one used by, say, the editorial side of a magazine, because whatever is paid for the art or design represents but a fraction of the total cost of the ad. Its space in a magazine can run to tens of thousands of dollars, its time on TV to hundreds of thousands.

One answer to the question "What to charge?" might be: whatever the advertiser or agency is willing to pay. Sometimes the employer will mention a figure. "Can you do the job for $300?" In most cases you will set your own rate. It could be by the hour, or it could be by the assignment. Obviously, you will charge less at the beginning because you are less sure of yourself, and you will make more false starts. Furthermore, one of your selling points may be that you are less expensive than established designers, illustrators, or copywriters.

As you become better established, your rates go up.

Whatever you charge, it should be at least as much as a semiskilled working person gets. Twenty dollars an hour for a person with talent is not an unreasonable starting figure.

If you must give a price ahead of time, do not underestimate the amount of time involved. And if the job is for a client who demands a lot of your time explaining things and asking for changes, that should be figured in, too.

If you work fast, you might want to avoid hourly rates because you would be working against yourself. The current edition of *Pricing & Ethical Guidelines* (Graphic Artists Guild, 11 West 20th Street, New York, New York 10011) can help you fix your prices, although your experience and location may make your prices quite different from those shown in the book.

At first you will take any jobs that come along. Eventually you will stay away from jobs that do not pay well enough or that can't be done adequately under the limitations set for them. You will also avoid jobs you don't like doing.

On any one job, you and your client will come to an understanding of what's possible for the price. Often this involves a contract or at least a letter of agreement signed by both of you. You will have to know whether the job calls for camera-ready copy or just a rough or roughs and a comprehensive.

Outside typesetting and photostatting charges are usually sent directly to the client. If you include them as part of your costs, you would add a 15 percent handling fee.

If selling yourself is distasteful, or if you want to concentrate on what you do best—creating beautiful and useful designs or illustrations—you may want to hire an agent or sales representative. Such an agent usually takes 25 percent of your billings. This compares to the 10 percent taken by literary agents, but what literary agents have to sell are whole books with greater earning potential.

In the beginning you will work out of a studio at home. Then you will rent an outside studio (too many distractions at home and not enough room). Then you will hire a secretary and an assistant or two. You will become a studio head or partner, not just a freelancer.

Freelancing as a Copywriter

Freelancing is not just for artists and designers. Copywriters freelance, too. Before she became a university professor, Ann Keding wrote advertising copy as a freelancer in southern California for several years. But she established herself first as a staff copywriter at several agencies.

There were some disadvantages, she found, in freelancing, including the lack of a paid-up medical plan, but she found she could make twice what she made as a 9-to-5 writer. She also got around much more, meeting various clients and taking on a variety of assignments.

Why would an agency hire a freelance copywriter? For one thing, jobs sometimes pile up. The agency needs temporary help. For another thing, the creative juices at the agency sometimes cease to flow. The agency needs some new ideas and a fresh approach.

A freelance copywriter would probably work closely with the agency's art director, the resulting advertising emerging as a team effort, making what Don Harbor calls "a fusion of art and copy that together forms a more powerful impression than either could do alone."[21]

A freelance copywriter typically charges $500 a day in a big city, sometimes more. An assignment may take a week or more and involve moving into an agency office temporarily. Another way of figuring the fee is to charge the agency a per-day fee of 1 percent of what a yearly salary would be for the same work.

An hourly rate for a freelance copywriter in a small town might be as low as $15, especially when there isn't much experience.

Working with Agencies

A penalty for doing work for an agency is that the agency is always in a hurry. Deadlines are often unreasonable. Charles Saxon, *The New Yorker* cartoonist, did a lot of advertising cartooning but didn't like all the rush. Once he questioned an art director about the genuineness of a deadline. "I'm coming in town next Tuesday. Couldn't I bring it in then?"

"Look," said the art director, "if I wanted the job next Tuesday, I would have *called* you next Tuesday!"[22]

Unlike other professionals—freelance writers for magazines, for instance—you work anonymously in advertising. Even as an illustrator you may not be able to sign your work. You ask for high rates in lieu of public recognition for your work.

While the public does not recognize your contribution, the people in advertising do, and often one good piece of work results in other assignments given you by the same advertiser as well as by other advertisers and agencies.

One of the discouraging things about freelancing—and about staff work with an advertiser or agency, for that matter—is subjecting what you do to several layers of critics, many of them uninformed in matters of design and language.

Jeanine Holly stimulated many phone calls from potential clients and agencies with this folder announcing her services as a freelance copywriter. The copy suggested three tongue-in-cheek advantages she could offer: a money-back guarantee, a freeze on her rates (her "humble contribution to the de-escalation of these depressing, inflationary and inflammatory times"), and a free bottle of Lancers Vin Rosé with any first order for her services ("It makes the bill easier to swallow"). This message was stamped at the bottom: "DIAL 297-1264 NOW! Operators are standing by."

A light-hearted poster used for self-promotion by Marc Advertising, Pittsburgh, offers illustrated advertising terminology in chart form. Note, for instance, that "Deadline" is a floor outline of a murder victim and "Air Date" is a pumped up rubber doll. "Self-Mailer" is a man crowded into a rural mailbox. Design and art by Joe Kowal, the agency's art director.

An Illustrated Compendium of Advertising Phraseology

CAPS AND LOWERS · MECHANICAL ARTIST · KEY ARTIST · STORYBOARDS · CROP MARKS

MASTHEAD · SUBHEAD · ROUGH PENCIL · FLUSH LEFT · FLUSH RIGHT · SNIPE

BRAINSTORMING · TIME BUY · SPACE BUY · DOUBLE TRUCK · TYPEFACE

SELF MAILER · SELF LIQUIDATOR · LIP SYNC · 60 SECOND SPOT · 30 SECOND SPOT

DUMMY · DEADLINE · MEDIA ANALYST · TYPE SPEC · SPOT COLOR · PICA

DOLLY GRIP · TV DONUT · RADIO DONUT · AIR DATE · FINISH ART

MARC. advertising

To be successful, you will have to master the art of compromise. Sometimes you will decide that your critics are right.

Working with the Client

Designers work differently with their clients. Some designers show only tight comprehensives, others show lesser works. Jack Summerford shows only loosely executed pencil or marker layouts to his clients.[23]

It's possible to overwhelm the client with choices. Result: indecision and stalemate. And you may find that the one or two fill-out-the-batch roughs are the ones that appeal to the client. They will be the ones you really didn't want to finish. It is better to weed out the designs that don't work well and present only two or three for client selection or approval.

You should be prepared to make changes required by the client. Art direction requires compromises. One of its challenges is to work under what may appear to be impossible conditions.

And, of course, another challenge is deciding which clients—and which jobs—deserve your attention. Alexander Woollcott said that "the worst sin of all is to

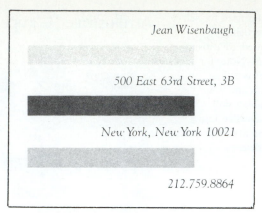

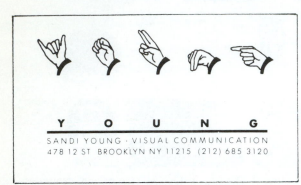

Sandi Young's business card, which she designed, uses sign language, "one of the strongest forms of visual communication," to spell out her name. The name is also printed, in red, below. All the other printing is in black. Her letterhead uses the same basic design.

Designer-illustrator Jean Wisenbaugh, who maintains a studio in New York, uses a narrower card than usual to make it stand out and also because its design, as she conceived it, dictated the size. Three color stripes (blue-green, orange, and purple-magenta) mark her card and all her business stationery.

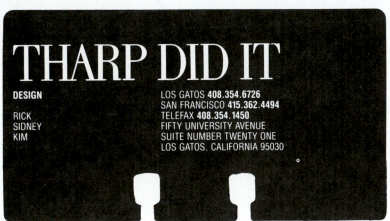

Like every other design studio, Tharp Did It, Los Gatos, California, passes out business cards that are coordinated in design with its business stationery. But it also has sent out cards that fit clients' and potential clients' Rolodex files. Designers: Rick Tharp and Karen Nomura. Art director: Rick Tharp.

do well that which shouldn't be done at all." Some of the least worthy products get the best design. Like a good lawyer, good design can work for any kind of client.

Designers must constantly make ethical decisions about whom to serve and what a design should communicate. As a public service, some designers, without pay, devote after-hours free time to nonprofit clients and causes they can identify with.

Becoming a Specialist

As your career progresses you will, no doubt, begin to specialize. Sometimes the specialty will come about because of an accidental succession of clients. You do a special kind of job for one; another sees it and requests a similar job.

Sometimes the specialty comes as a result of a talent that leads in a single direction. Adrien Frutiger, a prolific type designer best known for developing the face called Univers, found that in art school he had "a much stronger affinity for abstract designs than for naturalistic or representational ones. And so I discovered that calligraphy and type design are the disciplines in which I can excel."

Letha Wulf of Letha Wulf Design uses her signature, which has enough flair to qualify as calligraphy, as the art for her business card. The signature is in gold, the type in turquoise.

Frutiger thinks young artists and graphic designers should move into a specialty early: "Focus on one field; our world needs specialists more and more."[24]

Pitching Clients

What's involved in lining up a client? The Duffy Design Group, which makes about 40 pitches a year, figures it puts in from 25 to 40 hours to make one. The typical Duffy proposal runs from 15 to 20 pages and carries, in addition to an introduction, background information, situation analysis, a statement of the marketing challenge, key design issues, the studio's proposed approach, cost estimates, timing, relevant case studies, brief biographies of members of the design group, references, standard terms of work, and a conclusion.[25]

Hungry Dog Studio, Atlanta, Georgia, run by Bob and Val Tillery, specializes

Dear
Mr. Murdock,
is Dole
bananas?

Dole had already picked finalists in its look for a new agency, but that didn't stop Ketchum Advertising, Los Angeles, from making this last-minute pitch to the food company in a trade-magazine ad. The urgency of the appeal precluded the use of art or decoration. (The ad earned Ketchum a hearing, but the account went to another agency.) Art director: Dennis Lim. Copywriters: Scott Aal and Brent Bouchez.

It's late in the game.

The finalists have all been selected and the presentation dates have been set.

But, with all due respect, we believe that Dole may have overlooked the one agency in Los Angeles that makes the most sense for the job.

Ketchum, Los Angeles.

An agency opened five years ago to launch and build the Acura Division of American Honda. A marketing success story that more than speaks for itself.

Since then, Ketchum's advertising for Health Net, one of California's largest HMO's, more than doubled their awareness in less than 90 days. And from a tiny 800-number buried in the copy of a print ad, we generated more than 3,000 calls a week for Kids by William & Clarissa, a new line of fresh, clean children's shampoos, lotions, oils and sunblocks.

But, more important, our people have food in their blood.

We've worked on everything from Safeway to Hunt-Wesson, from Pizza Hut to Capri-Sun Juices to Gilbert H. Brockmeyer's Natural Ice Cream. Craig Mathiesen, President of Ketchum, Los Angeles helped Orville Redenbacher's Gourmet Popping Corn explode to number one in the category.

We know food, we know image-building and, if you're reading this ad, then we know how to get the consumer's attention.

A combination that, to our way of thinking, seems perfect for Dole.

If you agree, please give Craig Mathiesen or Brent Bouchez a call at Ketchum's Wilshire Boulevard offices. (213) 444-5000.

Ketchum Advertising
Los Angeles

C A R E E R S

in funky music industry design work. A presentation by this studio usually consists of some work by Bob, some by Val, and some resulting from collaboration. "We offer our clients two minds instead of one, and . . . [clients] seem to respond favorably. . . . We tell our clients to decide which one of us they want to do the job."[26]

The inside three panels of a self-promotion folder for Bronson Leigh Weeks, a Portland advertising agency with a reputation for lively design as well as good copy. "Playing it safe is not our style." "The Works" is one of a series, each with its own title.

Defending Design Choices

The ability to sell yourself, to exude confidence in your design choices, will do more, perhaps, than anything else to lift you from the ranks of the also-rans to the ranks of the big-name designers. Your confidence develops as your record of successful campaigns grow.

The skeptical client needs reassurance from the designer. The protesting client needs reasons.

In *The Relations Explosion,* William L. Safire discussed that important man in any political campaign, Charlie Regan. "In every headquarters, there is a certain amount of gentle turning down that must be done without offending well meaning volunteers. Horrible campaign songs, meaningless slogans and painful pamphlets are submitted and must be rejected in a way that will not diminish enthusiasm. . . . Strategic delays are necessary." So the campaign manager says, "Sounds great to me, but have you checked it with Charlie Regan?" Or, "I'll give you a firm go-ahead just as soon as Regan gets back." Charlie Regan has a place on the organization charts all right, and there is a sure-enough desk; his raincoat may be draped over a chair or sometimes neatly hung up. But he never seems to get back. When someone calls, he is "down at the printers." The truth is *there is no Charlie Regan.*

" 'The little man who isn't there' is indispensable to any political effort," explained Safire.[27]

Unfortunately, designers have no Charlie Regan. They can't very well put off clients who make what may be unreasonable and impossible suggestions. ("Can you squeeze one more item and price in that blank corner there?" or "Why can't you use some Old English for the headings?") Either designers must defend their layouts or they must make adjustments, however distasteful that may be.

How does one defend an arrangement of elements or a choice of type or art? Is not good layout a matter of taste? When there are disagreements, can designers be sure their tastes are superior to those of the clients?

For each decision made while working on an assignment, the designer formulates a reason for self-assurance if not for client approval. Of course, the rightness and wrongness of the final design *is* a matter of taste, a taste cultivated through hours and then years of observation, study, practice, and experimentation. "It seems to me," said Daniel Berkeley Updike, "that a right taste is cultivated . . . by knowing what has been done in the past and what has been so esteemed that it has lived."

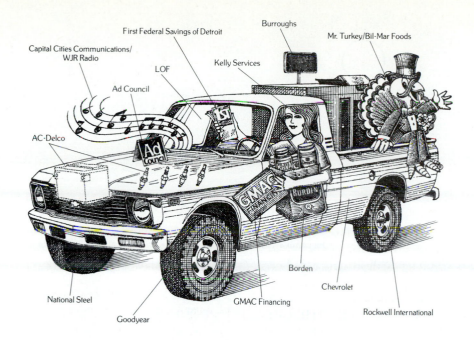

Capital Cities Communications/
WJR Radio

First Federal Savings of Detroit

Burroughs

Mr. Turkey/Bil-Mar Foods

Kelly Services

LOF

Ad Council

AC-Delco

National Steel

Goodyear

GMAC Financing

Borden

Chevrolet

Rockwell International

Campbell-Ewald, Detroit, dramatizes the variety of its clients in this "company car" drawing by Ron Rae used in an ad in *Advertising Age*. To do the job the illustrator had to let a few products hang outside the car and go to a partial cutaway for others. The pointing lines make this art as much a diagram as a cartoon drawing. The accompanying copy made the point that Campbell-Ewald is "a broad and balanced agency, qualified to perform in a variety of markets."

"Your personality shows through in the ads you do," said Amil Gargano, president of the Ally & Gargano agency. "If you're shallow, or dull, or self-indulgent, it shows." Gargano also says that ad makers must be responsive to people. "Don't waste your time in advertising unless you respect people. You can't hide what you are. You're revealed through your work."[28]

NOTES

1. THE WORLD OF ADVERTISING

1. "Big Business Shuns Corporate Responsibilities," *Media: The Asian Marketing and Communications Magazine,* May 30, 1983, p. 10.

2. See Anne-Marie Wright Ninivaggi's "When High Standards Cost Ad Sales," *Folio,* January 1992, p. 62.

3. Robert L. Shayon, "Advocacy Advertising," *Pennsylvania Gazette,* May 1979, p. 9.

4. Restructured from an article by Ted Morgan, "New! Improved! Advertising!" *The New York Times Magazine,* January 25, 1976, p. 52.

5. Martin Mayer, *Whatever Happened to Madison Avenue?* (Boston: Little, Brown and Company, 1991), p. 9.

6. "Laptop Presentations Pitch Products," *Communication World,* December 1991, p. 38.

7. John S. Meskil, "The Media Mix," *Media Letter,* American Association of Advertising Agencies, January 1979, p. 2.

8. Peter Kerr, "Ads Targeting 'Forever Young' Grumpies," New York *Times,* reprinted in the Eugene, Oregon *Register-Guard,* August 27, 1991, p. B1.

9. Interview with J. Craig Mathiesen, February 27, 1991.

10. Steven Waldman, "The Tyranny of Choice," *The New Republic,* January 27, 1992, p. 23.

11. Judith Alder Hennessee and Joan Nicholson catalog offenses in "NOW Says: TV Commercials Insult Women," *New York Times Magazine,* May 28, 1972, p. 12ff.

12. Barbara Lippert, "Agencies, Marketers Woo Postfeminist Woman," *Adweek,* March 7, 1983, pp. 17, 20.

13. Quoted by Jennifer Foote, "The Ad World's New Bimbos," *Newsweek,* January 25, 1988, p. 45.

14. John O'Toole, "Out, Damned Political Spot," *Newsweek,* October 29, 1984, p. 20.

15. "Cigarette Ads and the Press," *The Nation,* March 7, 1987, p. 283.

16. Martin Mayer, "What Merger Era, and Going Public, Cost Ad Agencies," *Advertising Age,* May 20, 1991, p. 24.

17. Bruce Horovitz, "Furor Over Smoking Camel," Los Angeles *Times,* October 11, 1991, p. D1.

18. Barbara Lippert, "War on the Spokes-Genitals," *Adweek,* October 28, 1991, p. 33.

19. Quoted by Skip Wollenberg, AP dispatch, Eugene, Oregon *Register-Guard,* June 14, 1991, p. 7C.

20. Skip Wollenberg, AP dispatch, Eugene, Oregon *Register-Guard,* February 14, 1992, p. 5B.

21. Saul Bass, "Creativity in Visual Communication," *Creativity: An Examination of the Creative Process* (New York: Hastings House, 1959), pp. 122, 123. Quoted by permission.

22. Marc Trieb, "Critic's Notebook: The Lesson of Lessen," *AIGA Journal,* Vol. 5, No. 1, 1987, p. 5.

23. Jerry Fields, "Art Directors' Salaries," *Art Direction,* January 1976, p. 46.

24. Peter Adler, "The Best of Both Worlds," *Advertising Age,* June 4, 1979, p. 60.

25. Dugald Stermer, "Design as a Fashion Statement," *AIGA Journal,* Vol. 5, No. 1, 1987, p. 1.

26. Steven Heller, "The Abuse of Style," *AIGA Journal,* Vol. 5, No. 1, 1987, p. 2.

27. Quoted in a 1979 *Wall Street Journal* ad, "Korey's Story," reprinted in *Advertising Age,* March 26, 1987, p. 69.

28. Quoted in a 1983 *Wall Street Journal* ad, "Krone Alone," reprinted in *Advertising Age,* March 26, 1987, p. 70.

2. THE CREATIVE PROCESS

1. Art Kleiner, "Master of the Sentimental Sell," *The New York Times Magazine,* December 14, 1986, p. 52.

2. Stephen C. Kopcha, "Misconceptions About Creativity," *Adweek,* November 16, 1987, p. 50.

3. Wes Perrin, *Advertising Realities,* (Mountain View, California: Mayfield Publishing Company, 1992), p. 132.

4. Steven Penchina, "Gone Are the Glory Days," *Adweek,* March 4, 1991, p. 32.

5. Quoted by Kenneth Jacobsen, "David Ogilvy," *Adweek,* January 28, 1991, p. 16.

6. Quoted in "Words from the Wise," *Art Product News,* September/October 1986, p. 40.

7. John S. Straiton, "The Fey Cult of Cutie-Pie Creativity," *Marketing/Communications,* November 1969, p. 64.

8. William Bernbach, "Bill Bernbach Defines the Four Disciplines of Creativity." *Advertising Age,* July 5, 1971, pp. 21–23.

9. "Creativity TV Style," *Advertising Age,* October 13, 1975, p. 14.

10. Quoted by Kathryn Sederberg, "Top Agency 'Creatives' Take a Closer Look at Creativity," *Advertising Age,* June 4, 1979, p. S–10.

11. *Ibid.,* p. S–10.

12. Quoted by John F. Baker in "Dr. Rollo May," *Publishers Weekly,* December 1, 1975, p. 12.

13. Kathryn Sederberg, *op. cit.,* p. S–3.

14. Ray Valek, "Humorist Gives Tips for Creativity," *Communication World,* April 1991, p. 11.

15. John Carambat, "What Drives the Creative Personality?" *Step-by-Step Graphics,* November/December 1989, pp. 144–149.

16. John Leo, "The Ups and Downs of Creativity," *Time,* October 8, 1984, p. 76.

17. "Melancholy's Creative Side," *U.S. News & World Report,* March 5, 1990, p. 51.

18. Quoted by Baker in "Dr. Rollo May," p. 13.

19. Quoted in "Design '64: Directions and Dilemmas," *CA: The Magazine of the Communications Arts,* September/October 1964, p. 81.

20. Ron Hoff, in Maxine Paetro, *How to Put Your Book Together and Get a Job in Advertising,* (New York: Executive Communications, 1979), pp. 77, 78.

21. Paul Waddell, "Try Creativity—It Sells," *Advertising Age,* December 13, 1982, p. M–36.

22. Sharon Churcher, "A Hitch in Hitchcock's Credits," *New York,* January 17, 1983, p. 12.

23. In a letter to the editor, *Advertising Age,* March 20, 1972, p. 88.

24. From "True Gage," a 1978 ad sponsored by *The Wall Street Journal.*

25. Quoted by *Time* in its "People" column, December 18, 1978, p. 85.

26. "Winners," *Adweek,* March 23, 1987, 38-page insert.

27. Quoted by Trip Gabriel, "Bill Evans's Twilight Zone," *Vanity Fair,* January 1992, p. 59.

28. Kurt Andersen, "Nouvelle Cuisine for the Eyes," *Time*, June 8, 1987, pp. 88, 89.

29. Massimo Vignelli, "From Less Is More To Less Is a Bore. Is More the Better?" *U&lc.*, December 1982, p. 10.

30. Randall Rothenberg, "In Ads, Simple Is Replacing Slick," New York *Times*, reprinted in *APA Magazine*, Winter 1991, pp. 32–35.

31. Ann Keding and Thomas Bivins, *How to Produce Creative Advertising*, (Lincolnwood, Illinois, NTC Business Books, 1990), p. 23, 24.

32. Letter to the author from Jack Fund, March 20, 1991.

33. As quoted in a *Wall Street Journal* ad in *Advertising Age*; July 15, 1985, p. 15.

34. Ann Keding and Thomas Bivins, *op. cit.*, p. 6.

35. John Canaday, *Mainstreams of Modern Art*, (New York: Holt, Rinehart and Winston, Inc., 1981), Second Edition, p. 6.

36. Quoted by Digby Diehl, "Q & A: Bill Lear," *West*, April 23, 1972, pp. 30–31.

37. Jack Roberts, "The Ten-Letter, X-Rated, Gold-Plated Word," *Art Direction*, July 1971, p. 78.

38. Bruce Kurtz, *Spots* (New York: Arts Communication, 1977), p. 70.

39. Hanley Norins, *The Young & Rubicam Traveling Creative Workshop*, Englewood Cliffs, N.J.: Prentice Hall, 1990), p. 45.

40. J. L. Marra, "Using Analogy to Teach Idea Generation in Advertising," *Communication: Journalism Education Today*, Fall 1978, pp. 2–5.

41. Kyle Heger, "The Automation of Creativity," *Communication World*, November 1991, pp. 18–21.

42. Martin Mayer, *Whatever Happened to Madison Avenue?* (Boston: Little, Brown and Company, 1991), p. 255.

43. Quoted by D. Morgan Neu, "Creativity: Its Meaning for Researchers," *Art Direction*, August 1984, p. 10.

44. Alexander Lindey, *Plagiarism and Originality* (New York: Harper & Brothers, 1952).

45. Herb Lubalin, "Herb Lubalin's Typography Issue," *Print*, May/June 1979, p. 43.

46. Quoted by Amy Saltzman and Edward C. Baig, "Plugging in to 'Creativity,' " *U.S. News & World Report*, October 29, 1990, p. 96.

3. PUTTING IT INTO WORDS

1. "Brand Image, Character Termed All-Important," *Advertising Age*, August 30, 1982, p. 14.

2. Wes Perrin, *Advertising Realities*, (Mountain View, Calif.: Mayfield Publishing Company, 1992), p. 17.

3. Quoted in a 1986 *Wall Street Journal* ad, "How Now, Hal?" reprinted in *Advertising Age*, March 26, 1987, p. 82.

4. Quoted by Bruce Stockler, "Thoughts That Count," *Millimeter*, February 1990, p. 112.

5. In a speech to the Association for Education in Journalism and Mass Communication, Corvallis, Oregon, August 8, 1983.

6. Quoted by Martin Mayer, *Whatever Happened to Madison Avenue?* Boston: Little, Brown and Company, 1991), p. 152.

7. John W. Crawford, *Advertising*, 2d ed. (Boston: Allyn & Bacon, 1965), p. 173.

8. Steve Haggard in a letter to the editor of *Advertising Age*, August 6, 1990, p. 16.

9. "Food Ads: A Recipe for Confusion," *University of California at Berkeley Wellness Letter*, December 1991, p. 1.

10. Hanley Norins, *The Compleat Copywriter* (New York: McGraw-Hill, 1966), p. 6.

11. "Hellbox," *Media People*, November 1979, p. 12.

12. "Lifestyle of the '80s," *U.S. News & World Report*, August 1, 1983, p. 45.

13. Quoted in a 1981 *Wall Street Journal* ad, "Mike's Likes," reprinted in *Advertising Age*, March 26, 1987, p. 85.

14. "Ad Follies of 1989," *Advertising Age*, January 1, 1990, p. 37.

15. Bernice Kanner, "Tobacco Road," *New York*, January 17, 1983, p. 16.

16. Nancy L. Croft, "Enticing the Customer," *Nation's Business*, July 1987, p. 64.

17. Quoted in "Quotes," *Marketing/Communications*, January 1972, p. 54.

18. Quoted in a 1980 *Wall Street Journal* ad, "Very Jerry," reprinted in *Advertising Age*, March 26, 1987, p. 61.

19. Otto Kleppner and Norman Govoni, *Advertising Procedure*, 7th ed. (Englewood Cliffs, N.J.: Prentice-Hall), 1979.

20. Quoted by Joseph Seldin in *The Golden Fleece* (New York: Macmillan, 1963), chap. 13.

21. David Greenberg, "Washington Diarist," *The New Republic*, March 25, 1991, p. 46.

22. Volney Palmer, "The Final Say," *Advertising Age*, January 28, 1980, p. 44.

23. Reva Korda, "How to Break the Rules," *Advertising Age*, March 5, 1979, pp. 47, 48.

24. Quoted in a Magazine Publishers Association ad in *Advertising Age*, February 18, 1991, p. 49.

25. Gail Bronson, "In Advertising, Big Names Mean Big Money," *U.S. News & World Report*, July 4, 1983, p. 60.

26. From a Los Angeles *Times* story appearing in the Eugene *Register-Guard*, September 16, 1987, p. 9B.

27. "Freeberg: Humor's No Laughing Matter," *Advertising Age*, January 20, 1992, p. 52.

28. Jack Broom, "Hollywood Cuts in on Ivar's 'Dances,' " Seattle *Times*, April 5, 1991, p. 1.

29. "MADD Leader Backs Ad Curbs," *Advertising Age*, July 18, 1983, p. 74.

30. "Mac the Bod Ads Lifts Eyebrows," *Advertising Age*, July 25, 1983, pp. 3, 86.

31. John Blumenthal, "Is Truth Bar to Creativity?" *Advertising Age*, October 9, 1978, p. 75.

32. Quoted by Gertrude Synder and Alan Peckolick, *Herb Lubalin*, American Showcase, Inc., New York, 1985, p. 17.

33. You can see a collection of the ads in *The Wall Street Journal's* reprint of them in the March 26, 1987 issue of *Advertising Age*.

34. To be consistent, the text for this chapter shows all advertising headlines in caps and lower case even though a large percentage of headlines these days are set in all lowercase. The chapter shows slogans in lower case.

35. Quoted by Elaine F. Weiss, "King of the Chews," *Harper's Magazine*, October 1982, p. 23.

4. THE PRINCIPLES OF DESIGN

1. Gillian Naylor, *The Bauhaus* (London: Studio Vista/Dutton Paperback, 1968), p. 7.

2. Harvey Offenhartz, *Point-of-Purchase Design* (New York: Reinhold, 1968), p. 195.

3. James Miho of Needham, Harper & Steers in the foreword to the catalog of the 1970/1971 Communication Graphic Show sponsored by The American Institute of Graphic Arts.

4. Milton Glaser in *Graphic Designers in the USA/3*, Universe Books, New York, 1972, p. 53.

5. Philip C. Beam, *The Language of Art* (New York: The Ronald Press, 1958).

6. Called the "divine proportion" by Fra Luca Pacioli in 1509 and the "golden mean" by nineteenth-century artists, it figures out mathematically at exactly 1.681 to 1.

7. Quoted in Mary Anne Guitar's *22 Famous Illustrators Tell How They Work* (New York: David McKay, 1964), p. 108.

5. LAYOUT APPROACHES

1. Actually, the Chinese proverb has it that one picture is worth *more than* ten thousands words (see *Bartlett's Familiar Quotations*), which makes his point even stronger.

2. "Place Company Logo Higher in Ad . . .," *Folio*, August 1982, p. 39.

3. Developed and expanded over a period of years in the writing of succeeding editions of this textbook, the highly arbitrary list has been treated by some other writers as definitive. Readers should understand that the list is nothing but a temporary crutch. It can't possibly cover all the permutations that advertising design can take.

4. Interview with Robert Keding, July 3, 1992.

5. "Why Ask Why?" *Print* (Computer Art and Design Annual 1), Vol. XLV, No. VII, 1991, pp. 6, 7.

6. Marjorie Spiegelman, "Design for the '90s: New Directions," *Graphic Arts Monthly*, January 1990, pp. 101, 102.

7. Carol Terrizzi, "Desk-top Publishing: Starting Small, Thinking Big," *Folio,* November 1986, pp. .104, 109.

6. PRODUCTION

1. Pauline Ores, "Changing Times," *Desktop Communications,* May–June 1992, p. 4.

2. James Craig, *Production for the Graphic Designer* (New York: Watson-Guptill, 1974).

3. Interview with Robert Keding, July 3, 1992.

4. Of course, there wasn't any paste in the old system, either; it's been rubber cement, or wax, or glue sticks.

5. Betsy Spethmann, "Print Ads Read Into Computer Revolution," *Advertising Age,* May 25, 1992, p. 43.

6. Gary Olsen, *Getting Started in Computer Graphics* (Cincinnati, Ohio: North Light Books, 1989), p. 123.

7. Ronald Labuz, "Catch the PC Wave," *Magazine Design & Production,* January 1987, p. 32.

8. Wayne Robinson, *How'd They Design and Print That?* (Cincinnati, Ohio: North Light Books, 1991), p. 6.

9. Ann Keding and Tom Bivins, *How to Produce Creative Advertising* (Lincolnwood, Illinois: NTC Business Books, 1990), p. 156.

10. Norman Sanders, *Graphic Designer's Production Handbook* (New York: Hastings House, 1982), p. 189.

7. TYPOGRAPHY

1. David Ogilvy, *Confessions of an Advertising Man,* Atheneum, New York, 1987, p. 93. (Paperback edition of 1963 book.)

2. Type scholars distinguish between the "newer" old-style letters of Caslon (English) and Garamond (French) and the older letters of the incunabula (Venetian), but such distinction is not necessary for our purposes.

3. Quoted in "Zapf on Tomorrow's Type," *Communication World,* November 1983, p. 20.

4. Quoted by Lisa Hooker, "Designing Type by Observation," *Magazine Design & Production,* June 1986, p. 23.

5. "Zapf on Tomorrow's Type," p. 21.

6. Allan Haley, "The ABC's of Alphabet Design," *U&lc.,* May 1986, pp. 2 and 3.

7. Quoted by Noreen O'Leary, "Legibility Lost," *Adweek,* October 5, 1987, p. D7.

8. *Ibid.,* p. D8.

9. See Don Finck's "Why a Type Director?" *Art Direction,* June 1990, pp. 74–76.

10. Letter to the author from David A. Wesson, Milwaukee, Wisconsin, undated. Quoted by permission.

11. This segment, like several others in this book, appeared in a slightly different form in the author's "Look of the Book" column in *Communication World,* a publication of the International Association of Business Communicators. Reprinted by permission.

12. Howard Fenton, "In Pursuit of Typographic Quality," *Pre-,* May 1990, p. 10.

8. ART

1. Watson Saint James, "Art Directors Drawn to Macintosh," *Advertising Age,* March 13, 1989, p. 50.

2. Interview with David Foster, June 29, 1992.

3. Quoted by Art Schlosser, "Fine Art vs. Commercial Art: Will the Twain Ever Meet?" *Print,* September/October 1964, pp. 52–61.

4. "Fine Arts," *Adweek,* March 23, 1987, p. 3.

5. Marjorie McCloy, "Is It Art Yet?" *Publish!* July 1989, p. 47.

6. Reported by Roy Pinney in *Advertising Photography* (New York: Hastings House, 1962).

7. David Deutsch, "When Do Suggestions Interfere with Job Creativity?" *Advertising Age,* January 28, 1980, pp. 43, 44.

8. "Ads Show Few Blacks," *Editor & Publisher,* August 10, 1991, p. 35.

9. Veronique Vienne, "Money Can Buy You Love," *Metropolis,* December 1991, p. 48.

10. Jonathan Alter, "When Photographs Lie," *Newsweek,* July 30, 1990, p. 44.

9. COLOR

1. Jan White, "Using Color to Carry the Message," *Folio,* April 1, 1991, p. 86.

2. "The Post-Modern Palette," *Art Direction,* October 1983, p. 39.

3. "The Bluing of America," *Time,* July 18, 1983, p. 62.

4. Liz Horton, "Colour Eschews Black-and-White Advertising Rates," *Folio,* March 1, 1991, p. 34.

5. Color blindness seems to be mostly a male phenomenon. John Adkins Richardson in *Art: The Way It Is* (New York: Harry N. Abrams, 1973) reported that 8 percent of men and only 0.5 percent of women are color-blind.

6. Some scholars consider green as a fourth primary.

7. Violet is called "purple" when on the bluish side.

8. GDS Books, P.O. Box 9464, Providence, Rhode Island 02940, offers a book of 20 of her full color covers reproduced on Kromekote paper and on oversize pages. Price: $55.

9. "The Color Purple," *American Demographics,* June 1987, p. 24.

10. Fran Lebowitz, *Metropolitan Life* (New York: E. P. Dutton, 1978), p. 130.

11. See Alyce Kaprow, "Color and Computer Graphics," *Magazine Design & Production,* November 1987, pp. 53–56.

12. Eliot DeY. Schein, "Twenty Tips," *Folio,* February 1980, p. 78.

10. NEWSPAPER ADVERTISING

1. Figures from *Editor & Publisher International Year Book 1992.*

2. Lisa Bennenson, "The Data Chase," *Adweek,* Special Report: The Newspaper Business May 4, 1992, p. 6.

3. From 1992 rate cards.

4. Anna America, "Housing Ads Are Inviting More Scrutiny," *Presstime,* January 1992, p. 29.

5. Martin Mayer, *Whatever Happened to Madison Avenue?* (Boston: Little, Brown and Company, 1991), p. 117.

6. *Editor & Publisher,* December 3, 1983.

7. George Garneau, "ANPA-Ad Bureau to Merge," *Editor & Publisher,* January 18, 1992, p. 3.

8. Local advertising in other media will be considered in later chapters.

9. Detailed in a talk given at an advertising workshop sponsored by the Federation Publicitaria de Puerto Rico in San Juan.

10. Letter to the Editor, *Advertising Age,* March 7, 1983, p. 48.

11. Interviews with Paul Burke and Dan Villani, July 9, 1992.

12. Interview with Tom Chastain, July 22, 1992.

13. Interview with Kelly Shively, January 21, 1988.

14. "Grand Illusion," *Newsweek,* October 6, 1975, p. 96.

15. Bill Gloede, "What's Black & White and Red All Over?" *Editor & Publisher,* September 24, 1983, p. 15.

16. Wayne Kelly, "Newspapers Can Use Color Inappropriately," *Editor & Publisher,* October 22, 1983, p. 24.

17. *ANPA Newspaper Information Service Newsletter,* August 31, 1971, p. 2.

11. MAGAZINE ADVERTISING

1. J. K. G., "Man's Best Friend," *New Republic,* November 28, 1983, p. 43.

2. Daniel Harris, "Lovely to Look At," *The Nation,* December 2, 1991, p. 711.

3. Theodore Peterson, "The Modern Magazine at Age 90," speech delivered at the University of Illinois, Urbana, October 18, 1983.

4. Norman Hart, *Industrial Advertising and Publicity* (London: Halsted Press, 1978), pp. 148, 149.

5. "On Accepting Ads," *Commonweal,* October 1966, p. 7.

6. All ads from the June 15, 1992 issue of *Advertising Age.*

7. "Magazines versus Television," *Folio,* November 1979, pp. 77–79.

12. BROADCAST ADVERTISING

1. Hooper White, "Has the Tide Run Out on New Wave?" *Advertising Age,* March 7, 1983, p. M-4.

2. Piet Verbeck, "Technographics: A New Ripple," *Advertising Age,* July 15, 1985, p. 18.

3. Thomas Sowell, "We May Yet Return to Decency," column circulated by Creators Syndicate and published in *Conservative Chronicle*, November 6, 1991, p. 29.

4. Rochard Zoglin, "It's Amazing! Call Now!" *Time*, June 17, 1991, p. 71.

5. Based on observations made by Bruce Kurtz in *Spots* (New York: Arts Communications, 1977), pp. 86–93.

6. Stephen Battagilo, "Forget Zapping; Viewers Now Zip," *Adweek*, March 4, 1991, p. 22.

7. Ann Keding and Thomas Bivins, *How to Produce Creative Advertising*, (Lincolnwood, Illinois: NTC Business Books, 1990), p. 67.

8. Peter Ognibene, "TV Advertising for Books," *Publishers Weekly*, April 12, 1976, p. 50.

9. Erik Lacitis, "Long-Playing TV Ad Is a Record Maker," *Seattle Times*, February 4, 1980, p. B2.

10. Bill Abrams, "If Logic in Ads Doesn't Sell, Try a Tug on the Heartstrings," *Wall Street Journal*, April 8, 1982, p. 27.

11. Dan Kelly, "Where Mood Speaks Louder Than Words," *Advertising Age*, August 23, 1982, p. M–2.

12. Joe McKnight, AP dispatch, Eugene, Oregon *Register-Guard*, July 28, 1991, p. 5B.

13. Noting the limitations of earlier attempts to classify TV commercials, including the attempt in this book, Ibrahim M. Hefzallah and W. Paul Maloney in *Journal of Advertising Research*, August 1979, pp. 57–62, suggested thirteen categories.

14. Frank Romano, "Frank Talk," *Type World*, April 1989, p. 2.

15. Clio Awards at 30 East 60th St., New York, maintains an archive of more than fifty thousand radio and TV commercials available—at a price—for showing to public gatherings.

16. Bradley Johnson and Cleveland Horton, "QuickTime Boosts Mac's Ad Ability," *Advertising Age*, January 13, 1992, p. 3.

17. Howard Sutton, "TV Animation Isn't Just Cartoons," *Advertising Age*, January 31, 1972, p. 51.

18. Quoted by Jeff Greenfield, "Down to the Last Detail," *Columbia Journalism Review*, March/April 1976, p. 17.

19. *Ibid.*

20. Roger D. Rice, "Baby Medium, Television Grows Up Since 1940s," *Advertising Age*, April 19, 1976, p. 112.

21. Lynn Hirschberg, "When You Absolutely, Positively Want the Best," *Esquire*, August 1983, p. 53.

22. Bruce Kurtz, *Spots* (New York: Arts Communications, 1977), p. 80.

23. "Art Directors Who Direct," *Art Direction*, November 1987, p. 76.

24. Arthur Bellaire, "Animation and Closeups Can Save Your TV Spot Dollars," *Advertising Age*, January 11, 1971, p. 70.

25. "Abbott Television Advertising Follows Strict Guidelines," *Commitment*, Abbott Laboratories, Fall 1982, p. 7.

26. W. Keith Hafer and Gordon E. White, *Advertising Writing* (St. Paul, Minn.: West Publishing Company, 1977), pp. 133, 135.

13. DIRECT-MAIL ADVERTISING

1. *Direct Marketing* comes out monthly to serve the users of this medium.

2. Ralph Whitehead, Jr., "Direct Mail: The Underground Press of the '80s," *Columbia Journalism Review*, January/February 1983, p. 44.

3. Bob Stone, "Creativity in Direct Marketing and Direct Response Advertising," in Hadley Norins' *The Young & Rubicam Traveling Creative Workshop* (Englewood Cliffs, N.J.: Prentice Hall, 1990), p. 158.

4. Jeffrey H. Birnbaum, "After Eros . . . ," *The Wall Street Journal*, March 18, 1980, p. 16.

5. "Kind of Crooked," *Time*, July 30, 1979, p. 33.

6. Eliot DeY. Schein, "Twenty Tips," *Folio*, February 1980, p. 77.

7. Elinor Selame, "Simplicity and Other Key Design Considerations for Business Stationery," *Printing Paper* 64, no. 3 (1978), pp. 10, 11.

8. Quoted by John D. Klingel in "Open Me: The Art of the Envelope," *Folio*, March 1983, p. 128.

9. Kimball R. Woodbury, *Printing Paper* 64, no. 3 (1978), p. 14.

10. From a 1991 J. Peterman catalog.

11. Bob Stone, *op. cit.*, p. 159.

12. *Marketing with Newsletters*, E. F. Communications, 5721 Magazine Street, Suite 170, New Orleans, Louisiana 70115.

13. *90 Ways to Save Money on Newsletters*, 50092 Kingscross Road, Westminster, California 92683.

14. Barbara Marsh, "Enterprise," *The Wall Street Journal*, July 12, 1991, p. B1.

15. Elizabeth Howard, "Preparing Annual Reports for the 1990s," *Public Relations Journal*, May 1991, p. 26.

16. Stephanie Schorow, AP dispatch, Eugene, Oregon *Register-Guard*, April 3, 1991, p. 6B.

17. Richard A. Lewis, "Gone Is the Golden Age," *DA*, Second Quarter. 1975, p. 10.

18. Dan Danbom, "Annual Reports Deemed Challenging Opportunity," *Communication World*, September 1991, p. 21.

19. Mary De Lisi, "The Changing Landscape of Annual Report Design," *Communication World*, September 1991, p. 18.

20. David Owen, "Rest in Pieces," *Harper's Magazine*, June 1983, pp. 70, 71.

14. POSTERS AND DISPLAYS

1. "Ladybird's Bill," *Newsweek*, March 5, 1979, p. 18.

2. Peter Allen, "Editor's Galley," *American Advertising*, Winter 1990–91, p. 2.

3. Quoted by Stuart Tomlinson in an interview in *The Oregonian*, November 9, 1987, p. B1.

4. For a collection of full-color reproductions, see their book: Hayward Cirker and Blanche Cirker, *The Golden Age of the Poster* (New York: Dover, 1971).

5. Kenneth Wylie, "What's Good, What's Bad, What's Beautiful," *Advertising Age*, August 8, 1983, p. M–15.

6. B. Roland McElroy, "Billboards: Clean, Effective, Efficient, Endangered," *American Advertising*, Winter 1990–91, p. 27.

7. See *The Big Outdoor*, an undated booklet published by the Institute of Outdoor Advertising.

8. See Jean Murphy and Patricia McCullough, "Markings: Reflecting on Your Fleet," *Heavy Duty Trucking*, June 1987, pp. 46–56.

9. From a POPAI press release, October 14, 1987.

10. *P-O-P: The Last Word in Advertising*, Point-of-Purchase Advertising Institute, Inc., New York, n.d., p. 2.

15. LONG-TERM DESIGN

1. Barnard Rudofsky, "Notes on Early Trademarks and Related Matters," in Egbert Jacobson, ed., *Seven Designers Look at Trademark Design* (Chicago: Paul Theobald, 1952), p. 28.

2. Ernst Lehner, *Symbols, Signs & Signets* (Cleveland: World Publishing Company, 1950), p. 119.

3. Isaac E. Lambert, *The Public Accepts: Stories Behind Famous Trade-Marks, Names and Slogans* (Albuquerque: University of New Mexico Press, 1941), p. 168. Frank Rowsome, Jr. retells some of Lambert's stories in his entertaining *They Laughed When I Sat Down: An Informal History of Advertising in Words and Pictures* (New York: McGraw-Hill, 1959); see chapter 7, "The Trademark Menagerie."

4. The term *logotype* or *logo* also applies to the special lettering or typesetting of the name that goes at the top of page 1 of a newspaper or on the cover of a magazine. *Flag* and *nameplate* are other terms also used in this connection.

5. "P&G Gets Satanism Rumor Settlement, Changes Logo Anyway," *Skeptical Inquirer*, Fall 1991, p. 22.

6. Elwood Whitney, ed., *Symbology: The Use of Symbols in Visual Communications* (New York: Hastings House, 1960), p. 116.

7. J. E. Cirlot's *A Dictionary of Symbols*, 2d ed. (New York: Philosophical Library, 1972), contains a thorough listing of symbols and their meanings. So does Henry Dreyfuss's *Symbol Sourcebook: An Authoritative Guide to International Graphic Symbols* (New York: McGraw-Hill, 1972). A more compact list can be found in the author's *Publication Design*, 5th ed. (Dubuque, Iowa: Wm. C. Brown Company, 1991).

8. "Humor Value Permits Jeans' Similar Name," *Insight*, December 7, 1987, p. 54.

9. Scot Haller, "Checkout Time at the Roach Motel," *New York*, July 9–16, 1979, p. 71.

10. Jacob Weisberg, "Washington Diarist," *The New Republic*, October 14, 1991, p. 54.

11. B. G. Yovovich, "In Search of a New Corporate Label," *Advertising Age*, March 7, 1983, p. M–23.

12. Joan Kron, "Alphabet Scoop," *New York*, January 26, 1976, p. 48.

13. Gertrude Snyder, "Pro-File: Helmut Krone," *U&lc.*, June 1979, p. 13.

14. Wolf Von Eckardt, "Heraldry for the Industrial Age," *Time*, October 18, 1982, p. 85.

15. See Barbara Knight, "Trademarks Live!" *Journal of The American Institute of Graphic Arts* 16:2, p. 13.

16. Requoted in *New York*, January 26, 1976, p. 48.

17. John Revett, "Corporate Logos Are His Game, Bass Is His Name," *Advertising Age*, January 8, 1979, p. 38.

18. Mark Muro, "The Man Who Makes Book Covers," *Boston Globe*, March 12, 1983, pp. 20, 21.

19. "Cover Art: Heating Up," *Publishers Weekly*, October 2, 1987, p. 70.

20. "100 Classic Album Covers," *Rolling Stone*, November 14, 1991, pp. 91–154.

21. Dugald Stermer, "Packaging Sound," *Communication Arts*, January/February 1974, p. 51.

22. "Fire and Ice-T," *Time*, July 27, 1992, p. 23. The artist later asked Time Warner to remove the song from the album.

23. Milton Glaser, "Signs in the Supermarket," *Harper's*, March 1986, p. 26.

24. Maxine Brady, *Bloomingdale's* (New York: Harcourt Brace Jovanovich, 1980), p. 110.

25. Quoted by Walter McQuade, "Packages Bear Up Under a Bundle of Regulations," *Fortune*, May 7, 1979, p. 189.

26. Theodore J. Gage, "Agencies Want Involvement, But Only in Design Process," *Advertising Age*, December 17, 1979, p. S–1.

27. Joan Chatfield-Taylor, "Designing the World Around Us," *San Francisco Chronicle*, July 27, 1979, p. 25.

28. Don E. Forest, "Simple Rules for Success in Package Design," *Adweek*, August 23, 1983, p. 26.

29. "High Hopes in a Black Box," *Newsweek*, August 22, 1983, p. 51.

30. Alan D. Fletcher, *Yellow Pages Advertising*, booklet published by American Association of Yellow Pages Publishers, Chesterfield, Missouri, 1986, p. 3.

31. "Yellow Pages Myth: Claims and Truth," *Yellow Pages Update*, Summer 1987, p. 5.

16. CAREERS

1. Quoted by Martin Mayer, *Whatever Happened to Madison Avenue?* (Boston: Little, Brown and Company, 1991), pp. 158, 181.

2. Letter from Don Harbor to a student, March 7, 1986. Reprinted by permission.

3. Quoted in "Color Trends in Graphic Design," by Helene Eckstein, *Step-by-Step Graphics*, November/December 1987, pp. 149, 152.

4. Don Harbor, "Hot Hints from Harbor," *How. . . Ideas & Techniques in Graphic Design*, March/April 1986, pp. 46–50.

5. "Tracy Wong," *Art Direction*, June 1990, p. 61.

6. Letter to the author from Tracy Wong, February 8, 1988.

7. From an ad sponsored by *The Wall Street Journal, Advertising Age*, May 16, 1983, p. 18.

8. "Jack Summerford," *Communication Arts*, September/October 1983, p. 32.

9. "How Much Does He Make? How Much Does She Make?" *Step-by-Step Graphics*, May/June 1991, p. 23.

10. Don Harbor, *loc. cit.*

11. Candance Dempsey, "Designers: Don't Miss the Boat!" *Monthly News of the Northwest Advertising Industry*, September 1982, p. 11.

12. LoriBeth Skigen, "Cashing in Their Chips," *Advertising Age*, February 25, 1991, p. 28.

13. Laurie Freeman, "A Byte of a Problem," *Advertising Age*, February 25, 1991, p. 28.

14. Apple Computer, Inc., estimates that its Macintosh is used in about 70 percent of United States advertising agencies and design studios.

15. Wes Perrin, *Advertising Realities* (Mountain View, Calif.: Mayfield Publishing Company, 1992), p. 149.

16. Jim deYong in a speech to students at the University of Oregon, Eugene, January 21, 1988.

17. Maxine Paetro, *How to Put Your Book Together and Get a Job in Advertising* (New York: Executive Communications, 1979), p. 42.

18. Martha Metzdorf, *The Ultimate Portfolio* (Cincinnati, Ohio: North Light Books, 1991), p. 28.

19. *Ibid.*, p. 38.

20. James Craig, *Graphic Design Career Guide* (Watson-Guptill, New York, 1983), p. 135.

21. Harbor, *ibid.*

22. Told by Mort Walker in *Backstage at the Strips*. (New York: Mason/Charter, 1975), p. 102.

23. "Summerford" *op cit.*, p. 32.

24. From a page devoted to Adrien Frutiger in James Craig's *Graphic Design Career Guide* (New York: Watson-Guptill, New York, 1983), p. 110.

25. Nancy Kullas, "Pack Your Proposals with Power," *How*, September/October, 1990, pp. 148, 149.

26. Quoted by Martha Metzdorf, *op. cit.*, p. 118.

27. William L. Safire, *The Relations Explosion* (New York: Macmillan, 1963).

28. "Go, Gargano!" ad sponsored by *The Wall Street Journal, Advertising Age*, August 22, 1983, pp. 12, 13.

29. Sid Bernstein, "Keep Them Graphic Artists in Check!" *Advertising Age*, February 27, 1978, p. 16.

30. Martin Mayer, *op. cit.*, p. 27.

ASSIGNMENTS

CHAPTER 1. THE WORLD OF ADVERTISING

Assignment 1. Search through newspapers and magazines to find examples (one each) of national, retail, mail-order, trade, industrial, professional, and institutional advertising. Evaluate the copy approach and design of each.

Assignment 2. Clip the following from magazines: a seven-word headline; a block of copy 2″ wide by 3″ deep; a printed photograph 3″ by 4″ (vertical or horizontal); a piece of line art occupying a space no bigger than a 2″ square; and a signature. (Do not waste time hunting for pieces that are these exact sizes; pick pieces larger than necessary and trim them to size.) Arrange these elements in a rectangle 6″ wide by 9″ deep. Move them around into as many formations as you can; then settle on one.

Seeing how your fellow students solve the same problem, you will be surprised at the variety of arrangements possible, even with so many restrictions spelled out.

Assignment 3. For this assignment and others to follow, you might want to skip ahead in the textbook and read chapter 4, "Layout Tools and Techniques."

A square (or rectangle), a triangle, and a circle are the three basic shapes a designer works with. What do they symbolize to you? Create an ad using as *the only art* a filled-in square (or rectangle) with a headline that refers to the art. Do the same for the triangle and the circle. These three ads should be 8½″ × 11″ rough sketches, all for different clients of your choosing, with the art occupying whatever proportion of the space you think is appropriate.

An example of the kind of ad you could come up with: The American Heart Association shows a ¼″-diameter circle with this headline: "A Blood Clot the Size of This Dot Can Cause a Heart Attack."

Assignment 4. Sanity Enterprises, Inc., New York, puts out something called an "Anger Banger," a high-impact absorbent pad in a booklike case. The harried executive simply opens the "book" and pounds away with a fist, easing tension that has built up.

It's not an entirely serious or needed product; at $10 it is probably more a gift item than anything else.

The case is covered with a suedelike material and has the words "Anger Banger" centered on its face.

Design an ad 4¾″ wide by 5″ deep for a magazine like *New York,* using the headline "For Fast Relief, Punch the Pad," and include a coupon (this is mail-order advertising) and some photographic art of your choosing plus a copy block of about 130 words.

At this point in the course, your layout can be very rough.

Assignment 5. During the Clarence Thomas–Anita Hill hearings, Morton Kondracke came up with an idea for a product, which he described in a column in *The New Republic* (Dec. 2, 1991). It would be a Harassment Stopper, a tiny transmitter disguised to look like a pin that a woman could wear at the office. It would broadcast to a receiver-type recorder back at her desk, providing her with proof that her boss was harassing her. Assume that the pin is in production and that you have the job of designing a one-column by four-inch magazine ad selling it by mail ($69 plus $4 for postage and handling). Make it a butterfly pin. The ad is in black and white.

CHAPTER 2. THE CREATIVE PROCESS

Assignment 1. Come up with a visual metaphor to show that Apple's PowerBook computer can do anything a regular-size personal computer can do. Design a full-page, full-color ad for the newsmagazines, building it around the metaphor you develop. Leave room for only a small amount of copy. The art with a headline should pretty much take care of the selling job.

Assignment 2. In 1987, *Harper's* magazine, "in the interest of moral instruction and clarification," asked several leading advertising agencies to develop ads promoting the seven deadly sins—wrath, lust, avarice, gluttony, sloth, envy, and pride—and ran the ads in the November issue.

The ad for greed, created by The Martin Agency, showed Santa Claus in a serious mood wearing a suit. The headline read: "The World's Foremost Authority Speaks Out on the Subject of Greed." An ad promoting lust, created by TBWA Advertising, Inc., showed an ancient love scene with the headline: "Any Sin That's Enabled Us to Survive Centuries of War, Death, Pestilence and Famine Can't Be Called Deadly." The secondary headline (there was no copy) read: "Lust. Where Would We Be Without It?"

Now it's your turn. You have a more difficult assignment, in a way. Do a full-page magazine ad selling some virtue. What's in it for the reader of your ad?

Assignment 3. Here is an in-class exercise used by Professor Robert M. Anservitz at the University of Georgia School of Journalism to help copywriting students build "adjective banks" and develop "a more incisive awareness of the roles shape, color, and texture" play in the identification of objects:

One to three students leave the room; then a relatively common item is brought out and shown to the remaining students. They take three to five minutes to write down descriptions. (The descriptions cannot mention the function of the item.) The instructor then puts the item back out of sight and calls in the students who left the room. Using only descriptions (adjectives or adjective phrases) furnished by their classmates, the returning students individually but simultaneously draw the item at the blackboard. The exercise ends when one of the returning students figures out what the item is.

Assignment 4. Take a TV station or newspaper in your hometown and see what you can come up with as an appeal to media buyers who probably know nothing about the medium. What can you say about it that would convince media buyers it is a good medium for the agency's clients? Work up a series of rough sketches of ads. Then narrow in on one and finish it off as well as you can. The ad would appear in *Advertising Age.* You make the space decision.

Assignment 5. Let us say that your college is feeling the pinch: fewer students are enrolling because there are fewer students out there. The situation is serious because it costs about as much to run a half-empty college as one that is filled. So the college is going to do some advertising.

For a regional magazine or for a regional edition of a national magazine, design three 2¼″ × 9½″ ads—deep, one-column ads—that position your college against the others in your area. Stress its strengths—or at least one of its strengths—and try to recruit some new students: recent or about-to-be-graduate high school students as well as people who have been out of school for a while.

Perhaps you will want to deal with the fact that going to your college will make people more employable in desirable jobs. Or maybe you will want to say that the education will make students better rounded, better able to cope with and enjoy life. Maybe in one of your ads you will want to appeal to college dropouts. You can deal with part-time or full-time possibilities.

Write the headlines and leave room for copy. Design ads (in rough layout form) that in each case make use of some art (whatever you think is appropriate). Let each ad make a different point. Keep them related. Do not use color.

CHAPTER 3.   PUTTING IT INTO WORDS

Assignment 1. A trade rumor in the early 1990s had Trident switching to an edible paper for the inner wrapper of each stick of gum in the package. With less wasted paper and less litter, it would have been a "green marketing" coup.

Assume that Trident really *is* going to use edible paper and write the copy for a half-page magazine ad announcing the fact. Do a rough layout to show where the copy would go in the ad and what kind of art you would use. Include a headline.

Assignment 2. Gary Anderson, a printmaker and designer, has toyed with the idea of putting out a line of infant wear—in basic black. He would call his line Uncle Gary's Black Baby Clothes.

Assuming a complete line, possibly even including diapers, work out a copy approach—it could be humorous—for upper-middle-class parents (and relatives) and write some copy (any reasonable length) and suggest art. The ad would appear as a full page in magazines.

Assignment 3. Select a nonprofit organization you can identify with and familiarize yourself with it. It can be a religious, educational, health, ecological, trade, or political organization. Pick a cause it espouses and do some research into that cause. Then write an all-copy ad on the subject, making a single major point, and do it without being preachy. End with the notation: "For further information write to . . ." or something similar.

Type out your copy on regular sheets of typing paper, double-spacing it, and keeping it at three or four pages. Double-space between lines as you would for any copy written for publication. Write the headline and several subheads (headlines within the copy at natural breaks). Do not bother to do a layout for this assignment.

Assignment 4. Professor Willis L. Winter, Jr., as an assignment for his Advertising Copywriting class, asks students to pick out a current ad they greatly admire and write the next ad in the series.

You now have the assignment. Pick an ad that is the current one in a series and study it. Then work up *your* ad, continuing the theme or introducing a new theme. Write both the headline and the copy. Do a quick rough, too, to show what kind of art and design you have in mind. (Your new ad should bear a family resemblance to the existing ad.)

Assignment 5. One of the copywriter's main jobs is to organize material into a logical, easy-to-follow sequence. This would include the writing and arranging of subheads for a direct-mail piece.

Let us say that you are helping put together a folder promoting landscape architecture as a career. The cover carries the not-very-original title: "So You Want to Be a Landscape Architect!" Good enough, unless you can come up with something better. The inside panel carries the main subtitle "Career Opportunities" and this set of sub-subtitles: "Self-Employed," "Forest Service or BLM," "Teaching," "Architects or Engineers," "Cities and Counties," "Nursery," "College," "Start Early," "High School," and "Experience." Quite a hodgepodge.

See if you can reorder these headings, rewriting some of them, perhaps even dropping some and adding others. Keep the idea of parallel structure in mind.

Then relist them in outline form, showing which should be main subtitles and which should be sub-subtitles. Keep to three levels of importance, including the main title of the folder, which, of course, would be the top level.

Presumably, under each subtitle would be some copy and possibly some art, but you can skip all that. This is simply an exercise in making headings clear.

CHAPTER 4.   THE PRINCIPLES OF DESIGN

Assignment 1. Study the several early examples of advertising shown in the opening chapters and, taking one of them, adopt its basic design and create a new ad that could appear in today's media. Do whatever updating you feel is necessary, but don't lose too much of the early feel. Let your ad wallow in nostalgia.

Your product is Bayer Aspirin, and you have a vertical one-third of an 8½″ × 11″ magazine page available to you. Black only.

Assignment 2. Professor Robert Bohle of the School of Mass Communications at Virginia Commonwealth University gives his students one assignment that asks them to design the worst-looking ad they can. With the ads on display, students enthusiastically enter into a discussion about what makes the designs ugly and ineffective.

That's your assignment this time: Do an 8½″ × 11″ ad for a national magazine (you pick the client) that violates all the design rules as you understand them. Make the ad ugly. Then be prepared to explain why the ad is ugly and why it doesn't work.

Assignment 3. The Virginia Division of Industry Development paid $50,000 to two nationally known research organizations to make a study of its prime water sites for industry. Now it wants to make the study available to industrial firms who might want to locate in the commonwealth.

It will buy space in *Chemical Week* and other trade journals likely to be read by industrial executives. The ad, in black-and-white, will occupy two-thirds of a page, or a space 4½″ × 10″. A copywriter offers this headline: "Get a $50,000 Water Study for 29¢" (or whatever a first-class stamp costs at the time you do the assignment).

Do a rough layout to include the headline, about seventy words of copy, a coupon, and a picture of the book containing the study: *Virginia Prime Water Sites for Industry.* Try to put the principles of good design to work.

Assignment 4. Do a 1-col. × 1″ ad for a new correspondence cartoon course. The ad will run in black-and-white in *Popular Mechanics.*

The school is North American School of Cartooning, P.O. Box 678, your town. The course, written by a "well-known cartoonist," features thirty-six lessons. It stresses today's techniques and current markets for cartoons. It takes a practical approach. But there is no individualized instruction. The purpose of the ad is to get inquiries. The price ($69.95) and other details will be covered in follow-up direct mail, which you are not designing.

See if you can work some kind of cartoon illustration into the ad along with the information you think is vital. You cannot do much, of course, in so small a space. This is the challenge of the assignment.

If you wish, you may do your rough in a larger size, but in proportion to the printed size. Make your rough reasonably comprehensive. Keep your lines and type strong enough to take the reduction.

Assignment 5. Assume that the ad for Napier shown in this chapter was one of a series of five. Design the other four, making them related to each other in size and appearance.

Indicate art clearly enough so that you can develop a tie between headlines and art. Use color if you wish but keep your layouts rough.

CHAPTER 5. LAYOUT APPROACHES

Assignment 1. The Real Poop is an organic fertilizer from poultry manure, produced by Harmony Products Inc., Chesapeake, Virginia. Prepare a 1 col. × 2″ ad, to be run back-of-the-book in environmentally conscious magazines, that sells this product by mail order. $7.00 per 4-pound bag, postpaid.

Harmony Products says that the product has no bad odor and is excellent for all house and garden plants.

Your ad can be a rough layout. Ruled lines or greeking for copy. What you use as an illustration and what you say in your headline are up to you.

Assignment 2. Pick out a full-page black-and-white ad from a consumer magazine and a newspaper ad the same size or larger and trace them, taking great care to show graduation of tones. Bear down on the pencil when you trace your headlines, keeping them as near to black as you can. Indicate body copy by ruling parallel lines. If in a copy block you find some boldface type, try to show this in your tracing. When you have finished, put the originals with your tracings and decide for yourself how close you came to a faithful rendering.

Assignment 3. Do three 2-col. × 8″ and one 4-col. × 15″ ads promoting your local newspaper's classified ads.

The ads will be run at two-day intervals in the sponsoring paper (not in the classified section), small ones first. Use art in each ad. Letter in the headlines; indicate the body type in the usual way. You do not have to write the copy, but your roughs should indicate copy approach.

Points you may want to cover: minimum words accepted in classified, rate per word, deadline for copy. The classified advertising manager is interested in plugging especially the Lost and Found, Houses for Sale, Personals, and Miscellaneous for Sale sections.

Tie your series together so that the reader will see a relationship.

The final ad could be summary in nature. Or you could plan a teaser campaign, using the last ad as the focus.

Your layouts can be very rough. Your client in this case does not need pampering.

Assignment 4. You're doing an ad for Sony Handycam camcorders. Several models. Playback directly on any TV. "The People's Choice." Try doing ten thumbnail roughs—one each for all the formats described in the chapter. Use real headlines, if they suggest themselves to you; otherwise, just scribble down some zigzag lines. These thumbnails can be very rough, and at this stage can be black-and-white.

Do them in a size that would, when blown up to full size, occupy a full page in a magazine like *Time*. Be sure your thumbnails are kept in correct proportions. Make them all the same size and arrange them neatly on one page of your layout pad. You might want to do several of each format and cut out the best ones and paste them down on another sheet. Label each of the thumbnails as to format so your harried instructor will not have to guess.

Assignment 5. Pick any one of the thumbnails in this chapter showing various ad formats and, quadrupling the size, do a rather finished rough layout, substituting real words (of your choosing) for the display type and real art (you decide what the ad is to sell) for the crude art shown. Make whatever adjustments you think necessary, but try to capture the feel of the thumbnail you choose.

CHAPTER 6. PRODUCTION

Assignment 1. Find an example of (1) offset lithography, (2) letterpress, (3) gravure, and (4) silk-screen printing. Examine each under a magnifying glass (8-power, if possible), looking especially at the reproduction of the type, and describe the differences in the blackness and crispness of the printing.

Assignment 2. Take a headline from one 8½″ × 11″ (full-page) magazine ad, a piece of art (photo or illustration) from another, a block of copy from another, and a logo from still another and paste them down on an 8½″ × 11″ sheet as though you were preparing camera-ready copy. Be exact in your placement. Use a computer, if possible. While this is an assignment in doing a finished pasteup, and will be graded on that basis, try to create a good design.

Assignment 3. Create a format for a newsletter on nutrition—a newsletter that can be produced and made camera-ready on a computer. Show a first page and an inside page (8½″ × 11″). Let these pages stand as models for pages in future issues. Plan for some art. Make up a name for it and show the nameplate or logo. Assume that the newsletter is sponsored by a foundation.

Assignment 4. How many different uses—preferably new and imaginative—can you come up with for Scotch brand Post-it Note Pads?

Design a multipanel double-page ad for a magazine showing these new uses, and include a headline and a bit of copy to introduce the ad.

Assignment 5. The Bettendorf, Iowa, public library, when it was to move to a new building, asked patrons to make a special effort to check out books at the old library and return them to the new. If each of the more than eighteen thousand cardholders checked out 3.4 books, the director figured, all sixty-five thousand books could be moved without having to hire the job done. The library would save an estimated $1000.

Assume that you have drawn the assignment to design a 5½″ × 8½″ sheet, to be printed on one side in a single color, horizontal or vertical, that will be passed out to patrons during the month before the move. The piece would urge patrons to participate and to get other cardholders to participate, too. Rough in the elements your ad would contain. Plan to include one small piece of art.

CHAPTER 7. TYPOGRAPHY

Assignment 1. From among ads shown in the chapters up to now, pick one that is directed to consumers and re-do it as an ad directed to retailers. Duplicate the type style in order to tie the ads together. Tell the dealers why they should stock plenty of the units. Mention a heavy advertising and promotion program to bring already-sold customers in.

Write the headlines and figure out your copy approach. You don't have to write the copy itself. But be sure to indicate headline, art, and copy of the comp you create.

Assignment 2. From a type-specimen book or from this book pick an old-style roman alphabet, a modern roman alphabet, and a sans serif alphabet in 36-point size and trace the letters (both caps and lower case) and numbers with a sharp pencil. Use the fill-in method, being careful to show how the letter strokes join one another and how serifs fit. Before you begin tracing, draw in some light guidelines.

This exercise, although tedious, will familiarize you with how each of the letters in the major typefaces is constructed.

Assignment 3. Take any one of the three original alphabets in assignment 2 and trace the letters to form this American Lung Association headline, using three or more lines: "Take Care of Your Lungs. They're Only Human." Use caps and lower case or all lower case. You will be making decisions about letter and word spacing as well as line spacing. Break your lines into logical takes.

Assignment 4. Take another of the alphabets and, using it merely as reference, *hand letter* the headline in Assignment 3, increasing (by eye) its size to about 60 points and breaking it into three lines.

Assignment 5. A number of packages and book jackets have featured display lettering built of cartoon animals or people, bent and combined, sometimes with props, to spell out words.

See what you can do with Wheatreats, a good-tasting and nutritious breakfast food (fictitious) in flake form marketed mainly for children. Use happy, healthy-looking children to build your all-cap letters. Use single figures when possible, but use two (or more) in combination when necessary. Throw in a prop or two if you have to.

CHAPTER 8. ART

Assignment 1. Looking through current advertisements in magazines, find examples of six—any six—of the art styles listed in the chapter. Tell why you think the styles are appropriate to the advertisements.

Assignment 2. Consider the Office Pavilion ad in chapter 3 and create a new ad in the series. Use photography and the same general format. Your job is to convince readers that Office Pavilion does a better job than other office-furniture dealers.

Assignment 3. Consider the following qualities that could be attached to organizations and see if you come up with an idea for a symbolic picture for each:

well established	sturdy
trustworthy	progressive
vigorous	dedicated
prompt	friendly
considerate	fast growing

Sketch out and label your ten symbolic pictures. Do not worry about how well drawn they are. Use stick figures and other shortcuts. If necessary, include descriptions so your instructor will understand your drawings. For this assignment the ideas are much more important than the renderings.

It might help to have a specific organization in mind, such as a bank or utility. Indicate this to your instructor.

You do not have to design any ads. Just draw the symbols.

Assignment 4. Pick out any quote from any book of quotations and come up with an illustration idea. Rough it out. Have in mind either halftone or line art. It may be a photograph or drawing. You will be graded on your concept, not on how well you have drawn your art. But do *design* the art. Consider its composition. Be sure to include the quotation with what you submit to your instructor.

Assignment 5. You're designing an ad for Varig Brazilian Airlines and the Brazilian Tourism Authority to encourage a vacation in Rio and Brazil. You'll point to a low-price airfare and hotel package, and you'll play up the "world-famous Copacabana and Ipanema beaches" and the night life in Rio, a city that "gets hotter at night." The ad, in color, will cover two pages in an 8½″ × 11″ travel magazine published in the United States.

You may use any or all of the photos on the next pages (they were taken by Steve Lorton, a magazine editor and writer). You may crop them, if you wish, and of course you can change their sizes. Assume that they are available in both color and black-and-white. Two of the photos involve dancers at an annual Rio carnival. The third photo shows a woman in Bahia selling street food. Another photo shows an outdoor "dress shop" in Bahia; another shows Bahia boys pausing in their play.

Pick the photo or photos that will work best for you and add others, if you wish. Work out a theme and headlines and include a coupon in your ad for readers who will want to send for further

information. You may want to read about Brazil in an encyclopedia before doing your ad.

What you'll turn in to your instructor will be a rough layout.

CHAPTER 9. COLOR

Assignment 1. Design an 8½″ × 11″ full-color ad for Crayola Washable Crayons (eight-crayon box) that plays up the colors as well as the washable feature. "Now you can let your child enjoy the fun of coloring without the worry." The ad is to appear in women's magazines.

Assignment 2. Design a full-color ad for women's magazines for Lubiderm Lotion and Lubiderm Body Bar that features the products up close. Even though you have full color, use it subtly to give your ad a monochromatic feel.

Take off from the line, "Think of them as shampoo and conditioner for your skin." The lotion is for dry-skin care; the body bar moisturizes. You write the headline.

Assignment 3. As a class assignment, Kathy Rotramel tried her hand at rearranging the elements in the "Get Cracking" ad shown in chapter 5, not necessarily to improve the ad but to see what other arrangements are possible.

Pick another ad shown in this book and see what you can come up with. Turn in three different rough layouts in whatever size and shapes you want. Use a second color.

Assignment 4. A few years ago *The Wall Street Journal* reported an upsurge in sales of a product called "Bag Balm," which farmers had used as an ointment for cows with scratched or irritated udders since 1908. The upsurge at first puzzled company officials, because, apparently, the cow population was down from what it had been. It turned out, according to the *WSJ* story, that some people were using the product as a cheap and effective treatment for their own minor cuts and scratches. Some doctors had been recommending the product.

In 1983 Charles Kuralt discovered Bag Balm and featured it on his "On the Road" TV show.

Although officially extending the product's market to include human use might involve legal, packaging, and perhaps even manufacturing problems, let us assume, for the sake of this assignment, that the manufacturer has taken care of these matters

and intends to capitalize on the new use and to launch an advertising campaign encouraging it. And the campaign will be directed to the middle classes.

Your job is to turn out a full-color, full-page ad for *Family Circle* and similar magazines to announce the "new" product. Let us assume that the company will not change the product itself (including its turpentine smell) or its container (a metal can with a drawing of a cow's udder on the side, as shown in the rough sketch nearby). Let us further assume that the company does not intend to cover up the fact that the product has long been used for animals.

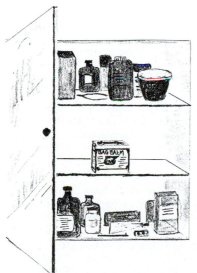

An old remedy is found in new places.

You may want to play the assignment straight. Or you may want to have some fun with it. The client is open minded—so long as the advertising increases the market base.

Work out your theme, write your headline, and decide what you want for art. It will be necessary to show the container (about the size of a three-inch cube, with a lid that lifts off and pushes back on), but if you do not want to show the udder, you can change the viewing angle. Indicate the copy block in the usual way. Do your comp in full color. The container is in magenta, dark green, light green, and white.

Here's one student's solution to the design problem. The student is Scott Loos of Newport Beach, California. He nicely isolates the product from others and uses white space effectively to create an ad with a silhouette format.

Assignment 3. Until the 1960s the Hershey Chocolate Corporation did no national consumer advertising—at least it did none in the United States. Now it does do some. Assume you have drawn the assignment to design a full-page, full-color ad for *Boys' Life* promoting both the plain and almond candy bars. Do a comp. The idea for selling the bars and the appropriateness of the ad to the medium are important parts of this assignment.

CHAPTER 10. NEWSPAPER ADVERTISING

Assignment 1. You are working for a newspaper's display advertising department, and you are about to pitch a new account: Evergreen Tree Spray Service, Inc. Do a rough layout (or comp, if you wish) for this outfit, on speculation, carrying the following information (it does not have to be worded like this): "In business since 1947. Radio-dispatched trucks. Same-day service in most cases. Modern equipment and methods. Free estimates by phone. Call 313–5005. One-time service or contract service available. Topping, pruning, trimming, removal, fertilizing, root and leaf feeding, poison oak and poison ivy control, insect and disease control." Maybe you can come up with a good theme and an inviting headline.

The ad will be 6¼″ wide by 8″ deep. Letter in—or punch in—the headlines and any subheadings, and use ruled lines or greeking for the smaller type. Include a logo and any art you think appropriate.

Assignment 2. A quality men's store, carrying such brands as Oxxford (with two *x*s) suits and Allen Edmonds shoes, cashmere sweaters, expensive after-shave lotions and colognes, and so on, is going out of business. The store has the same name as your last name.

Design an ad that reflects both the image of the business and the urgency of the prices. These are once-in-a-lifetime bargains. All sales final. But quantities are limited, so be there early.

Four columns × 15″, with some illustrations.

Assignment 3. You are working in the display advertising department of a medium-size newspaper, and you have two ads to knock out before closing time. The ads can be pretty rough. (Your grade will be based partly on the quality and appropriateness of your work and partly on speed. Indicate at the bottom of your roughs how much time you spent on each.)

    a. The Organic Terrace, a health food store in your town, is celebrating its first anniversary with a 20 percent markdown on all items in the store. The prices will remain in effect for one week. Do an ad that would occupy about 30 column inches in the local newspaper. (This means the ad can be 2-col. × 15″, 3-col. × 10″, or 4-col. × 7½″.)

        Include some art in your rough layout. Indicate where headlines and copy are to go, but do not bother to do any of the writing. Show where the logo and slogan go. The ad will be in black-and-white.

    b. Music City U.S.A., a chain of music stores in your town, is clearing out floor samples of stereo component sets, Panasonic and Pioneer brands.

        In an ad occupying roughly 60 column inches (you choose the shape of the ad), announce the clearance and show some sample sets. Play prices big—but use 000s. (Exact figures can be filled in at the last minute.)

        Show where headlines and copy go—but do not bother writing them. The logo is an expanded script. Make sure you include a store address. The sale is for three days only.

Assignment 4. Do these two newspaper "shop roughs," limiting yourself to twenty minutes for each one:

    a. An ad, 40 to 50 column inches, any shape, for Coolside Swimming Pools Co., 156 Cieloha Blvd., your city. You are selling all-concrete swimming pools, $5,995, installed, with labor and materials. Easy terms. Make up a headline and dream up a drawing.

    b. An ad, 1-col. × 2″, for Chandler Travel Agency, Inc., 1450 Broadway, your city. The client wants to remind local newspaper readers it can handle any travel problem, business or pleasure; and the customer pays nothing more than regular transportation prices.

Assignment 5. Maybe someone will do it someday, but it probably is not a practical idea. Nevertheless it might be interesting to come up with a theme and to design an ad for a new kind of shoe store. (Come up with a name for the store, too.)

It is a store that sells shoes singly, so that people with feet of different sizes can be properly fitted: maybe a 9B for the left foot and a 9½B for the right. If you want to get playful, you could mention that peg-legged people can get by on half of what they'd pay elsewhere. This would also be the preferred store for three-legged people.

People who tend to wear out one shoe before the other (stick-shift drivers who do a lot of clutching with their left foot) might be sold on buying two left-foot shoes to go with one right.

Use a second color in designing your half-page newspaper ad announcing the new store. Mention brand names and competitive prices.

CHAPTER 11. MAGAZINE ADVERTISING

Assignment 1. You're doing a 1-column (a third of a page) magazine ad for Used Rubber USA, San Francisco, which manufactures and markets purses, drawstring pouches, knapsacks, belts, vests, and sandals made from old tires and intertubes. Very chic. And environmentally sound.

Rivets and clasps help fasten the rubber pieces together. Many of the pieces retain the stamps of the tire companies: Michelin, Pirelli, Goodyear, etc. The prices range from $150 to $200.

Crowd as much as you can into the ad, write the copy, and include a coupon for a catalog. The ad will be in black and white.

Assignment 2. The fountain pen is back, after nearly disappearing from the market with the coming of the ballpoint pen. The makers have largely solved the problem of leaking, improved the ink-loading mechanism, and introduced ink cartridges. The new popularity of fountain pens also reflects the influence of the arts-and-crafts movement and represents, to some extent, a protest against the computer age.

Dream up a new theme to sell pens for Parker, which is introducing a new model with European styling to compete with Lamy or Mont Blanc. Do a series of three one-third-page ads to run in news magazines.

Assignment 3. Take an existing full-page magazine ad and redesign it to fit two other sizes: (1) a one-column ad and (2) a two-page ad. Hold onto the same elements, and keep the same mood. You may enlarge, condense, and rearrange the elements, and, if necessary, you may recrop the art.

Assignment 4. Pick a time in your state when tourism is down, and create an ad for placement in a city or regional magazine outside the state to lure visitors. Play up what might be attractive to visitors during this "down time." Obvious advantages would be smaller crowds and off-season prices. But find something really positive to say.

Do versions of your ad in three sizes to fit the magazine.

Assignment 5. This is an assignment Professor William Ryan of the University of Oregon gives his students:

Study the editorial design of a magazine to see if you can imitate the style in a full-page ad going into the magazine. Pick a company likely to advertise in the magazine and create a comp for that company's sponsorship. Develop your own theme, pick out appropriate art, and write a headline. Indicate body copy in the usual way.

Some magazines do not allow advertising that comes too close to duplicating their basic design. Let's assume, for the sake of the assignment, that the magazine does not object. At the worst, it asks you to run "An Advertisement" across the top in small letters.

CHAPTER 12. BROADCAST ADVERTISING

Assignment 1. Pick a current TV commercial that defies logic or makes a claim that, upon analysis, actually works against the sponsor, and work out your own commercial for a competitor. Capitalize on the weakness of the original commercial but don't mention it or its sponsor.

For this assignment, just describe your commercial. You don't have to work out a storyboard or script.

Assignment 2. Depend Undergarments for the incontinent has used an actress remembered for her romantic roles in the 1940s to sell the product in no-nonsense TV commercials.

Let's assume that the client wants an entirely different approach. Do a rough storyboard for a thirty-second spot that has flair but is also perfectly serious and is in no way offensive.

Assignment 3. Pick a new, best-selling book, fiction or nonfiction, and assume it is about to go into a paperback edition. Do a storyboard for a 30-second commercial to be shown in major cities. Keep your production costs down, but use color, of course.

Assignment 4. Pick out an obscure recording artist, assume that a record company is packaging a cassette and CD of the artist's best numbers, and do a sixty-second, hard-sell TV commercial to sell them. They will not be available in stores. Have the viewer send for the product to an address in your hometown. Plan to play samples of the music. Crowd a lot into the commercial.

Assignment 5. Using the theme "Shoplifters take everybody's money," the merchants of Philadelphia a few years ago got together to launch what turned out to be a successful ad campaign against shoplifting. Figuring that teenagers account for a large percentage of shoplifting, the merchants directed their campaign largely to that audience.

A good way—perhaps the best way—to reach that audience was through radio. Commercials directed to teenagers mentioned the facts that stealing resulted in higher prices and that shoplifters faced criminal charges if caught. Commercials likely to be heard by parents asked the question: "Was today the day you were going to warn your daughter [or son] about shoplifting?"

It is time to relaunch the campaign—in Philadelphia or whatever big city you are in or near.

Write a sixty-second radio commercial (about 150 words if it is all talk) using any technique you wish. You may pick up the theme from the earlier Philadelphia campaign. Direct your commercial either to teenagers or adults.

CHAPTER 13. DIRECT-MAIL ADVERTISING

Assignment 1. Pick the tourist attraction nearest where you are, and, to promote it, design a direct-mail piece of a kind found in racks in motels. Include enough photographs to fully explore what's offered at the place. If the place already has a piece, study it; and look over pieces for similar attractions. But don't be overly influenced by them. Most are poorly designed.

Give your piece a contemporary feel.

Assignment 2. Your client is the imaginary International Insurance Group, which, as a public service, is putting out a series of folders for parents on career opportunities for their youngsters. You have drawn the assignment to design one for the field of advertising.

Do a comprehensive rough of a three-fold folder that will fit a no. 10 business envelope. You should work out a theme and some headings, but you need not write the copy. Doubtless you will want to use subheads to break the copy into readable chunks. You can indicate these with scrambled consonants or sets of *M*s and *W*s. Allow for any halftones and drawings you think are needed.

Plan on using black and a second color throughout.

Paper stock is white offset.

Assignment 3. With more competition coming to hospitals and health-care centers, advertising in this area has increased and become more sophisticated and, in some cases, more emotional. The health services industry is an industry acutely aware of the power—and need—of communications of all kinds, including advertising. Direct-mail pieces, for instance, endlessly roll off of in-house presses.

Typical of the advertising campaigns directed to the public are those that announce weight and fitness programs, physical therapy, and drug- and alcohol-abuse treatment. Design a direct-mail piece that promotes one of these programs sponsored by a hospital or clinic in your area. Any format. Black plus one color.

Assignment 4. Pick out some product for which an advertising program involving consumer direct-mail, general-circulation magazine, and dealer trade-magazine advertising would likely be used. Work out a master ad for use in a general-circulation magazine (a column wide by the page-length deep) that could be used in part in the other two media. Do comprehensive roughs of all three ads. Use any direct-mail form you think appropriate. Full color is available for both the general-circulation and the direct-mail ads; use black-and-white for the trade-journal ad.

The trade-journal ad should have a good deal of the character of the general-circulation ad, because one of the purposes of the trade-journal ad is to remind the dealer of the national advertising program. The direct-mail piece, to be mailed to selected lists, may or may not look like the general-circulation magazine ad. But for economy reasons, you may want to use some of the art from the general-circulation ad.

Assignment 5. You have the job of coming up with a format for a catalog that sells designer carpenter tools: high-priced tools that are as much for show as for work. Made of stainless steel and chrome and featuring rosewood handles, they are more for collectors than for people who really work with their hands.

You don't need to design the whole catalog. Just the cover and a sample spread. Your catalog should use coated paper and look expensive. Full color, if you like. Make up names and products. Play down prices.

CHAPTER 14. POSTERS AND DISPLAYS

Assignment 1. Pick a new-car dealer in your city and do a billboard (pick a size from among those listed in the chapter) that stresses service. Move in close on any art you use. Make your poster bold but elegant.

Assignment 2. Do a 24-sheet poster for (a) a political candidate of your choosing or (b) a public cause or crusade that you believe in. If you choose the latter assignment, include the sponsor's name. If the name is part of the message (as in "Give to the Red Cross"), play it up large. Otherwise put it in small type off to one side. Move in close on the art. Use big, thick letters for your type. Apply color generously.

Assignment 3. The Starlight Restaurant in your city is renting a 43′ × 10′6″ painted bulletin two miles out on the main highway leading into the city. It will be illuminated. A family-style restaurant, it specializes in steaks and fried chicken at moderate prices. It is open from 8 A.M. to midnight. Closed Mondays.

Design the bulletin, using full color. If you use artwork, it should be "posterized." Keep the panel within the frame; no extensions.

Assignment 4. The American Bank, with four locations in a medium-size city, is buying a 100-showing of 24-sheet posters. Frankly, it has nothing to promote but the usual services and the fact that it is locally owned.

The purpose of the advertising is to help the bank get its fair share of the business. (Three other banks operate in the area.)

Design the poster. You have no limitation on color.

Assignment 5. Bearing in mind that better-educated people are turning away from smoking and that its appeal these days seems to be mostly to blue-collar classes and to some younger people, work up an outdoor poster that could conceivably be sponsored by one of the antismoking groups. Indicate a small credit line on the poster, naming an anti-smoking organization.

CHAPTER 15. LONG-TERM DESIGN

Assignment 1. The American flag, said by some to have been designed by Betsy Ross and said by others to have been designed by Congressman Francis Hopkins, undoubtedly will never change, except for new stars as any new states are admitted. Nor should it. But, as an exercise, design a brand new one, holding onto the character of the original, if you wish, or making drastic changes. Stay with the same colors, and be prepared to defend or explain any new symbolism you introduce.

Assignment 2. Take the words "Car Wash" (caps and lower case, all lower case, all caps—it doesn't make any difference) and make a logo, working a car into it. One solution would be to make a car—a generic car—out of one of the letters.

Assignment 3. Take the three initials of your name and make a well-designed monogram of them. Include with the initials a piece of art that symbolizes your personality, your intended occupation, or one of your interests; for instance, a sun, a palette, or a ski pole. (Avoid astrological signs.)

Do not let the art overpower the initials. Instead, let it help unite them. Keep it flat, decorative, on the abstract side.

Work in a size big enough so you will not be cramped. But render the monogram boldly enough so that it will reduce to about a one-inch square. Use black only.

You may place the initials and art inside a circle, shield, or other field; or—better—you can let the initials and art stand by themselves. Be sure you end up with a nicely unified whole.

Student Brian P. Wimberly, a music major, shows you how he would handle the assignment.

Robin J. Campbell, a dancer, designed her monogram by converting a *J* to a ballet shoe.

Christine G. Schloe's interest in cooking comes out in her three-initial monogram. The outline style of her letters carries over to the outline style of her art.

the advertiser needs a new one, design an ad in an appropriate size. Make the ad a comprehensive, putting enough into its execution to impress an art director you might want to approach for a job.

Assignment 2. Jim deYong, an advertising agency principal, tells of an assignment he had in a copywriting course taught by Professor Max Wales. It was to write a letter to an agency asking to be interviewed for a job. Most of the letters turned in by the students followed an expected format and used familiar themes. There was barely-under-control bragging about campus publications work and soft peddling of inexperience. deYong composed a letter confessing to being one of life's losers but making the point that the agency might find him useful anyway. The letter was unusual enough for Wales to show it to his teaching colleagues for their reactions. deYong got the letter back from Wales with this notations: "I like it. Others didn't. That's the hell of writing copy."

Try writing your own letter asking for an interview. Make it serious, clever, whatever; it should be in a style you are comfortable with.

Assignment 3. Work up a résumé to be used in your hunt for a job in advertising, whether you are applying as a potential designer or art director, copywriter, or other worker. Organize it tightly and use parallel structure. Follow the advice contained in this chapter.

Assignment 4. Do a newspaper ad of approximately 12 column inches (1 column × 12″, 2 columns × 6″, or 3 columns × 4″) announcing the opening in town of your design (or design and copy) studio to serve local advertisers, agencies, and printers. Stress the services you do best and include some art. Design the ad to single out the few readers of the paper who could use your services.

Don't make up facts. Be realistic. If you are short on experience, play up something else in the headline and copy. Concentrate on the quality of your work and, perhaps, on your reasonable fees.

The design of your ad will demonstrate what you can do.

Assignment 5. Design a business card, letterhead, and envelope to use in your new business.

Assignment 4. From among the thousands of grocery store packages, select one you think needs redesigning—and redesign it.

Assignment 5. Pick out an ad from this book with a sponsor likely to be listed in the Yellow Pages (see, especially, the chapter on newspaper advertising) and design a 6″-wide-by-2½″-deep ad for a Yellow Pages directory published in the advertiser's home city. Do not use any color.

Study the ads in a Yellow Pages directory to get an idea of what to include. Pick out the right section for the ad and design the ad to stand out from other ads in that section.

CHAPTER 16. CAREERS

Assignment 1. Pick a product or service you admire but whose advertising, from a design standpoint, is uninspired. Using the advertiser's existing theme, or one of your own if you think

GLOSSARY

A

abstract art   simplified art; art reduced to fundamental parts; art that makes its point with great subtlety. Opposite of realistic or representational art.

accordion fold   a direct-mail piece with panel that fold alternately inward and outward so that the piece opens and closes like an accordion.

account   what the advertising agency or medium calls the advertiser. An agency also refers to the advertiser as a *client*.

account executive   person in the agency in charge of advertising for the account or client. This person may also be called an "account supervisor."

acetate   clear film used for overlays, especially when the artist is preparing art for a color plate.

AD   short for *art director*.

advertising   communication from an advertiser to a potential buyer in printed, broadcast, painted, or some other form.

advertising agency   organization that prepares and places advertising for various clients.

Advertising Council   nonprofit organization of advertisers, agencies, and media that creates and places public service advertising.

Advertising Review Board   self-regulating organization set up by the advertising industry.

agate line   line of type set in 5½-point type. Also, a unit of measurement. Newspapers sometimes measure ad depths by agate lines: fourteen to a column inch.

agent   business representative for freelance artists of all kinds who offer advertising services.

airbrush   tool that uses compressed air to shoot a spray of watercolor pigment on photographs or artwork. Used for retouching.

align   arrange elements so that they line up with other elements.

all caps   all-capital letters.

animation   in TV commercials, action accomplished through the use of cartoon characters or puppets.

annual report   booklet issued each year by an organization to summarize its activities and financial situation.

antique paper   rough-finish, high-quality, often bulky paper.

art   all pictorial matter in an ad; photographs, illustrations, cartoons, charts and graphs, typographic effects.

art deco   the look of the 1920s and 1930s: simple line forms, geometric shapes, pastel colors, rainbow motifs.

art director   person in charge of all visual aspects of an ad, including typography.

art nouveau   sinuous, decorative, curvy art associated with the turn of the century.

ascenders   portions of letters that rise above the top of the x-height.

asymmetric balance   balance achieved by strategic arrangement of unequal elements in an ad. A heavy item on one side does not require a corresponding element directly across from it. Informal balance.

audio   the part of advertising you can hear, especially in a TV commercial.

availability   time that an advertiser can buy on radio or television.

axis   imaginary line used to align visual elements and relate them.

B

bait advertising   advertising that lures people into stores for bargains or would-be bargains. Often it is difficult to buy the product advertised.

balance   stability in design; condition in which the various elements on a page or spread are at rest.

bank   see *deck*.

bar chart   art that shows statistics in bars of various lengths.

basis weight   weight of a ream of paper in standard-size sheets. Standard size for book papers is 25″ × 38″.

Bauhaus   school of design in Germany (1919–1933). It championed a highly ordered, functional style in architecture and applied arts.

BCU   big closeup, as used in television.

Ben Day   process by which engraver or printer adds pattern or tone to a line reproduction.

billboard   poster panel used in outdoor advertising.

billing   amount of money an agency charges its clients. Includes charges for services rendered plus production and media bills.

binding   that part of a magazine, book, or booklet that holds the pages together.

bird's-eye view   view from above.

bit   basic unit of information in a computer's binary system.

bit map   image made from bits and stored in the computer's memory.

black letter   a close-fitting, bold, angular style of type that originated in Germany. Also known as *Old English* and *text*.

bleed   a picture printed to the edge of a sheet (technically, to achieve this effect, the sheet is trimmed after the printing). Used also as a verb.

blind embossing   embossing without printing.

blowup   enlargement. "Blow up" when used as a verb.

blueline   see *Vandyke*.

blurb   copy found on a book jacket, usually extravagant in its praise of the book.

body copy   column of type set in a relatively small size.

body type   type 12 points in size or smaller.

boldface type   heavy, black type.

bond paper   crisp paper used for business stationery, often with rag content.

book   bound publication of forty-eight pages or more, usually with a stiff or heavy cover. Some magazine editors call their publications *books*.

booklet   a publication of between eight and forty-eight bound pages, sometimes with a cover of a slightly heavier stock. Often in a size to fit a no. 10 envelope.

book paper   paper, other than newsprint, used in the printing of books, magazines, and direct mail. Includes many grades and finishes.

border   rule or other art that surrounds an ad and defines its edges. Not all ads need or use borders. Mostly for newspaper ads.

box   design element composed usually for four rules, with type or art inside.

brainstorming   meeting in a group in the hope that members will stimulate each other to create or make discoveries.

bridge   music or sound effect linking two scenes in a commercial.

broadside   direct-mail piece that unfolds to a large sheet about the size of a newspaper page.

brochure   high-quality, expensive direct-mail piece.

brownline   see *Vandyke.*

burnish   smooth down paper letters or pattern sheets so that they will adhere to a pasteup.

business paper   see *trade magazine.*

busy   condition in design in which elements are too numerous for the space and compete with each other for attention.

byline   the author's name set in type, usually over the author's story or article. Ads seldom carry bylines.

byte   eight contiguous bits; the equivalent of one character of type.

C

CAD   computer-aided design. Program more for architects, engineers, industrial designers, etc., than for graphic designers.

calender   polish, as in a finishing step in the making of some paper.

calligraphy   beautiful handwriting or hand lettering used in place of type in some advertising.

camera lucida   lens system for tracing and enlarging. Most artists today prefer using a full projector or viewer, such as the Goodkin or Artograph.

camera-ready copy   a pasteup ready to be photographed by the platemaker.

camp   art so bad it is good

caps and small caps   all capital letters, with the initial letters of words set in larger capitals.

caption   legend accompanying a photograph used as editorial material in a magazine; newspapers use *cutlines.* Advertising photographs usually do not require captions, except in some direct mail.

caricature   drawing that exaggerates or distorts a person's features.

cartoon   humorous drawing, done usually in pen or brush-and-ink or in washes.

cartouche   fancy border.

casting off   copyfitting.

cathode-ray tube   system of phototypesetting making use of a televisionlike tube.

center spread   two facing pages at the center of a saddle-stitched magazine. Elements in an ad can cross the gutter in a center spread without any problems or register.

character   any letter, number, punctuation mark, or space in printed matter.

checking copy   copy of a publication sent to an agency or advertiser for proofing or to prove that the ad was actually run as ordered.

chroma   color intensity.

circular   vague term for a direct-mail piece.

circulation   number of copies sold or distributed. Can be accurately measured. *Readership* used in this context refers to the number of people who actually see the publication—a number two to three times higher than circulation in many cases. Readership is harder than circulation to measure.

classified advertising   small-type, usually all-type, small-space ads, sponsored by private individuals as well as companies, arranged by category in one section of the newspaper.

cliché   something used too often, hence boring and no longer effective.

client   see *account.*

clip book   pages of stock art usually on slick paper, ready for photographing by the platemaker.

clip sheet   see *clip book.*

close up   move together.

closeup   picture made with camera so close to subject that only the head and shoulders show.

closing date   deadline for submitting ad to medium if it is to be printed in a specific issue.

coated paper   paper covered with a smoothing agent, making it stiff and, usually, shiny. Good for reproducing photographs.

cold type   type composed by typewriter, paper pasteup, photographic, or electronic means.

collage   piece of art made by pasting various elements together.

collateral   noncommissionable media used in an advertising campaign.

collating   gathering and arranging printed sheets or signatures into the desired sequence. Usually done by machine.

color separation   negative made from full-color art for use in making one of the plates.

column   section of the text matter (when the text matter is extensive) that runs from the top to the bottom of the copy area. An ad or page can carry more than one column of type.

column inch   area that is one column wide by 1 inch deep. A column-inch ad in a newspaper can be referred to as a fourteen-line ad. See *agate line.*

column rule   thin line separating columns of type.

combination cut   printing plate made from superimposition of a line and halftone negative.

comic strip   comic drawing or cartoon that appears in a newspaper on a regular basis; a series of drawn panels. Characters in comic strips have been enlisted for advertising campaigns. And the comic-strip format has been popular with some advertisers, especially those appealing to young audiences.

commercial   advertisement on radio or TV.

commercial art   illustrations, typography, and design used in advertising. Thought to be different from *fine art,* but actually much advertising—or commercial—art ranks with fine art in quality.

commission system   system of payment to an advertising agency: The agency gets 15 percent of what the client spends for time and space with the media. See also *fifteen-and-two.* The system has sometimes come under fire. Another system is for the agency to charge a fee or retainer for its services.

comp   comprehensive layout. Sometimes a preliminary sketch before painting or final illustration is made.

company magazine   see *house organ.*

composition   type that is set. Also, in art or design, the arrangement of elements.

compositor   craftsman who sets type.

comprehensive layout   layout finished to look almost as the printed piece will look.

condensed type   type series with narrow characters.

consumer magazine   advertising person's terminology for *general-circulation magazine.*

continuity   script for a radio or TV commercial.

continuous-tone art   photograph or painting or any piece of art in which tones merge gradually into one another. Requires halftone reproduction.

contrast   quality in design that permits one element to stand out clearly from others.

controlled-circulation publication   publication sent free to interested subscribers. Usually a trade magazine. For benefit of advertisers, the circulation is audited, as it is for paid-circulation publications. Some controlled-circulation publications now call themselves "qualified-circulation" publications.

cool colors blue and green colors that tend to recede from the viewer. Restful colors.

cooperative advertising advertising paid for by both the national (brand-name) and the local advertiser. Also, advertising in which several normally competing firms get together to do a common selling job.

copy written material or text matter for an ad, both before and after it is set in type. Includes the ad's headline. The nonheadline part of the copy is called the *copy block.* Also, the pasteup from which the platemaker makes the plate.

copy area that part of an ad inside the border or margin. Sometimes called "type area."

copy block text part of an ad; column of copy; all of the copy in an ad except the headline, captions, and logo.

copy chief head of the copy department of an agency or company.

copyedit see *copyread.*

copyfit estimate how much space copy will take when it is set in type.

copy platform the basic idea for an advertisement or an advertising campaign.

copyread check the manuscript to correct errors made by the writer.

copyright protection available to the owner of a manuscript, piece of art, or publication, preventing others from making unfair use of it or profiting from it at the expense of the owner. Most ads are not copyrighted, but publications in which they appear usually are. Still, the advertiser, not the publisher, owns the advertising.

copy testing research into the effectiveness of advertising copy.

copywriting writing copy for advertisements.

corporate advertising see *institutional advertising.*

corporate identity the look and recognition factor of a corporation; the corporation's image.

cost-per-thousand cost to reach one thousand readers with a full-page ad; CPM.

cover stock heavy or thick paper used as covers for magazines or paperback books.

CPM see *cost-per-thousand.*

creative director person in charge of both copy and design at an advertising agency.

credit line the photographer's name set in type, usually right next to the picture. Ads on occasion carry credit lines.

crop eliminate unwanted areas in a piece of art, usually by putting marks in the margins to guide the platemaker.

CU closeup shot, as in a TV commercial.

cursor a movable spot of light that appears on a computer display terminal. Controlled by a key on the keyboard, it shows where corrections, insertions, deletions, and other changes can be made in copy.

cut art in plate form, ready to print. For the letterpress process.

cutlines see *caption.*

cut to abruptly change a scene in a TV commercial.

D

dealer imprint dealer's name and address added onto an already-printed advertisement or placed on an advertisement prepared elsewhere.

dealer tie-in manufacturer's advertisement that includes names of dealers.

decal ad, symbol, or sign in the form of a sticker that attaches itself to glass, metal, or other material.

deck portion of a headline, consisting of lines set in the same size and style type.

deckle edge ragged, feathery edge available in some of the quality paper stocks.

deep etch plate used in offset lithography on which the image is slightly recessed.

delete take out.

demographics statistics on a particular market, covering age, sex, education, occupation, and so on.

descenders portions of letters that dip below the baseline of the letters.

design organization; plan and arrangement of visual elements. A broader term than *layout.* Used also as a verb.

designer person who plans and arranges elements in an ad. The art director (an executive) is also often the designer.

"designer's block" temporary suspension of creative facilities.

desktop publishing personal computer and printer setup allowing word processing, art creating, makeup, and the printing of camera-ready copy.

die-cut hole or other cutout punched into heavy paper. Used also as a verb.

digitizing changing type or art to small dots that can be manipulated by the computer.

dingbat small typographic decoration.

direct advertising printed advertising other than that appearing in newspapers and periodicals. It comes in many forms, but it does not include posters or point-of-purchase advertising.

direct halftone halftone made by the platemaker photographing the object itself rather than a photograph of the object.

direct-mail advertising same as direct advertising. More narrowly, direct advertising circulated by mail.

director for a TV commercial, the person immediately in charge of casting, filming, and other details. Works under the producer.

directory advertising advertising in directories such as telephone directories.

display ad local ad in a newspaper that makes use of design or random placement of elements of various sizes to attract attention.

display type type larger than 12 points, used for titles in direct mail, headlines for magazine and newspaper ads, and posters. See also *titles.*

dissolve effect of one scene coming into a TV commercial while another goes out. Used also as a verb.

dividers an instrument used to measure distances on a proof or piece of art so that the measurement can be transferred and duplicated.

dolly move camera gradually either in to or back out from the subject, as in a TV commercial.

dot etching correcting color separation negatives by making halftone dots smaller.

double truck newspaper terminology for *spread.*

downstyle style characterized by the use of lowercase letters in headlines except for first letters of first words of sentences and for first letters of proper names. Exaggerated downstyle uses no capital letters anywhere.

dpi dots per inch.

draw program computer graphics program using object-oriented graphics to produce line art.

dropout halftone see *highlight halftone.*

drybrush rendering in which only partially inked brush is pulled across rough-textured paper.

dry-transfer letters see *transfer type.*

DS abbreviation for *dissolve,* as in a TV commercial.

dubbing adding pictures or sound after film or recording is made, as in a commercial.

dummy the pages of a publication in its planning stage, often unbound, with features and pictures crudely sketched or roughly pasted into place.

duotone halftone printed in two inks, one dark (usually black), one lighter (any color).

duplicate plates copies of the original plates prepared for distribution to several publications.

duplicator machine that reproduces a limited number of copies. Large pressruns require regular printing presses.

dust jacket see *jacket*.

E

ECU extreme closeup, as in a TV commercial.

edit change, manage, or supervise for publication. Also, as a noun, short for *editorial*.

edition part of the pressrun for a particular *issue* of a publication. Space in regional or demographic editions of magazines is available to advertisers at rates less than the rates for an entire issue.

editorial short essay, usually unsigned, stating the stand of the publication on some current event or issue. Also used to designate the nonbusiness side of a publication. Sometimes the advertiser designs the advertising to look like editorial rather than advertising matter.

editorial matter anything appearing in a publication that is not advertising.

electric spectacular outdoor advertisement making extravagant use of electric lights and, in most cases, a form of animation.

electrotype duplicate plate.

element copy, headline, art, rule or box, border, spot of color—anything to be put into an ad.

elliptical dot screen screen that permits a greater range of middle-value grays in halftone reproduction than is possible with a regular dot screen.

em width of capital *M* in any type size. Spacing equal to the *square* of the type size.

emboss print an image on paper and stamp it, too, so that it rises above the surface of the paper.

en width of capital *N* in any type size. Spacing equal to *half the square* of the type size.

English finish smooth finish. English-finish papers are widely used by magazines.

engraving see *photoengraving*.

expanded type type series with wider-than-normal characters.

exploded view an illustration in which parts of an object are separated so that they can be better read.

F

face style or variation of type.

fade let a scene in a TV commercial gradually disappear from the screen. Used also as a noun.

family subdivision of a type race.

FCC Federal Communications Commission. A federal agency that licenses broadcast stations.

FDA Food and Drug Administration. A federal agency that regulates advertising of foods, drugs, and cosmetics.

feature play up. As a noun, a quality or characteristic of the ad.

feedback reader's or viewer's expressed response to an advertisement.

felt side best side of a sheet of paper for either printing or drawing. It is the side that, in the manufacturing process, came in contact with felt rollers.

fifteen-and-two standard discount a medium gives an agency for advertising placed. The 15 percent (of the gross bill) is kept by the agency, the 2 percent (of the net bill) is often passed on to the client.

film clip short section of film that can be inserted into a TV commercial.

fine art art created primarily for aesthetic rather than commercial purposes. Art used for advertising is usually referred to as *commercial art*.

fixative clear solution sprayed onto a drawing to keep it from smearing.

flatbed press letterpress press that prints from flat base. Slower than rotary letterpress.

flat color see *spot color*.

flop change the facing of a picture. A subject facing left in the original will face right in the printed version. Not a synonym for *reverse*.

flow chart art showing a manufacturing process.

flush left aligned at the left-hand margin.

flush left and right aligned at both the left- and right-hand margins. Justified.

flush right aligned at the right-hand margin.

folder direct-mail piece folded at least once. Of a size, usually, to fit into a no. 10 envelope.

font complete set of type characters of a particular face and size.

foreshorten exaggerate the perspective.

formal balance see *symmetric balance*.

format size, shape, and appearance of an ad or publication.

formula editorial mix of a publication. Of importance to the advertiser in that it determines the audience the advertiser reaches.

foundry type hand-set metal type.

four color full range of colors obtained by printing red, yellow, blue, and black.

fourth cover back cover of a magazine. Most expensive space in the magazine, unless the advertiser can buy the front cover.

frame in film, a single picture from among the many making up the action.

freelancer artist, photographer, designer, or copywriter called in to do specialized jobs for the advertiser.

freeze action action in a TV commercial that stops suddenly, causing actor to appear as though frozen in place.

French fold direct-mail piece printed on one side of a sheet, which is folded into a four-page folder with the blank side of the sheet hidden.

frisket paper that shields part of a drawing or pasteup from ink or exposure. Liquid frisket is also available.

FTC Federal Trade Commission. A federal agency that regulates advertising to some extent.

full color see *four color*.

full position preferred position in a newspaper, next to editorial matter or at the top of a column of ads.

full showing the poster-ad shown on all units in a public transportation system. It can also mean a *100 showing* in outdoor advertising.

"funky" art amateurish, 1930-ish, sometimes outrageous art. Art associated with the underground press of the 1960s and underground, adult, and corner drugstore comic books. Also, art with a polished but primitive charm.

G

gag cartoon humorous drawing, usually in a single panel, with caption, if there is one, set in type below. Gag cartoonists appearing regularly on magazine editorial pages have occasionally been enlisted by advertisers to help sell products or ideas.

galley tray on which type is assembled and proofed.

galley proof long sheet of paper containing a first printing from a galley—or tray—or type.

ganging up arranging forms in printing so that several different jobs can be printed at the same time on single sheets.

gatefold magazine cover that opens out to two additional pages. Makes possible an ad three pages wide.

gelatin duplicating reproducing a limited number of copies from a gelatin surface. A paper master is used to put the image on the gelatin surface.

general-circulation magazine magazine with popular appeal, usually with a large circulation, usually available on the newsstands. Sometimes called a "slick."

gimmick a sometimes clever, sometimes phony idea or device put into an ad to gain attention or sway the reader.

gingerbread design design with an overabundance of swirls and flourishes; cluttered design.

glossy print photograph with shiny finish. For reproduction purposes, better than a matte-finish print.

golden rectangle classic shape with a width-depth ratio of approximately 3:5 (or 5:3).

gothic term applied to various typefaces that have challenged the traditional. Currently, modern sans serifs.

grain the way cellulose fibers in a sheet of paper line up, giving direction to the paper. You would design a direct-mail piece to fold with the grain, not against it.

grainy dim, distracting pattern in a photograph, lessening its impact and clarity. Like "snow" in a television picture.

graph see *bar chart, line chart,* and *pie chart.* Also, short for *paragraph.*

graphic design design of printed material and—stretching the original definition—broadcast material.

graphics tablet input device that permits drawing with an electronic pen on an electronic tablet.

gravure method of printing from incised plate. For magazines, a rotary press is involved, hence *rotogravure.*

greeking making the body copy in a comprehensive layout look like real copy—but copy that cannot be read. You can buy *greeking* that has been printed on waxed transparent sheets.

grid carefully spaced vertical and horizontal guidelines that define areas in a layout; a plan for designing an ad.

gutter separation of two facing pages.

H

hairline very thin rule or line.

halftone reproduction process by which the printer gets the effect of continuous tone, as when reproducing a photograph. It is done with dots.

hand lettering lettering done with pen or brush. Used infrequently now that photolettering is available.

handle small back dots in an object-oriented computer graphics program that surround an image to allow the artist to change its size or position.

hardware the computer, ready to accept the appropriate software program.

head short for *headline.*

heading headline or title.

headline display type in an ad. An ad can be all headline. On the other hand, some ads do not have headlines.

head-on position in outdoor advertising, the placement of an ad so that it directly faces oncoming traffic.

hed short for *head,* which is short for *heading* or *headline.*

hidden offer special offer buried in ad in order to test readership.

high camp see *camp.*

highlight halftone halftone in which some parts have been dropped out to show the white of the paper.

hot press paper smooth paper without much "tooth." Used for line drawings.

hot type type made from metal.

house ad advertisement promoting the publication in which it appears.

house agency advertising agency established by advertiser to handle its own advertising. Unlike an advertiser's advertising department, a house agency is a complete unit, often eligible for media discounts.

house organ publication of an organization or business released regularly for public relations reasons. Usually it does not carry ads. The publication is itself an advertisement doing an institutional job.

house style style that is peculiar to an agency or that remains the same from ad to ad.

hue quality in a color that allows us to recognize it—by name. The name of the color.

I

icon on-screen symbol that represents a computer program function.

illustration drawing or painting. Although a photograph can be used for illustrative purposes, it is not usually called an *illustration.*

illustration board cardboard or heavy paperboard made for artists, available in various weights and finishes to take various art mediums.

imagesetter professional typesetting machine like Linotronic and Agfa Compugraphic that produces quality output on photographic paper or film with dpi of 1,200 or more.

imprint print local name or material on an already printed piece of advertising. Used also as a noun.

india ink waterproof drawing ink, usually black.

industrial advertising advertising designed to reach industry rather than the general public.

industrial designer designer of products. Packages are sometimes designed by industrial designers, sometimes by graphic designers.

informal balance see *asymmetric balance.*

initial first letter of a word at the beginning of advertising copy, set in display size to make it stand out.

insert advertising page or pages printed elsewhere and delivered to publication for inclusion in an issue or edition. As a verb it means "to put into place."

insertion order authorization from an agency to publish an ad.

inset art placed inside other art or art surrounded by type.

institutional advertising advertising designed to create an image or build goodwill rather than sell a product.

intaglio see *gravure.*

integrated commercial one that is broadcast as part of the program; not stuck in at a break or tacked on at the beginning or end.

intensity strength or brilliance of a color.

intercut quick change of the camera from one scene to another in a TV commercial.

interface link two or more electronic devices to make them work as a unit.

intermediate blueprint detailed sketch giving directions to the producer of a TV commercial.

interrobang combination exclamation mark and question mark. Available in several faces but not widely used. Also spelled "interabang."

Intertype linecasting machine similar to Linotype.

island display a point-of-purchase display out in the aisle, away from shelves and other displays.

island position placement of an ad in a publication so that it is entirely surrounded by editorial matter.

issue all copies of a publication for a particular date. An issue may consist of several *editions.*

italic type type that slants to the right.

J

jacket paper cover that wraps around a book to protect and advertise it.

jaggies jagged, stair-like lines resulting from use of low-resolution printer.

jingle musical commercial, especially for radio.

job press printing press used for small or short-run jobs. Not for periodicals.

justify align the body type so it forms an even margin on the right and the left.

K

kerning in typesetting, arranging a letter so that it fits into another letter's area to improve spacing.

keying   putting a code number or letter on a coupon so when it is mailed in the advertiser will know which of several publications used triggered the response. Also, coding the typewritten copy to show where it fits in the layout.

keyline drawing   drawing done partly in outline to use in making more than one plate for a spot-color job.

kilobyte   basic unit of measurement for computer memory, equal to 1,024 bytes.

kraft paper   heavy, rough, tough paper, usually tan in color.

L

lap dissolve   in a commercial, the fading of one scene into another; both can be seen for a second or two.

laser printer   printer using laser beam to create dot pattern on paper that reproduces what is on the computer screen.

lay out   put visual elements into a pleasing and readable arrangement.

layout   noun for a *lay out*.

lead   (pronounced "ledd") put extra space between lines of type.

leaders   (pronounced "leeders") dots or dashes used to carry eye across white space usually to a column of numbers.

leading   (pronounced "ledding") extra space between lines of type.

leaf   small sheet of paper.

leaflet   small sheet of paper, printed on one or both sides. One of the least pretentious of direct-mail forms.

legibility   quality in type that makes it easy for the reader to recognize individual letters.

letterpress   method of printing from raised surface. The original printing process.

letterspace   put extra space between letters. Periodically a popular practice for advertising headlines.

letterspacing   extra spacing between letters.

libel   published defamatory statement or art that injures a person's reputation.

lift   shorter version of a TV commercial.

ligature   two or more joined or overlapped characters on a single piece of type.

light table   table with frosted glass or plastic top with illumination underneath. Used for tracing purposes or for viewing, retouching, and arranging negatives.

linage   amount of advertising space expressed in agate lines: fourteen to the column inch.

line art   in its original form, art without continuous tone, done in black ink on white paper. Also, such art after it is reproduced through *line reproduction*.

linecasting machine   see *Linotype* and *Intertype*.

line chart   art that shows trends in statistics through a line that rises or falls on a grid.

line conversion   continuous-tone art that has been changed to line art. A screen of any one of several patterns is involved.

line reproduction   process by which the printer reproduces a black-and-white drawing.

Linotype   linecasting machine that produces type for letterpress printing or type from which reproduction proofs can be pulled. A trade name.

lip sync   synchronization of an actor's lip movements with sound that is recorded separately.

list broker   agent who rents out lists of potential buyers to direct-mail advertisers.

lithography   originally, process of making prints from grease drawing on stone. See also *offset lithography*.

live action   action in a TV commercial involving real people.

live area   ("live" with a long *i*) the interior part of an ad that must be left intact. Area outside of this area can be cropped so ad can run in a magazine with a smaller page size.

local advertising   advertising placed by local retail firms rather than by national manufacturers.

logo   short for *logotype*. The name of the advertiser in art or type form that remains constant from ad to ad. Usually available in more than one size.

long shot   picture taken from far away, as in a TV commercial.

loose art   informally drawn, relaxed art. The impression is that it was done in a hurry.

loss leader   item advertised at a cost below what retailer paid for it. Purpose is to increase store traffic.

lowercase   small letters (as opposed to capital letters).

LS   long shot, as in a TV commercial.

Ludlow   machine that casts lines of display-size letters from matrices that have been assembled by hand.

M

magazine   publication of eight pages or more, usually bound, issued on a regular basis at least twice a year. Also, storage unit for mats for linecasting machine.

mail-order advertising   advertising designed to sell products by mail. Can make use of direct-mail advertising as well as other media of advertising.

mainframe   computer with a number of users to meet the needs of a large organization.

make good   ad run free by a medium to compensate for significant error made by the medium in content or placement of the original ad.

makeready   all the work involved in preparing printing materials and the press for a particular job.

marketing   the whole system by which seller and buyer do business. Advertising is one step in the process.

market research   research conducted to determine nature and extent of audience for which product is designed.

mass media   units of communication: newspapers, magazines, television and radio stations, books, and others.

mat   short for *matrix*. Cardboard mold of plate, from which a copy can be made. Also, brass mold from which type can be cast.

matrix   see *mat*.

mat service   organization that supplies ideas, complete ads, and—most important—mats and proofs of artwork that can be used in ads by the few remaining letterpress papers.

matte   combine two scenes into one, as in a TV commercial.

matte finish   dull finish.

MCU   medium closeup, as in a TV commercial.

measure   length of a line or column of type.

mechanical   see *camera-ready copy*.

mechanical spacing   nonadjusted spacing between letters; opposite of *optical spacing*.

media   see *mass media*.

media buyer   person in an advertising agency who selects the media and decides the schedule for the clients' ads.

medium   singular for media. Also paint, ink, or marking substance used in drawing or painting. In this context, the plural of medium can be "mediums."

medium shot   in television, a picture taken not from far away, but not close up either.

megabyte   unit of measurement that equals 1,048,576 bytes.

merchandising   any activity designed to stimulate trade.

microcomputer   single-user computer small enough to fit on a desktop.

mockup   facsimile of product or package.

model release   signed statement by person authorizing the use of that person's picture in an ad.

modem   device that allows a computer to communicate with other computers over telephone lines by converting the digital binary code to analog form.

modular design   highly ordered design, marked by regularity in spacing.

moiré   undesirable wavy or checkered pattern resulting when an already screened photograph is photographed through another screen.

Monotype   composing machine that casts individual letters. Used for high-quality composition.

montage   combination of photographs or drawings into a single unit.

mortise   a cut made into a picture to make room for type or another picture. Used also as a verb.

motivational research   research that attempts to explain why buyers and potential buyers act as they do.

mouse   device, hooked to the computer, that, moved across a flat surface, moves a pointer. There is also a roller-ball mouse that stays in place in a base.

MS   medium shot, as in a TV commercial.

mug shot   portrait.

Multilith   duplicating or printing machine similar to offset lithography presses, but on a small scale. Multilith is a trade name.

N

national advertising   advertising sponsored by manufacturers designed mainly to build interest in specific brands.

news hole   nonadvertising space in a newspaper.

newsprint   low-quality paper stock lacking permanence; used by newspapers.

next-to-reading-matter   placement of the ad next to editorial matter. Thought to give the ad greater readership.

O

object-oriented graphics   graphics that have been formed from lines, circles, boxes, etc., using draw software programs. Also called *vector graphics*.

off-camera   not shown, although the voice may be heard, as in a TV commercial.

offset lithography   method of printing from flat surface, based on principle that grease and water do not mix. Commercial adaptation of *lithography*.

offset paper   book paper made especially for offset presses.

Old English   see *black letter*.

100 showing   in outdoor advertising, a showing for one month of enough posters to reach the entire market. The number of posters for a 100 showing would vary from city to city.

op art   geometric art that capitalizes on optical illusions.

optical   any special photographic effect used in a TV commercial.

optical center   a point slightly above and to the left of the geometric center.

optical illusion   art that plays tricks with the eye; art that can be interpreted in different ways.

optical spacing   spacing in typesetting that takes into account the peculiarities of the letters, resulting in a more even look.

optical weight   the visual impact a given element makes on the reader.

organization chart   art that shows how various people or departments relate to each other. Used occasionally in annual reports.

overlay   sheet of transparent plastic placed over a drawing. The overlay contains art or type of its own for a plate that will be coordinated with the original plate.

P

paint program   computer graphics program by which artist paints by adjusting pixels that make up a bit-map screen display.

page   one side of a sheet of paper in a publication.

pagination   the use of a computer to design and lay out pages, eliminating pasteup.

painted bulletin   outdoor poster painted on a panel.

painterly look   the look in art that stresses technique, tool, or medium used. The strokes show.

painting   illustration made with oil, acrylic, tempera, casein, or watercolor paints. Requires halftone reproduction; if color is to be retained, it requires process color plates.

pan   move camera to right or left, as in making a TV commercial.

panel   board on which poster is posted. Also, a box, rectangle, page, or other definable unit of display in print-media advertising. Also, a group of persons observed systematically by advertising researcher.

Pantone Matching System   standard color-selection system in computer graphics.

paper stock   paper.

parallel structure   organization in writing or design that gives equal treatment to each item, making it easy for the reader to comprehend and compare. Each item is introduced with the same phrasing or art device.

pass-along readers   readers of a publication who did not buy it.

pastel colors   soft, weak colors.

pastel drawing   drawing made with gray or color chalks.

paste up   verb form of *pasteup*.

pasteup   see *camera-ready copy*.

PC   personal computer, using MS DOS, developed by IBM and now manufactured by other companies as well. "PC" does not refer to the Macintosh, although it is, of course, a "personal computer."

pencil drawing   drawing made with lead or graphite pencil. Usually requires halftone reproduction.

penetration   extent to which a medium or advertisement reaches a market.

perfecting press   rotary press that prints on both sides of a sheet or roll of paper in a single operation.

perspective   quality in a photograph or illustration that creates the illusion of distance.

photoboard   a TV storyboard after the fact, used for promotional purposes when the commercial is actually on the air.

photocomposition   composition produced by photographic means.

photoengraving   cut or plate made for letterpress printing.

photolettering   display type produced photographically.

Photomechanical Transfer   copy print. Referred to as a PMT.

photostat   photographic copy. Also called *stat*.

phototypesetting   body copy set photomechanically or photoelectronically.

pic   short for *picture*.

pica   12 points, or one-sixth of an inch.

pictograph   a chart or graph in picture form.

picture   photograph, drawing, or painting.

pie chart   art that shows statistics—usually percentages—as wedges in a pie or circle.

piggyback commercial   commercial run right after another commercial by the same sponsor but promoting a different product.

piggyback type   printed type with no space between lines. Sometimes used for headlines.

pix   plural of *pic*.

pixel   smallest picture element that can be displayed on a computer screen.

plate   piece of metal from which printing is done. See also *cut*.

plug   mention of a product in nonadvertising time, as on a TV program, presumably without the advertiser's having to pay for the mention. Used also as a verb.

PMS   Pantone Matching System, used by designers to pick colors according to a scale.

point   unit of measurement of type; there are 72 points to an inch.

point-of-purchase advertising   advertising that attempts to do a selling job in or near a retail establishment.

P-O-P   point-of-purchase advertising.

pop art   fine art inspired by comic strips and packages. See also *camp*.

positioning   using advertising to give a product its own personality in the mind of the potential customer; segregating the product from competing products.

posterization   the conversion of continuous-tone art to black-and-white art. Middle grays are dropped; or multiple colors are reduced to a few simple, flat colors.

poster panel   standardized structure on which poster is pasted.

poster plant   local organization that erects and maintains poster panels.

PostScript   sophisticated page description language for medium- to high-resolution printing devices.

preferred position   desirable place in medium for which advertiser pays a premium rate.

Preprint   ad in a sort of wallpaper design printed in rotogravure in another plant for insertion in a letterpress or offset newspaper.

press-on type   letters printed on transparent paper or thin plastic that can be cut out and pressed into place on a pasteup.

press run   total number of copies printed during one printing operation.

printer   craftsman who makes up the forms or operates the presses.

printing   the act of duplicating copies of ads or pages.

process color   the effect of full color achieved through use of color-separation plates; way to reproduce color photographs, paintings, and transparencies.

producer   for a TV commercial, the person put in overall charge after the storyboard has been approved. The producer is not usually connected with the advertising agency.

production   process that readies an ad for publication after copy has been written and ad has been designed. Can also include the typesetting and printing.

production house   for commercials, an organization that takes over after the storyboard (or, in the case of radio, the script) is approved. For point-of-purchase, an organization that designs and supervises the printing of the advertising.

progressive proofs   set of platemaker's proofs of a full-color ad, showing each color plate separately, what happens as each color is added, and finally all four colors in combination.

proofread   check galley proofs against the original copy to correct any mistakes the compositor makes.

prop   item to be placed on a set for a TV commercial to give it authenticity.

proportion   size relationship of one part of the design to the other parts.

psychedelic art   highly decorative art characterized by blobs of improbable colors, swirls, and contorted type and lettering.

publication   product of the printing press, consisting of bound or unbound pages circulated on a regular basis.

public relations advertising   see *institutional advertising*.

publisher's representative   organization representing media to advertising agencies.

publishing   act of producing literature and journalism and making them available to the public. Printing is only one small part of the operation.

pub set   composition supplied by the publication in which the ad is to appear.

R

race   major category of typefaces.

ragged left   aligned at the right but staggered at the left.

ragged right   aligned at the left but staggered at the right.

rate card   card, folder, or booklet listing various rates for time or space in a medium. It also lists mechanical requirements for ads.

reach   what *readership* is to the print media, *reach* is to television.

readability   quality in type that makes it easy for the reader to move easily from word to word and line to line. In a broader sense, it is the quality in writing and design that makes it easy for the reader to understand the ad.

readership   number of readers of an ad or of a publication. See also *circulation*.

ream   five hundred sheets of paper.

rear projection   technique that allows actors to be filmed in front of a screen on which is projected a still or moving background.

register   condition in which various printing areas, properly adjusted, print exactly where they are supposed to print. Used also as a verb.

release   see *model release*.

relief   raised printing surface.

render   execute, as in making a drawing.

rep   short for publisher's representative, which is a firm that sells space for publications it represents.

reprint   copy of an ad reprinted after its original appearance in a publication. Often used as a form of direct advertising.

repro   short for *reproduction proof*.

reproduction   a copy.

reproduction proof   a carefully printed proof made from a galley, ready to paste down so it can be photographed.

residuals   payments paid to performers for repeated showings of programs or films in which they play roles.

resize   rearrange and change elements so that the ad can appear in another size.

retail advertising   advertising by retail establishments directed to customers and potential customers.

retouch   strengthen or change a photograph or negative through use of art techniques.

reverse   white letters in a gray, black, or color area. Opposite of *surprint*. Mistakenly used for *flop*. Used also as a verb.

rococo   complicated, crowded, elaborate, overly decorative.

roman type   type designed with thick and thin strokes and serifs. Some printers refer to any type that is standing upright (as opposed to type that slants) as "roman."

ROP   run of paper. Anywhere in the paper, not just on certain pages.

rotary press   in letterpress, a press that prints from plates curved around a cylinder. All offset presses are essentially "rotary," although the term is not generally applied to them.

rotogravure   see *gravure*.

rough   see *rough layout*.

rough layout   more or less crude, preliminary sketch, showing where type and art are to go in the ad.

rout   cut away.

rule   thin line used either horizontally or vertically to separate lines of display type or columns of copy.

runaround   section of text set in narrow, sometimes irregular measure to make room for art.

run in   let the words follow naturally in paragraph form.

S

saddle stitch   binding made through the spine of a collection of nested signatures.

sans serif type   typeface with strokes of equal or near-equal thickness and without serifs.

saturation   concentrated media coverage.

scale   quality in a photograph or illustration that shows size relationships.

scaling   working out measurements for art that is being enlarged or reduced to fit a given space.

scanner   device that digitizes art and photographs and stores them or presents them on screen for manipulation by a computer artist or designer.

scene   in a commercial, the action and dialogue taking place continuously with the same background.

schedule   list of media to be used for an advertising campaign.

schlock   vulgar, heavy, tasteless.

scoring   crease or partial cut in a piece of cardboard allowing it to be folded easily.

scotch print   photographic proof from a plate negative. Used for reproduction purposes.

scratchboard drawing   drawing made by scratching knife across a previously inked surface. The English call it a "scraperboard drawing."

screen   cross-hatched lines on a glass plate used between the camera lens and the film in the halftone process. Also, tint block in a dot pattern. Also, the concentration of dots used in halftone process. The more dots, the finer the screen.

screen capture   print exactly what's on the computer screen, including the descriptive frame. Use also as a noun.

scribing   ruling a line by using a special tool to lift a thin layer of emulsion from a negative. Useful for printing forms.

script   type that looks like handwriting.

second color   one color in addition to black or the basic color.

second cover   inside front cover.

self-cover   booklet cover made from same paper stock as the inside pages.

self-mailer   direct-mail piece that does not need an envelope.

sequence   series of related elements or pages arranged in logical order.

series   subdivision of a type family.

serifs   small finishing strokes of a roman letter found at its terminals.

serigraphy   silk-screen printing.

set   that unit in a studio that forms the background for the actors in a TV commercial.

set solid   set type without leading between lines.

SFX   abbreviation for sound effects (because "FX" is pronounced "effects").

shade   variation of a color.

shading sheets   line or dot pattern printed on transparent paper or thin plastic that can be pressed down or transferred onto original art, creating the illusion of tone. Zipatone is one brand. There are several others.

sheet-fed press   press that takes individual sheets of paper rather than rolls of paper.

shelter magazine   magazine dealing with homemaking and maintenance.

shop rough   very crude rough layout.

side stitch   stitch through side of publication to act as its binding.

signature   all the pages printed on both sides of a single sheet. The sheet is folded down to page size and trimmed. Signatures usually come in multiples of sixteen pages. A magazine or book is usually made up of several signatures. Also, the name of the advertiser at the bottom of the ad, sometimes called *sig cut*.

silhouette   art subject with background removed.

silk-screen printing   stencil printing through a silk screen.

silver print   photographic print made from the negative used for making a plate.

slab serif type   type designed with even-thickness strokes and heavy serifs. Sometimes called "square serif" type.

"slice-of-life"   description applied to commercials featuring ordinary people in ordinary situations.

slick magazine   magazine printed on slick or glossy paper. Sometimes called simply "slick."

slipcase   a display cardboard box open at one end to receive a book or books.

slogan   phrase or sentence used regularly in advertising to summarize or sell. Run usually at bottom of the ad, with the logo.

slug   line of type produced by linecasting machine. Also, material for spacing between lines, 6 points or thicker.

small caps   short for *small capitals*. Capital letters smaller than the regular capital letters in that point size.

sneak   mood music in a TV commercial that comes in almost unnoticed and establishes a mood.

software   the program that fits the computer and makes possible word processing, art creation, makeup, etc.

sort   what a printer calls a piece of type.

SpectaColor   ad printed in rotogravure in another plant for later insertion in a newspaper. Unlike a Preprint ad, a SpectaColor ad has clearly defined margins.

split fountain   technique of printing in two colors at one time by using two colors of ink in the press's ink fountain.

split-run   publication of two similar ads in a periodical; half the copies contain one of the ads, half contain the other. Used to compare effectiveness of ads.

split screen   the picture is divided so that two scenes can be shown at the same time, as involving a couple on the telephone.

spot   time segment on TV of sixty seconds or less used as a commercial.

spot color   color other than process color. Usually printed as solid areas, in screened tints, or in line.

spot illustration   drawing that stands by itself, unrelated to the text, used as a filler or for decorative purposes.

spread   two facing pages. "Two-page spread" is redundant but sometimes necessary for clarity.

square serif   see *slab serif type*.

SRDS   *Standard Rate & Data Service.*

Standard Rate & Data Service   series of regularly issued publications that carry production requirements for advertising in the various media: size limitations, plate requirements, and so on.

stat   see *photostat*.

station representative   to the broadcasting industry what a *publisher's representative* is to the publishing industry.

stereotype   plate made from a mat that in turn was made from a photoengraving or from type.

stet   proofreader's notation to the typesetter or printer to ignore the change marked on the proof.

stick   metal holder into which type or Ludlow mats are placed during hand-setting operation.

stock   see *paper stock*.

stock art   art created for general use and stored until ordered for a particular job.

stop motion   series of pictures in a film in which changes are minor but abrupt, as in the filming of an inanimate object from several angles.

storyboard   series of rough sketches of scenes for a TV commercial in its planning stage, along with description of the scenes and wording of the dialogue.

straight matter   text matter that is uninterrupted by headings, tables, and so on.

strike-on composition   cold-type composition made with a typewriter or typewriterlike machine.

strip-in   one negative fitted next to another (but not over it) so the two together can be used to make a single plate. Also used as a verb: "strip in" (two words).

style   distinct and consistent approach to art or design as well as to writing.

subhead   short headline inside the copy. Also "subhed."

substance weight   weight of one thousand sheets of paper in a standard size.

supergraphics   huge, colorful letters and typographic art used both to decorate building interiors and exteriors and to identify or give directions.

superimposition   a showing of one camera image over another, as in a TV commercial.

surprint   black letters over gray area, as over a photograph. Opposite of *reverse*. Used also as verb.

swash caps   capital letters in some typefaces with extra flourishes in their strokes, usually in the italic versions.

swatch   color sample.

GLOSSARY

"swipe file" artist's or designer's library of examples done by other artists; used for inspiration.

Swiss design design characterized by clean, simple lines and shapes, highly ordered, with lots of white space; based on a grid system.

symbol picture or abstract graphic device that suggests or stands for a product, service, or idea.

symmetric balance balance achieved by equal weights and matching placement on either side of an imaginary center line.

T

table list of names, titles, and so on. Particularly used in annual reports.

tabloid newspaper with pages half the usual size; about 11″ × 15″.

tag in a TV commercial, something added, such as an invitation or identification from a local announcer.

take a part of the text matter or, in television, a part of the film or tape. Also in television, a switch from one camera to another.

talent the actors, musicians, and others involved in the making of a TV commercial.

TCU abbreviation for tight closeup, as in a TV commercial.

tear sheet publication page showing the ad.

teaser ad that withholds information, including in some cases the name of the sponsor, until a later ad in the campaign.

technique way of achieving style or effect.

tempera show-card color or poster paint. Unlike watercolor, it is opaque, but it is water-soluble.

text see *body copy.*

text matter see *body copy.*

text type see *black letter.*

theme central idea in an ad or campaign.

third cover inside back cover.

thumbnail very rough preliminary sketch of an ad in miniature.

tight art art done with precision and clarity.

tight shot in a commercial, a frame that shows only the subject, with no distracting background.

tilt move camera up or down, as in making a TV commercial.

tint weaker version of tone or color.

tint block panel of color or tone on which something else may be printed.

tissue rough layout done on thin paper.

tissue overlay thin paper covering over art, copy, or the entire ad. Used as a place for noting corrections or simply as protection for what is underneath.

title crawl effect created by titles in a commercial moving up and out of the picture.

titles type used as superimpositions for TV commercials.

tone darkness of the art or type.

tooth ability of a paper or board to receive a drawing medium.

trade advertising advertising directed to retailers or wholesalers, not to the general public.

trade magazine magazine published for persons in a trade, business, or profession.

trademark symbol which identifies product or organization and which is consciously developed and adopted by that organization.

transfer type letters printed on the underside of transparent paper or thin plastic that can be rubbed off and onto a pasteup.

transparency in photography, a color positive on film rather than paper.

TrueType page description language competing with PostScript that includes new outline font technology.

two-color usually black plus one color. But it can mean two separate colors without black.

two-up a printing form in duplicate to permit two copies for each printing, cutting press time in half.

type printed letters and characters. Also, the metal pieces from which the printing is done.

typeface particular style or design of type.

type specimens samples of various typefaces available.

typo typographic error made by the compositor.

typography the type in an ad. Also, the art of designing and using type.

U

unity design principle that holds that all elements should be related.

upper case capital letters.

V

value in color, the degree of lightness or darkness.

Vandyke photographic proof from a negative of a page to be printed by the offset process. Sometimes called *brownline* or *blueline.*

Velox photoprint with halftone dot pattern in place of continuous tone, ready for line reproduction.

video visual portion of a TV commercial.

videotape tape for use in broadcasting that contains both audio and video material. Unlike film, it permits immediate playback.

vignette oval-shaped halftone in which background fades away gradually all around.

visual having to do with the eye.

visualization the process by which an artist or designer changes an idea or concept into visual or pictorial form.

VO voice-over in a TV commercial.

voice-over sequence in a TV commercial during which an announcer's or actor's voice is heard, but the person is not seen.

VTR video tape recording.

W

warm colors red and orange colors that tend to project toward the viewer. Stimulating colors.

wash drawing ink drawing shaded with black-and-white watercolor. Requires halftone reproduction.

web-fed press printing press that uses a roll of paper.

weight variation of type that involves the thickness of its strokes: light, medium, bold, ultrabold, and so on.

wf wrong font. Typographic error in which a character from another font is mistakenly used.

whip shot in a TV commercial, fast pan shot that blurs the action on the screen. Also known as "whiz shot," "blur pan," and "swish pan."

white space space in an ad not occupied by type, pictures, or other elements.

wide-angle shot picture made with lens that allows more to be seen at the right and the left than would otherwise be possible.

widow line of type less than the full width of the column.

wild track second track for a TV commercial added after the filming.

wipe optical effect in a TV commercial in which a blade appears to move across the picture, wiping it clean, while another picture takes its place.

wipe over optical effect in which one picture moves into another, often geometrically.

wire side the poorer side of a sheet of paper. It is the side that rested on a traveling wire screen during the manufacturing process.

woodcut engraving cut in wood. Also, the impression made by such a plate.

worm's-eye view view from low vantage point.

WSIWYG   acronym for "what you see is what you get."

X

XCU   same as ECU.

Xerography   inkless printing making use of static electricity.

x-height   height of lowercase *x* in any typeface. An *x* is used for measuring because its top and bottom would rest exactly on the guidelines, if they were drawn.

Z

zinc   slang for *photoengraving*.

Zipatone   see *shading sheets*.

zip pan   see *whip shot*.

zoom   a rapid change in camera distance from subject. Used also as a verb.

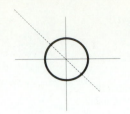

BIBLIOGRAPHY

This bibliography, with a few exceptions, covers volumes published during the past decade. The arrangement follows as closely as possible the organization of material in *The Design of Advertising*. Obviously, any one volume might fit into more than one category, but it is listed only in the category that has the greatest claim on it. To keep the list manageable, this edition omits general books on advertising and marketing, including textbooks, and concentrates on creative aspects, media, and production.

Creativity

Amabile, T. M. *The Social Psychology of Creativity*. New York: Springer-Verlag, 1983.

Baker, Steven. *Systematic Approach to Advertising Creativity*. New York: McGraw-Hill, 1983. (Paperback edition of 1979 book.)

Buzan, Tony. *Use Both Sides of Your Brain*. New York: E. P. Dutton, 1983.

Cleary, David Powers. *Great American Brands: The Success Formulas That Made them Famous*. New York: Fairchild Books, 1990.

Hammer, Emanel. *Creativity, Talent and Personality*. Malabar, Florida: Krieger Publishing Co., 1984.

Heller, Steven, and Chuast, Seymour, eds. *Sourcebook of Visual Ideas*. New York: Van Nostrand Reinhold, 1989.

Ideas on Design. London and Boston: Faber and Faber, 1986.

Jewler, A. Jerome. *Creative Strategy in Advertising,* 4th ed. Belmont, Calif.: Wadsworth, 1992.

Keil, John M. *The Creative Mystique*. New York: John Wiley & Sons, 1985.

Levinson, Bob. *Bill Bernbach's Book: A History of the Advertising That Changed the History of Advertising*. New York: Villard Books, 1987.

Marra, James L. *Advertising Creativity: Techniques for Generating Ideas*. Englewood Cliffs, N.J.: Prentice Hall, 1990.

Milton, Shirley, F., and Winters, Arthur A. *The Creative Connection: Advertising Copywriting & Idea Visualization*. New York: Fairchild Books, 1981.

Moriarty, Sandra E. *Creative Advertising*. 2d ed. Englewood Cliffs, N.J.: Prentice-Hall, 1990.

Newcomb, John. *The Book of Graphic Problem-Solving*. New York: R. R. Bowker, 1984.

Norins, Hanley. *The Young & Rubicam Traveling Creative Workshop*. Englewood Cliffs, N.J.: Prentice Hall, 1990.

Patti, Charles H., and Moriarty, Sandra E. *The Making of Effective Advertising*. Englewood Cliffs, N.J.: Prentice-Hall, 1990.

Perkins, D. N. *The Mind's Best Work: A New Psychology of Creative Thinking*. Cambridge, Mass.: Harvard University Press, 1983. (Paperback Edition.)

Resnick, Elizabeth. *Graphic Design: A Problem-Solving Approach to Visual Communication*. Englewood Cliffs: N.J.: Prentice-Hall, Inc., 1984.

Rothenberg, Albert. *The Emerging Goddess: The Creative Process in Art, Science, and Other Fields*. Chicago: University of Chicago Press, 1982.

Rothenberg, Albert. *Creativity and Madness*. Baltimore: John Hopkins University Press, 1990.

Strong, 3rd, Leonard V. *The How To Book of Advertising*. New York: Fairchild Books, 1990.

VanGundy, Arthur B. *108 Ways to Get a Bright Idea and Increase Your Creative Potential*. Englewood Cliffs, N.J.: Prentice-Hall, 1983.

White, Jan V. *Graphic Idea Notebook*. Rev. ed. Cincinnati: North Light Books, 1991.

Wilde, Richard, and Wilde, Judith. *Visual Literacy: A Conceptual Approach to Solving Graphic Problems*. New York: Watson-Guptill Publications, 1991.

Winters, Arthur A., and Milton, Shirley F. *The Creative Connection: Advertising Copywriting and Idea Visualization*. New York: Fairchild Books, 1990.

Wolf, Henry. *Visual Thinking: Methods for Making Images Memorable*. New York: Rizzoli International, 1988.

Young, James Webb. *A Technique for Producing Ideas*. New ed. Chicago: Crain Books, 1975. (A classic.)

Copywriting

Albright, Jim. *Creating the Advertising Message*. Mountain View, Calif.: Mayfield Publishing Company, 1991.

Bayran, Richard. *Words That Sell*. Chicago: Contemporary Books, 1987.

Bly, Robert W. *The Copywriter's Handbook*. Updated ed. New York: Henry Holt and Company, 1990.

Book, Albert C., and Schick, C. Dennis. *Fundamentals of Copy & Layout*. 2d ed. Lincolnwood, Illinois: NTC Publishing Group, 1990.

Burton, Philip Ward. *Advertising Copywriting*. 6th ed. Lincolnwood, Illinois: National Textbook Company, 1990.

Crompton, Alistair. *The Craft of Copywriting*. Rev. Am. ed. Englewood Cliffs, N.J.: Prentice-Hall, 1982.

Keding, Ann, and Bivins, Thomas H. *How to Produce Creative Advertising: Traditional Techniques and Computer Applications*. Lincolnwood, Illinois: NTC Business Books, 1991.

Malickson, David L., and Nason, John W. *Advertising—How to Write the Kind that Works*. Rev. ed. New York: Charles Scribner's Sons, 1982.

Meeske, Milan D., and Norris, R. C. *Copywriting for the Electronic Media*. Belmont, Calif.: Wadsworth Publishing Company, 1987.

Milton, Shirley F., and Winters, Arthur A. *The Creative Connection: Advertising Copywriting and Idea Visualization*. New York: Fairchild Books, 1982.

Monnot, Michel. *Selling America: Puns, Language, and Advertising*. Washington, D.C.: University Press of America, 1982.

Norins, Hanley. *The Compleat Copywriter,* 2d ed. Melbourne Florida: R. E. Krieger Publishing, 1980.

Ogilvy, David. *Ogilvy on Advertising.* New York: Crown, 1983.

Parker, Robert B. *Mature Advertising: A Handbook of Effective Advertising Copy.* Reading, Mass.: Addison-Wesley, 1981.

Parker, Roger C. *From Writer to Designer.* Emeryville, Calif.: Serif Publishing, Publishers Group West, 1990.

Schwab, Victor O. *How to Write a Good Advertisement.* North Hollywood, Calif.: Wilshire Book Co., 1980.

Schultz, Don E. *Strategic Advertising Campaigns.* 3d ed. Lincolnwood, Illinois: NTC Business Books, 1990.

Urdang, Laurence, ed. dir. *Slogans.* Detroit: Gale Research Company, 1984. (More than 7,000 slogans listed.)

Weaver, J. Clark. *Broadcast Copywriting as Process.* New York: Longman, Inc., 1984.

Design and Layout

Alejandro, Reynaldo. *Classic Menu Design.* Glen Cove, N.Y.: PBC International Inc., 1988.

Arntson, Amy E. *Graphic Design Basics.* New York: Holt, Rinehart and Winston, 1988.

Berryman, Gregg. *Notes on Graphic Design and Visual Communication.* Rev. ed. Los Altos, Calif.: William Kaufmann, 1983.

Blatner, David, and Stimeley, Keith. *The QuarkXPress Book.* Berkeley, Calif.: Peachpit Press, 1991.

Bockus, Jr., William H. *Advertising Graphics.* 4th ed. New York: Macmillan, 1986.

Borgman, Harry. *Advertising Layout.* New York: Watson-Guptill, 1983.

Campbell, Alastair. *The Graphic Designer's Handbook.* Philadelphia: Running Press, 1983.

Carter, David. *Evolution of Design.* New York: Art Direction Book Company, 1985.

Chajet, Clive, and Shactman, Tom. *Image by Design.* Reading, Mass.: Addison-Wesley Publishing Company, Inc., 1991.

Chwast, Seymour. *The Left-Handed Designer.* New York: Harry N. Abrams, 1985.

Collier, David. *Collier's Rules for Desktop Design & Typography.* Boston: Addison-Wesley, 1991.

Colton, Bob. *Basic Desktop Design & Layout.* Cincinnati, Ohio: North Light Books, 1989.

Conover, Theodore E. *Graphic Communications Today.* 2d ed. St. Paul, Minn.: West Publishing Company, 1990.

Craig, James, and Barton, Bruce. *Thirty Centuries of Graphic Design: An Illustrated Survey.* New York: Watson-Guptill Publications, 1987.

De Sausmarez, Maurice. *Basic Design.* New York: Van Nostrand Reinhold, 1983.

Denton, Craig. *Graphics for Visual Communication.* Madison, Wis.: Brown & Benchmark, 1992.

Dorfsman & CBS. New York: Showcase, Inc., Publishers, 1987.

Frankel, Annabel, and Morton, Rocky. *Creative Computer Graphics.* New York: Cambridge University Press, 1985.

Friedman, Mildred, and Giovanimi, Joseph. *Graphic Design in America.* New York: Harry N. Abrams, 1989. (Various essays)

Garner, Philippe. *Twentieth Century Style and Design: 1900 to Present.* New York: Van Nostrand Reinhold, 1985.

Gill, Bob. *Forget All the Rules You Ever Learned About Graphic Design. Including the Ones in This Book.* New York: Watson-Guptill, 1981.

Gosney, Michael; Odam, John; and Schmal, Jim. *The Gray Book: Designing in Black and White on Your Computer.* Emeryville, Calif.: Ventana Press, distributed by Publisher's Group West, 1990.

Great Menu Graphics. Glen Cove, N.Y.: PBC International Inc., 1989.

Heller, Steven, and Chwast, Seymour. *Graphic Style.* New York: Harry N. Abrams, Inc., 1988.

Heller, Stephen, and Fink, Anne. *Low-Budget/High-Quality Design.* New York: Watson-Guptill Publications, 1990.

Holland, D. K., et al. *Graphic Design: New York.* Cincinnati, Ohio: North Light Books, 1992.

Hurlburt, Allen, *The Grid System.* New York: Van Nostrand Reinhold, 1978.

———. *The Design Concept.* New York: Watson-Guptill, 1981.

Ishioka, Eiko. *Eiko by Eiko.* New York: Callaway Editions, 1983. (Graphic design examples by a famous Japanese art director.)

Is the Bug Dead? New York: Stewart, Tabori & Chang, 1982. (Reproduction of all the great VW ads.)

Isaacs, Reginald. *Gropius: An Illustrated Biography of the Creator of the Bauhaus.* Boston: Bullfinch Press, Little, Brown and Company, 1991.

Jervis, Simon. *The Penguin Dictionary of Design and Designers.* New York: Penguin, 1984.

Kleinman, Philip, ed. *International Advertising Design.* Glen Cove, N.Y.: PBC International, Inc., 1989.

Labuz, Ronald. *Contemporary Graphic Design.* New York: Van Nostrand Reinhold, 1991.

Laing, John, ed. *Do It Yourself Graphic Design.* New York: Facts on File, 1984.

Margolin, Victor, ed. *Design Discourse: History, Theory, Criticism.* Chicago: University of Chicago Press, 1989.

Meggs, Philip. *A History of Graphic Design.* 2d ed. New York: Van Nostrand Reinhold, 1991.

Meyerowitz, Michael, and Sanchez, Sam. *The Graphic Designer's Basic Guide to the Macintosh.* New York: Allworth Press, 1990.

Morgan, Ann Lee, ed. *Contemporary Designers.* Detroit: Gale Research Co., 1985. (Biographies of some 600 designers, along with essays and 400 illustrations.)

Morgan, John, and Welton, Peter. *See What I Mean: An Introduction to Visual Communication.* Baltimore: Edward Arnold, 1986.

Muller-Brockmann, Josef. *A History of Visual Communication.* New York: Hastings House, 1981.

———. *The Graphic Designer and His Design Problems.* Rev. ed. New York: Hastings House, 1984.

Nelson, George. *George Nelson on Design.* New York: Whitney Library of Design, 1979.

Olsen, Gary. *Getting Started in Computer Graphics.* Cincinnati, Ohio: North Light Books, 1989.

Passuth, Krisztina. *Moholy-Nagy.* New York: Thames and Hudson, 1987.

Pedersen, B. Martin, ed. *The Graphic Designer's Green Book.* New York: Watson-Guptill Publications, 1991. (Designing with attention to the environment.)

Print Casebooks 8, Print, Washington, D.C., 1989. (Multivolume set showing 266 award-winning design projects.)

Prohaska, Ray. *A Basic Course in Design.* New York: Van Nostrand Reinhold, 1980.

Rand, Paul. *Paul Rand: A Designer's Art.* New Haven, Conn.: Yale University Press, 1985.

Remington, R. Roger, and Hodik, Barbara J. *Nine Pioneers in American Graphic Design.* Cambridge, Mass.: MIT Press, 1989.

Shoshkes, Ellen. *The Design Process.* New York: Watson-Guptill Publications, 1989.

Siebert, Lori, and Ballard, Lisa. *Making a Good Layout.* Cincinnati, Ohio: North Light Books, 1992.

Smith, Robert Charles. *Basic Graphic Design.* Englewood Cliffs, N.J.: Prentice-Hall, 1985.

Snyder, Gertrude, and Peckolick, Alan. *Herb Lubalin: Art Director, Graphic Designer and Typographer.* New York: American Showcase, Inc. 1985.

Squibb, Sharon. *Studio Techniques for Advertising Agencies and Graphic Designers.* New York: Watson-Guptill Publications, 1991.

Swann, Alan. *How to Understand and Use Grids.* Cincinnati, Ohio: North Light Books, 1989.

————. *Graphic Design School.* New York: Van Nostrand Reinhold, 1990.

————. *How to Understand and Use Design and Layout.* Cincinnati, Ohio: North Light Books, 1991.

Thompson, Bradbury. *The Art of Graphic Design.* New Haven, Conn.: Yale University Press, 1988.

Walker, Lisa, and Blount, Steve. *Getting the Max from Your Graphics Computer.* Cincinnati, Ohio: North Light Press, 1991.

Ward, Dick. *Creative Ad Design & Illustration.* Cincinnati, Ohio: North Light Books, 1988.

Warren, Jack. *Basic Graphic Design & Paste-Up.* Cincinnati, Ohio: North Light Publishers, 1985.

West, Suzanne. *Working with Style-Traditional and Modern Approaches to Layout and Typography.* New York: Watson-Guptill Publications, 1990.

————. *Comping Techniques: Visualizing and Presenting Graphic Design Ideas.* New York: Watson-Guptill Publications, 1991.

White, Jan V. *Graphic Design for the Electronic Age.* New York: Watson-Guptill Publications, 1988.

Whitney, Patrick. *Computers in Design.* New York: Random House, 1985.

Production and Printing

Aldrich-Ruenzel, Nancy, ed. *Designer's Guide to Print Production.* New York: Watson-Guptill Publications, 1990.

Bann, David. *The Print Production Handbook.* Cincinnati, Ohio: North Light Publishers, 1985.

Beach, Mark; Shepro, Steve; and Russon, Ken. *Getting It Printed.* Portland: Coast to Coast Books, 1986.

Beach, Mark, and Russon, Ken. *Papers for Printing.* Cincinnati, Ohio: North Light Press, 1991.

Bove, Tony, and Rhodes, Cheryl. *Desktop Publishing with PageMaker.* New York: John Wiley & Sons, 1987. (Two volumes: one for Macintosh, one for IBM.)

Conover, Theodore E. *Graphic Communications Today.* 2d ed. St. Paul: West Publishing Company, 1990.

Craig, James. *Production for the Graphic Designer.* 2d ed. New York: Watson-Guptill, 1990.

Crow, Wendell, C. *Communications Graphics.* Englewood Cliffs, N.J.: Prentice Hall, 1986.

Hulme, Kenneth S. *An Introduction to Desktop Publishing.* Cincinnati, Ohio: Boyd & Fraser Publishing Company, 1990.

Johy, Lynn. *Preparing Your Design for Print.* Cincinnati, Ohio: North Light Books, 1988.

Kleper, Michael L. *The Illustrated Handbook of Desktop Publishing and Typesetting.* Blue Ridge Summit, Pa.: TAB Books, 1987.

Lem, Dean P. *Graphics Master No. 4.* Los Angeles: Dean Lem Associates, 1988.

Lippi, Robert. *How to Buy Good Printing and Save Money.* New York: Art Direction Book Company, 1987.

Marquand, Ed. *How to Prepare and Present Roughs, Comps and Mock-ups.* New York: Art Direction Book Co., 1985.

McDonald, Duncan, et al. *The Graphics of Communications.* 6th ed. Ft. Worth, Texas: Harcourt Brace Jovanovich, 1993.

Murray, Ray. *How to Brief Designers and Buy Print.* Brookfield, Vt.: Business Books, Brookfield Publishing, 1984.

Parnau, Jeff. *Desktop Publishing: The Awful Truth.* New Berlin, Wisconsin: Parnau Graphics, Inc., P.O. Box 244, 53151, 1989.

Pocket Pal: A Graphic Arts Digest for Printers and Advertising Production Managers. New York: International Paper, published periodically in new editions.

Robinson, Wayne. *How'd They Design and Print That?* Cincinnati, Ohio: North Light Books, 1992.

Sanders, Linda S. *47 Printing Headaches (And How to Avoid Them).* Cincinnati, Ohio: North Light Press, 1991.

Sanders, Norman. *Graphic Designer's Production Handbook.* 9th ed. New York: Hastings House, 1990.

Tilden, Scott W. *Harnessing Desktop Publishing: How to Let the New Technology Help You Do Your Job Better.* Pennington, N.J.: Scott Tilden Inc., 4 West Franklin Ave., 08534, 1987.

Vince, John. *Computer Graphics for Graphic Designers.* White Plains, N.Y.: Knowledge Industry Publications, 1985.

Type and Letterform

Bauermeister, Benjamin. *A Manual of Comparative Typography: the PANOSE System.* New York: Van Nostrand Reinhold, 1987.

Beaumont, Michael. *Type: Design, Color, Character & Use.* Cincinnati, Ohio: North Light Books, 1991.

Binns, Betty. *Better Type.* New York: Watson-Guptill Publications, 1989.

Brady, Philip. *Using Type Right.* Cincinnati, Ohio: North Light Press, 1988.

Bruckner, D. J. R. *Frederic Goudy.* New York: Harry Abrams, 1990.

Carter, Rob; Day, Ben; and Meggs, Phillip. *Typographic Design: Form and Communication.* New York: Van Nostrand Reinhold, 1985.

Carter, Rob. *American Typography Today.* New York: Van Nostrand Reinhold, 1989.

Craig, James. *Basic Typography.* New York: Watson-Guptill Publications, 1990.

————. *Typography: A Manual for Designers, Non-Designers & Desktop Publishers.* New York: Watson-Guptill Publications, 1990.

Dair, Carl. *Design with Type.* New ed. Buffalo, New York: University of Toronto Press, 1982.

Dewsnap, Don. *Desktop Publisher's Easy Type Guide.* Cincinnati, Ohio: North Light Books, 1992.

Digital Typeface Library. New York: Art Direction Book Co., 1985. (Shows 1,350 digital typefaces.)

Elam, Kimberly. *Expressive Typography: The Word As Image.* New York: Van Nostrand Reinhold, 1990.

Felici, James. *How to Get Great Type Out of Your Computer.* Cincinnati, Ohio: North Light Books, 1992.

Goines, David Lance. *A Constructed Roman Alphabet.* New York: David R. Godine, 1983.

Gottschall, Edward M. *Typographic Communications Today.* Cambridge, Mass.: The MIT Press, 1989.

Haley, Allan. *ABC's of Type: A Guide to Contemporary Typefaces.* New York: Watson-Guptill Publications, 1990.

Hermann Zapf & His Design Philosophy. New York: Society of Typographic Arts, 1987.

Hess, Stanley. *The Modification of Letterforms.* Rev. ed. New York: Art Direction Book Co., 1986.

Hinrichs, Kit. *TypeWise.* Cincinnati, Ohio: North Light Books, 1991.

King, Jean Callan, and Esposito, Tony. *The Designer's Guide to Text Type.* New York: Van Nostrand Reinhold, 1982.

Kleper, Michael. *Desktop Publishing & Typesetting,* 2nd ed. Pittsford, N.Y.: Graphic Dimensions, 1991.

Krasucki, Cheryl Adams. *The Art of Professional Typography—Mac Style.* Virginia Beach, Virginia: TypograMac Publishing, 1990.

Labuz, Ronald. *Typography and Typesetting: Type Design and Manipulation Using Today's Technology.* New York: Van Nostrand Reinhold, 1987.

Lawson, Alexander S. *Printing Types: An Introduction.* Rev. ed. Boston: Beacon Press, 1990.

————. *Anatomy of a Typeface.* New York: David R. Godine, 1990.

————. *The Compositor as Artist, Craftsman, and Tradesman.* Athens, Georgia: Press of the Nightowl, 320 Sandfinger Drive, Athens, Georgia 30605, 1991.

March, Marion. *Creative Typography.* Cincinnati, Ohio: North Light Books, 1988.

Meggs, Philip B., and Carter, Rob. *Typographic Design: Form and Communication.* New York: Van Nostrand Reinhold, 1985.

Morrison, Sean. *A Guide to Type Design.* Englewood Cliffs, N.J.: Prentice-Hall, 1986.

Ogg, Oscar. *The 26 Letters.* Rev. ed. New York: Van Nostrand Reinhold, 1983.

Perfect, Christopher, and Rookledge, Gordon. *Rookledge's International Typefinder.* Mount Kisco, N.Y.: Moyer Bell Limited, 1991.

Romano, Frank. *Practical Typography From A to Z.* Arlington, Va.: National Composition Association, 1984.

Rosen, Ben. *Digital Type Specimens: The Designer's Computer Type Book.* New York: Van Nostrand Reinhold, 1990.

Solomon, Martin. *The Art of Typography: An Introduction to Typo-icon-ography.* New York: Watson-Guptill Publications, 1985.

Spencer, Herbert. *Pioneers of Modern Typography.* Cambridge, Mass.: MIT Press, 1983. (Paperback edition of 1969 book.)

Stone, Sumner. *On Stone: The Art and Use of Typography on the Contemporary Computer.* San Francisco: Bedford Arts, Publishers, 1990.

Torre, Vincent, ed. *A Tribute to William Addison Dwiggins on the Hundredth Anniversary of His Birth.* New York: Inkwell Press, 1983.

Type Specimen Book, The. New York: Van Nostrand Reinhold, 1974. (544 faces, 3,000 sizes.)

Updike, Daniel Berkeley. *Printing Types: Their History, Forms and Use.* New York: Dover Publications, 1980. (Two volumes. Reprint of a classic.)

White, Alex. *How to Spec Type.* New York: Watson-Guptill Publications, 1987.

Wolfe, Gregory. *Type Recipes: Quick Solutions to Designing with Type.* Cincinnati, Ohio: North Light Books, 1991.

Art and Photography

Beakley, George C. *Freehand Drawing and Visualization.* Indianapolis: Bobbs-Merrill, 1982.

Bernstein, Saul, and McGarry, Leo. *Making Art on Your Computer.* New York: Watson-Guptill Publications, 1986.

Brown, Nancy. *Photographing People for Advertising.* New York: Amphoto, 1986.

Colyer, Martin. *How To Find and Work with an Illustrator.* Cincinnati, Ohio: North Light Books, 1990.

Frankel, Annabel, and Morton, Rocky. *Creative Computer Graphics.* New York: Cambridge University Press, 1985.

Gombrich, E. H. *The Image and the Eye.* Ithaca, N.Y.: Cornell University Press, 1982.

Green, Michael. *Zen & the Art of the Macintosh.* Philadelphia, Running Press Book Publishers, 1987.

Heller, Steven, ed. *Innovators of American Illustration.* New York: Van Nostrand Reinhold, 1986.

Heller, Steven, and Pomeroy, Karen. *Design with Illustration.* New York: Van Nostrand Reinhold, 1990.

Herdeg, Walter, ed. *Graphics Diagrams: The Graphic Visualization of Abstract Data.* New ed. New York: Hastings House, 1982.

Holmes, Nigel, *Designers Guide to Creating Charts & Diagrams.* New York: Watson-Guptill Publications, 1984.

Holmes, Nigel, and DeNeve, Rose. *Designing Pictorial Symbols.* New York: Watson-Guptill Publications, 1990.

Marcus, Aaron, *Managing Facts and Concepts: Computer Graphics and Information Graphics from a Graphic Designer's Perspective.* Washington, D.C.: National Endowment for the Arts, 1983.

Melot, Michel. *The Art of Illustration.* New York: Skira/Rizzoli, 1984.

Miller, Ernestine, comp. *The Art of Advertising: Great Commercial Illustrations from The Early Years of Magazines.* New York: St. Martin's Press, 1980.

Nelson, Roy Paul. *Humorous Illustration and Cartooning: A Guide for Editors, Advertisers, and Artists.* Englewood Cliffs, N.J.: Prentice-Hall, 1984.

Newcomb, John. *The Book of Graphic Problem-Solving: How to Get Visual Ideas When You Need Them.* New York: R. R. Bowker, 1984.

Reed, Walt, and Reed, Roger. *The Illustrator in America 1880–1980.* New York: Watson-Guptill Publications, 1990.

Roskill, Mark, and Carrier, David. *Truth and Falsehood in Visual Images.* Amherst: University of Massachusetts Press, 1983.

Sacharow, Stanley, *Symbols of Trade.* New York: Art Direction Book Company, 1983.

Salomon, Allyn, *Advertising Photography.* New York: Watson-Guptill Publications, 1987.

Satterwhite, Joy, and Satterwhite, Al. *Lights! Camera! Advertising! How to Plan and Shoot Major Advertising Campaigns.* New York: Watson-Guptill Publications, 1991.

Saunders, Dave. *Professional Advertising Photography.* Lincolnwood, Illinois: NTC Publishing Group, 1990.

Schlemmer, Richard M. *Handbook of Advertising Art Production.* 4th ed. Englewood Cliffs, N.J. 1990.

Sobieszek, Robert A. *The Art of Persuasion: A History of Advertising Photography.* New York: Harry N. Abrams, 1988.

Szarkowski, John. *Photography Until Now.* New York: Museum of Modern Art, 1990.

Thompson, Philip, and Davenport, Peter. *The Dictionary of Graphic Images.* New York: St. Martin's Press, 1980.

Truckenbrod, Joan. *Creative Computer Imaging.* Englewood Cliffs, N.J.: Prentice-Hall, Inc., 1988.

Tufte, Edward R. *The Visual Display of Quantitative Information.* Cheshire, Conn.: Graphics Press, 1983.

————. *Envisioning Information.* New Haven, Conn.: Graphics Press, 1989.

White, Jan V. *Using Charts and Graphs.* New York: R. R. Bowker Company, 1984.

Wilson, Mark. *Drawing With Computers.* New York: Perigee Books, Putnam Publishing Group, 1985.

Color

Agogton, G. A. *Color Theory and Its Applications in Art and Design.* New York: Springer-Verlag, 1979.

Binns, Betty. *Designing with Two Colors.* New York: Watson-Guptill Publications, 1991.

Durrett, H. John, ed. *Color and the Computer.* San Diego: Academic Press, 1986.

Ellinger, Richard G. *Color Structure and Design.* New York: Van Nostrand Reinhold, 1980.

Guide to Quality Newspaper Reproduction. Washington, D.C.: Newspaper Advertising Bureau, American Newspaper Publishers Association, 1986.

Itten, Johannes. *The Art of Color.* Rev. ed. New York: Van Nostrand Reinhold, 1990.

Sidelinger, Stephen J. *The Color Manual.* Englewood Cliffs, N.J.: Prentice-Hall, 1985.

Stockton, James. *Designer's Guide to Color.* San Francisco: Chronicle Books, 1984. (Two volumes.)

White, Jan. *Color for the Electronic Age.* New York: Watson-Guptill Publications, 1990.

Wong, Wucius. *Principles of Color Design.* New York: Van Nostrand Reinhold, 1986.

Retail Advertising

Garcia, Mario; Bohle, Robert; and Fry, Don, eds. *Color in American Newspapers.* St. Petersburg, Fla.: The Poynter Institute for Media Studies, 1986.

Milton, Shirley F. *Advertising for Modern Retailers.* New York: Fairchild Books, 1981.

Ocko, Judy Young. *Retail Advertising Copy: The How, the What, the Why.* Wheaton, Ill.: Dynamo, 1983.

Rosenblum, M. L. *How to Design Effective Store Advertising.* Rev. ed. Wheaton, Ill.: Dynamo, 1983.

Spitzer, Harry, and Schwartz, F. Richard. *Inside Retail Sales Promotion and Advertising.* New York: Harper & Row, 1982.

Watkins, Don. *Guide to Newspaper Ad Layout.* Wheaton, Ill.: Dynamo, 1983.

Broadcast Advertising

Baldwin, Huntley. *How to Create Effective Commercials.* Lincolnwood, Ill.: NTC Business Books, 1989.

Bergendorff, Fred L., and others. *Broadcast Advertising & Promotion.* New York: Hastings House, 1983.

Conrad, Jon J. *The TV Commercial: How It Is Made.* New York: Van Nostrand Reinhold, 1983.

Kaatz, Ron. *Cable: An Advertiser's Guide to the Electronic Media.* Chicago: Crain Books, 1983.

Orlik, Peter B. *Broadcast/Cable Copywriting.* 2d ed. Needham Heights, Mass.: Allyn & Bacon, 1990.

Schulbert, Bob. *Radio Advertising: The Authoritative Handbook.* Lincolnwood, Ill.: NTC Business Books, 1989.

Stewart, David W., and Furse, David H. *Effective Television Advertising: A Study of 1000 Commercials.* Lexington, Mass.: Lexington Books, D.C. Heath, 1985.

White, Hooper. *How to Produce Effective TV Commercials.* 2d ed. Lincolnwood, Ill.: National Textbook Company, 1986.

Woodward, Walt. *An Insider's Guide to Advertising Music: Everything You Must Know for TV and Radio.* New York: Art Direction Book Co., 1982.

Wurtzel, Anal, and Acker, Stephen. *Television Production.* 3d ed. New York: McGraw-Hill Book Company, 1989.

Direct-Mail Advertising

Annual Report Planning Book. Chicago: Alexander Communications, Inc., 1988.

Arnold, Edmund C. *The Making of Flyers, Folders, and Brochures.* Chicago: Lawrence Ragan Communications, 1983.

Bivins, Thomas, and Ryan, William E. *How to Produce Creative Publications.* Lincolnwood, Illinois: NTC Business Books, 1991.

Direct Marketing Creative Guild. *Direct Marketing Design.* Glen Cove, N.Y.: PBC International, Inc., 1985.

Direct Marketing Design: The Graphics of Direct Mail and Direct Response Marketing. Glen Cove, New York: PBC International, Inc., 1985.

Herrin, Jerry. *Annual Report Design.* New York: Watson-Guptill Publications, 1990.

Hicks, Donna E. *Business Card Design.* New York: Art Direction Book Co., 1990.

How to Create Successful Catalogs. Colorado Springs, Colo.: Maxwell Sroge Publishing, 731 N. Cascade Avenue, 1985. (With contributions by 39 catalog industry experts. Expensive.)

Nelson, Roy Paul. *Publication Design.* 5th ed. Dubuque, Iowa: Wm. C. Brown Publishers, 1991.

Sroge, Maxwell. *101 Tips for More Profitable Catalogs.* Lincolnwood, Illinois: NTC Business Books, 1991.

Stone, Bob. *Successful Direct Marketing Methods.* 4th ed. Chicago: Crain Books, 1988.

Sutter, Jan. *Slinging Ink: A Practical Guide to Producing Booklets, Newspapers, and Ephemeral Publications.* Los Altos, Calif.: William Kaufmann, 1982.

Winter, Elmer, *Complete Guide to Preparing a Corporate Annual Report.* New York: Van Nostrand Reinhold, 1985.

Posters and Point-of-Purchase Advertising

Ades, Dawn, et al. *The 20th Century Poster.* New York: Abbeville Press, 1984.

Berger, Arthur Asa. *Signs in Contemporary Culture.* New York: Longman, 1984.

Grushkin, Paul D. *The Art of Rock: Posters from Presley to Punk.* New York: Abbeville Press, 1987.

Konikow, Robert. *Point-of-Purchase Design 2.* Glen Cove, N.Y.: PBC International, Inc., 1989.

Wellington, Duke. *The Theory and Practice of Poster Art.* Cincinnati, Ohio: ST Publications, 1987. (Reissue of 1934 book.)

Trademarks, Logotypes, Book Jackets, Record Covers, Packages

Bereswill, Joseph W. *Corporate Design: Graphic Identity Systems.* Glen Cove, N.Y.: PBC International Inc., 1987.

Blount, Steve, and Walker, Lisa, eds. *Primo Angeli: Designs for Marketing.* Cincinnati, Ohio: North Light Books, 1991. (About package design.)

Carter, David. *Designing Corporate Identity Programs for Small Corporations.* New York: Art Direction Book Co., 1982.

———. *How to Improve Your Corporate Identity.* New York: Art Direction Book Company, 1986.

Dreyfuss, Henry. *Symbol Sourcebook.* New York: McGraw-Hill, 1972. (Eight thousand universal symbols and signs.)

Duncan, Hugh Dalziel. *Symbols in Society.* New York: Oxford University Press, 1974.

Errigo, Angie. *Rock Album Art.* New York: Mayflower Books, 1979.

Great Packaging Graphics. Glen Cove, N.Y.: PBC International, Inc., 1989.

Jones, John Philip. *What's in a Name? Advertising and Concepts of Brands.* Lexington, Mass.: Lexington Books, D.C. Heath, 1986.

Logoz, Michel. *Wine Label Design.* New York: Rizzoli International, 1984.

Martin, Douglas. *Book Design.* New York: Van Nostrand Reinhold, 1990.

Mendenhall, John. *High Tech Trademarks.* Vol. 2. New York: Art Direction Book Co., 1990.

Morgan, Hal. *Symbols of America.* New York: Penguin Books, 1986.

Murphy, John, and Rowe, Michael. *How to Design Trademarks.* Cincinnati, Ohio, 1988.

Pattison, Polly. *How to Design a Nameplate.* Chicago: Lawrence Ragan Communications, 1982.

Pfeifer, Ken. *CD Packaging & Graphics.* Cincinnati, Ohio: North Light Books, 1992.

Radice, Judi. *The Best of Shopping Bag Design.* Glen Cove, N.Y.: PBC International Inc., 1987.

Roth, Laszlo, and Wybenga, George. *The Packaging Designer's Book of Patterns.* New York: Van Nostrand Reinhold, 1991.

Sacharow, Stanley. *Packaging Design.* New York: Photographic Book Company, 1982.

Sonsino, Steven. *Packaging Design.* New York: Van Nostrand Reinhold, 1990.

Thorgerson, Storm; Dean, Roger; and Howells, David, eds. *The Second Volume Album Cover Album.* New York: A & W Visual Library, 1983.

Whitburn, Joel. *The Billboard Book of Top 40 Albums.* New York: Watson-Guptill Publications, 1987.

Williamson, Hugh. *Methods of Book Design.* 3d ed. New Haven, Conn.: Yale University Press, 1984.

Wong, Wucius. *Principles of Three-Dimensional Design.* New York: Van Nostrand Reinhold, 1990.

Careers

Barry, Ann Marie. *The Advertising Portfolio.* Lincolnwood, Illinois: NTC Business Books, 1990.

Berryman, Gregg. *Designing Creative Resumes.* Rev. ed. Los Altos, Calif.: Crisp Publications, 1991.

Brackman, Henrietta. *The Perfect Portfolio.* New York: Amphoto, Watson-Guptill Publications, 1985. (Mostly about selling photographs.)

Craig, James, *Graphic Design Career Guide.* New York: Watson-Guptill, 1983.

Craig, James, and Bevington, William. *Working with Graphic Designers.* Lakewood, N.J.: Watson-Guptill Publications, 1989.

Crawford, Tad. *Legal Guide for the Visual Artist.* Rev. ed. New York: Robert Silver Associates, 1987.

Davis, Sally Prince. *The Graphic Artist's Guide to Marketing and Self Promotion.* Cincinnati, Ohio: North Light Books, 1987.

Ganim, Barbara. *The Designer's Commonsense Business Book.* Cincinnati, Ohio: North Light Books, 1991.

Gold, Ed. *The Business of Graphic Design.* New York: Watson-Guptill Publications, 1985.

Gordon, Barbara, and Gordon, Elliott. *Opportunities in Commercial Art and Graphic Design.* Lincolnwood, Ill.: VGM Career Horizons, National Textbook Company, 1985.

Graphics Artists Guild. *Handbook of Pricing & Ethical Guidelines.* Cincinnati, Ohio: North Light Books. (Published periodically in new editions.)

Heller, Steven, and Talarico, Lita. *Design Career.* New York: Van Nostrand Reinhold, 1988.

Herring, Jerry, and Fulton, Mark. *The Art & Business of Creative Self-Promotion: For Graphic Designers, Writers, Illustrators & Photographers.* New York: Watson-Guptill Publications, 1987.

Ito, Dee. *The School of Visual Arts Guide to Careers.* New York: McGraw-Hill Book Company, 1988.

Jones, Gerre L. *How to Market Professional Design Services.* 2d ed. New York: McGraw-Hill, 1983.

Lewis, William, and Cornelius, Hal. *Career Guide for Sales and Marketing.* New York: Monarch Press, 1983.

Metzdorf, Martha. *The Ultimate Portfolio.* Cincinnati, Ohio: North Light Books, 1991.

Mogel, Leonard. *Making It in the Media Professions.* Chester, Conn.: The Globe Pequot Press, 1987.

Montaperto, Nicki. *The Freelancer's Career Book.* New York: Arco Publishing, 1983.

Morgan, Jim. *Marketing for the Small Design Firm.* New York: Watson-Guptill Publications, 1984.

Moriarty, Sandra E., and Duncan, Tom. *How to Create and Deliver Winning Advertising Presentations.* Lincolnwood, Ill.: NTC Business Books, 1989.

Stewart, Joyce M. *How to Make Your Design Business Profitable.* Cincinnati, Ohio: North Light Books, 1992.

Weilbacher, William M. *Choosing and Working with Your Advertising Agency.* Lincolnwood, Illinois: NTC Business Books, 1991.

Weinstein, David A. *How to Protect Your Creative Work: All You Need to Know About Copyright.* New York: John Wiley & Sons, 1987.

Werenko, John D., ed. *Guide to American Art Schools.* Boston: G. K. Hall & Co., 1987.

Yeung, Mary. *The Professional Designer's Guide to Marketing Your Work.* Cincinnati, Ohio: North Light Books, 1991.

INDEX